D0085800

THE ARCHAIC STYLE IN GREEK SCULPTURE

THE ARCHAIC STYLE IN GREEK SCULPTURE

By Brunilde Sismondo Ridgway

PRINCETON UNIVERSITY PRESS
PRINCETON, NEW JERSEY

Published by Princeton University Press, Princeton
In the United Kingdom: Guildford, Surrey

This book has been composed in Linotype Caledonia

Printed in the United States of America
by Princeton University Press, Princeton, New Jersey

Library of Congress Cataloging in Publication Data

Ridgway, Brunilde Sismondo, 1929–
The archaic style in Greek sculpture.

Includes bibliographies and index.
1. Sculpture, Greek. I. Title.
NB90.R56 733'.3 76–19655
ISBN 0–691–03920–8
ISBN 0–691–10052–7 pbk.

Preface

My interest in Archaic Greek sculpture started in 1953–54, when, as a graduate student at Bryn Mawr College, Rhys Carpenter suggested that I write an M.A. thesis on this subject "without bibliography, using only illustrations and your own eyes." The following year I was fortunate in receiving an Ella Riegel Fellowship from the Department of Archaeology, which enabled me to spend the period 1955–57 at the American School of Classical Studies in Athens, researching the same topic in direct contact with the monuments. The result was my Ph.D. dissertation for Bryn Mawr College, "Observations on Style and Chronology of Some Archaic Sculptures" (April 1958). Yet the present book bears no resemblance to my earlier efforts; in seventeen years of teaching and of discussion with my students, I have learned a great deal, and though my indebtedness to my early training will never be cancelled, my approach and thinking have changed considerably. In particular, while my dissertation was a rather dogmatic expression of personal opinions, the present book attempts a formulation of questions meant to reopen old problems and to encourage further thinking. It is my hope that this work will be particularly helpful to students, to whom it is directed, since they will have to provide some of the pending answers.

As early as 1909 the bibliography on Archaic Greek sculpture was defined by W. Déonna as "enormous." Since then it has increased in geometric progression. In addition, finds have multiplied and many new sites have been excavated or published. To give a comprehensive listing of all articles and books on the period 650–480 BC, or to mention all major monuments and fragments seems an impossible task. I have therefore relied on the excellent tools provided by Gisela M. A. Richter with her basic books on Kouroi, Korai, and Attic Gravestones, and I have attempted to focus instead on geographical trends and patterns of distribution for the various Archaic sculptural types. I have refrained from describing individual statuary, except in cases where comments seemed helpful for a better understanding of style and chronology. I have also tried to avoid specific dates in favor of more general definitions.

Following the format which proved satisfactory for my *Severe Style*, I have put all documentation in individual bibliographies at the end of each chapter; here too only the most important or the most recent works have been cited, the handiest sources of illustration noted. Books easily accessible to students have been selected when possible, and English translations of illustrated books have been preferred over the original editions. Likewise, J. J. Pollitt, *The Ancient View of Greek Art*, is quoted in its Student, rather than in its Unabridged, edition. I have tried to mention at least one photographic reproduction for each piece discussed, but I have kept my plates to a minimum since I want this to be a teaching tool within a student's limited financial reach. Whatever illustration I have included is either little known or meant to support a specific point. Finally, I have used footnotes solely to expand on arguments pertinent to the discussion in progress, or to present additional evidence which could not be woven into the main text. This last function had been absorbed by the Appendices in my *Severe Style*, but the idea had to be abandoned here because of the already excessively long manuscript.

My text was written in the period from September 1974 to August 1975, during my Sabbatical Year. A generous grant from the Simon Guggenheim Memorial Foundation enabled me not only to devote this year to my project but also to travel to some key museums in England and Greece in November-December 1974. I wish here to record my sincere gratitude and very real debt to the Guggenheim Foundation. I elected to stay at Bryn Mawr College during the rest of my leave, in order to profit from the stimulating discussion and unstinting help I received from all my colleagues, in particular those of the Greek and the Archaeology Departments. To Richard S. Ellis, Machteld J. Mellink, Carl Nylander, and Kyle M. Phillips, Jr., I am grateful not only for their patience with my queries and their constructive answers but especially for opening my horizons both toward the East and toward the West, through their own interest in the Oriental and the Etrusco-Italian world. To my students, and in particular to Carlos A. Picón, I am indebted for preliminary readings of my text, and for the verifying of specific details abroad. Nancy Bookidis and Nancy Winter supplied not only their own indispensable works but also many specific and valuable comments. Eileen Markson pruned my English and challenged my obscurities and woolly thinking. But many other people should be remembered here, with my thanks: our former student Lauren T. Adams, who let me read her Harvard dissertation on Soft Limestone; Judith Perlzweig Binder, who pointed out to me many important details and also read and criticized my Chapter 2; Lanny Bell, of the University Museum in Philadelphia, who provided some Egyptian references; John Boardman, who discussed with me the problem of the diffusion of the Daedalic style; Robert A. Bridges, who commented on my architectural chapters; Michael M. Eisman, who applied his knowledge of vase painting to the comparable issue of sculptural workshops; L. H. Jeffery, who was the inspiration for the entire Chapter 10, which she kindly consented to read and correct; Judith Schaeffer, who sent me her doctoral dissertation on the costume of the korai and critically read my pages on the subject; Nicholas Yalouris and several other archaeologists overseas, who opened to me the storerooms of their museums and gave me the benefit of their stimulating ideas. I consider myself very fortunate in having once again had Harriet Anderson of Princeton University Press as my editor. Mary Lou Zimmerman has been of great help in proofreading and indexing. Finally, my gratitude goes to my mother-in-law, Louise M. Ridgway, who typed the most confusing section of my original manuscript, and to my husband and four sons, who managed to live with an absentee wife and mother.

B.S.R.

Bryn Mawr College
August 27, 1975.

Contents

PART IV: SCULPTORS AND PROBLEMS OF STYLE

List of Illustrations and Photographic Sources

List of Abbreviations

Works most frequently cited have been abbreviated according to the list below. For German books of large scope, the English edition is used, where available, to accommodate students with limited libraries at their disposal. Comments on individual works, both on editions and on ways of referring to catalogue entries, will be found below, as necessary.

AA: *Archäologischer Anzeiger*, Beiblatt zum *JdI*.

AAA: *Athens Annals of Archaeology*.

AbhBayerAk: *Abhandlungen Bayerische Akademie*.

ActaA: *Acta Archaeologica*.

Adam: S. Adam, *The Technique of Greek Sculpture*, BSA Suppl. no. 3, Oxford 1966.

Adams: L. T. Adams, "Orientalizing Sculpture in Soft Limestone from Crete and Mainland Greece," Harvard University Ph.D. Dissertation 1974.

AGA: G.M.A. Richter, *The Archaic Gravestones of Attica*, London 1961.

Agora xi: *The Athenian Agora*, vol. xi-E. B. Harrison, *Archaic and Archaistic Sculpture*, American School of Classical Studies at Athens, Princeton 1965.

AJA: *American Journal of Archaeology*.

Åkerström: Å. Åkerström, *Die architektonischen Terrakotten Kleinasiens* (Skrifter Utgivna av Svenska Institutet I Athen, Acta Instituti Atheniensis Regni Sueiciae, 4°, xi) Lund 1966.

AltSt: E. Buschor, *Altsamische Standbilder*, 5 vv., Berlin 1934–1961.

AMA: *Die archaischen Marmorbildwerke der Akropolis*, Franfurt am Main, 1939. (In this work, the korai have been published by E. Langlotz, the other sculptures in the round and the reliefs by W.-H. Schuchhardt, and the architectural sculpture by H. Schrader.)

Ancient View: J. J. Pollitt, *The Ancient View of Greek Art, Criticism, History and Terminology*, Student edition (Yale Publications in the History of Art, 26) New Haven 1974.

AntCl: *L'antiquité classique*.

AntDenk: *Antike Denkmäler*

AntJ: *Antiquaries' Journal*.

AntK: *Antike Kunst*.

AntP: *Antike Plastik*, ed. W.-H. Schuchhardt, 1962–1972; F. Eckstein, 1973–

Archaeology: *Archaeology*, Magazine of the Archaeological Institute of America.

"Archaic as Survival": C. M. Havelock, "The Archaic as Survival versus the Archaistic as a New Style," *AJA* 69 (1965) 331–40.

"Archaistic Reliefs": C. M. Havelock, "Archaistic Reliefs of the Hellenistic Period," *AJA* 68 (1964) 43–58.

ArchCl: *Archeologia Classica.*

Archeologia: *Archeologia, Fouilles et Découvertes*, Paris 1964–

ArchEph: *Archaiologike Ephemeris.*

ArchHom: *Archaeologia Homerica: Die Denkmäler und das frühgriechische Epos*, ed. F. Matz and H.-G. Buchholz, 3 vv., 1967– (German Archaeological Institute).

Aristodikos: Chr. Karouzos, *Aristodikos. Zur Geschichte der spätarchaisch-attischen Plastik und der Grabstatue*, Stuttgart 1961.

Art and Experience: J. J. Pollitt, *Art and Experience in Classical Greece*, Cambridge 1972.

ArtB: *Art Bulletin.*

Art of Greece: E. Akurgal, *The Art of Greece, Its Origins in the Mediterranean and Near East* (Art of the World Series) 1966 (New York 1968).

ASAtene: *Annuario della Scuola Archeologica di Atene.*

Aspécts: N. Kontoleon, *Aspécts de la Grèce Préclassique*, Paris 1970.

AthMitt: *Mitteilungen des Deutschen Archäologischen Instituts, Athenische Abteilung.*

AttiMGrecia: *Atti e Memorie della Società Magna Grecia.*

BABesch: *Bulletin van de Vereeniging tot Bevordering der Kennis van de Antieke Beschaving te 'S-Gravenhage*, Amsterdam.

BaghdMitt: *Mitteilungen des Deutsches Archäologischen Instituts, Baghdader Abteilung.*

BASOR: *Bulletin of the American School of Oriental Research.*

BCH: *Bulletin de Correspondance Hellénique.*

BdA: *Bollettino d'Arte.*

Bedeutung: N. Himmelmann-Wildschütz, *Über einige gegenständliche Bedeutungsmöglichkeiten des frühgriechischen Ornaments*, Mainz, Akademie der Wiss. und der Liter., Abhandlungen der Geistes- und Sozialwissenschaftlichen Klasse, no. 7, 1968, 261–345 (also paged independently, as monograph).

Belleten: *Belleten Türk Tarih Kurumu.*

Berger: E. Berger, *Das Basler Arztrelief, Studien zum griechischen Grab- und Votivrelief um 500 v. Chr. und zur vorippokratischen Medizin* (Veröffentlichungen des Antikenmuseums Basel, 1) Basel 1970.

Berve & Gruben: H. Berve, G. Gruben, M. Hirmer, *Greek Temples, Theatres and Shrines*, New York 1962.

Blümel: C. Blümel, *Die archaisch griechischen Skulpturen der Staatlichen Museen zu Berlin*, Berlin 1963.

BMMA: *Bulletin of the Metropolitan Museum of Art, New York.*

Boardman: J. Boardman, *The Greeks Overseas, The Archaeology of their early colonies and trade*, Pelican Books, 2d ed., 1973.

Boersma: J. S. Boersma, *Athenian Building Policy from 561/0 to 405/4 B.C.*, Gröningen 1970.

BonnJhr: *Bonner Jahrbücher.*

Bookidis: N. Bookidis, "A Study of the Use and Geographical Distribution of Architectural Sculpture in the Archaic Period (Greece, East Greece and Magna Graecia)," Bryn Mawr College Ph.D. Dissertation 1967 (University Microfilms no. 68–4690). (In her Catalogue: P = Pediments; M = Metopes; F = Friezes.)

Boston Cat.: L. D. Caskey, *Catalogue of Greek and Roman Sculpture, Boston, Museum of Fine Arts*, Cambridge, Mass., 1925.

BrBr: H. Brunn, F. Bruckmann, P. Arndt, and G. Lippold, *Denkmäler griechischer und römischer Skulptur*, Munich 1888–1947.

BrMusCat: *British Museum, Catalogue of Sculpture in the Department of Greek and Roman Antiquities*, vol. 1, part 1, by F. N. Pryce, London 1928; vol. 3, by A. H. Smith, London 1904.

Brouskari: M. S. Brouskari, *The Acropolis Museum, A Descriptive Catalogue*, Athens 1974.

BSA: *Annual of the British School at Athens.*

BSR: British School of Archaeology at Rome, *Papers.*

BullClev: *The Bulletin of the Cleveland Museum of Art*, Cleveland, Ohio

Bundgaard: J. A. Bundgaard, *The Excavation of the Athenian Acropolis 1882–1890, The Original Drawings edited from the papers of Georg Kawerau* (University of Copenhagen, Institute of Classical and Near Eastern Archaeology Publication 1), Copenhagen 1974.

CSCA: *California Studies in Classical Antiquity*, Berkeley.

Collignon: M. Collignon, *Les statues funéraires dans l'art grec*, Paris 1911.

Cook: R. M. Cook, "Origins of Greek Sculpture," *JHS* 87 (1967) 24–32.

Corfu: G. Dontas, *A Guide to the Archaeological Museum of Corfu*, Athens, 1972.

Crd'A: *Critica d'arte, rivista di arti figurative.*

CronArch: Università di Catania, *Cronache di Archeologia e di Storia dell'Arte*

Cummer: W. W. Cummer, "Phrygian Roof Tiles in the Burdur Museum," *Anatolia* 14 (1970) 29–54.

CVA: *Corpus Vasorum Antiquorum.*

Dädalische Kunst: *Dädalische Kunst auf Kreta im 7. Jahrhundert v. Chr.*, Museum für Kunst und Gewerbe, Hamburg, Mainz 1970.

Davaras: C. Davaras, *Die Statue aus Astritsi, Ein Beitrag zur dädalischen Kunst auf Kreta und zu den Anfängen der griechischen Plastik*, *AntK* Beiheft 8, Bern 1972.

Dedications: A. E. Raubitschek, *Dedications from the Athenian Akropolis*, Cambridge (Mass.) 1949.

Delivorrias: A. Delivorrias, *Attische Giebelskulpturen und Akrotere des fünften Jahrhunderts v. Chr.*, Tübinger Studien zur Archäologie und Kunstgeschichte vol. 1, Tübingen 1974.

Delos: *Exploration archéologique de Délos, faite par l'École française d'Athènes*, Paris 1909–

Delphes: P. de la Coste Messelière & G. de Miré, *Delphes*, Paris 1947.

Deonna: W. Deonna, *Les "Apollons archaïques,"* Geneva 1909.

Deyhle: W. Deyhle, "Meisterfragen der archaischen Plastik Attikas," *AthMitt* 84 (1969) 1–64.

Dinsmoor: W. B. Dinsmoor, *The Architecture of Ancient Greece*, London 1950.

Dörig: J. Dörig, "La Tête Webb, l'Harmodios d'Anténor et le Problème des Copies Romaines d'après des chefs-d'œuvre archaïques," *AntK* 12 (1969) 41–50.

EAA: *Enciclopedia dell'Arte Antica, Classica e Orientale*, Rome 1958–1966; Suppl. vol. 1970; Atlas vol. 1973.

Edlund-Gantz: I. Edlund-Gantz, "The Seated Statue Akroteria from Poggio Civitate (Murlo)," *Dialoghi di Archeologia* 6 (1972) 167–235.

Erzählung: N. Himmelmann-Wildschütz, *Erzählung und Figur in der archaischen Kunst*, Mainz, Akademie der Wiss. und der Liter., Abhandlungen der Geistes- und Sozialwissenschaftlichen Klasse no. 2, 1967, 73–101 (also paged independently, as monograph).

ÉtTh: *Études Thasiennes*, École Française d'Athènes, Paris 1944–

Expedition: *Expedition*, The Magazine of Archaeology/Anthropology, The University Museum, University of Pennsylvania, Philadelphia (Pa.).

FA: *Fasti Archaeologici.*

FdD: *Fouilles de Delphes*, École Française d'Athènes, Paris 1902–

FdX: *Fouilles de Xanthos*, Institut Français d'Archéologie d'Istanbul, 1958–

Foce del Sele: P. Zancani Montuoro and U. Zanotti Bianco, *Heraion alla Foce del Sele*, Rome, vol. 1, 1951; vol. 2, 1954.

"Frieze": B. S. Ridgway, "Notes on the Development of the Greek Frieze," *Hesperia* 35 (1966) 188–204.

Gabelmann: H. Gabelmann, *Studien zum frühgriechischen Löwenbild* (Berlin 1965) with catalogue.

Gauer: W. Gauer, *Weihgeschenke aus der Perserkriegen, IstMitt* Beiheft 2, 1968.

GBA: *Gazette des beaux-arts.*

GdD: Ph. Bruneau & J. Ducat, *Guide de Délos*, École Française d'Athènes, 2d ed., Paris 1966.

GdTh: *Guide de Thasos*, École Française d'Athènes, Paris 1968.

GGA: *Göttingische gelehrte Anzeigen.*

Gortina: G. Rizza & V. Santa Maria Scrinari, *Il Santuario sull'Acropoli di Gortina*, Rome 1968.

"Grabmalbasen": F. Willemsen, "Archaische Grabmalbasen aus der Athener Stadtmauer," *AthMitt* 78 (1963) 104–53.

"Gravestones": L. H. Jeffery, "The Inscribed Gravestones of Archaic Attica," *BSA* 57 (1962) 115–53.

GRBS: *Greek, Roman and Byzantine Studies.*

Greek Art: R. Carpenter, *Greek Art, A Study of the Formal Evolution of Style*, Philadelphia 1962.

Greek Sculpture: R. Carpenter, *Greek Sculpture, A Critical Review*, Chicago 1960.

Guralnick: E. Guralnick, "Kouroi, Canon and Men: A Computer Study of Proportions," *Computer Studies in the Humanities and Verbal Behavior* 4 (1973) 77–80.

Hanfmann: G.M.A. Hanfmann, *From Croesus to Constantine*, Ann Arbor (Mich.) 1975.

Herdejürgen: H. Herdejürgen, *Untersuchungen zur thronenden Göttin aus Tarent in Berlin und zur archaischen und archaistischen Schrägmanteltracht*, Waldsassen-Bayern 1968.

Hesperia: *Hesperia*, Journal of the American School of Classical Studies at Athens.

Hiller: H. Hiller, *Ionische Grabreliefs der ersten Hälfte des 5. Jhrh. v. Chr., IstMitt* Beiheft 12, 1975. (In her Catalogue: O = Ostionische Grabreliefs; K = Kykladisch-Ionische Grabreliefs; N = Nordionische Grabreliefs; I = Italisch-Ionische Grabreliefs.)

Himera I: A. Adriani et al., *Himera I, Campagne di Scavo 1963–1965*, Rome 1970.

Hölscher: F. Hölscher, *Die Bedeutung archaischer Tierkampfbilder*, Beiträge zur Archäologie 5, Würzburg 1972.

Homann-Wedeking: E. Homann-Wedeking, *Die Anfänge der griechischen Grossplastik*, Munich 1950.

Hrouda: B. Hrouda, *Die Kulturgeschichte des assyrischen Flachbildes*, Bonn 1965.

HSCP: *Harvard Studies in Classical Philology*.

IG: *Inscriptiones Graecae*.

Isler-Kerenyi: I. Isler-Kerenyi, *Nike, Der Typus der laufenden Flügelfrau in archaischer Zeit*, Zürich/Stuttgart 1969.

IstForsch: Deutsches archäologisches Institut, *Istanbuler Forschungen*, 1932–

IstMitt: *Mitteilungen des Deutschen Archäologischen Instituts, Istanbuler Abteilung*.

Jacob-Felsch: M. Jacob-Felsch, *Die Entwicklung griechischer Statuenbasen und die Aufstellung der Statuen*, Waldsassen/Bayern 1969.

JdI: *Jahrbuch des Deutschen Archäologischen Instituts*.

JEA: *Journal of Egyptian Archaeology*.

JHS: *Journal of Hellenic Studies*.

JHS ArchR: *JHS Archaeological Reports*.

JOAI: *Jahreshefte des oesterreichischen archäologischen Instituts*.

KAnat: E. Akurgal, *Die Kunst Anatoliens von Homer bis Alexander*, Berlin 1961.

Karouzou: S. Karouzou, *National Archaeological Museum, Collection of Sculpture, a Catalogue*, Athens 1968.

Kerameikos: *Kerameikos, Ergebnisse der Ausgrabungen*, Berlin, various dates.

Kleine: J. Kleine, *Untersuchungen zur Chronologie der attischen Kunst von Peisistratos bis Themistokles, IstMitt* Beiheft 8, 1973.

Korai: G.M.A. Richter, *Korai, Archaic Greek Maidens*, London 1968.

Korkyra 2: G. Rodenwaldt, *Korkyra, Die Bildwerke des Artemistempels*, Berlin 1939.

Kouroi: G.M.A. Richter, *Kouroi, Archaic Greek Youths*, 1st ed. 1942, 2d ed. 1960, 3d ed. 1970. (The second edition is completely different from the first, but the third differs from the second only in a number of addenda, both to the catalogue of statues and to the bibliography. The numbers in my text basically refer to those of the 2d ed., but the numbers accompanied by a, b, or c indicate additions to be found in the third edition.)

Kranz: P. Kranz, "Frühe griechische Sitzfiguren—Zum Problem der Typenbildung und des orientalischen Einflusses in der frühen griechischen Rundplastik," *AthMitt* 87 (1972) 1–55.

Kurtz & Boardman: D. C. Kurtz and J. Boardman, *Greek Burial Customs*, Oxford 1971.

Kyrieleis: H. Kyrieleis, *Throne und Klinen, JdI* Erganzungheft 24, Berlin 1969.

Langlotz: E. Langlotz & M. Hirmer, *The Art of Magna Graecia*, London 1965.

Local Scripts: L. H. Jeffery, *The Local Scripts of Archaic Greece*, Oxford 1961.

Lullies & Hirmer: R. Lullies & M. Hirmer, *Greek Sculpture*, 2d ed., New York 1960.

Mallwitz: A. Mallwitz, *Olympia und seine Bauten*, Munich 1972.

"Man-and-Dog": B. S. Ridgway, "The Man-and-Dog Stelai," *JdI* 86 (1971) 60–79.

MarbWinckPr: *Marburger Winckelmann-Programm*.

MdI: *Mitteilungen des Deutschen Archäologischen Instituts* (1948–1953).

MélRome: *Mélanges d'archéologie et d'histoire de l'École Française de Rome.*

MemAcInscr: *Mémoires présentés par divers savants à l'Académie des inscriptions et belles lettres.*

MemLinc: *Memorie della Accademia Nazionale dei Lincei.*

Mendel: Musées Impériaux Ottomans, G. Mendel, *Catalogue des Sculptures Grecques, Romaines et Byzantines*, 3 vv., Istanbul 1912–1914.

Meola: E. Meola, *Terrecotte Orientalizzanti di Gela ("Daedalica" Siciliae), MonAnt* serie miscellanea 1:1 (vol. 48 of general series) 1971.

MittKairo: *Mitteilungen des Deutschen Instituts für ägyptische Altertumskunde, Kairo.*

MMA: G.M.A. Richter, *Catalogue of Greek Sculptures in the Metropolitan Museum of Art*, Oxford and Cambridge (Mass.) 1954.

MMS: *Metropolitan Museum Studies.*

MonAnt: *Monumenti Antichi* (Accademia dei Lincei).

MonPiot: *Monuments et mémoires publ. par l'Académie des inscriptions et belles lettres, Fondation Piot.*

MUSE: *MUSE*, Annual of the Museum of Art and Archaeology, University of Missouri, Columbia 1967–

MusHelv: *Museum Helveticum.*

NSc: *Notizie degli Scavi di Antichità.*

Ny Carlsberg: F. Poulsen, *Ny Carlsberg Glyptothek, Catalogue of Ancient Sculpture*, English ed., Copenhagen 1951.

OlBer: Deutsches archäologisches Institut, *Bericht über die Ausgrabungen in Olympia*, Berlin 1937–

OlForsch: Deutsches archäologisches Institut, *Olympische Forschungen*, 1944–

OpRom: *Opuscula Romana, Acta Instituti Romani Regni Sueiciae.*

Opus Nobile: P. Zazoff, ed., *Opus Nobile. Festschrift zum 60. Geburtstag von Ulf Jantzen*, Wiesbaden 1969.

Papaspyridi: S. Papaspyridi, *Guide du Musée National d'Athènes*, Athens 1927.

Paribeni: E. Paribeni, *Catalogo delle Sculture di Cirene*, Rome 1959.

Payne: H. Payne & G. Mackworth Young, *Archaic Marble Sculpture from the Acropolis*, 2d ed., London 1950.

Poggio Civitate: Soprintendenza alle Antichità d'Etruria, *Poggio Civitate, The Archaic Etruscan Sanctuary*, Catalogue of the Exhibition, Florence-Siena 1970.

ProcPhilSoc: *Proceedings of the American Philosophical Society.*

Ptoion: J. Ducat, *Les Kouroi du Ptoion*, Paris 1971.

QuadLibia: *Quaderni di archeologia della Libia*, 1950–

RA: *Revue archéologique.*

REA: *Revue des études anciennes.*

RendNap: *Rendiconti della Accademia di Archeologia, Lettere ed Arti*, Naples.

RendPontAcc: *Atti della Pontificia Accademia Romana di Archeologia, Rendiconti.*

Ruinen: G. Kleiner, *Die Ruinen von Milet*, Berlin 1968.

S. *&* S.: G.M.A. Richter, *The Sculpture and Sculptors of the Greeks*, New Haven 1950 edition.

Samos XI: B. Freyer-Schauenburg, *Bildwerke der archaischen Zeit und des strengen Stils*, *Samos* vol. XI, Bonn 1974.

Schefold: K. Schefold, *Die Griechen und ihre Nachbarn*, Propyläen Kunstgeschichte vol. 1, Berlin 1967.

Severe Style: B. S. Ridgway, *The Severe Style in Greek Sculpture*, Princeton 1970.

Sicile Grecque: G. & V. de Mirè, F. Villard, *Sicile Grecque*, Paris 1955.

Signatures: J. Marcadé, *Recueil des Signatures de Sculpteurs Grecs*, vol. 1, Paris 1953; vol. 2, 1957.

Stähler: K. Stähler, "Zur Rekonstruktion und Datierung des Gigantomachiegiebels von der Akropolis," *Festschrift Hans Erich Stier*, Münster 1972.

"Stelen": F. Willemsen, "Stelen," *AthMitt* 85 (1970) 23–44.

StEtr: *Studi Etruschi.*

Strommenger & Hirmer: E. Strommenger & M. Hirmer, *5000 Years of the Art of Mesopotamia*, New York 1964.

"Theräisches": N. Kontoleon, "Theräisches," *AthMitt* 73 (1958) 117–39.

Travlos: J. Travlos, *Pictorial Dictionary of Ancient Athens*, New York, Washington, 1971.

Tuchelt: K. F. Tuchelt, *Die archaischen Skulpturen von Didyma, Beiträge zur frühgriechischen Plastik in Kleinasien*, Istanbuler Forschungen 27, Berlin 1970. (Numbers preceded by K refer to items in the Catalogue, for which Tuchelt provides full discussion. Numbers preceded by L refer to the List of works cited by Tuchelt for comparanda, which gives bibliography. Though Tuchelt's list is quite comprehensive, it is not all-inclusive because of its specific comparative scope.)

Van Buren: E. D. Van Buren, *Greek Fictile Revetments in the Archaic Period*, London 1926.

Wallenstein: K. Wallenstein, *Korinthische Plastik des 7. und 6. Jahrhunderts v. Chr.*, Bonn 1971.

Wiegand: T. Wiegand, *Die archaische Poros-Architektur der Akropolis zu Athen*, Cassel and Leipzig 1904.

Willers: D. Willers, *Zu den Anfängen der archaistischen Plastik in Griechenland*, *AthMitt* Beiheft 4, Berlin 1975.

Winter: N. Winter, "Terracotta Representations of Human Heads used as Architectural Decoration in the Archaic Period," Bryn Mawr College Ph.D. Dissertation 1974.

PART I

DEFINING ARCHAIC SCULPTURE

Chapter 1

Problems of Chronology, Geography, and Typology

In both modern and ancient Greek, from which the term archaic derives, the adjective is used to indicate anything belonging to the remote past, without any qualitative judgment. It is only in the archaeological sphere that the word has acquired a technical meaning, to indicate that specific period of Greek culture from ca. 650 to 480 BC.

This archaeological use of the word began in the last decades of the Nineteenth century. Scholars like M. Collignon, J. Overbeck, and H. Brunn, avoided the term in publications prior to 1882 but used it in its new, restrictive meaning after 1885. Nonetheless, no complete agreement has as yet been reached either on the chronological span or on the artistic fields covered by the expression. P. Ducati, for instance, included the Geometric phase within his definition of Archaic, thus stretching the chronological brackets to 1000–480 while more recent studies primarily concerned with vase painting would place the beginning of the Archaic period at about 720, thus making it coincide with the phase of Orientalizing influence on Greek art.

Were it true by definition that a period should represent that span of time during which a specific style prevails and that therefore a change in style should mark the end of that period, it would be accurate to say that an Archaic period extending from 650 to 480 cannot properly accommodate vase painting and architecture. Our more refined understanding of pottery styles and wares allows much greater subtlety in dating. We also know that styles changed at different times in different areas and that no unity can be assumed even in one region alone within the conventional 650–480 span. In Attica, for instance, the Orientalizing style began around 700, changed to Black Figure around 620–610, and to Red Figure around 525, but while both techniques continued well into the Fourth century, the style itself changed at different points, e.g., ca. 460. The same situation applies to Lakonian, Rhodian, and other wares. As for architecture, we now know that imposing peristyle temples built entirely, or primarily, of stone were erected as early as ca. 700, in a continuous line of development which seems undisturbed by the 650 watermark. Nor does history, in any one area *of Greece*, justify the adoption of this specific date. It would seem, therefore, as if the Archaic period as canonically defined could refer only to sculpture.

Richter, in *Archaic Greek Art Against its Historical Background* (1949), seems thus to restrict the term despite her more inclusive title. In her Introduction (p. xxii) she discusses in fact the beginning of monumental stone sculpture, which, largely through relative chronology, can be placed approximately around the middle of the Seventh century. Here too, however, some further refinement is necessary since the so-called Daedalic style, which appears primarily in the minor arts, has produced some large-scale works in stone which can be dated toward the very end of the Seventh century or even later. It should therefore be recognized at the outset that a more accurate discussion of ancient art should refer to it by centuries rather than by periods or styles, and that no definite evidence exists for setting the beginning of the Archaic period at mid century.

This conclusion applies specifically to the chronological limits given to the term; yet there is a second, more important connotation, a stylistic one, which transcends the more refined subdivisions and seems to apply to the period as a whole. We do mean something specific when we speak of Archaic style, even if the picture conjured up by the word fits by and large only the production of the Sixth century. From a stylistic, especially a sculptural, point of view, the expression is therefore capable of precise definition.

Etymologically, archaic means "from the beginning or origin," and thus serves well to characterize those early stages in Greek sculpture which were to lead to the famous Classical masterpieces. If large-scale sculpture in other media existed in Greece prior to 650 (and this will be discussed in Chapter 2), it is only from ca. 600 onwards that a common interest in stone statuary spread throughout the Greek cities, promoting a style which can be easily identified despite all possible variations in region or time. This phase had all the excitement of a true beginning, with artists traveling from place to place sharing innovations and technical information, dedicating and signing their own work in a novel display of professional pride which cannot be overemphasized.

Other manifestations of Greek art from this period exhibit the same traits of style—if these traits be isolated in their most general application—and perhaps the most significant trait of all is the relative rapidity with which changes occurred within a given medium or class. Demand increased production, and increased production resulted in increased skill and technical development, be it in poetry, painting, or metal work. Every form of artistic expression seemed to find impetus in those pregnant years of the Sixth century, and even utilitarian objects, such as coins, tools, or weapons, seemed to partake of an increased artistic interest. From the Sixth century onward every artistic change can be understood and the next step predicted, with a fair amount of accuracy on our part, down to the Fourth century (and perhaps we might venture even beyond this point, if our knowledge of the Hellenistic period were greater) because we are now in the mainstream of what is usually called Classical art. The beginning of this artistic mode cannot be found, for instance, in the Daedalic or Orientalizing styles, which represent dead-end streets. In contrast with Archaic art, all preceding manifestations of Greek artistic activity neither explain nor adequately prepare us for the specific outburst of the Sixth century, and they remain more easily classified under regional headings and typological categories.

In speaking of stylistic changes, it is difficult to avoid such terms as development and evolution, yet they imply a sort of organic growth that moves from an imperfect or incomplete beginning to later fruition and fulfillment, and thus involve an element of judgment. Evolutionary theories on art already colored the ancient Roman sources, and both Quintilian and Cicero described Greek sculpture as moving from a rigid, unnatural style to a more realistic and softer expression. In recent times, Richter's pioneering work has helped crystallize a conception of Archaic sculpture as consistently striving toward increased naturalism and anatomical faithfulness. These criteria are useful in determining relative chronology and groupings; they may become dangerous, however, when too strictly applied or when seen as the single motivating factor behind the sculptor's expression. Though the general principle of increasing naturalism may apply to Archaic art as a whole, the degree of naturalism attained at any given time could vary not only from area to area but even from type to type. Nor can one work be considered more or less aesthetically successful than another because of its greater or lesser degree of naturalism. In my approach I shall therefore attempt to avoid qualitative judgments based exclusively on evolutionary principles, and will try to speak of changes rather than development. This task is relatively easier now, when Archaic art strikes a positive response in a modern generation attuned to primitive sculpture. It would have been proportionately harder in the aesthetic climate of the Nineteenth century, which appreciated only Classical Greek art, or of the Eighteenth century, when Classical sculpture meant essentially Roman classicizing and the Elgin marbles could be found crude and disappointing.

It is, however, helpful that such negative judgment on Archaic sculpture prevailed in Roman times, since it meant that there was little demand for originals of that period, and consequently little demand also for replicas of such works. Our understanding of later periods is greatly complicated by the fact that original Greek works are often totally lost and must be studied exclusively through the Roman replicas. Without such Roman copies, it is true, we would have no knowledge whatever of major masters like Polykleitos or Myron, and hardly more of Pheidias and Praxiteles. On the other hand, the Roman copyist inevitably distorted the original in transposing its medium or in introducing stylistic traits and techniques proper to his own time. It is often impossible to decide what is Classical and what is Hadrianic or Antonine in a Roman copy of a Greek work, and it is not always clear whether a statue reflects a lost Greek prototype or is an actual Roman creation echoing earlier styles.

This problem does not arise for Archaic sculpture. Although a few pieces exist which may perhaps be considered copies of Sixth century originals, these are so few as to be unnecessary for our understanding of the style. We have still suffered a grievous loss through the almost complete disappearance of Archaic bronze sculpture of large scale, yet what remains in marble or limestone, though fragmentary, has come down to us directly, without later intermediaries.

It is difficult to explain the Roman copyists' discrimination against Archaic works, especially since Archaistic statues seem to have been fashionable during the early Empire. Nor can the attitude be explained by the theory that Sixth century statues were no longer visible by the First century of our era. Many of them still stood in the great panhellenic sanctuaries, and even the Athenian Akropolis, which had been so severely damaged by the Persians in 480–479, displayed at least one Archaic Athena at the time of Pausanias' visit in the Second century AD. We can therefore only assume that taste was primarily responsible for this Roman omission. A second factor may be the relative anonymity of Archaic sculpture, which tended to concentrate on generic types and may not have suited the propagandistic and pedagogical inclinations of the Roman patrons. People like Cicero would have found little inspirational value in anonymous statues of kouroi and korai, while they could respond to the religious symbolism of divine images or to the historical and anecdotical value of an anarchical group like the Tyrannicides. For purely decorative purposes, the Severe style may have seemed more appropriate and dignified for statuary in the round. The reasons for the creation of Archaistic sculpture will be discussed in a later chapter.

CHRONOLOGICAL LIMITS OF THE PERIOD

The advantage of dealing directly with original works is offset by the almost total lack of chronological information on the sculptures themselves. Archaeological and literary evidence is minimal, historical connections are few and mostly unsafe. In placing the beginning of monumental sculpture around 660, scholars have focused on the date of Psammetichus I's conquest of Egypt. In his efforts to rid his country of the Assyrian invader, the first Egyptian pharaoh of the XXVI Dynasty had been greatly helped by Ionian and Karian mercenaries, whom he rewarded by assigning them two "camps" on either side of the Pelusian branch of the Nile. This correlation is, however, based on the assumption that Greek monumental sculpture could not have originated without direct influence from Egypt. Although this theory may be basically valid, the very nature of the settlements suggested by their military name (Stratopeda) seems unlikely to promote artistic exchange. Unfortunately, these two sites have not yet been identified and therefore archaeological evidence is lacking. Subsequent Greek foundations in Egypt are given considerably later dates by the historical sources; that these sources are unreliable is shown by archaeological finds of much greater antiquity at those sites in Egypt which have so far been identified. But if we disregard the literary sources and follow archaeological evidence alone, we lose the fixed date provided by Egyptian history. It should moreover be noted that very little sculpture has been found in the Greek sites in Egypt: basically only statuettes, much more Egyptian in appearance and medium than anything from other Greek areas.

The lower limit for the Archaic period seems much more solidly established by the date of the Persian destruction of the Athenian Akropolis. But it is at once obvious that this historical disaster involved Athens alone; yet the change in style, from Archaic to Severe, occurred throughout the Greek world and is therefore not determined by a specific *tabula rasa* condition which might have forced the artists to replace damaged monuments and might have spurred them to greater stylistic experimentation. The true significance of the Athenian disaster is that it gives a definite *terminus ante quem* for all the statues buried within the so-called *Perserschutt* (Persian debris), in vast trenches dug along the south and north sides of the Akropolis to contain the votives damaged by the Persians. Within these deposits, however, were placed objects made at different times; though none of them could postdate 480, we have no way of knowing how much earlier they had been dedicated. The problem is further complicated by the fact that some of the trenches have yielded a mixed fill, with some definitely post-Persian material. Other sculptures seem to have been buried at an earlier time, perhaps with the purpose of modernizing the sanctuary under the Peisistratids, and are therefore called *Tyrannenschutt*, tyrant debris. Under these circumstances, the validity of this chronological fixed point becomes somewhat more limited. It is perhaps worth noting that a more reliable indication of stylistic changes in Athens is given by a work known only through Roman replicas, namely, the Tyrannicides made by Kritios and Nesiotes in 477 (as dated by the Marmor Parium); although marble copies of bronze originals, these statues clearly show that the Archaic style had by that date been superseded by what is traditionally called the Severe style.

Nothing comparable to this Persian destruction can be found outside of Athens; the invasion did not touch the Peloponnesos, and at Eleusis very little can be associated with enemy action. In Eretria, the Persian attack of 490, just before Marathon, gives a *terminus ante quem* for the pedimental sculptures of the temple of Apollo Daphnephoros; but again, neither a *post quem* nor other Archaic material is available. In Asia Minor and the islands the Persians' hostility was felt earlier, around 494, but no statuary has been directly connected with these historical events.

METHODS OF DATING

Within these two chronological brackets—650/480—fixed points are very rare, and most of them debatable. All attempts at dating Archaic sculpture have had to fall back largely on relative chronology, that is, what can be established by placing all available statues in a "logical" sequence, where each piece *looks* later than the preceding but earlier than the following. Sufficient time is then allowed for "development" from one step to the next; and since the total chronological span involves merely 160 years, a great deal of time is given to presumably slow beginnings while the quickened pace of the late Sixth—early Fifth century is measured by ten or even five year intervals. This approach is, of course, defensible as a working method; it is nevertheless open to several dangers: 1) It starts from a preconceived theory of naturalistic development which tends to put at the beginning of the series what looks less, and at the end what looks more, natural; yet we cannot be sure that this corresponds to the actual order of production by the ancient sculptors. The arrangement appears logical because it has been logically organized by the modern researcher, according to assumed premises, but nothing forced the Archaic master to strict adherence to logical principles, be it even that of ever closer imitation of nature. 2) When naturalistic development is seen specifically in terms of individual anatomical details, it is possible to place excessive importance on single features at the expense of a more comprehensive vision of the whole. Some masters may have been especially interested in certain anatomical traits while disregarding others. 3) Regional preferences, outside influences or even individual tempo from sculptor to sculptor cannot be properly assessed through such a procedure. 4) Scholars differ in their evaluation of what constitutes early or late features, so that relative chronology remains largely subjective.

Richter, whose impact on Archaic studies will always remain considerable, has been the strongest supporter of this method of dating based on internal, naturalistic development. She has nonetheless tried to support her suggestions with all available external evidence and has conveniently summarized her dating criteria in introductory chapters to her groupings of Kouroi and Korai in her well-known books by the same name. In general terms, her comparative material is represented by: 1) stylistic correlations between male and female statues (where, of course, the same sequential principles prevail since both series were established by the same author); 2) comparison with Proto-Corinthian, Corinthian, and Attic vase painting (which may have limited value for sculpture produced in Asia Minor or Sicily); 3) comparison with plastic heads adorning Middle and Late Corinthian pyxides. Here again the sphere of influence may be limited, and the correlation between a monumental statue carved in stone and a miniature head modeled in clay may be questioned; 4) correlation with epigraphy; 5) with history or historical figures, and 6) with architecture.

Before discussing these last three categories, a word of caution should perhaps be added to the comments concerning the correlation between sculpture and vase painting. In this approach Richter had been preceded by other scholars, notably Ernst Langlotz in his fundamental study, *Zur Zeitbestimmung der strengrotfigurigen Vasenmalerei und der gleichzeitigen Plastik* (Leipzig 1920). The strictures inherent in this method can be summarized as follows: a) the difference in media, and more specifically the difference between a three-dimensional and a two-dimensional representation, is bound to affect stylistic renderings, thus invalidating the comparisons; b) it cannot be proved that sculpture and vase painting proceeded at the same pace of development; in some areas of experimentation (e.g., foreshortening, rendering of folds, etc.) the painter seems ahead of the sculptor, while at times the opposite situation appears to prevail; c) the chronology of Attic vase painting is also largely based on stylistic analysis and is therefore a relative chronology with few objective points. Proto-Corinthian and Corinthian are more reliably dated by correlation with the foundation dates of the Western colonies but these latter are still open to dispute, and the evaluation of the evidence is subject to the chance of the finds. Although we have, in general, a better grasp of the development of vase painting than of sculpture, thanks to J. D. Beazley and Humfry Payne, what is still tentative and theoretical in such chronology should not be forgotten.

A similar problem undermines the validity of dating sculpture through *epigraphy*. Here the most important contributions have been made by A. E. Raubitschek, *Dedications from the Athenian Akropolis*, 1949, and L. H. Jeffery, *The Local Scripts of Archaic Greece*, 1961. The former has analyzed the inscribed bases from the Athenian sanctuary and has suggested connections with the extant sculptures, while the latter has extended her analysis to other areas of the Greek world, devoting great attention to inscriptions on statuary. Yet in both cases external information remains tenuous; absolute dates are largely based on letter forms (thus on a stylistic analysis of sorts) and at times even on the appearance of the sculpture, so that a somewhat circular argument is established.

Correlating monuments with *history or historical figures* may be equally dangerous or, at best, vague. In many cases, what we know of sculptural development seems at variance with our historical information, and ancient sources do not always agree on the dates of battles and events. A case in point is the battle of Pallene, which has been variously assigned to 547, 541, 536 or even later; yet the well-known kouros (erected for a man named Kroisos, who is supposed to have died in that battle) seems to have been carved after 530, and we cannot even be sure that the deceased met his fate in that event. Examples could easily be multiplied and will be mentioned in later chapters at the appropriate point in the discussion.

The last chronological criterion, a correlation with *architecture*, is perhaps the soundest since more than one category of evidence (stratigraphy, history, architectural style, at times even epigraphy) can be brought to bear on each instance. The one absolute date we have for an Archaic monument is that of the Siphnian Treasury at Delphi, fortunately a small building abundantly decorated with sculpture, which is dated before 525. This date is ultimately based on the historical coincidence of a Greek with an Egyptian event since the Samian attack which caused, or contributed to, the end of Siphnian prosperity, occurred at the time when King Cambyses of Persia invaded Egypt. This event is dated to 525/4, the fifth regnal year of the monarch, whose entire reign spans the years from 530 to 522. More uncertain is the actual erection of the Siphnian Treasury, so that 525 remains basically another *terminus ante quem*. We do know that Siphnian affluence was short-lived, and the Treasury is small enough to have been built with relative speed. It should nonetheless be stressed here that even this one landmark in Archaic chronology contains an element of uncertainty.

Another reference point, whose validity has been overemphasized, is the Artemision at Ephesos, which is usually referred to as Kroisos' temple. Its importance for sculpture lies in the ivory and bronze figurines found under its foundations, and in the relief decoration of its column drums and parapet. According to ancient Greek sources, King Kroisos of Lydia paid for most of the columns and in general made generous contributions to the temple treasure. Since Kroisos reigned from 561 to 547, the Artemision has usually been dated around 550. But such enormous buildings as the Ephesian temple or other comparable Asia Minor structures remained under construction for several generations, and in some cases were even left unfinished. Since Kroisos contributed only financial help, the actual execution of the donated columns could have taken place considerably later. As for the parapet sculpture, it shows unmistakable signs of differing styles, as one would expect in a building which took over a hundred years to complete. The figurines under its foundations come from a mixed context which allows only stylistic dating, and we cannot anchor the beginning of the "Kroisos' Artemision" to any specific moment in Kroisos' reign. The enterprise is likely to have been a collective one as suggested by some ancient sources, and it could conceivably have started before Kroisos' accession. This problem too will be discussed in greater detail at another point. Suffice it here to stress, in summary, that very little evidence exists for absolute dates within the Archaic period, so that Richter's stylistic analysis has been largely responsible for our ideas on the dating of Archaic sculpture. Her position has been recently challenged by Harrison, who has made a strong case for substantially lowering most of Richter's dates. But Harrison's work is primarily concerned with Attic sculpture, and specifically with sculpture from the Athenian Agora, so that her discussion tends to omit monuments in East Greece or Magna Graecia. Himmelmann-Wildschütz and Tuchelt have attempted a corresponding study, this time slanted exclusively in the direction of Asia Minor. The Western Greeks, despite Langlotz's work on their art, still present a cloudy picture in need of clarification.

Chronology is a very natural preoccupation of art historians and archaeologists. It should nonetheless be stated that within the general context of Archaic sculpture little can be gained by shifting a monument one or two decades up or down the chronological scale. Given our present lack of fixed points, it seems more profitable to concentrate on determining general trends rather than on attempting to write the Annals of Archaic Greek sculpture. I shall therefore try to refrain from dating individual monuments precisely. On the other hand, history remains of primary importance in determining sculptural demands and stylistic changes, but history seen as social conditions rather than as specific (hence datable) events.

INFLUENCE OF GEOGRAPHY ON STYLE

If sculptural output is indeed influenced by general conditions, it follows naturally that different areas of Greek territory under different rule or different foreign influence should produce different forms of sculpture. Local sculptural schools have often been advocated, but never successfully isolated, for the Archaic period, so that only a general distinction between Greek and Asia Minor sculpture is easily defined and acknowledged. Further refinement is usually confined to specialized studies and has found virtually no echo in handbooks or reference works. Richter, with her emphasis on a cultural *koine* and on shared aims and sculptural techniques, has further contributed to obliterating the dividing lines between regional productions by dividing kouroi and korai into chronological rather than geographical groups. Her position seemed all the more defensible in view of the fact that much of Archaic statuary falls within distinctive types ubiquitously appearing throughout the Mediterranean basin.

Here again a more cautious position should be taken. Admittedly, Archaic sculptors traveled so frequently from place to place that it is difficult to isolate veritable schools; and the find spot of a statue cannot assure us of its nationality since monuments traveled almost as easily as the sculptors. On the other hand, a different approach can perhaps be tried by cutting across categories and by grouping sculpture geographically, as far as possible, since the chronological approach has already been extensively explored with ambivalent results. Each geographical area responded to different stimuli and had different interests, resulting in distinct iconography and style. It is not always possible, given the present state of our knowledge, to determine causes or discern effects, but the specific location of a city should always be kept in mind in examining its sculpture. It is, for instance, obvious that a site like Cyrene in North Africa, which did not possess marble quarries and was surrounded by Libyans with little or no interest in sculpture, should rely on imports for its Archaic art, at least as long as a local school of carving could not be established. On the contrary, cities like Miletos and Samos, with easy access to marble supplies and in close contact with the highly developed Oriental kingdoms, were bound to be influenced by the artistic production of their neighbors. The people of Poseidonia/Paestum must have rubbed elbows with the Etruscans; the inhabitants of Sicily must have been somewhat affected by Punic and native practices, as well as by the occasional waves of East Greek immigrants. In such complex contexts it is obviously difficult to identify what constitutes the local and what the imported element, but the attempt at analysis should be made.

The difficulty is compounded when the site itself is not in Greek territory but belongs to a Hellenophile community which presumably "imported" Greek masters. The obvious example for the Classical period is provided by the Karian Maussollos, who had his splendid tomb at Halikarnassos adorned by mainland Greeks. The Archaic Lycians and Lydians may have recruited their sculptors closer to home, but they seem to have anticipated Maussollos' practices.

THE SCOPE OF THIS BOOK

It is therefore necessary to outline the scope of this book, both in geographical and in chronological terms, and to explain its semantics and its basic method of approach. I shall here accept, for practical purposes, the conventional span 650–480 to define the Archaic period; hence Archaic, in the following pages, will denote either persons or objects belonging somewhere within the second half of the Seventh, the entire Sixth, and the first two decades of the Fifth century. In particular, Archaic will apply to the style of those years, yet it should be made clear that no abrupt conversion from the Archaic style is postulated at the fateful date of 480. Elements of the Severe style had already infiltrated works antedating 480 while a sort of "lingering Archaic" continued into the Severe period, and a new form of archaism appeared during Classical times. However, different terms will be used to describe such survivals or revivals of Archaic style. Conversely, monuments in Daedalic style or outside the mainstream of Archaic sculpture which fall within the selected time span will also be discussed. Geographically, I shall consider any sculpture found within Greece proper, including Macedonia; on any of the Greek islands, with the sole exclusion of Cyprus; and in all the Greek colonies, both East and West, with specific attention to Magna Graecia and Asia Minor. But while "Magna Graecian" will refer to both Sicilian and South Italian material, "Ionian" (or East Greek) will not mean exclusively from Asia Minor but also from the islands. Selected non-Greek material will be discussed when it seems either made by Greeks or under such strong Greek influence as to repay analysis, but I shall not attempt to consider either Persian or Etruscan sculpture in any depth, nor to stray too far afield from my main topic and area of competence. Yet I shall try to evaluate foreign elements and stimuli on Greek production, discussing in particular the problem of the origins of Archaic monumental sculpture. I shall proceed by types, not necessarily to outline their chronological development but rather to acknowledge their existence and diffusion throughout the Greek world, and to ask relevant questions concerning their adoption, appearance, and meaning. A tendency toward imitating nature will be taken for granted, but not as the primary aim of Archaic sculptors. Rather, I visualize the Greek sculptural process as starting from the premise that a statue depicts man in his physical (*not* metaphysical) reality, yet it remains a statue and as such is given a base. From such a premise would have developed the different types according to the different needs, meanings, and techniques. As sculptors perfected their techniques or changed their objectives, they may periodically have "checked" against nature, as it were, thus producing more naturalistic renderings. But this would remain only a secondary concern, so that discrepancies in anatomical accuracy or in the treatment of drapery may have occurred at any point, and certain types (e.g., the Korai) may actually have looked *less* realistic with the passing of time. Technique and its strictures will also be considered in analyzing both monuments and stylistic changes.

I shall restrict my analysis mainly to large-scale monuments in stone or bronze, excluding statuettes or works in terracotta unless their evidence contributes to the discussion. I shall not try to be encyclopaedic in my approach but shall select representative monuments, confining the analysis of additional pieces to footnotes. I shall focus on the production of the Archaic period proper, but a last chapter will be devoted to the difficult problem of Archaistic and Archaizing sculpture, that is, works carved after 480.

Since such works existed and could conceivably be mistaken for genuine Archaic sculpture, and since we proceed on the assumption that the Archaic period witnessed the emergence of a distinctive and widespread style, it seems profitable to isolate the most characteristic elements of such a style and to find the most general common denominator of these elements so that they may apply regardless of chronology and geographical origin. A certain amount of overlapping, or a causal relationship among traits, will at times be evident.

BASIC TRAITS OF ARCHAIC SCULPTURE

Frontality

This is possibly the most distinctive trait of statuary in the round. The term implies not only that the statue directly confronts the viewer but also that it obeys the *Law of Frontality*. This can be formulated as follows: if a line were drawn through the vertical center of a statue, the two resultant halves would be perfectly symmetrical and the weight of the figure would be evenly distributed on both legs. This formulation must allow, however, for different positions of the limbs, but never to the extent of altering the static balance of the torso. In particular, Archaic statues show little or no sign of experimentation with the *mechanism* of motion, understood as the shifts and changes in musculature commensurate with the action portrayed. Such interest in muscular movement and balance is here considered a distinctive trait of incipient Severe style.

Frontality may at times result in the reduced depth of a composition in the round, so that only the frontal and rear views may appear plausible in naturalistic terms, and the side views seem aesthetically irrelevant. In other cases, frontality may result in *quadrifaciality*, that is, each side of the statue is conceived as an entity to be viewed for itself, with individual features belonging to one or the other side with no crossing over. But this quadrifaciality is a phenomenon more limited in time and place, while frontality as here defined applies to completely rounded statues as well.

In terms of relief sculpture, frontality means that a frontal torso may be joined to legs in profile, but the rule of even distribution of weight should obtain. However, relief work is largely narrative by nature and allows greater freedom of positions which cannot all be included under such law.

This trait is closely connected with:

Symbolism

The activity which is not represented through inner motion is expressed instead through schematic poses. For instance, running is not realistically portrayed but symbolically shown by a figure bending one leg at a right angle while the knee of the other leg almost touches the ground. The human body is therefore transformed into something comparable to a hieroglyph for speed. Since symbolism needs to be explicit in order to be understood, much of Archaic sculpture results in exaggerated postures, like sign language. This trait may also be partly responsible for the creation and persistence of:

Standardization

Technical considerations and foreign influences may have contributed to the adoption of types: the seated figure, the naked male, the draped female, the guardian animal. Or they may represent another aspect of symbolism. These various motivations will be considered for each category. Here we need only isolate the trait. Statues vary in individual details, but they can still be grouped according to general characteristics. Only the inclusion of specific attributes (usually separately added to a more or less standard image) or of inscriptions serves to differentiate and identify the subject represented, if indeed greater characterization is attempted. By and large, however, the dedicant is mentioned but the statue itself is anonymous.

Decorativeness

This trait can be defined in more than one way, but my selection of the word focuses on the rich and ornate appearance of an Archaic work, be it in matter of details or in total impression. Ultimately this decorativeness stems from something comparable to symbolism: each feature, anatomical or otherwise, is rendered by means of patterns which only approximate, or allude to, the physical aspect of the detail portrayed. The most obvious example in this context is the representation of hair (human or animal) for which no single pattern is adopted, but all patterns used are more or less artificial and therefore result in elaboration and ornateness. The same applies to the rendering of drapery or of individual muscles.

Linearity can be listed as a sub-trait in this context. The term is here used to express the concept that each feature, or pattern, is given specific contours which serve as guidelines to the sculptor in carving. The result is often a series of grooves cut *into* the surface of the stone; even a ridge is rendered by depressing and enlarging the furrows which delimit it on either side. This technique is particularly obvious in the treatment of folds, whose flat ridges usually lie all at the same superficial level, while thin grooves separate them from one another. The effect of volume and greater plasticity is conveyed by undercutting the horizontal edges rather than by increasing the vertical depressions. In other words, Archaic sculpture relies largely on a sort of engraving technique and employs little modeling. By modeling I mean the rendering of volumes and individual features through the rise and fall of the surface, with smooth transitions between heaving and sinking planes. In drapery, modeling results in a rippling surface where folds are rendered farther apart and therefore fewer in number, as typical of the Severe style. On the other hand, Archaic drapery consists of closely packed (ironed out) *pleats* and superimposed flat layers separated from one another by undercutting.

Fractioning, a second sub-trait, is a consequence of the linearity just described, in that each feature is isolated through engraved contours and does not "organically" connect with the other features. The lack of transitional planes between features and the hieroglyphic determination of each trait result in a fractioned rendering, so that the whole appears as the sum total of various parts rather than as the fusion of correlated elements. This additive process increases the decorative effect of both sculpture in the round and relief.

Rapid Rate of Change Toward Naturalism

Since naturalism is here *not* considered an aim of Archaic sculptors, it can be recognized as a trait, that is, as an objective result. To formulate it differently, we can say that constant and rapid experimentation on the part of the Archaic masters produced an ever increasing appearance of naturalism in their statues, which however never attained complete realism. Paradoxically, the Archaic style ends when the rendering of sculptural anatomy ceases to be a recording of as many parts as are available in the human body and becomes a selective process whereby only significant features are included.

The Quality of Agalma

As a last characteristic of Archaic sculpture some authors would list the Archaic smile, or at least that appearance of bursting vitality and cheerful joie de vivre which seem to permeate Sixth century statues. While the Archaic smile is a definite rendering which can be graphically plotted and demonstrated, its ultimate origin has been attributed to different causes: some authors would reduce it to a mere technical device to translate the curvature of the human mouth, others see it solely as part of a more general exuberance. The answer may lie somewhere in between these two extreme positions, and the problem will be discussed later in more detail. Suffice it here to say that the trait is not widespread enough to be isolated as a general characteristic. On the contrary, a naive excitement would seem a more common component, though its detection is so subjective as to make definition difficult. Perhaps the easiest way to point out this characteristic is to contrast an Archaic with a Classical statue: the latter appears dignified and idealized, while the former, for all its physical mass and artificial details, seems light and gay, regardless of the presence or absence of the Archaic smile. Nor can this effect be attributed to residual polychromy, since all ancient sculpture was painted and the practice is not limited to Archaic statuary alone. This same effect, moreover, is conveyed by a totally white marble. Some authors believe that we acknowledge, in this perception, the very excitement which must have imbued the Archaic sculptor at the dawn of his art, his feeling of pride in breaking new ground through a new artistic medium. Others consider all Archaic sculpture as the physical expression of a golden age which ends with the Persian threat. I cannot subscribe to this latter theory, nor can I completely concur with the former, though I would readily acknowledge that Archaic statues have a different spiritual content from Severe or Classical, and come perhaps closest to the original meaning of the word *agalma*: that which delights, a pleasing gift.

FOR PAGE 1

For the introduction and use of the term Archaic in modern times, see *EAA* s.v. *Arcaico, Stile* (L. Vlad Borrelli). For the ancient use of the word, see *Ancient View*, 255–59.

For an Archaic Period 1000–480, see, e.g., P. Ducati, *L'Arte Classica* (Torino 1927); for one beginning ca. 720, see, e.g., R. M. Cook, *Greek Art* (New York 1972) 12.

FOR PAGE 4

Quintilian: *Inst. Oratoria* 12.10.1–10; Cic. *Brutus* 70.

FOR PAGE 5

On the problem of differentiating the Roman from the Greek contribution in Roman copies, see, e.g., P. Zanker, *Klassizistische Statuen: Studien zur Veränderung des Kunstgeschmacks in der römischen Kaiserzeit* (Mainz 1974). With specific reference to Archaic, see infra Ch. 11.

FOR PAGE 6

The most recent attempt to pinpoint absolute dates is by Kleine.

On the Greeks in Egypt, see M. M. Austin, *Greece and Egypt in the Archaic Age* (Cambridge 1970); Boardman, 108–58, esp. 112.

On the *Perserschutt* and the *Tyrannenschutt*, see W. B. Dinsmoor, *AJA* 38 (1934) 425. However, many standard assumptions will probably need revision in the light of Bundgaard's recent publication and future work. See especially, Bundgaard, 10–16. For the traditional version, see *Korai*, 5–6.

Tyrannicides by Kritios and Nesiotes: *Severe Style*, 79–83.

FOR PAGE 7

Some of the criticism expressed here can be found in Carpenter's review of Richter, *Kouroi*[1], *AJA* 47 (1943) 356–58.

FOR PAGE 8

For recent attempts at correlating sculpture with vase painting, see, e.g., Kleine, 78–93, 99–100, 113–16; cf. also A. W. Byvanck, *BABesch* 38 (1963) 84–88.

On the relative independence of sculpture from other forms of art, see also *Agora* XI, 16 (at end of entry no. 65).

The latest discussion of the Battle of Pallene is in Kleine, 15–16 and 53–56.

The chronological evidence for the Siphnian Treasury is summarized in *Korai*, 63, and Kleine, 31–32.

FOR PAGE 9

Artemision at Ephesos: Kleine, 30–31 (too high); Tuchelt, 131–36 (two phases, ca. 550–540 and 540–530 BC, for the column sculptures).

Harrison: *Agora* XI, 3–13.

Himmelmann-Wildschütz: *IstMitt* 15 (1965) 24–42.

Tuchelt: 131–65, and Chart, 224–25.

FOR PAGE 10

For recent attempts to establish local schools, see *Ptoion* and *Samos* XI. J. G. Pedley's work on Archaic Cycladic sculpture is forthcoming.

FOR PAGE 12

Frontality: S. & S., 24 n. 8, ". . . a perfect symmetry in the two sides of the body, i.e., the equal distribution of weight on the two legs. This admits of the torsion of the body which we find adequately rendered in some Egyptian sculptures."

Deonna, 7, gives the definition established by J. H. Lange, *Darstellung des Menschen in der älteren griechischen Kunst* (Strassburg 1899) with French translation of the first part, as for the 1st ed. of 1892, xi–xii: "Le plan médian qu'on peut concevoir passant par le sommet de la tête, le nez, l'épine dorsale, le sternum, le nombril et les organes sexuels, plan qui partage le corps en deux moitiés symétriques, reste invariable, ne se courbant ni ne se tournant d'aucun côté." See also *Greek Art*, 99–100, and *EAA*, s.v. *Frontalità*.

Art and Experience, 6, in a more general context describes what I call "standardization" as the "representation of the specific in the light of the generic." My "decorativeness" with its subtraits is discussed by Pollitt on p. 5 as "the analysis of forms into their component parts." His entire Ch. 1 should be read in conjunction with my remarks.

FOR PAGE 13

On anatomical evolution and naturalism, cf. *Ptoion*, 464 for a strong defense of different regional developments.

FOR PAGE 14

Archaic smile as meaningful: See, e.g., J. Charbonneaux, *La Sculpture Grecque Archaïque* (Paris 1938) 29. *Art and Experience*, 9, defines it as "not so much an emotion as a symbol, for they (the kouroi) are beyond emotion in the ordinary sense of the word."

Carpenter (*Greek Art*, 191) considers the Archaic smile "a purely physical indication of inner well-being, intended to remedy the morose lifelessness of the earlier straight-lipped representation." Yet on pp. 97–98 (and also in *Greek Sculpture*, esp. 36–37, and in *The Esthetic Basis of Greek Art*, rev. ed. 1959, 64–67) he has perhaps given the most lucid description of how the Archaic sculptor projected unforeshortened and linear shapes onto the surface of his statuary. In general, Carpenter's works include the most comprehensive treatment and the only truly theoretical discussion of the formal principles of Greek Archaic art.

Art of Greece, 214, attributes even the Archaic smile to Oriental influence.

Chapter 2

The Problem of the Origins: The Daedalic Phase

THE THEORIES OF ORIGIN

Two main views of the origin of Archaic sculpture are current. One sees it as a sudden and unprecedented event triggered by outside stimuli; the other considers it the culmination of a long process of experimentation in other media and on a smaller scale. According to the first theory, the Egyptians taught the Greeks how to carve monumental stone blocks and gave them the inspiration for the basic sculptural types; according to the second theory, Eighth and Seventh century bronze and terracotta figurines in Geometric and Daedalic style ultimately provided the forms susceptible of being translated into large-scale statuary. There is supporting evidence for both of these views, but there is also reason to think that in neither case is the evidence conclusive. Moreover, both positions fail to take into account the question of the monumental, the over life-size, which seems to be such a distinctive trait of the first Archaic statues.

Not all peoples have experienced a need for monumental sculpture, and those who did seem to have been variously motivated. In antiquity the availability of stone may have had great importance in promoting sculpture, yet human ingenuity was always able to substitute a suitable medium when stone was not available and the impulse for statuary did exist. Conversely, people who employed stone extensively for their architecture did not necessarily use it for sculpture, and even the widespread practice of stone relief (as exemplified in Assyria and Persia) does not automatically assure a corresponding production in the round. Yet we should bear in mind that monuments portraying divinities or rulers might conceivably have been made in precious or perishable materials[1] which have not survived, and that new discoveries may at any moment appreciably change the picture we see now.

The Minoans and the Mycenaeans were thought to have developed to a very high artistic level without making use of monumental sculpture. In recent years, however, the discovery of terracotta statues on the island of Kea and on the Akropolis at Mycenae has provided valuable fresh evidence, especially because at both sites the statues were found in sanctuaries and so must have had religious significance comparable to that of later Greek sculpture. Though neither the Kea nor the Mycenae idols have been fully published, enough is already known about them to allow some preliminary comments in this context.

[1] That this theory is not as far-fetched as it might seem is shown by ancient Mesopotamian (Assyrian) texts which speak of statues of Lamassu and other figures in gold and silver, as well as copper and bronze. Cf. *The Assyrian Dictionary* A/1 (Chicago 1964) under *Aladlammu*, L/9 (1973) under *lamassatu* and *Lamassu* 2b and 3; cf. also D. D. Luckenbill, *Ancient Records of Assyria and Babylonia* (reprint 1968), vol. I no. 528; vol. II nos. 367 and 413. I am grateful to M. de J. Ellis for these references.

The Mycenaean figures, though larger than statuettes, are still not large enough to rank as monumental sculpture. The tallest are between 0.50 and 0.60 m., and their technique and decoration relate them to pottery rather than to statuary. Even the most naturalistic among them have atrophied arms and unarticulated, wheel-made bodies. Moreover, we have no evidence that any of them survived in a context accessible to the historical Greeks.[2]

It is otherwise with the Kea figures. They are almost life-size, some of them, without feet, attaining a height of ca. 1.50 m. Their wide skirts are largely undetailed, but taper realistically at the waist and set off the magnificent breasts, which are often shown bare within an open jacket or covered only by a garland. The figures (at least 30 in number) have been found in Fifteenth century levels within an isolated structure which was obviously a shrine; but fragments joining the same statues were excavated in later strata: some were in a Twelfth century fill, and one head was set on a ring base of terracotta and stones in a late Eighth century context. Obviously this head had been considered worth salvaging and had remained an object of veneration for generations, while the shrine itself continued in use through Classical Greek times.

The history of Bronze Age sculpture has been changed by the discovery of these Kea statues, and it is possible that excavations in years to come hold equally superb surprises. The statues are now badly weathered, but originally their surfaces were coated with a thin layer of finer clay over which traces of paint still remain in a few spots. The total effect may have been surprisingly naturalistic. The isolated head from the Eighth century level has been compared by some to an Archaic kouros, an analogy suggested by the arched eyebrows flowing into the nose and by the pinched cheeks. But it is dangerous to draw comparisons from such weathered features. It is, nonetheless, important to recognize that, contrary to previous beliefs, the Greeks of the Seventh century may have been exposed to large sculpture in the round from earlier periods, of which we have as yet no knowledge.

Ancient terminology for statuary includes such pre-Greek words as *kolossos* and *bretas*. Although we cannot be sure of their exact meaning in the Bronze Age, these terms were certainly used in the Classical period to describe cult statues and other images. Genuinely Greek, on the other hand, are words like *andrias* and *xoanon*, both of which suggest a carved, most likely wooden, image; the first term, moreover, specifically indicates that such images were anthropomorphic. Ancient sources refer to several such xoana noted for the great veneration attached to them, though not perhaps for their aesthetic appeal. In addition, many wooden statuettes have now been found, though none is earlier in date than the second half of the Seventh century. Large-scale statuary in wood is therefore a class to be reckoned with in discussing the antecedents of Archaic stone sculpture, al-

[2] Some rather large terracotta idols, wheel-made, have been found in Siphnos in an Archaic context and have been dated early in the second quarter of the 7th century, on the basis of their fabric and painted decoration, which resemble Naxian pottery. One example, preserved only to the top of the waist, reaches a height of 0.405 m. Cf. J. K. Brock and G. Mackworth Young, *BSA* 44 (1949) 19–20 nos. 1–2 pls. 6–7.

A similar wheel-made figure was found in Gortyna (*Gortina*, no. 59, pl. 11, a proto-Daedalic Athena, ht. 0.362 m.). Neither the Siphnian nor the Gortyna idols, however, can be connected with the beginning of monumental sculpture in stone because of their obvious ceramic quality. They are important to my subject mostly because their existence (especially the Siphnian examples) indicates a considerable interest in statuary at Naxos during the early 7th century.

For wheel-made figures and various types of bodies in the Daedalic period, see also Meola, esp. 11–47.

though such figures have not survived or have as yet escaped recognition. (None, however, is likely to have been much over life-size.)

In particular, it is important to determine how influential wooden statuary may have been in the formation of the Daedalic terracotta figurines as the immediate inspiration for stone statuary. Yet it is necessary to view the evidence anew, especially since a large body of material—the Daedalic sculpture from Cretan Gortyna—was published after Cook's article had appeared.[3]

Daedalic Style

The Gortyna Material. Figures in Daedalic style have distinctive features. The most characteristic is the head: rather flat on top, with a low forehead and a trapezoidal or triangular face considerably wider at the temples than at the chin. This facial triangle is balanced on either side by wedges of hair in inverse position, so that they end at chin level on a broad, flat "base"; in horizontal section, a Daedalic head is also triangular, the two sides of the face being set at an angle to each other (Fig. 1). Up to the discovery of the Gortyna material, Daedalic art consisted mostly of isolated heads, either broken off from a body or made separately as busts or attachments to vases. Jenkins, who wrote the first book on this subject, illustrated heads only, even in cases of stone statues whose bodies are still preserved, simply because the identifying traits of the style were deduced from that one feature. G. Rizza, in publishing the material from the sanctuary on the Gortynian Akropolis, has made a detailed study also of bodily forms[4] as represented by the many terracotta plaques and statuettes from a votive deposit connected with a many-roomed temple and a large altar. Unfortunately, none of this material was found in a stratified context, and the criteria for the arrangement remain the greater or lesser naturalism of the rendering. To be sure, Rizza finds that his classification is confirmed by the fact that each bodily type is constantly associated with a specific head type, and that each formula for the human body presupposes that immediately preceding.[5] Again, one is tempted to doubt a "sequence" based on purely typological grounds, even when the material is abundant enough (214 Daedalic pieces) to justify the establishment of such a sequence and the hypothesis of a local school. Specifically, Rizza's dates are higher than Jenkins' and high in general; for him, Proto-Daedalic starts ca. 700, the Early Daedalic goes from ca. 690 to 670, Middle from 670 to 640, and Late Daedalic from 640 to 620, this last date being partly established according to current theories of the inception of the Archaic style. At the end of the Seventh century, Rizza believes, the Gortynian sanctuary experienced a decline, with very little material extant from the Sixth and Fifth centuries, but

[3] This material is, however, taken into account by Kranz, who enlarges upon Cook's position to include also the seated type in a Geometric tradition that is a forerunner of the Archaic renderings. His refutation of Cook (who had accepted the seated type as coming from the Orient) is particularly developed on pp. 33–43. According to Kranz, therefore, all three basic Archaic types: the kouros, the draped female figure, and the seated figure, would derive from Geometric art, and even, ultimately, from the Mycenaean past. In general, certain German scholars, following the teachings of N. Himmelmann-Wildschütz, have taken the lead in advocating continuity in Greek art, if not always from Mycenaean, at least from Geometric times.

[4] See especially his figs. 284–89 on pp. 220–21, which illustrate the sequence from Proto-Daedalic to Late Daedalic. More discussion of Daedalic bodies in Meola.

[5] See p. 213. Yet he is aware of the persistence of certain facial types, p. 226.

more preserved from the Fourth century and the Hellenistic period. The temple, according to Santa Maria Scrinari, dates before 750, though adorned with sculpture which is attributed to the Middle and Late Daedalic periods; but again all this material was found re-used and out of context, so that only stylistic analysis provides the dating.

The most important contribution of the Gortyna finds is that for the first time we have large-scale stone carving of types which occur also in the local terracotta productions. Among the 17 limestone pieces are the lower part of a large seated figure broken below the waist to a height of ca. 0.80 m. (no. 7), two large plaques with (presumably) three figures each (nos. 8 and 9; restored height of each slab, ca. 1.50 m.); and the torso and part of the head of a sphinx (?) of possible architectural origin (no. 14; preserved ht. 0.64 m.). One of the stone plaques, badly fragmentary, shows two naked female deities, identified as such by their tall headdress, presumably to be integrated with a third figure, also female; this plaque is assigned by Rizza to the Middle Daedalic period, ca. 650. The second plaque shows a male personage grasping at his left a woman who is naked except for a polos; the position of his fragmentary right arm suggests that a similar figure once existed at his right. This second panel is considered Late Daedalic, yet both plaques are assigned to the temple as parts of a lower border of decorated orthostats, in Oriental (Neo-Hittite) fashion. The naked women of the stone reliefs hold their arms along their sides, while some of the comparable terracottas place one hand on the pubic area and, at times, one hand just below the breasts. The terracottas include several draped female figures, either on plaques or in the round, many wearing the characteristic cape over the shoulder and a tall polos on their heads.

I have dwelt at some length on the Gortyna material because it has not yet found its way into the handbooks and is therefore relatively little known. I believe moreover that this group of limestone and terracotta sculpture is of the greatest significance for our understanding of the Daedalic style and that it may be open to different interpretations. What concerns us here is whether the clay figurines may have sparked the creation of large-scale stone sculpture in similar style, which in turn produced the Archaic kouros and kore types.

To begin with the terracottas, I am especially struck by the variety in hairstyles within the four Daedalic groups. We see triangular masses with horizontal striations ending at the level of the collarbones, similar masses ending at a lower level, wedges articulated by vertical as well as by horizontal grooves which therefore produce beaded tresses, and in some cases even tresses separated from one another and scattered over the breasts, clearly diverging from the hair hanging over the back. In particular, one fragmentary naked figure (presumably from a plaque: no. 186 a-b) holding one hand to the chest and the other to the pubes, has a distinctive herringbone pattern to her tresses, which lie one on either side of her face and two on either breast. Rizza places her in the late Daedalic group, yet a similar hair pattern occurs in figures whose clothing and features mark them as post-Daedalic (Archaic: no. 213 a-c). The naked bodies selected by Rizza to illustrate the development from Proto- to Late-Daedalic form a convincing progression, but we cannot be sure that crudity (especially in terracottas) always corresponds to an early date. As for the draped figures, anatomical analysis is once again confined to the face, and virtually no account has been taken of what may constitute an important element in determining chronology: the presence or absence of feet.

Moving from the terracottas to the material in stone, one notes that the Gortyna temple itself is dated approximately a century earlier than the three-figured panels, and that even the latter are assigned to two different periods. But is it logical to assume that decoration at the base of the walls (as reconstructed) would be introduced so long after the initial construction, and would then be repaired and replaced after ca. 20 years? I cannot claim to have a ready answer to this problem, but I would suggest that the two plaques, which seem to belong together because of their dimensions and material, be removed from the temple, or at least be brought closer together in time. If the two reliefs are indeed more or less contemporary and only reflect two different hands and approaches, then one may wonder about the validity of the dates assigned to some of the terracottas.

As Rizza noted, the type of the naked goddess pointing to her reproductive organs comes from the Levant. It was presumably brought to Crete with the influx of foreign workers who must have been responsible for the great flourishing of Orientalizing art in the island. According to Boardman's recent studies, these were probably jewelers and metal workers who might have fled from Tell Halaf, in Northern Mesopotamia, when their site was attacked by the Assyrians in 808. North Syrian cities must also have contributed a great deal to the waves of new iconography and techniques which swept Crete at the end of the Ninth century and later. These Oriental craftsmen established workshops in the island, presumably not only for metalwork but also for terracotta figurines and for stone sculpture, which was of course being carved at this time in their home territory though largely for reliefs. The Daedalic head type, together with the technique for fashioning figurines in molds, must have come in with one of these waves, or at least through the importation of Syrian material, in the late Eighth to early Seventh century. The style is largely preserved in terracottas, but it also occurs abundantly in gold jewelry.

I am inclined to doubt the postulated sequence from clay figurines to stone statues. Carpenter has emphasized the vast difference in conception and manufacture between objects in small and those in large scale, and nothing need be added to his argument. The more logical sequence, which certainly obtained in Classical times, was for the life-size statuary to influence the minor arts, and not vice versa. Yet we have no evidence for monumental sculpture providing the inspiration for the Daedalic style, and the North Syrian material does not seem to supply the missing link.

The rapid and widespread diffusion of the Daedalic style must have been connected with terracotta production because only highly standardized manufacture allows for the consistent repetition of features. Carving, because of its very individual nature, results in slightly different traits for each object produced while terracotta figurines and plaques, made from a mold, would tend to perpetuate and diffuse a uniform style. I believe, however, that features typical of wood carving can be detected in some of the Daedalic terracottas.

I would consider specifically suggestive of a hard medium the sharp lines which terminate the hair wedges, before beaded tresses were introduced into the repertoire. Equally wooden in appearance is the "facet" marking the pubic triangle in some of the naked bodies from Gortyna.[6] The sharp definition of the groin suggests the insertion of the torso

[6] See especially *Gortina*, fig. 284 on p. 220. R. S. Ellis has pointed out to me that a similar rendering can be found in ivories, but there too what is used is a carving rather than a modeling technique. It is true that sharpness of contours and inner lines can be obtained by intaglio carving of the mold, but I believe that the *desire* to produce such sharp forms could only have been prompted by observation of similar renderings in other media.

between separately carved legs, a technique highly probable in wood, where addition of limbs must have been part of normal procedure. Finally, the straight flanks of some clay figurines are surprising in a medium which relies on modeling even for the making of the mold, but are understandable in a style imitating a carved prototype. It is not inconceivable that the original image from which the clay mold was taken was carved in wood. This wooden prototype would produce a sharper mold and permit the taking of many imprints, a factor of some importance in the mass production of terracotta figurines and plaques. But beyond this immediate wooden prototype, I suspect that sizable sculpture in wood might have given the inspiration for some of the figurines as well as for the contemporary statuary in soft limestone. We have no evidence for Syrian wood carving though obviously the cedars of Lebanon provided an ample supply of primary material. What can be said, however, is that in carving limestone the North Syrian masters used the same methods and tools required for wood carving, with somewhat similar results. It is conceivable, therefore, that the Daedalic style, brought to the Greeks and Cretans from the Orient together with techniques and tools, spread by means of terracotta molds and figurines, but at the same time produced sizable wooden statuary which "fed" inspiration to the concomitant lines in soft stone and the minor arts.

It is perhaps safe to assume that all statues or figurines in Daedalic style were meant to represent divinities. With typical religious conservatism, this style must have continued beyond 600, obviously abetted by the practical use of the same mold through the years in the case of the figurines and by the considerable cost of large-scale wooden statuary, which must have prevented frequent experimentation. Since we know that Lingering Archaic and Lingering Severe style traits were possible in later times, we may reasonably assume that Lingering Daedalic overlapped with the true Archaic style. For reasons which are not yet clear, the Archaic style did not catch on in Crete as it did elsewhere in Greece, and Cretan sculpture, far from providing the impetus for monumental sculpture, merely petered out. Perhaps Crete, as some scholars maintain, was still too strictly tied to its Minoan past.[7] More probably, the new stylistic trends did not find favor because they were associated with a different medium, marble, and with a less popular male divinity. Yet this Cretan rejection of the Archaic style should not surprise; in comparable situations, the Persians and Etruscans assimilated and imitated certain early Greek sculptural styles but refrained from imitating Classical sculpture.

If it is true that Lingering Daedalic carried on well into the Archaic period, some of the "Daedalic" pieces in the Gortyna sanctuary may even be later than 600, and thus the scarcity of truly Archaic objects from this sanctuary may be accounted for. Specifically, I would lower the date of the terracotta torso of a youth (no. 161), which Rizza rightly compares with the bronze kouros from Delphi. He dates both within the Middle Daedalic

[7] Crete seems to have had a special interest in two-dimensional, rather than in three-dimensional, representations. Typically Cretan, for instance, are the bronze cut-outs, of which so many have been found recently: *JHS ArchR* 19 (1973) 30–31; *AAA* 6 (1973) 109–14. Though the people represented by these bronzes are often shown in complex poses, the sheet-like thinness of the metal reduces them to mere silhouettes. The same approach is visible in the Cretan relief pithoi, where figures within registers or panels give the same impression of being flat appliqués, despite, at times, their considerable relief from the background surface. This penchant for two-dimensional forms may have encouraged Cretan rejection of the Archaic style, with its more voluminous shapes.

period, therefore ca. 650. To my eyes, the Delphi statuette is not the forerunner but the contemporary of the early Archaic kouroi in marble, and should be dated ca. 600. The presence of a belt, rather than complete nakedness, is not per se proof of an earlier date, since minor arts often tend to imitate large-scale prototypes; the bronze may therefore echo a cult image like the gigantic Naxian Apollo in Delos which wore a similar belt, an accessory perhaps to be read as an identifying attribute. And Rolley, who has recently written an extensive analysis of the Delphi bronze, points out that the position of its arms closely resembles that of Kleobis and Biton. The Cretan terracotta kouros which Rizza compares to the Delphi statuette bears indeed a strong resemblance to the latter, but I believe it betrays rather a dependence on wooden prototypes, still visible, especially in profile, in the sharp curve of the nose and the simplified treatment of the hair mass ending along a straight edge.[8]

The Gortyna terracotta kouros is remarkable especially because it represents the single specimen of this popular Archaic type from the entire Gortynian deposit: a surprising fact which may perhaps corroborate the lower date I propose for the object. Unfortunately, the statuette is preserved only to the waist, and therefore we cannot gauge its stance. In the Delphi bronze it is interesting to note not only that the legs are separated but that the left is slightly advanced. This is the typical (though here somewhat subdued) pose of the marble kouroi, which may supply a clue to the complex problem of origins and influences.

Wooden Statues. As already mentioned, the word *kolossos* is of pre-Greek origin, and the philologists have postulated that it may come from the Asia Minor area because the radical *kol-* occurs frequently in the onomastics of that region. This radical expresses the idea of "thing erected, built," and *kolossos* would therefore be the semantic equivalent of the Latin *statua.* In a recent article, Roux has further argued that the term carried no implication of size until the erection of the Colossus of Rhodes, indeed enormous, in the Hellenistic period. Prior to that time, the word was simply used to indicate a statue, yet not indiscriminately any statue but a statue of a specific kind. By reviewing all pertinent ancient sources, Roux has come to the conclusion that the term applied only to those images which were column-like, or were tightly wrapped in a sheath-like garment, or even simply held their legs close together.[9] By extension, the word could be used in the Fifth century by Aischylos to indicate what Roux suggests may have been herms in front of a palace.

If Roux's hypothesis is correct, the term *kolossos*, taken in conjunction with *bretas* and *xoanon*, which specifically refer to wooden images, may allow us to postulate that pre-Archaic statues were often, if not always, wooden images represented tightly enveloped in their clothes or with their legs close together. This position would be the almost inevitable consequence of wearing a female dress with a narrow skirt, which is indeed the

[8] Compare, for instance, the wooden kouros from Samos illustrated by Richter among the forerunners (*Kouroi*, figs. 17–19).

[9] A typical example, although hammered rather than cast and although Archaic in date, is the Apollo Amyklaios, which stood over Hyakinthos' grave. Perhaps somewhat the same type of statue is reflected in the so-called Kimolos stele; a slab surmounted by human shoulders and arms, now headless (see infra, Ch. 6).

rendering we see in the Daedalic figurines.[10] If such rendering was dictated by contemporary fashions, the Daedalic craftsmen were simply imitating the daily costume of real life. On the other hand, a second, technical explanation would also be possible. A terracotta figure thrown on a wheel tends to have a rounded contour, and therefore an ample skirt like the Gortyna idols nos. 103–104. But a wooden figure derived from a beam or a board offers less scope for a garment flaring out at the hem, and therefore appears to have a taut skirt or a columnar profile. Exactly this type of figure is represented by the three wooden idols from Palma di Montechiaro in Sicily, which belong to the Archaic period.

It has often been said that the so-called Nikandre in the Athens National Museum is plank-like and therefore shows that marble sculpture must have derived from wooden prototypes. Cook, in his defense of a terracotta origin for Greek stone sculpture, maintains that "till the power-driven saw came into use logs were easier to produce than boards, and no less convenient as blanks from which to carve a human semblance of largish size." Yet boards must have been employed extensively in the Geometric period for the making of ships, and the spectacular Royal tomb at Gordion has shown that very substantial beams and planks of great length and excellent finish were employed in architecture by the late Eighth century. It has long been postulated that the Doric and Ionic orders reflect, in their details, previous stages of wooden origin, yet no such building has come down to us. To the same chance of preservation we must therefore attribute our almost total lack of monumental Greek sculpture in wood, of which at least a remote echo must be preserved in the tradition of the Trojan Horse.[11]

Similar inferences may be drawn from different clues. Davaras has suggested that the seated figure from Gortyna, at present preserved only from the waist downward, was built up from at least two separate blocks, of which the upper, forming the torso, is now lost. The opposite situation prevails with the statue from Astritsi, which remains only down to the waist, while the lower block with buttocks and legs is now missing. This technique seems surprising for seated figures. It has been ingeniously suggested that Cretan craftsmen of the time must have been unable to quarry a single block large enough for the entire statue or unable (or unwilling?) to do the deep trimming into the block required by the pose. In either case, their approach has been seen as a Cretan response in limestone to the monumental marble sculpture of the Cyclades or East Greece. To this definite possibility

[10] On the basis of Roux's argument, it can safely be said *only* that by the time of Aischylos and Herodotos the word *kolossos* carried this meaning. There is no assurance that this meaning obtained also in pre-Archaic times. Later authors, for instance Pausanias, refer to aniconic images, which they describe as column-like or pillar-like, without using the term *kolossos*, but we may safely assume that by the 2d century AD the second connotation, of gigantic size, had taken over and therefore pre-empted the usefulness of the term for smaller works. Such column-like images continued to be made even at a time when stone was the normal medium employed, and obviously co-existed with anthropomorphic renderings of divinities. For a recent discussion of these aniconic idols, see, e.g., N. Yalouris, *Olympiaka Chronika* 1 (1970) 1–17, esp. 11–17. Not only were goddesses shown in this fashion but also gods, such as Apollo Agyieos and Dionysos Dendrites.

[11] An over life-size wooden statue was postulated by A. Evans at Knossos on the basis of some bronze locks and fragments of carbonized wood: *The Palace of Minos* III (London 1930) 522–23, figs. 365–66. Davaras, 39 and n. 191 has further bibliography. See also *EAA*, s.v. *legno*. An article by H. V. Hermann ("Zum Problem der Entstehung der griechischen Grossplastik," *Wandlungen, Studien zur antiken und neueren Kunst* [Waldsassen-Bayern 1975] 35–48) has appeared too recently to be taken into account here; the author, however, has made many of the same points and he produces a strong argument for early statuary in wood of elaborate and sophisticated appearance.

I should like to add the alternative that the Cretan technique reflects here the practice of wood carving, which would find it economical and feasible to make a statue out of different parts.

A second clue is offered by the stone base, which Buschor and Schleif suggested would have been the pedestal for a Geometric cult statue in the Samian Heraion. Reckoning from the cutting on the surface, the image could have been at least life-size if not taller. We are, of course, told by some ancient sources that the first Samian xoanon was aniconic, but Pausanias (7.4.4) mentions a wooden statue made by Smilis of Aegina, of the age of Daidalos, and perhaps its reflection can be seen in a spectacular wooden figurine ca. 28 cm. high which was probably influenced by a more sizable image in the same medium. The statuette represents a woman in a tight skirt, wearing a most elaborate headdress (polos or mitra), which marks her unquestionably as a divinity. Her date has been placed tentatively around 640, but her prototype must be earlier, and of wood, since by her time over life-size sculpture in marble was already being carved in the islands and has survived, though in a sadly fragmentary state. The decoration of the statuette's garment could be conceived also on a stone statue, but the intricate carving of the headdress would have been possible only on a wooden prototype, not on a marble image, at a period when stone sculpture was just beginning.[12] The statuette wears the distinctive cape of Seventh century female figures, which has often been considered typically Cretan but should instead be seen as "typically early": a fashion of Daedalic times. Davaras has recently reviewed the literature and the evidence for this garment, concluding that it was called *epiblema* and may have had a hieratic character which made it appropriate for divine images.

To summarize: these various clues, taken in conjunction with the ancient literary sources and with Greek vocabulary for sculpture, seem to support the theory that large-scale statuary in wood existed at least during the entire Seventh century. Some traits of the Daedalic style, moreover, seem to me more easily understandable in the framework of woodcarving than that of terracotta molding, as Cook suggested. The Daedalic style, carried by foreign craftsmen and represented in the major as well as in the minor arts, must ultimately have come from the Levant, but must have spread throughout Greece, Asia Minor, and the islands, including the Western colonies. It is not necessary to postulate a single source of influence nor to assume (as is generally done) that the Northern Pelopon-

[12] The idea of a wooden prototype has been suggested by the German excavators on the basis of the literary sources, the excavational evidence, and the appearance of the wooden statuette. It is, of course, conceivable that this figure reflects not a carved polos but a real one, perhaps richly woven or embroidered, since early cult statues were often adorned with real clothes. Even in this case, however, the prototype should be of wood since it is unlikely that a stone image would be given added garments. To be sure, the wood carver, having at his disposal a conducive medium, might have elaborated beyond what appeared in his prototype. However, this supposition is equally questionable since statuettes tend to simplify and subtract, but not to add, ornament from the model they copy (see, e.g., the replicas of the Athena Parthenos in Classical times).

Another interesting type of divine image is reflected in terracotta figurines from South Italy, of which two replicas are now known. The rather large impression (reconstr. H: ca. 34 cm.) shows a female with an elaborate skirt whose registers contain several scenes: Ajax carrying the body of Achilles, a *choros* of women, and two sphinxes. Unfortunately the top of the statuette is not preserved. See P. Zancani Montuoro, *AttiMGrecia* NS 11–12 (1970–71) 67–74, reconstruction p. 68 fig. 1, and pls. 27–28. Works of this nature confirm the suspicion that elaborate cult images like the Ephesian Artemis, Artemis Pergaia, or the Aphrodite of Aphrodisia may go back not to a Hellenistic but to a Late Daedalic or early Archaic prototype. Cf. *AJA* 79 (1975) 107–8, M. J. Mellink's review of R. Fleischer.

nesos was the main stronghold of a style which penetrated elsewhere in the wake of Proto-Corinthian and Corinthian pottery. Crete was particularly receptive to this form of art and continued to use it even after the introduction of the Archaic style and of monumental sculpture in marble. In fact, Crete seems to have rejected Archaic style per se and seems never to have employed marble on any appreciable scale until the late Classical period. The fragmentary marble kouros from the temple of Apollo Pythios at Gortyna remains so far unique and should probably be considered an import or a "foreign" dedication. Moreover, whatever architectural sculpture has survived from the island seems to belong to none of the canonical Greek orders, but rather to partake of Oriental forms and ideas of decoration which did not find general acceptance elsewhere in Greece.[13]

Seen from this point of view, Crete cannot claim to have been the birthplace of Greek monumental stone sculpture, as has recently been reiterated. Whereas the Archaic style seems to have had as one of its characteristics an evolutionary trend towards naturalism, the hieratic Daedalic was unable (or unsuited) to develop along more naturalistic lines, and therefore was discarded. Moreover, Archaic sculpture seems to have been wedded to marble from its inception, and material can almost be considered a trait distinguishing true Archaic from true Daedalic. To be sure, soft limestone continued to be used well into the Sixth century for economic or practical reasons, but it was carved in imitation of contemporary marble sculpture. On the other hand, marble statues (like Kleobis and Biton) could retain some features of Daedalic style, but as part of a Lingering Daedalic tradition rather than as full expression of the style itself. Finally, the beginning of Archaic sculpture is characterized by over life-size statuary. This desire to express the superhuman, at least in scale, was strong enough to overcome the difficulties inherent in the quarrying and carving of suitable blocks and must have represented one of the motivating forces away from Daedalic, which seems never to have attempted equally large statuary.

STONE SCULPTURE

If I maintain that Daedalic works could not have been the true forerunners of Archaic sculpture, and that Cretan statuary therefore represents a dead end rather than the beginning of the road, I must supply an alternative theory to explain the inception of Archaic, or even to define the style at its start, so that we can recognize its first appearances: I would suggest tentatively that these are connected with the widespread cult of Apollo during the late Seventh century.

Several scholars believe that this deity is of Anatolian origin, probably to be equated with the sun-god, and with specifically virile if not war-like character. The Greeks associated him with sudden death, and Homer gives us a frightening picture of him in the first Book of the Iliad (1.43–53) when he descends from Olympos in great strides to bring pestilence and disaster to the Achaeans. Perhaps the aftermath of the colonization movement, and a renewed wave of influence from the Orient, stressed a new conception of the god as a figure of action. Certainly the fact that the Greeks could adopt at this time a new

[13] N. Kontoleon (*Aspécts*, 86–87) has advanced the hypothesis that Cretan sculpture virtually came to an end during the Archaic period because the island did not develop the *polis* structure typical of Greece proper. But, given the great differences among Greek cities of the 7th and 6th centuries which nonetheless developed their own forms of Archaic statuary, I wonder whether such sociological explanation represents a total answer to the question.

technique and a new medium must be more than a happy coincidence since certainly Egypt and its sculpture were known throughout the Aegean well before the mid Seventh century. I believe that the new technique was actually sought because this new popular cult and this new conception of Apollo suggested a different expression from the traditional static figures of Daedalic art.

Undoubtedly Apollo could continue to be represented with legs joined together even in later times. We know that there was one such statue in Delos, which a building account of 302 calls a "kolossos," and that the enormous sphyrelaton at Amyklai was column-like in its lower part. But it is perhaps significant that the male figure in the Gortyna triad-plaque should be shown with legs divaricated in an action pose made possible by the relief technique. Almost at the same time appeared the marble kouros in a medium which could withstand the stress of the striding pose in a sculpture in the round,[14] and with its enormous size which removed it from the human sphere and implied divinity at a glance.

My suggestion is based indeed on my belief that the early kouroi are not generic representations of youths, but portray Apollo himself. This point will be argued in the chapter on Kouroi; suffice it here to say that the unorthodox nakedness, the exceptional size, the occasional presence of attributes, the hairstyle, the very function of the type, all support, or at least do not contradict, the theory that this new statuary form was originally created to depict the god. Most important of all is the action pose. Contrary to present belief, I am convinced that the kouroi do not simply stand with one leg advanced: they walk. To enforce this "hieroglyph" of striding, the Greeks even removed the back support of their Egyptian prototypes, and the stone screen between the body and the advanced leg, which to their eyes froze their male figures into statuesque immobility.[15] Ironically enough, this Greek innovation was attributed to Daidalos, yet it marked the rejection of the static Daedalic style, and it produced over life-size statues which were, however, not *kolossoi* at all in the original meaning of the word.[16]

Certainly, the stance with an advanced foot may have created as much of an impression in its time as the Polykleitan Canon did almost two centuries later. Yet in neither case did the departure from previous practices represent a great aesthetic leap. Therefore, its impact must have lain in its theoretical basis and its potential. Polykleitos' Doryphoros represented the sculptural embodiment of mathematical harmony and the ideal beauty of human musculature in its two potential aspects, tension and relaxation. The Archaic kouros, with its left leg forward, expressed the release from immobility and the potential-

[14] Virtually the same point, that of the kouros being "born" in marble, is made in *Aspécts*, 81 and n. 2 with additional bibliography. See also *Ptoion*, p. 453, where the relative paucity of kouroi in limestone is attributed to technical difficulties.

[15] To be sure, Egyptian male figures in wood had neither such a back screen nor the "membrane" connecting the advanced leg to the background because no such support was needed in a different medium. However, even these freer representations of a human figure are not meant to convey the idea of movement but simply the fact that the statue has two legs visible from any point of view. How similar such wooden figures can be however when compared to a Greek kouros, especially if naked, is shown by Fig. 2, a Sixth Dynasty statuette in the British Museum. Note in particular the protruding hips.

[16] On the basis of this theory, obviously none of the Late Geometric figurines of men or youths can qualify as a true predecessor of the Archaic kouros, not even the so-called Mantiklos Apollo nor the many fighting warriors from Olympia, despite their active poses. Note, in particular, that in Geometric bronzes the legs may be *separated*, but the feet are aligned in the *same* plane, without the foot-forward stance symbolic of motion.

ity for action. Although such statues appear to us (as to the Romans) stiff and immobile, their contemporaries must have seen them as daring and innovative because they broke with previous tradition and opened up other avenues of development. That it took over a century for such a potential to be realized should perhaps be attributed to conservatism and "standardization," that is, to the desire to repeat a form to ensure recognition. But the movement away from rigid "attention stances" had started and would eventually result in extreme animation.

The excitement produced by these first statues can perhaps be recaptured in the ancient sources which describe Daidalos' works as lifelike, or indeed so lively that they had to be chained to be prevented from running away. This obviously rhetorical exaggeration has at times led to the suggestion that no true sculpture need correspond to these descriptions. They were solely meant to convey the idea of imaginary miraculous creations by legendary, semi-divine, or divine beings like Prometheos or Daidalos. On the other hand, these over-imaginative statements may simply reflect the surprise felt at the time in seeing statues which stepped forward, as contrasted with the obviously immobile stances of previous works. It may not be amiss, at this point, to make a comparison with events of our own era, because the human mind reacts somewhat similarly through the ages. The movies of the Teens and early Twenties could only show people walking very rapidly, with mincing steps and wooden motion, which seem now thoroughly removed from normal experience, yet at the time these motion pictures were hailed as entirely naturalistic and lifelike. Because they represented such an innovation over still photography, these films appeared realistic, and the human mind suspended judgment, or stretched credibility, because it could translate the unusual vision into the familiar experience. Similarly, Greeks living in the Sixth century might have seen the early kouroi as lively and moving, despite their obvious stiffness and rigidity, simply because they represented a definite advance over previous renderings. Daidalos was then credited with the innovation because of the typical Greek need to find a definite source for any new technique and formula; thus the "Daedalic question" may closely compare with the Homeric question, and the term may hide several nameless artists under one name.

Because a male figure could be shown naked,[17] the legs could be more easily separated. The female figure, hampered by attire, took longer to "move." Yet eventually the walking kore made its appearance within the repertoire, together with the fuller, pleated skirt which could allow such movement. It is interesting, in this respect, to outline a possible sequence of development. At first, the goddesses were shown with no feet (e.g., Samian Hera in wood, Gortyna seated figure), or with mound-like feet compressed against the hem of the skirt. As male figures began to be produced in action poses, female skirts began to form a niche-like opening over the feet, which then appeared as if framed within a window.[18] This rendering may have corresponded to actual fashions. A trailing skirt,

[17] The problem of male nakedness will be discussed in Ch. 3 on kouroi.

[18] A somewhat similar arrangement can be found in three of the terracotta idols from the Cretan sanctuary of Karphi, dated to the sub-Minoan period around 1000 BC (J.D.S. Pendlebury, *The Archaeology of Crete* [London 1939] 312 and pl. 41:1-2). Here, however, each foot has its own niche and is modeled separately as if to provide for motion. Similar bell-shaped idols (e.g., from Gazi, Gournia, and Knossos, S. Hood, *The Minoans* [New York 1971] 134, figs. 116–17, see also p. 138 pl. 115) have no provision for feet, and the Karphi figures may perhaps be considered exceptional. In any case, their chronological distance from the Archaic examples precludes their inclusion in this discussion.

shorter over the front and thus revealing the feet, seems indeed suggested by comparable rendering of profile figures in vase painting. On the other hand, it is also possible that sculptors were reluctant to undercut their female statues to expose their ankles all around, and therefore reverted to a technical device which appears to us as a change in fashion. Other solutions made the kore lift and gather her skirt on one side to allow movement for the leg, or tried to produce such movement within the tight skirt itself. An example of the first solution occurs in the Samian Philippe, whose right foot advances beyond the left in conjunction with the lifting of the skirt. Another statue from Samos (Fig. 21) in comparable style attempts the opposite position, by lifting her hem beside the retracted foot. The second solution is perhaps to be seen in the still unpublished kore from Klaros, whose peculiar twist could be interpreted as a miscutting; yet her flat and misshapen feet emerging from a fairly straight skirt barely arching in the center are obliquely aligned and in keeping with her turn toward the proper right. The total appearance is still rigid and generally awkward, so that in the preliminary reports the statue has been dated too early and contemporary with the Nikandre. A closer assessment would place it in the second quarter of the Sixth century, a date perhaps corroborated by the letter forms of the dedicatory inscription which runs along the left thigh. The final stage was reached at some time after 550 in statues where more clinging drapery outlines the entire advanced leg though korai never step as far forward as their male counterparts. But I suspect that the inhibiting contour of the female garment was initially responsible for the persistence of "colossal" traits in female figures, which may therefore have been dated too early by modern scholars.[19]

Foreign Influence

Egypt. If "colossal" Daedalic continued to inspire female figures into the Archaic period, did Egyptian statues provide the prototype for the kouros? This question has been greatly debated, with answers ranging from complete denial to entire consent. Most recently, several German archaeologists have defended the theory of spontaneous internal development for all the Greek types, without dependence on foreign sources. Yet significantly, the ancient sources on Daidalos state that his statues had the same *rhythmos* as those of Egypt, and the Greek word here should perhaps be taken to mean not simply form or pattern but also movement, or rather motion stance or walking pose. If this translation is correct, it would corroborate my theories on the inception of the Archaic style. Another passage explains at great length the method employed in carving by the Egyptians, stating that it was adopted also by the Samian masters, Theodoros and Telekles. To the studies by Erik Iversen and Kim Levin we should now add the research by Eleanor Guralnick, whose "cluster analysis," carried out with the help of stereo-photogrammetry and computer, has shown that the Greek kouroi traditionally assigned to the first half of the Sixth century show consistent similarities with the Second Egyptian Canon.

[19] Egyptian female statues have equally tight skirts, yet they can be represented with one foot slightly ahead of the other. However, this pose is accompanied by a rendering of the garment which reveals the body beneath as if it were naked. Probably the Greeks did not like such immodest representations for their women and therefore rejected the Egyptian prototypes. Cf. *Greek Sculpture*, 20. It is interesting to note that some indication of the female body was nonetheless given, but for the *back* of the statues.

Briefly summarized, the situation is as follows: It seems certain that during the 26th Dynasty (663–525) Egyptian sculptors adopted a canon of proportions slightly different from that previously used, and which is therefore known as Canon II. It consisted of establishing a grid based on a division of the standing human figure in twenty-one and one-fourth parts, with twenty-one squares from the soles of the feet to a line through the eyes. Major anatomical points were located on the grid lines or at the intersections of grid lines, and the grid itself was applied to the surface of the block which was to be carved, so that the size of the unit forming the squares was a variable determined by the size of the block. The grid represented a true canon of proportions because the number of square units of height remained constant, and the lines invariably crossed the body at the specified places. Such grids have been preserved on unfinished statues in the round, on reliefs, and even in papyrus drawings and plans. Iversen compared the proportions of the New York Kouros, as deduced from the published measurements, with the proportions of the Egyptian Canon II and was able to show that the Greek statue had the same ratio as that based on the contemporary Egyptian grid. Iversen, however, did not extend his studies to other Archaic kouroi, and other scholars were quick to point out that the New York Kouros could not be considered the norm, but was rather the exception since he appeared different from all others. Guralnick has now shown that this visual impression is not totally correct. By applying the method of cluster analysis, she has compared three whole and unrestored Greek kouroi (the New York, the Tenea, and the Melos kouroi) with the Egyptian Canon II, on the one hand, and with real human beings on the other, taking her measurements from a NATO survey of Greek Air Force personnel. Her computer analysis showed that each of the three kouroi clustered with the Egyptian Canon in 75 percent of their opportunities, and that one or more clustered with it in 30 percent of the 32 opportunities offered, while their clustering with true human beings was not statistically significant. On the other hand, three more kouroi of the second half of the Sixth century showed increasing points of comparison with true human beings, the most "natural" being Aristodikos. It seems logical to conclude that the Greeks adopted the Egyptian canon initially as a technical device, then proceeded to alter it according to their own inclinations and eventually according to nature because of that penchant for realism which was never a primary concern of the Egyptian sculptor. This very manipulation and correction are reflected in general throughout Greek art, whether applied to finding the most pleasing shape for a vase or the system of proportions for a Doric temple, and they result in the thorough "Graecizing" of any imported element.

The above statement partially answers the often formulated objection that Greek kouroi cannot really derive from an Egyptian prototype because the finished products do not look Egyptian. The Egyptian counterparts of the early kouroi seem far more sophisticated and anatomically correct. Similarities and differences between Egyptian and Greek male statues have often been listed and discussed; Levin has published perhaps the most extensive recent analysis; Guralnick has given it in outline form; I have presented elsewhere comments on balance and technique and will reopen the question below, in Chapter 3 on kouroi. Suffice it here to speak to the most general and important points applicable to the specific problem of the origin of Greek Archaic sculpture.

I am not suggesting that the impetus for Greek Archaic statuary came solely or even primarily from Egypt. The situation must have been far more complex, and other strands of influence will be isolated later in this discussion. I have already intimated that the Daedalic style, as seen especially in large-scale wooden sculpture, must have continued for some time to form a component in the representation of Archaic female figures. But what seems to me entirely convincing is that the *technique* of carving large blocks of stone and the *system of proportions* necessary to magnify life-size into a much larger scale came to the Greeks from the Egyptians.

First of all, no amount of practice in the making of terracotta or solid bronze figurines is conducive to the kind of magnification evidenced in Archaic stone statuary. Even very large wooden statues would not have compared with their marble contemporaries if they were indeed colossal in their lower parts, either columnlike or tightly sheathed in a skirt. The piecing technique possible in wood seems quite different from the kind of piecing adopted in Archaic marble works. Finally, the four-sidedness of early Greek statues is not only explainable through the Egyptian grid system applied simultaneously to the four main faces of a block but is also compatible only with stone carving in general, as contrasted with the more plastic appearance of a figurine modeled in clay or wax. The kouros figure, as we know it in the early Sixth century, is conceivable only in stone, and more specifically in the relatively hard medium of marble.[20] Soft limestone or basalt, as carved in North Syria (the other source of inspiration), produced different effects and aimed at different results, with definite emphasis on relief rather than on sculpture in the round.

Should Greek and Egyptian sculptures still seem too different for direct imitation to have existed, a glance at the limestone production of Cyprus and Rhodes will suffice to show how much greater the difference is between early Archaic Greek works in marble and contemporary limestone statuary elsewhere. Perhaps the most striking difference lies in the fact that these other places did not attempt anything in the way of the enormous sizes made possible for the marble carving Greeks by the direct teaching of people who had long since transcended the human scale in their art.[21]

It is also generally acknowledged that Egypt gave Greece some of the stone-cutting tools (e.g., the drove)[22] and the two basic architectural moldings (the cavetto and the half-round) from which Greek architects were able to derive all their multiple variants. Other specific details, such as the upward-tapering doorways and the lion-head water-spouts, were probably also taken over from the Egyptian architectural repertoire even if a water-spouting lion must have made very little sense to the literal-minded Greeks. If such borrowings in the field of architecture can be accepted without discussion despite the fact that Greek buildings as a whole bear no resemblance to Egyptian structures, one fails to see why borrowings of technique, proportions, and typology in the field of sculpture should seem improbable on the strength of formal dissimilarity alone.

[20] Note, moreover, that even Egyptian sculpture in limestone, for all its protecting screens in the back and between the legs, tended usually to be small; and harder stones, like granite or diorite, were chosen for statuary of much greater size.

[21] It could even be suggested that the very idea of indicating divinity or importance by means of superhuman size came to the Greeks from the Egyptians.

[22] In unfinished Egyptian monuments one can detect also the same working practices which prevail in Greek sculpture; for instance, the use of drilled channels to separate areas of stone. See, e.g., Br. Mus. 1165, an unfinished false door from the tomb of Bateta at Sakkara, 5th Dynasty, which retains traces of such drill work all along the edge of the first recessed panel of the doorway. Among the Greeks such drill channels were in use very early, and are quite noticeable, for instance, between the toes of the gigantic Naxian Apollo in Delos (foot in the Br. Mus.; *Kouroi*, fig. 90).

One final objection, that the Egyptians never used marble for their statuary and therefore could hardly have taught the Greeks how to work in that crystalline medium, can be refuted on two counts. First, a pier of stone lends itself equally well to the application of proportional grids be it marble, granite, or some other variety of rock. Secondly, the Egyptians did in fact use marble, though never to a great extent: large statues in that medium were made during the 18th and 19th Dynasties, and presumably more would have been made had the supply of material been plentiful. It is understandable that the Greeks, who had easy access to excellent marble quarries, should transpose Egyptian techniques into the medium at their disposal which best lent itself to being quarried in sizable blocks.

This consideration of supply might explain why so little Archaic sculpture has been found at Naukratis, and why what was found is in alabaster or limestone and looks far more Egyptian than Archaic Greek statues from elsewhere.

The few Naukratite kouroi, largely in alabaster and of very small size, are characterized by a low-slung, bulging lower abdomen, the complete absence of abdominal partitions and, often, a different arm position. Limestone works from Naukratis are mostly in diminutive scale and share with contemporary Rhodian pieces a definite "minor arts" appearance. Significant in this respect is the treatment of the back, which is usually left thoroughly uncarved and flat, so that the entire statuette is abnormally thin. This practice recalls that of terracotta figurines, where the mold-made front is sealed off with a plain slab of clay smoothed by hand. Whatever detail is given in these limestone pieces is much more reminiscent of wood than of marble carving, and all in all the entire soft stone production of both Naukratis and Rhodes seems much more strictly connected with Cyprus and Egypt than with Greece. This is particularly noteworthy for Rhodes, which also produced sizable works in marble and Archaic (East Greek or Cycladic) style. It is tempting to infer from such evidence that the makers of limestone statuettes remained independent from sculptural workshops in marble and that their products represented merely a cheap alternative to terracotta figurines, perhaps only remotely influenced by contemporary large-scale statuary.

The question therefore arises as to where specifically the Greeks could have learned Egyptian techniques, and where in Greece they could have developed them. To be sure, this complex question cannot have a single solution, and the state of our knowledge is still too incomplete to allow us to answer with assurance. The most likely possibility is that Greek travelers learned stone carving techniques in Egyptian centers, and then developed them either in Samos or in Naxos, or perhaps in both places at more or less the same time. As already mentioned, the ancient sources speak of Samian masters learning their methods in Egypt, and Samos seems an ideal candidate for the birthplace of Greek sculpture. Not only had it been the site of a major sanctuary since the Eighth century but it was also a major crossroad for Egyptian and Oriental influences, and it had easy access to marble from the Cyclades and probably from its own local quarries. Naxos also had its own immediate supply of material and the added impetus of the nearby sanctuary at Delos, which seems to have furnished a ready market for sculptural dedications —significantly, to Apollo.[23]

[23] According to ancient sources (e.g., Paus. 8.14.8; 10.38.6; Plin. *HN* 34.83), Samos seems to have been important as a bronze-casting center in the Archaic period, while Naxos is not mentioned in this connection. It would be tempting to assume that the more rounded appearance of some Samian kouroi,

Some modern scholars prefer to see the birthplace of Greek sculpture in the Northeastern Peloponnesos, largely because of Corinthian prominence in trade and pottery. The evidence available so far, however, does little to substantiate this claim, and the marble supply, though possible, seems to have been somewhat limited, so that much of Corinthian sculpture continued to be in limestone or terracotta well into the late Archaic period. The entire Peloponnesos, moreover, seems to have been a stronghold of the minor arts and of the Lingering Daedalic style. It has yielded only nine or ten kouroi; two of these, the Argive Kleobis and Biton which were found at Delphi, retain significant Daedalic traits. If Archaic sculpture ideologically began with the introduction of the kouros type, as well as with the use of marble, Corinth or the entire Peloponnesos can hardly claim to have been the birthplace.

To return to the initial question (where the Greeks could have learned the Egyptian technique), I have intentionally spoken of travelers. It would seem perhaps more logical to assume that a mixed center like Naukratis, where Greeks and Egyptians lived together though in separate quarters, might have been more favorable ground for the emergence of common workshops. An interesting theory, which originated in a Bryn Mawr College seminar, actually suggested that the reason why the Greek kouroi do not more closely resemble their Egyptian prototypes may lie in the workshop hierarchy of Egyptian centers. According to this hypothesis, the Greeks would have served as apprentices, and would have been in charge of the preliminary roughing out of the figures from the quarry blocks. They would therefore have learned the technique and the principle of the grid, but they would never have given those final touches which produced the finished statue and which were reserved for the chief sculptor, the head of the workshop, who was presumably an Egyptian. This suggestion finds support in the known practices of Classical masons in Athens, where the apprentices would carve out the preliminary fluting of columns but the master himself would reach the final surfaces and complete the work. Attractive as this hypothesis is, it does not explain why the apprentices were never promoted nor how the technique could move on to Greek territory. Moreover, according to a recent study, the Greeks and Karians who settled in Egypt did not do so in the same way as other Greek colonists elsewhere, and did not establish regular relations with their cities of origin. The Greeks in Naukratis did not have the right of intermarriage with Egyptian women and seem to have been prevented from mixing freely with the native population. The mercenary settlements might have fared differently in that the Pharaoh encouraged intermarriage to increase the population and to assure a loyal army, but again there was virtually no contact between the mercenaries and their mother cities, and no finds attest to the popularity of stone sculpture at the few excavated sites. It seems best to visualize Greek traveling artists as men who could have moved somewhat more freely within Egypt than colonists but who would have stayed there a relatively short time, absorbing the general principles of stone carving and proportional canon without acquiring the refinements which would have made their work look unmistakably like the Egyptian.

Adam has treated Greek stone carving techniques so comprehensively that it is unnec-

---

as contrasted with the sharp and flat contours of their Naxian counterparts, was due to influence from the clay modeling which formed the preliminary step in bronze casting. However, large-scale sculpture in bronze was probably not produced before the middle of the 6th century (the time of Rhoikos and Theodoros) and therefore cannot have influenced the *inception* of monumental sculpture on Samos.

essary here to make more than a few specific points. It is important to remember that the application of guidelines to the four sides of a stone pier resulted in the progressive removal of layer after layer of marble, in a process somewhat comparable to the unwrapping of a mummy from its encasing bandages. Therefore the more superficial layers represented only a rough approximation to the desired shape, but entailed the trimming away of corners and of excessive stone, thus considerably reducing the weight of the entire block. Adam has made the interesting suggestion that trained quarrymen might have carried out this trimming process to a very advanced stage before shipping the block to the commissioning sculptor. If a standard canon of proportions was in existence, it would have been simple for the sculptor to send to the quarry his specifications for type and size, and the masons there could proceed on their own to do the preliminary carving. Only the final touches, therefore, would have been left to the master, those being nonetheless the most important for the statue's individuality. This theory would explain the Archaic tendency to adhere to standard types, especially in the case of the male figure, and would highlight the relative lack of Greek interest in originality, in the modern meaning of the word. On the other hand, it is conceivable that sculptors traveled to the quarries in person, so that any preliminary shaping could be done under their supervision.[24] Certainly, sculpture must have been a relatively rare luxury in the Archaic period, so that we cannot visualize the kind of mass production which obtained at the quarries in Roman times. It is nonetheless useful to remember that "international styles" might be the result of technical requirements and expediency, and it is useful also to see the relative uniformity of Archaic Greek sculpture as a possible result of a newly learned technique which had a binding as well as a creative effect.

Anatolia. It is perhaps significant, in this respect, that the many unfinished Archaic statues left behind in the Naxian quarries should all be male. Adam postulates the application of the canon also for the female figure, with the proviso that enough stone be left over the front to leave scope for variation in the carving of the garment.[25] On the other hand, if the Egyptian influence was largely limited to the male figure and the female type remained under some influence from the Daedalic tradition, the variety of renderings in this latter can be explained on the grounds of several different components from elsewhere. Although the analogy is not quite cogent, one may compare the evolution of the kouros type to that of the Doric order, and the evolution of the kore to that of the Ionic. This parallel is not based on the presumed masculinity of one order as contrasted with the femininity of the other, as Vitruvius explains. It refers rather to the Oriental components

[24] It is interesting, in this respect, to note that the same practice of preliminary shaping in the quarry seems to have been followed by the Assyrians, who also attempted statuary of enormous size. Two famous reliefs from the palace of Sennacherib (704–681 BC) at Nineveh, now in the British Museum, show the king supervising the moving of a guardian figure from the quarry onto a barge and to his palace. The shape of the human-headed monster is discernible within the block, but an ample frame of unworked stone seems to have been left all around it and people are shown walking over it without apparent fear of damaging a finished surface (Slabs nos. 124820–124824, the quarry is at Balatai, as mentioned in the inscription, the approximate date 690). Illustrations: R. D. Barnett and W. Forman, *Assyrian Palace Reliefs in the British Museum* (London 1970) pl. 8; for a drawing, see Hrouda, pl. 54:1.

[25] I understand that Guralnick is now trying to apply the Egyptian canon to some female statues, and that the results may be positive, at least in some cases. It has also been pointed out to me that not much weight could be eliminated by pre-trimming a standing female statue.

that must have been active in the creation and the many variations attempted in Ionic temples. No two Archaic Doric temples are the same, to be sure, but the degree of experimentation from building to building does not affect the basic elevation and the total appearance of the structures in the same way in which different details in the anatomy of the kouroi do not affect their basic stance or the tectonic whole. On the contrary, it is very difficult to describe the kore in more than the most general terms (if the definition is meant to apply to the entire type) because variations in garments and poses defy standard formulation. Asia Minor and the islands seem to have been the home territory par excellence of the female figure, and it is in their hinterland that one should look for influences.

This problem will be discussed in greater detail in Chapter 4 on Korai. Here I can only point out that recent discoveries of over life-sized statues in neo-Hittite territory have considerably enriched our understanding of the artistic production and, in particular, of the treatment of drapery in non-Greek areas. I refer specifically to the headless statue (3 m. high) of a man from Kululu, near Kültepe, in Anatolia, which can be dated on historical grounds around 700. The statue shows a mantle with zigzag folds worn in a fashion comparable to the Greek himation and a sleeved chiton such as we find in some korai, with seams running along the outer contour of the arm. Another find from Kululu is a sphinx with inlaid eyes, which may suggest another source for this technique in some Greek sculptures usually considered to be under Egyptian influence. One more statue, this time from Palanga, must be approximately contemporary with the Kululu man; it is also of monumental size, though not quite as large. Its mantle has more numerous zigzags at the edges, thus corroborating the presence in freestanding sculpture of a motif which had already been noticed largely in relief or the minor arts. Akurgal has written extensively on the subject of Oriental inspiration for Greek motifs, though his relatively low chronology for some of the Near Eastern material tends to give the Greeks a more innovative and influential role than they might have played in reality. Yet even more than individual motifs and fashions in clothing and accessories, which could easily have traveled independently of sculptural techniques and influences, it is life-size or over life-size sculpture in the round, though carved in the local basaltic stone, which suggests neo-Hittite inspiration for early Greek sculpture. By contrast the better known North Syrian reliefs look somewhat removed from Greek typology and techniques.[26]

The Orient is also responsible for having given Greek Archaic art its content of monsters and its narrative iconography. According to a recent study, Oriental art presented the Greeks with alien images without content since the mythology connected with the representations was unknown to the Greeks. However, they gave their own content to the Oriental pictures and used them to illustrate their own traditional stories. If this hypothesis is correct, no representations of myth or legend are possible in Greek art before the

[26] F. R. Grace (*AJA* 46 [1942] 341–59, esp. 343–48) suggested, and Richter agreed (*Kouroi*, 2–3), that Assyrian renderings may also have provided inspiration for specific motifs. Aside from the details of musculature and hair patterns, there is a definite hairstyle which may also have reached the Greeks from Assyria. It consists of looping the long hair mass over a fillet, so that it folds over it, spilling down again almost to the level of the nape (Br. Mus. 118917, from the palace of Sennacherib at Nineveh, Hrouda, pl. 39:2). It is, however, difficult to see how direct contacts between Greeks and Assyrians could have taken place, so that Assyrian sculpture per se cannot be considered influential in sparking the inception of monumental statuary in Greece.

beginning of the Late Geometric period, and not many may have appeared before the end of the Eighth century. In this context it is interesting to note the great variety and richness of subjects and iconography which occur in the art of the Cyclades, especially on the spectacular relief pithoi. They seem to confirm the fact that the islands could be particularly receptive to ideas and motifs coming from elsewhere, and that they provided fertile ground for concepts of monumentality and narrative.

Again, in the context of origins, the question arises whether such creatures as the lion and the sphinx passed into the Archaic monumental repertoire from the Oriental minor arts: ivories, metalwork, and textiles. To accept this suggestion would be to accept for such types a magnification process—from two-dimensional figurine to large-scale sculpture in the round—which has been rejected for the human figure on technical and conceptual grounds. Here, too, the basalt sphinx from Kululu and the many Hittite and Egyptian lions in stone encourage me to think that the Greeks must have seen monumental renditions of such subjects although they might have long been familiar with similar representations in much smaller scale. On the other hand, our undisputed acceptance of foreign prototypes for both the sphinx and the lion makes it seem more remarkable, to my eyes, that a similar origin for the kouros type, or even for the female figure, should be disputed or debated.[27]

A Domestic Influence: Armor

Before concluding, one more source of influence on Greek statuary should be isolated: Greek armor. With very convincing arguments, J. F. Kenfield has advanced the hypothesis that bell-corselets and greaves, as made since the Late Geometric period, may have had great impact on Archaic stone sculpture of almost a hundred years later. This influence is to be seen in the anatomical details which characterize both front and back of the metal corselets, and which can be found, in almost unchanged form, in some Greek kouroi—not only the Argive Kleobis and Biton and other members of Richter's Sounion Group but also the later Cleveland kouros (Figs. 3–4). Kenfield attributes the similarity to the aesthetic conservatism of hoplite armor, which retained certain anatomical patterns for over two centuries. He also makes the important point that armorers may have been the monumental sculptors of the late Eighth–early Seventh century, as shown by the Dreros *sphyrelata*, which bear such close similarity to armor in both technique and detail. The three under life-size statues from this Cretan site—a naked male and two female divinities, made of bronze sheets hammered and riveted over a wooden core—have been generally dated to the Seventh century. Most recently, Schäfer has favored a date within the Middle Daedalic phase, rejecting Rizza's attribution to the Early Daedalic between 690 and 670. However, Boardman has convincingly argued for a late Eighth century date, on the basis of comparative material from other sites, thus vindicating Pendlebury's original dating of the Dreros bronzes on the basis of their context.

Kenfield is probably correct in attributing to influence from armor that "much greater

[27] It is, of course, understood that men and women formed part of the Greeks' daily experience, while the same cannot be said for the sphinx and the lion. Yet it is noteworthy that the griffin, which appeared so often in the minor arts, both Greek and Oriental, seems to have found little or no favor with monumental stone sculptors of the Archaic period.

feeling for the true volume of the human figure" which Greek statues seem to have as contrasted with their Egyptian prototypes. Indeed, armor "has to conform to the true volume of the human figure in order to be worn." Since a corselet consisted of a plastron and a dos, it provided the guidelines also for that part of the human body which was not fully visible in an Egyptian statue, the back. Greaves supplied the pattern for the rendering of the calf muscles and the shin bone. And the engraving technique used to delineate muscular details on armor could be applied almost unchanged when carving in stone. To these points made by Kenfield, I should like to suggest the addition of another: that the distinctive pattern of eyebrow arches flowing uninterrupted into the straight nose of an Archaic face may have its origin in the noseguard and orbital cavities of a Corinthian-type helmet.[28] Finally, Kenfield thinks that Greek armor remained relatively conservative in anatomical details, while stone sculpture advanced rapidly toward naturalism. I would see armor, especially as shown on vase painting, as not remaining stationary but as becoming increasingly stylized in the rendering of musculature (for instance, the volutes which replace the more organic curves delimiting the pectorals). Is it too far-fetched to suggest that such stylization set in as a distinguishing mark to differentiate an armored from a naked body in contemporary "naturalistic" sculpture?

SUMMARY

The complex problem of the origins of Greek monumental stone sculpture can be outlined as follows:

1) Large-scale wooden statuary seems to have existed even in prehistoric times and was probably made during the Eighth and Seventh centuries. Presumably ill-shaped at first, it eventually became anthropomorphic but colossal in that the lower part was column-like or shown as if tightly enveloped in a garment. Since religion was probably dominated by female deities, such renderings were highly appropriate for female figures.

2) At the beginning of the Seventh century, the Daedalic style was introduced from the Syro-Phoenician world. It spread throughout Greek territory and flourished particularly in Crete. It was easily applied to the iconography of female divinities and found its best expression in wood, although it was also adopted by the minor arts in other media and translated into soft limestone statuary around 650. Large-scale wooden images of goddesses provided inspiration for the early kore type in marble, and some traits of the Daedalic style continued well into the Sixth century, partly because of religious conservatism and partly because of iconographic expediency.

3) At approximately the same time, Greek armorers must have developed the body armor, with its complement of anatomical details, and some armorers may have attempted sculpture, significantly over a wooden core.

[28] This rendering may seem an obvious solution to the problem of carving two features so directly connected as nose and eyes; its originality emerges only when comparison is made with Egyptian, Near Eastern, or even Daedalic solutions, which result in an entirely different treatment of eyebrows and nose. Particularly interesting is the fact that Greek Archaic statues do not attempt to indicate the hairs of the eyebrows, while both Egyptian and Assyrian faces have most prominent renderings which look almost like appliqués.

Another detail which may possibly derive from armor is the tripartite division of the upper arm (at the deltoid muscle), as seen, for instance, in the Sounion Kouroi. Similar engraved lines occur on upper-arm guards in bronze, as preserved at Olympia.

4) Around the middle of the Seventh century, Greek travelers were exposed to Egyptian techniques and statuary. They must have adapted their acquired information to suit their specific need: the making of male figures, possibly in action, as representations of male divinities, presumably Apollo. This sudden need could be explained on the basis of the increasing importance of this god both at Delphi and Delos, as well as in areas of Asia Minor where he was associated with Artemis. The "walking" statues were made in marble, with the grid technique learned from the Egyptians, and they marked such a departure from previous methods and iconography that they could truly be considered to signal the inception of a new, naturalistic style, the Archaic. The patterns employed by armor may have supplied some of the anatomical details for the new type.

5) The "walking" kouros presumably sparked attempts to make the female statues move too. This desire could be achieved only through the elimination of the confining Daedalic costume and the adoption of new garments, for which the neo-Hittite areas provided the East Greeks with patterns and inspiration, and possibly even daily fashions. Monumental statuary in the round from North Syrian territory must also have further influenced the creation of comparable Greek sculpture.

6) This fusion of elements, local (i.e., armor and Daedalic, even if the ultimate inspiration for both was also Oriental in origin), Anatolian/Phoenician, and Egyptian, came to complete fruition in the areas which were most open to foreign contacts and closest to the supplies of marble: Samos and the Cyclades, specifically Naxos and Paros. In either case, close proximity to a sanctuary must have promoted experimentation and created demand. The iconographic ferment produced by the infiltration of anonymous Oriental motifs within the Cycladic sphere must also have contributed to the creation of other statuary types like the monumental sphinx and lion.

7) The restricting effects of a technique and canon imported from abroad and hardly susceptible of variation, combined with the material difficulties of supply and transportation, may have resulted in the widespread adoption of certain general types and of a common style, although individual regions and sculptors managed to put their imprint on their products. Certainly the new style was hailed as exciting and pleasing though certain areas, like Crete, never fully accepted it. Marble remained the main medium throughout the Archaic period, with bronze becoming a serious competitor only toward the end of the phase. Poros and limestone were used seldom, and solely as a cheaper substitute, even for architectural sculpture, and wood was confined to statuettes or to the occasional cult image. Size, enormous at first, was gradually reduced to normal, and the Late Archaic period even produced some marble figures at a scale less than life-size.

These seven points condense my previous discussion, but two more need briefly to be made. First, we should acknowledge the fact that, for all its various sources of inspiration, Greek sculpture managed to acquire almost from the very beginning a quality and style which set it entirely apart from the production of other countries. It is perhaps more profitable, and more difficult at the same time, to investigate not what the Greeks borrowed from elsewhere, but in what way they managed to transform these foreign elements into something uniquely their own and to do it so successfully that their very sources were later influenced by Greek art. Despite extensive borrowings from foreign cultures, the end product of Archaic sculpture is unmistakably Greek and thoroughly coherent, without a trace of eclecticism to betray its multiple origins. This process of selection and transformation needs further clarification and analysis.

The second point is that Archaic marble statues were not made as cult images, not even the over life-size monuments. The idols worshiped in the temples remained relatively small and presumably wooden because of the great veneration that is usually attached to antiquity and tradition. Therefore Archaic sculptural production was not triggered, as is often said, by the need for providing a focus for the newly erected stone temples. Even as late as the Fifth and Fourth centuries, shrines were built to house cult statues of much greater antiquity and little aesthetic value—and the first gigantic image within a temple (though perhaps not a cult statue in the true sense of the term) may have been the Athena Parthenos by Pheidias. Yet there is no mistaking the religious content of Archaic statues, which must have been made solely as civic and public art to please the gods and honor the dead. As such, they represented the divinities themselves, often in enormous size, or anonymous human beings as offerings. Why these religious feelings found expression in anthropomorphic statues at that specific time is probably impossible to fathom completely. Certainly, historical conditions, the presence of a wealthy aristocracy or a powerful tyrant, must have contributed to the financing of this new form of art whenever technical knowledge and foreign examples became available. At the present state of our knowledge, it can only be stressed how different the purposes and motivations of the Greek sculptors seem to have been from those of their contemporary sources.

BIBLIOGRAPHY 2

FOR PAGE 17

Exponents of the first theory are, e.g., Carpenter and Richter, in their various writings. For the second theory, see Cook or Kranz, with added bibliography.

Kea statues: *Hesperia* 33 (1964) 328–31; *Archaeology* 15.4 (1962) frontispiece for color reproduction of head K 3.511. Some of the original estimates on numbers of statues and their chronology have been revised through further research; most of my information comes from a lecture-seminar held by Miriam E. Caskey at Bryn Mawr College in the Spring of 1975. Her publication of the Kea statues is in preparation.

Mycenae idols: *JHS ArchR* 15 (1969) 11–12; *AAA* 3 (1970) 72–80; G. E. Mylonas, *The Cult Center of Mycenae* (Monographs of the Academy of Athens 33) 1972, 29–30, 39; *AAA* 6 (1973) 189–92.

FOR PAGE 18

Terminology for sculpture: V. Müller, *MMS* 5 (1934–36) 157–69, especially n. 5. See also H. Frisk, *Griechisches Etymologisches Wörterbuch* (1954–70) under the various entries.

On wood and wood carving: *EAA* s.v. *Legno* (with some literary sources); M. J. Mellink, *Dark Ages and Nomads ca. 1000 B.C.* (Istanbul 1964) 63–70, esp. 69; Davaras, 39–40, with bibliography. For literary sources mentioning *xoana* in materials other than wood, see *JHS* 10 (1890) 133–34. See also infra, 23–26.

FOR PAGE 19

Daedalic sculpture: the classic work is R.J.H. Jenkins, *Dedalica. A Study of Dorian Plastic Art in the Seventh Century B.C.* (Cambridge 1936). G. Kaulen, *Daidalika* (Munich 1967) has advanced some new theories which have not met with general agreement; see, e.g., the reviews by C. Rolley, *RA* 1970, 133–34, and D. G. Mitten, *AJA* 74 (1970) 107–10. For a broader compass, see *Dädalische Kunst*; cf. also P. Demargne, *La Crète Dédalique* (Paris 1947) and id., *Naissance de l'art grec* (Paris 1964).

For a review of *Gortina*, see J. Schäfer, *Gnomon* 44 (1972) 185–95.

Rizza's chronology: *Gortina*, 46 and 148; for the date of the temple, see p. 26; cf. also p. 244.

FOR PAGE 20

Some of the Gortyna material is illustrated by Davaras; see also Demargne, *Naissance* (supra, bibl. for p. 19) fig. 459.

FOR PAGE 21

For the theory on the replacement of the plaques, see *Gortina*, 52.

On Oriental origin of the iconography of the naked goddess: *Gortina*, 248–49.

For workmen coming from Tell Halaf, J. Boardman, *BSA* 62 (1967) 57–75, especially 66–67.

For the introduction of the mold: Cook, 28.

From figurines to large-scale sculpture: *Greek Art*, 60–66; *Greek Sculpture*, 5–7.

FOR PAGE 22

Crete tied to its Minoan past: Demargne, *Crète Dédalique* (supra, bibl. for p. 19), passim, and especially p. 353. See also infra, p. 26 n. 13.

For a critical summary of recent bibliography on early Crete, see P. Demargne, *RA* 1974, 301–6.

Terracotta kouros compared to bronze from Delphi: *Gortina*, 231 and figs. 314–15 on p. 235. On Delphi kouros, C. Rolley, *FdD* 5:2 (1969) 111–13 no. 172. Rolley lowers the traditional chronology (645–640) to ca. 620, but I would favor an even lower date. Rolley seems to accept for his kouros the Cretan origin postulated by many, and he seems to doubt the "island Ionic" provenience suggested by Schefold 161 pl. 13. To me the presence of the belt on the bronze kouros suggests a connection with Delos and Naxos.

FOR PAGE 23

On the meaning of *kolossos*, G. Roux, *REA* 62 (1960) 5–40; see also J. Servais, *AntCl* 34 (1965) 144–74. Also supra n. 10. J. Ducat, *BCH* 100 (1976) 239–51.

FOR PAGE 24

Wooden idols from Palma di Montechiaro: Best illustrations in *EAA* 4, fig. 624 on p. 531. On

Sicilian Daedalic and various types of bodies, see Meola, esp. 11–47 for comments on Daedalic in general. To her bibliography add now E. Paribeni, *AttiMGrecia* NS 9–10 (1968–69) 61–63.

Cook's quotation is from p. 27, where he maintains that wood carving had no special importance on the formation of the Daedalic style. For the opposite position, which sees the origin of monumental sculpture in wood, see H.-V. Hermann, *AA* 1974, 636–38.

Royal tumulus at Gordion: *AJA* 62 (1958) 147–54, especially 148–49.

On technique of Gortyna statue: Davaras, 18–20.

Cretan technique as response to Cycladic marble carving: Adams, 56.

FOR PAGE 25

Samian base for cult statue: D. Ohly, *AthMitt* 68 (1953) 25–50; E. Buschor, *AthMitt* 58 (1933) 152–58.

For a commentary on Pausanias, see P. Levi, *Pausanias' Guide to Greece* (Penguin Books 1971) vol. 1, 237–38 and n. 24.

Wooden Hera statuette from Samos: D. Ohly, *AthMitt* 82 (1967) 89–99; G. Kopke, *ibid.*, 100–48, especially 107 for the date (ca. 640). This is considered too late by Kranz, 21 n. 75, who believes the figurine is Cretan, even Gortynian.

For the *epiblema*, see Davaras, 59–64, with bibliography.

FOR PAGE 26

Marble kouros from Gortyna: *Kouroi* no. 177 figs. 525–26 (ca. 490–480 or later).

Crete as birthplace of monumental stone sculpture: Davaras, 50.

On the Oriental origin of Apollo, see, e.g., H. Cahn, *MusHelv* 7 (1950) 185–99; E. Simon, *Die Götter der Griechen* (Munich 1969) 122–36; E. Vermeule, *ArchHom* 3 part v (1974) 88–89.

FOR PAGE 28

On Daidalos: H. Philipp, *Dädalische Kunst*, 5–13, esp. 9 for a discussion of 5th century sources on the liveliness of Daidalos' statues. See also Davaras, 41–43, with different conclusions.

On the motion of kouroi, see the stimulating comments in *Erzählung*, 88–89 and n. 1.

FOR PAGE 29

Trailing skirt of women on vase painting: *Art of Greece*, 203, attributes it to influence from North Syrian and Hittite art.

For Samian korai, walking korai, and the kore from Klaros, see infra, Ch. 4.

On the meaning of *rhythmos*, see *Ancient View*, 133–43; however, Pollitt does not include my suggested meaning among the translations for the term. Another possibility would be that walking is taken to be a rhythmical alternation of steps. The major ancient source on this point is Diod. Sic. 1.97.6. On Telekles and Theodoros see Diod. Sic. 1.98.5–9; cf. *Ancient View*, 13–14 and nn. 3–4, with bibliography. See also infra, Ch. 10.

E. Iversen: *MittKairo* 15 (1957) 134–47; id., *Canon and Proportion in Egyptian Art* (London 1955).

Kim Levin: *AJA* 68 (1964) 13–28.

FOR PAGE 30

Guralnick, esp. 78 for an outline of similarities and differences. See also her "Kouroi and the Egyptian Canon: A Study of Proportions," Ph.D. Diss for the University of Chicago, 1970.

Against the theory of Egyptian influence on Greek sculpture, see, e.g., R. Anthes, *ProcPhilSoc* 107 (1963) 60–81; also Cook and Kranz, passim.

For comments on the balance and technique of kouroi: B. S. Ridgway, *AJA* 70 (1966) 68–70.

FOR PAGE 31

On Greek carving techniques, the most important work is Adam, *Technique*; see also B. S. Ridgway in *The Muses at Work*, ed. C. Roebuck (Cambridge 1969) 96–108.

Limestone works from Rhodes: *BrMusCat* 1:1, 156–70; on Cypriot works, most recently, *Salamine de Chypre* vol. 5, M. Yon, *Un dépôt de sculptures archaïques* (Paris 1974).

Greek moldings derived from Egypt: L. Shoe, *Profiles of Greek Mouldings* (Cambridge 1936) preface; *Greek Art*, 234.

Lion-head waterspouts: I.E.S. Edwards, *The Pyramids of Egypt* (Penguin books, 1961) 184; A. Badawy, *A History of Egyptian Architecture* 1 (Giza 1954) 188–89.

Sculpture from Naukratis and Egypt: *Kouroi* nos. 28–30, 59–61, 81–85; figs. 129–31, 204–7, 264–72; cf. also *BrMusCat* 1:1, 180–200.

FOR PAGE 32

On Egyptian use of marble: A. Lucas, *Ancient Egyptian materials and techniques* (London 1962) 414–15.

Cyclades as birthplace of Greek sculpture: Homann-Wedeking; *Aspécts*, 80–81.

FOR PAGE 33

A recent summary of opinions and bibliography on the various theories over the birthplace of Greek sculpture, in Davaras, 44–45.

For Corinthian sculpture in particular see Wallenstein; note, however, that for the 7th century and the first half of the 6th he can list only 8 pieces (or groups of fragments) from the entire Corinthia, and of these only one was actually found at Corinth. The others are: 1) the "metopes" from Mycenae; 2) the architectural sculpture (pediments and metopes) from the temple of Artemis at Corfu; 3) the Laganello head in Syracuse; 4) a male head in Boston, presumably from Greece; 5) a fragmentary kouros from Aktion; 6) a complete kouros from Aktion; 7) the Tenea kouros. Yet in 1951 F. Poulsen (*Ny Carlsberg*, 18–19) could write: "The best Archaic kouroi were created by Peloponnesian and Attic art, but Ionia and the Islands were not long in sharing in the develment."

Greek apprentices in Egyptian workshops: The theory was advanced by Karen Vitelli, who has kindly allowed me to mention it in this context.

On the Greeks in Egypt, see M. M. Austin, *op. cit.* (supra, 15, bibl. for p. 6) 43, and the discussion of Naukratis, 22–33.

FOR PAGE 34

Adam's suggestion: p. 7. But note the comments by E. B. Harrison, *ArtB* 54 (1972) 536–37, especially regarding sculptors traveling to the quarries.

FOR PAGE 35

Kore predominant in Ionia: See B. S. Ridgway, review of Richter's *Korai*, in *ArtB* 52 (1970) 195–97.

Kululu draped statue: T. Özgüç, *Kultepe and its vicinity in the Iron Age* (Ankara 1971) 102–9. See also for the sphinx with inlaid eyes, pls. 41–42; and for illustration of the statue from Palanga, pl. 39.

Moschophoros eyes under Egyptian influence: K. Levin, *AJA* 68 (1964) 18. See also *Art of Greece*, passim, and *KAnat*, e.g., 220. The article by F. R. Grace, *AJA* 49 (1942) 341–59, can still be read with profit.

On Oriental iconography and its use by the Greeks, see J. Carter, *BSA* 67 (1972) 25–58.

FOR PAGE 36

J. F. Kenfield, III, *OpRom* 9 (1973) 149–56; id., *AJA* 78 (1974) 70–71.

On the Dreros bronzes, see Kenfield, *OpRom*, 152 n. 10 with extensive bibliography; add *Gortina*, 224 (between 690 and 670) and J. Schäfer, *Gnomon* 44 (1972) 185–95. Boardman, *BSA* 62 (1967) 61; J.D.S. Pendlebury, *The Archaeology of Crete* (London 1939) 338.

FOR PAGE 37

The quotations are from Kenfield, *OpRom* 9 (1973) 156.

Corinthian helmets: See, e.g., *OlBer* 7 (1961) pls. 14–52, passim.

PART II

SCULPTURAL TYPES

Chapter 3

Kouroi and Related Male Figures

In the previous chapter I have suggested that the Archaic style was strictly connected with the inception of the kouros type, which dictated both an iconography of movement and the use of a medium capable of standing the technical stresses of the pose. It is therefore appropriate to begin a systematic analysis of Archaic sculpture by focusing on the kouros.

The term applies to Archaic statues of naked youths (that is, beardless men) standing with one leg forward, feet flat on the ground parallel to each other, and arms along the sides. Such statues began to come to light and attract interest during the Nineteenth century, and their number has considerably increased in recent years. Initial controversy about their meaning and origin has given place to almost passive acceptance. We have come to view all kouroi as similar and to take for granted their ubiquitous presence in both cemeteries and sanctuaries, their nakedness, their chronological sequence. I believe, however, that many problems still deserve discussion, and I hope to reopen many seemingly closed questions.

THE GENESIS OF THE TERM

Perhaps the first kouros to receive scholarly attention was the enormous Apollo dedicated by the Naxians in Delos. The fragments, seen and described by European travelers as early as 1416 (Buondelmonte), were finally recovered by L. Ross in 1835. Yet this first example was not a typical kouros in that he wore a belt, and his surviving hand (the left), pierced by a hole, held an attribute, probably a bow. This statue must have engendered the belief that all such Archaic statues represented Apollo, so that subsequent finds were given this name regardless of their purpose. The identification was suggested on the basis of the Homeric Hymn to Apollo, where the god is characterized as youthful and athletic, with flowing long hair. Inscriptions on kouroi dedicated to that deity and ancient sources describing early statues of Apollo contributed to the theory.

By 1895, however, it had been recognized that not all such statues represented the god, and the Greek archaeologist V. I. Leonardos, in discussing the youth from Keratea, could suggest that the generic term kouros be used instead. From the native Greek the word passed, untranslated, to the French when Lechat adopted it in 1904, regretting that no equivalent existed in his own language. By 1909, when Deonna wrote *Les "Apollons Archaïques,"* he placed the earlier definition within quotation marks, and in 1942 Richter made the new term a byword by publishing the first edition of her *Kouroi*, which has since appeared in two revised and enlarged issues.

It should be emphasized that her book by no means purports to describe and illustrate all known Archaic statues of this type. It attempts only to include the most important or complete examples available, dividing them into chronological groups based on the rendering of anatomical details. Richter did not formulate regional groupings because she firmly believed in a common style which spread with even pace throughout the Greek world of the Sixth century. Moreover, artists and their works traveled with great ease at all times, as attested by literary sources and epigraphic evidence.

This chronological approach has tended to blur regional variations and especially all possible difference in the meaning and purpose of the kouroi within the Greek world. More recent publications are now approaching the material within closed groups, therefore trying to establish not only relative but also internal chronology for all the finds from specific sanctuaries or sites. Though excavation has not been systematic enough to allow firm conclusions, some comments in general can here be attempted. In contrast to Richter, I shall not include kouros-like figures in the minor arts, but shall concentrate exclusively on large-scale statuary.

THE DISTRIBUTION OF THE KOUROS

The island of Naxos seems to have been the most productive source of kouroi, if not the only one, from their inception through the first half of the Sixth century. This assertion is based on the large number of statues in Naxian marble and fairly distinctive Naxian style which have been found scattered through the island itself and in many other Greek sites. It is also supported by the pattern of distribution which, when plotted on a map, appears to radiate in ever widening circles from this Cycladic center. Of the other marble quarries, Paros acquired prominence in the second half of the Sixth century, virtually replacing Naxos as a source of sculptural material but also establishing some stylistic influences of its own. Samos started by importing Naxian marble, but by the early Sixth century, when the first kouroi appeared, the island had its own source of supply in a local quarry; it certainly should rank as an important center for the making of kouroi in distinctive style. After the initial impulse had come from abroad, presumably from Naxos, local marble or even limestone was used in many places. Attica did not utilize its own resources until late in the Archaic period, importing both marble and stylistic ideas from elsewhere during the Sixth century. Note, however, that the Moschophoros and kore Akr. 593 are in Attic (Hymettian?) marble.

This brief sketch applies virtually to all Archaic sculpture. Looking at the kouros in particular, we find that the type seems to have spread with different rhythm from area to area, in some cases reaching very far from the place of origin, and in others almost ignoring neighboring territory.

The earliest kouroi have been found on Naxos, Delos, and Thera, and belong to the Seventh century. In Asia Minor the kouros seems not to have arrived before the second quarter of the Sixth century, a rather late date when compared with the inception there of other Archaic types. On the other hand, it is perhaps premature to write at this point the history of Archaic sculpture in Asia Minor. Since finds have been largely sporadic and inconsistent, we have notable gaps in our knowledge and some excavation material is still unpublished.[1] On the basis of present evidence, however, it would seem that Archaic

[1] Perhaps much will be learned from the publication of the Erythrai finds, which is still pending. Some of the Archaic sculptures from the site were shown at the 10th International Congress in Ankara/Izmir, in September 1973. There are also oral reports of a limestone kouros from Bayrakli/Old Smyrna.

Ephesos concentrated exclusively on architectural sculpture. This site, so rich in Orientalizing ivories and bronzes, has not yielded a single kouros or, for that matter, any other kind of freestanding statuary at a large scale. The absence of the kouros could be explained on the grounds that only the Ephesian Artemision, not the town itself, has as yet been found and excavated, and that male figures may not have been considered appropriate dedication for a goddess. On the other hand, some kouroi were dedicated to Artemis in Delos; and one would expect, if not kouroi, at least other statuary types from such an important sanctuary.

By contrast, Didyma has yielded a wealth of Archaic sculpture, including approximately 20 kouroi, thus ranking as one of the major centers of concentration for the type. Miletos was probably the seat of an important school of carving, and may be responsible for the spreading of the kouros to non-Greek areas, such as Xanthos in Lycia, or various other sites in Karia where the type seems to have been popular. Miletos also introduced the kouros to her own colonies, for instance Theodosia on the Krim (toward the eastern end of the Crimea) and Istros, near the delta of the Danube. In the wake of Greek colonists, and perhaps traders, the kouros spread far and wide within the Mediterranean basin. Some come from Olbia, from the Propontis on the Sea of Marmara, from Macedonia (Figs. 5–6) and Thrace. Along the coast of North Africa, the important Greek colony of Cyrene has produced many kouroi; and one small limestone torso, headless but with long hair down the back, is in the museum of ancient Utica, therefore in Phoenician/Punic territory. Kouroi occur in Sicily and South Italy, but not as abundantly as one would expect from such rich areas, perhaps because suitable stone was locally unavailable while clay was plentiful. Some kouroi have been found in Spain; a strange head is in Jugoslavia.

Of the Greek islands, most of the Cyclades—and, of course, Samos, as well as Chios, Rhodes, Thasos, Euboea, Aegina and Corfu—have yielded kouroi in greater or lesser numbers, some of them, which must in some cases be considered "imports," in distinctive Ionic or Cycladic style. The only surprising exception is Crete, where only one late example of the type has been found; this paucity is, however, compatible with the general picture from that island, since the typical marble kore in Ionic garb is also totally absent.

In Greece proper, the pattern of distribution is uneven and unexpected. I begin with the Peloponnesos because the Daedalic style seems to have found fertile ground in that area, at least in the minor arts, and Corinth is often considered the birthplace of Greek monumental sculpture. Yet, if the kouros is truly indicative of Archaic art, this claim can hardly be maintained. There are only nine or ten kouroi known to me from the entire Peloponnesos, and this figure includes Kleobis and Biton, which were set up in Delphi but were carved by an Argive master. That their style is local seems supported by Lingering Daedalic features, the engraved pattern of their musculature so reminiscent of corselets, and finally their similarity to the lower part of a bronze statuette from the Argive Heraion. Yet they are not the typical kouroi, since they wear boots, and their slightly bent arms, more angled than in standard figures, suggest action. Similarly, the so-called Phigalia kouros does not conform to the general type because he holds his arms flexed and his hands forward, at different levels, presumably with attributes; it is therefore likely that this statue represents an Apollo, as suggested also by the hair rendering. The grand total can be further reduced by at least one example, the Epidauros kouros, which seems an Ionic import. The head from Corinth is late enough (ca. 490–480) to have belonged to a body in action, and provides inconclusive evidence. Finally, two items on the list, two fragmentary male figures from Corinth and Isthmia, are not in marble but in local limestone.[2] The Tenea kouros alone, therefore, represents Peloponnesian production in canonical form and medium, and perhaps also the fragmentary statue from Pheia, which is, however, suspect as a "native" because it was found in a harbor town and, specifically, the harbor of Olympia.

The case of Olympia is in fact the most striking of all. Except for a fragment of Archaic hair, Ionic in appearance, and too small to reveal whether it belonged to a male or female figure, Olympia to this day has produced no example of a kouros, despite intensive excavation. Even granting the lack of good local marble and the possibility that such an important sanctuary may have rated expensive bronze statues now lost, the absence of the type seems surprising. Bronze was not used extensively for large-scale figures until at least the second half of the Sixth century, and one would therefore expect some marble kouroi to have been dedicated prior to that date. Amandry has shown that Olympic victors followed unpredictable patterns in commemorating their feats with votive monuments, and that the practice did not become common until after the Persian wars. We also know that at least two Sixth century winners chose to have their statues in wood. One may wonder whether this medium was preferred to marble because it allowed more active poses—therefore the apparent rejection of the kouros type as a victory monument may have been due to its rather neutral appearance. On the other hand, the statue that the Olympic pankratiast Arrichion of Phigalia set up in his home town is described by Pausanias (8.40.1) as a typical kouros. But here it is perhaps significant that Arrichion's image stood in Phigalia and not at the site of victory.

All in all, Olympia, like Ephesos, has produced very little Archaic sculpture aside from what can be attributed to architectural decoration—a fact which seems all the more puzzling in view of its many Geometric bronzes representing warriors and charioteers which could have found some counterpart in Archaic marble sculpture. Sparta, on the contrary, has yielded a relatively high number of Archaic stone statuary, including a Seventh century warrior torso and a bearded man with a tail, but no kouroi. We must conclude that the presence or absence of a certain type is not directly connected with the total sculptural patrimony of an area, with the relative wealth of the site, or even with the identity of the site itself, whether town or sanctuary. The explanation must lie in the specific meaning attributed to each sculptural type. The situation in the Greek mainland, and in Attica in particular, confirms this assumption.

Although isolated examples appear almost everywhere, two regions have produced the greatest number of kouroi: Attica and Boeotia. The estimated figures for the Ptoan sanctuary alone approximate 120 kouroi, and others were found in Boeotian towns. At the Ptoion, some statues were imported from elsewhere, especially from Naxos and Paros, but a local school of sculpture also existed and worked in a distinctive style, often in local material. In Attica, well over 30 kouroi are attested, either through preservation of the statue itself, or of its base. Most of them come from the fertile area of the Mesogeia, where the rich aristocratic families of the Sixth century had their estates, but many have also been found in the cemeteries of Athens. With the single exception of the kouroi from Cape

[2] One more limestone kouros may be represented by the fragmentary legs found in the Argive Heraion (*JOAI* 19–20 [1919] 144 no. 1 fig. 82); the scale is under life-size, and I have been unable to trace the fragments; therefore I cannot vouch for their attribution solely on the basis of a photograph.

Sounion, which seem to have been votive, the Attic kouroi are either funerary or of unknown nature. No true kouros, apparently, stood on the Athenian Akropolis.

This categorical statement may seem contradicted by the many fragments of male figures in the Akropolis museum, but on close analysis the evidence is either inconclusive or negative. Though male and naked, the statues do not conform to the standard kouros type because of their poses or attributes; moreover, none of them attains the over life-size scale of contemporary funerary monuments. The Akropolis had a rich population of male statues, but they were shown as riders, draped youths, mythological characters, seated treasurers, clothed offering-bearers, cuirassed warriors, and athletes in active poses.[3]

To be sure, the apparent lack of Akropolis kouroi may simply result from too narrow a definition of the type, which eliminates possible candidates because of minor shifts in weight, head turns, or arm positions. Yet these different poses, taken in conjunction with the relatively late date of the works involved, lead me to believe that the changes are significant harbingers of the Severe style, which witnessed the disappearance of the anonymous kouros. Even the earliest kouros candidate, Akr. 665, held his hands at different levels, and may therefore have represented an athlete. Toward the end of the Archaic period, bronze statues considerably outnumbered contemporary marble dedications. We might therefore be missing a good deal of destroyed evidence. But this situation would still not account for the omission of the type in marble in the earlier Sixth century, nor do the extant bases of the missing bronzes suggest the possibility that many kouroi did in fact once exist.

THE MEANING OF THE KOUROS

Why is the true kouros absent from the Athenian Akropolis? Certainly not because Athena is a goddess; not only have kouroi been found in sanctuaries of other female deities (Artemis, Aphrodite, Hera) but many other male figures were deemed appropriate for the Akropolis. Perhaps the standard kouros was too neutral a figure for the literal-minded

[3] Statistics on Akropolis male figures, derived from *AMA*, are as follows: 11 more or less complete statues or torsos, 8 male heads, 6 hands, 19 fragments of arms, 10 legs, and 6 feet. Besides the torso Akr. 665 (*AMA* no. 298), which also is not canonical because of its hand position, there are two male heads, Akr. 653 (*AMA* 323) and perhaps Akr. 306 (*AMA* 326) which could qualify; but since their bodies are not available, it is difficult to decide whether they belong to real kouroi. Of the other male figures, Akr. 692 (*AMA* 300) had both arms bent and held away from the body; to this statue Schuchhardt has also attributed a fragmentary left arm with open hand which would further differentiate the work from the standard kouros type. Akr. 689 (*AMA* 302) is the famous Blond Boy, whose lifted right heel, slanting hips, and bent head remove him from the category of frontal youths. The same can be said of the so-called Kritios Boy (Akr. 698, *AMA* 299), who may no longer be Archaic. The torso Inv. 4075 (*AMA* 305) is identified by Schuchhardt as a possible diskophoros because the remains of arms and neck, as well as the treatment of the musculature, suggest athletic action. All the other more or less preserved pieces are disqualified because of active poses or attributes (wings, corselets, etc.). Among the heads, Akr. 617 is considered male by Richter (*Kouroi* no. 65), but female by Langlotz (*AMA* 86). Akr. 663 (*AMA* 322) is turned slightly to the proper left and probably belongs to a rider. There are fragments of 6 hands, of which two are open, one resembles a rider's, and two held objects; 19 fragments of arms, of which many are impossible for kouroi, while some may not even be Archaic; 6 feet (one unfinished), and 10 fragmentary legs, of which one surely belonged to a rider. Most of these works date from the very end of the Archaic period, and all of them are at least no earlier than the second half of the 6th century.

Athenians, who preferred greater characterization in their dedications. However, the kore type seems to be as anonymous as the kouros, yet it was greatly favored as an Akropolis dedication. Here the answer may lie in the suitability of the female offering for Athena; moreover, what seems generic to our eyes may have carried a definite connotation for the contemporary Greek. A kore could have represented an attendant to the goddess, a priestess, an *ergastine*, or an *arrephoros*; and it could be dedicated by anyone, either man or woman. This is one of the main differences between Greek and Oriental practices; in Egypt or in the Near East the votive statue was the representative of the worshiper, meant to stand perennially in front of the divinity as a constant reminder of the offerer. Rather than seeking favors, Archaic Greek statues seem to have been largely thank-offerings after the favor was granted, even when they took the form of first fruits or a tithe at the beginning of a career or at the completion of a successful enterprise. As sculptural skills progressed, the dedicants may have become more demanding and may have expected to see some definite allusion to their profession or their achievement in their votive offerings. Statues of athletes, warriors, and treasurers were then set up, together with the more general "pleasant gift," the kore, which in earlier times could suffice precisely because it was visually divorced from its dedicators, who could be identified only through the votive inscription. But this answer also is not entirely satisfactory, especially since the Moschophoros shows that a certain amount of characterization was possible at a relatively early date.

One more possibility should be explored: that the kouros came to Attica primarily as a funerary monument, and remained largely limited to that function alone. This theory finds a certain amount of corroboration in the large number of Attic kouroi whose funerary nature is certain.[4] In addition, the two attested Athenian dedications at the Ptoan sanctuary in Boeotia, where kouroi were the offering par excellence, seem to have been a charioteer and perhaps a kore. One further detail may be significant. Attic male figures of the mid Sixth century (for instance, the Rampin Rider, the Zeus of the Introduction Pediment, even the Bluebeard from the Hekatompedon) wear their hair relatively short, clearing their shoulders. By contrast, both earlier and later Attic kouroi—from the Dipylon head to the Kroisos—wear theirs long and down their backs.

In general terms, it is correct to assume that male hairstyles became progressively shorter with time. The long tresses of the late Seventh–early Sixth century were gradually rolled up or cut short by the end of the Archaic period, and finally replaced by what we would call the crew cuts of Severe athletes. Within the sequence of Attic kouroi, this progressive shortening seems to have begun around 520; after that date, long curls were apparently limited to gods and heroes, perhaps to suggest that they were not mortals or had lived in earlier times. Some individual renderings of loose strands may have been meant to convey strenuous activity in disheveled athletes or warriors, or affectation in members of the *jeunesse dorée*. But what significance, if any, attaches to the discrepancy between the short-haired men and the long-haired kouroi of mid Sixth century Athens?

We can perhaps surmise that status, both social and chronological, was implied through

[4] Their figure is particularly relevant when contrasted with the general percentage of votive versus funerary kouroi. According to B. Freyer-Schauenburg (*Samos* XI, 9 n. 38), ca. 10 percent of all kouroi are surely funerary, ca. 47 percent come from sanctuaries, while ca. 43 percent are of unknown provenience.

hairstyle, but in the first case the situation appears the opposite of what one would assume since the aristocratic rider and the divine Zeus wear the shorter coiffure. It is more probable that youths cut their long locks upon entering manhood, and I believe this point should be stressed since we have tended to use the kouroi as standard example of sculptural evolution and contemporary fashions.[5] But if it is true that only beardless youths, and not men, wore their hair long after ca. 560, can we therefore assume that all later funerary kouroi stood upon the graves of young men? Or should we rather believe that Attic kouroi, because of their funerary nature, represented the deceased as heroized and therefore with "heroic" hair?[6]

The Funerary or Cult Purpose

This question opens up the entire problem of characterization in funerary sculpture. Some early theories suggested that the Archaic Greeks commemorated with expensive monuments only those relatives whose premature death seemed to violate the laws of nature, therefore not elderly parents, but only young sons and daughters. These theories are now superseded; both epitaphs and statues of seated matrons and men have shown that age was not a factor in the erection of funerary monuments.[7] In addition, Attic grave stelai present a wide range of subjects: bearded and beardless warriors, old and young athletes, even women with infants. This characterization in relief sculpture, however, makes all the more remarkable the apparent uniformity and anonymity of the funerary kouroi.

If the kouros type was considered too generic to represent an athlete or a warrior on the Akropolis, how could it be chosen to portray Kroisos or Aristodikos, when it stood on their graves?

The exclusive and expensive nature of such statues precludes the possibility that they were mass-produced, like late Fourth century gravestones. These funerary kouroi were specifically commissioned by wealthy aristocrats or foreigners from sculptors who seem to have advertised their work quite openly, since considerably more signatures of masters appear in funerary than in votive inscriptions. The deceased being commemorated by the monument was obviously not available as a sitter for the sculptor since his death was the prerequisite for the commission, yet some distinguishing factors could easily have been added by any master. Are we to think, for instance, that Kroisos went to battle naked and unarmed? A spear or a javelin, added to the clenched fists, or a metal helmet placed on the head, if not the actual rendering of a cuirassed torso, were certainly within the possi-

[5] See, e.g., *S. & S.*, 73–74. Karouzos (*Aristodikos*, 39) considers short hair (on both votive and funerary statues) as typical of an athlete and therefore "anomalous" in the general context of Archaic art. Note, however, that long-haired Spartan soldiers are mentioned in ancient sources and depicted on Lakonian vases.

[6] Such theory finds some confirmation in the over life-size dimensions of the funerary (as contrasted with some of the votive) kouroi, and in the fact that Aristotle (in Plutarch, *Consol. ad Apollon.* 27) calls the dead *kreittones*, "better, greater" than the living (cf. *Aristodikos*, 30).

[7] See, e.g., the comments by Karouzos (*Aristodikos*, 27–28). It has been pointed out to me that it is not the absolute age of the deceased but his or her failure to be immortalized through physical descendants that seems to require representation by a statue or stele. However, the monument of Therylides was erected by his children, as specified by the epitaph; Karouzos (*Aristodikos*, 66, B 5) suggests it was a grave statue, and Jeffery ("Gravestones" 122, no. 14) an equestrian group. See also infra p. 141.

bilities of any sculptor of the second half of the Sixth century and would have provided easy allusion to the form of death and the valor of the youth so clearly expressed by his epitaph. On the other hand, can we be sure that the youthful Kroisos statue really marked the grave of a young man?

The Sounion Kouroi. It is perhaps impossible to find answers to these various questions. Suffice it here to stress again that no Attic kouros, with the exception of those from Sounion, has ever been excavated from a votive context, as contrasted with the many found either within temples or in sanctuary areas outside of Attica. Yet many Attic shrines are known. The Sounion evidence must therefore be examined with care.[8]

Two enormous kouroi, many fragments, and four bases were found in a pit east of the Temple of Poseidon, on the promontory. Moreover, fragments from at least five more kouroi, ranging from life-size to half life-size, were excavated from a second deep pit near the Temple of Athena. Two of these fragments, presumably from thighs, carried inscriptions which, though now mostly obliterated, made clear that Sounians had dedicated the statues. This is incontrovertible evidence that the kouros could be used as a votive offering in Attica, and even presumably as an offering to Athena. Several other points, however, need consideration.

First of all, the Athenaion is not the only ancient temple within the precinct; a second building, smaller but contemporary with the Temple of Athena, stood to the north of it. Since both structures are now thought to belong to the second half of the Fifth century, neither can be connected with the Archaic kouroi, but they may well represent the Classical phase of an earlier cult. While the Athenaion is identified on the basis of ancient sources, we have no information as to the other shrine. It has been suggested that it could belong to a hero, but it is of standard temple form and was probably for a divinity.[9] The same (second) pit which yielded the kouroi also produced two iron swords, other votive offerings of military character, some objects appropriate to Athena, and finally the well-known relief of a naked youth perhaps crowning himself. If indeed some of the material from this pit can be connected with a god or a hero, rather than with Athena, the fragmentary kouroi could also have belonged to the same cult and therefore have, at least in part, chthonic or funerary connections. Can this be the case also for the kouroi found near the Poseidonion?

These enormous statues were at first identified as the Dioskouroi because of the peculiar star pattern around their nipples, but this theory has not found general acceptance. More

[8] That some kouroi at Sounion may have been funerary is shown by an inscribed block from a stepped grave monument made by Epistemon, son of Hippostratos. Karouzos (*Aristodikos*, 66, B 6) assumes that the statue was a kouros, but no definite evidence exists for this surmise. For a different reading of the inscription see "Gravestones" 143 no. 56.

[9] The statue base at present within this second temple once obviously held a kouros, which, to judge from the plinth cavity, must have been approximately as big as the two giants from near the Poseidonion. The base is of Eleusinian limestone, which was not imported into Attica until the end of the 6th century. We know from this that enormous kouroi were erected at Sounion at that late a date. The base was re-used in the temple, presumably as the first course of a more complex arrangement, since the original front of the plinth cavity now faces toward the rear of the cella, and it is unlikely that such a cavity would have been left exposed. We do not know where the base and its kouros originally stood; they may well have been brought down from the Poseidonion to their present location. The same may be true of the kouroi found in the pit fill. In fact, some capitals, and other blocks from the late Archaic temple of Poseidon, were also re-used in the Athena precinct. If this surmise is correct, all the Sounion kouroi would then be dedications to the same god.

probably all the kouroi from the same deposit (some seventeen of them) represented the same type. The current theory is that they were early offerings to Poseidon, buried after the Persian destruction of 480. There is no archaeological evidence for an *early* Archaic temple to the sea god, but the date of some of the kouroi has been used to argue that the cult on the promontory was already established by the beginning of the Sixth century. However, what cult?

Homer (*Odyssey* 3. 278–82) mentions the pilot of Menelaos, Phrontis, who was killed by Phoebus Apollo and buried at Sounion. A hero cult centered on a mariner could easily have changed with time to a worship of Poseidon, the sea god. The kouroi could have been dedicated to the hero at first, then to Poseidon, in a continuing tradition. Or they may have represented a heroized version of the dead Phrontis, appropriate as an offering to Poseidon himself. As a final possibility, the kouroi may have been images of Apollo, not only as the slayer of Phrontis but as a chthonic divinity who is also a patron of sailors and a seafaring god himself, often associated with Poseidon. As Aktaios and Delphinios, Apollo might even have preceded Poseidon on the Cape, to be assimilated by him in later times. I personally prefer the theory that the Sounion kouroi are funerary/votive offerings to the Hero Phrontis, and that they represent him or a funerary Apollo. I believe that the Sounian statues, more than any other Attic kouroi, were set up under strong Naxian influence (perhaps even by "emigré" Naxian artists) and therefore followed not only the aesthetic but also the religious practices common on that island and all over the Cyclades.

This theory finds support in: 1) the fact that no other kouroi have been found in Attic sanctuaries; 2) the actual location of the promontory, which is an almost obligatory stop for all sail traffic from the islands and the East to Athens; 3) the Naxian marble used for the kouroi; 4) several stylistic features, which compare closely with Naxian works, such as the hair pattern, the presence of jewelry, the schema for the fisted hand, the hip muscle which continues as a ridge above the buttocks; 5) the inscriptions engraved directly over the body of the kouroi, which seems common practice in Asia Minor and Ionian territory in general but is highly unusual in Attica. This last point deserves special consideration since it conceives of the statue as an object that can carry an inscription rather than as a human portrait. Obviously Egyptian and Near Eastern sculpture, which were primarily meant as inscription-carriers, must have influenced the Greeks of Asia Minor and the islands, while the Athenians, with their seemingly more literal approach to statuary, confined the inscriptions to the neutral base.

The stylistic features of the Sounion kouroi will be examined later in greater detail. Here it remains to see why the Athenians elsewhere preferred to use the type as funerary rather than in its double purpose as votive offering and grave monument. I believe the answer lies neither in the deities worshiped nor in the ritual of the cults. I suspect that the kouros, arriving in Attica from elsewhere, was understood as a heroic representation of sorts, perhaps because of its nakedness, and therefore was automatically assigned to the commemoration of the dead.

Nakedness

We do not quite know why the kouroi are naked. It is generally assumed that theirs is an athletic nakedness, that these youths are immortalized as they appeared in the palaestra—but it then seems surprising that Olympia, the athletic ground par excellence, should be devoid of such images. Attic stelai, which often commemorated athletes, always included some piece of equipment to clarify the allusion; therefore nakedness alone might not have been sufficient indication.[10] Since the standing draped youth existed side by side with the kouros type, and was indeed fairly common in Asia Minor where nakedness was considered shameful among the neighboring barbarians (Herod. 1.10), special significance may have attached to the nude rendering. It may, for instance, have been further indication of age. Youths who still retained their long hair and were beardless could have been shown disrobed (as indeed they were even in Egyptian sculpture), whereas a bearded man may have had to be clothed. Yet the mature but naked Rampin Horseman seems to invalidate this conjecture.

To assume that the Greeks "undressed" the draped prototype they had derived from the Egyptians because of a specific Greek interest in human anatomy seems invalidated by the observation that not all regional schools of carving showed a similar scientific inclination. In fact, Attic kouroi alone display structural coherence and definite interest in musculature. All other kouroi present abstract renderings of anatomical forms which may pass for natural but are rather simplifications of more or less convincing stylizations of the human body. It has never been suggested that the Greeks may have taken from the Egyptians a naked type. Yet Egyptian representations of nude male figures, though uncommon, do exist. Aside from the ithyphallic god Min, whose (unusual) nakedness carries a fertility connotation, children in general, and the child Horus specifically, were always shown unclothed, as a sign of youth. More important, wooden statuettes of a person's *ka* (soul) were naked as a sign of eternal youthfulness and can therefore be seen as divine/funerary. If the Greeks specifically meant to portray a youthful god rather than a mortal, they may have fastened onto nudity as a distinguishing trait and may have, at a later time, extended the originally divine type to include dead and heroized men. This hypothesis does not, however, explain why the kouros was excluded from the Akropolis. Could it be that nakedness was considered improper in an Attic sanctuary? While the cloaked Moschophoros and the heavily draped youth Akr. 633 may lend support to this theory, scores of other naked figures from the Akropolis suggest that this was not the case.

Perhaps this problem cannot be solved, or perhaps no such problem exists and we should continue to take the kouroi's nakedness for granted. I suspect nonetheless that it was a significant trait, almost an attribute, whose meaning may have varied from area to area in Archaic Greece, and which in Attica (and perhaps even in the Peloponnesos) might have been interpreted as definite heroization, appropriate solely for actual gods (Apollo) or for funerary purposes. Obviously vases and the minor arts showed naked people in a variety of contexts, but monumental statuary apparently obeyed different rules and was more conservative and limited, both in content and context. It is therefore legitimate to raise the issue of the meaning of the naked kouros, even if an answer is not yet available.

The Function of the Belt

However, not all early kouroi were naked. Though corresponding to the general type in all other details, a few statues exist to which a belt was added, either plastically or

[10] Deonna (52–53) in discussing the nakedness of the kouroi, explains it "par des raisons propres à l'art," and gives secondary importance, if at all, to palaestra practices.

separately in metal. Here again the traditional answer has been to assume that the belt is an abbreviated symbol of a more complex costume, and in fact the same type of belt appears worn by fully clothed women or by partly draped men. Yet this very fact shows that a total costume could be shown when desired, and therefore the elimination of all clothes but the retention of the belt on a naked figure must have had its own significance.

A series of bronze statuettes of the Geometric period, some from Olympia and some attributed to that site, show naked men wearing helmets and brandishing spears in action poses; around their waists are wide belts, made either of flat bands or of a tubular ribbon wound spirally several times. Similar, also, are the belts worn by bronze figurines of charioteers. In these cases perhaps the belt stands indeed for the entire costume, as the helmet stands for a panoply.[11] On the other hand, the belts shown on the kouroi are quite different: they are wide, presumably of metal with a leather lining, and come together with a narrow clasp in the center. Often a raised border runs around the edges.[12] This rendering may simply be a more detailed portrayal of the same item which appears simplified on the Geometric figurines, and in fact the larger scale of the marble kouroi would allow greater elaboration. But we find the same type of belt in the bronze statuette of a kouros from Delphi and in the kneeling ivory youth from Samos, which may once have formed part of a lyre. Perhaps this type of belt was introduced only in the Seventh century and replaced the simpler Geometric type, so that chronological significance alone attaches to the difference.

The presence or absence of belts on kouroi may also have chronological import. Some of the earliest kouroi (Thera A) seem entirely naked, while slightly later ones from the same site wear the accessory, around 640–630. The rendering disappears shortly after the turn of the century, and it has been suggested that its elimination is caused by the new desire to adhere to nature and naturalistic representations. Yet I doubt that naked youths were a more normal sight than a bare youth with a belt, and helmets or spears continue to stand for more complex armor all the way into the Classical period. Perhaps another explanation could be ventured. To my knowledge, seven marble kouroi, all of natural or over life-size, wear belts, and they all seem to come from Naxos; even the very large ones on Thera were imported from the neighboring island. One of the seven, the gigantic statue dedicated by the Naxians in Delos, surely represents Apollo, and it is legitimate to ask whether the addition of the belt was meant to characterize that god.

Support for this theory comes from a Red Figure vase which shows a suppliant (Kassandra? Helen?) grasping a belted statue in the kouros schema who must therefore

[11] Note, however, that in E. Kunze's interpretation (*OlBer* 4, p. 123), the Geometric warriors would represent the youthful Zeus, therefore another divinity.

[12] The so-called Mantiklos Apollo in Boston (*Kouroi*, figs. 9–11) is often described as wearing a belt (see, e.g., Erika Simon, *Die Götter der Griechen*, [1969] 123 and figs. 117–18). I believe, however, that this is an erroneous impression since the "band" around the waist is actually recessed in relationship to the torso. Though this effect could result from the indentation created by a tight belt, it is more probable that the "belt" is purely the strip of body visible below a corselet. Though the bronze statuette is generally considered naked, the strong median line and the incised dots which follow the line of the clavicles could be more easily explained as part of some body armor, which might even include a neck-guard. The position of the left hand, to my mind, is explainable only if the figure held a bow; a spear, as sometimes suggested, would extend in front of the face, thus obscuring the composition from a frontal viewpoint. For a recent publication of the piece, see M. Comstock and C. C. Vermeule, *Greek, Etruscan and Roman Bronzes in the Museum of Fine Arts* (Boston 1971) no. 15 pp. 16–17.

represent a god, probably Apollo. In addition, all the belted kouroi come from areas associated with the cult of Apollo. Even the bronze statuette was found in Delphi, and the ivory youth, if indeed part of a lyre, may have been an allusion to the musical god or to his following.[13] On the other hand, one of the Thera kouroi (Δ) was probably set up in a cemetery. Is this sufficient evidence to exclude the Apollo identification?

Not all statues found in funerary contexts stood for the deceased.[14] We have at least one instance, at Aeolic Kyme, where divine figures were erected in a cemetery, perhaps as protection for the burials. While Cybele, Demeter, or Kore would seem more appropriate divinities for such a function, Apollo has a strong association with death, or even with protection of the dead. Not only was sudden death inflicted by him, but he was the god who protected Hektor's corpse from Achilles' abuses. In at least one instance we know of a statue of Apollo standing over a grave, even if it is that of a mythological character, Hyakinthos, and the god is portrayed in his column-like aspect, in a gigantic sphyrelaton. Moreover, in the tradition of his annual trip to the Hyperborean regions, Apollo is comparable to Demeter and Kore, whose appearance and disappearance coincide with the vegetation cycle. Finally, it has recently been suggested that Etruscans knew Apollo in a funerary function, a conception of the god which they may have adopted in the belief of their Trojan ancestry. It seems more likely to me that they may simply have received this idea, as many others, from Asia Minor Greeks who could in turn have absorbed Anatolian cults and credence. If early kouroi were introduced to Attica as representations of a funerary Apollo, it could explain why the Athenians seem to have limited their use to graves. But why should Apollo be shown wearing a belt?

Those who postulate continuity from the Geometric figurines to the Archaic statues accept the belt as a war-like attribute. This military aspect could easily be reconciled with Apollo, who was the virile god par excellence and therefore could be shown with the attributes appropriate to a strong man even if no immediate connection with war was implied. In fact, Apollo appears helmeted in an early depiction of the Struggle for the Delphic Tripod on an Olympia tripod-leg, and dedications of a military character have been found in several of his shrines (e.g., on Corfu, at Bassae, etc.).[15] The belt would have been

[13] One further instance of a belted Apollo may have occurred in Cyprus. Today only the head, the so-called Chatsworth Apollo in the British Museum, survives. But accounts by Cypriot peasants who found and carried off the bronze fragments relate that the statue wore something comparable to their own cartridge belts—a colorful detail which sounds convincing because of the homely parallel. On the other hand, a 5th century Cypriot example, though very Greek in style, is hardly evidence for early Archaic Greek practices. Cf. *Severe Style* 40 no. 8 with discussion of date and previous bibliography.

It would be interesting to know the reason for the epithet Zoster given to Apollo, as he was worshiped at Cape Zoster, in Attica, a site which had obvious connections with the Cyclades. Also the cult of "Belted" Apollo may have come to Attica from the islands. Pausanias (1.31.1) explains the name with reference to Leto loosening *her* belt there, but the temple excavated at the site seems to belong to Apollo; see K. Kourouniotis, *Deltion* 11–12 (1927–29) 9–53.

On actual Greek bronze belts, see S. Karouzou, *Deltion* 16 (1960) 60–71 pls. 25–34; examples of the second quarter of the 7th century.

[14] In support of this point, one of my readers has called my attention to the anonymous Greek epitaph (*Greek Anthology* 7.153) which describes a bronze statue of a maiden standing over the tomb of Midas. Whether the deceased was indeed the famous king Midas, or simply a private individual with the same name is irrelevant; the fact remains that a female figure could be considered an appropriate memorial for a man.

[15] Naked men or demigods wearing belts appear on Early Bronze age seals in Mesopotamia. They are often engaged in fighting monsters, and in some cases they may have a possible association with the

eliminated from the kouroi when the Greek conception of Apollo began to emphasize the more civilized aspects of his character. Since, however, the same type of belt is shown on contemporary female statues, one hesitates to attribute a definite virile meaning to it, especially when the earliest kouroi (Thera A) appear without it. The same objection would apply to interpreting the belt as part of athletic equipment, especially since Archaic representations of wrestlers or other athletes show them completely naked. Allusions in literary sources suggest that magic significance may have attached to belts, but since we do not know exactly how, it is best at present to suspend speculation. The iconographic question of the early kouroi, belted or unbelted, should however be reopened.[16]

It may seem a definite step backward from present progress to return to the old identification, but I suspect that the kouros type did indeed begin as a representation of Apollo, and that only at a later time did it acquire a more generic meaning which made it appropriate dedication for other divinities, including goddesses. Even when increased sculptural skill would have allowed greater characterization of Apollo statues, this was achieved solely through minor changes (in arm position and hairstyle), but the basic kouros schema was retained as late as the end of the Archaic period. Meanwhile the more generic kouros continued his basic association with the god.

This assertion is based on statistics; some kouroi have been found in sanctuaries of other deities, but by and large the vast majority come from areas traditionally connected with Apollo. Though the grand total of over 120 kouroi from the Ptoan sanctuary still remains unmatched, approximately 20 kouroi, as already mentioned, are documented for the sanctuary of Apollo at Didyma, and at least 15 for Delos. Several isolated examples were found within temples of the god, others carried dedications to him, and we may perhaps include also some which stood in sanctuaries of his divine relatives: his sister, Artemis, his son, Asklepios, his double, Helios.[17] To be sure, the distribution of finds remains uneven.

---

sun god. The difference in space and time seems, however, too considerable to postulate their connection with the Greek representations. Closer in time is an Iranian practice which continued from the First Millennium BC well into our era, and which was shared by Mitannians and Assyrians alike. According to G. Widengren (*Iranica Antiqua* 8 [1968] 133–55, especially 148–50; id. *Der Feudalismus im alten Iran*, Cologne 1969, 56 and n. 53), certain societies of warriors worshiped a god or hero killer-of-dragons and styled themselves friends or *mairyas*. They fought "naked" but with a leather belt, braided their hair, and used the image of a dragon on their standards and helmets and in their decorative art. The belt worn by these warriors was seen as a symbol of their connection with a hero or ruler, a mark of their feudal dependence, and a fidelity link with the master. From this initial connection, the belt in general became symbolic of a feudalistic society, so that seizure by the belt was the equivalent of the death penalty, through dissolution of the link with the ruler, while the awarding of a belt was a sign of honor.

How much of this Oriental meaning can be transferred to the Greek kouroi is questionable. It would be tempting to associate the dragon-slaying Iranian god with the Python-killing Apollo since the latter is the only Greek divinity (besides the heroes) who kills animals. The belted kouroi would symbolize their association with the divinity, or the very god would be personified with one of the attributes of his followers, as he later appears with a libation phiale commonly used by mortals. Unfortunately the parallel of the braided hair cannot be pushed too far because beaded tresses are not typical of male figures alone, and in Greek statuary may simply reflect contemporary fashions. Also Celtic warriors of the 6th c. BC went into battle naked except for a belt, but again this association seems remote.

[16] I cannot subscribe to G. Kaulen's theory (*Daidalika*, 113–15) that the Ionians started wearing belts in sympathy with Babylon, destroyed by Assurbanipal in 648.

[17] *Kouroi* no. 117 = from pronaos of Temple of Apollo, Gortyna (torso).

129 = temple of Apollo, Kalymnos, Dodecanese (Head).

187 = temple of Apollo Lykeios, Metapontum, Magna Gr. (Torso). (One foot of this kouros was

We may not be surprised that Klaros, still virtually unexcavated and unpublished, has yielded only one offering-bearer and one kouros head, though it was one of the most important oracles of Apollo in antiquity. On the other hand, the much more thoroughly excavated Delphi has produced only 5 kouroi, since Kleobis and Biton cannot be included in a canonical list.[18] We can only assume that not all sanctuaries of Apollo accepted the kouros type with equal enthusiasm, but this consideration alone does not disprove the basic identification of the kouros as a possible image of Apollo.

The Summary of the Meaning

A synthetic statement can be formulated as follows: From a study of distribution and an analysis of the kouros it would appear that the type was created around 650 to replace, though not entirely, a colossal or column-like representation of Apollo. The Greeks adopted the Egyptian schema (including perhaps the divine and youthful characteristic of nakedness), but wanted it to carry a definite suggestion of movement, so that some technical changes had to be made. They eliminated the backrest and the stone screen connecting it with the advanced leg; thus the center of gravity of the statue, for stability's sake, had to be shifted forward so as to fall between both feet. From its inception, the kouros had a funerary as well as a votive function, both of which can be reconciled with an identification of the type as Apollo. This identification is based on the fact that the great majority of kouroi with known provenience come from sanctuaries of Apollo or were dedicated to that god. In addition, some Seventh century kouroi wear a belt, which may have served further to characterize that god, perhaps as a symbol of virility and war-like qualities, or may have been simply an additional ornament. Even total nakedness, far from being purely an athletic allusion, must have carried iconographic meaning while the over life-size dimensions of the early statues definitely removed them from the human sphere. In its votive function, the kouros stood for the god himself or for his followers. Thus, in time, it could become appropriate dedication for divinities related to Apollo, or for sanctuaries in general, though not all areas of the Greek world were equally receptive to the spreading

---

found in more recent excavations along the east facade of the temple of Apollo, and a vague suggestion is made that the statue may have belonged to that building's pedimental decoration, which seems to have consisted of both limestone and marble pieces, *RA* 1967, 10–13.)

108 = temple of Apollo, Aliki, Thasos (Deonna; Richter uncertain).

168 = temple of Apollo Daphnephoros, Eretria (prob. Apollo).

114 = temple of Apollo area, Thera (another, more complete kouros from sanctuary of Apollo Karneios, not in *Kouroi*: *AthMitt* 73 [1958] Beil. 93–4).

Also, most of the kouroi from Naxos, Paros, Thera, Cyrene, Aktion, and Naukratis must have been associated with the prominent sanctuaries of Apollo at their respective sites.

A kouros' legs found at Miletos must have come from Myus, because the dedication mentions Apollo Termintheus, worshiped there (*Belleten* 35 [1971] 201–12). A Samian kouros (*Kouroi* no. 77) was dedicated by Leukios to Apollo (inscription on thigh).

Two kouroi (*Kouroi* nos. 124 and 154) were found in Kamiros, Rhodes, leaning against an altar of Helios; some kouroi from Naukratis and Paros come from shrines of Asklepios. Some kouroi from Delos were found in the Artemision. *Kouroi* no. 124 may go with a head excavated nearby (*AAA* 6 [1973] 116, fig. 4 and p. 118).

[18] It is interesting to note that all the kouroi in Delphi (*Kouroi* nos. 103, 104, and 149) look Cycladic in style, and the base which preserves a kouros' feet (*Kouroi* no. 105) was inscribed by the sons of Charopinos the Parian. The head (*Kouroi* no. 46), now in Delphi, is actually from Trikorphon and probably female (*AAA* 5 [1972] 317 n. 3); the strange head from Delphi in Athens (*Kouroi* no. 150 figs. 438–39) is limestone.

of the type. In its funerary function the kouros probably symbolized Apollo as protector of the dead and as the divine traveler to the Hyperborean regions. This was the aspect which the Athenians chose to emphasize, thus utilizing the kouros almost solely as grave monument. It is not impossible that such funerary statues may have portrayed the dead himself, but in this case we should either assume that all dead thus commemorated were young, or that they were immortalized in a perennially youthful appearance. It is at any rate significant that the Attic kouroi are usually over life-size and wear their hair long even at a time when bearded male figures wear theirs shorter; both size and hairstyle may be heroizing traits, though the latter may only imply that the wearer had not yet reached manhood status. The Sounion kouroi, being the only Attic examples of a votive nature, must have been set up under outside influence or for a heroic cult. Elsewhere, the kouros was particularly popular in Boeotia, Asia Minor, and the Greek islands, and, to some extent, even in non-Greek territory under Greek influence. Crete and the Peloponnesos seem to have resisted the diffusion of the type, perhaps because of Lingering Daedalic style or because of a preference for the aniconic Apollo.

KEYS TO CHRONOLOGICAL ASSESSMENT

Before embarking on an attempt to draw thumbnail sketches of regional styles for kouroi, it may perhaps be useful to risk a few tentative generalizations on changes which may have chronological significance.

Plinths

One of these changes can be observed in the development of the kouros' plinth. This term applies to that island of stone, part of the original block from which the statue was carved, which was left under and between the feet of the figure and served to anchor it to a separate base. At first the contour of the plinth was roughly oval, with the stone island large and massive. In a later phase the plinth appears smaller, approximately following the outline of the feet. In the next two or three decades, the edge was trimmed closer to the statue's feet, curving in between them to form a narrow "isthmus." The final stage of the plinth, toward the end of the Sixth century, returned to the oval. However, a hexagonally shaped plinth seems also to have occurred concomitantly throughout all these various phases. Since the latter has been consistently found in association with Naxian or Naxian-influenced kouroi, it may perhaps be considered typical of that island, though not all Naxian plinths have the same shape. This observation is interesting for the lead it offers in trying to group kouroi by provenience and regional style. A comparable observation has shown that Samian kouroi often stand on a square or rectangular plinth which, instead of being trimmed close to the feet, is almost as large as the base into which it is set, and forms a virtual slab on which the statue rests. This peculiar feature is found also in Samian bronze statues, and seems to have purely regional rather than chronological meaning.

Anatomy

Anatomical renderings have been taken as date indicators, but they too may have a significance that is largely topographical. Nonetheless, some general changes apply in a roughly chronological progression. For instance, the arms, which at first look awkwardly attached to the torso, as if held by strings, and extend too far down the thighs, later become shorter and more organically connected. The epigastric arch can be either pointed or rounded into a narrow oval, but becomes progressively wider and flatter, following the rib cage toward the flanks. The abdominal partitions within such an arch seem to have been a mainland discovery which eventually spread to the islands, perhaps along the routes of the marble trade. If indicated at all, they are at first a series of ripples or flat areas marked by as many as four or more transverse lines intersecting the *linea alba* in the center. These horizontal divisions finally dwindle to the canonical two, forming four globular masses. At first, the back is as straight as a board and the buttocks protrude excessively, but gradually the curve of the upper spine and the fuller back counterbalance the glutei. Hips, thighs, and calves progressively acquire bulge and mass. In more general terms, whatever was rendered by grooves and ridges earlier in the Sixth century, toward the end of the Archaic period is suggested by modeling, that is, by the gradual sinking and rising of surfaces within the major forms, in a subtle articulation which is often betrayed solely through the play of light and shadow.

Hairstyles

Hairstyles can be useful for dating when considered within the closed group of the kouroi rather than on all Archaic male figures in general. From the Daedalic style the early kouroi seem to have inherited the long locks which part over the shoulders to fall both over the chest and the back; yet no true Daedalic *male* figurine displays the same arrangement. One wonders whether this is basically a female hairstyle which was adopted by certain kouroi for a specific reason, or, and this is a very tentative suggestion, whether this abundant hair was in itself, from the beginning, that sign of a divinity or a hero that it became later on, because it had been borrowed from another context. In particular, one may hesitantly suggest that the Greeks misunderstood or mis-translated into hair the lappets of a typical Egyptian royal headdress which they saw either directly or through North Syrian intermediaries. Horizontal striations are in fact a common Daedalic stylization for hair, which continues, however, well into the Sixth century (cf. Fig. 4). Recently Naxos has yielded a very attractive head of a kouros with this layered hairstyle, which should be dated to the second quarter of the Sixth century, and even Akr. 665 shows traces of this coiffure, though confined to the back, as late as ca. 530. If this idea of Egyptian borrowing has any validity, it would imply that no Greek male, in everyday reality, ever wore such a hairstyle and that it had therefore purely iconographic and artistic significance. On the other hand, the fashion may have been real enough but simply limited in time and diffusion.

In chronological terms, we find that long locks over the chest occur largely during the Seventh century but seem to peter out with the inception of the Sixth century, or at least to undergo changes indicative of the later date. Important in this respect is the position of the ear in relationship to the hair mass; during the Seventh century it lies in front of the strands without affecting their fall, but in the Sixth the hair at the temples appears lifted and pulled back by the ear in a more natural rendering.

As for regional distinctions, I know of no Attic kouros with tresses over the chest, but this exclusion of the front locks may simply imply that the fashion was superseded by the time the kouros reached Athens. Naxos and Paros, and indirectly Thasos and Thera, seem to pioneer even in this rendering, during the Seventh century, and the fashion appears occasionally also in Sixth century Asia Minor. The sporadic Sixth century instances in Greece proper are either early enough to be considered cases of Lingering Daedalic, or late enough to be using an old-fashioned coiffure to characterize Apollo. This must be the case of the Phigalia and the Eretria "kouroi," for instance, while various mythological figures in architectural sculpture are thus differentiated from common mortals and projected back into a conservative past, e.g., the Dioskouroi of the Sikyonian metope (Fig. 59) or the Zeus of the Siphnian pediment at Delphi. Only Herakles, by and large, supplied the exception to this iconographic rule and is almost invariably portrayed as the wrestler par excellence (and perhaps even as a peasant?) and therefore with small curls hugging his cranium, whereas the more aristocratic Theseus appears with long locks down the shoulders. Around 520, kouroi start to roll their hair up over the nape, and by the beginning of the Fifth century short hairstyles are the norm. A typical late Archaic hairstyle, which is frequently found on charioteers, loops the long hair back under the fillet and then lets it spill over it. The arrangement is distinctive enough that it may be significant to find it used earlier for divinities in Assyrian reliefs.

The variety of hair renderings is so great that it is impossible to list all the patterns or to divide them into chronological and regional groups that are strictly consistent. In some areas certain renderings appear to prevail over others, and specific changes within the same hair pattern may indicate different dates, but there are too many gaps in our knowledge to draw up a consistent picture. Attic kouroi, for instance, prefer globular beads or pearls which in the earliest statues are large and round, often evenly aligned, but tend to become oval, more compressed, less sizable and orderly as time progresses. The Cyclades may have invented the opposite pattern, which has been defined as negative pearls. This motif could also be termed the vertebrae pattern, because it recalls the slightly concave sections of the spinal cord. A simpler design, which has been called chocolate squares, is a flat simplified grid which may also have island origin but is greatly favored in Boeotia. Examples of horizontal striations, which were common in Daedalic works, occur in several kouroi of varied provenience, while vertical strands, beaded or wavy, which were used by Cycladic masters as early as the Seventh century, become increasingly frequent everywhere after the mid Sixth century. A Samian variant of the strand pattern starts as a mass of wavy ribbons which end in corkscrew curls with extra tresses brought in to fill the interstices. Despite its apparent naturalism, this rendering can also be misleading; for instance, a small head in Cyrene has been described as wearing a knitted cap bordered by pearls because the alternation in the level of the strands resembles the purl pattern of wool (Figs. 7–8).

This ambivalence is typical and brings up an important point. Of all the human features, hair is the most elusive and can be rendered only by approximation, either by being impressionistically blocked out as an undetailed mass or by being converted into a pattern which necessarily tends to look abstract and decorative. This need to translate strands or curls into guidelines which could be reproduced over the flat surface of a stone block is largely responsible for the unreal appearance of many Archaic coiffures; yet we may have tended to dismiss Archaic hair as pure pattern a bit hastily. Tightly braided hair, as we see today in "corn rowing," for instance, may result in a series of beads or pearls closely approximating the effect on the kouroi. On the other hand, motifs which have been traditionally interpreted as patterns of natural hair may depict diadems or other forms of artificial ornament as appropriate for male as for female figures. Two photographs taken from contemporary life in Turkey may serve to illustrate my point (Figs. 9–10).

While renderings in later statuary are usually susceptible of only one interpretation, Archaic patterns toe the thin line between artifice and naturalism, so that it is often impossible to tell whether a natural feature has been converted into a decorative design or whether an ornament merges in appearance with the anatomical details. For instance, the Sounion kouros may be wearing a metal diadem over his forehead, somewhat like an Assyrian nobleman[19]—or the similarity in pattern with the hair over his back may suggest that the "snails" are actual curls visible between two fillets; by the same token, the rounded shape of his earlobes may indicate an earring or an overstylization of a physical detail. More puzzling is perhaps the hair arrangement of a Samian head in Istanbul. The peculiar wings above the ears cannot be reconciled with any natural flow of hair, and it has been suggested that they are an applied ornament. Yet they closely resemble a fairly common coiffure pattern of East Greek kouroi, in which a short layer of tresses, at times ending in spiral curls, is combed back over the forehead and lies over the similar but longer tresses covering crown and nape.

Pubic hair

Equally ambiguous is the pattern for the pubic hair, which may represent purely artistic fashions rather than daily reality but which seems to change with time. An attempt to classify the various renderings breaks into a variety of groups and subgroups, some supported only by examples on vases and bronze statuettes. On marble kouroi pubic hair is seldom plastically indicated, though small "life-savers" curls appear on one of the earliest kouroi (Delos A 333), and others may have had this detail added in paint. The increased instances of sculptural renderings toward the end of the Archaic period may have been influenced by the concomitant line of bronze statues, where paint could not be employed. Although types overlap in time and distribution is uneven, the development of pubic hair patterns can be roughly outlined as follows: The earliest shape starts in the Seventh and continues to the last quarter of the Sixth century. It is trapezoidal, with the longest side at the top, and is at times articulated into curls but is more often simply a raised plane. The latest examples may have a slightly concave upper edge. Around 520 a new pattern occurs: the upper edge breaks into two shallow concave curves which rise to a central point, while the sides cave in. This eventually develops into a star- or leaf-shaped pattern, three-pointed, with the fourth tip resting broadly on the base-ring of the penis (e.g., Aristodikos). A further development prolongs the two side tips and tones down the upper point, so that eventually the pubic hair is again rendered with a straight upper edge from thigh to thigh and narrowing sharply toward the penis, but the resulting trapezium is much lower than the Seventh century shape and usually wider. This last is the shape favored by the Severe style.

[19] A relief from Khorsabad (Strommenger & Hirmer, pl. 227) shows the same combination of waves over the temple and superimposed diadem, which is here clearly tied at the back of the head and studded at intervals with snail-like rosettes which closely resemble those of the Sounion kouros. Interestingly enough, a similar "diadem" with upright hook-spirals between two fillets appears on the monumental head from Naxos now in Copenhagen (*Kouroi* no. 50).

Hands

One other pattern may have regional and chronological significance: the schema for the clenched hand. There are two basic variants of this rendering: the simpler one turns the fist into a triangle almost fused with the thigh; the second, and more complex, articulates it into four facets rather than the normal three. In the first variant, the exposed surface of the hand consists of two inclined planes which meet along the line of the knuckles, and the fist is turned inward, as it were, toward the leg. In the second, the fist turns outward and stands out from the body even when it still adheres to it; two lines of knuckles and three inclined planes are therefore revealed, and only the back of the finger tips touches the thigh with a fourth plane. In the earliest Attic kouroi this geometric fist is actually incorrect, and the fingers have been given one extra joint; a faintly engraved line separates the padding of the tip from the next section, giving each finger a total of four, rather than the natural three, phalanges. As time progresses, the fist is shown less tightly clenched, with the thumb often resting against the middle phalange, so that the squarish outline is retained without violating the anatomy.

Unfortunately these two fist types do not correspond to two equally well-defined regional groups. Indeed, one kouros in Delos (A 1742) seems almost to exemplify both types at once; yet his triangular left hand looks more clearly four-sloped from behind. In some cases, instead, the squarish pattern is visible only from the front, and the shorter fingers seen from the rear approximate the triangular shape. In addition, hands have often broken off from the bodies, so that evidence is lacunose at best. I venture to suggest that the triangular fist is more at home in Asia Minor and Samos (and perhaps, by extension, in Boeotia and the Peloponnesos), probably under the more direct influence of Egyptian renderings or simply in keeping with East Greek preference for unbroken contours and flowing lines. The squarish schema may have originated in Naxos. From there it was transmitted to Attica, which adopted it with special enthusiasm since it appealed to the Athenian sense of structure and appreciation of clearly articulated forms.[20]

Knees

Before approaching the kouroi regionally, one more comment in general should be made. From the earliest examples, regardless of provenience, sculptors seem to have given great attention to the knees of their male figures. Patterns vary, but even the most abstract

[20] Several kouroi in Delos, which have the four-faceted form of the fist, have been attributed stylistically to Naxos, but definitive proof of such rendering there is presently unavailable. The extant left hand of the gigantic Apollo in Delos retains only three of its fingers, and corresponds to neither pattern; the fingers look actually jointless and somewhat rubbery. However, this effect may be caused by weathering, and the hand might have shown a more fully articulated outline had the thumb and index finger been preserved. As mentioned above, this is the case for the Delos kouros, A 1742. Another Delian figure (A 4048, also considered Naxian) resembles the colossal Apollo in the appearance of its hands as they are seen from the back of the statue.

A Naxian origin for this four-faceted fist pattern is also postulated by Harrison (*Agora* XI, 15 n. 6), who notes that it appears also on the kneeling ivory youth from Samos (Schefold, pl. 19).

An unusual fist rendering occurs on a Samian kouros (*Samos* XI no. 37 pls. 24–25): the left hand is turned outward so that both index and middle finger are visible from the frontal view; even their nails are carefully indicated. The general outline of the fist is four-faceted, but the schema is different from the traditional version.

kouroi, with highly simplified torsos, have powerful knees rippling with muscle and bone effectively rendering functional articulations. Specific renderings have been traced back to Egypt and Assyria, but the universal emphasis, even in areas with largely no interest in body structure, may suggest that the Greeks themselves attached particular significance to this anatomical detail. Though kouroi seem to stand in a "locked-knee" position, the early sculptors might have recognized the need for this natural hinge in the mechanism of walking. Such powerful knees in kouroi may therefore have emphasized their striding potential, or even their action pose.

Finally, it should be noted that around 530, if not earlier, Archaic sculpture in general, and kouroi in particular, begin to share in what may be termed the International Style. While I believe that I can distinguish regional differences and traits in the early kouroi, I find the picture blurring as we move toward the end of the Sixth century. Late Archaic statues often combine details typical of several areas. Although a basic distinction between works from East Greece and those from Greece proper can still be drawn, Asia Minor and the islands seem to fall under increasing mainland influence, and Athens takes a definite lead in sculptural style. In addition, the Delphic sanctuary must have functioned as a virtual melting pot for all trends, while the Cyclades loosened somewhat their monopoly on marble and lost some of the markets for their products. An almost manneristic, Archaizing phase ushered in the end of the Archaic period proper and paved the way for the surprising sweep of the unified Severe style.

REGIONAL DIFFERENCES AMONG KOUROI

Naxos[21]

Naxian kouroi should be analyzed first since they are the earliest preserved (kouros A in Thera is dated ca. 650) and considerably influenced production of the type elsewhere. The evidence from some closed contexts (Delos, for instance, and the Ptoan Sanctuary in Boeotia) points to Naxos as having been the chief source of marble and statuary until replaced by Paros, both for material and style, around 540.

Naxian kouroi tend to be thin and flat, the early ones still retaining something of the plank in their torsos. A certain attention to anatomy results in decorative patterns: grooves outline shoulder blades (Naxian Apollo in Delos), ridges frame the elbow (Delos A 4083) or continue the line of the hips over the flanks and back, dipping in a point over the buttocks (Naxos Mus. no. 5520). The earliest kouroi (Naxian Apollo; Delos A 333) when seen in profile, show a marked recession of the groin area, which almost caves in between the thighs, but this rendering disappears in later statues. Perhaps the most distinctive feature is the way in which the sharp contour of the torso, flaring upward from a narrow waist, virtually collides with the edge of the arms. Equally stylized is the V-shaped groin splayed to continue to the sides of the torso. Even in bodies where the hip muscles swell,

[21] Before embarking on descriptions of regional styles, it should be stressed once more that my comments should be considered only tentative and provisional. They may point out traits which fall short of universal occurrence within the regional group or which are limited in time. Given the many traveling masters and the extent of cross influences, any attribution of an Archaic statue to a definite geographical school must be considered tentative.

they do so on the prolongation of the groin line, not as a horizontal interruption to it. Yet for all this angularity, lower abdomens can swell slightly and epigastric arches be faintly rounded. Though the *linea alba* is at times marked, the abdominal partitions are usually absent and, in general, anatomical details are merely suggested. The single exception to this rule may be the pronounced knee muscle, in two parts. Naxian sculptors seem to have loved smooth surfaces carefully worked, to have preferred ample curves to knobby musculature, to have tended toward harmonious and decorative stylization rather than naturalistic imitation. The hair, as already mentioned, is often of the negative pearls variety, but the beaded tress is also employed, usually ending in a point. The hair mass over the back terminates along a straight horizontal line, and tapers off into the stone to such an extent that weathering can easily eliminate all traces of the back hair below the neck. In one of the early kouroi from Thera, which are usually considered Naxian products, the vertical strands lie at different depths, and the fillet encircling them is tied with a loose rounded knot which is found again on the Kriophoros in Thasos. The features of few Naxian kouroi are well preserved, but a very large head now in Copenhagen may be considered representative, especially for the decorative diadem between two fillets (which recalls the Sounion kouros), the engraved vertical lines at the corner of the mouth, the high swinging eyebrows, below which the orbital cavities angle sharply inward before rising into the parallel plane of the lids.

A surprising trait of these Naxian kouroi is the frequent use of metal attachments. Traces of lead over the pubic area may have resulted from the practice of gluing the separately carved penis with a mass of molten lead, rather than fastening it with a pin (Delos A 333, perhaps also A 4052), but some kouroi have metal pins over the buttocks (Naxos 5520) or at the waist (Delos A 4085), at times even when a belt is plastically rendered (Delos A 334). Perhaps extra ornaments were added in metal: studs over a pre-existing belt, or an entire belt in bronze. Be that as it may, this practice is sufficiently different from sculptural renderings in Egypt or Anatolia (or, for that matter, from other Greek kouroi) to deserve attention.[22]

[22] It has generally been assumed that the gigantic Naxian Apollo in Delos had metal front curls and a metal belt (*Kouroi* no. 15 p. 52, under *Hair* and *Torso, front*). D. Pinkwart (*BonnJhr* 172 [1972] 12–17) has now correctly noted that the holes for the presumed bronze curls over the chest occur *below* the traces of spiral ends for individual locks, and that such spirals correspond exactly to the hair rendering on the Apollo's back. She concludes that the holes, and the presumed bronze curls, must have been a later addition to a coiffure once entirely in marble. The same suggestion is made for the belt, since a marble ridge is still visible just above the break on the upper fragment of the torso. Since this plastic rendering of the belt would have been unnecessary as an underpinning for a bronze accessory, the metal belt should also be considered a later addition. In a second note (*BonnJhr* 173 [1973] 117) the same scholar accepts the theory suggested to her by W. Koenigs and F. Eckstein that some larger holes vertically arranged on the lower half of the torso were probably made in mediaeval times, in an attempt to break the enormous statue into smaller fragments. She also tries to answer Eckstein's query about the discrepancy in the plastic rendering of the belt, which in the upper fragment appears as a ridge, while in the lower section of the torso appears as a groove. Pinkwart suggests that the difference is produced by the bulging body below the belt.

Important as these observations are, I would suggest that the holes below the chest curls on the Apollo may have carried ornamental pendants or weights, rather than being for later additions or repairs. Pinkwart herself seems to accept the theory that bronze ornament decorated the center of the spiral curls over the back, and therefore the idea of original metal attachments on the statue cannot be entirely discarded. Furthermore, the metal additions to the plastically rendered belt of Kouros A 334 make me think that the two renderings are not mutually ex-

Paros

Parian style produces more athletic kouroi. They have long torsos with thick waists, narrow hips, arms and shoulders pulled back, and chests thrust forward. Particularly distinctive is the rendering of the muscles which connect pectorals and back to the arms and are often deeply undercut. Ducat has defined them as "tense as ropes." Whereas a Naxian torso climbs steeply and collides at an angle with the edge of the arms, a Parian torso swells out into the curve of the rib cage and loops down into the arms, with this U-turn overshadowing, as it were, the edge of the armpit. This rendering at times creates the impression that the shoulders are too broad for the torso. The groin lines tend to be strongly oblique and may form an initial V topped by two diverging strokes marking the hip muscles. The groin itself can be slightly undercut, so as to form almost a ridge over the thighs. In general, despite their solid form, these Parian kouroi have a fluidity which is typical of Archaic sculpture from the islands.

One more detail which may tentatively be considered Parian, though it occurs on the Naxian Apollo in Delos and on some Attic kouroi, is the rendering on the back of a long vertical groove on either side of the spinal furrow (cf. Figs. 4 and 6). The standard schema shows curves at the shoulder blades, and perhaps tense swelling muscles at the waist, but here the emphasis on the vertical depression from top to bottom of the torso is clear.

Despite their more massive build, Parian kouroi are as stylized as the Naxian. Their rounded surfaces may look more natural but are still oversimplified. The Parian love for curves shows at times in the slightly sloping contour of the shoulders, the elliptical edge of the hair over the back which rises and sinks with the spine, the cavetto shape of the throat merging gradually into the face. These kouroi were greatly in demand during the Sixth century and must have been exported widely since we find them at the Ptoion as well as, probably, in Cyrene. The few heads preserved vary a great deal but have a certain prettiness and rounded forms which recall Samian or East Greek traits, though with a straighter profile and more marked features.

East Greece

Because of these basic affinities, one should look next at the kouroi from Samos and Asia Minor. Within the East Greek territory, the Ephesian school can usually be distinguished from the Milesian, but mostly in ivories, figurines, the treatment of drapery or of the female face. In addition, no freestanding statuary of any size has as yet been found at Ephesos, and specifically no kouroi. Therefore my stylistic sketch applies basically to Milesian works, either domestic or colonial. Here too the female figures are more distinctive, but the kouroi, several of which are two or three times larger than life, seem to have derived inspiration from Samos, especially for the hairstyles and the apparent disinterest in abdominal partitions. What were faint curves in the island kouroi become rounded volumes in the Milesian statues. The head in particular looks spherical and in profile forms a continuous curve from crown to chin, with the nose lying just within or at the approxi-

---

clusive. The metal pins on the *glutei* of some Delian kouroi are more difficult to explain. Note the comments in *Bedeutung*, 274, with particular reference to similarly positioned decoration in proto-Attic vases. See also *Art of Greece*, 194–96 and 203, with reference to Luristan bronzes.

mate apex. The full throat suggests fatness and a double chin, while no marked jaw line emphasizes the junction of the head to the thick, short neck. The wide shoulders usually slope and flow with unbroken contour into almost cylindrical arms and bulging pectorals; the lower abdomen swells. The entire build is portly and massive without being muscular, fleshy without being fat. In general, all sharp definitions are avoided and structural transitions, from trunk to limbs and from neck to face, are blurred and minimized. The V-shaped groin can be felt rather than seen and, in some cases, almost disappears before reaching the hips; at times, it seems to connect with the edge of the rib cage, thus virtually bringing out the almond-shaped island of the swelling abdomen in the center of the body. The *linea alba* and the spinal groove are the two main accents within the torso, and even these are understated. This lack of emphasis on the underlying bone and muscle structure results perhaps from the attempt at a unified composition: some kouroi look almost as if they had been turned on a lathe. But because waists are not stressed, some torsos seem slightly too long, and the total effect is obviously stylized despite the apparent naturalism of the fleshy rendering.

Hair patterns vary, but one often sees elongated beads within vertical tresses; horizontal ripples may space the beads so that they resemble peas within a pod because of the typical East Greek blurring of transitions. A second layer of wings over the temples occurs fairly frequently. In Ionia, according to Tuchelt, strands are commoner in the south, diagonal grooves in the north. A similar differentiation can be detected in the profiles, the northern ones jutting farther forward, thus increasing the forehead slope.[23] Of the features, the eyes are large and almond shaped, the mouth large with a thicker lower lip, the cheeks very full and usually wider than the temples, but merging without break into the continuous curve of the almost moon face. One should note the affinities, if not the strong similarity, between these East Greek heads and those from Rhodes. But the Rhodian body structure, to judge from the few examples of marble kouroi preserved, is much more clearly articulated, more Cycladic in general appearance, more nervous and muscular.

Samos

Samian kouroi, as already mentioned, may have influenced the rendering of the Milesians. What is difficult to realize from the extant fragments is that some of the Samian youths were so enormous that the Sounion kouroi would have looked small beside them. Naxos and Samos are therefore linked by this unusual tendency to produce statues on a scale well beyond any human experience. A kouros standing over 5.50 m. tall (and Samos had more than one such monument) can hardly have been understood as the portrayal of a normal human being even if dedicated to a divinity, but must have suggested the divinity itself. The Naxian Apollo in Delos, which matches the Samian youths in scale, confirms that such proportions were considered appropriate for a god. Unfortunately the two largest statues from Samos are so fragmentary that we cannot tell whether accessories prompted specific identifications, though this does not seem to be the case. It should be noted further that the Samian kouroi are considerably later than the Naxian Apollo, and probably even later than the earliest Attic examples. Even in Samos, therefore, as in Asia Minor in gen-

[23] Could this receding forehead be an Anatolian trait? It vaguely recalls the Amarna sketches of Hittites. Surprisingly enough, it is found again in many Etruscan works.

eral, the male type seems to have followed the first female statues, though appearing earlier on the island (first third of the Sixth century) than on the coast (about the middle of the Sixth century). Since the earliest Samian kouroi are already in local marble, one can perhaps assume Cycladic influence to have been diluted if not entirely absent, yet some fragments show what I would call Naxian traits, others Parian. By and large there is the same emphasis on rounded forms prevalent in Asia Minor, the same lack of interest in abdominal partitions, the same softening of all transitions. The epigastric arch is basically rendered as the edge of the rib cage: it therefore projects almost like a step from chest to abdomen, across the entire torso, rather than describing a calligraphic curve in its center. Arms tend to be cylindrical, but a few examples show a swelling biceps; among the few preserved fists the triangular, rather than the squarish, outline predominates, with one remarkable exception which so turns the hand as to reveal not just the index but also the middle finger from the front. Next to the simplified, fleshy modeling of most kouroi, others appear more muscular and structurally defined: their groin lines are clearly cut, or even undercut, and one surprising torso shows unmistakable abdominal partitions. But this unique example already reflects the International Style (ca. 540–530). One peculiar kouros, probably a funerary statue, has folds of flesh on its lower abdomen, delimited by engraved lines.[24] All preserved knees seem strongly articulated, though with different stylizations.

Hair patterns are beads (even the pod variety) or vertebrae, and include some wavy strands and horizontal striations; by and large, Samian hair seems to reach lower down the kouroi's shoulders than in other regional styles, but this is not always the case. There are several instances of added wings over the temples; and the most complex example of this coiffure, the monumental head in Istanbul, belongs to a Samian giant (probable total H. ca. 3.25 m.). The local variant of the strand pattern has already been mentioned.

All these kouroi—from Naxos, Paros, East Greece, and Samos—are remarkable for their lack of abdominal partitions. When these occur, the total statue looks late enough to have been open to outside influences, with Naxos perhaps the most receptive at the earliest date. The thin and abstract kouros from Melos (Fig. 11), often considered under Naxian influence, is peculiar in having a triangular fist and a rippled stomach. Kouroi found in the other Cyclades or considered "imports" share the absence of this latter feature. It is therefore all the more surprising to meet with the strongly muscular youths from the Greek mainland.

Boeotia

The Boeotian school, or the school of Akraiphia as Ducat calls it, is readily isolated through the use of local stone, identifying inscriptions, and the abundant documentation from the Ptoan sanctuary. The kouros type seems to have arrived around 590–580, and the earliest examples are in local style, though possibly under Attic influence, and often larger than life. This style remains pure until approximately 550; it then falls under the influence of various sources, producing kouroi in Naxo-Boeotian and Paro-Boeotian style, until, after

[24] One wonders whether such a peculiar rendering occurred under Egyptian influence. That the island was open to outside inspiration and perhaps even fashions is shown by the limestone torso in a foreign costume, which is considered a Samian work imitating Cypriot iconography (*Samos* XI no. 76 pl. 63: the only Samian freestanding statue in poros).

530, these foreign influences are so thoroughly assimilated that no local trend can be isolated. Though Ducat calls these late Ptoan kouroi fully Cycladic, I would rather see them as part of what I call the International Style.

It is interesting, however, that the earliest impulse for the kouroi may have reached Boeotia from Attica since the first complete torso we can examine, Thebes no. 1, has an overabundance of abdominal partitions. Except for kouroi in island style, or under predominant influence from the Cyclades, all Boeotian works retain this interest in the muscular divisions of the stomach. In addition, despite the sharp, engraved quality of many details, this particular rendering is almost invariably modeled, so that the rippled abdomens of the Akraiphian kouroi, with as many as five horizontal divisions, strongly resemble an old-fashioned washboard.

Another distinctive feature of the Akraiphian style is the sharp definition of planes—rather, of facets—which once suggested the idea that the sculptor carved with a knife. These Boeotian kouroi have shoulders that are more like epaulets; their breasts are angular, their backs flat, their thighs squared. Anatomically, they seem all wrong: the Orchomenos kouros has an epigastric arch which climbs in between the breasts, and five abdominal divisions do not exist in nature. As Ducat points out, these kouroi are made of bits and pieces, each part treated for itself; they are assembled almost according to geometric formulae, yet they manage to achieve a strong stylistic unity. They may look brutal but are also elegant and vigorous, almost like colonial art, and in many ways are closest to modern sculpture.

A true masterpiece in this style is the head Nat. Mus. 15, which is entirely made of flat planes and sharp edges. The thin-lipped mouth cuts like a slash across the lower face and, together with the quizzical lines of the flaring eyebrows, lends it an enigmatic expression. The total structure of the head is so simplified and abstract that one tends to overlook how deeply the features sink into the block and penetrate the profile view. This stylization has usually been responsible for the high dates traditionally given to early Boeotian sculpture. Yet it is the whole statue in every case which exemplifies how advanced traits and modeled features can coexist with engraved details and flat planes. Recent studies have assigned much lower dates to specific pieces; in particular, the Orchomenos kouros, under strong Naxian influence, is now dated ca. 550; Thebes no. 1, in purer Akraiphian style, around 560.

The Boeotian material is more difficult to assess when outside influences dilute the local traits. Kouroi in island style may have little or no indication of abdominal partitions or even omit the epigastric arch. This latter, in Boeotian style, is sharply angular, but Naxian inspiration produces some elliptical curves; Parian sources introduce bulging hip muscles.[25]

[25] According to Ducat (*Ptoion* 453–54 and 459–63) the total picture of the kouroi at the Ptoion seems to form a chronological pattern, with the local school active from the inception of the kouros series, ca. 590–580, to ca. 540–530, and producing its purest style between 580 and 555. Naxian imports began only around 560 and seem to have disappeared by 540–530, even in terms of marble, when Paros took over in both medium and style; in particular, after 540, Parian marble seems to have been used by all masters, regardless of nationality. This was true also at Delos, where Parian kouroi apparently arrived after the Naxian and continued longer than they (*GdD*, 39–46). There are relatively few Attic imports throughout the 6th century (14, including statues other than kouroi) and they seem to fall within the period 570–490, with concentration in the decades around 550. None of these Attic sculptures represents a masterpiece, and they were probably the work of minor artists. Other imports are regarded as South Cycladic and Ionic.

Since kouroi from the Ptoion, which form a closed group, show such variety of influence and admixture of traits, one may legitimately ask whether there is any point in trying to distinguish regional styles. I believe there is because, as already mentioned, apparently discrepant anatomical renderings can appear on the same statue and no longer surprise or condition our chronological assessment if they can be traced to a specific school or influence. Kouroi very different in appearance can be recognized as contemporary if produced by different areas.

Mainland Greece

Other schools of mainland Greece are difficult to isolate, except for Attic. Maybe our evidence is still too scanty or, more probably, no other definite school existed and imports took care of other markets. An Argive style is often claimed for Kleobis and Biton, which look different from other kouroi. Their faces seem Daedalic at first glance but lack the typical triangular section and are quite flat, with features sketched on the front plane. To all intents they are meant as twins to look alike; yet it has been suggested that one was made by the Argive (Poly)medes, the other by an Ionian sculptor. I cannot subscribe to this theory: whatever differs from statue to statue must be caused by the lack of a specific model and by the nonmechanical technique of reproduction. The emphasis in both is on musculature: note the heavy thighs, the short torsos, the powerful arms definitely bent in action, not simply held at the sides. The engraved epigastric arch looks more than ever like the pattern on a metal corselet, and the striations on legs and arms recall other pieces of protective armor, but the backs are surprisingly empty. Could this imitation here simply mean that their maker was not too familiar with marble carving? The pose, eagerly tilted forward, the position of the arms, the presence of the boots, the emphasis on physical strength make me think that these are narrative statues, heroized characters, not just standard kouroi. They seem early, but they may just be provincial.

The Corinthian school may be equally elusive. If, as already mentioned, marble was not a favored medium in an area rich in soft limestone and clay, kouroi had little chance for development there. The few instances in poros (the Corinth fragments, the Isthmia legs) have a simplified style largely conditioned by the material. The emphasis was probably on contours and surfaces rather than on anatomical articulation. The elegant Tenea kouros, usually considered the exponent of such a school because the only complete find from the general region, has a touch of island style in his sloping shoulders, lack of abdominal partitions, dorsal striations. But the face could be Corinthian, especially in the pointed nose and squarish chin. The other marble youth from Corinth, just a head, is too late to be truly typical and useful. We need more monumental evidence from Corinth, and perhaps we have it in the Peiraeus Apollo, which shows many of the same facial features, a simplified anatomy based largely on contours, and a familiarity with clay in his doughy locks. But this remarkable statue, surely late Archaic, was found out of context and cannot be counted in a Corinthian check-list. Nor is it fair to include examples from the so-called Corinthian colonies, some of which seem to have looked rather farther afield for their sculpture.[26]

[26] Often included within the Corinthian production are, for instance, the kouroi from Aktion. But at least one of them (*Kouroi* no. 40 figs. 154–56) has been called Cycladic (*Samos* XI, 71), and the second one (*Kouroi* no. 74 figs. 255–57) seems Parian to me. For the artistic tendencies of Corfu and Syracuse, see infra Chs. 7 and 9, respectively.

Magna Graecia

Magna Graecian style is more easily identified in architectural than in freestanding sculpture. Langlotz has suggested that all marble statues found in Sicily or South Italy were carved where the stone itself was quarried, that is, abroad, but a certain provincialism in some of the pieces makes me doubtful. In any case, none of the extant examples is larger than life, so transport may have been a hampering factor for a region which otherwise loved the gigantic. The preserved kouroi are so few that generalizations are difficult. Of the six pieces in Sicily, most are late and International in style; the earliest, dedicated to the doctor Sombrotidas, is inscribed along one thigh in the Ionic fashion; it may well be Naxian though the toning down of the knee muscle results in apparently overlong thighs which do not seem typical. South Italian kouroi are bulkier, with almost inflated torsos. Their musculature is rendered, but they do not look athletic or clearly articulated. They were probably under East Greek influence, perhaps Samian or Cycladic, rather than Peloponnesian or Attic.

Attica

The most distinctive style of all is that of the Attic kouroi, for which we have the greatest number of complete examples. The overriding interest seems to be not so much in anatomy per se as in the problem of structure. The Attic sculptor seems to want to know how a body is put together, tends to stress the tectonics of a statue, marks the joints with ridges and grooves as if they were moldings in a building. Even at their most abstract, Attic statues have a clarity of form which commands immediate belief. Because of this clarity, perhaps more than because of the specific technique, early Attic statues tend to be four-sided, with features which clearly belong to a single plane, either front or back, or the two sides. In early works, like the New York Kouros or the Dipylon head, all the facial traits could be shaved off the front without considerably affecting the thickness of the entire head. They lie so superficially on the face that proper lighting brings out the point where the cheek "turns the corner" to begin the side plane.

Contours are largely angular, often broken by protruding musculature, yet they do not have the abruptness of the Akraiphian "facets." The four-sloped hand is the only Attic schema, made even more geometric than necessary, with the fist trying to break its link with the thigh as soon as possible. Abdominal partitions, as well as the tensors of the spine, reveal the sculptors' absorbing interest in anatomy below the surface. Shoulders are almost consistently straight, upper arms swell with muscle, the full calves often seem out of proportion.

The impulse for the type may have come to Attica from Naxos, but in the Dipylon/Agora fragments and the New York kouros we see how every element has been integrated and reinterpreted in an Athenian way. This is not quite so for the Sounion kouroi. Though unmistakably Attic in many ways, they do not quite fit into the early sequence, and attempts to reconcile them with the others succeed for details but not for the total statues. I would suggest that foreign influences are much more apparent in the Sounion statues, and that even their (votive/chthonic) function may be exceptional, prompted by foreigners perhaps at a sailor's sanctuary where many ships stopped. To mention specific details, the vertebrae pattern in the hair of the Sounion kouroi is different from the traditional Attic pearls; the so-called Sounion torso has the same ringlets ending in spirals which we see on the Naxian Apollo in Delos; the complete kouros wears a double fillet with ornaments similar to the diadem on the equally sizable Naxian head in Copenhagen.[27] The peculiar ridge which carries the line of the hips to the buttocks is present in at least one torso in Naxos, and so is the raised curve framing the elbow. The four-sloped hand looks at home in Attica but also in Naxos, and the wide face of the Sounion kouros has different proportions and structure from the other more or less contemporary examples. Of all the early Attic kouroi, moreover, the Sounion statues are the most decorative, not only in the star-like engraving of their nipples, but also in the markings of the many abdominal partitions in the front, the ribs (?) in the back,[28] the double lines for the shoulder blades, or the bifurcated ends of the diadem fillet. I suspect that some of these features are dictated by size. The sculptor had comparatively larger surfaces available because of the gigantic size of his kouroi and did not want to leave such vast expanses blank. Even the abdominal partitions might have been the brainstorm of an artist who no longer could include the (Apolline?) belt on a statue given to Poseidon/Phrontis. As it is, no major surface of the statues is devoid of plastic action. Finally, note that the kouroi stand straight on plinths which fit into their bases at a slant, so that the total figure seems, to the viewer who faces the front of the pedestal, about to stride. The Naxian Euthykartides may have aimed at somewhat the same effect when he set his kouros (with a slight twist) on a triangular base in Delos.

Island influence on details of Attic sculpture may have continued intermittently. An interesting comparison is between the Attic Kroisos and Delos A 4048, the first Naxian example with some indication of the abdominal partitions. Though Kroisos is athletic and powerful, unmistakably Athenian, and the Delos statue is abstract and decorative, especially in its groin pattern, they both share an unusual detail. Their forearms have been freed from the torso but look like an outer mold for the thighs, since their inner surfaces cave in exactly along the curve of the bulging legs.[29] The vertical grooves on the back of the Kroisos have already been mentioned as a possibly Parian feature.

The Volomandra kouros deserves brief comment because of the peculiar reduction in depth. Instead of being formed from the meeting of four planes (front, back, and the two sides) no matter how skillfully integrated, this kouros in section would appear to be made

[27] This over life-size head (*Kouroi* no. 50; *Ny Carlsberg* no. 11a, 29–30) at one point was even considered Attic, before its origin from Naxos was demonstrated. It has somewhat the same clear-cut look of the Sounion kouroi, the same firm chin and relatively wide forehead.

[28] I know of no other example of the starred nipples of the Sounion kouroi, but the newly found kouros from Myrrhinous (Merenda, the "brother" of Phrasikleia) has a circle of tiny dots surrounding his nipples, and some kouroi, surprisingly, seem to have had inserted nipples (Nat. Mus. 3757, Karouzou, 23).

For this kind of rendering on the metopes of the Athenian Treasury in Delphi, copper insertions have been suggested (see infra, Ch. 8).

A similar rendering of ribs (?) on the back occurs on the naked torso of a guardian deity on an Assyrian relief from the Palace of Sennacherib at Nineveh (Br. Mus. 118917, Hrouda, pl. 39:2).

[29] A kouros from the Ptoion, Thebes no. 6 (*Ptoion* no. 161, *Kouroi* no. 96) which Ducat considers Naxian in style, has his forearms still attached to the thighs, but the thin layer of stone in between does not conceal the fact that one shape is the negative of the other.

On the Kroisos, see the comments by W.-H. Schuchhardt (*AntP* 6 [1967] 17 and pl. 7b), who finds the same rendering in the seated "Dionysos," NM 3711.

out of two shallow arcs of a circle joining in a thin ridge at the flanks. This rendering is not apparent from a photograph since the arms cover this sharp meeting point and since the curve of the biceps in profile hides the deeply indented back. But the statue looks abnormally thin on direct examination, especially in proportion to its wide front, with its tense shoulders which give it almost the look of a padded football player. The new kouros from Merenda has helped to convince me that the pattern of flames over the Volomandra's forehead is an added ornament, obviously favored by Attic youths since several examples now are known from this area.

RELATED MALE FIGURES

Offering bearers

One more group of male statues usually is included with the kouroi because these statues resemble kouroi in many ways. They vary from the standard formula in that they carry objects or animals. In all other respects—nakedness, youthfulness, hairstyles, anatomical treatment—they rank with the kouroi and seem to fall within the same regional stylistic divisions. They are not nearly as numerous and occur in Asia Minor and the islands rather than in Greece proper. In Attica only one definite example of the animal carrier is known, and it is not a kouros: the Moschophoros. On the other hand, a statue from Didyma, one from Klaros, one from Samos, are so close to the canon that we could easily mistake them for kouroi were it not for the obvious addition. Usually they carry the animal in front of their chest, with both arms thrust outward at more or less the same level. One fragment from Didyma shows a kouros whose animal, rendered in low relief against his body, seems to be slipping down, since it is approximately level with the boy's genitals. The gigantic Kriophoros in Thasos holds his ram upright, flat against his body and to one side. Only in such cases, when the offering is carved in one piece with the human figure, can we definitely identify its nature. In cases where struts connect offerings to torsos, the object has usually broken off and its original appearance remains a matter of conjecture. An earlier reconstruction of a Samian kouros as leading a young bull or calf standing by his side has recently been questioned, and the fragments are now interpreted as a mythological group, perhaps Theseus struggling with the Minotaur. This interpretation may be equally doubtful: the total absence of muscles in the tubular arm of the kouros, his everyday coiffure, hardly suggest the heroic efforts of the Athenian prince. Some limestone statuettes from Kamiros and Naukratis carry animals, but they are either mythological (Herakles) or genre (hunters). In either case they are too obviously products of the minor arts to be considered in this chapter. One more kriophoros, from Erythrai, has not yet been published.

Other kouroi may not have carried animals but may have held something in their hands. A poros torso in Geneva, unusual also in stepping forward with his right leg, seems to have something in his right hand pressed against his thigh. His left hand must have been stretched forward, since it did not touch the thigh. A kouros from Paros now in Copenhagen has lost both his arms, but the position of his shoulders indicates that he held both arms away from his body and outstretched. His left hand, as shown by a break, was carved against his chest in a gesture typical of some kouroi from Naukratis but more popular among Ionic korai. His right supposedly rested on his hip (an almost Classical pose); some extra stone near the inserted genitals suggests however that he may also have carried something against his right side. The Phigalia kouros, as already mentioned, may have stretched his arms forward at different levels, perhaps holding attributes appropriate to an Apollo. More unusual is a torso found on Naxos in 1972; this life-size kouros folds his arms across his chest, palms flat against the body and thumbs up, but not joining in the center, since his *linea alba* is still visible between the hands.[30]

One may raise the question whether the offering bearer is a representation of the worshiper coming with his offering or whether it may portray the divinity himself, with the sacrificial animal. Though the latter seems hardly the case for the Klaros kouros or the Didyma youth, this alternative is valid for the Thasian kriophoros because of his uncommon size and divided hairstyle. Literary sources describe wooden or bronze statues of Apollo holding a deer in his outstretched hand, perhaps because the medium allowed a freer pose. The Thasian kriophoros, presumably for reasons of equilibrium, holds his animal in what might be termed the most economical pattern for an animal bearer in stone;[31] yet his enormous size makes me doubt that expense was of primary consideration. More plausibly his gesture, taken from Egyptian art, may imply protection. He could therefore be Hermes, Apollo, or another male divinity in his function as patron of the herds and protector of animal life.

The Athenian Moschophoros certainly represents Rhonbos, a human being, and it is a masterpiece of Attic art. Made of local (Hymettian) marble, it has some traits of carving which recall contemporary sculpture in soft limestone, for instance, the grooves delimiting nostrils and naso-labial lines. His hair, to my eyes, is not divided but pushed forward by the presence of the animal on his back. All the small asymmetries of the composition bring out the liveliness of the group: one wonders whether the mantle contour is kept flowing to emphasize the different distance of the two elbows from the body. Though a real calf's joints would have to be broken to allow the position, the arrangement in marble looks plausible and natural, with a great cross of human arms and animal legs forming the dominant pattern in the center. The mantle, once painted, must have provided an emphatic frame for the abdominal partitions, of which there are too many, but surprisingly well modeled at this early stage. The inserted pupils and the calf-bearing pattern itself go back to the Egyptian 5th Dynasty (ca. 2500); but this muscular man is an Athenian, one of the earliest monumental dedications on the Akropolis, around 550.

[30] Another Naxian sculpture is so anomalous that it defies classification. It consists of a life-size head, somewhat weathered and damaged, resting on a strong cylindrical neck which is in turn set on a totally columnar body almost like a cippus, the whole 1.55 m. high. The strange "idol" was at first considered a kouros and as such was included by Deonna in his corpus. It later disappeared, to be found again some forty years later, built into the steps of a private house on the island and covered by a thick layer of whitewash. The head was then described as female (*BCH* 71–72 [1947–48] 440, fig. 16; for the very first mention of the piece, see L. Pollak, *AthMitt* 21 [1896] 226). The peculiar shape of the body cannot be due to recutting because of the great projection of the pillar from the base of the neck: the column is too large to result from a finished torso which had been cut down. Perhaps its true affinities are with the Kimolos stele (see infra, Ch. 6). Unfortunately, the statue was not available for inspection in December 1974 when I visited Naxos. For another peculiar kouros from Naxos (partly in the round and partly in relief) see also Ch. 6, 149, 172 n. 28.

[31] I.e., the outline of the marble block, if reconstructed around the figure, would show very little waste of material caused by the addition of the animal, which fits within the same tight contours as the man.

Draped Figures

We do not know whether the so-called Ilissos kouros, who wears a chlamys over his shoulders, was a man or a youth. A short beard would not have touched the chest, and in its present state the headless torso gives no indication of age. The short mantle was carved to accommodate a metal fastener, to be inserted separately and strung from edge to edge, as if to keep the mantle in place. It must have resembled the chained clips with which we secure a sweater thrown over the shoulders. It has been suggested that the kouros may be Hermes, but since the same kind of traveling cloak is worn by the human Moschophoros, this identification is not compelling. The remains of his outstretched arms would suggest ranking him rather with the offering bearers. The statue looks Attic in the rendering of drapery and abdominal partitions. Even more Athenian is the over-dressed youth from the Akropolis (Akr. 633), who, despite his three garments, manages to reveal a great deal of his musculature. He too bends his right arm in the offering bearer's pose, though his elaborate attire would seem to class him with the draped youths. On the Athenian Akropolis he is an oddity since the type, until now, has been found exclusively in Asia Minor and Samos, with one example in Sicily where the scantily draped male figure looks like an Ionic foreigner (Figs. 13–14).[32]

It has recently been suggested that these dignified, plump East Greek figures—some of them larger, some smaller than life—might be the "portraits" of important people who, however, did not rank high enough for a seated statue. This supposition is supported by the inscription on the draped man in the Louvre, "I am [the statue] of Dionyshermos, son of Antenor," and by the draped youth from Pitane, which was found in a cemetery. Inscriptions on votive kouroi, on the contrary, give the donor's name in the nominative, with the addition of *anetheke* (dedicated) and sometimes even a qualifying epithet for the statue (e.g., *perikalles agalma*, a very beautiful object). In these youths the drapery would therefore be used as a status symbol and consequently represent the worshiper or the deceased rather than generic statues to please the gods. One wonders, however, whether a draped rendering is enough to confer a sort of cadet dignity on a person, or whether instead the clothed version is simply a reflection of everyday attire in contrast to heroized nakedness.

The draped youths usually stand in the same position as the naked kouroi, with arms

[32] Didyma alone accounts for 14 examples, and there are five in Samos. There are, of course, many draped kouroi in Cyprus, some of them even with transparent drapery (e.g., Nat. Mus. 4505, Karouzou, 10; Deonna, no. 140 p. 237), but we cannot take them into account except as evidence of the Oriental preference for this draped type. Much more important, however, are the many terracotta statues, some of them almost life-size, which have been found within the last decade in the Sanctuary of Demeter and Kore on the slopes of Acrocorinth. Though not as heavily draped as their Ionic counterparts, and extending in time well into the Classical period, these young men are wrapped in a himation, carry an offering (which is often an animal) and, when Archaic in date, have long curls hanging over the chest. It has been suggested that these statues cannot represent common worshipers, since the sanctuary was largely frequented by women, but must portray some mythological hero associated with the two Eleusinian deities. (R. Stroud, *Hesperia* 37 [1968] 324–25; N. Bookidis, *Hesperia* 41 [1972] 317).

A headless limestone figure from a cemetery near Tanagra in Boeotia has been published both as male and as female and will be discussed below in Ch. 4. Here it should be noted that Adams (172–76) compares it to a group of Cretan and Cypriot "snake priests," thus implying that the draped figure is male (cf. Pharaklas, *Deltion* 24 [1969] 66–73, pls. 43–44).

along their sides and fists clenched; in a few instances the right hand may touch the edge of the mantle, in a gesture reminiscent of the korai pulling their skirt aside. Their most common attire is a long chiton with short sleeves, and a mantle draped around the body in what may be considered the reverse of the arrangement for the female figures. In fact, the voluminous himation is looped below the right arm, leaving it free for action, and is then tossed over the left shoulder with a heavy fall of folds hanging vertically on the left side of the back. This vertical arrangement is distinctive for men and often helps settle the question whether a fragment belonged originally to a male or female statue since the korai wear their mantle diagonally both front and back. This consideration should help to identify the torso from Sardis as male, despite the rich jewelry and the fact that a Lydian monument may not reflect the fashions of the Greeks. A few male statues wear only a mantle without the chiton.

Warriors

A final category of male standing figures could represent specific individuals: the armed warriors. The type is common in the minor arts but relatively rare in monumental sculpture, perhaps because of a certain uneasiness in rendering metal armor in stone. Large-scale bronzes must have existed in the late Sixth century but have largely vanished except for a bearded helmeted head from the Athenian Akropolis (Fig. 12; Nat. Mus. 6446). The earliest stone example, to my knowledge, is a Spartan cuirassed torso in local (Taygetan) marble which belongs still within the Seventh century; the left arm was down, the right probably held a spear. This warrior is headless, but a later helmeted head also from Sparta, though badly weathered, suggests the same type. It must have been particularly popular in Lakonia, since the Severe period produced the spectacular "Leonidas," now reconstructed as part of a duel, with a central figure, presumably Athena, changing the monument into an epic or a mythological group.

Elsewhere, Samos has produced an over life-size example, and the Athenian Akropolis accounts for a cuirassed torso (Akr. 599) of an archer in action, to judge from the position of the arms and the attached quiver. Holes for metal insertions over the buttocks suggest that some free drapery from a chitoniskos was attached separately, though part of the garment was simply painted over the naked body below the corselet. The roughly worked crown of the head in some kouroi has, at times, been interpreted as evidence that the statue originally wore a metal helmet; in most cases, however, I have found the evidence unconvincing.[33]

[33] Another theory suggests that to such rough crowns more elaborate coiffures were once added in stucco. In particular this suggestion has been made for the so-called Sabouroff head in Berlin: C. Blümel, *RA* 1968, 11–24 and especially 19–23, figs. 8, 10, and 12. This interesting sculpture is usually considered a portrait of the tyrant Peisistratos, erected either posthumously by his sons after 528 or during his life time but without attempting a true depiction of Peisistratos' advanced age. Other theories have suggested that the Sabouroff head represents Theseus, or even simply an athlete, and the dates proposed for it range from ca. 550 to after 480 (cf. Kleine, 40–42 with bibliography). I believe that our dating difficulties stem partly from the fact that we expect long hair on men around 540; but if we realize that this was not necessarily the case, then even the postulated stucco additions can be eliminated. The Sabouroff head remains a most interesting and unusual piece of sculpture, as are all the various heads of Archaic bearded men. Several have come down to us as heads alone, and it would be interesting to make a study of them as a group. In such a group I would include, for instance, the

SUMMARY

It would seem that the traditional kouros was not generally considered appropriate to represent a living being, either because too anonymous or because its nakedness removed it from the sphere of everyday reality. The type was specifically used to represent the divinity, the heroized dead, or even a "pleasing offering," an agalma. This last function would extend to the offering bearers, except in cases where greater characterization was attempted. Draped or cuirassed statues could instead stand for specific individuals and could carry dedicatory inscriptions in the first person; in East Greece they seem to have been adopted also for some funerary monuments. Toward the end of the Archaic period the type of the naked athlete could replace the kouros, presumably because its nakedness was by then used as a characterizing element, in conjunction with active poses or even because the original meaning had become diluted or forgotten.

---

bearded Fauvel Head in the Louvre (no. 2718) and the head in Delos (A 4108) most recently discussed by V. Regnot in *BCH* 87 (1963) 393–403 pls. 9–11. Its complicated fillet arrangement makes me think that a special personage, perhaps a divinity, may have been intended.

BIBLIOGRAPHY 3

FOR PAGE 45

Kouroi as representations of Apollo: This theory finds an early expression in *GBA* 33 (1886) 418. *Contra* see A. Furtwängler in W. H. Roscher, *Ausführliches Lexikon der griechischen und römischen Mythologie* (Leipzig 1884–1937), s.v. *Apollon* (p. 450).

Naxian Apollo in Delos: *Kouroi* no. 15, figs. 87–90. For an account of early travelers to the island, see E. W. Bodnar, *Archaeology* 25 (1972) 210–15. Most recently, on the statue, D. Pinkwart, *BonnJhr* 172 (1972) 12–17; 173 (1973) 117.

Homeric Hymn to Apollo: see, e.g., vv. 133 and 448–50. Note, in particular, the allusion to "uncut hair" (v. 133).

Leonardos: *ArchEph* 1895, col. 75 n. 1.

H. Lechat, *La Sculpture attique avant Phidias* (Paris 1904) 251. Deonna includes some pieces not discussed by Richter in *Kouroi.*

FOR PAGE 46

Pattern of distribution for the kouros type: *Aspécts,* 79–83.

Arrival of the kouros in Asia Minor: Tuchelt, 171–72. See, however, H. P. Laubscher's review of Tuchelt, *Gnomon* 46 (1974) 500–6, where a history of Archaic sculpture in Asia Minor is considered premature and additions to Tuchelt's list are made.

FOR PAGE 47

Didyma kouroi: Tuchelt, K 1—K 20.

Xanthos: *FdX* 2 (1963) pl. 51:1–3; Tuchelt, L 55.

Karia: E.g., Tuchelt L 66, 68, 69 and addenda at bottom of the list. A kouros from Iasos was shown at the 10th International Congress in Turkey, Sept. 1973.

Theodosia on the Krim: *AA* 1928, col. 90 fig. 10.

Istros: *Kouroi* no. 86a figs. 602–4.

Olbia: *Kouroi* no. 178 figs. 522–23; also head fragment, *JHS* 44 (1924) 46 fig. 1.

Propontis (Erdek, ancient Artake): *Kouroi* no. 127c figs. 628–31; Tuchelt L 67 (with added bibliography).

Macedonia (Europos): *Makedonika* 9 (1969) 179 pls. 85–86; *JHS ArchR* 16 (1970) 21 and fig. 36 a–b.

Thrace (Tekirdag): *Belleten* 34 (1970) 347–51.

Cyrene: Most recently, *Kouroi* no. 63b figs. 593–96; *AJA* 75 (1971) 41–42 pl. 8. Others in Paribeni.

Utica: As far as I know, this piece is not published, but I saw it in July 1974.

Sicily and South Italy: Besides *Kouroi,* passim, and Langlotz, see G. De Luca, *AntP* 3 (1964) 33–60.

Spain: Madrid, Prado Museum, A. Blanco, *Catalogo de la Escultura* (Madrid 1957) no. 437 E pl. 80.

Jugoslavia (Dubrovnik/Ragusa): *Kouroi* no. 86b figs. 605–8; *AA* (1960) cols. 22–26 figs. 1–4.

Greek islands: *Kouroi,* passim, but add: *Samos* XI nos. 29–57, 139.

Chios: *ArchEph* 1939–41, Chronikà p. 26 and figs. 4–5 on p. 25.

Corfu: *Kouroi* no. 135a (correct height to read 8.4 cm.) fig. 639; *Corfu* 44, MR 817, from Mon Repos (said to be in Naxian marble but probably made by a Samian).

Crete: *Kouroi* no. 177 figs. 525–26.

Kleobis and Biton: *Kouroi* no. 12 A–B figs. 78–83 and 91; see also infra, p. 70 and bibliography.

Bronze statuette from Argive Heraion: *Hesperia* 21 (1952) 176–79 no. 71 pl. 45; *RA* 1975, p. 8 figs. 11–13.

Phigalia kouros: *Kouroi* no. 41 figs. 144–46.

Epidauros kouros: *Kouroi* no. 91 figs. 293–96; it is considered Cycladic work in *Ptoion,* 263.

Head from Corinth: *Kouroi* no. 163a fig. 640; *Severe Style,* 59 fig. 75.

FOR PAGE 48

Poros legs from Corinth: *Hesperia* 39 (1970) 319–20 nos. 6–7 pl. 78.

Poros kouros from Isthmia: *Hesperia* 44 (1975) 426–30.

Tenea kouros: See infra, p. 70.

Pheia kouros: *EphArch* (1957) 39–40 pl. 11.

All the Archaic sculpture from Olympia is in course of publication (P. Bol).

P. Amandry: *Charites,* Festschrift E. Langlotz (Bonn 1957) 63–87, esp. 67–70.

Wooden statues of Olympic victors: See, e.g., Mallwitz, 56–57.

Arrichion of Phigalia: P. Levi (*Pausanias' Guide to Greece* [Penguin Books 1971, vol. 2], 471 n. 294), is convinced that the Phigalia kouros is

Arrichion, but the position of the statue's arms makes this theory impossible.

Sparta: Besides the *Catalogue of the Sparta Museum* by M. M. Tod and A.J.B. Wace (1906), see *Deltion* 24:2[1] (1969) 131–35.

Estimates on kouroi at the sanctuary: *Ptoion*, 451; the maximum total would give 135 kouroi (126 of marble, 9 of poros); the minimum possible total is 90 kouroi (83 in marble and 7 in poros). 120 is considered the most likely number.

For the Attic kouroi, besides *Kouroi*, passim, see also *Aristodikos*, Catalogue 2, pp. 59–71, and, to some extent, also Catalogue 1, pp. 44–58.

FOR PAGE 49

Akr. 665: *Kouroi* no. 137 figs. 406–8; *AMA* no. 298; Deyle, 29–31; Brouskari, 61–62. The fragmentary inscribed base attributed to this statue, if pertinent, confirms that it was a votive offering. Bundgaard, 16, states that the kouros was built into the Byzantine wall.

On the meaning of the kouroi, see recently *Samos* XI, 8–11, where most of them are considered representations of mortals.

FOR PAGE 50

Athenian dedications at the Ptoion: *Ptoion* nos. 141–42 pp. 242–58.

FOR PAGE 51

On characterization in funerary sculpture, see *Aristodikos*, 26–43, and esp. 32 and 39.

Kroisos: *Kouroi* no. 136 figs. 395–98; also called the Anavyssos kouros from its find spot, on which see E. I. Mastrokostas, *AAA* 7 (1974) 217–28; cf. also C.W.J. Eliot, *Coastal Demes of Attika* (*Phoenix* Suppl. 5, 1962) 70–72. For a discussion of the epitaph, cf. Ch. W. Clairmont, *Gravestone and Epigram* (Mainz 1970) 16–17 no. 2. For Kroisos' connection with the Alkmaionid family, see C.W.J. Eliot, *Historia* 16 (1967) 279–86. Kleine, 53–56, accepts the connection but does not relate Kroisos' death to the Battle of Pallene.

FOR PAGE 52

Sounion kouroi: *Kouroi* nos. 2–5 figs. 33–49; add the inscribed fragment, B. Staïs, *EphArch* 1917, 202–3; *Local Scripts*, 73–74. For finds from the Temenos of Athena, see Staïs, *op. cit.*, 201–4.

See also W. B. Dinsmoor, Jr., *Sounion* (Keramos Guides 1971) 37–51, for structures within the temenos. For the relief of a youth crowning himself, see *Severe Style*, 49 fig. 70; *Aspécts*, 14, explains the youth's gesture as devotional, the athlete confronting the deity that has given him victory.

Sounion kouroi as Dioskouroi: Staïs, *op. cit.*, 191 fig. 6a.

FOR PAGE 53

For the maritime character of Apollo, see L. R. Farnell, *The Cults of the Greek States* (Oxford 1907) vol. 4, pp. 145–47; see also 317.

Statues carrying inscriptions engraved on the body itself have been collected in *Samos* XI, 71–72 and nn. 30–35. From this category I would exclude statuettes since the small size of both figure and base may have imposed restrictions; moreover, we have no assurance that such statuettes were always given with a base. For the Attic dislike of inscriptions directly on statues, see *Local Scripts*, 73.

FOR PAGE 54

Kouroi, 3, suggests that the nakedness of the kouroi was introduced by the Greeks because it "served best their purpose of anatomical study and . . . corresponded to their athletic ideal."

Although the god Min is usually represented as a mummy, for a naked statuette in adult shape, see, e.g., a bronze figure in the Fitzwilliam Museum, Cambridge (6th century, EGA 4376.-1943), in a walking pose. That nakedness could also be a sign of youth is shown by the many representations of the child Horus with the long lock of childhood (another reason for the long hair of the kouroi?).

FOR PAGE 55

Belts as abbreviated symbol of entire costume: Deonna, 49.

Geometric bronzes with belts: F. Willemsen, *AthMitt* 69–70 (1954–55) 12–32; on the belt, see 19 and 30. *Art of Greece*, 190, considers the belt a kind of sash known from Hittite, neo-Hittite, Assyrian, and Syrian art.

Bronze kouros from Delphi: supra, pp. 22–23, 40.

Ivory youth from Samos: *AthMitt* 74 (1959) 43–47; Schefold, pl. 19 and pp. 73, 163–64. *Art of Greece*, 215, compares the belt to a form of sash shown on the Ivriz rock relief (his pl. 30), neo-Hittite, ca. 730. On Phrygian belts and their use by the Greeks, see J. Boardman, *Anatolia* 6 (1961) 179–89.

On belted kouroi and chronology see "Theräisches," 123–24; the statement on naturalism is on p. 124. The seven belted kouroi are: 1) Thera kouros B (?), "Theräisches," Beil. 87–89b; 2) Thera kouros Γ, Beil. 90–91a; 3) Thera kouros Δ, Beil. 91–92, funerary; 4) Delos A 333; 5) Delos A 4085 (in metal?); 6) Delos A 334 (in marble, perhaps with metal attachments); 7) Naxian Apollo in Delos. For the belt of this last statue see infra, p. 65 n. 22. The kore from Thera (Theräisches," 117–21, Beil. 81–82) had her belt added in metal.

RF vase: E 336, British Museum *CVA* Fasc. 5, III, 1, C, pl. 65, 2a; *Kouroi* fig. 1 opposite p. 16; by the Dwarf Painter.

FOR PAGE 56

Cybele from cemetery at Kyme: Collignon, 65–66; Mendel, 2 no. 522; Tuchelt, 89. For two naiskos reliefs from the same cemetery, reproducing the same iconographic type, see Tuchelt, L 89–90, with bibliography. See also infra, Chs. 5 and 6.

Apollo as protector of corpses and funerary god: E. Simon, *JdI* 88 (1973) 27–42, esp. p. 33.

Apollo Amyklaios over Hyakinthos' grave: Paus. 3.18.9–19.5. Note that the statue had a helmet, spear, and bow, attributes of a warrior. Cf. Schefold, pl. 265a and commentary on pp. 245–46.

On Apollo and the Hyperboreans: N. Yalouris, *Olympiaka Chronika* 1 (1970) 1–17.

On the helmeted Apollo, see comments in *Erzählung*, 18 (86) nn. 1–3.

Olympia tripod-leg with Struggle for the Tripod (?): F. Willemsen, *OlForsch* 3 (1957), B 1730 pl. 63; *Art of Greece*, pl. 59 and p. 190.

FOR PAGE 57

Magic significance in literary sources: S. Marinatos, *ArchHom* I Ch. A (1967) 38.

FOR PAGE 58

On the technical changes made by the Greeks to the Egyptian prototype, see B. S. Ridgway, *AJA* 70 (1966) 68–70.

FOR PAGE 59

Kouroi's plinths: *Ptoion* 455 (note the reservations about the plinth shape of the New York kouros, the only one which does not seem to fit the outlined development). Also *Kouroi*, 13–16. For a Samian base, see, e.g., *AthMitt* 78 (1963) 123–25 no. 5 Beil. 69.

For anatomical descriptions and tables, see *Kouroi*, 17–25.

FOR PAGE 60

Naxos kouros with striated hair: N. Kontoleon, *Praktika* 1972, 145 pls. 126–27; id., *Ergon* 1972, 98–99 figs. 94–95.

Position of ear in relationship to hair mass: Contrast, e.g., Thera kouroi A and B, and Kleobis and Biton; see "Theräisches," 122 and nn. 23a–25.

FOR PAGE 61

Eretria "kouros": *Kouroi* no. 168 figs. 494–96.

For the "loop hairstyle," see, e.g., *Kouroi* no. 164 figs. 485–88, or no. 171 figs. 509–10. For Assyrian comparison, cf. supra, p. 35 n. 26.

For the definition negative beads or pearls, see G. Schmidt, *AthMitt* 86 (1971) 38 (e.g., Sounion kouros). Chocolate squares; see *Ptoion*, 127 and passim (e.g., *Kouroi* no. 96).

Cyrene head: Paribeni, no. 13; L. Polacco et al., *Sculture Greche e Romane di Cirene* (Padova 1959) 10–25; see esp. pp. 14–19 for the discussion of a knit cap and literary sources; the head is considered female by E. Langlotz, *AthMitt* 77 (1962) 111–20.

On Archaic hair, see *Greek Sculpture*, 48–50.

FOR PAGE 62

On the Sounion kouros, see also *Bedeutung*, 15 and nn. 2–5.

For the discussion of Samian hair, see F. Eckstein, *AntP* 1 (1962) 47–57, esp. 50 and n. 11.

Pubic hair: *Aristodikos*, 72–83.

Delos A 333: *Kouroi* no. 17 figs. 94–95.

Aristodikos: *Kouroi* no. 165 figs. 492–93.

FOR PAGE 63

Delos A 1742: *Kouroi* no. 113 (no ill.).

For the Attic rendering of the four-faceted schema, see *Kouroi* figs. 60–68 (various kouroi).

FOR PAGE 64

My comments on Naxian kouroi are largely based on the perceptive analysis by J. Ducat in *Ptoion*, 453–54, 459–63, and in *GdD*, 39–46. I was able to examine personally many Naxian kouroi in December 1974.

For a good detail of the elbow of kouros Delos A 4083, see Adam, pl. 2a.

FOR PAGE 65

Copenhagen head: *Kouroi* no. 50 figs. 172–73.

Many of the Naxian and Delian kouroi are still unpublished.

Delos A 4085: *Kouroi*, figs. 20–21.

Delos A 334: *Kouroi*, figs. 22–24; *BCH* 83 (1959) 559–63 pl. 28.

FOR PAGE 66

My comments on Parian kouroi are based on Ducat's analysis in *Ptoion*, 311 and *GdD*, 42, as well as on direct observation (December 1974).

Examples of the "Parian" treatment of the back are: Paros Mus. nos. 157, 167, 311 (to my knowledge, unpublished); Kroisos; Nat. Mus. 3757 (Karouzou 23, unknown provenience); to a certain extent also the Cleveland kouros (*AJA* 78 [1974] pl. 21:1–2) and the Parian kouros in the Ny Carlsberg Glyptothek (*Kouroi* no. 117 figs. 347–49). For a Parian head, see *Kouroi*, no. 116 figs. 356–58.

Cyrene kouros (from Paros ?): *AJA* 75 (1971) pl. 8:3–4.

East Greek kouroi: Besides Tuchelt, see also F. Eckstein, *AntP* 1 (1962) 47–57; H. P. Laubscher, *IstMitt* 13–14 (1963–64) 73–87.

For a very peculiar head in Izmit (Nikomedia, Bithynia), see *Belleten* 31 (1967) 331–34 figs. 1–5.

The gigantic kouroi from Didyma are Tuchelt, K 1 to 5, 7, 9bis, 10, 11.

FOR PAGE 67

Tuchelt on hairstyles: See p. 185.

Rhodian kouroi: E.g., *Kouroi* nos. 124 and 154 (figs. 365–68 and 447–49); Rhodian head: *Kouroi* no. 125 figs. 373–75.

Samian kouroi: *Samos* XI nos. 29–57, 139; see pp. 9–10 for the statement that even the most gigantic examples must be considered "human." That Samian kouroi could be exported is perhaps shown by the leg found in Myus, *IstMitt* 15 (1965) 64 no. 4 pl. 29:1; and the fragmentary head in Corfu, *JHS ArchR* 16 (1970) 19 fig. 30.

FOR PAGE 68

The unusual hand belongs to *Samos* XI no. 37 pl. 24.

Abdominal partitions appear on *Samos* XI no. 52 pls. 36–37; see *ibid.*, p. 100 for a statement of Cycladic influence on the Samian statue.

Funerary (?) kouros with fleshy abdomen: *Samos* XI no. 57 pls. 42–43.

Head in Istanbul of the Samian giant: *Samos* XI no. 47 pls. 30–33.

Melos kouros: *Kouroi* no. 86 figs. 273–79; cf. also *Ptoion*, 455, on his plinth and Naxian influence.

On Boeotian kouroi: *Ptoion*, passim. For the various schools and influences represented, see pp. 453–54 and 459–66; the school of Akraiphia is defined especially on pp. 462–66.

FOR PAGE 69

Kouros Thebes no. 1: *Ptoion* no. 63 p. 132, dated ca. 560, as contrasted with *Kouroi* no. 34 figs. 141–43, where it is dated early in the 590–570 group. Note also the comments on the entire Orchomenos-Thera group in *Agora* XI, 4.

Orchomenos kouros: *Kouroi* no. 33 figs. 138–40 (dated within the same time span as Thebes 1); *Ptoion*, 132 and 464, ca. 560–550, with the latter date the more probable, and some Naxian influence observed in the statue.

Head Nat. Mus. 15: *Kouroi* no. 10 figs. 72–75, dated 615–590; *Ptoion* no. 58, ca. 580. (Could it be later?)

FOR PAGE 70

Kleobis and Biton: *Kouroi* no. 12 A–B figs. 78–83, 91–92. For the inscription, see *Signatures* I, 115. For the sculptor, see also infra, Ch. 10. For the theory of two different masters, see G. v. Kaschnitz-Weinberg, *Studies presented to D. M. Robinson* (St. Louis, Mo., 1951) 525–31; a rebuttal by P. de la Coste Messeliere, *BCH* 77 (1953) 177–78. The latest discussion of the statues is by H. Drerup, *MarbWinckPr* (1970) 1–6, who reviews previous studies and suggests a reversal of the position of the statues; see also Cl. Rolley, *RA* 1975, 3–12 and esp. p. 10 and n. 3 for chronology.

For Corinthian sculpture, see supra, pp. 47–48; cf. also supra pp. 33, 42.

Tenea kouros: *Kouroi* no. 73 figs. 245–50; latest, D. Ahrens, *JOAI* 49 (1971) 117–31.

Peiraeus Apollo: *Kouroi* no. 159bis figs. 478–80; N. Kontoleon in *Opus Nobile*, 91–98.

FOR PAGE 71

Magna Graecian statues as imports: Langlotz, *Magna Graecia*, 40–41.

Kouros to Sombrotidas, from Megara Hyblaia: *Kouroi* no. 134 figs. 388–90; Langlotz, *Magna Graecia*, pl. 7 p. 260 (Naxian); Berger, figs. 162–63 and p. 155, where he suggests that the family of Sombrotidas came from East Greece. For Samians in Megara Hyblaia, see G. Dunst, *AthMitt* 87 (1972) 156–58 (Excursus A).

Attic kouroi: For the early group, see *Ptoion*, 103–6; *Agora* XI, 13–16 no. 65; K. Schefold, *AntK* 4 (1961) 76–78; *Kerameikos* 6:2 (1970) 411.

New York Kouros: *Kouroi* no. 1 figs. 25–32, 60–62.

Dipylon Head: *Kouroi* no. 6 figs. 50–53, 65–67.

FOR PAGE 72

Euthykartides' base: *Kouroi* no. 16 (not illustrated) and G. Bakalakis, *BCH* 88 (1964) 539–53; against the attribution of the kouros to the base see, e.g., J. Marcade, *RA* 1975, 14. See also infra, Ch. 10.

Delos A 4048: *Kouroi* no. 112 figs. 343, 346.

Volomandra kouros: *Kouroi* no. 63 figs. 208–16.

FOR PAGE 73

Kouros from Merenda (Myrrhinous): *AAA* 5 (1972) 298–324; *AAA* 6 (1973) 367–69.

On offering bearers in general, see *EAA* s.v. *Moscoforo e Crioforo.*

Statue from Didyma: Tuchelt, K 16 pls. 18–19.

Statue from Klaros, Izmir inv. 3504: Tuchelt, 130 (Addenda to the List).

Statue from Samos: *Samos* XI no. 45 pls. 28–29 (cf. no. 46).

Didyma fragment: Tuchelt K 17 pl. 20:2.

Kriophoros in Thasos: *Kouroi* no. 14 figs. 84–86; *GdTh*, 115; *AJA* 68 (1964) 17–18.

Samian "bull-leader": *Samos* XI no. 64, pl. 54; for the suggestion of Theseus and the Minotaur, p. 134. A more plausible suggestion, that the torso may belong to an archer, is on p. 135.

Kamiros statuettes: *BrMusCat* 1:1, 163–64, B 340–B 346; Naukratis statuettes, *ibid.*, 189–90, B 448–B 450.

Kriophoros from Erythrai: Shown at the 10th International Congress of Classical Archaeology, Turkey, Sept. 1973.

Torso in Geneva: *Kouroi*, no. 90 figs. 288–90; W. Deonna, *BCH* 75 (1951) 38–59.

Parian kouros in Copenhagen: *Kouroi* no. 117 figs. 347–49; *Ny Carlsberg*, no. 1a pp. 18–19.

FOR PAGE 74

Torso from Naxos: N. Kontoleon, *Praktika* 1972, 144 pls. 124–25; *Ergon* 1972, 97–98. For a "prediction" of finds showing Cycladic continuity, *Aspécts*, 57.

Ancient sources on Apollo holding deer: Pliny, *NH* 34.75; Paus. 9.10.2. See also E. Bielefeld, *IstMitt* 12 (1962) 18–43.

Moschophoros: Akr. 624; Payne, 1–3 pls. 2–4; *AMA* no. 409; Brouskari, 40–41. Egyptian influence: K. Levin, *AJA* 68 (1964) 18 and nn. 39–41; see also her p. 17. Oriental parallels from Carchemish and Karatepe: *Art of Greece*, 113 fig. 81 and pl. 34a opposite p. 141.

FOR PAGE 75

Ilissos kouros: Nat. Mus. 3687; I. K. Konstantinou, *Deltion* 14 (1931–32) 41–56, with drawing of metal attachments; BrBr 781–2 (text by H. Riemann); for the Hermes identification, *Aristodikos*, F 1; *Severe Style*, fig. 17.

Akr. 633: Payne, 46 pl. 102; *AMA* no. 308; Brouskari, 72–73; *Severe Style*, figs. 49–50.

Didyma draped men: Tuchelt K 21–35; see also L 70, L 102bis, L 104–5; for K 30, see *IstMitt* 21 (1971) 96–97.

Samos: *Samos* XI nos. 72–75 and, in poros, no. 76; no. 66 may have belonged to a group. See comments on pp. 151–52 for general type and for the suggestion of "second rank" people, who did not quite rate a seated statue.

Sicily: Syracuse Mus. no. 705; P. Orsi, *Antike Plastik*, Festschrift W. Amelung (1928) 168–71 no. 1 figs. 1–2; *Sicile Grecque*, pl. 45.

Dionyshermos in the Louvre: Tuchelt, L 102bis; *Kouroi*, no. 124a figs. 616–19; for the correct reading of the inscription, see G. Daux, *BCH* 91 (1967) 491–93.

Youth from Pitane: Tuchelt, L 104; *KAnat*, 229–31 fig. 195.

For an example of "perikalles agalma," see *Samos* XI no. 49, the kouros dedicated by Cheramyes; *Ptoion* no. 238; cf. also no. 141. For a specific analysis of this formula, see Ch. Karouzos, *Epitymbion Ch. Tsountas* (1941) 535–78. For first-person inscriptions on monuments, consult (with some caution) M. Burzachechi, *Epigraphica* 24 (1962) 3–54.

FOR PAGE 76

Draped man touching edge of mantle, from Cape Phoneas: *Samos* XI no. 72 pls. 59–60.

Torso from Sardis: Tuchelt, L 105; G.M.A. Hanfmann and K. Z. Polatkan, *Anatolia* 4 (1959) 55–65.

Male statues wearing only himation: *Samos* XI no. 75; Syracuse kouros (supra, bibl. for p. 75). See also supra, p. 75 n. 32, for the terracotta statues from Corinth.

Bronze head from the Akropolis: Nat. Mus. 6446; Papaspyridi, 195; BrBr 2.

Spartan torso: *Deltion* 24:2[1] (1969) 131–32 no. 2 pl. 121a–b.

Sparta, helmeted head: *ibid*, no. 3 pl. 120b. Leonidas, *ibid.*, 132–33 no. 5; *Severe Style*, 39 no. 5.

Samos warrior in Berlin: *Samos* XI no. 78 pls. 65–67.

Akr. 599: *AMA* no. 307; Brouskari, 128–29 (dated 470–460).

For roughly worked head crowns, possibly covered by helmets, see e.g. Akr. 621, Payne, pl. 103:1–2; *AMA* no. 315 and comments in the text, with further references; Brouskari, 96. See also infra, Ch. 5, p. 141.

Chapter 4

Korai and Other Female Figures

CHARACTERISTICS OF THE KORE

The generic Greek term for girl (daughter, maiden) has been adopted for the female counterpart of the Archaic kouros. Yet if the definition of the youth type was relatively simple and implied a standard pose, that for the female figure is considerably more complex. A kore is basically a standing, draped female statue made during the Archaic period, that is, between 650 and 480. But these are the only constant terms of the definition. As for pose, she may be shown with legs joined together or with one foot forward; with arms at the sides, or with one arm against the chest, or with one hand holding her skirt in the center or to one side; and finally, with one arm or both outstretched, presenting an offering. As for the objects she holds, they can be animate or inanimate: birds, hares, flowers, fruits, wreaths. Her costume may vary; her head may be bare or veiled, surmounted by a polos or by a diadem. Her hair may be of different lengths and patterns, it may be spread over both front and back or be limited to her shoulders. Her feet may be shod or bare.

To this bewildering variety of possibilities, other problems should be added. Are these differences chronological, geographical, or both? What is the relationship between the kore type and the beginning of marble sculpture? What is the relationship of the freestanding korai to the female figures supporting holy water basins (perirrhanteria)? What garments are the korai really wearing and how? Should we try to find explanations for all apparent discrepancies in the rendering of the attire, or should we attribute them mostly to artistic freedom and arbitrary choice for variety's sake? In particular, do specific costumes identify specific personages and, in general, who are the korai?

Until fairly recently only the korai recovered from the Athenian Akropolis were well known as a group; the rest seemed sporadic material, and even the intermittent publication of Samian statuary did not manage to convey a systematic picture of female sculpture in that island. In 1968 the publication of *Korai* provided a very useful grouping of the most important examples, conveniently illustrated in one volume. The catalogue followed the same guidelines established for the kouroi, emphasizing chronological over topographical divisions and using both the rendering of drapery and anatomical development as dating criteria. Included are a considerable number of statuettes in terracotta, bronze, and ivory, some architectural sculpture, mirror supports, and even some bronze plaques and jewelry, so that the total of 206 items is misleadingly close to that obtained for the kouroi. However, some actual examples of marble korai were omitted, and more finds have occurred since the appearance of the book. In addition, several sites have now received thorough publication and can help reshape our picture of the development of the Kore type in Greek sculpture.

At the present stage of our knowledge, the korai seem not to have been quite as numerous as the kouroi and seem never to have attained the gigantic size of some of their male counterparts, though several maidens are well over life-size. In addition, several kouroi outside Attica could be shown to have had a funerary function, but only two Attic korai are definitely connected with tombs. Others from that region can reasonably be surmised to have served the same purpose, but outside Attica all evidence is missing. Two figures from Samos, which had been originally published as funerary, are now being considered votive; and a peculiar limestone statue holding a ribbon (or a snake?) which was found in an archaic cemetery in Tanagra, Boeotia, is preserved only from neck to lap. It is difficult to determine whether its cylindrical body is male or female. The Attic evidence may mean that the Athenians were especially eager to honor their dead with outstanding monuments; or again, it may simply reflect the possibilities of a wealthy and powerful aristocracy. But since other territories with less prominent citizens or imperfectly known social history have yielded good evidence for funerary kouroi, it is perhaps safer to assume that the kore was less popular as a grave marker or that our evidence is still incomplete. Specifically in Asia Minor, where the status of women was supposedly more prominent than in Greece proper, one would expect to see funerary sculpture reflect these conditions, but the finds from Miletos suggest that the seated matronly figure was preferred over the youthful standing type. As a result, most of our korai must have been votive in character or meant to represent a divine being.

PROBLEMS OF TYPE AND DATE

Nikandre

One of the earliest marble korai to represent a specific divinity is known as Nikandre, the name of the Naxian woman who set her up in Delos as a dedication "to the far-darter." She was found near the Artemision, and her inscription suggests that she was an offering to the goddess rather than to her brother Apollo. It has been argued that the over life-size statue must have portrayed Artemis herself since the fisted hands were pierced for the insertion of metal objects, which are usually taken to be arrows, on the basis of the dedicatory inscription. Another theory, however, would like to see the goddess in her role as Mistress of Animals, therefore holding the leashes of two lions, now lost, which would have formed part of the original offering. This restoration would also bring the Nikandre considerably close in spirit to the figures supporting large holy water basins on their heads while standing on lions, an important category of marble sculpture which will be discussed presently. However, I feel that the hypothesis is weakened by the fact that the dedicatory inscription runs along the left side of the statue and would have been partly obscured by an object which extended below the level of the fist. Nor is it completely certain that the statue portrays Artemis since the phrasing of the dedication seems to distinguish between the recipient of the offering (Artemis) and the offering itself, which speaks in the first person. An image of the goddess might rather have been inscribed: "Nikandre dedicated me, *the* far-darter. . . ."

The controversy over the interpretation and identification of this statue is important in highlighting our difficulty in distinguishing between a generic kore and a specific representation. Cases exist in which the inscription, giving the name of the dedicant in the nominative, makes it clear that the statue stands for the worshiper. This seems to be particularly true for Asia Minor sculpture, where the tradition of identifying the offering with the dedicant was perhaps influenced or reinforced by Oriental practices. In other cases, the statue is donated by a man and excludes the identity of the dedicant with dedication. Finally, in cases where there is no inscription to help settle the issue, I believe that the costume may allow us to perceive possible shades of meaning in the various types. It is in fact significant that, of the various anonymous korai known to us at present, only the Nikandre and a group of figures from Delos have been proposed as divine images in the full sense, the Delian group largely because of association with other gods and goddesses clearly identified through specific attributes like the aegis for Athena or an animal skin for Artemis.[1] Even in such cases, therefore, it is the costume which furnishes the clue since Athena's aegis represents a definite extra garment added to a typical kore attire.

The Nikandre wears a belted costume with sleeves and (a detail which is usually unnoticed)[2] a short cape which appears mostly as a link between her back and her arms since the way in which it was fastened over her chest is no longer clear. I believe I can discern two faintly rounded depressions at the point where a continuation of the cape's edges over the upper arms would make them join between her breasts. Theoretically, one could assume that the cape is an animal skin, with paws tied over the chest, but this trait is perhaps too sophisticated for the early period. More probably, the Nikandre wears one of the many capes one finds on Daedalic female figures (cf. Fig. 1), whether in limestone, wood, or other media, though none of those comes down as low as the faint traces on the Nikandre suggest. If a real cape, hers was perhaps held in place by a "spectacles fibula" fastening the two edges of the cloth.

The cape, as well as the style, definitely link the Nikandre with Daedalic works and times, yet the material and the considerable size indicate that Archaic marble sculpture had already started in the Cyclades. If our chronological assessments are correct, how does this early dating of the korai affect the theory that the impulse toward marble carving was largely determined by the desire to produce *male* figures in a striding pose? Since in effect the earliest extant female figures (Nikandre and the kore from Thera) are very nearly contemporary with, or only slightly earlier than, the earliest kouroi, this evidence would support, or at least not contradict, my suggestion because we can hardly imagine that good luck has preserved for us the very first products of such carving for both male and female types. Yet two possible objections exist: an even earlier date has been assigned to the fragment of an over life-size kore in Samos (second quarter of the Seventh century), and a considerable number of perirrhanteria, in a variety of local marbles, seems early enough to imply that carving in that medium was already practiced before the advent of the kouros. Both these facts, however, are open to other interpretations.

The Samian Kore

The Samian kore is preserved only in her lower part, comprising the bottom of her block-like skirt, from which two rather shapeless feet emerge and a tenon, projecting below the plinth, for fastening onto a base. This latter is particularly interesting since it

[1] This statement, to be sure, does not mean to imply that there are no other statues of archaic goddesses but only that they are clearly identified.

[2] This detail was pointed out to me by Judith P. Binder, but the main published descriptions of the statue, including *Korai*, speak of her dress as a one-piece costume. However Meola, 40 fig. 13a draws Nikandre with such a cape, and on p. 44 n. 124 refers to it as part of her modular divisions. Meola gives no reference to her source for this detail.

would be more appropriate for a wooden statue and should therefore represent a survival in stone of earlier practices.[3] As for the figure proper, though flat and quite similar to the Nikandre from the front, it has considerable depth in profile view and is therefore an example of that massiveness of body which characterizes all later Samian korai. Yet so little of the figure is preserved that no absolute precision can be claimed in dating it. Its importance lies mostly in its very large size, its material (Naxian ? marble), and its wood-like tenon with all its implications. It could easily be reconciled with the dates suggested for Nikandre and the Naxian kouroi. The fact remains that all kouroi from Samos seem to be considerably later and made of local marble. One would therefore tend to postulate that monumental sculpture started in Samos under impulse from the Cyclades but concentrated on the kore type. Yet the perirrhanteria may already be in the local bluish-gray marble. I am strongly in favor of considering Samos one of the birthplaces of Archaic sculpture, independent of Naxos, and I would hesitate to attribute very high dates to the early korai since their similarity to wooden xoana proportionately increases their appearance of great antiquity and may not correspond to actual calendar years. As for the kouroi, we may not yet have found the earliest Samian examples—or we may have to accept the fact that Samos, because of its strong veneration of the goddess Hera, used the general impulse coming from Egypt and the Orient to carve female rather than male statues.

Perirrhanteria

The perirrhanteria are less of a problem since the highest date assigned to them coincides approximately with the highest date for an extant (Samian) kore, ca. 660. It is perhaps significant that the earliest example was found in Samos though a recent study suggests that it could not be a true prototype for the entire series, which shows too many stylistic differences.[4] The iconography of a human figure standing on a lion is obviously imported from the Orient. But the idea of the female figure supporting a basin on her head may also have come from outside sources, specifically Egypt. A fragment from a large granite offering bowl in the Fitzwilliam Museum, Cambridge, has on the outside of its rim part of one support in the form of a Hathor's head. Given the large dimension of the bowl, more than one leg would have been needed, and presumably the Hathor's head should be integrated with a complete body. The bowl is inscribed to the gods Re and Horus of Hermopolis Magna, and dates from the Thirteenth-Twelfth century. Though such Egyptian

[3] The Nikandre also has such a tenon though illustrations usually show her at plinth level. Cf. Picard, *Manuel* I, 567 fig. 196. See also Jacob-Felsch, 8 and n. 21.

[4] F. W. Hamdorf, *AthMitt* 89 (1974) 47–64, lists over 16 examples of the type; he argues that the marbles employed vary and that stylistic traits are so different from item to item that one cannot think in terms of a single prototype but rather of an invention (sparked from the Orient) which gave impetus to the adoption of the type in different places simultaneously. Though Oriental influence is stressed, Lakonia is proposed as the possible birthplace for the type since so many of the extant examples are in Lakonian marble and were found in that area. This article goes further than previous studies by G. Hiesel and J. Ducat in suggesting also that the female figures probably represent servants of the gods, comparable to the Charites, Horai, or Nymphs. The geographical range for the diffusion of the type has been recently increased by the recognition of one more example from Selinus. The marble statuette seems closest to the figures of an Olympia perirrhanterion (E. Paribeni, *AttiMGrecia* NS 9–10 [1968–69], 61–63).

objects are not common, they may have caught the fancy of the Samians since precisely such votive and religious furnishings are likely to have been exported to an island which has been found full of Egyptian and other Oriental material. Note that the Greek perirrhanteria have been found in greatest concentration (4 items) at Olympia, which was itself open to all kinds of Oriental and Orientalizing imports, while the other basins all come from major Greek sanctuaries. Both the perirrhanterion from Samos and that from Isthmia are particularly revealing of Oriental influences in the way in which the women's hair protrudes on either side of the neck, in a manner reminiscent of the so-called siren-attachments to metal cauldrons, and the prototype for the entire vessel should perhaps be sought in bronze work.

In a book on Archaic sculpture, the perirrhanteria are important only insofar as they attest to marble carving at an early date. Despite the considerable size of some of them (Isthmia, h. of each kore ca. 50 cm.), they remain confined to the realm of the minor arts and can throw no specific light on contemporary sculpture because of their innate conservatism. There is no reason to believe them earlier than the inception of monumental marble sculpture, and they should be considered influenced by it, rather than vice versa. To my knowledge, none of the women from marble perirrhanteria wears a cape, and this detail should further remove them from the sphere of Daedalic art.[5]

DISTRIBUTION

The available evidence would suggest the following history for the kore type. A considerable tradition of large-scale female figures (cult images?) in wood and in bronze or other metals found its translation into marble around 660 when kouroi were also being carved in that medium. The centers of origin for the type seem to have been both Naxos and Samos, with the East Greek island following an independent tradition of its own until approximately the turn into the Sixth century. At this time the arrival of the kouros (if indeed it was thus delayed) must have opened the way to Cycladic influence when active trade in marble had stopped because of the exploitation of local quarries in Samos. The earliest korai in Asia Minor seem to date from around 600, and their foldless garments still appear in the Daedalic tradition, but it should be emphasized that a plain straight skirt may continue until 560, so that absence of folds should not per se suggest a high chronology, nor should "Daedalic Style" be postulated on the basis of relatively small fragments. Although the kore type seems to have found its most fertile ground in East Greece, our next examples come from Attica, Chios, and the Cyclades, with Samos experiencing an apparent pause until about the second quarter of the Sixth century when a new veiled type is introduced, presumably through some Anatolian influence I believe. On Samos then began an uninterrupted series of korai which was at its richest from ca. 560 to 540 and petered out around 520. Naxos virtually disappeared from the scene after 550, with Paros and the other Cyclades offering sporadic evidence until about the third quarter of the Sixth century. At that time the Athenian Akropolis began its own series, under strong in-

[5] The two terracotta examples included in *Korai*, nos. 12–13, show female figures with capes, but they are standing on a simple base and are holding their breasts, so that their tradition connects more readily with Oriental Astarte plaques than with the women-on-lions of the stone perirrhanteria.

fluence from the islands, and managed in turn to influence production on Samos and in Asia Minor around 530–520, thus contributing to the creation of an International Style even within the kore type.

Basically, only Athens has yielded examples of the latest (early Fifth century) korai. Corinth has produced none for the entire Archaic phase though it began to carve peplophoroi in the Severe period. The whole Peloponnesos is, as usual, very poor in freestanding sculpture: aside from fragments of two korai in Sparta (in local marble, and at least one of them wearing a peculiar, transitional form of the diagonal mantle) and four pieces in island marble from a statue in the Argive Heraion, we have only limestone works. These are the head of a kore allegedly from Sikyon[6] and the gigantic head in Olympia which has been variously considered Hera or a sphinx. Even Boeotia, so rich in kouroi, has produced few examples of female figures; of the three from the Ptoion, one is obviously an import from Attica. Delphi has no korai, though the type was known through the Karyatids of the various Ionic treasuries and the pedimental figures from the Temple of Apollo. A head in the Delphi museum, which has generally been considered male, is more probably female because its diadem is comparable to that of the "Attic" Phrasikleia, but it comes from Trikorphon in Naupaktia. Sicily, which had imported or produced a few kouroi, has fewer korai, which include the strange terracotta statue in Catania. Some more traditional but often unfinished products appear in Tarentum. Non-Greek territories in Asia Minor (Lydia, Karia, Phrygia) have a few examples, and so do some of the neighboring territories (Kalchedon on the Bosphoros, the area of the Black Sea, the islands of Skyros and Thasos, Thrace) which obviously received the type from East Greece or the islands. Even Cyrene, with no marble quarries of its own, has several korai in different styles, which must have come from different workshops.

Basically, therefore, the distribution chart suggests a very strong tradition for the kore in Asia Minor and Samos, with some important workshops located also in other islands: Naxos, Paros, and perhaps Chios. From these centers the type spread to Greece proper, where Attica was particularly receptive but not the other areas despite an obvious production of female figurines in the minor arts. Though this may seem somewhat the same pattern of distribution as that available for the kouros type, chronologically and iconographically East Greece is shown to be in the lead, with considerable lag, or lack of evidence, elsewhere.

COSTUME

The archaic female attire is more complex and varied than usually acknowledged. The earliest korai wear tight-fitting tunics, belted at the waist, with relatively short sleeves either sewn or buttoned along the outer edge of the arms. This costume is variously called a chiton or a peplos, but this latter term is misleading because it evokes images of the Severe costume by the same name. The Archaic peplos, if the name be retained, cannot be described in Richter's words[7] but must have resembled a modern dress, though at times

[6] V. Karageorghis, *Sculptures from Salamis* I (Nicosia 1964) no. 1 pp. 7–8, reports that J. Marcadé had suggested associating the headless Cypriot kore under discussion (illustrated on pl. 7:1–4) with the head "from Sikyon" in Boston, but that unfortunately the connection could not be proved.

[7] *Korai*, p. 7. S. *&* S. p. 90, gives a slightly different definition, under "chiton": "The Doric one, known as the peplos, was made of wool spun and woven by Greek women in their houses all in one piece; it was

the sleeves are connected with the bodice, as if a belt were worn with a fitted version of the present-day poncho. It is difficult to determine whether this detail corresponds to the actual appearance of the garment or whether the sculptor in his reluctance to cut away the stone between arms and torso created the impression of a one-piece top. In Phrasikleia, for instance, the patterned border edging the sleeves stops when it reaches the body, and the left upper arm seems entirely surrounded by material, as if emerging from a circular opening; yet the rear view in particular suggests that no division exists between sleeves and blouse.

A tentative division between chiton and peplos could be drawn on the basis of the sleeve arrangement. If sewn along the arms and shoulders, the costume is a peplos; if buttoned, it is a chiton. Yet this distinction is not completely foolproof. A better indication is perhaps provided by the rendering of the garment around the belt. If this latter is completely exposed, with little or no bunching of material over it, the costume should be the heavier peplos, perhaps made of wool. If, instead, the dress partly overlaps the belt, creating the so-called kolpos, because of its gulf-like shape, then the costume should be the chiton, which, being thinner, would allow for such movement of the material. But this is only a tentative suggestion. Distinction between peplos and chiton becomes easy after the mid Sixth century, when the East Greek convention of thin grooves and ridges, often wavy, is generally adopted to convey the crinkly texture of the fine linen tunic.

Both the chiton and the peplos can be worn by themselves. Often, however, the chiton is covered by a short diagonal mantle (himation) buttoned along the right arm and passing under the left armpit. This type of mantle first appears around 580, presumably in the Cyclades. Conversely, the peplos can overlie a thin chiton. I know of no diagonal mantle worn over a peplos, but a relatively long, or a short, shawl-like cloak can be worn symmetrically on both shoulders over the peplos and, in some cases, even over the chiton/diagonal himation combination. Shorter, cape-like wraps must also have existed, though they are often confused with the overfold (apoptygma) of the peplos since the rendering is similar to the Classical arrangement.

Such a cape is worn, I believe, by the so-called Peplos Kore (Akr. 679: Fig. 15), though it is ignored by all recent descriptions. No possible folding and overfolding of the one-piece costume could in fact explain the continuous edge over her right arm, as contrasted with the tight-fitting "blouse" visible under it. We should visualize this kore as wearing a thin chiton (now apparent only at the lower part of the figure, below the hem of the peplos), a heavier peplos, and then a small cape pinned over the left shoulder; her outstretched arm on that side causes the cape to open over the biceps. The hole for a second metal pin, over her right shoulder, may mean that the cape was fastened also at that point, to prevent slipping.[8]

At times this type of cape must have been more or less circular and unbroken, with only a central opening for the head, like a small Mexican poncho. Only this rendering can ex-

often worn open on one side and was regularly fastened over each shoulder with a brooch, button, or long pin." Note that in this "classical" arrangement the length of cloth, whether single or folded double, was wrapped around the body passing *under* both arms, but slack enough to be pulled up and fastened over the shoulders, leaving both arms bare.

[8] On the possible meaning of the "Peplos Kore" and her costume, see infra, p. 110. Cf. also my forthcoming article in *The Journal of the Walters Art Gallery* (1977).

plain, for instance, the appearance of the small kore from Eleusis. Richter describes her costume as a belted peplos with overfold, and an epiblema with edges showing along either side in front. Yet the vertical lines framing the front of the "skirt" could easily represent the bunching of the material under the tight belt, somewhat like the arrangement on the Peplos Kore, while the uninterrupted edge running parallel to the belt and continuing across both arms can hardly be reconciled with an overfold, since the "blouse" below has a much tighter fit. The only—though unlikely—way in which such a costume (and that of the Peplos Kore) could be explained as an overfolded peplos would be to assume that openings for the arms had been made just below the folding point of the apoptygma, so that the upper part of the peplos could fall in a cape-like covering, while the lower part could be independently tied around the waist. Were this the correct interpretation of the costume, the fashion would still be quite different from the Classical peplos, where the overfold remains firmly under the arms, which are both uncovered.[9]

The short mantle may also be made in two pieces and may be worn in a symmetrical arrangement, buttoned over both arms and hanging equally from the front and from the back. It usually has a horizontal neckline and a shorter central fold, so that the lower edge describes an inverted V (i.e., a swallowtail pattern) over both abdomen and buttocks. Examples of this fashion (which Langlotz calls "Koren mit Mäntelchen") are Akr. 605, 611 (Fig. 17), and 678 (Fig. 16), while a similar rendering has been recognized on a Samian piece, which is probably influenced by mainland works. Characteristic of this rendering is the similar appearance of both front and back. By contrast, another way of wearing the one-piece mantle (Langlotz's "Koren mit auf beiden Schultern gehefteter Mantille") is to drape it as if it had to have a diagonal edge, buttoning it over the right arm, but then pinning it also at one point over the left shoulder. This arrangement results in a horizontal neckline and an inverted-V hem over the front, but the back is dissimilar, with a long tip in the center of the figure, reaching down to the buttocks, flanked on either side by the so-called swallowtail pattern. A typical instance of this arrangement appears on korai Akr. 600 and 673 (Fig. 18).

Finally, a long mantle, for which the name himation should perhaps be reserved, follows more or less the same conventions as the equivalent costume for men, by leaving the right arm free and covering the left shoulder to hang over the back. The main difference consists in the fact that men usually gather the extra material into a many-layered bunch falling behind the left shoulder and leaving the left arm partly free, while the female figures cover both arm and shoulder with it, letting the heavy cloth hang from their left arm. The

[9] Another peculiar costume, which at first glance looks like a peplos with an overfold, occurs on some terracotta busts which may have decorated the pediments of the so-called Basilica at Paestum. They seem to be wearing a tight-fitting blouse with long sleeves. From below the breasts a loose panel of cloth (with a scalloped edge) hangs free, so that it can be lifted by the wearer; it is, however, sewn to the underlying blouse along the flanks. Two ruffles, corresponding to the edge of the panel, occur over the sleeves, one at mid-biceps and one at the wrist. The neckline is boat-shaped, with a wide opening (*BdA* 48 [1963], 212–20).

For a good Archaic example of an overfolded peplos, cf. the Goddess just beside Hephaistos on the north side of the Siphnian frieze. Two tips of her overfold are clearly visible at the opening on her left side, and while her right arm is partly hidden by the god's head, her free gesturing and the obvious vertical fall of her drapery along her right flank suggest that no continuous edge could have run along her right biceps, as in the Peplos Kore, or the cloth would have stretched obliquely in the direction of her raised arm.

draped youth Akr. 633 in this respect represents an exception, wearing his himation more in the female manner. A typical result of this way of draping the long mantle is that a diagonal edge runs from left shoulder to right armpit, in a reversal of the pattern created by the short diagonal himation. This fashion is exemplified by a Samian kore dated ca. 550. An alternative rendering, popular especially in the Severe and Classical periods, is to start wrapping the mantle from the left shoulder, carrying it diagonally across the back and below the right arm, to fling the rest of it over the left forearm so that the upper edge of the himation forms an almost horizontal line across the middle of the body, from right armpit to left forearm (e.g., Akr. korai 584 and 615).

Chronological and regional differences can be determined by the way in which korai wear their diagonal mantles or their chitons. But before embarking on topographical distinctions, three more items of clothing need to be mentioned: the chitoniskos, the skirt, and the veil.

The first two have been recently propounded on the basis of renderings not only in monumental sculpture but also in vase painting and the minor arts. The more obvious of the two seems the chitoniskos, which is also attested through mention in literary sources. It consists of the same type of material which forms the long chiton, but it is shorter, so that it does not reach the feet and may stop as high as the hips of the wearer. Akr. 670, 671, and 683 (Fig. 19) may be examples of this garment. An earlier instance is perhaps provided by a still unpublished kore from Erythrai, on display in the Izmir museum,[10] yet her chiton, instead of ending in an edge, seems to bend into a kolpos, as the rendering of the folds emphasizes. Other examples, especially in vase painting, are more explicit, at times giving a separate border to the edge of the short chiton.

The chitoniskos must be worn with some kind of skirt to cover the legs. It has recently been suggested that this was indeed a separate item of Archaic clothing, to be found not only in conjunction with the short chiton, but at times also over the long one, as an added element fastened at the waist. Certainly Mycenaean and Minoan figures wore independent skirts, as we see for example on the Kea terracotta statues (and on men and gods in Assyrian reliefs), but no term in ancient Greek sources has as yet been identified as meaning "skirt." Yet recognition of this garment would explain why many statues in diagonal himation have "blouses" differing in texture and color from the rendition of the fabric covering the lower body. The traditional explanation of a long chiton appearing under the short diagonal mantle attributes such changes to artistic whim or to the desire to provide for variety and contrast. It is, in fact, quite true that sculptural renderings of clothing are not

[10] The Erythrai kore probably dates around 560–550 and is well over life-size. She stands with her left leg slightly ahead of the right and holds her skirt with her right hand, thus producing a group of folds which run diagonally over her right thigh to merge and disappear against the heavy paryphe which so emphatically marks the central axis of the figure. This rendering may indicate some influence from Samos, though perhaps through intermediate sources and therefore somewhat misunderstood. Milesian connections may be suggested by the use of specific techniques; for instance, her head was inserted separately, a practice which is so far attested only for the Milesian area. However, her left arm, which is bent across the chest, was either repaired in antiquity or attached separately, and so was the outer portion of the right hand holding the skirt. This amount of piecing may indicate either an advanced technique, or relative scarcity of marble and skill, such as one might expect from a provincial workshop. E. Akurgal (whose oral opinion is quoted in *Samos* XI 112 n. 31) considers the kore Milesian.

always consistent. Some of the Akropolis korai display tips of garments that cannot be accounted for in terms of what they are wearing, but should be seen purely as balancing elements for a rich composition (e.g., Akr. 685). Similarly, the newly found Phrasikleia has a richer repertoire of patterns over the back than over the front of her one garment though it is unlikely that two different pieces of material were here envisaged by the artist. On the other hand, I find the possibility of a separate skirt quite plausible and even convenient to distinguish between indoor and outdoor apparel. A girl who would move around the house in a thin and semi-transparent chiton would find it practical before going out to step into a heavier skirt and to cover her shoulders with a diagonal mantilla of the same heavy material as the separate skirt. Examples of such combinations would be found on most of the Akropolis korai, e.g., korai 675, 680 (Fig. 20), 682, etc. According to the originator of the theory, this three-piece costume appears on terracottas of the Aphrodite Group (therefore of East Greek origin) by at least 550, earlier than any instance in Attica. If the kore from Erythrai is indeed wearing a chitoniskos and a skirt, she would provide a monumental example of such fashion at an even earlier date, and terracottas from Samos seem to show the difference between the upper and lower parts of the garment at least two decades earlier. Yet none of the extant marble korai from that island clearly exemplifies the same practice.

What is overwhelmingly represented in Samos is the veil. It consists of a single piece of cloth, presumably light and perhaps transparent, which must have been oblong. It is usually folded double lengthwise and worn over the head, so that it falls in two layers over the back. One layer (at times the upper, at times the lower) is pulled forward and tucked under the belt over the left hip (Fig. 21). On the right side, the veil is either held by the hand, or is flung over the shoulder, thus creating a long vertical line. This veil, never found on mainland korai, appears very frequently on Milesian statues, both standing and seated. According to B. Freyer-Schauenburg, the veil becomes progressively shorter and covers less and less of the figure. Its first appeareance on a Samian kore is dated around 575, and too little is preserved to determine all details. We can see, however, that its lower edge is higher than the hem of the chiton, and that the veil covers part of the left leg. The same arrangement prevails on the best-known of all Samian statues, the so-called Hera dedicated by Cheramyes, now in the Louvre, and on her "sister" in Berlin. In later works, however, the right side, and eventually also the left, are progressively uncovered, until the veil hangs over only the back of the wearer but not over the flanks. In some cases the veil is also worn doubled in such a way that a short but broad overfold is created across the back above the waist. The veil is usually rendered as entirely smooth, thus being clearly differentiated from the other plissé parts of the costume. Unfortunately, none of the extant statues clearly reveals how the veil was fastened over the head, and whether in some cases it was accompanied by a polos. Some heads, which cannot be joined to any of the extant bodies, seem to wear a diadem over the veil, or another head ornament in conjunction with it. One major distinction is that the Samian veil seems to hang straight from the head down the back, while the Milesian rendering makes it fall forward in two small "lappets" flanking the neck, so that the presence of the garment is obvious from a frontal view. Around 540 Samian korai began to wear their veils in a similar fashion, obviously under Milesian influence.

REGIONAL TRAITS

Samos

The Samian korai form the most distinctive and complete series. The three earliest examples are very large in scale but too fragmentary to tell us much about their garments. After these, which are currently dated to the Seventh century, there seems to be a gap until the second quarter of the Sixth, and one wonders whether the chronology of some of the early pieces should perhaps be lowered. Yet unlike all later works, not local but imported marble was used for them. The first Sixth century piece provides the first example of that bell-shaped skirt which is so typical of the Hera of Samos and which has been variously interpreted as an imitation of a tree trunk or of an ivory tusk. To my mind, this is simply a pleasing stylization in an area where contours and surfaces, rather than structure and articulation, are of primary concern to the carver.[11] This rounded body seems to go out of fashion around 550, to be replaced by an equally massive but more block-like shape.

Samian korai wear pleated costumes whose fullness is indicated by thin serrated grooves that do not penetrate deeply but cover the surface. If a horizontal section were cut from a Samian statue, its core would be compact, and only the outer "skin" would be affected by the rendering of the folds. Yet such folds are used sparingly; even on a chiton, they often alternate with blank areas, and veils inevitably create smooth surfaces next to the "permanent press" appearance of chiton and himation. When the chiton is worn alone, it is usually pulled over the belt to form a deep kolpos, both front and back, with a distinctive rounded bay in the center. The deep pouches on either side reach down to the level of the hips. The chiton is buttoned over the arms, but the groups of thin folds branching off from each fastening tend to run vertically as soon as they merge with the bodice, and strictly vertical accents dominate the entire chiton.

When a short diagonal mantle is worn, its upper edge is linear, without a border, often difficult to distinguish from the branching folds of the fastening over the right shoulder. This edge runs diagonally across the kore's chest, covering both breasts and looping under the left arm. Over the back the edge often disappears, because the veil covers everything as if it were made of a much heavier material. The entire mantle is textured with engraved folds, wider than those of the chiton, and running obliquely throughout or, in the second Cheramyes dedication in Berlin, turning to vertical from right shoulder to the end of the long mantle tip. The short mantle is so arranged that it forms a wide arc over the stomach, leaving part of the belt exposed but with no indication of a chiton's kolpos. After ca. 540, Milesian influence changed the course of the mantle folds, which run almost horizontally to the left breast and then fall vertically, while the chiton kolpos is visible as another series of folds under the lower edge of the himation. The International Style brings ever-widen-

[11] To be sure, the rendering may also be the sculptor's way of imitating an earlier (Daedalic?) cult image of the xoanon or *kolossos* type, while at the same time suggesting something of the body contour in a "modern" style. Interestingly enough, the later (Hellenistic?) cult images of the Artemis of Ephesos or the Aphrodite of Aphrodisias show the same tightly clinging skirt which opens up at the bottom to reach almost the edge of the roughly circular plinth, thus, in my opinion, clearly betraying their derivation from a much earlier prototype. See R. Fleischer, *Artemis von Ephesos und verwandte Kultstatuen aus Anatolien und Syrien* (Leiden 1973) and the review by M. J. Mellink, *AJA* 79 (1975) 107–8.

ing pleats, zigzag edges, even swallowtails to the lower hem of a longer himation, and finally wavy engraved lines for the chiton which contrast with the original vertical rendering. But undercutting of hems and folds is always kept to a minimum.

The Samian korai keep their arms and hands close to the body. When an offering is added, it is pressed against the breasts (usually below them), most often with the fully opened left hand.[12] This gesture makes the elbow project outside the general contour of the figure, but efforts are often made to link it with the rest of the body by means of the garments. The idea of having the kore hold her skirt aside with one hand—in Samos, usually the right—has been tentatively attributed to Geneleos, who introduced it in his famous family group, thus establishing a highly influential prototype for all later renderings. If this is the case, and if the Geneleos group has been correctly dated just before 560, then the Erythrai kore who performs the same gesture would have been erected under Samian influence and must be later than the group.[13] The thin texture of the chiton gathered by the hand produces an almost ropelike effect, which is not immediately identifiable with the presence of a raised ornamental border in the center of the chiton (the paryphe), since only one edge, that closer to the gathering hand, marks a possible distinction of areas on the costume. Later korai, following Milesian prototypes, have a clearly defined paryphe, but as late a piece as *Samos* XI no. 25 (ca. 530) returns to the single-edged convention, despite its obvious foreign influences.

As the kore holds her skirt with the right hand, so does she step forward with her right foot. This is the reverse of the kouros' stance, and is perhaps conditioned by the desire to make the active hand pull the garment. Attempts to put the left foot forward go either with an unlifted chiton or with a skirt still held by the right hand, so that the motion looks awkward, and too strong a diagonal emphasis makes the front of the figure slant to its right (Fig. 21). Toward the end of the Archaic period, influence from the kouroi, or from other sources, causes a shift in pose, so that both left hand and left leg are active. Fisted hands seem largely triangular, and adhere to the thigh even when holding the skirt aside.

The heads of the Samian korai are almost entirely missing. None of the extant bodies has the head preserved intact, and not a single head has been successfully reunited with its body. By and large, Samian heads are rounded, softly modeled, with prominent noses and slightly receding foreheads. Since the few extant examples are veiled, we get no information on hair patterns, but the heads of the Geneleos sisters must have been bare; a mass

[12] M. Yon, *Salamine de Chypre* v (Paris 1974): *Un dépôt de Sculptures Archaiques*, 114–15 no. 5, has suggested that the schema of the hand held against the chest, which is attested on Cypriot sculpture since the end of the 7th century, is of Egyptian origin. The Samian statues could have adopted this gesture either directly from Egypt or, more probably, from Cyprus, with which the East Greek island had very close contacts.

[13] A statuette of a kore that appears to be very early has been found in Aegina, in the sanctuary of Aphaia (Furtwängler, *Aegina*, fig. 285). She wears a smooth costume, but holds her skirt toward the center front, forming a heavy fold in the material. If this piece should really be dated early, it would precede the Samian examples. It is, however, more likely that the Aegina piece should be placed around 550 thus representing an adaptation rather than an innovation, especially since Aegina does not seem particularly prominent in sculpture at this early stage in the 6th century. Oriental, or perhaps Cypriot, influences may also be at work, in that the statuette apparently holds her right breast with her left arm. Note also the mantle or veil which bridges the gap between the bent left elbow and the body. If indeed a veil, it would be the only one yet found on a mainland Greek statue (cf. *Samos* XI, comment on p. 25) since Aegina usually shares in the artistic climate of nearby Attica. Unfortunately, I have been unable to find an illustration of the back of the Aegina statuette.

of hair cascades down their backs and over the breasts of one of them.[14] The prevalent pattern seems to be that of the elongated pearls.

In general, Samian korai are of superior quality; they are feminine, full without being fat, with no obvious display of musculature but with a great deal of modeling to suggest bodily forms under drapery. Light and shadow play an important role in the most typical figures, despite the apparent lack of penetration of the carving. Their textured surfaces are enormously rich and strongly recall metal engraving.

East Greece

The Milesian korai resemble those from Samos in many ways. Some of them have foldless, smooth garments; some wear veil and diagonal mantle. This himation has no upper border and covers both breasts; but while the Samian mantle tends to have oblique direction from right to left, the Milesian one, as already mentioned, emphasizes the vertical fall of the folds, which virtually describe an angle over the left breast. In addition, part of the material is pulled up from behind and around the left arm, though I am not sure how this is accomplished since the mantle describes the usual catenary folds over the left hip. The Milesian veil seems longer, as long as the chiton, and it is also pulled forward and tucked under the chiton's belt. Chitons often have a broad and flat central pleat and a wide kolpos articulated into folds, which is usually visible under the arch of the himation whose curve it parallels.

Korai from Miletos and Didyma (which stylistically are fundamentally related) show an unusual plasticity of folds, which comes close to the rippled modeling of the Severe style. Perhaps the best example is the fragmentary figure from the Ephesos column drum, in which the tip of the himation over the right hip shows this distinctive modulation. The kolpos, visible under the arch of the mantle, is also grooved to suggest folds, with a thickness and feeling for cloth quite different from Samian surface decoration but typical of Milesian works. Yet with this keen sense of plasticity goes also an interest in smooth areas which were perhaps detailed in paint. As in Samos, the International Style around 530 introduces more zigzag folds, greater interest in the bodily forms under the garments, and an appearance of movement. The parallel arches of kolpos and himation become wider.

Many of the Milesian statues wear a veil which tends to curve over both shoulders, surrounding face and neck before falling down the back. Around the temples the veil swells to suggest the hair underneath, in contrast with the tighter Samian arrangement. The Didyma figures often wear special ribbons, supposedly a mark of their priestly function. Hair, when shown free, can have negative pearls or elongated pearls as pattern. Facial features and the general shape of the head closely resemble those of the Samian statues; the smile is pronounced, probably because the lower lip is longer and thicker than the upper, rather than because of any definite curve to the mouth. Cheeks and chins are prominent, noses short and merging with the high-swinging curves of the eyebrows. Eyes are usually long and narrow, bulging between the tight lids, or at times only faceted rather than completely articulated into the component parts. Some instances of inserted eyes

[14] A third "sister" (*Samos* XI no. 60) seems to have worn her hair tied in a bun or at least gathered in such a way as not to cover the shoulders. The entire group is characterized by a desire to change details within the same general schema (see comments on p. 125 of *Samos* XI).

must reflect Anatolian rather than Egyptian practice (Fig. 22), and one cannot help seeing a resemblance between some of these East Greek korai and the so-called Eunuch in Berlin, an Urartian work dated to the early Seventh century.

The above comments may be extended virtually to all korai from Asia Minor. Indeed, it is plausible to assume that one famous statue now lost but probably made in Miletos, on the evidence of its stylistic traits, influenced the creation of closely comparable korai in Samos and Karia. All these East Greek korai hold their offerings close to the chest, and their preferred gift is a bird. The limestone kore from Klazomenai also holds a bird, but she is late enough (ca. 520) to have already absorbed influences from the Cyclades and perhaps even Attica. Her diagonal mantle has a flat upper border which runs in between, not above, both breasts; its lower edge describes a swallowtail pattern, rather than the usual arch. This kore has also reversed the standard Ionic pose, so that she holds her bird with her right hand, her skirt with her left. Her smooth chiton, with its doughy fall over the mantle border near the left arm, is almost a forecast of Euthydikos' kore.

Two more East Greek korai deserve special, though brief, mention because they are both still unpublished: the dedication by the priest of Artemis, Timonax, from Klaros, and the headless kore from Erythrai. The first has been dated too early because of her awkward pose and the simple garment she wears. But her peculiar twist is probably an attempt to show her as stepping forward with her right leg, and the folds engraved on the central portion of her skirt show that advanced renderings of drapery were already known. Also the letter forms of the dedicatory inscription, which, if not yet true stoichedon, at least is no longer boustrophedon, would be in agreement with a date in the second quarter of the Sixth century, ca. 560. The massive, over life-size Erythrai kore is mostly remarkable because of her chiton, unprecedented among East Greek examples in describing a downward curve hiding the belt rather than an upward swinging arch revealing it in the center. This frontal "pouch" rises steeply over the hips, so that the belt is visible in the rear above the prominent buttocks, within a squarish "opening" of the kolpos.

The Islands

This squarish-rear kolpos seems to be typical also of a kore from Chios, but unfortunately her front is damaged so that we cannot tell what the front rendering looked like. There are two of these Chian korai, remarkable because of the purely decorative rendering of the wavy folds branching off the chiton buttons over the arms. These folds are so stylized that they might not have been understood as such had we not had experience with other buttoned sleeves. They recall the engraved lines meant to suggest water on some Mesopotamian statues, though the distance in time makes this parallel relatively useless. Yet the gesture of one of the korai, who hides her hands under the tresses falling freely over her breasts, finds no parallel among Greek works but may have one in the Oriental sphere.[15]

[15] A Neo-Hittite torso in Copenhagen shows a woman holding both hands flat against her chest. Since her locks are quite long, in falling forward they cover her wrists also. Admittedly, this is not the same as the gesture of the Chian kore, but the latter may be a partial misunderstanding of the Oriental prototype. F. Poulsen, who illustrates the Copenhagen torso (*Der Orient und die frühgriechische Kunst* [Leipzig 1912] 98 fig. 100) compares it with several Etruscan representations of women holding their tresses, which may be a further elaboration of the neo-Hittite motif.

This distinctive squarish form of the kolpos is found again in a type which seems widely diffused around the Aegean and is difficult to localize since it shares Samian and possibly Milesian traits. It consists of a column-like lower body with tight skirt flaring out at the hem over the feet, spreading almost to the edge of a rounded plinth. This modulation of the lower part shows that the type dates well after the Daedalic period with its unarticulated bodies, and must be roughly contemporary with the Hera from Samos. It is belted at the waist, and at times has a squarish or barely rounded kolpos both front and back, notable because of the short extent of its "pouches." The simple top may have either buttoned or sewn sleeves. There are minimal indications of folds and when they do occur, they are simply engraved, much more widely spaced than in the typical Samian figures. In addition, most of the korai belonging to this general type (Figs. 23–24) have a maeander-ornamented paryphe in the center of the skirt, which in some cases also bisects the bodice, starting at the neckline. In one particular kore, in Paros (no. 802), the pattern runs vertically down the sides as well, so that a total of three borders decorate her skirt. All these korai hold the right arm down, the left bent against the chest, except for one muscular torso from Aegina, which has both arms lowered.

Given the wide distribution,[16] it would seem risky to make any regional attribution for this type, yet it is tempting to suggest that it may have originated in Paros. Particularly interesting in this respect is a comparison with the "Attic" Phrasikleia, which, as we now know, was made by Aristion, a Parian sculptor. Though this statue is still virtually unpublished, its open display in the Athens National Museum and the photographs which have already appeared allow a few comments. Her costume is probably a peplos, since it has no overfold but just a fullness above the belt which looks very naturalistic. Her left arm is also against her chest, the hand holding a flower, but her right hand pulls the skirt aside, an innovation for this group of column-like korai. Yet the sculptor may have felt the need to emphasize the difference between the thin Samian chiton which the hand could grasp almost like a rope, and the heavier peplos which should have more vertical pull. Or he was perhaps reluctant to disturb the subtly swinging contour of the lower body. The resultant effect suggests stretchable material that can momentarily be pulled out of shape before it returns to cling immediately below the hand. A comparable stage may be illustrated by the Erythrai kore, where the chiton is thin and the folds disappear into the paryphe. Not much later should be the Lyons Kore (Figs. 27–28), who is also holding her skirt with a slightly misunderstood and somewhat mannered rendering of the gesture. In Phrasikleia other details may be of Parian origin: the engraved lines above the belt, the zigzag hem of her skirt, the loose curl following the contour of the shoulders down to the upper arm.

The Cycladic Diagonal Mantle. Cycladic style is easier to distinguish when the diagonal mantle is present. Yet, surprisingly enough, this rendering appears relatively early and then disappears until approximately 530, or at least we seem to have lost all intermediate

[16] Besides the two korai from Chios, I would include in this group the two recently found korai from Cyrene (*AJA* 75 [1971] 42–46, pls. 6–8); the kore from Haghios Ioannis Rendhis in Athens (*AAA* 1 [1968] 34–35 fig. 3); the torso from Moschato (Attica) Nat. Mus. 3859 (*Korai* no. 40 figs. 132–34); the torso from Aegina (Nat. Mus. 73); the lower part of a kore also from Aegina (*Deltion* 22 [1967] 148, pl. 112); a kore in Delos, A3996 (*GdD*, 43); and some unnumbered examples in the Paros Museum storerooms. The kore from Lindos (Rhodes) may also belong with this general type (*Korai* nos. 76–77 figs. 244–52).

examples. In effect, the korai from the islands are either quite early or fairly late within the Sixth century, with a gap which is hard to explain and which is only partially filled by some of the imports to the Athenian Akropolis or the Delphic Karyatids.

The earliest example of a diagonal mantle appears on a Delian kore, A 4062, which unfortunately is so badly weathered that her attire is not easy to discern. Some recent descriptions say that she wears a one-piece garment, while others have pointed out the presence of a short himation. This statue is particularly interesting because she may be a sort of link between the column-like type wearing only the peplos/chiton and the more heavily dressed type with the diagonal mantle. The connection with the first group is suggested by the engraved paryphe on her skirt and by the exposed belt. As for her mantle, it forms a curve, like the Samian mantle, but seems to climb higher than on the Hera of Cheramyes and only one tip is visible since the entire back of the Delian statue is left fairly undetailed. No folds are recognizable. She must date from ca. 580 because of the contoured shape of her garment and the slight depression of her back along the spine; but earlier dates have also been suggested. If this chronology is correct, she precedes the entire series of Samian korai and may indicate that the diagonal mantle originated in Naxos or Paros.

In its developed form, the Cycladic diagonal mantle looks very rich because it is articulated into many stepped folds on either side of a central pleat. This latter can be relatively long and narrow, originating almost from the top button over the right arm, near the neck, and crossing the chest more or less obliquely. Or it can begin on the central axis of the figure, run vertically, and be distinctively wide and short, usually terminating well above the belt, which it leaves exposed. A similar fold occurs also on the back of the statue, in a parallel position. The idea for this rendering may have started from the desire to rationalize the change in direction from the vertical folds of the tip to the slanted ones created by the looping of the mantle under the left arm—a conflict of movement which is already explicit in the Milesian kore with the bird, in Berlin. It is more difficult to determine how the central pleat is formed. The most logical explanation is that the cloth is tucked in behind the border at the point of origin of such a fold, but this is not clearly visible on the statues.

The mantle now has an upper border, or crossband, usually formed by two or three tubular ridges or layers, which at least by 525 (on the evidence of the Siphnian Karyatid) can be overlaid by a series of ripples, as if the material below the crossband had been pulled up from behind. This rendering seems to occur only on the front; when the border is visible on the back, it usually shows only the horizontal ridges without overlay. More significantly, this crossband runs between the breasts, so that the left one is covered only by the crinkly chiton. The lower edge of the mantle has no trace of the arching pattern seen on the earliest Cycladic example (Delos A 4062) but forms an inverted V which at times climbs steeply between the tips of a garment apparently quite a bit longer than the East Greek version. In addition, these late Cycladic korai lift their skirts with the left hand held well away from the body and proffer the gift with the outstretched right. The mantle hangs freely from the arm along which it is buttoned, thus creating decorative tips and masses which widen the total composition considerably.[17]

[17] For examples of these Cycladic korai, see Delos A 4064 (*Korai* no. 147 figs. 468–71); Delos A 4067 (*Korai* no. 149 figs. 476–79); Delos A 4063 (*Korai* no. 150 figs. 480–82); a kore in New York from Paros (*Korai* no. 151 figs. 483–86); and one in Copenhagen, from Andros (*Korai* no. 152 figs. 487–90).

These are basically the attire and pose of the Akropolis korai, but the Cycladic ones can be distinguished by a certain extra fussiness of the folds, an engraved quality which allows a closer spacing of the ridges, a greater love of plastic ornament and metal attachments, and in general a search for decorative effects rather than naturalism. Toward the end of the Sixth century or early in the Fifth, this propensity for richness results in more than one central pleat over the front of the himation, or in more than one mantle, with a consequent multiplication of swallowtail patterns. The bodies, for all their feminine elegance, are powerful and bulky, with prominent breasts and massive thighs clearly defined by the clinging drapery. Yet one senses that their sculptors were not primarily interested in the articulation of the body beneath the garment nor in the proper relationship of trunk to legs and abdomen. The voluminous mantle, moreover, prevents any clear indication of the waist, which was so emphatically marked in earlier peplophoroi. In these late korai the vertical versus the horizontal accents are stressed, and excessive slimness is avoided through bent arms and widespread skirts and himatia.

Unfortunately the korai of this entire Cycladic group lack heads. Some exist in the local museums but are unpublished and usually poorly preserved. Only the Delphi Karyatids give us some inkling, and their prettiness and elaborate coiffures are in character with the richness of the Cycladic bodies. The so-called ex-Knidian Karyatid has many curls added separately, with a technique apparent on the bodies of some of the korai in Delos, while her inserted eyes indicate her possible connection with Asia Minor. The Siphnian Karyatid has many patterns and extra strands, as well as many added ornaments; that she was made by a Cycladic master is shown not only by the wide and short central fold of her himation but also by the typical Cycladic pithos which is carved in relief on her decorated polos.[18]

Once these Karyatids are accepted as works of island masters, they can be very useful. To begin with, they show that the direction of the diagonal mantle can be changed and the position of the legs reversed when the monument requires a duplication of figures, which are therefore rendered in mirror image. It may have been this ornamental need that broke the spell on the Asia Minor right-foot-forward stance.[19] The Knidian Karyatids seem transitional between island and Asia Minor works. In the way in which the hand grasps the paryphe, they are indebted to Samian prototypes: the fist appears in profile and is held close to the body. The mantle is fastened only on one arm, yet covers both breasts and curves in a wide arc over the abdomen in the East Greek fashion. But the central vertical pleat, the stepped folds, the zigzag edges of the swallowtail are definitely Cycladic. A more

[18] E. C. MacNeil Boggess, "The Development of the Attic Pithos" (Bryn Mawr College Ph.D. Dissertation, 1972) 278–79: "The pithos shown on the polos of the Siphnian Karyatid (*FdD* 4:2, 1928, hors-texte IV and V, pp. 58–64) has the typical shape used in the Cyclades in the 7th and 6th centuries B.C.: high neck, rounded shoulder, ovoid body, remnants of fenestrated handles from shoulder to rim."

Two more heads are sometimes attributed to the Cyclades because of their decorativeness: the so-called Boulgaridis head in Saloniki (*AMA* 35 fig. 3; W. Darsow, *MdI* 3 [1950], pl. 3:1); and a head in Thasos (*GdTh*, 117 no. 3 fig. 55). In general, Cycladic heads of ripe Archaic style are characterized by a love for contrasting movements of strands, so that often tresses of hair are pulled forward from under the diadem, to emerge over the forehead and contrast with the horizontal pattern of the forehead waves. As usual, H. Payne has written a most perceptive analysis of this style (p. 58).

[19] The earliest Samian example with the left foot forward is *Samos* XI no. 22, dated ca. 540–530. The Knidian Karyatids are usually dated before 540 though Herdejürgen (pp. 44–45) would lower this date to ca. 535, leaving open the question of whether this later chronology still allows attribution of the figures to the Treasury. The two matching korai from Cyrene (*Korai* nos. 168–69 figs. 536–39) may also have been Karyatids. The rendering of their hair may suggest Samian connections.

peculiar arrangement occurs on the Siphnian pediment: the female figure behind Artemis seems to have her left arm free, yet the crossband of her himation dips under both breasts before climbing to her left shoulder.[20]

The Rhedesto Kore. A few comments are needed about a most unusual kore which was not included in Richter's book and remains little known (Figs. 25–26). It comes from Rhedesto, ancient Bizye, a Thracian site between the Samian settlement of Perinthos and the Milesian foundation at Apollonia on the Pontos. The kore combines the influences one would expect from these two different sources but adds quite a touch of Cycladic style, perhaps received secondhand. The long tresses that fall only down her back are Samian, and perhaps also the crinkly skirt of her chiton, though no Samian garment ever had this continuously rippling surface, broken only by the flat band of the paryphe. This trait may perhaps be attributed to Milesian influence, which may have affected also the purely ornamental spacing of the groups of thin lines of the upper part of the chiton. The same rendering, unconnected with the points of fastening, occurs in some of the seated male figures from Didyma and may represent a sewn pattern rather than a logical suggestion of bunched cloth. Finally, the entire arrangement of the diagonal himation is Cycladic: its length, its zigzag lower edge which climbs into an inverted V of unequal sides, the vertical course of the folds arranged on either side of a central pleat, both front and back, and especially the lack of a crossband to the upper edge, which, however, runs in between the breasts, leaving the left uncovered. The way in which the skirt is pulled aside may be Cycladic: it is held on the left and at a distance from the body, so as to interrupt the continuous contour of the leg. The missing left hand was perhaps turned forward; the right, also missing, held an offering against the chest with the arm in the same horizontal position which we find in the Lyons kore, that is, below both breasts. Indeed, the two statues may show how the same Cycladic influence could be interpreted in two territories used to different sculptural traditions: East Greek for one, Attic for the other. The date of the Rhedesto kore, usually set around 540–530, should perhaps be slightly lowered (ca. 520?), because of the mixture of her influences and the remoteness of her place of origin.

Attica

To my knowledge only six of the Attic korai were found outside the Akropolis. Those from the Agora should belong with the citadel dedications; one fragment has even been found to join kore Akr. 683. The Kerameikos, surprisingly enough, has yielded no examples, perhaps because it became a public cemetery after the early Sixth century when it could still house monumental funerary kouroi.[21] Since these too seem absent after Solon, one may envisage the wealthy aristocrats setting up their own private graves near their country estates, away from the inner city. Some korai from Eleusis could be considered Attic, and there is an Athenian import at the Ptoion, but these are not important additions. The six non-Akropolis korai are more interesting: the earliest is the famous Berlin "goddess,"

[20] A comparable and perhaps provincial or misunderstood example occurs on the Dorylaion stele, the winged Mistress of Animals: *KAnat*, 241 fig. 210.

[21] Or perhaps even because of different funerary practices at an early stage. In fact, one of the earliest tomb monuments (middle or second half of the 7th century) was for a woman, Keramo, but a stele was used (see infra, Ch. 6, pp. 167–68 with possible reasons for the choice).

which is said to have been found near Keratea and was probably a funerary statue. The same may be true for the torso from Moschato which, together with the headless statue from Haghios Ioannis Rendhis, belongs to my tentative "Parian" group. Phrasikleia, perhaps a later member of the same group, was definitely a grave monument, from Merenda (ancient Myrrhinous), and so was Phile, of whom only feet and inscribed base are preserved, a work of Phaidimos. The kore from Lavrion, in New York, could also have been funerary because of her alleged provenience and since she was repaired and provided with a new head at some time in antiquity. All the other Attic korai, having been found in sanctuaries, must be votive in nature.

Few as they are, these funerary korai contribute some important information. They show that over life-size grave statues could be erected for women also, and throughout the Sixth century. It may be a coincidence that none of the six wears the diagonal himation; certainly the fashion was already known at least by the time of the Lavrion kore, who wears the crinkly chiton and, perhaps, an added skirt held almost in center front. Her offering,[22] pressed with the right hand (the left is restored) against her chest, still makes her part of the Asia Minor/Cycladic tradition, but after the switch in pose, therefore later than the Phrasikleia. Yet her legs are aligned and she seems immobile, as may be fitting for a grave monument or perhaps because korai "walk" later in Attica than elsewhere. The squarish outline of her kolpoi, both front and back, combined with the relatively deep pouches, show how influences could intermingle by ca. 530. Given the absence of the diagonal himation, one may wonder whether funerary korai are shown in an indoors attire, as contrasted with the more elaborately dressed votive figures. Yet the heavy symmetrical mantle of the Berlin kore, and the abundant jewelry and headdresses of the group contradict this hypothesis.

The Berlin kore has at times been questioned as a forgery, but such doubts should certainly be dismissed. It is more interesting to determine the various influences at work in her composition. Her face has the clarity and squareness typical of Attic kouroi, but her profile is deeper, her mouth more protruding and angular, her forehead somewhat more receding. Her offering is in her right hand, but I know of no other kore who holds it so low against her body; her left across her chest (with the peculiar, "Napoleonic" gesture of thumb behind the mantle) is perhaps a diluted, misunderstood version of the same tradition that produced the Hera of Samos. The steep vertical folds and the wide zigzags of the shawl-like mantle recall Asia Minor prototypes, especially the Branchidai, or even earlier Anatolian statues, like the draped figure from Kululu.

For all her massive and over-broad shoulders, the Berlin kore shows sensitive modeling around the hips; her contour, subtly narrowing at waist and ankles, should make her perhaps a bit more advanced than usually considered, around 570–560. But despite good workmanship and impressive appearance, this is not a successful statue. Its head is out of proportion both within itself and in relationship to the body. Note how high the cranium swings, how large the eyes are for the face. Even more puzzling are the steeply sloping feet, which not even high heels could put in that position (an East Greek trait?). The

[22] It is probably incorrect to speak of offering for the objects held by these funerary korai. As for the kouroi, these grave monuments probably represented the deceased in heroized form, and therefore the objects in their hands could be considered attributes, or even symbols of resurrection (fruits, pomegranates) or of gentility (flowers).

piece could be a truly Attic work but under considerable influence from Asia Minor and perhaps even the Cyclades. Phrasikleia has been a delightful surprise also because she seems the obvious next step after the Berlin kore, yet shows the same mixture of foreign and local elements, and we know for a fact that she was made by a Parian. Perhaps the answer lies in a local workshop which absorbed foreign artists and traded traditions. Phrasikleia's Attic ancestry is particularly visible in her high-sloping feet and her jewelry.[23]

The Athenian Akropolis. The Akropolis korai are a mixed bunch, unevenly distributed in time. The earliest group has at least two foreigners (Akr. 619 and 677) which have been called Samian but are more likely to be Naxian. Since these would therefore be among the earliest preserved Cycladic korai in diagonal mantle, a few more comments may be directed at pointing out their characteristics, rather than at arguing for a specific origin. Akr. 677, moreover, has the great good fortune of having kept her head, an unusual feat for an Ionic kore.

Akr. 677 shows better than 619 how the practice of a ridged crossband for the diagonal himation may have originated; on her one can still see that these ridges are the vestigial folds branching off from the first himation button near the neck, which the Naxian master renders with greater plasticity and relief than his Samian counterpart. At this early a stage, during the first half of the Sixth century, both breasts are still covered by the mantle. A seam, rather than buttons, closes its edges together over the right arm (as true also for 619), while another seam forms the chiton sleeve to the left. As a result, not a group of folds, but an entirely corrugated surface suggests the thin material of the undergarment. The hand wraps around the apple (?) instead of pressing it against the chest with a flat palm; the ulna protrudes visibly from the wrist, recalling the Berlin kore. The head tops a sloping neck clearly angled forward, with the back hair running a parallel slope, as contrasted with the nearly vertical arrangement of the Berlin kore. Similarly, the face in profile seems to flow toward the apex of the nose, with forehead and chin receding from the climax almost along continuous lines. Frontally, the eyes are emphasized by thin engraved lines which duplicate the contour of the upper lid, and occur again in the Naxian sphinx in Delphi. Akr. 619, of which the head is missing, shows basically the same traits but adds an almost Milesian form of the mantle, with folds running vertically before turning abruptly into the wide catenaries over the left hip. Neither figure wears a veil, so that the backs appear as engraved as the fronts.[24]

These two "Naxian" korai should not be much removed from 560. Even Langlotz, who dates them in the first quarter of the Sixth century, considers them later than Cheramyes' Hera, which more recent studies place 570–560. Contemporary, or later, should be the Pomegranate Kore, Akr. 593 (Fig. 29), which is traditionally dated ca. 580–570, probably because her relative lack of depth, in proportion to her broad frontal appearance, recalls the plank-like Nikandre. Her knobby wrist resembles that of the Lyons kore, and the left arm against the chest is horizontal, like the Moschato torso, rather than angled like the

[23] According to L. Blanck (*Studien zum griechischen Halsschmuck der archaischen und klassischen Zeit* [Köln 1974] 129), Attica and Boeotia prefer abstract objects, such as vessels, for their jewelry pendants, instead of the vegetal motifs favored in the East Greek area.

[24] The Akropolis has yielded fragments of another kore in the same style, but too poorly preserved for useful discussion. It is nonetheless important to note that there were at least three such imports at such an early date on the Athenian citadel (*AMA* no. 24 p. 65).

East Greek or Samian examples. In addition, the skillful way in which the mantle bridges the span between arm and torso has already been seen in the Attic Moschophoros. Yet she wears a finely folded chiton the buttoned sleeve of which is visible over her right arm. Since this rendering has not appeared among the "Naxian korai," an intermediate step in time must be postulated. Zigzag folds are apparent at the hem both of her mantle and of her peplos, on the right side. And the Pomegranate kore is the first sculptural work to show traces of the tooth-chisel, which in architecture did not appear until around 540. I believe that her sculptor was trying to imitate an earlier image. In any case, he knew that his work was to be placed in a position where the back was not fully visible since he did not carve it in detail.[25] Nor did he trouble to articulate the draping of the mantle, which at present is not clear though paint must once have helped clarify it. If the statue had to stand against a specific background, the sculptor may have intentionally sacrificed depth to frontal width, thus making his statue look far earlier than it may be. She must be holding a pomegranate by an invisible stem, not a lekythos as is sometimes suggested, since the object above her hand is faceted, as no lekythos would be. Akr. 593 is an interesting example of an Attic kore such as an Athenian master might have carved under some outside influence in the 550's.

The Lyons kore (Figs. 27–28) must herself date around 540, if not later, and she too is an Attic effort, showing an obvious misunderstanding of the diagonal mantle. As previously pointed out, not only does its upper edge go from left to right, in a reversal of the fashion admissible only in a Karyatid,[26] but it does not button over the arm and has only one tip. It is difficult to decide whether this garment reflects the influence of Ionia, as the lack of border would suggest, or of the islands, as the shallow inverted V of the lower edge implies. An Ionian master perhaps is suggested by the presence of a bird (a favorite East Greek offering) held with the right hand, and by the wide arch which the himation forms curving over the buttocks. Equally "East Greek" is the apparent transparency of the chiton skirt, which clings tightly and smoothly to the back of the powerful legs. But the Attic master, with his interest in bodily forms, has carried this rendering also to the pleated front, so that the division between the legs is revealed, and the massive shoulders of the kore resemble those of a padded football player. Note how muscular her arms are, and how unfeminine her breasts, which recall pectoral muscles—a rendering made more obvious by the peculiar smooth "chiton" she wears. Her left hand does not know how to hold the skirt, which it does in a half-hearted, fisted position, and the tightly pressed pleats are uncertain how to behave under the pull, forming peculiar angles after the initial slant from the waist. The mantle border running between rather than over both breasts is perhaps an Attic innovation which may have influenced the Cyclades, since none of the extant island korai with this rendering is earlier than the Akropolis statue. Some plastic vases in the shape of korai show this fashion at what may be an earlier date, and they have been attributed to Rhodes, but I am always reluctant to believe that major stylistic changes go from the minor arts to the major, or even to daily practices. Certainly

[25] Note how the sculptor started to carve more vertical grooves to separate the hair strands in the back, and gave up after beginning the second tress on either side. Obviously this was as far as the kore could be seen when in its proper setting.

[26] Yet see also the comments on the Nikai and kore Akr. 672. The question of whether the Lyons kore could have been a Karyatid was raised with me by Judith P. Binder in 1974; the point will be developed below.

the marble korai we have from Rhodes at present do not support the terracotta evidence.[27] It would also seem more plausible for the Cyclades to be the source of an innovation which could influence Attica, but here again, proof is missing. Be this as it may, all these traits combine to make the Lyons kore a most unusual statue, which only the genius of Humfry Payne could reassemble from such widely separated fragments. I shall return below to her possible function.

Most of the other Akropolis korai are distinctly later. The imports continue, as kore 675, in Chian marble, seems to demonstrate. Akr. 595 could be Parian. Others were probably made by "foreign" masters working in Attica. Basically they are all influenced by the Cyclades, especially in the rendering of the diagonal mantle and its ridged border with added "ruffles." But the Attic masters by and large tend to make the central pleat longer, somewhat slanted; and relatively few statues, or only korai with symmetrical mantles, have emphatic central accents. It is difficult to decide whether it is Attic inventiveness or advanced dates which determine the bewildering variety of combinations and drapings within the standard clothing repertoire. Certainly a strong feeling for plasticity prompts the undercutting of all edges, and even the drilling inside folds, so that they look inflated and hollow like the pipes of an organ. Instead of single curves to the pleated edges, the late Archaic period (after ca. 510 ?) uses double curves, adding an intermediate twitch to the linear stretch of each zigzag, which therefore becomes an S-shape rather than a dash. This double curve at the edge means an extra ridge within the pleat, so that folds become increasingly richer and progressively more artificial (e.g., Fig. 20: Akr. 680; 685, 598, etc.). After 500 the Akropolis kore is so removed from reality, so incredibly ornate in its plastic texture and polychromy, that some masters begin to experiment with smooth surfaces and quieter compositions (Akr. 615, Euthydikos' kore).

Gifts are no longer held against the chest, but separately carved arms allow outstretched offerings, sometimes with both hands. When the left holds the skirt, it pulls it well away from the body, at first to the side, but then, increasingly forward. How far this can go can only be understood by trying to reconstruct mentally the missing parts between the torso and the legs of Euthydikos' kore, one of the latest Akropolis maidens. The intact kore, seen in profile, must have looked somewhat like the standing maiden in the relief Nat. Mus. 36, who seems to stretch her skirt forward to the limit of its possibilities. Obviously by the 480's the gesture had lost its meaning, perhaps even its counterpart in reality, since women may already have started wearing the "Severe" peplos which made such a sudden appearance in art after the Persian destruction. If this suggestion is correct, one can imagine that the skirt-pulling gesture could turn into a mannered, almost an archaizing, coquetry. Note, in addition, that the few preserved hands are rendered in a different position: no longer turned sideways, with fingers towards and against, the thigh, but palms down (e.g., Akr. 683).

To comment selectively about heads and facial features, the earliest preserved (espe-

[27] A small torso from Lindos (*AAA* 6 [1973] 119, fig. 8) does indeed show this same trait, but its date cannot be earlier than ca. 530, to judge from the photograph. It is interesting to note that her chiton is smooth; her right arm holds the offering somewhat below the breast, but not so close to the body as to obscure the outline of the torso. Her left arm, apparently, was also at a certain distance from her side but is broken off at the shoulder, and it is now difficult to tell from illustrations what its original position was. The mantle has a three-banded cross-border, an almost vertical but moderately long central pleat and, at the break, the beginning of a swallowtail.

cially the Peplos kore) show clear traces of "negative carving." The general formula could be Cycladic or Ionic, but in an Attic desire to articulate the face, sculptors hollow out circular areas around eyes and mouth, so that cheeks and chin project not of their own accord, but because they are like islands emerging from the surrounding low waters. This "pinched cheek" effect disappears gradually, either into an appearance of true cheek bones or with a more integrated, smoother face modeling. Eyes and mouths tend to slant upward, perhaps because the sculptors are trying to give greater depth to the profile; when eyes look downward, almost bulging between the tight lids, one wonders whether the angle of vision for the statue in its final setting, on a high pedestal or column, might have been considered. At viewer's level, such korai tend to look shy or modest; from below they have a more enigmatic, smiling appearance, and the change is considerable. One should always try to look at these statues from different levels.

Though hair patterns vary in combinations, the basic motif of tresses falling forward over the breasts is found in almost all the korai, the surprising Akr. 683 (Fig. 19: "the Red Slippers kore") being exceptional also in this trait.[28] Though forward locks were useful in strengthening the neck (and at times in hiding its excessive elongation), the sculptor may have had trouble in working out how to separate them from the main hair mass over the shoulders. In some korai this split occurs low over the shoulders and looks natural and flowing; in others, it is high and an awkward triangle is left blank in between. This is particularly obvious in the attractive kore 674 (Fig. 30), where the marble has been left uncarved and at a considerably more superficial level than the neck would be, thus functioning as the equivalent of a strut between the locks. Wavy or plissé strands are preferred; long spiral locks are unusual, and one finds them so seldom in Greek stone sculpture that they are worth a second look. They appear, for instance, on kore 682, a puzzling piece also in other respects, and on the Athena from the East Pediment of the Temple of Apollo Daphnephoros at Eretria, on the island of Euboea. Yet they become common as an archaizing trait, so that we find them again as early as the Erechtheion Karyatids. Over the temples korai often wear roundels, which should convey the idea of long hair combed forward from the crown and looped over the ears to be gathered under diadem or fillet and then let fall forward over the breasts. Yet often the roundel has difficulty in climbing the ear against which it may collide, as for instance it does in kore 674 (Fig. 30), in a thoroughly unnatural manner. In between the roundels, over the forehead, often run horizontal strands without part, in an equally impossible arrangement, which only a wig could duplicate. But a certain amount of undercutting from strand to strand, and between hair and forehead, tries to convey the idea of volume and mass. Toward the very end of the Archaic period, and at the beginning of the Severe style, a new hairstyle develops, both for men and women: a shelf of snail curls over the forehead, most often in two rows, which

[28] A. Raubitschek (*Dedications*, no. 292, pp. 313–14) has connected this kore with a base inscribed by two men (Lysias and Euarchis) and meant to support two statues, as shown by the double cavity for the statues' plinths. The combination of two figures may explain why Akr. 683 advances the right leg rather than the left. One also wonders whether any special meaning was conveyed by the juxtaposition. Certainly the attire (for indoor activities?) and the slippers may have suggested a special function or character which the complete monument would have made clear to contemporary viewers. Ch. Karouzos (*BSA* 39 [1938–39], 102–5, III) has suggested that Akr. 683 is Sikyonian on the basis of her gesture, which leaves the vertical fall of the paryphe undisturbed; however, since the same schema appears much earlier in the definitely East Greek kore from Erythrai, this theory cannot be confirmed.

will be very popular in archaizing works such as herms. This style is equally effective in terracotta renderings (e.g., the Athena at Olympia). Its chronology may perhaps speak for Oriental (Persian?) influence.

The hair over the back is usually rendered as a series of pleated ribbons, often stepped outward on either side of a central strand or "part"; but wavy vertical lines are also possible and even impressionistic horizontal striations. The Lyons kore shows both her earlier date and her derivation from non-Attic style in retaining the beady pattern typical of East Greece or of very early Attica. Finally, a word about head structures. Diadems often conceal how the cranium swings upward and back, in peculiar ovoid shapes which are clear only in profile views. Faces remain basically oval, with the widest point at cheek level. Smoother cheeks and wider foreheads mark the inception of the Severe style.

THE MEANING OF THE KORAI

Though most of the Akropolis korai wear a diadem, only three wear poloi, and the question arises whether this headdress carries special meaning. The usual answer has been negative: a polos or a diadem is considered almost an interchangeable ornament. Yet the question should be reopened. Of the Akropolis examples, no. 654 is the earliest and should be considered a sphinx, not only because of its peculiar appearance but also because the hair arrangement, climbing to a peak at the part in the center of the forehead, seems typical of sphinxes or non-human beings, rather than of korai, especially at this early date. The strong asymmetry of the face could also be explained by the twisted position of sphinxes' heads, rather than by supposing the head to be part of a relief. A polos would be appropriate ornament for a sphinx, as shown by many extant examples, and it might strengthen the identification. It might also indicate that the headdress is worn by non-human, semi-divine creatures.[29]

The other two examples of poloi[30] occur on the Lyons kore (Figs. 27–28) and on a fragmentary head of peculiar beauty to which parts of a body have also been attributed, Akr. 696. The former used to be called an Aphrodite, mostly because of the polos and the presumed dove in her hand. Payne, by showing that her torso joined other fragments from the Athenian citadel, convinced scholars that she was just one more anonymous kore. The latter seems to have held her skirt with her right hand, close to her body or toward the front, and to have worn her mantle almost like a man, with a vertical zigzag edge over her left shoulder. Also the mantle of the Lyons kore is unusual, as already mentioned, and the possibility should be considered that these two figures may be Karyatids. In this case, the polos would be a normal element of their architectural function,[31] and the latter would

[29] V. K. Müller (*Der Polos, die griechische Gotterkrone*, Berlin 1915) believes that the polos was never worn by mortals in profane life; see especially his pp. 81–84.

[30] Payne (p. 15 n. 2) mentions one more example of a polos-wearing kore, Akr. 669. I would eliminate her, a peculiar work in any case, because her ornament resembles a diadem more than a polos, since the crown of her head is clearly visible above the stephane. Also Langlotz (*AMA*, p. 69 no. 28) describes her as a diademed kore.

[31] Not enough is preserved of the polos of Akr. 696 to tell whether it had in its center traces of a dowel or a meniskos, the typical spike placed over the head of a statue meant to be displayed outdoors, to prevent birds from perching on it. The metal remains on the polos of the Lyons kore have been called a meniskos. However, a fragmentary meniskos may be difficult to distinguish from a dowel. On the difficult problem of meniskoi in general, see now J. Maxmin, *JHS* 95 (1975) 175–80. The upper surface of the Lyons's polos is described as rough, but it is

remove them from the ranks of the generic korai, perhaps to give them funerary meaning. A possible connection with the later Erechtheion Karyatids is tempting. It seems natural that the Erechtheion architect, as he did for so many other elements of his building, might have imitated in his south porch earlier elements of special significance. The tomb of Kekrops had existed, at least in the tradition, since the Geometric period, as a projection into the Athenians' Mycenaean past, and Karyatids could have been erected (as a sort of baldacchino) in the early 530's when influences from the Orient were particularly strong or perhaps even under the inspiration of the Delphic treasuries. We can no longer tell whether the Lyons kore suffered from the Persian destruction and was buried with the other war debris since at least part of her reached France in the late Seventeenth or early Eighteenth century. Her availability in Roman times may perhaps be very tentatively confirmed by a statue in Corinth, an archaistic Athena (Figs. 64–65) with an owl, who holds her dress with the same peculiar half-fisted hand as the Lyons kore. Since a fragment has survived from a possible statue in mirror image, the two figures together might have originally functioned as Karyatids in the Roman Odeion at Corinth. Though the Lyons kore is smaller than the Corinthian statue and quite different in total appearance, the Roman sculptor might have copied the one mannered detail and turned his composition into an Athena, perhaps as a very veiled allusion to his source of inspiration. The hefty build of the Lyons kore, and especially her squared shoulders and muscular arms, would be particularly appropriate for a supporting function.

As for the other kore, Akr. 696 is obviously considerably later than the Lyonnaise (ca. 490), but another structure with Karyatid supports on the Akropolis is not unthinkable, especially at the time of its greatest activity. Its Pentelic marble may strengthen this suggestion since Parian was usually preferred for freestanding statuary until well into the Fifth century.

If this interpretation of the Akropolis figures should be correct, the polos would remain an element outside the strictly human sphere. This idea is not contradicted by the evidence of the Berlin "goddess" or the Phrasikleia since funerary statues have heroic size and significance which would make their headdress as appropriate for them as for a sphinx.[32] If these

probably not too rough to prevent adherence to another surface. In its present position, it looks as if its upper surface slanted backward, but a superimposed echinos could have compensated for this inclination as the Doric abacus does with inclined columns. Moreover, a certain amount of marble is missing between the lower and upper part of the Lyons kore, so that a slight readjustment of the intermediate surface might eliminate the tilt of the headdress and bring it level.

One of the small Archaic buildings on the Akropolis has been reconstructed as apsidal, and some peculiarly shaped roof tiles, as complex as one would expect on a tholos, probably belong to such a structure. It would be tempting to associate Karyatids instead of columns with a building having only one facade, but its tristyle-in-antis arrangement would require more than the usual pair of maidens.

[32] E. Simon (*RA* 1972, 205–20) has discussed the polos in conjunction with Hera and the Nymphs. She suggests (p. 214) that the Berlin kore could represent a maiden who died before marriage, and that the polos worn by the statue is a bridal crown patterned after that of the marriage goddess Hera in Boeotia. She also stresses the funerary character of the 5th century Erechtheion Karyatids, which she would consider polos-wearing Nymphs.

For the assimilation of Phrasikleia to Kore, Demeter's daughter, see *Aspécts*, 53–55; this point of view has been rejected by Ch. W. Clairmont (*AA* 1974, 220–23), yet he himself argues that the statue of the girl is over life-size. I believe that an element of heroization is definitely present and that the use of the word kore is meant as an intentional double entendre to suggest both the unmarried state of the deceased and her hopes for the afterlife. On the other hand, see G. Daux, *ArchCl* 25–26 (1973–74) 239–42.

"korai" could then be shown through their attire to portray more than mere maidens, can the same be said for other Akropolis statues or for other female figures in general?

By and large the answer remains negative for lack of sufficient evidence, but some suggestions can be made. The Peplos kore (Fig. 15) must have held a metal object in her right fist, which is pierced by a small hole. Does this make her an Artemis with bow and arrow, or an Athena with a helmet in her left hand[33] and spear in her right? To be sure, a spear would have been held upright. Yet I am convinced that the statue is no "anonymous" kore, but must represent a divinity because of her unusual costume and peculiar appearance. Indeed, scholars have found it difficult to reconcile her relatively late style with the old-fashioned peplos which she wears although all the other korai on the Akropolis wear the Ionic chiton-and-himation combination. If, as I believe, the Peplos kore also wears a cape, her sculptor probably meant to represent a much earlier image, recognizable indeed through her out-of-date costume which turns her into a Sixth century version of a kolossos or a xoanon. Likewise, Classical masters used chiton and himation to make clear they were portraying a statue amidst peplos-wearing human beings.

If the Peplos kore depicts a Seventh century cult idol, we can also understand her apparent rigidity and lack of movement, which contrasts with her slight asymmetries and strong plasticity. Payne has pointed out with great sensitivity all the small details which make the kore so alive, but there is no denying the block-like impression she makes at first viewing, an impression which may have been fully intended by her sculptor. His contemporaries would have recognized a goddess through the hieratic costume as well as through her attributes and the unusual amount of added metal jewelry. Similarly, the other "peplophoros" from the Akropolis, the peculiar relief-like Pomegranate kore (Akr. 593: Fig. 29), could be considered a divinity, either because it imitates a xoanon in its plank-like appearance or because the sculptor knew its intended location—a specific, and therefore probably religious, setting. However, pomegranate and wreath are conventional enough as votive offerings, and are not sufficient evidence for a Demeter or a Persephone, nor is her unusually voluminous himation drawn over her head, as we would expect in a matronly divine figure.

This last may instead be a significant detail in a statue which is already recognized as Leto because it was found in Delos together with a group of other figures which are clearly identified through other attributes. The component members of the group are recognizable also through the technical peculiarity that their backs are often left undetailed, as if for a strictly frontal display. Nat. Mus. 22 is most richly dressed; besides her crinkly chiton and diagonal himation, she wears a long mantle which covers her back

[33] N. Kunisch (*AthMitt* 89 [1974] 85–104 pls. 40–48) has recently compiled extensive lists of Black Figure and Red Figure vases in which Athena appears holding her helmet and a spear, though the relative position of these objects may change. In these scenes the goddess is further characterized by her aegis, yet the relief of the so-called Mourning Athena or the Roman copies of the Frankfurt type (*Severe Style*, figs. 69 and 123–24) show that at least in the first half of the 5th century this item could be omitted. The Peplos kore, if completed with helmet and spear, would resemble somewhat the Palladion as it appears, for instance, in the Vivenzio hydria by the Kleophrades Painter (Schefold, pl. 211a). Perhaps other statues originally associated with Akr. 679 once provided a narrative context which ensured identification. The problems raised by the interpretation of the Peplos kore will be discussed in a forthcoming article; see supra n. 8.

entirely, and a veil which was worn between the two and covers her head. This veil seems to be held together over her chest by a chain ornament partly carved and partly added in metal. In addition, the Leto had several metal attachments, including separate pendants for the two chains. Her diagonal mantle is unusually rich in having two central folds. And her hair is so luxuriant that some locks appear under her left armpit, emerging from under the various wraps against her chiton sleeve. That the veil was drawn over the head is clear from the profile view, where the material is seen to surround the neck.

This detail raises the question of interpretation for all the East Greek and Samian veiled korai. It has recently been repeated that no significance can be attached to this item beyond that of regional fashions since so many statues cannot all represent Hera or other goddesses. On the other hand, since some heads are shown bare, the veil must at least stand for matronly status or even for outdoor versus indoor attire. That in some cases it may stand for more is suggested by the many non-Greek representations of Cybele, where the goddess invariably appears veiled under her tall headdress. Even headless statues, like the two fragmentary torsos from Midas City, show combinations of veils or mantles with either smooth or crinkly robes quite comparable to the Samian figures. It is currently maintained that these Phrygian renderings are all later than, and therefore influenced by, Greek works like the Hera of Samos. Yet details like the vertical pattern in one,[34] the carved hem border in both, are obviously Oriental characteristics. Dates for the Phrygian works are not certain since they are based solely on Greek comparisons, and not enough examples are available to establish local groupings or sequences: But why should influences inevitably go from East Greece to Anatolia? To my eyes, the Samian statues do not look particularly Greek in conception or form. Granted that terracottas may show the incipient stages of fold formation, the specific combination of surface patterns made of thin, engraved lines and the smooth veil tucked in at the waist seem to me too Oriental to be ignored. Even the column-like shape is represented in the statue from Palanga.

The heads of the Greek figures are no longer extant: but since the iconography of a tall headdress accompanied by a veil, and usually also by a mantle, is so firmly established throughout Anatolia and can be traced so far back into a Mesopotamian-Sumerian past, such a reconstruction would not be implausible even for the Samian/East Greek statues. That no immediate link is provided by almost contemporary freestanding sculpture from the Near East is perhaps due to the medium in which such statues were carved: either perishable, like wood, or precious, like metal. Rock carvings and reliefs certainly provide close enough parallels, though of disputed chronological priority. Individual details and specific renderings are instead easily duplicated in earlier Neo-Hittite or Urartian works. The present tendency, especially among German scholars, is to refute any indebtedness of Greek sculpture to Anatolian sources, and to favor influences from the East Greek world as giving new impetus to non-Greek works of the early Sixth century. As the Kululu statues have recently shown, new finds from Anatolia may considerably alter the picture as we

[34] This pattern is not quite the equivalent of a paryphe. It runs from the break to the bottom border, along the left leg. I cannot be quite sure whether there is a corresponding border on the other side. The arrangement of the three vertical borders on a Parian kore (Paros Mus. no. 802, supra p. 99) gives a different impression since the two additional stripes run straight along the flanks, so that they are almost invisible from the front.

now see it, and present evidence seems already sufficient to hypothesize that more links existed and may eventually be found.[35]

Even strict dependence upon Oriental religious iconography would not ensure a similar divine identification for all the veiled Samian and East Greek korai. The possibility however exists, and we should be open to it since we have too easily extended to all female figures that generic meaning of agalma which, to be sure, applies to many of them. Since none of the korai is as enormous as some of the kouroi, their divinity cannot be argued on size alone. However, many female figures are over life-size, and the gods of the Delian group are all of normal or slightly smaller height. It may be worth noting that none of the extant monumental korai is ever shown naked. Obviously the Greeks did not consider nudity appropriate for official sculpture of women, and nakedness did not become an attribute of Aphrodite statues until approximately the mid-Fourth century. That naked hetairai appear on Archaic vases, and a few bronze naked women as mirror supports, confirms the difference between minor and major arts. Similarly, the nude goddesses of the Gortyna triad-plaques remained without successors in Archaic Greek relief or architectural sculpture, a fact which further demonstrates Greek independence from Cretan prototypes.

NIKAI

One more category of statues can be considered with the korai because of their predominantly female aspect: the Nikai. This personification of an abstract concept is, however, mentioned by Hesiod as a Titan's daughter, therefore as concrete a person as any of the other minor deities. Its sculptural iconography seems to have started in the islands also since the first Nike statue is attributed to Archermos, son of Mikkiades, from Chios. To the inscribed base in Delos has sometimes been assigned the winged statue now in the National Museum in Athens, which, however, may not belong to it and may be simply an akroterion.[36] Many of the extant statues of victories may in fact have had an architectural function since as flying creatures they were particularly suited for lofty positions. In costume and appearance they follow the same chronological conventions of the korai, wearing the tight-fitting peplos until approximately 550–540, then the diagonal mantle and the chiton. Their wings are usually attached to their backs with no regard for a proper connection with the body through the garments. A basic characteristic is the flying pose, similar to the running, with bent legs, and one knee raised so that the skirt falls back from

[35] One such link may be the bird which East Greek korai so often hold. Several Phrygian statues of the Goddess Kubaba are characterized by the attribute of a bird of prey pressed against the chest, perhaps significantly with the left hand. In addition, it has been pointed out that in hieroglyphic Hittite, a bird is the second sign in Kubaba's name (*Expedition* 6 [1964] 28–32).

[36] Rubensohn (*MdI* [1948] 21–43), on the basis of a terracotta from Paros, has shown that the objects under the Nike's tresses are not a second pair of smaller wings, but rosettes used as ornaments. Though this point is probably correct, his further argument that the statue represents not a Nike but a winged Mistress of Animals is refuted by Hamdorf (*Griechische Kultpersonifikationen der vorhellenistischen Zeit* [1964] 58–62, Catalogue 112–16) on the grounds that no *Potnia Theron* is ever shown in *knielauf* pose (p. 60). Stucchi (*ASAtene* 30–32, NS 14–16 [1952–54] 39–41) argues that optical corrections in the figure demand a high position to the right of the viewer and that therefore the Nike was the right-hand akroterion of a temple. Isler–Kerenyi stresses that a Nike as lateral akroterion is inconceivable during the Archaic period since she is considered an "individual" unsuitable for a double (p. 103).

it, leaving the calf exposed. This arrangement usually allows the sculptor to lengthen the paryphe and the massed skirt between the legs so that they touch the ground and create a very substantial support for the figure between the widely separated feet.

The Athenian Akropolis has produced four full statues and 14 fragments which may belong to Nikai. Of these, Akr. 694 shows extensive traces of restoration that resulted in an unusual draping of the mantle, now pinned only over both shoulders and not along the arms. The suggestion that she may have been the akroterion of the so-called Peisistratid Temple gains suport from her lack of balance on a central axis, unlike other Nikai which stood as independent dedications. Akr. 691 and 693 have their diagonal mantles pinned over the left shoulder, rather than over the right; they too may have been balanced by corresponding statues, or may have been rendered as figures in action who therefore needed to keep the right arm free. Or possibly, for aesthetic reasons, the mantle was pinned on the side opposite the direction of flight so that the heavy hanging drapery could float free of the body out into space; in fact, both these Nikai move to their right.

The large and impressive Nike 690 has been connected with the column inscribed with Kallimachos' dedication, as a monument presumably erected posthumously, after the death of the general at Marathon in 490. Not everybody agrees with such connection; but if it is correct, the expression "messenger of the immortals" in the inscription may suggest a statue of Iris rather than of Victory. If this should be true, iconographically Nike and Iris would be practically indistinguishable, and perhaps only the presence of a caduceus would have made matters clear in antiquity. That the statue is in any case quite late is shown by the restrained hairstyle, with locks gathered over the nape, and by the more extended position of the legs, which no longer bend sharply at the knee.

Other Nikai[37] occur in Syracuse, Tarentum, Eretria, Delphi, and perhaps Karthaia on Kea; at all these sites they were probably akroteria, but this very limited distribution seems to imply that the type was not readily accepted elsewhere. On the other hand, the obviously Cycladic character of the Akropolis Victories (Akr. 693 greatly resembles the Siphnian Karyatid) leaves no doubt as to the popularity of the subject in the islands. Chance must be responsible for our relatively meager evidence.

Other female figures are shown striding rather than simply stepping forward or flying, but identification is no longer possible. An interesting kore in Delos (A 4066) moves definitely to her left and may have been part of a group. On the Athenian Akropolis, a fragmentary figure (Akr. 159) has been tentatively called a running Athena but on no definite evidence.[38] A very large, similar fragment in Paros (no. 91) is unfinished, but may have already belonged to the Severe style. Close to the end of the Archaic period is also the very fragmentary Athena Promachos in Delphi.

SUMMARY

The kore type seems to be the almost perfect counterpart to the kouros. Originating probably as a divine image, it was then considered appropriate to represent the heroized dead, and finally became also a pleasant gift, without direct relationship to the dedicant.

[37] Very close to a Nike in pose and details, such as the streaming hair, is the headless statue which was found in Athens, east of the Tower of the Winds, Nat. Mus. 3936; *AA* 1934, cols. 143 figs. 9–10; Karouzou, p. 33.

[38] For striding figures, cf. also *Agora* XI no. 85 pp. 24–25 and n. 50.

Yet its distribution is geographically more limited than the kouros', and its funerary function is positively attested only for Attica; Miletos commemorated its women with seated statues, while Samos, though it must have held a prominent position in the creation of the kore in Ionic costume, may have used neither the seated nor the standing type for funerary purposes. For the Cyclades our evidence is still too scanty to allow firm conclusions: all extant korai from the islands, to my knowledge, had a votive function, except perhaps the very early statue from Thera.

Iconographically, the kore type seems heavily indebted to Oriental prototypes, both in details of rendering and in items of clothing. Some of the body stylizations may also have been derived from Neo-Hittite art. East Greece and Samos led in the production of korai, even if the Cyclades may have provided some inspiration. Certainly the islands developed stylistic features of their own, which in turn influenced greatly both Asia Minor and the mainland, and Athens in particular. The Peloponnesos has fewer korai than kouroi to contribute: three fragmentary examples from Sparta and the Argive Heraion.

The kore type at times had an architectural function, as a Karyatid, but it then followed the stylistic trends of contemporary freestanding sculpture from the same region. The type was further exploited to portray specific goddesses, usually by the addition of an attribute or extra garment, such as the veil for Leto, an animal skin for Artemis, or the aegis for Athena. This last deity could also be shown striding, and there are a few Archaic statues in action poses, which cannot, however, be certainly identified. One final category, that of the Flying Victories, utilized the kore type both in apparel and in general appearance but added wings, the so-called *knielauf* pose, and occasionally wind-blown, streaming hair. Stylistically, all these types developed equally and along the same lines, with folds and swags increasing in number and elaboration toward the end of the Sixth century and ending almost in mannerism and illogicality before a final reaction toward simple surfaces and more sober decoration. The peak of the type seems to have been around 520–500; the year 480 saw its disappearance.

BIBLIOGRAPHY 4

FOR PAGE 85

The major sources on the subject are *Korai* (note glossary); *AMA* (section on korai by E. Langlotz); Herdejürgen, with special emphasis on the diagonal mantle; *Samos* xi, focusing primarily on the Samian material, but with many useful comments on outside parallels. Payne remains the most readable and penetrating analysis of the Akropolis korai.

For a review of *Korai*, see B. S. Ridgway, *ArtB* 52 (1970) 195–97.

FOR PAGE 86

Samian statues now considered votive: *Samos* xi nos. 25–26; cf. p. 9.

Statue from Tanagra: N. Pharaklas, *Deltion* 24:1 (1969) 63–73 pls. 43–44. This publication considers the statue male, but an earlier notice considered it female: *Deltion* 16 (1960) 148–49. See also supra, p. 75 n. 32.

Nikandre: *Korai* no. 1 figs. 25–28; as Mistress of Animals: H. Gallet de Santerre, *Delos Primitive et Archaïque* (Paris 1958) 256. For inscriptions in general, see supra, p. 75 and its bibliography (Burzachechi). For a good photograph of Nikandre's back, which reveals the cape, see *BCH* 74 (1950) pl. 30. For the cape in Daedalic sculpture, see Davaras, 59–64; however, he omits the Nikandre from his discussion.

FOR PAGE 87

Kore from Thera: "Theräisches," 117–21 Beil. 81–82 and 89:1.

Samian kore: *Samos* xi no. 1 pl. 1; *Korai* no. 21:2 figs. 80, 82, 83. For a sketch of the reconstructed figure, see *AltSt* 2 p. 23, or *AthMitt* 68 (1953) 79 fig. 1; but note that in both these publications more fragments are attributed to the statue than officially accepted in *Samos* xi. The other pieces are there given to kore no. 3.

FOR PAGE 88

Perirrhanteria: *Korai* nos. 5–13, with ancient sources on p. 27. The latest article on the subject is F. W. Hamdorf, *AthMitt* 89 (1974) 47–64; but see also J. Ducat, *BCH* 88 (1964) 577–606, and G. Hiesel, *Opus Nobile*, 77–81. See also *Ptoion* nos. 47–48; A. Delivorrias, *AAA* 2 (1969) 7–10; E. Paribeni, *AttiMGrecia* NS 9–10 (1968–69) 61–63; related also is F. Chamoux, *BCH* 94 (1970) 319–26. For Oriental comparisons, see, e.g., *KAnat*, 40–41 figs. 18–19, Urartian, end of the 8th century.

FOR PAGE 89

Isthmia perirrhanterion: *Korai* no. 5 figs. 35–37.

Earliest kore in Asia Minor (from Didyma): Tuchelt, K 36, pl. 35:1 and fig. 25 on p. 141, for a sketch reconstruction.

FOR PAGE 90

Corinthian peplophoroi of the Severe period: W.-H. Schuchhardt, *Mélanges Mansel* (Ankara 1974) 13–24 pls. 11–16.

Kore from Sparta with diagonal mantle: *BSA* 11 (1904/5) 99–101 figs. 1–2 (erroneously described as wearing only one garment which has become unpinned over one shoulder. The chiton was probably rendered largely in paint; cf. Herdejürgen, 45 and n. 245). Head of kore: *ibid.*, 102–3 figs. 4–5.

Kore from Argive Heraion: *JOAI* 19–20 (1919) 145–48 no. 2 figs. 83–85.

Kore from Sikyon: *Korai* no. 99 figs. 301–3; *Boston Cat.* 8–9 no. 5.

Hera at Olympia: *Korai* no. 36 figs. 118–21; for the sphinx theory, see D. K. Hill, *Hesperia* 13 (1944) 353–60; see also infra, Ch. 5, pp. 123–24.

Boeotian korai: *Ptoion* nos. 46 (?), 116, 138 (Attic = *Korai* no. 143 figs. 454–55). I am not fully convinced of the female sex of *Ptoion* no. 46 (= *Korai* no. 2 figs. 29–30; see also infra Ch. 10, pp. 295, 301.

Head in Delphi: *Kouroi* no. 46; see *AAA* 5 (1972) 317n. 3.

Catania kore: G. Libertini, *Il Museo Biscari* (1930) no. 879 pl. 101, preserved h. (from head to below belt) 0.72 m.

Tarentum korai: E.g., *Korai* no. 171 figs. 541–44; E. Paribeni, *AttiMGrecia* NS 1 (1954) 63–70; *Korai* no. 172 figs. 545–47.

Korai from Lydia (Sardis): *Korai* no. 62 fig. 206; Tuchelt L 42bis.

Kore from Karia (Theangela): *Korai* no. 167 figs. 532–35; Tuchelt, L 85.

Korai from Phrygia (Midas City): C.H.E. Haspels, *Phrygie* 3 (1951) 111–15 pl. 47 a–b (two torsos). See also K. Bittel, *AntP* 2 (1963) 7–22, and Tuchelt, 161 nn. 1–2 with further bibliography and discussion.

Kore from Kalchedon: *Korai* no. 73 figs. 232–34.

Kore from the Black Sea (Odessa): *AA* 1928, col. 82 fig. 1.

Kore from Skyros: *Deltion* 22:2[1] (1967) 287 and pl. 186.

Kore from Thasos: *GdTh*, 117 no. 3 fig. 55; *BCH* 73 (1949) 547.

Kore from Thrace: *Makedonika* 9 (1969) 136 pls. 17–18; Herdejürgen, 45 n. 242 with further bibliography; for discussion, see infra, p. 102.

Korai from Cyrene: Paribeni, nos. 6, 8–9 (= *Korai* nos. 168–69 figs. 536–39) 10. Add J. G. Pedley, *AJA* 75 (1971) 42–46 pls. 6–8.

For the costume of the korai, see, e.g., *Korai*, 6–10; the definition of the peplos is on p. 7; cf. also n. 12.

FOR PAGE 91

Phrasikleia: *AAA* 5 (1972) 298–324 and frontispiece illustration in color. See also *EAA* Suppl. vol. 1 (1970) for a similar color photograph, opposite p. VIII. For discussion, see infra, p. 99.

Peplos kore, Akr. 679: *Korai* no. 113 figs. 349–54; *AMA* no. 4; Payne, 18–19 pls. 29–33; Brouskari, 56–57. For recent articles, see Ch. Tsirivakou-Neumann, *AthMitt* 79 (1964) 114–26; Deyhle, 1–12.

Earlier authors who mention a cape-like garment are B. Staïs, *ArchEph* 1887, col. 131, and W. Lermann, *Altgriechische Plastik* (Munich 1907) 53–54 and n. 1. H. Lechat, *Au Musée de l'Acropole d'Athènes* (Paris 1903) 188 n. 2, observes the rendering but explains it as a simplification by the sculptor.

FOR PAGE 92

Kore from Eleusis: *Korai* no. 75 figs. 236–39.

Akr. 605: Payne, 36 pl. 94; *AMA* no. 12.

Akr. 611: Payne, 22 pl. 60; *AMA* no. 11.

Akr. 678: *Korai* no. 112 figs. 345–48; Payne, 21 pls. 34–35; *AMA* no. 10. L. Bonfante Warren, *AJA* 75 (1971) 279, suggests that the dress of the kore was misunderstood by an Attic artist not yet accustomed to the Ionic diagonal mantle. But the apparent misunderstanding can rather be explained as a different way of wearing the himation.

Samian kore: *Samos* XI no. 25.

Akr. 600: Payne, 36 pl. 93; *AMA* no. 52.

Akr. 673: *Korai* no. 117 figs. 368–72; Payne, 35–36 pls. 62–64; *AMA* no. 51; Brouskari, 63–64.

FOR PAGE 93

Draped youth Akr. 633: supra, pp. 75 and 82.

Samian kore with long mantle: *Samos* XI no. 13; *Korai* no. 60, fig. 201.

Akr. 584: Payne, pl. 96; *AMA* no. 53; Brouskari, 103.

Akr. 615: *Korai* no. 125 figs. 401–4; Payne, pl. 92; *AMA* no. 56; Brouskari, 69–70.

Chitoniskos and skirt: J. A. Schaeffer, *Summaries of Papers* at AIA 76th Meeting, Dec. 1974, p. 17; id., *CSCA* 8 (1975) 241–56; id., "*A Comparative Study of Archaic Costume in Greece and Italy*," Ph.D. Diss. submitted to the University of California at Berkeley, 1973. Richter (*Korai*, 9) uses *chitoniskos* as the equivalent of *ependytes* (cf. her pl. III fig. c); but I find it difficult to believe that the same term, in the diminutive, could be used to indicate something worn *over* the chiton itself; more likely, the two garments were mutually exclusive.

Akr. 670: *Korai* no. 119 figs. 377–80; Payne, 35–38 pls. 65–67; *AMA* no. 8; Brouskari, 70–71.

Akr. 671: *Korai* no. 111 figs. 341–44; Payne, 40 pls. 42–43; *AMA* no. 14; Brouskari, 74.

Akr. 683: *Korai* no. 120 figs. 381–84; Payne, 36 pl. 59; *AMA* no. 9; Brouskari, 81–82; see also infra, p. 107 and n. 28.

Kore from Erythrai: Tuchelt, 130, Addenda to his List; *AJA* 70 (1966) 157, where it is said to be from a Perserschutt deposit dated ca. 670–545. The kore is shown as part of an interior view in M. Yenim, *The Izmir Museums and the Archaeology of Some Ancient Cities* (Izmir 1969) pl. 3; cf. also his p. 17 no. 7 (inv. no. 5301). See also infra, pp. 96 and 98.

For examples of the chitoniskos in vase painting, see the stamnos by the Berlin Painter, Munich Antikensammlungen inv. 8738; Beazley *ARV*[2] 209 no. 161; *CVA* Deutschland 20 (München 5) pls. 259:1–2, 260:1–2, 261:1–2, 262:3. I owe this reference to Schaeffer.

Kea terracotta statues: See supra, pp. 18 and 40.

Assyrian costume, esp. separate skirts: Hrouda, 26–28, 30–32.

FOR PAGE 94

Akr. 685: *Korai* no. 181 figs. 573–77; Payne, 35 pls. 72, 74; *AMA* no. 47; read Langlotz's comments on p. 97; Brouskari, 73.

Akr. 675: *Korai* no. 123 figs. 394–97; Payne, 31 pls. 49–50; *AMA* no. 43; Brouskari, 65.

Akr. 680: *Korai* no. 122 figs. 389–93; Payne, 33–34 pls. 54–55; *AMA* no. 45; Brouskari, 73–74.

Akr. 682: *Korai* no. 116 figs. 362–67; Payne, 27–31 pls. 40–43; *AMA* no. 41; Brouskari, 67–68; see also supra, p. 107 and infra, Ch. 11 p. 316.

Terracottas of the Aphrodite group: R. A. Higgins, *Greek Terracottas* (London 1967) 30 n. 1, and pp. 32–35.

For the "development" of the veil, see *Samos* XI, 54.

First Samian kore with a veil: *Samos* XI no. 5.

"Hera" dedicated by Cheramyes: *Samos* XI no. 6; *Korai* no. 55 figs. 183–85.

Second kore dedicated by Cheramyes, in Berlin: *Samos* XI no. 7; *Korai* no. 56 figs. 186–89.

Veil doubled with fold high across back: see, e.g., *Samos* XI, no. 22; cf. also the kore from Theangela, supra, pp. 90:116.

Samian korai with "Milesian" veil: *Samos* XI nos. 20, 22, 24.

FOR PAGE 95

For marbles used on Samos, see *Samos* XI, 2–3.

Milesian influence on Samian mantle: See, e.g., *Samos* XI no. 20.

FOR PAGE 96

Geneleos as the inventor of the kore holding her skirt: *Samos* XI, 129 and n. 122; for the date of the Geneleos group, see p. 128.

Samian korai with clearly defined paryphai: *Samos* XI nos. 20, 22.

Left foot forward with unlifted chiton: *Samos* XI no. 12 (?) p. 34.

Left foot forward, chiton lifted by right hand: *Samos* XI no. 16; *Korai* no. 69 figs. 225–27.

For comments on the walking kore, see, e.g., *Samos* XI, 127 and n. 104; cf. also supra, pp. 28–29.

Samian heads: *Samos* XI nos. 17–19.

For comments on Samian hair patterns, see G. Schmidt, *AthMitt* 86 (1971) 31–41, especially p. 38.

FOR PAGE 97

Metal engraving: Cf. some Urartian bronze figures standing on animals, as part of thrones: *KAnat* 34 figs. 9–10; 7th century, from Toprakkale.

Milesian korai: Tuchelt, L 36, 37, 42, 43, 62, 108; many typical Milesian korai appear in reliefs.

Korai from Didyma: Tuchelt, K 36–42.

For a discussion of the Milesian way of wearing the mantle, see Herdejürgen, 40.

Fragmentary figure from the Ephesos column drum: Br.Mus. B 119; *Korai* no. 85 figs. 269; cf. *Samos* XI, 47 and n. 164. N. Himmelmann-Wildschütz, *IstMitt* 15 (1965) 28, believes that the fragments from the column drums show a unified style, ca. 550; *contra* Tuchelt, 136 (two phases, 550–540; 540–530). Br.Mus. B 119 should belong to Tuchelt's second phase.

Veiled heads from the Didymaion: Tuchelt, K 75–81; for comments on their headdress, p. 99; cf. G. Bruns, *IstForsch* 17 (1950) 30–34; also H. P. Laubscher, *IstMitt* 16 (1966) 96.

Inserted eyes: Kore head in Missouri, *MUSE* 4 (1970) 7, Acquisitions 1969, no. 4; Tuchelt, L 62bis; H. P. Laubscher, *IstMitt* 16 (1966) 95–99.

FOR PAGE 98

Eunuch in Berlin: *KAnat*, 29–30 figs. 6–7.

For the theory of a Milesian prototype and statues under its influence, see *Samos* XI, 47 and Korai nos. 20, 21; from Miletos, kore Berlin no. 1577, Tuchelt L 108; cf. also L 42 and 84.

Kore from Klazomenai: *Korai* no. 163 figs. 520–23; Tuchelt L 86.

Euthydikos' kore: See infra, p. 106.

Kore from Klaros: *Korai* no. la (no illustration); Tuchelt, 130 and 160, gives the same early date (700–620), but for a later date, see Herdejürgen, *AntK* 12 (1969) 109 n. 54. An opinion on the letter forms of the inscription was kindly expressed orally by L. H. Jeffery in September 1973. On the kore from Klaros, see also supra, p. 29.

Korai from Chios: *Korai* nos. 37–38 figs. 122–28; J. Boardman, *AntP* 1 (1962) 43–45; Mesopotamian parallel: Strommenger & Hirmer, pls. 162–63 (ca. 2040–1870).

FOR PAGE 99

Paros kore no. 802: To my knowledge, unpublished.

Aegina torso: *Korai* no. 39 figs. 129–31.

Lyons kore: Akr. 269+163+164; upper part in Lyons, France. *Korai* no. 89 figs. 275–81; Payne, 14–18 pls. 22–26; *AMA* no. 25; Brouskari, 60–61. An important contribution on her costume is W. Darsow, *MdI* 4 (1951) 85–102. Cf. Herdejürgen, 56. Supra, pp. 105–6, 108–9.

FOR PAGE 100

Delian kore A 4062: Described as wearing a peplos in *GdD* 42–43. Payne, 16 n. 1, vouches for the presence of the diagonal himation; cf. also W. Darsow, *Festschrift Rumpf* (1952) 44–45. For a poor illustration, see *JOAI* 12 (1909) 250 fig. 126. I was able to see this statue in November 1974 and can confirm the presence of the himation.

On the Cycladic mantle, see Herdejürgen, 54–56 and 59–61.

Milesian kore with bird in Berlin: *Korai* no. 57 figs. 190–93; Tuchelt, L 42.

FOR PAGE 101

Ex-Knidian head: *Korai* no. 86 figs. 270–74; P. de la Coste Messeliere and J. Marcadé, *BCH* 77 (1953) 346–53. For the Knidian Karyatids, see *Korai* nos. 87–88 figs. 282–83, and *BCH* 62 (1938) 286; also Herdejürgen, 44, for a low chronology.

Siphnian Karyatid: *Korai* no. 104 figs. 317–20.

FOR PAGE 102

Figures from the Siphnian pediment: *Korai* no. 105 fig. 321.

Kore from Rhedesto, Thrace: Supra, pp. 90 and 116.

Agora fragment joining Akr. 683: *Agora* XI no. 75; see also *ibid.*, comments on p. 1.

Berlin "goddess": *Korai* no. 42 figs. 139–46.

FOR PAGE 103

Torso from Moschato and kore from Haghios Ioannis Rendhis: infra, p. 99 n. 16.

Phile: Athens Nat. Mus. 81; J. Dörig, *AA* 1967, 15–28, especially p. 19 and figs. 1–3; *Korai* no. 91 figs. 284–85.

Kore from Lavrion: *Korai* no. 138 figs. 441–44.

FOR PAGE 104

Akr. 619: *Korai* no. 58 figs. 194–97; Payne, 9 pl. 20; *AMA* no. 22; Brouskari, 48 (wrist recently added).

Akr. 677; *Korai* no. 59 figs. 198–200; Payne, 12 pls. 18–19; *AMA* no. 23; Brouskari, 50. These korai have been called Samian, e.g., by Langlotz (*AMA*, 63–65) and by Ducat (*Ptoion*, 276 n. 3); Naxian by B. Freyer-Schauenburg (*Samos* XI, 26 and 28). Brouskari (pp. 48 and 50) leaves the question open.

Akr. 593 (Pomegranate kore): *Korai* no. 43 figs. 147–50; Payne, 9 pl. 12; *AMA* no. 2; Brouskari, 43–44. For the tooth chisel around 540, cf. C. Nylander, *AJA* 69 (1965) 54 and nn. 35–36; also Adam, 19, who suggests a date ca. 560 for the tool.

FOR PAGE 105

Plastic vases from Rhodes: The idea is Herdejürgen's, p. 44 and n. 236 (cf., e.g., C. Blinkenberg, *Lindos* I [Berlin 1931] no. 2106).

FOR PAGE 106

Akr. 595: Payne, 30 pl. 61; *AMA* no. 32; Brouskari, 72.

Akr. 598: *Korai* no. 115 figs. 358–61; Payne, pl. 92; *AMA* no. 40.

Euthydikos' kore, Akr. 686+609: *Korai* no. 180 figs. 565–72; Payne, 40 pls. 84–88; *AMA* no. 37; Brouskari, 127–28.

Relief Athens Nat. Mus. 36: *Korai* no. 141 fig. 445; see infra, Ch. 11.

FOR PAGE 107

Akr. 674: *Korai* no. 127 figs. 411–16; Payne, 34–35 pls. 75–78; *AMA* no. 44; Brouskari, 70.

Athena from Eretria pediment: S. & S., figs. 281, 442; infra, Ch. 11, n. 15.

FOR PAGE 108

Terracotta Athena from Olympia: Schefold, pl. 50; *OlBer* 6 (1958) 169–88 pls. 66–70.

Akr. 654: Payne, 4–6, 19 pl. 11; *AMA* no. 85; Brouskari, 58. For the theory that the head belongs to a relief, see *AMA*, p. 127.

Akr. 696; *Korai* no. 126 figs. 405–10; Payne, 39 pls. 82–83; *AMA* no. 20; Brouskari, 67.

FOR PAGE 109

Archaistic Athena in Corinth: *Corinth* X (1932) 117–24 nos. 1–2 pls. 15–16 figs. 111–14.

FOR PAGE 110

Leto from Delos, Athens Nat. Mus. 22: *Korai* no. 148 figs. 472–75; J. Marcadé, *BCH* 74 (1950) 181–217; *GdD*, 43–44 (D) with bibliography; Karouzou, 10.

FOR PAGE 111

For a recent statement on the meaning of the veil, see *Samos* XI, 10 and 25.

For Oriental fashions and their persistence, see M. J. Mellink, *AJA* 64 (1960) 188 and *AJA* 79 (1975) 107–8.

For terracottas showing the beginning of folds, see *Samos* XI, 21 and n. 36; also the comments by K. Vierneisel, *AthMitt* 76 (1961) 46–47.

For examples of the German theories against Greek indebtedness to Anatolian sources, see K. Bittel, *AntP* 2 (1963) 7–22; Tuchelt, 169; Kranz, 30 and 42.

FOR PAGE 112

Nike, daughter of the Titan Pallas: Hesiod, *Theog.* vv. 383ff.

For a catalogue of Archaic Nikai in stone, see Isler-Kerenyi, 143–44 nos. 129–47; cf. also her discussion on pp. 77–117.

Nike from Delos: *Severe Style*, fig. 55; for a discussion of the base, see *Signatures* 2 no. 21. Cf. also bibliography quoted here, p. 112 n. 36.

FOR PAGE 113

Akropolis Nikai: *AMA* nos. 67–84.

Akr. 694: Payne, 54 pl. 119; *AMA* no. 67, Brouskari, 66; Herdejürgen, 67. See also infra, Chs. 7 and 11.

Akr. 691: Payne, 62 pl. 119; *AMA* no. 69; Brouskari, 81.

Akr. 693: Payne, 62 pl. 120; *AMA* no. 68.

For the theory that the mantle should hang on the side opposite the direction of flight, see W. Darsow, *MdI* 4 (1951) 88–89.

Akr. 690 (Kallimachos' Nike): Payne, pl. 120; *AMA* no. 77; Brouskari, 125–26. Against the connection of statue and inscribed column: A.-B. Follmann, *Der Pan Maler* (Bonn 1968) 22–23. The latest discussion is by Kleine, who refutes Follmann, 116–19. See also E. B. Harrison, *GRBS* 12 (1971) 5–24. R. Hampe, *Die Antike* 15 (1939) 169–74, identifies the figure as Iris and attributes to it a bronze kerykeion ending in two heads of Pan.

Nike in Syracuse: Langlotz, *Magna Graecia*, pl. 43.

Nikai in Tarentum: *Die Antike* 14 (1938) 162; *NSc* 12 (1936) 196–200 pls. 12–13.

Nike from Eretria: Isler-Kerenyi, 143 no. 138.

Nikai in Delphi: *FdD* 2:4 (1967) 234–47 pls. 86–91; cf. also Isler-Kerenyi, Cat. nos. 132–34, 136, 141.

Nike (?) as central akroterion for temple of Athena at Karthaia (Kea): *Deltion* 18:2[2] (1963) 281–82 pl. 327c; *BCH* 89 (1965) 862 fig. 7.

Akr. 159: Payne, 47 pl. 123; *AMA* no. 411; Brouskari, 65–66.

Paros no. 91: Adam, pl. 3a, p. 20.

Athena Promachos from Marmaria, Delphi: *BCH* 79 (1955) 379–406.

FOR PAGE 114

On the demise of the kore, see *Greek Sculpture*, 55; *Greek Art*, 102–3. Cf. also infra, Ch. 11, passim, and p. 313.

Chapter 5

Seated, Reclining, and Equestrian Figures

SEATED FIGURES

The seated figure presents basically the same problems that we have already encountered in dealing with the kouros and kore—problems of origin and influences, chronology, and identification. Here too, the pattern of geographical distribution may be significant, and again we find Asia Minor in the lead numerically, with high totals which include many male figures. Other areas have fewer or no examples, and men are not represented as often as women.

A recent study distinguished three types of seated figures: 1) those that sit on elaborate chairs with arm- and backrests; 2) those with only a backrest; and 3) those with no arm- or backrest whatever. Types 1 and 3 occur in the minor arts as early as the end of the Eighth century. Type 2 is first attested only about a century later, at the end of the Daedalic period, when it occurs both in stone sculpture and in figurines. Yet it is assumed that it might have originated as early and under the same circumstances as the two other types. From these premises the study concludes that all Archaic monumental seated statues can be traced back to Late Geometric prototypes and are therefore completely independent of Oriental influences or conceptions. Even details which may look imported are not so closely paralleled in the Orient as to be accepted without challenge. Since at the time of the earliest examples large-scale sculpture, if it existed, could probably not correspond to the minor arts in typology and style, it is assumed that the seated type was invented for figurines, which only at a later period could find proper translation into monumental scale. Ultimately, type 1 goes back even to Mycenaean conceptions, which undergo a revival in the Eighth century because of a return to comparable conditions, or at least because of a specific Greek interest in the heroic past. Thus the creation of sculptural types, not only the seated figures but also the kouros and the kore, would be less the consequence of outside influence than the expression of a historical and cultural change of situation in Greece in the late Eighth century.

This is not the place to discuss the possible origin of kouroi and korai, which has been treated elsewhere. I have also expressed previously the difficulty I see in magnifying a statuette into something as large as, or larger than, natural size. Consequently, I hesitate to accept Geometric seated figurines as the true predecessors of the Archaic statues because both scale and medium prevented an exact translation into monumental format. To be sure, men and women must have sat on stools, chairs, or thrones even at a time when no sculptural representation was attempted, and one need not always look abroad for inspiration when life itself can provide the sculptor with his models. The fact remains, however, that the very conception of monumental stone sculpture seems to have been triggered by a combination of circumstances, not the least of which was direct acquaintance with foreign carving techniques and monuments. Once this premise is accepted, it would be unreasonable to reject all possible Egyptian or Oriental inspiration for the various types, and specifically for the seated one, which was so prominent in these autocratic countries. Inevitably, the Greeks assimilated and transformed these influences so thoroughly that their finished products differed considerably from any foreign prototype and managed to look unmistakably Greek. But I find an even stronger difference between the Late Geometric statuettes and the Archaic sculptures, despite their common Greek origin. As for the various seat forms, I would tend to consider them an expression of rank and function rather than true criteria for typological distinction, once the basic conception of a seated statue is accepted. I shall therefore treat them all as a group, discussing various seat types only when I believe they provide a clue for identification.

The Earliest Examples

In general, the seated type remains the same throughout the Archaic period. The human body is stiffly erect, with only a slight inclination forward or backward of the upper torso and, in a few of the latest examples, minor differences in the position of arms and legs. Even so, the so-called Endoios' Athena, with her retracted right leg and her momentary pose, remains an exception. No Greek seated figure ever slouches or relaxes in its seat; the angular pose is relieved only by the gentle sloping or curving of lap and thighs. Perhaps because of the sheer bulk of such a conception, none of the extant seated statues is enormous, but several are larger than nature, and one Samian torso, if the seated restoration is correct, would be twice life-size.

Our earliest examples come from Crete and are in limestone. Both the seated woman from Gortyna and the two from Prinias (Fig. 1) had a definite connection with architecture, though we cannot be entirely certain of the exact position within the building. In one sense, this architectural context lessens their importance as examples of sculpture, but to my mind it also strengthens their link with Oriental prototypes and widens their distance from Geometric figurines, which could hardly be visualized in tectonic function. However, several other statues, also from Crete, seem to have been independent monuments, so that these objections are not overriding. More significant is the fact that Cretan sculpture, as discussed elsewhere, represents a manifestation in itself, short-lived and unconnected with the development of Archaic statuary in marble, so that the occurrence of seated figures in that area is not of paramount importance.

More relevant is the appearance of seated statues in the Peloponnesos, since it has given rise to the theory that inspiration for the type came to Asia Minor from the Greek mainland, the Cyclades, and Crete, and that the typical massiveness of the Branchidai is actually a stamp of Doric style. To be sure, the Peloponnesian statues are relatively early, include a male figure, and are remarkable in an area which has yielded so little Archaic sculpture in general. But this very consideration and the isolated nature of the examples make me doubt that their influence may have been so strongly felt at such a distance. I find it much more plausible to assume Oriental influences and conceptions for a series of Asia Minor statues which look quite different from the Peloponnesian or Cretan "prototypes" except for the obvious trait of being seated. Even Geometric figurines of the same type as the Didyma statues (type 1) look different, in that they use their armrests and their feet do not reach the ground. Once it is admitted that the Branchidai do not fit into the development of the minor arts and that they show the typical East Greek preference for flowing contours and a general massiveness (rather than "a massive articulation"), I do not see why we should look so far afield for their origin. I would rather accept an independent invention in the various areas, each conditioned by different prototypes, though possibly the main impulse might have come from abroad in all cases.

Concentrating specifically on the Peloponnesos, since its seated figures are usually considered earlier than the earliest from Asia Minor, we find four possible candidates: the limestone figure from Haghiorghitica (Arkadia; Nat. Mus. no. 57); the very large limestone head from Olympia (Hera); the Hagemo from Asea (Arkadia; Nat. Mus. no. 6); and the man from Magoula (Sparta Mus. 576). Of these only the first may belong to the Seventh century, though early dates have been given by some to the other examples as well.

Mainly, the Haghiorghitica statue is dated still within the Daedalic period[1] because of its peculiarly shaped head with its flat dome, the springing masses of hair behind the ears and the pointed face. When already in its present battered state, eyebrows and eyes were presumably scratched in by local peasants and the present filling of the holes gives the impression of inserted pupils. But these should be disregarded in the stylistic evaluation of the whole. That the statue may not be as early as the hair makes it seem is perhaps shown by the slight turn of the head, the massive shoulders slightly hunched forward, and the strong arms which are particularly impressive from the rear view. The figure wears a fringed mantle ending in a tasseled tip behind the left shoulder, and this form of draping may suggest that the statue represents a man, an impression already given by the powerful build of the torso. On the other hand, the statue was found in the area of a sanctuary of Demeter, and it has been suggested that it once wore separately inserted earrings and necklace. The hairstyle would be appropriate for a male as well as for a female in a Lingering Daedalic tradition, and in general the statue may not be too far removed from Kleobis and Biton, with which it would share a certain provincial conservatism quite appropriate to Arkadia. The very use of soft limestone instead of marble would speak for such provincialism. Yet a touch of Oriental influence may be revealed by the mantle; if the manner of wearing it is Greek, the fringe and tassel look Oriental and find a possible parallel in a Neo-Hittite relief from Sakçegözü, of the end of the Eighth century, or even in some Assyrian genii from Nimrud. Another foreign detail may be its seat type, which could come from North Syria (Kyrieleis, Type I), but its form is so simple that perhaps not much should be made of this point.

The enormous face usually called the Hera from Olympia has been identified as the cult statue seen by Pausanias within the Heraion, and should therefore belong to a seated figure flanked by a Zeus, presumably standing. Yet agreement on this identification is far from having been reached. We should perhaps discard the possibility that the face was part of the pedimental decoration since a temple built largely of mudbrick and wood could

[1] Kranz, 23, dates it at the end of the Daedalic phase, just before the inception of the Archaic period; but Jenkins, *Dedalica*, 78, places it in the first quarter of the 6th century. The springing masses of hair on either side of the face occur not only in the post-Daedalic Kleobis and Biton but also, for instance, in conservative figures like the running Gorgon on the predella of a stele in Athens, Nat. Mus. 2687, *AGA* no. 27 fig. 84, ca. 560.

scarcely have supported the weight of such sizable sculpture in stone. Another, and still vital, theory would make it the head of a gigantic sphinx, like the Naxian dedication in Delphi. Even the face's strong asymmetry would be in keeping with such a restoration, and other fragments found together with the head would be the feathers of a wing tip. Those who prefer to consider the face as part of the cult statue interpret these fragments as folds. It should be noted, however, that the head was not found within the temple, as occasionally stated, but in front of the east facade of the Palaestra, in a layer of alluvial sand over which a stone channel had been built. This stratification would almost surely prevent identification with the cult image seen by Pausanias in the Second century AD. Even if the face were really that of the seated Hera, its date should be after 600; a recent suggestion would place it ca. 560.[2]

A more definite example of a seated statue is the Hagemo from Asea, whose name is inscribed on the plinth just below her feet. Remains of a four-legged creature, perhaps a sphinx or a lion, appear next to her right knee, with no corresponding carving on the other side to suggest an armrest. This creature has therefore been considered a sign of the statue's chthonic function, and the monument may well have been the image of a heroized deceased, rather than of a goddess ("Artemis-Hagemo"). Chronology is difficult; some scholars consider the undetailed, block-like body quite early, others late. Jeffery, on the basis of the epigraphic evidence, suggests a chronology toward the end of the Sixth century and therefore sees the statue as a clumsy, provincial work; Kranz places it after the turn of the century, but not before the end of the first quarter. The shape of its plinth, which was obviously not set into a base, may make a mid Sixth century date more probable.

Finally, the statue in Sparta. It is important because it is undoubtedly of a man and because, though a provincial work, it may incorporate an innovation. This consists in the pose of the torso, which is not completely straight or slightly forward like the Haghiorghitica statue; the figure seems to lean back in a pose which we find only in one of the advanced Branchidai, London B 276. The human figure is almost as undetailed as the Hagemo. The type of seat, with lion's paws for the front legs, also comparable to the Hagemo, suggests some influence from Egypt, which is amply evident in the many Laconian hero-reliefs.

If we therefore summarize all this evidence, we seem to have little proof that the seated statue may have originated in the Peloponnesos. The extant examples are either dubious representatives of the seated type (e.g., the "Hera"), or later than the beginning of the Sixth century, if not considerably so. The gap in time and typology with the Cretan monu-

[2] I cannot subscribe to L. Alscher's theory (*Griechische Plastik*, I [Berlin 1954] 93–99), which would reconstruct a gigantic Hera, seated frontally on a high throne so that the head with polos and accompanying tendrils could be carved in high relief against the back rest. The peculiar break which has eliminated the rear half of the head is not only typical of a limestone split, but may have been an intentional cutting up of the total statue to reduce it to manageable blocks. Note that no protrusion mars the present state of the stone, which could virtually be a piece of ashlar masonry.

It has often been said that the fine carving of the polos and other decorative details of the face are reminiscent of ivory carving and should therefore date the statue (or its prototype) well into the 7th century. This high date is no longer possible, if the cult-statue theory is accepted, given the lower chronology for the Heraion. In addition, I believe that such fine surface detail is conditioned by the nature of limestone, which lends itself to exactly this kind of embellishment. The downward slant of the eyes makes me think that the head was set up at considerable height, to be viewed from below. This would not be the case if the "Hera" were seated, even taking into account that it is over life-size.

ments is such that the two sets need not be considered together, and we cannot really assume that a strong tradition of seated statues is revealed through these scattered monuments. Certainly they do not form the continuous sequence one finds at Didyma; to some extent they too seem to be under a certain amount of Oriental influence but presumably from sources different from the one at work on the Branchidai, as is apparent from the shape of their seats. Finally, the revised, lower chronology which I favor for the Peloponnesian examples makes them roughly contemporary with the Asia Minor monuments and therefore does not allow sufficient time for influences to travel from the mainland to the outlying areas. One should consider on the other hand the strong tradition of rulers' images in seated poses which prevailed in the hinterland of all the East Greek cities.

I know of no other early examples. Even a statuette in Delos which has at times been considered a mid Seventh century representation of Hera, should more probably come down to ca. 560 since the goddess pulls her skirt with her left hand. This unexpected gesture, which finds true meaning only in a standing figure whose walking could be hampered by a long garment, is not attested in monumental art earlier than ca. 570, and it would be surprising if a statuette, seated at that, were to precede large-scale sculpture considerably in the development of motifs. On the contrary, one assumes the gesture to have been well established in another context, before being applied, with some inappropriateness, to a work in small scale.

To be sure, reliefs from the islands (specifically Paros) show seated figures at an earlier date, and we can safely assume several wooden cult statues to have been enthroned. The very number of seated statuettes found at the Heraion in Delos suggests that they reproduced, in a different medium perhaps, some aspects of the cult image. But the monumental evidence is as yet missing, at least until the second half of the Sixth century.

Examples by Region

Didyma. Against such small numbers, the totals from Didyma and Asia Minor are particularly impressive. Didyma alone has yielded 13 statues of seated men and 8 of women, one of uncertain sex and a fragment of a throne, for a total of 23 monuments.[3] Asia Minor, especially the area of Miletos, has produced 17 statues of seated women from ca. 550 to 494. Though very early examples are missing, those preserved are usually large or even heroic in scale, with only three true statuettes included in the total. Yet the complete absence of statues of seated men in Asia Minor, aside from the Branchidai, is puzzling and deserves consideration.

Of the total 23 seated statues from Didyma, 17 were found along the Sacred Way leading from the harbor of Panormos to the Temple of Apollo. These are traditionally called the Branchidai in the belief that they represent the priestly successors of the legendary Branchos, who established the cult of the god on that site. In effect, the name Branchidai is attested only for the site, interchangeably with Didyma, and, interestingly enough,

[3] This total may actually rise to 24 in that one female statue appears to have been part of a pair; the seat of K 56 is ampler than usual, suggesting that it connected with that of a second figure. A similar pair comes from Miletos and consists of two identical female figures; we cannot be sure, however, of the sex of the second member in the Didyma pair. For a discussion of such double images, see T. Hadzisteliou-Price, *JHS* 91 (1971) 48–69.

in the feminine gender. One inscription, on the statue of Chares (Fig. 31), identifies him as ruler of Teichioussa, rather than as a priest, and it is quite probable that all other enthroned male figures were the votive offerings of neighboring potentates. Only one monument, now in Istanbul, differs from the others in the man's attire and the cubic shape of his seat; he is also the only figure to have been shown with an attribute, a peculiar staff which he holds pressed against his left side. Because of this unusual detail, as well as for the simplified form of its seat, this is the only statue which may indeed represent a prophet, if not a priest.

The female figures, with one possible exception, seem later than the male, and are variously attired; two, and perhaps more, wore a veil over the head. This variation within the group has been taken as a sign that the statues do not follow a single prototype and therefore cannot reflect a cult image of a goddess. They may perhaps be priestesses, but no information is available as to the sex of their dedicators. Since Samos has produced a clear example of a family offering, a statuary group where both man and wife were represented, I wonder whether some of the Didyma seated ladies could not simply be the wives of the rulers portrayed in some of the other monuments. In particular B 272, which is usually considered the earliest of the Didyma seated women (ca. 580) seems to me reasonably close to the male figure B 274 to form a possible set and, at least, to join it in date (ca. 560, probably even slightly later). Her relatively low kolpos perhaps corroborates this chronology as well as the fine treatment of the crinkly folds on both chiton and veil, and the subtle contour of her legs, especially her right, beneath her garment. The position of her long veil with its curving edge along her left side recalls the "younger sister" of the "Hera of Samos," the second Cheramyes' dedication in Berlin (ca. 560). Unfortunately, the seated Phileia from the Samian family group is not well enough preserved to show whether her head was covered. Certainly a veiled head in Classical times basically meant matronly status and not exclusively divine status, though it was easily used as an attribute for mother goddesses like Cybele, Demeter, and the Oriental Artemis.

Tuchelt has suggested for the entire Didyma series a range from ca. 600–580 to ca. 520–510. Though this lower limit is defensible, the upper seems too high, especially in consideration of the relatively short stylistic distance which separates the Branchidai from the Samian Phileia of the Geneleos group. But even with a lower initial date (ca. 570), their very distribution in time makes a strong argument in support of the view that these monuments did not originally form part of a planned processional border to the Sacred Way but were placed there in a subsequent period, presumably in the Fifth or Fourth century. This point deserves stressing because it is often said that the approach to the Temple, with its avenue lined by statues of seated people and lions, forms a clear parallel to Egyptian practices.[4] Tuchelt argues that all monuments must have stood originally within the area of the sanctuary since Greek dedications are not usually placed outside temene and since the sculptures were found along the Sacred Way without bases and with no proper arrangement for them made on the terrain. This last point is not compelling: these seated figures often have a very shallow plinth which could not be lowered into a separate base, and they might easily have stood directly on the ground. This solution should at least be true for

[4] The very high total of ca. 60–70 statues which the early publications give for the Branchidai is based not on actual monuments but on calculations stemming from the erroneous assumption that the entire avenue was flanked by similar statues.

some of the comparable Archaic monuments, for instance, the Hagemo from Arkadia, whose name was even inscribed on the front of the plinth. On the other hand, most of the extant statues from the Sacred Way are not identified, and it is likely that the dedicator's name was engraved on a separate base. In support of Tuchelt's theory one may also add that a few figures have a roughly finished or hollow back, while others are completely carved in all details from all sides. This difference in finish should correspond to a difference in setting, which a uniform placement along the road would tend to deny.

Only one of the Didyma statues (B 271) retains its head, probably because it was supported by an extension of the backrest,[5] which is however invisible from the front. It is a typical East Greek male head, including the double layer of curls (the "wings") over the forehead so often found on the kouroi. Yet the rest of the figure, especially the curvilinear stylization of its garment, sets the statue apart from the other Branchidai. With these it shares only that often mentioned massiveness which relies heavily on contours to carry the impression of the human form. Another head, now in Florence, unfortunately extensively damaged and somewhat reworked, has been attributed to the female figure B 272, a theory which Tuchelt rejects because the statue is veiled while the head is not. Without stressing its attribution to a specific Didyma statue, I wonder whether the Florence head could be male rather than female since it seems to have the raised second layer of curls over the forehead which is usually associated with the kouroi. Even the peculiar raised "tresses" crossing the dome need not be an exclusively female ornament, especially if, as in the comparable kore head in Berlin, they are added bead-strings and not natural hair.[6]

In the Branchidai, garments are all-enveloping, with the exception of forearms and toes, which emerge from slightly flaring skirts. Men wear their mantles so that their right arm is usually free and a group of flat layered folds stretches from their left shoulder to their lap and in between the legs, where it terminates in a series of wide zigzags. These are quite linear, except in a few cases (Br. Mus. B 273 signed by the sculptor Eudemos; or B 279) which show some rippling and undercutting. Long diagonal lines cross from the right leg to this folded-over layer of the himation; they are treated strictly as pattern, though they may correspond to a natural tension-pull of a garment so draped. They provide the same contrast of diagonal and vertical accents, of rippled and smooth surfaces which we find in some of the veiled korai. Yet here this conflicting pattern is somewhat toned down by the surprising modeling of the diagonal folds; these are fewer and farther apart than in the korai and create an undulating surface rather than a flat one shallowly engraved.

This unusually plastic detail tends, however, to hamper comprehension of the human body underneath the garments. Try to correlate in your mind the lower contour of the figure and the emerging toes, or attempt to visualize the legs in relationship to the knees.

[5] Not all seats have backrests of equal height; in some statues the throne is level with the shoulders, in others it is lower, so that the figure's hair can be seen to reach down its back. In most cases the statue sits forward on its throne, and the distance between body and backrest is filled with a layer of stone which is meant to be purely neutral, a technical support rather than an actual cushion.

[6] It is admittedly surprising that all the male Branchidai should be beardless. This is apparent not only in the one statue which retains its head (B 271) but also in the headless figures which show no traces of beard over chest or neck. Yet the Branchidai were obviously not immature youths but rulers or noblemen of some stature in life. One must either admit that fashions were different in East Greece, so that a mature man could remain beardless, or that the headless statues wore short beards—in which case B 271, which retains its head, should be considered female. This second theory would therefore seem less likely.

It is immediately obvious how artificial and stylized the total conception is, despite the apparent plausibility of the arrangement. Even the heavy group of vertical folds, which suggest the gathering of the thin chiton in between the legs, and which emerge from under the layered end of the himation, result in a purely decorative effect and again bear almost no relationship to the position of feet and legs. On the contrary, this detail becomes quite convincing in statues where the lap also shows a slight indentation corresponding to the space between the knees, or when the vertical folds sink markedly down, so that the outlines of shins and calves emerge as if under transparent drapery.[7] This treatment is particularly emphatic in the female statues which are latest in date; but here too attempts to correlate legs and torso fail in the peculiarly amorphous area of the lap (see, e.g., B 280). The sculptors of these seated figures seem to have been primarily interested in effects of monumentality and richness, and only secondarily in the realistic rendering of a human body on a seat.

This richness is now almost entirely lost since we miss the painted details which simulated embroidered borders and elaborate furnishings. Engraved contours still suggest some of the edgings to the sleeves or the patterns on some throne cushions, but only close observation of the originals can reveal them. Certainly when newly erected the statues must have looked splendid, the dignity of their portly bodies set off by the decorated costumes and elaborate thrones. By and large, the thrones do not have the lion's paw legs of the Samian Phileia and of two of the Peloponnesian examples, but their shape seems to be a mixture of Assyrian prototypes and Greek ideas. Probably because of a difference in conception but also perhaps for practicality in carving, the thrones are not accompanied by footstools, as is the practice in Assyrian and Persian representations. For the Branchidai, the plinth under the seat has been extended forward and cut along the contour of skirt and feet, in an arc of a circle which in some of them projects considerably more than in others, according to the greater or lesser plasticity of the bodies.

Two chronological comments, in brief. Some statues display a random correlation between crinkly folds and their possible sources of origin. In the male chiton, the sleeve is often sewn rather than buttoned, yet small groups of thin lines suggest the gathering of cloth produced by individual fasteners. In addition, these folds appear not only over the shoulders, but also originating from the neckline, at a point where no reasonable explanation can be found for such bunching, which is therefore treated as pure pattern. I wonder whether this decorative use of an originally functional and explicatory detail should indicate for some statues a date lower than that traditionally suggested. Another useful dating criterion may perhaps be the position of the hands. The standard pattern (especially for male figures) is to have one hand fisted and held upright over one knee (with the result that this awkward projection has usually broken off), and the other hand flat over the other knee; women normally hold both hands flat. But in some statues the fingers barely reach the knees while in others the hands cup them in a more realistic rendering. It is, of course, impossible to tell whether realism was consciously sought, or even whether greater realism is necessarily the result of prolonged observation. But since in one of the latest statues in

[7] Note that this same manner of wearing chiton and himation appears in the standing draped males from East Greece. The Cape Phoneas man (Ch. 3, Bibl. for p. 76) looks like one of the Branchidai who has just risen from his seat, but because of the cloth adhering to his legs, the mass of folds in between manages to look more natural and successful in articulating the body.

the series, as shown by the drapery (B 280), the knees are cupped with both hands, one may assume that also B 275 (dated 570–560) and B 276 (dated 560–550) should not be too far removed in time, and that these date perhaps from ca. 540. Another possibility is that these last two statues, which also share the same pattern of the chiton folds and the decoration of the throne, may come from a set by the same artist, or at least by the same workshop.

Most of the other seated statues from Didyma, although not found along the Sacred Way, are in general similar to the Branchidai, and they clearly form part of the same sculptural environment. They were found scattered, two of them on the road to the Altar of Poseidon on Cape Monodendri. The first of these carried an inscription mentioning the dedication of several other statues by a certain Ermesianax, yet nothing else was found with the inscribed piece. One should assume that the offerings once stood together, so that one inscription accounted for all; we have therefore further proof that Archaic monuments at Didyma were moved from their original setting. The second statue, a woman, differs from the standard Branchidai in her heavy and undetailed central fold, which strongly resembles the Milesian examples. In general, the latest seated statues from Didyma, whether from the Sacred Way or from elsewhere, seem closer stylistically to the Milesian, presumably because their basic difference is one of chronology rather than of school.[8]

Miletos. Since Didyma was exclusively a sanctuary, there is no question as to the votive character of its monuments. The problem is more complex for the seated statues from Miletos since many of them were found re-used in a late Antique wall. We have, therefore, no positive information as to their original location though fragments of inscriptions to Artemis built into the same wall may suggest that the seated figures also came from a shrine of that goddess. For the three pieces in the Louvre, however, provenience from a cemetery is established.

The Milesian seated figures, of which Tuchelt lists 13, differ from the Branchidai in several respects. First of all, no seated males have as yet been found. This fact may suggest that although a local potentate may have considered it proper, or profitable, to set up his own image in an international sanctuary, he did not feel equally free to set it up in a local shrine (to a goddess?) or within his own town. Certainly the practice of erecting honorary statues of living persons is unknown throughout the Archaic period, and perhaps Milesians did not favor the seated type as a grave monument to a man. We shall see later what is known about funerary practices in Asia Minor.

Secondly, a distinctive technical difference is that all the Branchidai had their heads carved in one piece with the rest of the statue, while the Milesian figures often had theirs inserted separately. There are considerable differences in size, too. The Didyma statues are all life-size or over; the Milesians are smaller, and two are statuettes. One specific monument included two seated figures in one block, with their thrones individually detailed but carved together; it has been suggested that they may represent Leto and Artemis. The same type was perhaps present also at Didyma, where, however, only one member of the "pair" remains (K 56) and its sex is undetermined. By and large, the Milesian seats are less

[8] See, e.g., K 63, which recalls two statuettes from Miletos in having a very long chiton kolpos, reaching to the knees. On the basis of such stylistic details, it would seem almost as if Miletos' production started when the Didyma series ended. This of course is not a tenable theory and may be simply a coincidence.

elaborate and more uniform; several of them, including two of those in the Louvre (which according to their find spot should have served funerary purposes), have such a high plinth under the feet that it amounts to a stool, though it is left in rough shape; but the throne legs continue well beyond that level and must have been visible above ground.

Finally, in contrast to the certain variety in the Branchidai attire, the Milesian statues all tend to be dressed alike, with only two exceptions: the "pair" with joined thrones have no veils, and the two statuettes wear a simple chiton with very low kolpos and a veil. The other seated statues are so consistent in their costume that it has been suggested that they all reflect a specific prototype, presumably a cult image of Artemis. This basic attire, consisting of chiton, diagonal himation, and veil, has all the stylistic traits of Milesian korai. We find the same type of short mantle without border, whose folds tend to fall vertically after a brief initial diagonal course; it is pinned along the right arm and pulled over the left from behind, covering both breasts. We see the same rounded kolpos, which in most cases shows engraved folds contrasting in direction with those of the himation. The veil is also typically Milesian, in that it curves around the neck to form two "lappets" over the shoulders, visible from the front, before cascading straight down the back of the wearer. Yet chronological and stylistic differences can be detected within this apparent uniformity.

The hallmark of the group is the heavy bunching of the chiton skirt in between the legs of the seated women. It is not divided into many vertical folds, as in most of the Branchidai, but at first looks column-like in its undetailed appearance. Though isolated from the legs by means of two deep vertical grooves, such a central bundle is approximately level with the surface of the legs. Modeled tension folds, running obliquely over the shins from the outer edges of the skirt, recall the rippling surface of some male Branchidai; at the hem, the skirt flares slightly out in a bell-shaped contour also similar to the Didyma statues. The chiton kolpos under the himation is so low that no belt shows. Chronologically, the statues of this type should belong around 540.

In later examples, the central gather becomes a definite flat paryphe, as we have seen in standing korai. It is concave in surface, sinks considerably lower than the level of the legs, and is flanked by a few deep vertical ridges; this total group of folds may terminate at the hem in a shallow swallowtail pattern. Over the legs, linear catenaries take the place of the rippled oblique strokes,[9] and culminate at the ankles, where the skirt breaks over the feet, making the hem turn inward, rather than outward, in a reversal of the earlier motif. Similar changes occur in the upper part of the statues: the kolpos becomes higher, so that the belt shows underneath; the head is still veiled, but long curls appear, scattered over the breasts, as the head covering seems to be pushed farther and farther back. Finally, in what should be one of the latest examples, the vertical folds of the diagonal mantle become articulated on either side of a definite central pleat, so that the lower edge of the himation forms a swallowtail. This change reflects not so much a late date as the diffusion of motifs through the International Style, as well as influence from the Cyclades, around 530–520. The two

[9] The appearance of catenaries seems to suggest that, as for the rippling folds, East Greek sculpture was ahead of contemporary mainland production in concepts of modeling and transparency. Though such linear motifs remain rather calligraphic, they serve to emphasize the roundness of the forms beneath the drapery by cutting across them rather than by running along them, as more usual in the Archaic formal language. Cf. *Greek Sculpture*, 130–32 and 139–44.

statuettes with very low kolpos should instead continue the tradition one sees in the Erythrai kore, but at a much lower date, presumably at the turn of the century.

Of the remaining five seated statues from Asia Minor, the two from Cape Plaka fall easily into the Milesian sequence. The veiled figure from Myrina is still unpublished though on display in the Izmir Museum. The arrangement of her veil seems to connect her with Miletos, and perhaps the wider spacing of the vertical chiton (?) folds is conditioned by the soft medium, limestone. A very similar, fragmentary figure from Klazomenai, also in limestone, may come from a relief of the type called "Seated Cybele in a Naiskos." The limestone seated figure from Kyme should also portray the goddess since traces of a lion are visible in her lap; yet the statue was found in a cemetery. Her attire is much more difficult to explain aside from the veil and the chiton, since the catenaries across her lap cannot be organically integrated with the vertical folds falling over her shins. Perhaps the statuette should be visualized as wearing a mantle draped across her thighs, rather than tossed over her left shoulder in traditional fashion. In any case, the Cybele from Kyme seems different stylistically from all the other Asia Minor examples.

Samos. It is more difficult to assess the seated statues from Samos. This island, which has proved so rich in all other sculptural types, has preserved only five possible examples of the seated variety, one of which comes from the Geneleos group, that veritable sampler of Archaic types. The second is a fragmentary statuette of Cybele holding a lion in her lap. The third is a portion of a throne which is too small to allow speculation as to its occupant. The fourth is the controversial "Aiakes." Finally, the fragmentary upper torso of a bearded statue of enormous scale could be restored either standing or seated. Since the piece is approximately twice life-size, it may portray a divinity, whose identity remains uncertain; though dimensions alone would have made it an impressive monument, too little of it is preserved to permit surmise as to its total appearance. Note the horizontally striated hair, falling low over the back, and the peculiar outcurving contour of the beard in a profile view. Something in this statue reminded me forcefully of Assyrian sculpture when I first saw it in the Vathy Museum.

For the seated type in Samos we are therefore basically limited to the analysis of two monuments: the Phileia from the Geneleos group, and the Aiakes. The first fortunately belongs to an entire complex which can be assessed on the basis of various figures, as well as on epigraphical grounds. It was dedicated to Hera by the head of the family, a reclining statue which, despite some controversy, should definitely be identified as male. His name ended in [- - - -]arches and was probably preceded by a patronymic now missing.[10] Each of

[10] This is the position maintained in *Samos* XI. A recent study by G. Dunst (*AthMitt* 87 [1972] 132–35) has produced a new reading of the extant letters, by means of a squeeze. The [- - - -]arches is now read as [- - - -]ilarches and is therefore considered a title rather than a proper name. Dunst suggests that it should be integrated as *agelarches*, therefore "leader of a band" presumably of women or priestesses connected with the Heraion. Noting the better quality of the ductus in the inscription, as compared with the names written on each figure, he believes that this is exclusively the dedicatory inscription, not the identifying label for the reclining figure, which he would like to consider female. In my text I have shared B. Freyer-Schauenburg's opinion for the following reasons: 1) I don't see why [- - - -]ilarches should be integrated "ag*el*arches"; 2) I would find it very difficult to accept the reclining figure as female since in that case its pose would be unique; 3) a band of priestesses or women associated with the

the six figures forming the group was inscribed with a name. The seated matronly figure at the head of the row represented the mother of the family, and her name, Phileia, runs vertically down the left front leg of her throne; on the edge of her mantle the sculptor added, in two lines: Geneleos made us.

The seat is a throne comparable in general shape to the East Greek ones, but with legs ending in lion's paws. A sort of raised flat plinth under the figure's feet functioned as a stool since it projected over and beyond the cutting in the stepped base. Phileia's head, shoulders, and most of the torso are missing. She is wearing a large smooth himation, doubled and wrapped like a man's, so that its lower edge runs diagonally across her shins revealing part of the chiton's skirt—a typically Samian tunic, marked by thin engraved lines in its center portion over both feet, with a peculiar dip in between them. These fine central folds are flanked by smooth areas on either side, but a puzzling swelling of the surface on the left, close to the throne leg, suggests a further bunching of the garment, almost as if Phileia held her skirt to one side. This, however, is impossible since both hands rest in her lap. Her fisted right hand is held horizontally, rather than vertically like the hands of the Branchidai, so that its low projection has preserved it; her left hand lies flat, but the fingers barely reach the edge of the vertical drop and do not cup the knee. The total impression is cubic, but slight sinkings and swellings suggest the presence of the legs under the skirt, while wide deep-curving grooves mark the crossing of the mantle over the concave lap. Though her massiveness may recall the Branchidai, the treatment of her costume is typically Samian, and to my eyes the workmanship reveals more interest in bodily forms and less emphasis on stylized contours than the approximately contemporary figures from Didyma. The date, based on the style of the entire group, should be shortly after 560; the maker was a superior artist whose sculptures may have exercised considerable influence on later statuary.

The Aiakes was found built into a Byzantine wall near the Akropolis of ancient Samos, not far from where the palace of Polykrates might have stood. The left side of the throne carries a dedicatory inscription to Hera by Aiakes, son of Brychon, and we know that Polykrates' father was named Aiakes, though we do not know his grandfather's name.[11] The figure is impressive, somewhat over life-size and seated on a throne that has armrests supported by lions, an unusually detailed backrest, and painted ornament. There is almost no plinth except for a small ledge beneath the figure's feet, which was probably sunk into a base. The occupant of the throne, like the Branchidai, wears a long mantle folded over the left shoulder so that a zigzag edge falls between the legs; a thin chiton underneath clings to the ankles and gathers between them with many central folds. This heavy group of pleats recalls many of the Didyma examples, but in none of the male figures is so much of the skirt revealed by the climbing edge of the himation; in some of the female statues a comparable effect is obtained though usually with a different costume.[12] The whole lower

Heraion would probably consist of people more or less equal in age and rank; yet the matronly status explicit in Phileia, and the position of supremacy of the reclining personage, would set them off from the rest of the standing figures. I consider this hierarchical ranging far more appropriate for a family group.

[11] For Polykrates' genealogy, and for other possible dedications by his grandfather Brychon, see now G. Schmidt, *AthMitt* 87 (1972) 165–85, with an appendix on the Tyranny in Samos, and a genealogical chart on p. 166.

[12] See for instance K 58. The seated man in Istanbul who may represent a prophet, K 55, has a similar long group of folds, but the total costume is not comparable. Only the standing man from Cape Phoneas has a vaguely similar arrangement.

part of the Samian sculpture is articulated into three vertical masses, of which the central mass, though less protruding, is made more emphatic by its visual connection with the long folds of the himation coming from the left shoulder. The left hand cups one knee, the right hand was fisted and vertical, though now broken off. The entire right forearm must have lain on the armrest, an unusual pose for seated figures, at least to judge from the Asia Minor examples.

Despite the over-all massiveness of the enthroned Aiakes, the structure of the body comes through more forcefully than that of any of the Branchidai, yet there is no true articulation of the figure and no specific attention to anatomy, as comparison with Attic examples makes clear. Stylization, although not obvious, appears in a few details, such as the inconsistent behavior of the chiton, which seems at once both heavy and transparent, and the ornamental hem of the central folds with its unnatural loops. The asymmetrical rendering of the long strands on either side of the neck suggests that the head was slightly turned toward the left, a suggestion reinforced by other elements of the composition. However, this may not mean that the statue formed part of a group.

There are several puzzles. Not only is the text of the inscription open to different interpretations, but the letter forms seem considerably later than the statue itself, ca. 500. Here perhaps one could imagine that a painted dedication had in time become so faint that an engraved one was commissioned to replace it, but would a statue of such importance have been given such a temporary inscription to begin with? A second theory, that the original dedication was carved on the base and was transferred to the seat when the sculpture, for some unknown reason, became separated from its pedestal, seems contradicted by the well-known Samian practice of writing dedications directly on the sculptures themselves. But the main puzzle is whether the statue portrays the dedicant, Aiakes, or the recipient, the goddess Hera. The original publication favored this second interpretation, but the most recent discussions of the piece favor the first possibility. Neither the over life-size scale nor the elaborate throne are decisive proof of divinity since both attributes are found among the Branchidai. The draping of the mantle seems more specifically male though it can be found on female figures (*Samos* XI no. 13). The relative flatness of the chest suggests a male, but the point could be argued, especially in comparison with *Samos* XI no. 16, undoubtedly female. The argument that no other statue of an official would be known from Samos (and indeed from Asia Minor except for the Branchidai) can be countered on the strength of the fragmentary throne *Samos* XI no. 68. Since, however, nothing remains of its occupant, a divine one is as likely a candidate as a mortal. The lack of a head veil is perhaps more important, but we cannot be sure that the figure did not originally wear a high polos.

I am inclined to favor the Hera identification on two, or perhaps even three, counts: the presence of shoulder locks and of the lion supports for the throne, and maybe even form and content of the inscription. Though strands over the chest are seen on male figures, these, as I believe, usually represent Apollo or his youthful followers, or even other divine or heroic characters. They would be surprising in a mature mortal, even if the father of the local tyrant. The seated lions of the armrests are unusual, actually unparalleled. They would be appropriate for Hera, who can be associated with lions, as examples from Delos show. As for the dedicatory inscription, had the statue represented the dedicant, it would probably have spoken in the first person: "I am Aiakes," as Chares did at Didyma; it is also less likely that the dedication would have been re-inscribed at a later date, when both

Polykrates and his father had already disappeared from Samian politics. If instead this was a divine figure, it might have been considered important to keep its inscription legible, recording the selling of booty (or the exacting of tribute) in her honor.[13]

Admittedly, no argument is decisive; the inscription has been variously dated, and the arrangement of the himation is a strong point in favor of the Aiakes interpretation. The statue should have been made around 540 or shortly after. On the basis of comparison with the so-called Endoios Athena from the Athenian Akropolis, some authors have favored a lower chronology, ca. 525, a date which would almost certainly prevent connecting the Samian statue with Polykrates' father since the tyrant himself died in 521. Though neither point can be proven, and some authorities insist on disassociating the Aiakes of the inscription from Polykrates and his family, style would support the earlier dating. Similarity with the Branchidai is somewhat remote and best seen in the seated "prophet" in Istanbul, which is itself unusual. The catenaries of the transparent chiton over the Aiakes' legs find parallels among the more advanced Milesian seated ladies, but the relative prominence of the central folds recalls the earlier examples.

The Cyclades. Not many seated statues are preserved from the Cyclades, and the most impressive one, in Paros, has not been fully published since the addition of new fragments. The figure is over life-size and sits on a wide, elaborate throne with a footstool. The right forearm, now missing, was inserted separately and stretched forward, perhaps even upward; the left arm, broken off at the shoulder, seems to have been held away from the body. This animation of the upper torso, so different from earlier seated statues, is also reflected in the lower limbs: the left leg and foot are slightly forward, and the asymmetry of the skirt with wide paryphe is more pronounced than in either the Aiakes or the Phileia. The rich diagonal mantle, with abundant ripples over the crossband, must have partly concealed the excessive length of the thighs. Its tubular folds collapse doughily as they reach the seat, in an arrangement which forecasts the incipient Severe Style. The statue, probably Hera, must belong to the early Fifth century. Other seated statuettes from the island are as yet neither published nor displayed.

Delos has produced some statuettes of Hera (one with a lion), and a group of divinities, presumably from an Agora of the Gods near the area of the Hellenistic Dodekatheon, which include two seated statues (Hera and Zeus) and an Apollo Citharode, possibly seated. The Hera is the best preserved, though still very fragmentary. Her throne was built with separate armrests and parts, and the footstool was elaborate. Her very rich mantle, pinned over both shoulders with an overlap at the border, recalls kore Akr. 673. Unfortunately, all these statues are badly broken and too late in date to be truly representative of Cycladic seated types though their richness is distinctive.

[13] The booty or tribute mentioned in the inscription has been considered either a form of taxation on all goods entering the Samian harbor or an actual income from piracy, for which the Samians were notorious. Aiakes speaks of his "tenancy" (supervision), but it cannot be determined whether it was of a political or a religious nature, that is, limited to the sanctuary of Hera or to the entire government of the island, in a forecast of his son's tyranny. A new interpretation (published after the appearance of *Samos* XI) suggests that the inscription alludes to the establishment of the right of asylum, that it should be dated ca. 500–499, that it is later than the statue, and that the latter represents Aiakes. For all these points, and a thorough discussion of previous interpretations and positions, see G. Dunst, *AthMitt* 87 (1972) 116–21 no. VII pl. 50:3.

Magna Graecia. Of the Western colonies, Sicily has preserved a most unusual kourotrophos in limestone. It was found over a grandiose subterranean tomb in the cemetery of Megara Hyblaia, and the grave goods show that both burial and statue should be dated around the middle of the Sixth century. The figure is so different from any Greek work that it must represent indigenous art. Despite stumpy proportions, it is a most forceful conception: at her breast are two stiff hooded babies, arranged head to foot, whose toes she cradles tenderly in overly large hands. The continuous sweep of her mantle unites the total composition which the loss of her head renders almost spherical.

A limestone female torso from Monte Casale resembles high relief against a background that could be the elaborate backrest of a throne. The kore holds a bird against her chest with both hands, wears a smooth chiton, and is usually thought to represent Aphrodite though what seems a polos headdress is rather a shelf-like projection over her head, perhaps to prevent breakage.

Finally, a terracotta seated figure from Grammichele is large enough (96.8 cm.) to be included among the statues. She wears a crinkly chiton and a voluminous himation which lies across her lap but is draped from right to left as if it were a diagonal mantle. Though this particular statue was probably made after 480, it seems to reflect an earlier prototype, perhaps a cult statue of the late Sixth century.

In South Italy, another terracotta ranks among the statues: the seated Zeus/Poseidon from Paestum (90 cm.). The typically plastic treatment of the hair can be found also in some of the stone metopes from Foce del Sele, which betray a long tradition of clay modeling. The statue is typically Greek, even East Greek in clothing and appearance, yet it seems to have absorbed its share of local influence, perhaps coming from as far afield as Etruria. One more seated monument, the marble Goddess from Tarentum in Berlin, belongs to the Severe period and cannot be considered here.

Attica. The seated statues from Attica form a recognizable group of their own, with some imports which can be clearly distinguished from the local works.[14] The earliest examples (three) are funerary in nature and more typically local: but there are several seated statues from the Akropolis which were either votive offerings or cult images. One fragmentary sculpture of very large size, from the Attic deme of Ikaria, may portray the god Dionysos (Figs. 34–35). Two more examples, one probably female and large, one a small Demeter, come from the Agora.

Besides the three extant grave monuments, three or four more bases once supported similar seated figures. Out of these six or seven examples, four were certainly erected for men, as shown either by the statue or by the inscription; one, a statue in the National Museum, is presumably female. Since we now have several gravestones showing seated women, it is plausible to assume that the same subject was appropriate for freestanding sculpture over women's graves. Obviously this dignified type of monument was considered suitable for elderly people in general, and especially for heads of households, in a funerary extension of the same concept embodied in the Geneleos group.

[14] For instance, the torso of a seated man, probably Zeus, which looks Ionic and may have come to Athens as ship ballast, according to one theory: Nat. Mus. 3045: Figs. 32–33; G. Rodenwaldt *AthMitt* 46 (1921), 27–35. Its East Greek origin seems now confirmed by a good parallel in Samos (*Samos* XI no. 75, cf. p. 155 and n. 271).

The statues themselves are remarkable for their structural clarity and simplicity of forms. Folds are indicated basically by lines which cross the marble cube with little or no indication of layering or plasticity. That this is not the result of early date is shown by the chronological range of the three monuments. The earliest is the seated woman from the Dipylon, now in the National Museum. It has been dated as early as the end of the Seventh century, but another and more probable assessment suggests ca. 550 (?). The seated man in the Kerameikos Museum (Fig. 37) may belong around 530, and the so-called Dionysos (Figs. 38–39) from the Plateia Eleutherias should be later, around 520.[15]

This last statue deserves a few comments because the most complete publication considers it a divine image, yet recent excavations have shown that the piece was found near the Erian Gate, in a cemetery area. One of the main objections to a funerary identification has thus been removed. This is such an impressive sculpture that a divine identification comes spontaneously to mind. In addition, the camp stool on which the figure sits obviously recalls the similarly seated gods of the east Siphnian Frieze. Finally, the animal skin over the stool has been identified as a panther, therefore an attribute proper of Dionysos. Yet all these points can be countered. The impressiveness of the statue is certainly not greater than that of the Kroisos kouros, for instance, with which the "Dionysos" has been rightly compared, yet the latter was obviously erected for a mortal. The camp stools in the context of the Siphnian Frieze are understandable as hierarchical differentiation between the lesser Olympians and Father Zeus, who sits on an elaborate throne; but Dionysos alone should have rated a more luxurious seat. In addition, the Kerameikos man, unquestionably funerary, uses a similar stool. As for the panther skin, it may perhaps indicate that the deceased was a Dionysiac priest, rather than the divinity himself. Other objections can then be formulated. Granted that a krobylos or other forms of rolled hair would not leave traces over the figure's neck, a loose hairstyle would seem more appropriate for Dionysos at this time in the Sixth century, as shown by the statue from Ikaria (Fig. 35) and perhaps even a long beard. A god would probably also wear a chiton underneath the himation. But these are all speculative points.

To get an idea of the rich colors and the many patterns on the statue, one must look at the drawings in the official publication. Suffice it here to point out how deliberate the extension of the stool seat is, so that its vivid cover can contrast with the relative simplicity of the man's mantle. Note also how the garment has been toned down to allow the powerful body a greater share of attention. The cloth clings unnaturally to the legs, fully revealing the large calves and prominent knees; we almost have the impression that the grooves for the folds have been slashed through the flesh. The right leg is at a slight angle, diverging from the strictly vertical left shin. The pose is natural, but acts as a further reminder of the body under the mantle.

The Kerameikos man and the seated woman from the Dipylon are so similar to the "Dionysos" in basic conception that one wonders whether the same workshop, specializing in grave monuments, might not have produced all three through the years. The Kerameikos man is more block-like, less splendid, but here too paint played a great role in bringing out forms and details. He is entirely wrapped in his mantle, so that no flesh shows except

[15] This same style, translated into two-dimensional forms, could create the relief of the seated man from Velanideza, who looks like the "Dionysos" converted into a gravestone. Here, however, the folds have acquired vibrant, calligraphic lines which bespeak the manneristic approach of the late Archaic period. The Velanideza relief is discussed in Ch. 6.

for the feet, yet the clinging cloth models the pectorals and the genitals as it sinks over the lap. The woman's short himation is wrapped over an undergarment, and there are large smooth surfaces, but the technique for the folds over the left arm is the same, with no added volume. Her seat was carved separately.

Not far in conception from this funerary group are the three statues of the so-called scribes from the Akropolis. This name is based on the pose, which recalls Egyptian renderings, yet the figures do not squat but sit on straight-legged stools holding tablets on their laps. Of the three, the best preserved and most elaborate is Akr. 629 (Fig. 36), which has been connected with an Ionic capital and inscribed column. We know, therefore, that the statue represents Chairion and was set up to Athena by his son Alkimachos in fulfillment of a vow. Since this same Chairion is known from another inscription in which he identifies himself as a *tamias*, it is conceivable that the scribe pose symbolizes a treasurer of the goddess keeping his accounts.[16]

This is one of the few Archaic statues which can be fleshed out if its connection with the inscribed column is accepted. In fact, Chairion's tombstone was found at Eretria; this makes it probable that he was one of the Eupatrids who went to Euboea with Peisistrastos during his exile. It is therefore logical to suppose that Akr. 629 was dedicated on the citadel by the treasurer's son only after 539/8, at the end of the tyrant's second exile. The date may be further narrowed down by assuming that the period of truce between the Peisistratids and the Alkmaionids, when the latter were allowed to return to Athens, would have been a more likely time than war for such monuments to be erected. The span of time would then be from 527 to 514, and a date shortly after 520 is best in keeping with the style of the Akropolis statue.

In many ways the *tamias* resembles the "Dionysos," especially where the drapery, adhering tightly to his body, clearly but illogically outlines his entire left leg and arm. We find the same folds slashed as if through the flesh, the same technique of flat wide bands delimited by incision to indicate pleats, without any real differentiation in planes from one fold to the next. Only the area in front of each groove has been slightly recessed to suggest the prominence of the new layer. But this is a working pose, so there is much more movement in the human body: the torso leans forward and to his right; the arms are held at different levels, with elbows away from the body; the head was probably slightly turned. Worth mentioning is the fact that, despite its small size (61.5 cm.) the statue was made in three pieces; we do not usually find such major piecing in Attica.

The other two scribes, Akr. 144 and 146, are smaller and less detailed. They were probably patterned after Chairion's dedication, with progressive simplification of the seat, smaller size, and less piecing. Akr. 144 is as muscular as Chairion, but the different shape of his epigastric arch—less ogival, more expanded at the bottom—shows its later date, despite its lesser quality. The entire group, the scribes and the "Dionysos," should be compared with the draped youth Akr. 633, who is more thoroughly covered but makes equal use of his costume as a foil for his musculature.

Seven more seated statues are known from the Akropolis, plus three statuettes, and feet

[16] H. Cahn (*RA* [1973], 15 and n. 5) has raised the question whether the seated pose of the Akropolis statues should be compared to that of the *dokimastes* in Red Figure vases showing scenes of *dokimasia* (the appraisal of young men and their horses conditioning their admission into the state cavalry). In this case, Cahn suggested, some of the marble riders from the Akropolis could have belonged together with the "scribes" as part of a single monument.

from five more possible examples, all probably female. Of this group, the most interesting are Akr. 620, whom low kolpos and modeled folds reveal as a Cycladic import, and Akr. 625, the so-called Endoios' Athena. The name derives from the fact that the statue, obviously portraying the goddess because of her aegis, was not found in the Persian debris but had rolled down the north slope of the Akropolis, below the Erechtheion. Its extensive weathering indicates that it had stood outdoors for a long time, and it has therefore been thought likely that this is the sculpture mentioned by Pausanias (1.26.4) on his visit to the Akropolis. If this could be proved, we would know its sculptor, Endoios, who is sometimes identified as an Ionian, sometimes as an Athenian. Though the latter is probably the correct guess (cf. Paus. 1.26.4), the master is known to have worked extensively in Asia Minor. Certainly, as often mentioned, the Athena is heavily indebted to Ionic art yet her stylistic traits make me think more of East Greek art than of Cycladic, especially the way in which the long folds of the chiton are gathered in between the lower legs. The low kolpos of the crinkly chiton is found in some of the later Milesian statues, but of course also on the seated goddesses of the East Siphnian Frieze. The comparison with this latter monument has often been stressed, especially because of the lively pose of the Athena, with her right leg drawn back and her head forward, which suggests impending movement and lends the usually static, hieratic type a narrative quality. Since the goddess sits on a stool, she should be visualized as armed, in a war-like context; another suggestion would identify her with Athena Ergane, whose cult on the Akropolis is attested through Pausanias. She would then be spinning, an activity which the armrests of a throne would have made difficult.

Of the other seated statues from the citadel, one is somewhat puzzling. Reconstructed from two fragments (Akr. 158 and 4834), the statue must have had a separately worked seat, since the back of her skirt is as detailed as the front; yet it is unusual for a statue to sit so far forward that the back of the legs can be seen from the rear. Could the relatively small size of the piece (preserved H. 22.7 cm., from ankles to slightly above the knees) and the steep slope of the legs above the knee be reconciled with a figure on a swing? Two more fragmentary statues can be integrated with a left hand pulling the skirt aside, in a mannered gesture made incongruous by the seated pose.

None of these Akropolis statues is datable before ca. 530, with the possible exception of two statuettes, which may however be simplified because of their small size, and may thus look earlier than they are. Aside from the treasurers, they are all female, and many may therefore be representations of Athena since in most cases they are too fragmentary to allow us to verify the presence of an aegis or other identifying attributes.[17] On the basis of the Didyma evidence, the possibility of a female commemorative statue on the Akropolis cannot be rejected out of hand, but it would certainly be unusual, considering the relatively minor status of women away from East Greece. That they were honored as mothers and wives is shown by the funerary monuments. Even these, however, do not seem to begin before the advanced Sixth century, and presumably around 550 BC, if the lower chronology for the Dipylon woman be accepted. All in all, Attica seems to have been somewhat slow in accepting the seated type in stone though obviously some of its cult

[17] Herdejürgen (p. 21) has suggested that some Akropolis statues (inv. nos. 3514 and 3721, *AMA* nos. 65 and 66 respectively) and the two seated figures from the Agora (*Agora* XI nos. 83 and 84) may ultimately derive from the Milesian Artemis type. Akr. 655 may be Cybele.

images in wood may have been enthroned. Yet Athena, as a goddess of action, was probably more often represented standing, as suggested by the fact that the sacred xoanon in the Erechtheion could be dressed with a woven peplos at the Panathenaic festival. It seems therefore reasonable to assume that the seated type was the latest in reaching Athens from the East, and that it never achieved in Attica the popularity obtained by the kouros and kore types. On the other hand, at least two seated figures from the Akropolis are so late as to be manneristic.

RECLINING FIGURES

Eastern in origin, and equally unpopular for marble sculpture in Greece proper, is the type of the reclining man. All the extant examples in stone come from Asia Minor or Samos though terracotta and bronze statuettes are known from elsewhere, and the subject of the reclining banqueter appears in relief sculpture and most often on vases. In marble, the most prominent figure is the dedicant of the group made by Geneleos in Samos. Initially, and even recently, identified as a woman, it should definitely be recognized as male, not only because of the ending of the name, [- - - -]arches but because the pose is very unusual for women, who appear reclining only in the minor arts. All other known stone sculptures in this pose are later than the [- - - -]arches, and may easily have been influenced by this most important Samian monument.

Two schemata were employed during the Archaic period for this particular type: the first shows the figure with both knees together, leaning on his side, and it seems to be the pattern preferred in the East Greek area; the second may have originated in mainland Greece or in the Western colonies but is certainly predominant in Magna Graecian works, all belonging to the minor arts. In this type the banqueter raises his right knee, while the left leg remains stretched out, so that the garment, when present, forms a sort of tent between the two.

Only a total of eight possible statues can be attributed to this type. Besides the [- - - -]arches, Samos has preserved two fragments of a reclining youth with long locks over his chest and a vessel in his hand. Another fragment may come from the cushion of a similar monument. Two more pieces, from Didyma, are now lost, and one was a statuette. The last three pieces, in Berlin, come from Myus and are also relatively small; one of the "banqueters" has a long inscription engraved on his chest identifying him as Hermonax, who, together with [- - - -]eunon, set up the offerings as tithe to Apollo. The statuette was therefore part of a more elaborate dedication comprising several pieces. Several other statuettes, all in limestone, were found in Lindos and are so closely related to Cypriot works that they need not be considered here, but they serve to confirm the popularity of the type in the Eastern sphere.

Some of the small bronzes and terracottas represent satyrs or Herakles; the monumental examples, at least in two cases, stood for men, and it is reasonable to assume that so did the others. The long-haired fragmentary figure from Samos may have portrayed a youth or a youthful hero. The presence of drinking vessels in the left hand has suggested that they may be banqueters, and the type is obviously similar to the reclining figures of the so-called Funerary Banquet reliefs (*Totenmahl*). Whether the stone sculptures in the round may have at times served also a funerary purpose is now no longer known. Certainly the extant examples seem exclusively votive and as appropriate for Hera as for Apollo. It is logical to assume that the reclining pose for a man was as much of a status symbol as that of the enthroned matron. The [- - - -]arches is a typical example of how important and opulent such a figure could look. Sculpturally, the piece is especially interesting for the way in which the garment collapses over the plinth, while at the same time following and emphasizing the contour of the prominent abdomen. The thin chiton which covers the upper part of the body is offset by the heavy mantle over the legs, whose folds recall the earliest statue from the Branchidai (B 271). The object which [- - - -]arches holds against his full, heavy chest had been thought to be a bird; it is too badly broken to be definitely identified, but it could be a plastic rhyton, as appropriate for a man.

EQUESTRIAN FIGURES

One more group of statues can also, strictly speaking, be considered as seated: the riders. It has been said that this monumental type is an Attic invention, and certainly most of the examples come from Athens and environs; but a few have been found elsewhere though the pattern of distribution is as strictly limited as that of the reclining figures. Those on Delos must have been votive offerings: A 4098 and A 4099 preserve the men still on their mounts, the first wearing a smooth costume with thin belt and neck border, the second too fragmentary to tell. A similarly draped rider (A 4102) is without his horse, though it could probably be the large animal whose neck alone remains (A 4100). Another horse's head, A 4101, had an inserted ear and a top knot which recalls Persian horses. A life-size archaic horse, from Paros, does not seem to have carried a rider. Gela in Sicily is well known for its central akroteria in the shape of riders, with the horse's body forming the *kalypter hegemon*, the large rounded tile covering the ridge pole, but these count as architectural sculpture. Equally architectural seem two naked, fragmentary horsemen from the cemetery of Megara Hyblaia. They were carved out of a single block of limestone and rode what amount to half horses, which therefore must have stood against a background, perhaps of a funerary naiskos. But a freestanding equestrian statue, especially in marble, presents the problem of supporting considerable weight (not only the rider's but the horse's body as well) on four thin legs; the solution of placing a large strut under the animal's belly is functional but hardly realistic, and partly spoils the aesthetics of the composition. It was perhaps this technical difficulty which so severely limited the diffusion of the type. Certainly East Greece, steeped in the Oriental emphasis on the heroic rider, could hardly have failed to respond to its appeal, had the feat seemed feasible. Bronze and terracotta statuettes of horse and rider are certainly widely diffused. A particularly monumental group, in terracotta, including a dog running alongside the horse, comes from a grave in Sicily and dates from ca. 500.

The Attic examples are both votive and funerary. The latter are limited to a large horse with its rider from Vari and the smaller but more complete statue from the Kerameikos (Figs. 40–41), to which an inscribed base has now been attributed. From this we learn that the monument was erected for Xenophantos and was made by Aristokles. The man, now headless, is enveloped in a Thracian cloak and held reins and goad (?) added in metal. A small fragment of his horse's mane shows flame-like locks carved in relief against a smooth background, and a comparable rendering from the Akropolis belongs with the famous Rampin Horseman group. A small horseman monument has also been suggested for the Lamptrai capital, on the basis of the long rectangular cutting on its top surface, and a bigger equestrian statue is postulated for a large inscribed base in the Kerameikos, one of the few monuments erected by children for a parent.

All other riders come from the Akropolis.[18] Aside from several fragments of legs and arms which may belong to horsemen, eight equestrian statues have been found more or less complete; and one head which, because of its asymmetry and neck twist, has been tentatively identified as a horseman's (Akr. 663).[19] Among the riders, the bearded Akr. 621 is particularly interesting since the rough finish of his hair over dome and nape has suggested that he once wore a helmet. Not all roughly finished heads were thus covered, but in this case confirmation comes from other attributed fragments, one of which is a rider's leg wearing a greave, thus proving that the man wore armor. To my knowledge, this is the only monumental example of a mounted warrior. His hair is long, at a date close to the end of the Sixth century, if not later; therefore the rider may have represented a mythological character.

Other equestrian statues from the Akropolis might have portrayed local notables, and not all of them need necessarily be votive, since Peisistratos supposedly had his lodgings on the citadel.[20] In particular, it has been suggested that the Rampin Horseman with his companion piece may be the sons of the tyrant, yet this explanation is not entirely convincing. Nudity, especially at an early stage, should still be symbolic, and the beard and hairstyle of the Rampin head are remarkably complex for the place and period. In its treatment, his hair is comparable to the beard of the seated Zeus from the Introduction Pediment. Note in particular the way in which extra strands are added half way down the longer locks, to increase the width of the hair mass at its base. Perhaps this similarity implies only that early Attic sculptors were still dependent on carving techniques in poros; on the other hand, the connection may be more telling. The wreath on the Rampin head has been considered a sign of victory at the Nemean or Isthmian games, thus negating identification of the pair as the Dioskouroi. But might not a wreath be simply a festive symbol like that (of myrtle?) worn by the Dioskouroi of Exekias' Vatican amphora? The choice of oak might simply be meant to stress their connection with Zeus, whose sacred tree the oak was. The highly stylized leaves have also been called celery; perhaps no specific kind is represented but simply leaves—a wreath. In more or less contemporary sculpture, the Dioskouroi appear mounted in the metope from the Sikyonian Treasury at Delphi, and they are perhaps to be identified also in the above-mentioned limestone group from Megara Hyblaia because of the funerary context. In Magna Graecia, in fact, the Dioskouroi had a longstanding connection with immortality and the afterlife. Suggestive of the

[18] A small naked torso found in a well on the North slope of the Akropolis can still be considered from the citadel (O. Broneer, *Hesperia* 7 [1938] 246 fig. 74).

[19] As Payne has pointed out, "the turn of the head is probably the result of an attempt to harmonize the two principal views of the statue" (p. 7). Although a man's main aspect is frontal, a horse appears to its fullest extent from the side. Inscriptions on extant bases show that equestrian monuments were set up with narrow side forward, but presumably the viewer was expected to see the long side also, in order to gain complete comprehension of the composition. When the rider's head is turned slightly to one side, he is clearly visible from whatever position the viewer chooses.

[20] The theory that Peisistratos lived on the Athenian Akropolis is often mentioned but without real documentation. *Contra* see most recently Boersma, 14–15.

Dioskouroi is the beard of the Rampin Horseman, which is relatively short and adheres to the cheeks as one would expect in a young man. Though the divine twins are mostly shown smooth-faced, Black Figure vases often represent them with a beard.

There can be no question that the Rampin Horseman is early. Payne has perceptively described the peculiarly receding planes of the face and the summarily treated back, but a rear view of the rider can still come as a surprise, especially the flat carving of the shoulder blades and the width of the shoulders compared to the narrow waist. The abdominal partitions are enclosed in a "mandorla," and there are four horizontal divisions above the navel, as in the Moschophoros. Though by a different hand, the two masterpieces should be approximately contemporary, shortly before 550. Another equally early example of the type may be the head Akr. 617, which, because of the peculiar treatment of the left cheek, suggests to me the asymmetrical posture of a rider.

It has been suggested that the lean, marvelously abstract marble dog from the Akropolis (Akr. 143) is by the same man who made the rider. Though little similarity can be pointed out between a dog and a naked man, or even his horse, it may seem more than a coincidence that there were two such hounds (Akr. 550), as there were two horsemen. It is tempting to associate the four to form a single group: two young men, returning perhaps from the hunt (the Dioskouroi after the Kalydonian boar hunt?) accompanied by their dogs, almost like the Sicilian terracotta in Boston or the Vatican Amphora. Yet the find spot of the riders seems to be different from that of the hounds, which are usually attributed to the Brauronion on the Akropolis and dated much later than the horsemen, ca. 520. However, at least one author would date the dogs no later than 540, and some recent theories have even cast doubt on the early date of this Artemis sanctuary. After the Persian destruction, debris might have been moved around at random, and there is no absolute certainty as to the location of all Akropolis finds. The dogs were supposedly found south of the Parthenon, the horsemen west of the Erechtheion, but the Rampin head came to light earlier than the body (1877, as against 1886 for the torso), and went to France as part of the Rampin collection; it was donated to the Louvre in 1896.

Of the other horsemen, the best known is perhaps the so-called Persian rider, Akr. 606, though his colorful costume is more probably Thraco-Scythian. A suggestion that the horseman might have been a member of the Scythian police force is invalidated by the fact that these foreign policemen were not called in before the Fifth century. Nonetheless, the presence of a Scythian contingent of archers in Athens, as addition to the regular army, has been postulated on the basis of their frequent representation on Attic vases between 530 and 510. Archers fought on foot, but the Akropolis rider could be one of the Scythian officers, using the horse and costume as insignia of his rank. Also a Thracian cannot be excluded. Thracian connections were promoted by the elder Miltiades and his family, as well as by the Athenian colonization of the Thracian Chersonesos, and the Thracian manner of dress may have been fashionable. Even if this specific rider is no longer identifiable, it is important to note that he should represent a contemporary, not a mythological character. Note also his extensive metal additions: his footwear, the harness, and, surprisingly, the entire forelock of the horse, which was made of braided bronze wire.

Other horsemen seem to have been naked, and some are so small as to rank almost as statuettes. Among them the most intriguing is the certainly legendary character who rides a Hippalektryon. This monster, half horse and half cock, is perhaps the only *Mischwesen* not to have come from the Orient, if, as vase painting seems to show, it really is an Attic invention which spread to Boeotia and Etruria with the diffusion of Athenian pottery. This is the only stone example; though the rider is unprepossessing, at least in his present mutilated state, he could perhaps be identified with Poseidon, since no other legend is known and at least three vases show the sea-god on the monster, holding a trident and accompanied by dolphins. In the line of mythological riders, Syracuse has provided another unique monument, a terracotta gorgon riding a horse which seems to be springing from the ground (H. 19.8 cm.).

SUMMARY

The seated statues, both male and female, seem to me to have originated in Asia Minor, where they enjoyed a long tradition, both as funerary and as votive monuments. Yet the votive purpose may have been limited to statues of important people set up within important sanctuaries; the practice is unknown from Greece proper, where all available examples may have had heroizing overtones. Samos, usually so fruitful, has little to offer, but seems to fit within the Asia Minor picture. The evidence from the Cyclades, at present, points to seated deities, but not enough is known. The Cretan seated figures, probably also divine and often connected with architecture, do not develop in any traceable form and lead nowhere. The Peloponnesos, as usual, offers meager evidence, ambiguous in nature. Attica starts with funerary examples, then continues with votives on the Akropolis, during the last third of the Sixth century, probably setting up only mythological or divine figures.

The reclining type in the round originates later, presumably around 560, and in Samos, whence it spreads moderately, and only in East Greek territory. Figurines in this pose are more diffused, and a second type may have also come from the mainland, but the very absence of large scale stone sculpture in this second schema confirms once again the vast difference in repertoire between major and minor arts.

Conversely, the monumental horseman type may be a mainland invention which did not spread to East Greece, though Western examples look Ionic. Again we find the type used as funerary and votive, with heroic character, but one may even suspect that a few examples on the Akropolis had honorary meaning comparable to the seated-ruler statue in the East, since they seem to portray contemporary individuals. The horsemen from Delos may be particularly significant in this respect.

BIBLIOGRAPHY 5

FOR PAGE 121

There is no recent comprehensive work on Archaic seated figures, though a Ph.D. Diss. on this topic is being written for the University of California at Los Angeles by Ellen Lattimore Alford. The most recent article is that by Kranz, but it deals only with the early Archaic monuments. For the statement that the seated type was invented for figurines, see his p. 20. For the influence of the Mycenaean past and general conclusions on the establishment of types, see his pp. 51–55. The same suggestion, though on different topics, has been made recently by H. A. Thompson in several lectures, including one which he delivered at the R. S. Young Memorial Symposium in Philadelphia on May 3, 1975: see *Archaeology* 28 (1975) 201.

FOR PAGE 122

For a study of seat types, see Kyrieleis.

Gortyna seated figure: *Gortina*, 156 no. 7 pls. 2–3; Davaras, 52 no. 7 figs. 23–24; Kranz, 20–22 pls. 10–11.

Prinias seated figures: L. Pernier, *ASAtene* 1 (1914) 54–63, 86–91; *id.*, *AJA* 38 (1934) 171–77 pl. 18:1. For a different architectural reconstruction, see C. Gottlieb, *AJA* 57 (1953) 106–7. See also Kranz, 22 pl. 11:2; Davaras, 55 nos. 25–26.

For other seated statues from Crete, and especially the torso from Astritsi, see Davaras, figs. 1–7, 25, and passim; Kranz, 20 n. 70.

Branchidai influenced by Doric style: Tuchelt, 173 and 216.

Geometric figurines type 1: Kranz, 15 and 44.

FOR PAGE 123

Haghiorghitica statue: *BCH* 14 (1890) 382–84; additional bibliography in Davaras, 14 no. 28; Kranz, 23 pl. 13, and here, p. 123 n. 1. The suggestion of earrings and necklace appears in Papaspyridi, 21–22, but is not repeated in Karouzou, 2–3, though the statue is still described as female.

Oriental influence in mantle: Cf. relief from Sakçegözü, *KAnat*, fig. 29; cf. also Tuchelt, 173. Assyrian genii: Strommenger & Hirmer, pls. 191–93. Some Assyrian statuettes found on Samos show similar mantles with fringes: Cf. J. Börker-Klähn, *BaghdMitt* 6 (1973) 41–64, especially drawing (fig. 2 on p. 45). The Oriental and Egyptian bronzes from Samos are published by U. Jantzen, *Samos* VIII (1972).

Hera from Olympia: See supra, pp. 90 and 115. For its finding place, see Mallwitz, 146–47; for the fragment of feathers/drapery, *ibid.*, 148 fig. 118. The date of the Hera is given as 590–580, e.g., in *Agora* XI, 12. For ca. 560, and the theory that the head may have come from a pediment, see U. Jantzen, *EAA* s.v. *Olimpia*, p. 643. For the interpretation of the polos as a leaf crown, see Ch. Kardara, *AJA* 64 (1960) 345 pl. 99.

Hagemo from Asea: Kranz, 24–25 n. 86 pl. 14; *Local Scripts*, 209–10, no. 6. For the shape of the plinth, Jacob-Felsch, 11 n. 38.

Statue in Sparta: Kranz, 27 pl. 17; for the type of seat, Kyrieleis, 181–86.

London B 276: Tuchelt K 52, pls. 49–50; *KAnat*, fig. 191.

FOR PAGE 125

Statuette in Delos: A 3991; Kranz, 24 pl. 16:1. The mid 7th century date is still given in the museum label; Kranz dates it to the second quarter of the 6th century. For the identification as Hera, see *BCH* 73 (1949) 125–32. For other seated statues holding their skirt see here, p. 138.

Reliefs from the islands with seated figures (partial list): I. A. Papapostolou, *Deltion* 21:1 (1966) 112 n. 63; cf. also *Deltion* 16 (1960) 245 pl. 215.

For a list of wooden seated cult statues: Tuchelt, 218–19, n. 127.

Statuettes from the Heraion in Delos: P. Levêque, *BCH* 73 (1949) 125–32; Herdejürgen, 20–21.

Didyma seated statues: Tuchelt K 43–65.

Miletos: Tuchelt L 91–92, 94–98, 101, 112 (double)–115. From elsewhere in Asia Minor, Tuchelt L 93–93bis, 99–100; statuette from Kyme, Tuchelt, 89; see here, p. 131.

Didyma statues from Sacred Way. K 43, 45–49, 51–55, 57–60, 63, 65.

On the name of Branchidai: Tuchelt, 194 and n. 17a.

FOR PAGE 126

Chares, Br. Mus. B 278: Tuchelt K 47, pls. 43–46.

"Prophet" in Istanbul (no. 1945): Tuchelt K 55 pls. 53–55 and pp. 215–16; see also H. Möbius, *AntP* 2 (1963) 23–29.

Female figures as priestesses: Tuchelt, 219.

B 272: Tuchelt K 45, pl. 42.

B 274: Tuchelt K 51, pl. 49:1.

Chronology: Tuchelt, 158–59; for the objection to the upper limit, see H. P. Laubscher, *Gnomon* 46 (1974) 500–6. For a seated statue from Miletos found in 1967 and dated after 480, see infra, Ch. 11 n. 16.

Original location of the Branchidai: Tuchelt, 212–14.

FOR PAGE 127

B 271: Tuchelt K 43 pls. 40–41; *KAnat*, figs. 187–88 (*not* 188–89).

Head in Florence: C. Laviosa, *ArchCl* 16 (1964) 13–25 pls. 1–8.

Head in Berlin: Laviosa, *op. cit.*, pl. 7:2; Blümel, no. 57 figs. 156–58; Tuchelt, L 43; *Korai* no. 94 figs. 291–92.

B 273: Tuchelt K 46, pl. 43:1.

B 279: Tuchelt K 59, pl. 57:2.

FOR PAGE 128

B 280: Tuchelt K 60, pls. 59–60, 62.

For some of the decorated borders, see Tuchelt, pl. 45 and figs. 14 (p. 77) and 17 (p. 89).

On the thrones, Tuchelt, 71–72; the earliest statue, K 43 = B 271, is closest to Assyrian works of the 8th–7th centuries. See also Kyrieleis, 163–64.

For examples of crinkly folds from neckline, see B 276 = K 52, or B 275 = K 48, pl. 47:1; *KAnat*, fig. 190.

FOR PAGE 129

Statues from road to Cape Monodendri: Tuchelt K 50 (now lost) and K 61, pls. 59–62.

Three seated figures in the Louvre: Tuchelt L 94–96, pls. 85–86.

Two figures in one block: Berlin no. 1623; Tuchelt L 112; for a possible identification, see Th. Hadzisteliou-Price, *JHS* 91 (1971) 48–69.

Two statuettes: Tuchelt L 114–115; Blümel nos. 55–56 figs. 152–55.

FOR PAGE 130

Prototype in a cult image: Herdejürgen, 17; Tuchelt, 218.

For chronological discussion of the costume, see Herdejürgen, 18; N. Himmelmann-Wildschütz, *IstMitt* 15 (1965) 24–42; his pls. 2–24 illustrate many of the seated statues, especially pls. 2, 6–8, 10; see also Blümel nos. 50–54.

One of latest examples: Louvre Ma 2787; Tuchelt L 95, pls. 85–86; *IstMitt* 15 (1965) 24 pl. 10.

FOR PAGE 131

Statues from Cape Plaka: Tuchelt L 99–100, pls. 85–86.

Veiled figure from Myrina: Tuchelt L 93bis (unpublished).

Figure from Klazomenai: Tuchelt L 93, pl. 84.

Seated Cybele from Kyme: Collignon, 65–66; Mendel, 2 no. 522.

Samian statuette of Cybele: *Samos* XI no. 69.

Fragment of throne: *Samos* XI no. 68.

Upper torso of bearded statue: *Samos* XI no. 79.

Geneleos group: Samos XI nos. 58–63 and esp. pp. 123–30; Phileia is no. 58, [----]arches is no. 63.

FOR PAGE 132

Aiakes: *Samos* XI no. 67; for the detail of the hem see *IstMitt* 15 (1965) pl. 5:1, and pl. 4:2 for the damaged right side of the statue. On the inscription, besides the discussion in *Samos* XI, 143–44, and by G. Dunst, *AthMitt* 87 (1972) 116–21, see also R. Meiggs and D. Lewis, *Greek Historical Inscriptions* (1969) 30–31 no. 16; see also here, p. 134 n. 13.

FOR PAGE 133

Identification as Hera: *AltSt* 2 (1934) 40–41; 5 (1961) 91.

Identification as Aiakes: *Samos* XI, especially p. 145; also G. Dunst, *loc. cit.*

Lions appropriate to Hera: P. Levêque, *BCH* 73 (1949) 125–32. A possible lion armrest could be connected with Hagemo (?).

FOR PAGE 134

For the claim that Aiakes of the statue is not connected with the family of Polykrates, see, e.g., Meiggs and Lewis, *loc. cit.*

Seated statue in Paros: Berger, 44 and 172 n. 95 figs. 47–48; Herdejürgen, 20 n. 74, and 60–61; Hiller, 75 n. 28 no. 7.

Group of divinities from Dodekatheon at Delos: J. Marcadé, *BCH* 74 (1950) 181–215; *GdD*, 43 n. 1 for further bibliography.

FOR PAGE 135

Kourotrophos from Megara Hyblaia: Langlotz, pl. 17; *NSc* 1954, 99–104.

Limestone torso from Monte Casale: Langlotz, pl. 28.

Terracotta from Grammichele: Langlotz, pl. 39.

Seated Zeus/Poseidon from Paestum: Langlotz, color pls. III–IV; *BdA* 40 (1955) 193–202. For the metopes from Foce del Sele, see infra, Ch. 8.

Goddess from Tarentum in Berlin: See infra, Ch. 11.

Dionysos from the deme of Ikaria: C. D. Buck, *AJA* 5 (1889) 463–67 fig. 44; H. Möbius, *AthMitt* 41 (1916) pl. 11; *AA* 1943, 290; Herdejürgen, 64 n. 396; Karouzou, 29 (Nat. Mus. 3897).

Seated figures from the Agora: *Agora* XI nos. 83–84.

Bases for seated funerary statues: "Gravestones," 127 no. 2 and 128 fig. 9; no. 2 is the famous Hockey-Players base, Nat. Mus. 3477.

Additional bases: "Grabmalbasen," 139 no. 9, probably for the seated Kerameikos man; *ibid.*, 140 no. 10, and 141 no. 11, for Anaxilas of Naxos.

FOR PAGE 136

Seated woman from Dipylon, Nat. Mus. 7: H. Möbius, *AthMitt* 41 (1916) 163; Kranz, 25–26 pl. 15; "Gravestones," 125; *Kerameikos* 6:2, 411–12. For a date at the end of the 7th century, Karouzou, 3. The ca. 550 date is given by Jeffery.

Seated Kerameikos man: "Grabmalbasen," 139 no. 9; "Gravestones," 125 no. 2; *AntP* 6 (1967) 13 figs. 4–5.

"Dionysos" from Plateia Eleutherias, Nat. Mus. 3711: "Gravestones," 133 no. [1]; W.-H. Schuchhardt, *AntP* 6 (1967) 7–20. Recent excavations and identification of cemeterial area: *AAA* 2 (1969) 258 and plan; "Stelen," 38 n. 37; Kurtz and Boardman, 89.

FOR PAGE 137

Akropolis "scribe," Akr. 629: Payne, 47 pl. 118; *AMA* no. 309; A. Raubitschek, *BSA* 40 (1943) 17–18 pl. 7:1–3 and fig. 4 on p. 37; Brouskari, 64. The various exiles of Peisistratos and the Alkmaionids have been most recently discussed by Kleine.

Scribes Akr. 144 and 146: *AMA* nos. 310–11; Payne, pl. 118.

FOR PAGE 138

Akr. 620: Payne, 47 pl. 117; *AMA* no. 59; Brouskari, 47: "not from the Persian destruction level, probably a cult statue which survived the Persian destruction." However, on the difficulty of determining levels on the Akropolis, see now Bundgaard.

Akr. 625, "Endoios' Athena" : Payne, 46 pl. 116; *AMA* no. 60; Brouskari, 71–72. That the statue may have originally belonged with the Persian debris is suggested by Bundgaard, 16. On Endoios, see infra, Ch. 10. For a figure of the Siphnian Frieze in comparable pose, see, e.g., Lullies & Hirmer, pl. 48 top, both the Ares and the Zeus; cf. also Herdejürgen, 21. For the Athena Ergane identification, see S. Stucchi, *RömMitt* 63 (1956) 122–28.

Akr. 158 + 4834: *AMA* no. 63.

Fragmentary statues pulling skirt aside: 1) Akr. 618: Payne, pl. 117; *AMA* no. 61; Deyhle, 34; Brouskari, 49–50. The statue resembles the seated woman in the relief Nat. Mus. 36 (*AGA* fig. 174, for which see infra, Ch. 11. 2) Inv. no. 3721: *AMA* no. 66.

Simplified statuettes: 1) Akr. 655: Payne, pl. 125; *AMA* no. 57; Brouskari, 109 (Cybele ?); 2) Akr. 169: *AMA* no. 58.

FOR PAGE 139

On reclining figures, see the book (with catalogue) by B. Fehr, *Orientalische und griechische Gelage* (1971), which includes statuettes; see esp. pp. 107–27 and Catalogue, pp. 176–83.

For examples of the second schema, see, e.g., Langlotz, *Magna Graecia*, pl. 23 (TC from Tarentum).

Samian reclining youth: *Samos* XI no. 70.

Second Samian fragment: *Samos* XI no. 71.

Didyma reclining figures: Tuchelt, K 34–35.

Reclining figures from Myus in Berlin: Tuchelt, L 39–40 and 73; Blümel, nos. 66–68 figs. 212–16; Hermonax is no. 66.

On the funerary banquet reliefs, besides the book by Fehr, see J. M. Dentzer, *RA* 1969, 195–214, and R. N. Thönges-Stringaris, *AthMitt* 80 (1965) 1–99.

FOR PAGE 140

There is no comprehensive work on Archaic rider statues. For the theory of Attic invention, see H. von Roques de Maumont, *Antike Reiterstandbilder* (1958) 7; his pp. 7–17 cover the Archaic period.

Riders from Delos: *GdD*, 45. I was able to see the statues in November 1974. I am not aware of any publication for the horse in Paros.

Akroteria from Gela: See infra, Ch. 7, pp. 218, 223.

Megara Hyblaia horsemen: *NSc* 1954, 109–10 figs. 33–34.

Terracotta group from Sicilian grave, now in Boston: C. C. Vermeule, *AntP* 8 (1968) 7–11.

Horseman from Vari: "Gravestones," 136 no. 1, Nat. Mus. 70; *Aristodikos*, 64, A 21. N. Yalouris has kindly informed me that a new piece has recently been joined.

Kerameikos rider: "Gravestones," 125 no. 1; "Grabmalbasen," 136–39, no. 8; "Stelen," 29 and pl. 11:2.

FOR PAGE 141

Lamptrai capital: "Gravestones," 138 no. 1; *AGA* no. 20 figs. 66–69. See also infra, Ch. 6, pp. 167, 181.

Large base in the Kerameikos: "Gravestones," 122 no. 14; *Aristodikos*, 66, B 5.

All the Akropolis fragments of horsemen and horses: *AMA* nos. 312–21.

Akr. 663: Payne, 46 pl. 100; *AMA* no. 322; *Kouroi* no. 139 figs. 402–3; Brouskari, 101–2.

Akr. 621: Payne, 46 n. 3 pl. 103; *AMA* no. 315; Brouskari, 96.

Rampin Horseman, Akr. 590 + Head Rampin in the Louvre: Payne, 6–9 pl. 11; *AMA* no. 312; Brouskari, 55–56. H. von Roques de Maumont (supra, bibl. for p. 140) gives a line drawing of the two horsemen as a group. The latest discussion in Kleine, 36–40. For the comparison with the Introduction Pediment, see also Lullies & Hirmer, commentary on pls. 30–31. For the wreath worn by the Rampin head, which speaks against an identification as the Dioskouroi, see *AMA*, 216 and 225. On the iconography of the Dioskouroi, *EAA* s.v. *Dioscuri*; Exekias' Vatican Amphora (Vat. 344), see, e.g., J. D. Beazley, *The Development of Attic Black-Figure* (London 1951) pp. 65–67.

FOR PAGE 142

Akr. 617: Payne, 3 pls. 9–10; *AMA* no. 86; *Kouroi* no. 65 figs. 219–20; Brouskari, 53–54 (where the head is considered female).

Dog, Akr. 143: Payne, 51 pl. 131; *AMA* no. 377; Brouskari, 57–58. For the second dog, Akr. 550, see *AMA* no. 378. For a date no later than 540, see Deyhle, 10. For the dating of the Brauronion on the Akropolis, see C. Edmonson, *AJA* 72 (1968) 164–65; *contra,* Travlos, 124. For a landslide on that area of the Akropolis (South of the Parthenon) after 480, with thorough mixing of the strata, see Bundgaard, 24.

Persian rider, Akr. 606 ("Miltiades"): Payne, 52 pls. 134–35; *AMA* no. 313; Brouskari, 59–60. For a Red Figure plate in Oxford with a mounted Scythian archer inscribed "Miltiades kalos," see H. T. Wade-Gery, *JHS* 71 (1951) 212–21. For a discussion of the Scythian contingent in Archaic Athens, see M. F. Vos, *Scythian Archers in Archaic Attic Vase Painting* (1963) 61–69, especially p. 66 for mention of this statue; on p. 79, the possibility of mounted reconnaissance.

Rider on Hippalektryon, Akr. 597: Payne, 74 pl. 136; *AMA* no. 319; Brouskari, 82. On the Hippalektryon, see G. Camporeale, *ArchCl* 19 (1967) 248–68. Of the vases listed by him, his nos. 18, 24, and 25 show a connection of the monster with Poseidon.

FOR PAGE 143

Syracuse Gorgon rider: Langlotz, pl. 12.

Chapter 6

Funerary Monuments, Animals, and Monsters

GRAVE MARKERS IN THE ROUND

That kouroi, korai, and seated figures were used as grave monuments has already been mentioned in the previous chapters. The evidence may, however, be usefully summarized here.

Human Figures

Kouroi. The earliest preserved funerary kouroi come from the island of Thera, one of them an example of the rare belted type. The feet and plinth of another were found embedded in the natural rock, on a hill slope just in front of a cleft in the rock face which concealed an ash urn. Next in date come the funerary kouroi from Athens, especially those from the great Dipylon cemetery, but Attica is the only area to have yielded an unbroken sequence of male figures as grave monuments, from ca. 600 to ca. 490, the Aristodikos being perhaps the latest in the series. Other regions of the Greek world produce less definite evidence. Some of the Samian kouroi were certainly used as tomb statues, others were found in cemeterial areas but cannot definitely be associated with burials, and in one case, the Leukios kouros, the dedication to Apollo engraved on the figure shows that it was a votive offering despite its provenience from Glyphada, one of the largest Samian nekropoleis. The cemeteries of Miletos have not yet been published or completely excavated, but at least one Archaic burial ground (south of Kazar Tepe) has yielded a fragmentary unfinished youth, presumably of the draped variety. Another draped male figure was found in the cemetery of Pitane.

Of the islands, a cemetery in Naxos has produced a remarkable fragment of a male figure carved in high relief against a solid marble screen, somewhat in the fashion of Old Kingdom Egyptian statues. One publication suggests that the kouros was perhaps matched by a similar high relief figure advancing the opposite leg, in mirror image, though the suggestion was presumably made because of the comparable monument to Dermys and Kittylos from Tanagra in Boeotia. There, however, the twins give the impression of being statues in the round set against a background, with a protecting shelf over their head, presumably for a finial. The Naxos fragment seems more of a relief, though too little is preserved to know whether the total statue looked rather like a pillar-herm or like an architectural member. An interesting parallel from Sardis, a better preserved kouros against a stone screen, also served funerary purposes. Two possible examples from Samos will be discussed below, with the stelai.

The above mentioned Dermys and Kittylos are difficult to assess: Richter, for instance, included them both in *Kouroi* and in *Archaic Gravestones of Attica*, the latter on the assumption that they were influenced by contemporary Athenian stelai. Yet the two look so different from other Attic examples, especially in their frontal pose, that the association should be questioned. They are perhaps closest to Kleobis and Biton, because they were set up as what may be a commemorative as well as a funerary monument. Their inscription, in fact, states that the statues were erected by one Amphalkes, without further specification. Unlike the Delphic statues, Dermys and Kittylos stood in a cemetery, but, like the Argive twins, the two Boeotians also wear boots or at least their toes are undetailed. They are embracing each other, in a difficult pose which the sculptor must have adopted only by *force majeure* because its symbolism was of paramount importance to express relationship between the two. The parallel with Egyptian statues is so convincing, both in pose and content, that one need look no further, even if Guralnick's studies seem to show that this is the Greek Archaic sculpture which corresponds the least to the Egyptian canon. On the other hand, one can assume that the back screen and top ledge were adopted purely as safety measures, in an unconscious imitation of Egyptian prototypes; spontaneous invention, or simultaneous but independent occurrence, cannot always be excluded. The presence of a background consolidated the breakable poros and removed the difficulty of articulating the embrace pose in all its complicated details. As it stands now, a disembodied arm appears to descend from the "ceiling" on either side of the group, without any visible connection with the figures' shoulders. I find the Boeotian twins much more strictly related to statuary in the round than to relief, and such would be the case even if they did indeed reflect Egyptian prototypes. Another point of view assumes instead that the action pose of the two brothers (the embrace, the stepping forward of each with the opposite leg) is typical of narrative relief, while stelai decorated with frontal figures usually partake of the nature of freestanding statues. However, I shall discuss such stelai among the other reliefs.

The Archaic cemetery of Tanagra has also produced a limestone figure the sex of which is disputed. I believe that it is a draped man holding a snake, and therefore I include it here among the kouroi. Of finds from other areas, only those from the cemetery of Megara Hyblaia in Sicily are definitely funerary: a naked youth inscribed to a doctor, and another (of which only one fragment remains) which was set up within a most elaborately decorated naiskos erected over a grave, with an overtone of heroization which recalls the much later monuments from Tarentum.[1] The Tenea kouros was apparently found fallen over a grave, and the Keos kouros near a pyre of ash and bones, but this evidence is not conclusive.

Korai. Funerary korai are again attested for Attica, though in lesser quantity. Elsewhere, we are not so sure. None of the Samian korai is definitely associated with graves, though in the case of two from Myli the original publication had left the question open. Yet the total number of finds from that area, mostly votive in nature, may suggest the same purpose for

[1] The architectural elements of the naiskos include a Doric frieze with very beautifully decorated metopes. The complexity and beauty of the carving are such that a 4th century date has been proposed for the panels, disregarding the fact that the tomb context is definitely and exclusively late Archaic. If such elaborate reliefs could be created in Sicily at such a date, one wonders why no more sculpture in the round has been found in the area. In fact, the architectural nature of the metopes speaks for their local origin, as contrasted with freestanding statuary which is usually considered imported.

the two korai as well. Some Chian and a very early, Seventh century example from Thera, may have been grave markers, but information is vague. Much more plentiful evidence comes from Cyrene, though its monuments can hardly be considered korai in the usual sense of the word. These are more properly busts, at times including only head and shoulder, more frequently going down to the waist or a little below it. These busts stood over tombs, at times with special platforms built to accommodate them, so that the total effect was that of a figure rising from the grave. The ghostly effect is increased in those examples where the face has been left blank and shapeless, so that not even paint could have supplied the missing features. The series as preserved seems to begin in the first half of the Fifth century, but obviously goes back to the second half of the Sixth, as shown by hairstyles and drapery conventions. Since some of these peculiar busts were found over the tombs of men, they cannot be considered portraits of the deceased, but must be representations of Demeter, Kore, or another appropriate funerary divinity.

Seated Figures. Seated figures as grave markers occur in Attica (both male and female), at Miletos (at least three females), and again at Megara Hyblaia (the astounding kourotrophos which was erected over a grandiose subterranean tomb). The Hagemo from Arkadia, because of its inscribed name and the small animal next to her knee, could be a heroized deceased, and perhaps the same function could be attributed to the male figure from Sparta. Seated statues of Cybele have been found in the Kyme cemetery, but here again it is difficult to distinguish the funerary from the divine.

Riders. One more type of monument, the equestrian statue, closes the series of human representations. Here too we find that Attica is in the lead, and that here are preserved the only examples definitely associated with real people. Jeffery has suggested that such statues may have portrayed men who belonged to the socio-economic class of the Knights but could sometimes stand also for those killed in cavalry action. The monolithic group from Megara Hyblaia forms the only other example of such funerary monuments outside Attica, but here the purpose is less clear: the pair of horsemen belonged within an architectural frame, either a naiskos or its pediment, and could portray the Dioskouroi, as well as two human beings.

From a review of all these monuments, it seems therefore that among the Greeks the Athenians were especially eager to honor their dead with all existing sculptural types in heroized form; specifically, the idea of the funerary kouros may have come to them from the islands. The East Greeks may have preferred the draped male and the seated female; the Western Greeks, the Peloponnesians, the people of Kyme and Cyrene may have stressed the idea of divine protection rather than the commemorative, portrait-like quality of funerary monuments. Yet this picture is so incomplete as to be potentially misleading.

Animals and Monsters

Since all human statuary types had been previously discussed, a summary of the evidence for them as funerary monuments could suffice at this point. The situation is more complex for other grave markers in the round since, as usual, the Greeks utilized the same sculptural types for votive purposes as well. I shall therefore have to deal with each category as a whole, and not exclusively with those examples or types connected with graves. These non-human representations include not only animals, but also fantastic monsters such as the Gorgon, the sphinx, and the siren, which had entered the Greek world largely through the decorative repertoire of the minor arts and had become very popular in media other than monumental sculpture. Though kouroi, korai, and seated figures are represented in the whole range of sizes, from the gigantic to the diminutive, they are largely confined to three-dimensional format, since depictions on vases or relief tend to be either narrative or decorative and therefore need not employ a static pose. On the contrary, heraldic animals or monsters form the very core of two-dimensional decoration as preserved, and were probably even more frequently represented in textiles and embroideries which are now lost. It is therefore almost impossible to trace sources of specific renderings without including all instances of the given type; yet it is equally impossible, within the scope of this book, to treat the subject so thoroughly. Here too I shall confine my analysis to large-scale monuments.

This arbitrary decision can be justified, I believe, by showing that the distribution pattern of a specific statuary type is not determined by the mere knowledge of that subject in certain areas. Regions which have yielded not a single specimen of a stone lion in the round were nonetheless thoroughly familiar with the animal in relief sculpture, vase painting, or other contexts. One should therefore focus on the question why Sixth century Magna Graecians, for instance, never carved a three-dimensional stone lion rather than the question *how* the Magna Graecians portrayed the lion, for instance, as a water-spout or on terracotta altars. In other words, the problem at hand is not whether a certain area of the Greek world was familiar with a particular subject but whether it considered that subject appropriate for monumental expression.[2]

Lions. The lion is indeed an almost perfect example to consider. It can still be argued nowadays whether the Greeks knew the living animal at all, or whether they simply imported its iconography from abroad. Regardless of the answer, we know that the motif penetrated Greece during the Orientalizing period, therefore long before it found its expression in stone. The same is true of griffins, sirens, and sphinxes, which followed the same routes. If vases were the first to show the lion, plastic vessels, ivories, and small bronzes still preceded all sizable examples; and when these did appear, they were colossal, with a jump in size which makes the transition from figurines as hard to understand as for all human sculptural types.

Basically, there are three types of monumental lions. A reclining type lies with one hind paw under the body and visible on the opposite side, head turned toward the viewer at

[2] This is perhaps one of the most interesting considerations which can occur to one in reading H. Gabelmann's *Studien zum frühgriechischen Löwenbild* (Berlin 1965). Although the author concentrated largely on three-dimensional examples and eliminated all depictions on vases, his catalogue included almost 200 items, with virtually all areas of the Greek world represented. His reviewers objected that his conclusions were probably acceptable for the lions in the round, but that a much more complex picture could be derived from the inclusion of vases, bronzes, coins, and gems (J. Boardman, *Gnomon* 39 [1967] 99–101; see also Cristofani, *ArchCl* 19 [1967] 197–99). I would have the opposite objection: that the picture given by the catalogue is misleading for sculpture. For instance, Sparta and Corinth figure prominently, yet the former has produced no *monumental* lion in the round, the second only three, and from its territory, not the city proper. Similarly, Magna Graecian lion-head water-spouts can hardly represent production in that area, where not a single specimen of the entire animal has been found.

approximately a 90 degree angle to the body, and one front paw sometimes crossed over the other. This pose is obviously of Egyptian origin (Fig. 42) and seems limited to Greek lions from Didyma and Miletos. A second reclining type, which is also represented in the Milesian area but is more widely diffused, exhibits a mixture of Hittite and Assyrian elements. From the latter source come, for instance, the heart-shaped ears folded back like a cat's. The animal may look forward, with mouth closed or partly open in a more ferocious attitude. The entire pose is more alert than the Egyptian-inspired one, and the hind legs remain as if ready to spring, on either side of the rump, though the belly touches, or almost touches, the plinth. Both these reclining types predominate in East Greek territory. The mainland of Greece and, to some extent, the Cyclades, prefer a sitting pose which eventually turns into a springing attitude, with rump in the air and chest lowered. Other regional differences can be seen in the rendering of the name, which in the Ionic examples extends down the back, while the mainland prefers a ruff around the face; but these distinctions are not always easy to see. Toward the end of the Sixth century, the lions show the influence of the International Style also, and the intermingling of traits eliminates regional differences.

The pattern of distribution is peculiar, though perhaps predictable. The lion is best represented in East Greek territory, with nine examples, mostly colossal, from Didyma, and at least ten from other areas of Asia Minor.[3] Many more, in various sizes, come from Lydian Sardis.[4] Samos has yielded three, of which one is unfinished. There are many lions in the Cyclades, especially the impressive row at Delos connected with the Letoon, and later, heraldic pairs from the same island (A 4103 and A 4104). Of the other Cyclades, Thera has a reclining beast from the Agora, Siphnos a limestone head, and Keos a colossal rock-cut example. Corfu and Kythera are also represented.[5] In Greece proper we have monumental specimens mostly from Athens. Two confronted pairs from the Akropolis are matching and may therefore have been akroteria of the same monument. Five lions come from the Kerameikos, and one of them, in poros, probably had a companion. Of the three from the Agora, one, quite large, is sitting, one is in a springing pose, and the third is an unusually simple and most effective head of a lioness. Elsewhere in Greece, Corinth has produced three lions from Perachora/Loutraki (Fig. 43). An unusual limestone lion in Olympia, which was probably used as a spout for a fountain, is earlier than all other types; its scaly mane and body probably show the influence of metalwork.[6]

[3] Gabelmann's list for Asia Minor has many lacunae. My total of 10 breaks down as follows: 2 from Smyrna, 1 from Knidos, 1 from Bodrum, 2 from Pergamon, 3 from Miletos, and 1 on a column in the Ankara Museum, provenience unknown. Fragments of a lion closely comparable to those from Miletos and Didyma have recently been found at Aphrodisias (K. T. Erim, *Aphrodisias Excavations Bulletin* 75–1, Dec. 1975, p. 3).

[4] In a lecture on May 3, 1975, Prof. G.M.A. Hanfmann mentioned that 22 lions are now known from Sardis. He attributed a protective function to most of them, not only on altars but perhaps also along roads and near temples. Unfortunately, the majority of the examples has been found re-used in later contexts.

[5] Even Crete may have one example, which could however belong to a relief. It is a poros fragment including the rump and hind leg of a seated feline, which could be a lion or a sphinx, on a low plinth. Though the front of the haunch is quite well cut in the round, the rest of the fragment is flattened, as for relief. The date is late Archaic, and the provenience is Knossos. J. Boardman, *BSA* 57 (1962) 30, pl. 3c.

[6] In Olympia was also found a small lion paw with a human foot on it, which is clearly Oriental in inspiration. It has been suggested that it could be part of the armrest for the throne of the cult statue in the Heraion (Mallwitz, 88–89 figs. 75–76). A strange fragment of a lion mane in poros was found in Corinth, but it is not certain whether it was part of a large water-spout or of a relief (N. Bookidis, *Hesperia* 39 [1970] 325 no. 12 pl. 79).

This geographical picture would be enlarged if perirrhanteria were included. Yet once again conception and size are so different that the inclusion does not seem justified. One point worthy of note is the peculiar moonface of some of the perirrhanterion lions, with a slash for the mouth which parallels the curve of the chin. This type of head, with due variations, is also found in the earliest Samian lion and in the spectacular beast from Corfu, often but erroneously associated with Menekrates' tomb. Its reclining body is massive, rounded, simplified, but the head is a complete abstraction, especially when seen frontally and slightly from below. The curve of the total structure is echoed and multiplied by the many lines marking mouth and whiskers, nostrils and eyes. From that angle the face loses any possible resemblance to a lion.[7]

Most of the examples from Didyma and Miletos are colossal. Among them, the Egyptianizing ones are perhaps the most striking. The earliest (Br. Mus. B 281), ca. 600–580, was dedicated as a tithe to Apollo (together with a matching animal) by the five sons of Orion the Governor. It was found along the Sacred Way at Didyma, not with its twin (which was recovered from a late Byzantine wall) but with a later lion (Br. Mus. B 282). Their juxtaposition suggested Egyptian parallels but was obviously the result of later setting as both statues originally stood elsewhere, presumably near the temple. Note how the dedicatory inscription is engraved directly on the animal's body, like a gigantic tattoo. Note also the deliberate asymmetry in the placing of the ridge which stands for the lion's spine. It is placed off center, so that it is not visible to a viewer facing the inscription, but only to a person standing on the opposite side; that this displacement is intentional is shown by the half-slouching pose, which reveals not only the belly but also the genitals of the animal. The restful impression is increased by the nonchalant crossing of the front paws. Fur texture is cleverly conveyed by tool marks.

A somewhat comparable stylization was used for the two funerary lions which stood at the entrance of a rock-cut tomb in Miletos. The smooth surface of the block-like body is broken by islands of anatomical details, in a peculiar contraposition of active and dead surfaces. While little suggestion of skeletal structure is given to the main bulk of the animal, the haunches include such naturalistic features as the loose skin rippling over the leg and the soft pads of the under-paw. Yet this very paw, appearing from under the lion, can hardly be visualized as part of a total hind leg and remains visually disconnected, even if suggestive of a reclining posture. This relaxed rendering turns the body into a series of planes, sloping down, as it were, from the watershed of the spine, in marked contrast to the barrel-shaped forms of the Assyro-Hittite type. The better preserved lion of the Milesian pair, now in Berlin, still has its head, which is more canine than feline and

[7] Note that this marvelous animal bears no resemblance to the lions from the Corinthia, despite the alleged artistic influence exercised by Corinth over Corfu. The rounded knobs which appear near the lion's nose, as part of the total frown, occur also, in a detached and more ornamental way, over the noses of the "panthers" of the Artemision pediment, on the same island. Even these latter, therefore, may reflect a local artistic tradition rather than a strong Corinthian influence. Finally, though the lion may not belong to Menekrates' tomb but to another rectangular grave nearby, note that the former is a tumulus, closer in shape to Etruscan or East Greek examples than to Corinthian forms of burial, another instance of the many influences at work on the island. Because of a split in the limestone, the Corfu lion is now in two pieces joined along a horizontal section which runs just above the paws and stomach area of the animal. A photograph (F. Crome, *Mnemosynon Th. Wiegand* [Munich 1938] 50–53 pl. 13; *Korkyra* II, fig. 158 and p. 179) of the lower piece, taken during its installation in the Museum, is particularly useful in emphasizing the torsion in the lion's neck and the asymmetry in the position of the paws.

gives the impression of having been forcibly thrust through a lace collar so stylized and completely divorced from the rest of the body does the mane appear. Note the deep-set eyes, not meant to be inlaid, which occur also on another colossal specimen from Didyma, in Istanbul.

In terms of purpose, many of the archaic lions were surely votive, as appropriate for an animal sacred to Apollo, Hera, Cybele, and other divinities. But several were also funerary. This function is attested for the three lions from Miletos, including the colossal one in the Louvre, and for at least two of the three from Samos. Some of the Sardis examples came from the cemetery area, as did also one of those from Smyrna. A headless animal in limestone, presumably another lion, is in the Ankara Museum and may come from the interior. It is inscribed in Greek letters as the monument of Mikos, son of Metrodoros, and is quite important in that it lies atop an Ionic capital, with its paws hanging over the baluster side. It would therefore seem that the columnar monument was not exclusively votive but could be funerary as well.

Of the Attic lions, the small poros specimen in sitting position crowned a built tomb in the Kerameikos and was probably accompanied by a matching piece in heraldic pose, to judge from the extant fragments. Four more, in marble, were found re-used, but in the general area of the cemetery and therefore were also grave markers. Of the two best preserved, the earlier one sits, but the other crouches, ready to spring, as the defender of the tomb. At least two of the three animals from the Agora are likely to have come from the nearby cemetery. Probably funerary also were the two lions from Loutraki in Copenhagen. They remain unique, despite the obvious influence they (or their regional fellows) seem to have had as far afield as Samos and Sardis. They are so decorative and cheerful that any resemblance to the real animal is lost, even more so than in the simplified and drowsy but forceful Milesian examples. Note in particular the flame-like locks of the mane and the ornamental dots among the whiskers. The third lion from the Corinthia (Perachora), in Boston (Fig. 43), has a more serious expression and a long, narrow face, but basically it fits the same pattern. The two lions from Corfu were both found in a nekropolis. As for the Cyclades, their Archaic examples may be purely votive.[8]

It is impossible to determine exactly the causes behind the changes in the lion's poses. From a purely sculptural point of view, the reclining rendering was the best, since it ensured the marble against breakage, but a heavy lion almost sinking into its plinth in the Egyptian schema may have conveyed power and majesty rather than alertness. If a concept of guardianship came partly to replace one of nobility and strength, one can understand the preference for a more active pose after Near Eastern prototypes, head erect and belly not quite touching the ground, as in one of the Samian examples. The springing pose, with rump in the air, occurs earlier on coins but may have been the sculptural answer to the problem of having the lion standing on four thin marble legs; the lowered chest and the outstretched front paws had the same practical effect as the shapeless support under a horse's stomach and added a touch of ferocity to the monument. The sitting lion is unexplainable in terms of realism, since the live animal does not sit in this fashion.[9]

[8] A lion attacking a bull may have also been used as a funerary monument in the Archaic period, in Boeotia and in Athens. Cf. *Agora* XI no. 93. Certainly Classical grave lions are sometimes shown with just the head of a bull under their front paws.

[9] A sitting lion appears on one of the reliefs from Assurbanipal's Hunt scenes (see, e.g., H. Frankfort, *The Art and Architecture of the Ancient Orient*

Obviously the pose is derived from the world of dogs (or from the Egyptian seated cats?), and occurs (at Delos) as early as the earliest East Greek examples. The possibility should be considered that it was inspired by the sphinx which, because of its human head, may have looked more normal in an upright position.

Sphinxes. Like the lion, sphinxes may be both funerary and votive, and, again like the lion, when in their function as grave markers, the sphinx may have embodied concepts of guardianship and protection of the dead. But while the lion can specifically allude to a person's bravery, or even to a person's name, a sphinx never personifies characteristics of the dead and remains confined to the supernatural and mythological sphere, even if Sixth century Greeks may have met a lion in their daily life no more often than a sphinx.

The Orientalizing sphinx brought into Greece in the Eighth century could be either male or female, though the latter predominated. It combined a long-haired human head with a lion's body, the connection occurring abruptly at the base of the neck without any attempt at plausibility, yet the result was not unpleasant and commanded belief. Votive sphinxes tended to look forward, since they represented the total monument and the viewer could walk around them. Funerary sphinxes, at least in Attica, often stood atop decorated stelai, as only one element of the total grave marker.[10] They were therefore shown in profile, but with the head turned at a 90 degree angle from the body, toward the spectator, not in threat but simply in acknowledgment.

Richter has gathered together all major examples of Attic gravestones, including sphinxes which are preserved by themselves but which could once have been connected to a stele. Of her 17 examples, one (perhaps two) comes from Corinth and one from Aegina. The others are either in Athens, coming from the city or its environs, or in foreign museums with an alleged Attic provenience (9). Of the total 17, only 7 can be safely assumed to be funerary, though many of the remaining 10 are also probable candidates. In only 3 cases, however, can we be sure that the sphinx and its capital topped a decorated stele, as postulated by Richter for all of them. Though others could be included, certainty is lacking, and we cannot assume that the same funerary practices prevailed in Corinth and Aegina simply because both areas have produced sphinxes of a comparable type. To be strictly accurate, moreover, 2 of the 17 are only heads, and their identification as sphinxes is plausible but not proven.

Despite these strictures, Richter's work remains the only attempt to collect Archaic

---

[Baltimore 1954] pl. 111), but he is near death, spewing blood, and his hunched up position with lowered head has little in common with the alert poses of the Greek animals. Assyrian renderings may however have influenced the seated lion depicted on the chariots of the Kyzikos frieze (see infra, Ch. 9: 259).

Iconographically the seated lion, together with the seated sphinx, appears in the Near East as early as the 18th century. Cf., e.g., the Pratt ivories, probably from Acem Hüyük (P. O. Harper, *Connoisseur* 172 [1969] 156–62, esp. fig. 3) or the ivory lion from Altintepe, ca. 8th century (T. Özgüç, *Altintepe* [Ankara 1969] pl. A and p. 42 figs. 39–40). Seated lions occur early in Egyptian art, but remain rare; cf. U. Schweitzer, *Löwe und Sphinx im alten Aegypten* (Glückstadt and Hamburg 1948) 24 and pls. 4, 6, 12, 16.

[10] Sphinxes as finials may have been a familiar sight, given the early use of such monsters as temple akroteria. But even if the adoption of a sphinx to top a stele was prompted by association of ideas, both the sphinx akroterion and the sphinx finial may have served an apotropaic as well as a decorative purpose. In addition, the sphinx's wings make it a plausible figure to place on elevated positions, hence its great popularity as an akroterion.

sphinxes. Individual articles have appeared on the subject, but no comprehensive study has as yet been made and cannot be accomplished in this book. I have tried to collect other examples, with an eye to distribution and function, but any conclusion must be considered highly tentative and temporary.

Except for a fragmentary specimen from Karian Halikarnassos, I have been unable to find a single sphinx in the round from East Greece or Samos.[11] This result is particularly surprising in that the monster is of Oriental origin and appears on many Greek-influenced but non-Greek monuments, in both the Sixth and the Fifth centuries. Didyma, Myus, Assos, Erythrai, have all produced sphinxes carved on altars and temples, and in Samos several buildings had their antae protected by sphinxes in relief, but no freestanding example has come to light, especially from nekropoleis.

That this apparent absence of the monumental sphinx may be due to chance is perhaps suggested by two facts. Some of the earliest sphinxes preserved stood atop Ionic columns, and the very association with an architectural order originating in East Greece would suggest that the idea itself came from that territory. In addition, we know of votive capitals and columns of sizable proportions from Asia Minor sanctuaries. The sculpture they supported is now lost, but that they may, in some cases at least, have carried a sphinx is suggested by depiction of sphinxes on columns or piers in later reliefs, for instance, those of the Nereid Monument from Xanthos, where one slab shows a winged sphinx between two lions in a springing pose. The practice may reflect influence from Assyria, where statues of animals were placed in high position as protective symbols.

It has recently been argued that an Ionic capital is ill-suited to support a sphinx because of a basic disharmony between principal views: a sphinx facing straight ahead can be seen frontally only when the viewer faces the baluster, therefore the short side of the supporting Ionic capital. Yet this criticism can be countered in two ways: 1) a sphinx is perhaps more effective when seen from the side, with the great wings arching into the air and the lion body appearing in full stretch; therefore the main view for both capital and monster would coincide; 2) the exaggerated elongation of the early volute capitals may have been determined by the very need to support the length of a reclining feline body; therefore the earliest Ionic capitals may have been originally created for votive rather than for architectural purposes.

This last theory has already been advanced because our earliest examples of canonical Ionic capitals seem to come from sphinx-columns rather than from temples. At present the oldest is perhaps the large but sadly fragmentary capital and column from Aegina, which has been reconstructed as a sphinx monument. Its connection with the earliest phase of the (Doric) temple of Aphaia would place it around 600 or shortly after. Sphinxes must have been popular in Aegina; besides this impressive early monument, another equally large and early sphinx probably stood near the temple of Apollo, the head of a third one is preserved in the local museum, an almost complete sphinx is in Athens, and a masterpiece of the Severe style also comes from the island. It seems logical to assume that most, if not all, of these examples served a votive purpose.

[11] Some sphinxes have been postulated as akroteria of some Asia Minor temples, for instance at Assos, but the evidence usually consists only in lion's paws, which could equally well be integrated as total lions or griffins, not necessarily as sphinxes. Over life-size terracotta sphinxes may have formed the lateral akroteria of the Rhoikos temple at Samos.

Also votive is the famous Naxian Sphinx in Delphi perched atop her impressive Ionic capital, on a column that must have stood over 10 meters high. The sculpture is particularly remarkable because of the fine engraving of the feathers, which strongly recall metalwork, over both the chest and the wings of the sphinx. The face, with the large staring eyes and vertical lines at the corners of the mouth, is distinctively Naxian and allows a dating around 560. Somewhat later, but perhaps from the same island workshops, is the recently found sphinx from Cyrene (Fig. 46), which also stood on an Ionic column with elaborate capital. Its marble seems to come from the Greek islands but, if not Naxian or Parian, the monument should perhaps be considered Chian because of the simplification and stylization of the feline body, on which no feathers are engraved, combined with the unusual decorativeness of the volute capital.[12] In Delos we find a fourth sphinx on an Ionic column, this time with a capital that has now been recognized as typically Parian: the volute scroll is split in the center by an ornamental motif, and other examples of this rendering have been found on Paros. This is the best preserved and better known of the sphinx-columns from Delos, but others existed, all mounted on Ionic capitals. One, however, came from near the tomb of the Hyperborean Maidens (A 3842), and may have carried funerary allusions. The turning of the head to the side may reflect its date (third quarter of the Sixth century) as well as its function. As for Paros, the Delion has produced its own sphinx crouching on its haunches. Its head is broken off, but probably turned to the left, to judge by the arrangement of the hair over the right shoulder. Its wings are smooth like the Cyrene sphinx, but feathers would have been detailed in paint. Ribs are prominently carved on both sides. It is uncertain, unfortunately, whether the sphinx served as an akroterion for a building or as a stele crowning.[13]

From the islands the type probably moved to the peripheral areas, though examples are few and all somewhat late. A peculiar fragmentary sphinx in Odessa has a stone screen between its legs, despite its fairly secure sitting position; what remains of the feathers is so elaborate that the piece may well no longer be Archaic. A small headless sphinx from Al Mina, now in Oxford, is also dated to the incipient Severe period. A sadly fragmentary example came to light in Sicily, at Megara Hyblaia, and is the only one so far, outside of Attica, for which a funerary purpose can be definitely be claimed. A terracotta head from Akragas can be included here because of its considerable size (23.5 cm.), though the identification as a sphinx is based only on its facial asymmetries and the unequal fall of the tresses on either side of the face. Since the curls on the proper right look slightly displaced, the sphinx, if such it was, would have turned her head to one side. Another head (Figs 44–

[12] This latter is unique in having an echinos carved with two superimposed rows of egg-and-dart. This superimposition of identical moldings is often found on architectural members on Chios, and in triplicate in some Asia Minor sites like Didyma and Xanthos. Chios may have been particularly interested in sphinxes, since during the 6th century it even minted coins with a sphinx as a device.

[13] A very massive headless sphinx in Naxos, Museum no. 85, seems too elaborate to be Archaic; the fragmentary haunches of a feline in the same Museum could belong either to a sphinx or to a lion. Perhaps here should be mentioned also the peculiar engraved plaques, representing both male and female sphinxes, which were found on the Athenian Akropolis and are by some considered akroteria of a very early (7th century?) temple of Athena. This engraving technique occurs also on the marble antefixes of the Oikos of the Naxians in Delos (*BCH* 45 [1921] 234; the building may, however, have been wrongly identified; see *GdD*, 79 n. 4 and 85 n. 2; a change need not affect the Naxian provenience of the marble antefixes). Given Naxian influence on Athens, it would not be surprising to find such examples on the early Akropolis (nos. 232, 3709, etc.; Payne, pl. 17: 4–6; Wiegand, pl. 11 and p. 179).

45), but in marble, now in Cleveland, Ohio, has a greater claim to the identification because it wears a low polos and does not look like a normal kore. Its features are decidedly "Oriental," and its provenience is allegedly Soluntum, a Punic site near Palermo.[14] Finally, still in Sicily, the area of Caltagirone produced a relief with two sphinxes back to back on either side of a central floral ornament, one paw raised against the edge of the slab. The stele may be votive, but could easily be funerary, since the vegetal motif could be appropriate to both realms. Of particular interest is the line of dots along the wings, since these decorative details occur frequently not only on Corinthian vases (as white dots) but also on Corinthian sculpture, specifically sphinxes, as a recent study has shown.[15]

These are probably the only sphinxes that can at present be distinguished from their more abundant Attic counterparts, not only because of their medium, which is generally limestone, but also for a specific detail in the rendering which is easily due to the Corinthian propensity for decoration over structural analysis. Granted that the combination of a human head and a lion's body is awkward at best, the feat can be accomplished if no great attention is given to making the transition plausible. The Attic master, however, perhaps influenced by his subconscious thought of a human chest, tried to articulate the shoulders of the animal as separate from the chest, which appears recessed between them, while the head is set back from the shoulder. The Corinthian master stressed instead a continuous contour from neck to chest, so that the latter projects beyond the line of the shoulders and the result is somewhat bird-like and plausible, or at least pleasing. Only two sphinxes, both in poros, were known from Corinth, but at the end of 1972 a new example, in marble, came to light. The location of the find, not too far from a cemetery area, suggests a funerary function for this impressive animal, which in many stylistic details recalls the Tenea kouros. The somewhat excessive massiveness of the front legs suggests the sculptor's fear for his marble, but also the fact that the sphinx was not meant to be seen frontally. That the main view was with the body in profile is also suggested by the tresses on the left side of the face, which have been carved diagonally rather than perpendicularly, in order to make them visible when one faces the sphinx, whose head turns at a 90 degree angle from the body. Since no carved gravestone has as yet been found at Corinth, it is impossible to determine whether the Corinthian sphinx stood directly over a grave or surmounted a tall, decorated pier like the Attic examples.

As for the Attic sphinxes, aside from those listed by Richter, there are only six others from the Akropolis, more or less fragmentary.[16] They are useful in showing that not only

[14] According to information from the Museum, the sphinx was found around 1820 and had long been in the possession of an Italian family, before being put on the antiquarian market. A possibility exists therefore that the head may come not from Punic Solunto (Solus) but from Selinus, which in Italian is called Selinunte and was excavated much earlier than the Punic site. This provenience would still account for the East Greek traits of the Cleveland head, since Selinus, a colony of Megara Hyblaia, had strong contacts with the East, including some of the Punic/Phoenician centers. It has been noted that the Cleveland sphinx has the left ear higher than the right, perhaps as a consequence of a possible turn of the head to one side.

[15] I am indebted to James C. Wright, who has taught me how to distinguish an Attic from a Corinthian sphinx and has let me read his paper on the Corinthian sphinx *AGA*, no. 15, which he wrote for the American School of Classical Studies in 1974. My comments are largely based on his work. An article by him on this topic will appear in *Hesperia*.

[16] Presumably the strange head which O. Broneer found in 1938 is also from the Akropolis. It was in Well A, on the north slope of the citadel (*AJA* 42 [1938] 447 and fig. 4). Since the same well yielded a right forepaw and part of a tail, the excavator suggested that the battered marble head may have belonged to a sphinx. The head was carved separately and was once fastened to its body by means of a

funerary but also votive sphinxes turned their heads to one side, presumably when the pose had become fashionable. The number seems relatively high, and two of the sphinxes (Akr. 630 and 632) are dated ca. 560–550, which would place them among the earliest marble monuments from the Akropolis. Though this date should perhaps be lowered, it may not come down more than a decade or so. Another early head (Akr. 654) wears a polos and a parted hairstyle, and has often been considered a sphinx. As Payne recognized, it is stylistically very close to the Rampin Horseman, which it should precede in time. The erection of sphinxes on the Akropolis should therefore coincide with the beginnings of artistic activity in the sanctuary.

From this most imperfect picture, it would seem as if the sphinx originated in the islands, or perhaps, on circumstantial evidence, even in Asia Minor, through Oriental influences and for purely votive and protective purposes. By extension of this guarding function, the type was used in conjunction with graves, perhaps only in Attica, from which the practice might have spread to Corinth and then to Sicily, while the Cyclades continued to promote the erection of sphinx-column monuments in other peripheral areas. All these monumental sphinxes sit on their haunches with hind legs resting flat on the ground. As far as I can tell, none of the votive sphinxes crouches like the funerary examples around 560–550, and one wonders whether specific meaning attaches to the variation, perhaps purely in terms of visibility or stability. Other poses were obviously possible, but I know of no sphinx reclining on its capital, for instance, like the lion of the Ankara grave marker, or like some small bronzes.[17] What the pose of the Olympia Hera would have been, if the head really belongs to a monster, it is impossible to tell. Its dimensions are much larger than those of the Naxian Sphinx in Delphi, and the total monument would have been considerably bigger; there is the added difficulty of its being in relatively soft limestone rather than in marble.

Sirens. Another monster which combines a human head with an animal body is the siren, not the mermaid but the bird-woman renowned for its singing. This association made it a favorite tomb marker for poets, singers and orators in Classical times, as well as a typical and ceaseless mourner at the grave, but there is no assurance that such meaning obtained also in the Archaic period. Another of the Orientalizing motifs which appeared first in the minor arts, the siren was greatly favored on vases, mirror handles, and bronze vessels.[18]

---

large lead dowel. This technique, and the peculiar slope of the forehead, as visible in the available photograph, suggest to me that the piece may originally have come from Asia Minor or the islands.

[17] Some of the small bronzes are particularly interesting. For instance, there is a reclining sphinx on what appears to be a volute capital for a column, which was once attached to the edge or rim of some object; it was found in the Malophoros sanctuary in Sicilian Selinus (*MonAnt* 32 [1928] col. 351 fig. 148). Another bronze, in Olympia (B 5300) shows the monster *couchant*, front paws stretched forward, polos-wearing head turned toward the viewer, long wings extending horizontally over the entire body to reach the curl of the upright tail. One more bronze sphinx, from Samos, in Berlin, is wingless, probably in direct imitation of an Egyptian prototype. I could see no number for this object in the Museum, and I know a photograph of its head only (*AltSt* v, 97–98 figs. 398–99).

[18] Note in particular the bronze lamp in Naples, with a silenus mask attached to the outside of the three-spouted bowl and a siren atop the column-like shaft in the center. Does this rendering suggest that sirens were also erected on (Doric?) columns in the 6th century? The lamp in Naples has been considered a Magna Graecian product, but the applied silenus mask may recall the protruding heads on marble vases from the Cyclades (N. Valenza, *BdA* 57 [1972] 133–37).

Some terracotta containers are themselves in the shape of sirens; and one bronze askos, from Kroton in Magna Graecia, has a human figure stretched on its back, suggesting that the siren is transporting it to the other world. Certainly sirens and not Harpies are the winged female figures with ovoid bodies carrying in their arms small, doll-like creatures, depicted at the corners of the so-called Harpy Tomb in Xanthos. Why these souls should be shown as female, if the tomb was primarily erected for a Dynast, is not quite certain, but at least in Lycia and at least by ca. 500–490 this funerary connotation of the siren must have existed. If, as is often suggested, the idea of the human-headed bird was given to the Greeks by the Egyptian *ba* bird, the association with death could have come with the iconography, in that the *ba* represents the soul in its independent state after the death of its former owner. Another theory would derive the type from the Orient.

The first sizable examples in stone belong to the mid Sixth century. The most complete is an interesting siren in Copenhagen which presumably comes from Kyzikos. This provenience seems confirmed by the shape of the face with its receding forehead, undetailed prominent eyes, wide mouth. Two human arms emerge from under the wings and press a cithara against the shapeless chest, which projects well forward of the neck. The carving of the feathers lacks the extensive analytical detail of the Naxian Sphinx, for instance, but the total effect is decorative and pleasing. The original purpose of the piece is not known. That it could be votive is shown by the presence of a siren in Delos (A 3995) though without human arms and musical attributes. Another siren (Figs. 47–49), equally bird-like except for its head now missing, was found in the Potters' Quarter at Corinth, at the bottom of a pit which contained mostly late Fifth century pottery, thus showing that the Archaic siren was discarded only after a long period of use. Its original purpose is unclear: it could have been funerary as well as architectural, as akroterion for a small temple of the second half of the Sixth century. Were it not for the remains of human curls over one side, this fine piece of Corinthian poros sculpture could be taken for a true bird, and, had the break occurred lower, its proper nature would not have been suspected. From this example one wonders if the marble "bird" from the Athenian Agora may be a siren since it was meant to be seen only from the proper left. This obligatory viewpoint may well go together with a human head turned to that side. Though in marble, its two legs are carved as if in relief, with stone left between them, the right slightly advanced. Note how the more cautious sculptor of the Corinth siren left an entire wedge of poros stretching from legs to tail, to secure the stability of his piece. In the Agora bird, the wings were attached separately and were probably both raised; in the Corinth siren they lie against the body, in continuous flowing contour, but asymmetrically, to correspond with the head turned to her left, as shown by some strands of hair falling over on the right. Even if the Agora bird were indeed a siren, its provenience would not ensure its funerary function. It was found west of the Eleusinion, and it may well have been dedicated there. Unfortunately, many of these interesting minor sculptures, whether sphinxes, sirens, or lions, unless they attained considerable size, are likely to be overlooked in Museum storerooms, without even being published.[19]

[19] A fragmentary bird in trachyte, found in Gordion, had originally been interpreted as a siren because it wore a necklace, and was therefore thought to have been a possible akroterion for a temple on the city mound. A more recent interpretation shows that the fragment is indeed a bird and an appropriate dedication to the Phrygian goddess Kubaba, whose frequent attribute it was. (M. J. Mellink, *Expedition* 6 [1964] 28–32, especially 31–32; cf. Tuchelt, p. 164, under Gordion, for the earlier interpretation.)

Birds. With the sirens should perhaps be mentioned the birds, though none of them is likely to be funerary. The Athenian Akropolis has produced a certain number of owls, one of them (Akr. 1347) impressive for size if not for workmanship (H. 95 cm.). Another, equally large or larger, was superbly carved but is fragmentary beyond restoration. A small poros owl has sometimes been attributed to a hypothetical Athena to go with the so-called Bluebeard pediment; another, also in limestone and from Athens, is now in Berlin.

Other birds were found in Delos: doves (A 3122 and A 3123) and some sea birds which might have served as throne support, perhaps for Leto (A 4049 and A 4050). The goddess Hera also attracted birds: a very naturalistic bronze dove from Perachora might have been held by the hand of an early statue since the bird's feet would not allow it to stand on an even surface. Cast solid, the dove has been dated to the mid Seventh century, but it looks almost like one of the souvenirs one can buy today in Piazza San Marco, Venice. In fact, it is very difficult to judge the date of animal sculpture, and some pieces are considered Archaic almost by default. Given the many Samian and East Greek korai holding birds, one would expect a certain number of such animals in the round, as independent offerings; but none has as yet been reported from that region, perhaps for the reasons mentioned above though many bronze and ivory hawks in miniature size have been found at Ephesos.[20]

The Gorgon. To my knowledge, only one stone example of the Gorgon is preserved in the round:[21] Obviously the Gorgon appears free standing even if it is utilized as an akroterion, and the same applies to akroterial lions and sphinxes, though even their occurrence in architectural function is limited or more often simply conjectured. But the Gorgon mentioned above must have stood over a grave, perhaps even crowning a stele since it was found in the Kerameikos. Though badly fragmentary, enough of its wings is preserved to show that they spread out frontally rather than parallel and sideways, as is the case with sphinxes. The reconstruction as a running Gorgon is made plausible also by the many gravestones on which the monster appears in relief.

Other Creatures. Other creatures occur occasionally; there is a votive bull from the Akropolis, but in Classical times a bull, symbol of Dionysos, could be erected over the grave of a Dionysios as a symbol of fertility and vigor, but also as an allusion to the deceased's name. The same meaning applied to statues of goats, which in Classical times were often shown butting in heraldic confrontation. Whether this type of monument ever occurred in the Sixth century is not known, and the charming head of a goat (Fig. 50) in Cleveland is much more likely to have been a votive offering in a sanctuary, like the fragmentary cow from the Heraion in Samos. Other animals which later occur both in votive and funerary contexts are dogs, but I do not know of an Archaic dog as a grave marker, whether as a guardian or as a pet. I have already spoken of equestrian statues. Here I should add that

[20] As mentioned in the preceding note, several stone birds come from Phrygian sites, and their connection with the goddess Kubaba may have interesting implications for the cult of Ephesian Artemis, and, more generally, for the practice of dedicating female statues holding birds.

[21] For a riding Gorgon in terracotta, from Sicily, see supra. Ch. 5. Another terracotta Gorgon, presumably in the round, came from the excavations around the Athenaion in Gela, but it is too fragmentary to reveal its original function: *ASAtene* 27–29, NS 11–13 (1949–51) 87–90.

some horses were carved without riders; there were at least three of them on the Athenian Akropolis, and a big Archaic horse is in Paros, with a sizable strut under his stomach for support. In general, marble animals are few. Bronze animals are more numerous, but they are statuettes; the larger bronzes have not survived to our day, and only the stone bases or the literary sources attest to their existence. By and large, however, these expensive monuments were votive. It would seem that Archaic grave markers, when in the round, stressed concepts of protection or status rather than of grief and hope for resurrection, so that animals as fertility symbols or mourning pets and sirens could not have enjoyed the same popularity which they achieved in the Fourth century.

STELAI

The Origins

Freestanding sculpture in the round was used for markers, but the funerary monument par excellence, at least in Athens, was the stele. Here again the pioneering work was done by Richter, but her very careful collecting and the wealth of Attic examples have tended to oversimplify the picture and push evidence from elsewhere into the background. Moreover, much new material has been found since the publication of her *Archaic Gravestones of Attica* in 1961.

The origin of the Greek stele is disputed. One theory favors an uninterrupted sequence of grave markers from the Middle Helladic to the Late Geometric period, which eventually developed into the elaborate examples of the Archaic phase. A second theory recognizes the presence of stelai in the Orient and Egypt, and even for the Greek ones assumes foreign impulses comparable to those active for freestanding sculpture. Certainly early stelai exist, but some are so indefinite in nature that it is impossible to tell whether they are truly Geometric or Byzantine, or perhaps simply crude rather than early. In many cases, moreover, a funerary function cannot be proved. Among the early but doubtful examples is the peculiar object from Kymisala in Rhodes, a broken pillar surmounted by a disc set on edge, which in turn is topped by a rectangular member somewhat like the abacus of a Doric capital. On one face of the disc six birds facing left are rendered in low relief, while a rosette appears on the other side. Andronikos has claimed that it is funerary and Late Geometric, since the area where it was found houses a cemetery ranging from the Bronze Age to the Eighth century BC; other authors are doubtful. On the other hand, Andronikos rejects as funerary a stele from Kimolos which Kontoleon accepts since it was also found close to a Late Geometric nekropolis. It is a block of soft limestone carved as a plain stele in its lower part, but its upper part is virtually in the round, shaped like a woman's torso, now headless, with crossed arms. The total effect is almost like the later hip-herms. The bottom part, probably painted to represent a skirt, ends in a sort of tenon for insertion into a base. The suggested date is the end of the Eighth century, but this also has been doubted. Obviously objects of this nature can lead to endless speculation as to the nature of the funerary stele, the origin of the grave statue, and the meaning of the aniconic marker. It would be logical to assume that roughly shaped slabs or pillars inscribed with the name of the deceased, as are found in the Seventh century cemeteries of Thera, could lead to identifying the marker with the dead, so that a representation of him would next be given, either carved in relief on a flat slab or partly in the round. A transitional stage would give us peculiar pieces like the Kimolos stele or the relief kouros from Naxos, or even the small column from the same island, topped by a human head. On the other hand, such examples remain so scattered, isolated, and stylistically undefined, that it is better to suspend judgment at present. The only reliable fact that remains is that graves were marked with some kind of stone monument as early as the Seventh century and probably earlier.

Among the examples of uncertain nature are the stelai from Prinias in Crete (Fig. 51). These are soft limestone slabs decorated with figures rendered by means of incision, but one cannot speak of true carving or relief. Though this technique has at times been compared with woodwork, it is more likely to reflect metalwork. One peculiarity is that details are often rendered by means of a double line which is then painted in contrasting color, with the surrounding area left plain and smooth; even the profile of the human face is thus outlined, with startling effect. Since all objects depicted lie at the same level, superimposition of planes is rendered by cutting one detail into another, so that a warrior, for instance, appears as a head atop a shield which seems to be walking on two legs, with absolutely no stepping down from rim of shield to level of thighs. The subjects are warriors or women, in profile and often in action poses, though some figures stand on a small pedestal, which has suggested the theory that they represent statues.

The Prinias stelai have been traditionally considered funerary, but recent studies express some doubts. One suggestion is that they were part of a civic building or an altar, either standing between wooden posts or as part of an orthostat course. What is known of Cretan architecture, under some influence from the Orient, would tend to support this hypothesis.[22]

One more example of an early gravestone could be the marble relief slab from Paros depicting a seated woman. Though the carved front is smooth, the back of the slab is quite rough and curved, almost as if an originally rounded block had been cut in half. The figure on the front is difficult to see, and it has been said that it is unfinished; it certainly does not occupy the entire space on the slab. If the figure is indeed holding a scepter or a staff, the stele may be votive rather than funerary and represent a goddess though, of course, the possibility of a heroized deceased cannot be excluded. The relief has been dated ca. 650 or earlier. It would therefore seem that the tradition of relief sculpture, whether votive or funerary, began in the Cyclades, more or less at the same time as sculpture in the round; and it is perhaps from the islands that Athens received the idea of the decorated slab as a grave marker. On the other hand, it is quite possible that Attica developed its own tradition of gravestones, the relief version coming as an almost obvious consequence from the tall undecorated slabs used in the Seventh century once the funerary kouros had been introduced from elsewhere. It is startling, in fact, how closely the extant examples carved

[22] Two undoubtedly funerary stelai from Crete have been recently published as the last representatives of a series that began with the Prinias reliefs. Yet only the repertoire (a warrior, a woman) may speak for connections. Both the format and the technique are different; the warrior stele is thin and narrow, in relatively low relief, the girl's stele is in higher relief within a naiskos-like frame, and has wider and thicker format, with a socket on the upper surface presumably for a cavetto finial or other crowning ornament. Lebessi considers this latter under Attic influence, though in both gravestones the figures face to the left (A. Lebessi, *AntP* 12 [1973] 7–14). These Cretan stelai date from the very end of the Archaic period, ca. 490–480, at the time when the practice of such funerary monuments is best attested outside of Attica; therefore continuation from the Prinias reliefs is an unnecessary assumption.

with a human figure resemble the profile view of a kouros within its block. The profile outline which almost fills the frame of the stele, in low relief, may not be too far from the design which the sculptor drew as preliminary guideline on the side face of his block, before beginning to carve a kouros in the round.

The Attic Evidence

Since the Attic decorated gravestones form the only continuous sequence available for the Sixth century and have been thought to have influenced all other comparable monuments elsewhere, they should be examined first. According to Richter, the earliest type (Ia; ca. 610–575) consisted of a rectangular base, a tall thick shaft probably carved with a human figure in low relief, a cavetto capital and a seated sphinx as a finial in the round, each part usually cut separately and then connected with the others to form an impressive, tall monument. How sizable such early stelai might have been is shown by the very massive sphinx in New York (*AGA*, no. 1) which must have required a substantial pier to support it. This basic formula continued in the next period (Ib; ca. 575–545), but the shaft may now have included a decorated *predella*, a sort of platform under the human figure's feet; the sphinx on the capital no longer sat but crouched. In its final stage (Type Ic; ca. 550–525) the sphinx-pillar shaft stele remained basically unchanged, but the heavy cavetto of the capital turned into a more elegant, lighter-looking form, a double-tiered volute of lyre shape (Fig. 52). Around 530, on the wave of influence from Ionia, a new type of grave stele came to Attica, the thin slender slab in one piece with its finial, which consisted of a palmette above a double or a single pair of volutes. Since this type of monument was considerably smaller and obviously less expensive than the elaborate sphinx-pillars, Richter suggested that the change may have been encouraged by an anti-luxury decree. Certainly many stelai of this type were no longer decorated in high relief but simply by incision or even with paint alone; and some odd types—that is, funerary monuments of different format which Richter considered transitional between the two standard formulas —could occur at the same time.

Non-Canonical Stelai. This generally correct and clear picture suffers from its rigid definition of formats and periods, which makes little or no allowance for experimentation and differences. In the light of new evidence we can now modify and add to this basic schema. To begin with, we can be reasonably sure that palmettes and volute finials existed earlier than the last third of the Sixth century and presumably as early as some of the first decorated stelai. A fragmentary stele in Berlin with an incised head in profile had originally been restored as a standing youth though it showed an unusual amount of empty space around the design. A more recent restoration suggests that the head belongs rather to a seated woman, comparable in hairstyle to the Berlin Kore and approximately contemporary with it. The picture panel must therefore have been wider than tall; the engraved line above the woman's head is comparable to the upper border in the Paros stele, while the thinness of the Attic slab suggests a volute-palmette crown. This revised identification shows also that women were honored with funerary monuments and depicted on them as early as men, though previous theories held that this was not usually the case. Certainly the number of grave monuments for women remains smaller than that for men, but their occurrence may be significant since probably the matronly status of wife or mother suggested a seated image, thus requiring a broad format for any relief. The Anavyssos stele, with the partly preserved figure of a mother holding a child, is therefore not "unprecedented," as Richter comments, either in its shape or in its finial (probably a series of volutes terminating in a palmette) even if the date of the piece (ca. 530) could still place it within the range of the sphinx-pillars, according to her system.

Other gravestones for women, all of the wide format, are attested either through inscribed bases or fragments. To mention the most important, the Lampito base gives the additional information that a broad stele (for a seated woman?) could be made by a major master since it is signed by Endoios. Two more were made by Aristokles, one of which shows the leg of a throne and part of a lion-leg footstool with some hanging drapery. The total scene has been reconstructed with the help of a relief in the National Museum which Richter considered heroizing since it depicts a seated lady confronted by a standing maid. But the iconography is so similar to some Classical stelai that other scholars had been inclined to consider also the Archaic relief as funerary. Richter's main objections had been the form and content; now that new finds have considerably amplified the Attic funerary repertoire, such objections are no longer compelling even if nothing excludes a votive purpose for some of the examples, given the Greek propensity for using the same motifs or types for different functions.

This kind of wide format could be used for men as well as for women. Two fragments in low relief, from Velanideza, have been recomposed to form a seated man, facing right (Fig. 55). A second base signed by Aristokles may have been for a similar stele. Other subjects on broad slabs, which had hitherto been considered anomalous, or perhaps not funerary in character, can also be included, like the Copenhagen relief with two warriors, the athlete throwing a javelin (why a warrior, and why part of a frieze?), or the so-called Marathon Runner (Fig. 53), though the correct interpretation of this work is still disputed.[23]

Even within the tall and slender format reconsiderations are now in order. A new piece recently added to an old find shows that the bearded warrior on the shaft held a shield, not a spear, in his left hand; therefore the space in front of his face must have remained empty.[24] A tenon hole in the upper surface of the stele implies a separately added finial, as late as ca. 525–520. The total height of the monument has been calculated as ca. 3.30 m. with the human figure 2.20 m. tall, making it an exceptional gravestone even in a land of impressive tomb markers.

On such evidence, some early capitals which were listed in *AGA* as supporting sphinxes

[23] M. Andronikos (*ArchEph* 1953–54, Oikonomos Festschrift, II, 317–26) suggests that the broad plaque formed one end of a built grave, which, when complete, would have looked like a sarcophagus. H. Wiegartz (*MarbWinckPr* 1965, 46–64) claims that the relief is votive, that it was once fastened against a wall, and that it commemorates a victory in a Pyrrhic dance. The collapsing or running pose of the figure would therefore show a moment in a performance whose military character is suggested by the helmet. This interpretation may obtain even if the stele should be considered funerary, since it is unlikely, at least in Attica, that a gravestone of the 6th century would show the actual moment of death.

[24] More than the usual space is also obvious in *AGA* nos. 74 (behind the man), 50 (above) and 73 (all around). This last stele shows the painted head of a youth facing left, a reversal of the more common position to the right. Richter had assumed that the earliest figured stelai may have had their relief figures also facing left, since the New York sphinx headed in that direction. The painted stele mentioned above may suggest that positions could vary regardless of date.

because carved separately from the shaft can now be restored as bearing a palmette finial (nos. 42, 43). Likewise, some stele shafts had been included within Type I because the style of their relief placed them before 530, but they have now been integrated with a palmette finial because too thin to support a sphinx (nos. 30, 33, 50, 52). Conversely, not all sphinxes stood on capitals (some may have rested directly on the grave, like the lion) and not all capitals were surmounted by sphinxes. Jeffery has suggested that the Lamptrai cavetto once held a small marble equestrian statue and formed part of a different grave monument, comprising a short undecorated shaft and an inscribed base. A comparable reconstruction had once been proposed but has now been largely overshadowed by the new theories so forcefully exemplified by the impressive brother-and-sister monument reconstructed in all its tripartite splendor in the Metropolitan Museum in New York. F. Hiller has now argued for three types of finial from the second quarter of the Sixth century onward: 1) a cavetto capital, with or without sphinx; 2) a volute capital; and 3) a palmette and volute capital, with the volutes bound together by a fillet.

That other variations of the "plain base/relief shaft/capital with finial" arrangement also existed is now proved by the Kerameikos base decorated with four riders in relief, which once supported a gravestone, perhaps the so-called Diskophoros stele. Note the subtle ways in which the Archaic artist, as early as ca. 560, managed to obtain differentiation within apparent uniformity. For instance, the spacing of the horses varies, not enough to detract attention from the main part of the monument but certainly enough to prevent automatic repetition and monotony. Despite the small scale and the relatively low relief, the horses' muscles ripple, and the riders look as if they had to restrain their mounts. The horsemen themselves differ in costume, position of legs, even in age. The youngest, a beardless rider, leads the file. While the bearded men who follow him have short hair, he wears his long; he may perhaps be the deceased, commemorated on the stele above in another of his activities, since his hairstyle corresponds well with that of the Diskophoros, tied in a bun down the nape.

As for the Diskophoros stele, the addition of a new fragment with the youth's right leg shows that he was not simply standing but striding, a figure of action, as early as ca. 560. Almost as early is the startling head of a boxer with broken nose and swollen ear, from a similar gravestone, who raises his hand tied with a boxing glove, perhaps in a significant gesture. Another athlete, an Olympic victor who probably belonged to the Alkmaionids, had a more elaborate monument which must also have differed from the standard type, though erected around 550. An inscribed base from the Kerameikos shows a cutting for a central stele flanked on either side by a circular cavity, presumably meant to hold the bottom of two vases, or perhaps two columns in turn supporting other objects. Another such base has been found elsewhere in Athens, and its inscription shows that it commemorated two dead brothers. Since the Kerameikos base was probably for a father and his son, the missing stele might have shown two people, while the same message might have been conveyed by the two columns.

That stelai almost from the beginning could portray two people at once is perhaps shown by the Keramo stele, so called after one of the two names inscribed on the slab. This is likely to be one of the earliest examples of Attic gravestones, dated epigraphically to the middle or second half of the Seventh century and now broken into an irregular shape. When first discovered, traces of a relief could be discerned, but we now have only the evidence of the inscription. Though only one sentence, it is split into two separate lines, yet not for lack of adequate space. Jeffery has suggested that the arrangement may correspond to the positioning of two figures on the stele, Keramo and Enialos, both mentioned in the epitaph. Given the dimensions of the present fragment, the two personages may have been seated if the evidence has been read correctly and the piece is truly funerary. This very early occurrence, not only of a decorated gravestone but of one showing two seated persons, would place Attica at the forefront of the Greek areas producing grave reliefs. In general, Archaic Attic stelai commemorating two persons at once are not so rare as one might believe. Besides the examples already mentioned above (Copenhagen warriors, brother-and-sister stele, stele of Keramo) several inscribed bases or portions of slabs attest to the practice.

Not all stelai were decorated with human figures even after such practice had started. This is demonstrated by the well-known poros pillar in the Kerameikos, now better understood through a published drawing and dated in the 570's, and by a second example, fragmentary but inscribed vertically and decorated with moldings at the edges. These should be interpreted not as the predecessors of the relief variety but as concomitant though perhaps slightly unusual versions. We have to allow for anomalous pieces throughout the Sixth century: for instance, stelai with only the name of the deceased in the middle of the shaft, and a palmette finial; or stelai decorated, perhaps with paint, on only a portion of the surface (e.g., Theron's stele, or Antiphanes'). Finally among the odd types, three more formats should be mentioned: the panels which may have formed part of a built tomb, perhaps as a series of metopes or an orthostat decoration; the puzzling discs, decorated with paint or with inscription, and finally the square and low blocks, perhaps the trapezai of literary sources.

Other Types of Attic Funerary Monuments. The first type is at present best known through a series of four badly battered and fragmentary slabs, one of them decorated with a rider wearing a petasos and three with a beardless man in the same attire. Since the figures are not centered within their slab, the total scene must have been more complex, though any reconstruction remains hypothetical. In addition, part of each slab may have been covered by an overlapping architectural member, since the extant reliefs seem bordered on only three of their four sides. But no structure has as yet been recognized to which these panels may belong. The same applies to a Chian relief, also showing a horseman on a slab of similar appearance, which probably served the same funerary function. The Athenian series has recently been dated to ca. 550–540 and connected with an Ionic workshop on the basis of the similarity with the (later) horseman relief in Chios. Perhaps also the person buried within the structure in Athens was an Ionian, presumably a man of some standing. That this "Ionic" theory is not impossible is shown by an interesting round building, which at present has been restored within the Kerameikos museum. It belongs to the middle of the Sixth century and combines a Doric frieze with carved moldings uncommon for the order. Here only the workmen may have come from Ionic Asia Minor to work under Peisistratos; the interior of the structure they built was filled with earth, so that the architectural elements formed only the veneer for a burial mound, which might have been an actual grave or a Heroon or Cenotaph.

The discs are usually inscribed and must have been set up in such a way as to be readable by the passerby. It has not yet been determined whether they stood on pillars of their own, or closed the mouths of funerary urns or even of channels for offerings. One is pierced by holes, obviously for fastening though perhaps not for hanging like a Roman *oscillum.* It is not even quite certain whether the shape was functional (a stopper) or simply imitated actual athletic diskoi to symbolize victory in games (the funerary games?) or even just the athletic prowess of the deceased. Negating such a possibility perhaps is the disc painted with the seated image of a bearded man which the inscription identifies as the doctor Aineios. Though the majority of these marble discs carries only an inscription, they are not an obvious form of tomb sculpture, but deserve further attention and cataloguing.

Finally, there are the *trapezai,* though this may not be the appropriate name for the type. It existed outside of Attica, and examples are known from Classical Athens though we may have only one Archaic specimen now in New York. It is a low and square gravestone inscribed "Kalliades, the son of Thoutimides" and decorated on one face with a running Gorgon in relief. A comparable block, similarly decorated and probably funerary but later re-used as a water basin, is in the Paros museum. The Parian running Gorgon, enclosed on all four sides by narrow bands, is in low relief and must have been largely detailed in paint. Since this motif appears on the predella of a stele in Athens (*AGA,* no. 27), both the examples in Paros and New York could conceivably have been cut off from the bottom of a more complex monument, rather than being independent markers on their own. Trapezai proper, of course, served as offering tables on which to place lekythoi and other grave gifts, if not as sacrificial altars.

Canonical Stelai. After all the additions and changes, a few comments should be added about the canonical Attic gravestones. Unfortunately I cannot expand on their aesthetic appeal nor can I analyze some of the best examples in detail. They are superb pieces of carving, which would have appeared even more impressive when original colors were preserved. But a few points need to be made.

First of all, their size. Though the total monument stood, in some cases, over four meters high, the human figure carved on the shaft is usually life-size or only slightly larger; the only exception would be the already mentioned warrior with a shield, who can be restored as ca. 2.20 m. tall. Since kouroi used as grave statues could be much larger, one wonders why people on stelai could not be shown equally heroic in dimensions. Perhaps the answer lies in the fact that the kouros did not represent the deceased per se, as he was in real life, but as a sort of heroized image which had no immediate correlation with the dead, and may even originally have portrayed a funerary Apollo. On the contrary, people on stelai are shown with much stronger individualizing characterization, not only with different attire, hairstyles, or even attributes, but even differing in age and in activities. Though such representations still amounted to types, of which several replicas could be made—the warrior, the diskophoros, the naked athlete with spear or javelin—nonetheless variety was great and may have reflected specific wishes of the family. An interesting theory suggests that the desire to keep the human figure on the stele within natural scale without diminishing the total impressive height of the shaft resulted in the introduction of the predella, which was then decorated with suitable motifs out of a sort of *horror vacui.* That something could be added also above the heads of the figures is shown by examples like *AGA,* nos. 29 and 50. This subsidiary decoration may have been purely apotropaic, like the running Gorgon, or it may have served to characterize further the deceased, like the "departing warrior" scene on a stele in New York or the horseman of the Barracco predella. Note that this subsidiary decoration is carefully prevented from detracting attention from the main scene; either its relief is lower, or the entire panel is merely engraved or painted. Examples, however, do exist in which both the shaft and the subsidiary areas are decorated in the same technique, for instance the stele of Lyseas where both the deceased (a priest of Dionysos ?) and the galloping squire of the predella are painted. Similarly, both the shaft and the finial may be rendered entirely in paint, as in the athlete stele in the Kerameikos. Though the final effect may have been comparable, in their present state of preservation the engraved stelai look quite different from the painted, which have been more severely damaged by the loss of their color. Now the incised figures still stand out in all the purity of their design: the draped youth smelling a flower, a profile face on a fragmentary shaft in the Louvre, the naked boy with a staff and, among the latest finds, the sensitively depicted feet of a man.

Color on gravestones may have been important in more than one respect. Not only did it add life to the picture and details to the general outline, it also created the background. Most grave stelai have their background painted a vivid red, which has unfortunately faded away in most cases. How bright it originally was can still be seen in a newly displayed stele of a warrior in the National Museum in Athens. Certainly such color was important in bringing out the carved scene, but architectural relief usually had a blue background; why was a different color adopted for the gravestones? A metope or a frieze, way up on a building, needed higher carving and a uniformly colored background to be perceived from the ground; against a vivid blue, the lighter figures must have stood as if outlined against the sky, with a realistic touch. Perhaps funerary monuments were painted red for the opposite reason: to remove their content from any possible connection with reality—a daily scene painted against an otherworldly background.[25] This is, of course, pure speculation, but finds slight support in an early Hellenistic gravestone from the Kerameikos with a youth in three-quarter pose against a yellow or golden background, the color of heroization which was eventually taken up by Byzantine mosaics. Obviously inferences drawn from later evidence are unsystematic and dangerous, especially in the field of funerary art, where beliefs varied not only from place to place but from time to time. However, the question might as well be raised. It should also be stressed that considerable difference exists between architectural and votive or funerary relief. Pediments, metopes, friezes, as already mentioned, had to be seen from considerable distance and from a different angle of vision; they needed great projection, bold modeling, clear outlines. Votive or funerary reliefs usually stood approximately at eye level, and therefore needed little projection and subtle modeling. Given the narrow width of the standard grave stele, outlines were simple and narrative was of necessity limited. Some of the incised shafts have been compared with Red Figure or White Ground vases. I should prefer to think of them in terms of

[25] It is usually assumed throughout the world from antiquity to our time that the color red is associated with blood, and therefore with life. See, e.g., K. Friis-Johansen, *The Attic Grave Reliefs* (Copenhagen 1951) 116–17, and references there cited. On the other hand, Kurtz and Boardman (p. 217) state that only the Spartans seem to have used a red shroud, and that red paint on the inner surfaces of some Greek stone and wooden coffins may have signified fire rather than blood. Certainly red predominated on the costumes of the Berlin kore and Phrasikleia, two undoubtedly funerary statues.

sculptors' sketches,[26] since this was a specialized world, perhaps the monopoly of a few masters who signed their works to acquire clientele. This is not to say that each carver of grave monuments was a superior artist; some of the workmanship is hasty or poor, and quality seems to deteriorate toward the end of the Sixth century. Even the early stele of an athlete holding a javelin (*AGA*, no. 27) shows how the sculptor could miscalculate the space at his disposal, thus having to cut into the stele's border to accommodate the toes of the figure's left foot. In technical terms, of particular interest is the way in which the background often curves around the figure, since the sculptor started from an even plane and cut deepest in the center, where he attempted to convey the greatest number of superimposed or foreshortened levels, but rose gradually toward the edges, so that different parts of the relief figure lie against a background of differing depths.

Non-Attic Stelai

What is the relationship of the Attic gravestones to those of Ionia? The traditional position has been to claim that the shaft decorated with a human figure and surmounted by an elaborate capital was an Attic invention, which changed to a thinner slab crowned by a palmette around 530, under Ionian influence. F. Hiller's argument for palmette finials as early as ca. 560 and contemporary with other types of ornament would make the adoption of the motif a purely Attic idea independent of foreign influence, and perhaps stimulated solely by architecture. Since the Attic palmettes never achieved the luxuriant glory of the East Greek or Cycladic examples, one can easily accept the idea of spontaneous invention in different places producing similar but unrelated effects.[27]

Samos. More controversial is the problem of whether Attica was instrumental in diffusing the practice of decorated gravestones and, in particular, in introducing the human figure on stelai which had traditionally been left plain except for the elaborate palmette finial. That this could be the case is argued on the evidence of Samos, the only other area of the Greek world to have produced a coherent sequence of funerary monuments covering approximately two or three generations. According to the recent Samian catalogue of Archaic sculpture, poros stelai with anthemia began in the second third of the Sixth cen-

[26] Sculptors' sketches in this technique do in fact exist; see *Samos* XI no. 104 pl. 78, with a human face engraved in profile to the left. Not only does the outline show a correction for the rendering of the hair over the forehead but the total appearance of the block, with a socle-like projection at the bottom, suggests that the lower part of the figure was never intended to be drawn on the same surface. In addition, there is no room for the attachment of the arm, the breast lies too high, and the entire section below the neck was never "drawn" by the master who had sketched such an interesting profile face.

[27] In general terms, one can state that Attic palmettes rely especially on contour; their inner details are engraved or rendered in paint, and only exceptional cases have a low fillet separating the petals. All elaboration of design takes place in one plane. By contrast, the Samian petals of the Polykratean period have undulating surfaces, some concave, some convex, in alternation; after ca. 520, concave renderings predominate. Many other details (in the volutes, at the heart of the palmette) are either scooped out or in relief. The volutes on which the palmette rests extend their scroll to the very edge of the stele. The Cycladic palmette type is again different. There the volutes stop near the center, above a flat band; the heart of the palmette is left undecorated, and the petals are either smooth or convex, often with a central "spine." The Parian anthemion (infra) is unusual in having two superimposed palmettes above volutes.

tury, reached their peak between 530–510, and started to decline at the turn into the Fifth century.

Plain stelai with anthemia continued to be made after 500, no longer in poros but in marble; their finials became somewhat hybrid and overly elaborate despite their obvious derivation from previous monuments. At the same time a different form of palmette finial was introduced, presumably from the Cyclades, and a type of decorated gravestone, of which only five fragmentary examples remain, probably topped by a floral crown comparable to, if not identical with, the preserved "Cycladic" fragments. Yet the decorated shaft is called Samo-Attic and contrasted with a local experiment: two early Fifth century fragmentary reliefs showing naked youths in more or less frontal poses. These are considered independent of the "Attic" group because a like subject can be found in an amphiglyphon from Olbia (the Leoxos stele), and because the human figure is rendered in natural size, thus providing a sort of continuity with the funerary kouroi. By contrast, the other group of decorated stelai is considered Attic, not only because of its style and format but especially because the subject matter of at least one gravestone has been reconstructed into a man-and-dog scene—the deceased offering a tidbit to his hound—of which the earliest examples presumably come from Attica.

Granted that the idea of putting the human figure on a shaft seems alien to the Samian tradition, once the two experimental pieces with frontal youths were introduced into the island's repertoire, one need not automatically assume Athenian influence over the next group.[28] My reasons for doubting the Attic connection lie in the presumed Athenian priority for the motif of the man and dog. To my mind, Attic stelai tend to show the deceased in isolation, with inanimate attributes, even if in action poses; when other figures are introduced, they are either dead themselves, being commemorated in the same monument, or part of the secondary decoration, carefully distinguished from the main scene. The horse is not comparable to the dog in this respect since the former functions purely as a symbol of the dead man's rank, while the latter, in the man-and-dog scenes, interacts with the deceased in an affectionate relationship. Admittedly, our earliest examples of such a stele type, which became popular later in the Fifth century, seem to come from Athens, but at least one reconstruction is doubtful and the idea itself may have been introduced by Ionic sculptors, who were certainly active in Athens in the funerary line.[29]

A different viewpoint argues that juxtaposition of dead and living (whether animal or human) is an aspect in the development of the gravestone, which before 500 isolated the deceased but after the turn of the century introduced vignettes symbolic of his status and

[28] Indeed E. Buschor (*AthMitt* 58 [1933] 25 and 43) suggested connecting one of the relief youths with a "Cycladic" anthemion, and the recent find of a comparable relief from Naxos (supra) may also speak for an island origin. There are now several examples of this peculiar frontal rendering, and one wonders whether they should not be connected in some fashion. Their distribution (Naxos, Samos, Olbia [?], Sardis, and perhaps Tanagra in Boeotia) would still be compatible with a Cycladic origin for the motif. Perhaps also the stele from Giase-Ada (Thrace) with a frontal girl should be considered part of the same tradition. Her anthemion has obvious Samian affinities.

[29] A finer distinction is made by Hiller (137–39), who divides the man-and-dog group into two types. The first shows the man and the animal simply juxtaposed; and is considered of Attic origin; the second shows the two in interaction and is attributed to the East Greek sphere, probably Samos. According to this theory, the stele fragment *Agora* XI no. 104 would belong to Type I and be an Attic work; the second Athenian fragment, *Agora* XI no. 105, belongs to Type 2 and is considered Ionic also on stylistic and technical grounds.

interests. Yet even this position is based primarily on the apparent lack of such scenes in earlier stelai, and on the widely accepted assertion that very few decorated gravestones existed outside Attica. To be sure, evidence is still quite scanty, but attempts to collect it can produce a substantial total, and new finds begin to fill some gaps. Indeed, H. Hiller, who has compiled a catalogue of Ionic grave reliefs of the first half of the Fifth century, could state that approximately 21 of her 45 items were not known twenty years ago. Despite the chronological restriction, Hiller's work is very useful in showing the wide range of non-Attic stelai after 500. She favors the traditional position, that no true production of grave reliefs existed outside of Attica before that time, yet she makes a definite contribution in recognizing regional distinctions and in postulating original iconography not always derived from Attic prototypes.[30] Chronology however is most difficult to assess, and some of the works listed by H. Hiller within the Fifth century have at times been assigned to an earlier phase. Moreover, Hiller perhaps overemphasizes Attic influence, while minimizing the importance of earlier Ionic experiments. On the contrary, I suspect that the islands and Asia Minor may have played a greater role than is at present assumed in the development of decorated gravestones, and that the present dearth of examples is simply part of the same imperfect picture which we have of East Greek Archaic sculpture as a whole, as we have seen in the case of the sphinx. In addition, the very shape of a stele makes it handy for re-use and some existing monuments may have escaped detection.[31]

East Greece. My suspicion stems from various factors: 1) the presence of Graeco-Persian stelai, some of which may be still Archaic (although many are later) and which are not grafted onto a local Persian tradition;[32] 2) the wide diffusion of stelai in the Neo-Hittite

[30] Specifically, Hiller distinguishes: 1) an East Greek group, which includes Samos and the Ionic colonies outside Asia Minor, as well as Lydia, the Dodecanese, and the nearby Ionic coast (23 examples, O 1–23); 2) a Cycladic-Ionic group, which comprises also the neighboring islands and areas under Cycladic influence, such as Boeotia and Euboea (K 1–15); 3) a North-Ionic group, covering Thasos and Thrace (N 1–4); and 4) an Italic-Ionic group (I 1–3). The stelai thus catalogued are either tall and narrow, with a palmette finial, or wide and less tall, and crowned by a pediment. Iconographically, the draped man is a favorite type, single girls (unknown in Attic repertoire) are often portrayed, and the many-figured groups appear, often including interaction. These last types, including the man playing with his dog, though "unthinkable without the earlier Attic stelai" (p. 142), represent specific Ionic variations and innovations in the iconographic field.

[31] This is, for instance, the case of a stele from Amorgos, whose Archaic relief was cut down, and whose back and top were carved as the triglyphs and metopes of a Doric frieze, presumably for a Hellenistic funerary structure. What survives of the Archaic relief shows a draped youth in profile to right, holding a flower with his left hand, the right arm bent and crossing the body at waist level. Unfortunately a complete reconstruction of its action is impossible. The finial is missing. The stele has been dated to the turn from the 6th into the 5th century. Another, later, gravestone from the same island preserves only its upper part, with the head of a youth and a volute-palmette finial. Ph. Zapheiropoulou, *AAA* 6 (1973) 351–55; figs. 1–2 show the Hellenistic recutting; fig. 3 the present state of the Archaic relief, and figs. 4 and 5 are reconstructed drawings. Fig. 6 is stele no. 13 in Chora.

[32] Graeco-Persian stelai are still very difficult to assess and date, and scholars vary widely in their interpretations and chronology. In particular, some stelai from Daskyleion have given rise to the theory that an Archaic figureless shaft surmounted by a palmette was later utilized by non-Greek masters who carved on it complex figured scenes. Other scholars stress instead the unity of format-finial and carved registers. It is impossible to give here the rich bibliography on the subject; see, more recently, on the general subject of Graeco-Persian reliefs, Hanfmann, 18–19, and n. 21 with bibliography; H. Möbius, *AA* 1971, 442–55; J. Borchhardt, *IstMitt* 18 (1968) 161–211; H. Metzger, *AntClass* 1971, 505–25; E. Akurgal, *Mélanges Mansel* 2 (Ankara 1974) 967–70.

as well as the Egyptian world; 3) the sprinkling of Greek stelai with figured decoration which are found in relatively backward areas but in developed form, thus presupposing some kind of established tradition elsewhere. A few examples of the figured gravestone in Sixth century Asia Minor may be relevant here.

The Kalchedon stele has been variously considered votive or funerary, and therefore its many-figured scene has either been interpreted as the birth of Athena or the death of a woman in childbirth. Recent mentions have all favored a funerary explanation, which therefore makes this unprepossessing relief an important forerunner of the pathetic scenes of Fourth century Attic gravestones. The inscription supports this interpretation and helps date the slab to ca. 550. Not only is the scene unique for its date in its complexity, it is also clearly indebted to non-Greek prototypes in its broad format and silhouette relief. Comparable are Graeco-Egyptian or Egypto-Karian reliefs. One in Berlin shows a prothesis scene, four mourning figures standing around the deceased, who is laid out on a kline with a table which look very Greek in shape. But the whole scene is under the protection of a large winged-sun disc and uraei, despite a Greek inscription which identifies the dead man as a Milesian. A limestone gravemarker, inscribed in Karian and dated ca. 550–530, was found in a Karian cemetery near Nectanebo's temple at Sakkara and is now in the Fitzwilliam Museum in Cambridge. Under the usual winged-sun disc, a man and woman "in thoroughly Greek style" are parting, each extending a hand to touch the other's chin in a gesture of affection which recalls wooing scenes on Black Figured vases.[33] Obviously one cannot make much of such anomalous cases in foreign territory, but it is likely that funerary paraphernalia, even abroad, may reflect those of the land of origin.[34]

Influence from East Greece or the islands should also be responsible for the appearance of stelai in outlying areas of the Black Sea, Thrace, or the Anatolian interior. The Dorylaion stele, from Phrygia, has often been considered an anomaly and perhaps a votive relief. Certainly the presence of a winged figure holding a lion by a paw can only be considered divine, a Mistress of Animals. But the opposite side of the slab has two registers: one with a horseman accompanied by his servant and a dog, the other with a man in a two-horse chariot; these suggest a funerary purpose. The treatment of the goddess' costume recalls both the pedimental figures and the Karyatids of the Siphnian Treasury at Delphi, which should date the Dorylaion stele around 520. Evidence from Lydia is more ambiguous; the strange stele with a frontal "kouros" had no finial preserved, and a recently found marble anthemion from Sardis has not retained its stele. Theories that the Borgia stele came from Sardis have not found confirmation but Hiller has recently pointed out that the hole in the rear of the stele, for attachment to a background, would be appropriate

[33] It is interesting to note that the same gesture occurs on a relief from Persepolis where two noblemen greet each other: one of them touches the other's beard. The relief, also in the Fitzwilliam, comes from the east landing of the grand staircase in front of the Council Hall of Darius I and Xerxes. One therefore wonders whether the gesture is of Oriental or of Greek derivation in both the funerary and the architectural relief.

[34] Of particular interest also may be the amphiglyphon found at San Varano, Italy, near Forlì, on the direct route between the sea and the hinterland of Emilia, which suggests direct contacts between the Near East and the head of the Adriatic sea. The double stele shows on one side two rampant goats nibbling at a sacred tree, on the other a sphinx whose tail terminates in a deer head. Both sides are further decorated by a palmette-volute ornament which recalls Greek anthemia, but the figures are wholly Oriental in conception. The relief has been dated to the late 7th, first half of the 6th century (*JHS ArchR for 1967–68*, vol. 14, p. 47 fig. 24; *StEtr* 35 [1967] 655–58, pl. 143).

for a Lydian relief decorating a tomb facade, an ornamental practice limited to that geographical area.

The two stelai from Sinope should perhaps not be discussed here because already datable to the Severe Period, but the above-mentioned amphiglyphon of Leoxos from Olbia and the stele from Apollonia fit within the time range. A fragmentary stele, showing the middle portion of a man's naked body against the background of some drapery, was found near Phanagoria (Russia) the principal Greek city on the east side of the Straits. Two Thracian examples are of importance. The first is the amphiglyphon from Komotini, ca. 500, interesting not only because of the presence of the living servant boy and the dog but also because amphiglypha have been considered an Ionic invention. The second stele was found at Giase-Ada, southwest of Komotini, probably ancient Stryme; it is the fragmentary relief of a girl facing outward, the slab crowned by a volute-palmette anthemion which recalls Samian examples, though it has also been called Chian. The date of this piece should be around 525.

From Asia Minor proper come examples of tall and narrow stelai (e.g., the stele from Syme, which resembles Attic formulas), of decorated bases which may have supported them (the Loryma base), and of finials in the shape of stunted pyramids, which carry decoration on one side only and probably topped pillar gravestones. Finally, the doctor's stele now in Basel, showing a seated man facing a young attendant with medical equipment hanging in the background, has been variously considered Milesian, Samian, and even Koan. Scattered and vague as all this evidence may be, the possibility that Asia Minor Greeks used decorated gravestones should be considered.

The Islands. Similar funerary practices should have prevailed in the islands. Aside from the very early relief from Paros, already mentioned, others exist which share the same ambivalent appearance that qualifies them for both votive and funerary purposes. When the human figure is not seated, the interpretation of the relief as funerary seems more assured, but a certain touch of heroization may always have been included. Kos has produced two interesting fragments, one with a boy holding a cock, another with an apparently erotic scene comprising several people and a flute player, in a most unusual rendering.[35] Other fragmentary reliefs come from Rhodes, Chios, Kythnos, Tenos, and other islands. Paros, besides the Gorgon predella already mentioned, has also produced a spectacular anthemion with a double palmette over volutes with inserted eyes. Another comes from Thera. Two long slabs with complex scenes, also found in Paros, have been attributed to a Heroon, possibly of Archilochos, and belong to the realm of architectural sculpture.

Boeotia. In Greece proper, two areas in particular have produced more than occasional examples of decorated gravestones. Boeotia, after the unusual Dermys and Kittylos, seems to have followed the Athenian lead in several imitative gravestones which have been listed by Richter together with the Attic examples. Toward the end of the Archaic period a man in Orchomenos had his tomb marker carved with the man-and-dog motif by the Naxian Alxenor; this shows perhaps a renewed opening to the islands. None of the Boeotian stelai, to my knowledge, has preserved its finial, but the peculiar tenon over Dermys and Kittylos

[35] This latter, however, may be part of a larger frieze and will be discussed infra, Ch. 9.

speaks for a substantial crowning member. An early Fifth century fragmentary finial in Thebes has been reconstructed as a lyre-shaped capital; its volutes, which might have supported a bronze object, perhaps a small kantharos, are adorned by metal insertions in the eyes. It may have topped a gravestone like Alxenor's. A late Archaic stele from the vicinity of Thebes has a wide format, topped by a curving molding at the top, to accommodate a helmeted rider and his horse (Fig. 54). Note the unusual details of the man's flying mantle and of the horse's head which was turned outward to face the viewer.

Lakonia. The second Greek area with a considerable production of reliefs is Lakonia, though here too the debate over their proper function has been long and inconclusive. One of the latest opinions asserts that since a relief comparable to the famous Chrysapha stele in Berlin has been found within a sanctuary near the river Eurotas, the question is settled and the reliefs must all be considered votive. Certainly the traditional scenes—with a couple seated on elaborate thrones and confronted by diminutive human figures bringing gifts—imply some kind of worship. It is interesting to find this discrepancy in size, and therefore in visual importance, between humans and divine figures not only in reliefs so obviously inspired from Egypt (note the rendering of the thrones, with animals' legs, not just feet, and the bearded snake rearing behind the seat) but even in Attic works from the Athenian Akropolis like the well-known scene with Athena and a family of worshipers bringing her a pig. But if such comparisons with unquestionably votive compositions tend to stress the religious aspect of the Spartan reliefs, the chthonic symbols included in the latter suggest that ancestral worship is involved. Note in particular not only the frequent snakes but also the egg and the cock, which signify resurrection. The connection of some Lakonian reliefs with a scene from the Harpy Tomb monument from Xanthos, in Lycia, is intriguing since it suggests a common foreign source, perhaps in Egypt. Again, presumably the double purpose, votive and commemorative, obtained for both monuments without being mutually exclusive.

Besides the traditional seated-couple scene, other Lakonian stelai show seated men with dog and horse, youths, girls, and even mourning figures. The technique of the carving stresses outlines, which are carried straight back to the background plane or are superimposed on each other with a collage effect devoid of modeling or foreshortening. The rather simplified rendering of these works makes them look earlier than they may be; their appearance is probably due more to religious conservatism than to actual inability on the part of the sculptors, but this presumed retardation remains typical of Lakonian works in general. Among the grave markers should perhaps be included also the peculiar pyramidal pillar where two wider figured faces alternate with two narrower ones carrying a single snake. Each of the wider faces shows a man and a woman, and have been interpreted in terms of local epics: Menelaos first wooing and then threatening Helen. Schefold considers the monument funerary and dates it ca. 580–570.

Finally, two more regions have produced gravestones which continued into the Fifth and Fourth centuries: Thessaly and Macedonia. Since, however, the truly Archaic examples are few and difficult to date, they can be omitted here.

Magna Graecia. In Magna Graecia, evidence for decorated stelai is even poorer despite the fact that Sicily had known some native examples since the Bronze Age. As usual, the best information comes from Megara Hyblaia, which has produced a broad limestone stele, trapezoidal in shape, with sides tapering from top to bottom; traces of doweling show that it may have come from a naiskos. The main field depicts a horseman and is capped by a pediment decorated with triglyphs. A second stele from the same site, also in limestone, has approximately the same shape but carries a kneeling warrior in very low relief.[36] A gravestone showing a youth against a relatively wide background comes from Selinus, but is archaizing rather than Archaic—or even a forgery. A bearded head of a warrior comes from Camarina. The same Sicilian tendency for naiskos frames may have prevailed at Cyrene, where a late Sixth century stele with a youth (Fig. 56) was probably set into a separate architectural border.

SUMMARY

Greek funerary sculpture seems to have utilized the same types, both in relief and in the round, which were also used for votive purposes, with the sole exception of the tall and narrow stele. This, to my knowledge, was mainly used as a grave monument and reached its greatest development in Attica. However, it should be stressed that this was by no means the only format adopted there for the purpose and that several shapes and types of gravestones could exist simultaneously. Whether the broad format influenced, or was influenced by, the votive relief is now impossible to say, but I suspect that the former is the case. Unfortunately, a thorough study of Attic votive reliefs of the Archaic period has not yet been made, and those from other areas are often ambiguous and could usually serve both purposes.

It is also important to note that decorated gravestones may have existed outside Attica, and especially in East Greek or Ionic territory. Here too format could vary, and, both in Attic and non-Attic examples, content was given much greater scope and characterization than the standard funerary statue. As for the latter, aside from some regional preferences, types were the same as for votive offerings, and priorities are difficult to establish. Even apotropaic monsters like the sphinx may have been erected earlier as civic rather than as private monuments. Yet it should be stressed that the same theme may have had different meanings in different areas and that more local originality prevailed in the way people commemorated their dead than in how they worshiped their gods.

[36] From Megara Hyblaia comes also a lyre-shaped capital, with two palmettes of Cycladic type in between volutes, but one cannot surmise whether it belonged to a sculpted stele, although its funerary nature seems certain: *Sicile Grecque*, pl. 23.

BIBLIOGRAPHY 6

FOR PAGE 149

Belted kouros from Thera: "Theräisches," Beil. 91–92; see supra, p. 56.

Feet and plinth embedded in rock: *JHS ArchR* 12 (1966) 18 fig. 31; *Ergon* 1965, 124–25 figs. 157–58; Jacob-Felsch, 7 and n. 15, with further examples of the practice.

Samian funerary kouroi: *Samos* XI nos. 53, 56; found in cemeterial areas but uncertain: no. 57; Leukios kouros: no. 35.

Unfinished statue from Milesian nekropolis: *Ruinen*, 127 and fig. 94 on p. 128.

Draped male figure from Pitane: Tuchelt L 104; *KAnat*, figs. 195–97.

Naxos "relief-kouros": N. Kontoleon, *Praktika* 1960, 261 pl. 199 a–b; *Aspécts*, 52 pl. 22:1–2.

Dermys and Kittylos: *AGA* no. 9 figs. 31–33, 192–95; *Kouroi* no. 11 figs. 76–77; see also K. Levin, *AJA* 68 (1964) 17.

Stele from Sardis: Collignon, 47, fig. 20.

FOR PAGE 150

Guralnick, *CompSt*, 80.

"Action pose" as typical of relief: N. Kontoleon, *Opus Nobile*, 92–94; *Aspécts*, 52–53.

Tanagra limestone statue: supra, pp. 75 n. 32, pp. 86, 115.

Megara Hyblaia kouros inscribed to doctor: supra, pp. 71 and 82.

Kouros within naiskos: *NSc* 1954, 90–96; G. Vallet & F. Villard, *Mégara Hyblaea* 4 (1966) 55 n. 4 pl. 93 (for decoration of naiskos). Cf. Langlotz, who comments on pl. 129; he dates it to the 4th century, but finds from the tomb show that it must belong to the late Archaic period.

Tenea and Keos kouroi: Kurtz & Boardman, 237–38.

Samian korai: *Samos* XI nos. 25–26; cf. also p. 9. Original publication: *AltSt* 2, p. 37; 5, p. 95.

FOR PAGE 151

Kore from Thera: supra, pp. 87 and 115.

Cyrene busts: L. Beschi, *ASAtene* NS 31–32 (1969–70) 133–41; see especially p. 210.

Seated figures and riders: See supra, Ch. 5. For Jeffery's suggestion, see "Gravestones," 151.

On Athenian funerary practices in general, see *Aristodikos*, 26–43; I disagree on some points.

FOR PAGE 152

On the lion, see H. Gabelmann. See also *Art of Greece*, 176–83 and notes.

FOR PAGE 153

Lions from Didmya: Tuchelt K 66–74, K 85; the last is probably architectural. From the rest of Asia Minor, Tuchelt mentions only L 117–20. For some of the Sardis lions, see now Hanfmann, 14.

Samian lions: *Samos* XI nos. 81–83.

Cycladic lions: From Thera, "Theräisches," Beil. 95–96; from other islands, several are illustrated in *AthMitt* 76 (1961) 67–80. The lions from Delos have not yet been officially published; see, however, H. Gallet de Santerre, *Delos* 24 (1959) 23–36 and pls. 33–49; *GdD*, 112–14; *Agora* XI, 29 n. 70. Gabelmann, 74–76, dates the Sacred Lake lions ca. 550–540; *contra* see Jacob-Felsch, 11 n. 41.

For lions elsewhere, see references in Gabelmann, catalogue.

Akropolis lions: *AMA* nos. 382–84.

Kerameikos lions: Listed in "Gravestones," 126, nos. 1–5. For the poros lion with companion, see *Kerameikos* 6:2 (1970) 412–13.

Agora lions: *Agora* XI nos. 90–92.

Corinthian lions, in Copenhagen: *Ny Carlsberg*, nos. 5–6; in Boston: *Boston Cat.* no. 10.

Limestone lion-spout from Olympia: *Olympia* III, 26 fig. 23 pl. 5; Mallwitz, 89 fig. 77.

FOR PAGE 154

Perirrhanteria: See Ch. 4, pp. 88–89.

Corfu lion: *Korkyra* 2, pp. 176–88; cf. fig. 164 on p. 185 for an illustration of the lion's face from below. Note, however, how close the stylization of nose wrinkles can come to natural patterns in real lions: *JHS* 71 (1951) 89 and pl. 32.

Didyma lion B 281: Tuchelt K 66 pls. 63, 65–66. Its twin is K 67 pls. 65–66, 68.

Lion B 282: Tuchelt K 69 pl. 64.

Lions from Miletos, in front of tomb: *Ruinen*, 127 fig. 92; the tomb is dated by its content to the second half of the 6th century. Cf. also Blümel no. 62, figs. 179–83, and Tuchelt L 117.

FOR PAGE 155

Colossal lion from Didyma in Istanbul: Tuchelt K 71 pl. 70.

Lion from Miletos in the Louvre: Tuchelt L 119; Gabelmann, pl. 26 no. 127.

Funerary lions: *Samos* XI nos. 81 and 83; Sardis lion in *KAnat*, 279 fig. 245 on p. 275; from Smyrna, *KAnat*, 279 figs. 246–47.

Lion on column, in Ankara (monument of Mikos): *KAnat*, 279–80 fig. 249.

Samian lion in active pose: *Samos* XI no. 83. That the springing pose occurs earlier on coins is mentioned by J. Boardman, *Gnomon* 39 (1967) 101.

FOR PAGE 156

Sphinxes: *Art of Greece*, 187 with notes; N. M. Verdelis, *BCH* 75 (1951) 1–37; A. Dessenne, *Colloque de Strasbourg 22–24 Mai 1958* (Paris 1960) 155–61.

Sphinxes from Corinth: *AGA* nos. 14–15.

Sphinx from Aegina: *AGA* no. 40.

Sphinxes topping decorated stelai: *AGA* nos. 11, 37, 38.

Heads only: *AGA* nos. 17 and 18.

FOR PAGE 157

Halikarnassos sphinx: B. Ashmole, *Festschrift A. Rumpf* (1952) 5–9; Tuchelt L 65.

Didyma altar: *JdI* 79 (1964) 202–29; now in Izmir Museum.

Myus altar (found in Miletos): Blümel no. 64 figs. 186–92; for the attribution to Myus, see *IstMitt* 15 (1965) 62–63.

Assos, confronted sphinxes on architrave: *Boston Cat.* no. 8; fragments of a second architrave block with almost duplicate scene are in Paris and Istanbul; cf. *RA* 23 (1914) 220 fig. 45.

For drawings of the entire sculptural decoration at Assos, see *EAA*, Atlas vol., pls. 13–15; pl. 15 shows the sphinx metope.

Architectural terraccottas with confronted sphinxes were shown during a paper on Erythrai at the 10th International Congress of Classical Archaeology in Turkey, Sept. 1973.

Samos, anta sphinxes: Rhoikos altar (ca. 540): *Samos* XI no. 128; Temple of Hermes and Aphrodite (ca. 530–520): *Samos* XI nos. 129–32; Great Temple of Hera (520–510): *Samos* XI nos. 133–34.

Non-Greek monuments with sphinxes: See, e.g., the Phrygian rock-cut facade of Aslankaya near Afyon, *KAnat*, figs. 52–53; Xanthos, pediments with sphinxes in the British Museum: *FdX* 2 (1963) pl. 47 (details in *KAnat*, figs. 90–93); Sidon, Lycian sarcophagus: *KAnat*, fig. 96.

Votive capital from Didyma: Th. Wiegand and H. Knackfuss, *Didyma* 1 (Berlin 1941) 149 pl. 213, F 662, a poros capital of the end of the 7th century. Cf. also the Aeolic capital from Larisa, K. Schefold, *JOAI* 31 (1938–39) 42–43 fig. 17, and 50–51 for its function.

Nereid monument, siege frieze: pending the official publication of the sculptures (this particular frieze by W. Childs), see *EAA* Atlas, pl. 282 (U 161, bottom right).

For Assyrian animals on columns, see Hrouda, 64 pl. 12:1 and n. 67; besides mountain goats, a dog or lion as crowning is known under Tiglath Pileser III (744–727).

Ionic capital ill-suited for sphinx: Jacob-Felsch, 16 and n. 53; cf. also p. 15.

Ionic column started as votive pedestal: G. Gruben, *AthMitt* 80 (1965) 207–8.

Aegina column and sphinx: *ibid.*, 170–208; for the one near the temple of Apollo, see *ibid.*, fig. 5 and p. 187 n. 22.

Head of sphinx in local museum: A. Furtwängler, *Aigina* (Munich 1906) pls. 82–83, but Gruben (*op. cit.*, p. 187) thinks it is a kore.

The head of the sphinx from Aegina in Athens (*AGA* no. 40) has now been found and joined to the body (Nat.Mus. 77). For the Severe sphinx in Aegina, see *Severe Style*, 35–36 figs. 51–52.

FOR PAGE 158

Naxian Sphinx in Delphi: *FdD* 2:4 (1953) 1–32 pls. 1–15; see also Jacob-Felsch, 109–10 no. 5; Schefold, pl. 261a; *Korai* pl. XI: f-g-h, opposite p. 44. For a similar capital in Naxos, which probably supported a sphinx, see *FdD* 2:4 (1953) 21–22 pls. 15–17:5–7.

Cyrene sphinx: *AJA* 75 (1971) 47–55 pls. 9–10.

Delos sphinx: *GdD*, 44–45, pl. 6. Since there are more than one votive capital from the island, presumably several sphinx monuments once existed; see also Jacob-Felsch, 112–13 no. 8. For the type of capital, now considered Parian, see *AAA* 1 (1968) 178–81; also *AA* 1972, 379 and figs. 35–37 on pp. 376–78; cf. also *ibid.*, 358–60.

Delos A 3842: *BCH* 48 (1924) 254–58 and figs. 21–22 on p. 257. For the tomb of the Hyper-

borean Maidens, see *GdD*, 94 n. 32 and bibliography in n. 1.
Paros no. 194: O. Rubensohn, *Das Delion von Paros* (Wiesbaden 1962) 57–58 no. 7 pl. 9.
Odessa sphinx: AA 1928, cols. 87–88 fig. 9.
Al Mina sphinx: Boardman, 55 pl. 2a.
Sphinx from Megara Hyblaia: *NSc* 1899, 407 fig. 5; *Arte Antica e Moderna* (1960) 332.
Terracotta head from Akragas: Langlotz, color pl. VI.

FOR PAGE 159
Cleveland sphinx: M. Bieber, *Art in America* (July 1943) 112–26 fig. 1; Cleveland Museum of Art, *Classical Art Handbook* (1961) pl. 3.
Caltagirone relief: Langlotz, pl. 13.
Poros sphinxes from Corinth: *AGA* nos. 14–15 figs. 46–53.
Marble sphinx from Corinth: *AAA* 6 (1973) 181–88.
Akropolis sphinxes: *AMA* nos. 371–76.

FOR PAGE 160
Akr. 630: Payne, 10 pls. 7–9; *AMA* no. 371; Brouskari, 37.
Akr. 632: Payne, 10 pl. 56; *AMA* no. 372; Deyhle, 49–50 fig. 18:2; Brouskari, 47, where the sphinx is dated 540–530.
Akr. 654: supra, pp. 108 and 118.
Sirens: in general, see *EAA* s.v. *Sirena* (H. Sichtermann, 1966), where the Egyptian derivation is doubted. *Contra* see, e.g., J. D. Cooney, *BullClev* 55 (1968) 262–71. For Phoenician connections, see *Art of Greece*, 150–56 (tridacna shell sirens).

FOR PAGE 161
Askos from Kroton: G. Jacopi, *ArchCl* 5 (1953) 10–22 pls. 4–8.
Harpy Tomb: Latest discussion in Berger, 129–42 figs. 146–49. Cf. also the pediment from Xanthos in the British Museum, where a siren stands on a column: Berger, 135–36 fig. 152; *FdX* 2 (1963) pl. 48:2 (attributed to Building F and dated after 470).
Siren from Kyzikos: *KAnat*, figs. 226–28; *Ny Carlsberg* no. 4a.
Delos siren: unpublished ?
Corinth Siren: *Corinth* XV:1 (1948) 70–71 pls. 26–27; see p. 71 n. 56 for the mention of a terracotta siren, possibly akroterial.
Marble bird from Athenian Agora: *Agora* XI no. 89.

FOR PAGE 162
Owl, Akr. 1347: Payne, 51 pl. 131; *AMA* no. 380; Brouskari, 23.
Larger but fragmentary owl, Akr. inv. 1355 + 245, etc.: *AMA* no. 381.
Poros owl in Athens, Akr. 56: Brouskari, 34.
Poros owl in Berlin: Blümel no. 10 figs. 27–28.
Delos birds: *GdD*, 45; *BCH* 53 (1929) 188 fig. 2 and 196–97; *BCH* 62 (1938) 218–19, with lists of finds.
Bronze dove: H. Payne, *Perachora* I (1940) 133–34 pl. 41 (length, 19 cm.; height, 10 cm.).
Kerameikos Gorgon: D. Ohly, *AthMitt* 77 (1962) 92–104.
Bull from the Akropolis: *AMA* no. 379.
Monument of Dionysios, 345–338: Ch. W. Clairmont, *Gravestone and Epigram* (Mainz 1970) 151–52 no. 76, with bibliography, pl. 31.
Butting goats as Dionysiac symbol: Th. Kraus, *AthMitt* 69–70 (1954–55) 109–24.
Goat head in Cleveland: *Handbook of the Cleveland Museum of Art* (1966) 20 no. 3; inv. no. 26.538, limestone.
Samian cow: *Samos* XI no. 85.

FOR PAGE 163
Stelai. The theory of uninterrupted sequence is by M. Andronikos, *Deltion* 17:1 (1961–2) 152–210, French summary on pp. 292–95; the Kimisala stele: *Ibid.*, pl. 88; cf. also Kurtz & Boardman, 219.
Kimolos stele: N. Kontoleon, *Theoria*, Festschrift Schuchhardt, (1960) 129–37; *Aspécts*, 49–53 pl. 23. The date is doubted by Kurtz & Boardman, 220.

FOR PAGE 164
Column with human head at Naxos: See *supra*, p. 74 n. 30.
Prinias stelai: Good summary in K. Friis Johansen, *The Attic Grave-Reliefs* (Copenhagen 1951) 80–82; the most recent study (Adams) doubts the funerary purpose of the stelai and postulates architectural use.
For a recent acquisition of a Cretan stele, see *MUSE* 7 (1973) 9 no. 58 (ill.), dated ca. 650. Cf. also Hiller, 137 n. 62.
Relief from Paros: *Deltion* 16 (1960) 245 pl. 215; *AA* 1964, 274; *Aspécts*, 49–53.

FOR PAGE 165
On profile view of kouroi and similarity with stelai, see also "Gravestones," 153.

Attic stelai: Much of the following criticism is expressed in my review of *AGA*; see *AJA* 66 (1962) 419–22.

Stele in Berlin: *AGA* no. 24; new interpretation by F. Hiller, *MarbWinckPr* 1967, 18–26.

FOR PAGE 166

Anavyssos stele: *AGA* no. 59; *Aspécts*, 18; Hiller, 135 and n. 54a.

Lampito base: "Gravestones," 130 no. 24; see also 121 no. 12, to Melissa, and 131 no. 27, which probably reads Kleito; cf. also 149–50.

Monuments by Aristokles: 1) base for broad stele, epigram for Oinanthe: *Deltion* 20:2 (1965) 86; *BCH* 92 (1968) 738–39; "Stelen," 34–41; G. Daux, *ArchCl* 25–26 (1973–74) 242–43; 2) fragmentary stele from the Kerameikos: "Stelen," pl. 15:2. Relief in Athens (Nat.Mus. 36): *Ibid.*, pl. 15:1; cf. also *AGA*, fig. 174 and infra, Ch. 11, 309–10. For an interpretation of the latter relief as funerary, see "Gravestones," 148 no. 7, and 150.

Velanideza relief: *Deltion* 21:1 (1966) 102–15, summary on p. 213; pls. 43–46 and fig. 1; see especially p. 110 n. 49.

Base signed by Aristokles, for father of Oinanthe: "Stelen," 35. For another broad stele, see the base in the Kerameikos, "Grabmalbasen," 122–23 no. 4a, Beil. 74:2. Cf. also the painted seated figure on the base of Nelonides signed by Endoios: "Gravestones," 127 no. 19. On broad format, see also Andronikos, *ArchEph* 1956, 209; *Aspécts*, 18–19.

Copenhagen relief with two warriors: *AGA* no. 77.

Athlete throwing javelin: *AGA* no. 48; "Gravestones," 125 no. [10].

Marathon runner: Schefold, pl. 41. More bibliography supra p. 166, n. 23.

New piece added to old fragment: *AGA* no. 47; *AAA* 2 (1969) 394–97. The addition of palmette finials to the pieces mentioned is suggested by F. Hiller, *MarbWinckPr* 1967, 18–26.

FOR PAGE 167

Lamptrai cavetto: *AGA* no. 20; "Gravestones," 137 no. 45 and 138 no. 1, as part of the same monument. For an earlier reconstruction, see F. Winter, *AthMitt* 12 (1887) 105–18 and fig. 1. The reconstruction was corrected by W. B. Dinsmoor, *AJA* 26 (1922) 261–77 (he reproduced Winter's reconstruction on p. 270 fig. 8). Cf. *Aspécts* 11–12, for the interpretation of the side figures.

Brother-and-sister stele: *AGA* no. 37. New fragment in Athens: A. Greifenhagen, *Antike Kunstwerke* (Berlin 1965) 4 no. 3.

Kerameikos base with riders, Inv. P 1001: "Grabmalbasen," 105–9 no. 1. For an analysis of the relief, see also B. S. Ridgway, *Hesperia* 35 (1966) 195 n. 33. For the connection with the Diskophoros stele (*AGA* no. 25) see "Grabmalbasen," 109. New fragment added to the stele: "Stelen," 28–29 pl. 11:3. It was found not far from the find spot of the riders' base P 1001.

Boxer stele: *AGA* no. 31; *Aristodikos*, 44 no. A 1, and comments on p. 40; "Gravestones," 128 no. 1.

Grave monument of Olympic victor: "Grabmalbasen," 110–17, no. 2, Beil. 60 and fig. 1.

Similar base from Athens: *Aristodikos*, 68–69, C 4 and fig. 2.

Keramo stele: "Gravestones," 129 no. [22]. For other examples of double commemoration, see "Gravestones," 136 no. 41; 139–40 no. 48; 140–41 no. 50; 146 no. 60. See also *AGA* no. 76, the Lavrion stele.

FOR PAGE 168

Kerameikos pillar: *AGA* no. 7; "Stelen," 23–27 and pl. 9. Second example, *ibid.*, 27–28, fig. 1, pl. 10.

Theron's stele: *AGA* no. 60 A–B; the controversy over the identification is still rife; for the latest statement, see E. Vanderpool, *AAA* 5 (1972) 238–51, with previous bibliography.

Antiphanes' stele: *AGA* no. 54.

Built tombs, panels in National Museum: "Stelen," 30–34 pls. 12–13; S. Karouzou, *AthMitt* 76 (1961) pls. 70–71.

Chian relief: "Stelen," 33–34 pl. 13:2; Berger, 40 fig. 38. Hiller, 61, 166–67, Cat. O 22.

For built graves, cf. also the terracotta plaques discussed by J. Boardman, *BSA* 50 (1955) 51–66.

Round building in the Kerameikos: *AA* 1969, 31 and fig. 1 on p. 32.

Discs: "Gravestones," 147 nos. 64 and 66, with further bibliography; Berger, 155–58 figs. 164–65 for disc of Aineios.

FOR PAGE 169

Trapezai: G. Despinis, *ArchEph* 1963, 46–68 pls. 3–4; Kurtz & Boardman, 168, 235–37; "Trapeza" in New York: *BMMA* 16 (Feb. 1958) 187–88 fig. 1; *Aristodikos,* 91 n. 76, suggests that the piece may be a predella, possibly reused; Paros "trapeza" with Gorgon: inv. no. 172. Unpublished ?

For a good analysis of the Athens stele with Gorgon predella, see J. Dörig, *AA* 1967, 21–23.

Horror vacui: M. Andronikos, *Deltion* 16 (1960) 46–59.

FOR PAGE 170

Departing warrior scene on New York stele: *AGA* no. 45; for a color reproduction, see *AJA* 48 (1944) pls. 8–9, 11.

Barracco predella: *AGA* no. 64.

Stele of Lyseas: *AGA* no. 70; "Gravestones," 141 no. 53.

Athlete stele in the Kerameikos: *AGA* no. 58; see especially the drawing in *AthMitt* 73 (1958) 1–5, Beil. 1–2 pl. 1.

Draped youth smelling a flower: *AGA* no. 57.

Shaft in Louvre: *MonPiot* 41 (1946) 63–71.

Boy with staff: *AA* 1963, cols. 431–39.

Man's feet: *Deltion* 21:1 (1966) 115–21 pls. 47–48.

Warrior stele in Athens: Nat.Mus. M 1541; I am not aware that it has been published yet.

Hellenistic gravestone with yellow background: *AA* 1942, col. 253 and fig. 30 on col. 250.

FOR PAGE 171

Workmanship deteriorating toward the end of the Archaic period: E. B. Harrison, *Hesperia* 25 (1956) 34.

On technical details, see the comments by J. Frel, *AA* 1973, 196.

Samian stelai: 540–500, *Samos* xi nos. 88–100 (an occasional example in marble); 500–480, *Samos* xi nos. 150–52; Cycladic finials: *Samos* xi nos. 153–54; figured stelai: *Samos* xi nos. 145–49; for the term "Samo-Attic," see p. 216.

FOR PAGE 172

Youths in frontal poses (limestone): *Samos* xi nos. 143–44.

On Samian figured stelai, see also Hiller, 21–26, 148–51, Cat. nos. O 1–6.

Leoxos stele: Berger, 40 fig. 45 and bibliography in n. 83; Hiller, 154–55, O 9.

On the man-and-dog stelai, see B. S. Ridgway, *JdI* 86 (1971) 60–79. For a different viewpoint, see Berger, 109–14; Hiller, 137–39 with notes; cf. also her p. 129 n. 19 and 163–64 (O 18); 47–51.

FOR PAGE 174

Kalchedon stele: B. Schmaltz, *IstMitt* 19/20 (1969–70) 177–85; Berger, 103–4 fig. 124; *Aspécts,* 13; Hiller, 18 n. 17.

Graeco-Egyptian relief in Berlin: Boardman, 134 and pl. 9a.

Stele from Sakkara in Cambridge: *JHS ArchR* 17 (1971) 75 fig. 13 and 76 no. 26; *JEA* 56 (1970) pl. 10:2.

Dorylaion stele: Berger, 40 fig. 39, dated ca. 500; "Man-and-dog," 73–74 nn. 39–41; Hiller, 167–69 (O 23).

Lydian stele with frontal "kouros": Collignon, 47 fig. 20.

Anthemion from Sardis: *Archaeology* 27 (1974) 139 fig. 3, dated ca. 525–500.

Borgia stele: Hiller, 47–51, especially n. 136; cf. also 156–60, O 11.

FOR PAGE 175

Stelai from Sinope: Berger, 126 n. 321 and fig. 145; *Severe Style,* 97–98 figs. 133–34 and bibliography on p. 108; Hiller, 165–66 (O 20–21).

Stele from Apollonia: "Man-and-dog," 63 no. 2 fig. 2; Berger, figs. 26, 57; Hiller, 152–54 (O 8).

Stele from Phanagoria: *JHS ArchR* 9 (1963) 49 fig. 35; Hiller, 156 (O 10).

Amphiglyphon from Komotini: "Man-and-dog," 74–75; Berger, figs. 44, 133–34; Hiller, 151–52 (O 7).

Stele from Giase-Ada: *AJA* 61 (1957) 285 pl. 86:17.

Stele from Syme: Berger, 59 fig. 58.

Loryma base: Berger, figs. 35–36a; Hölscher, 21–23; Hiller, 159 (O 13).

Finials for pillar-stelai from Erythrai: *JOAI* 15 (1912) Beibl. cols. 64–66; *JOAI* 16 (1913) Beibl. cols. 57–60; are these truly finials or anta capitals? and what are their dates?

For an entire pyramid as a funerary monument (from Sinope), see Ch. W. Clairmont, *Gravestone and Epigram* (Mainz 1970) 33–37 no. 10 pl. 36; Hiller, 164–65 (O 19). The scene in low relief on one side of the pyramid resembles the Sinope stelai.

Doctor's stele in Basel: Berger, 49–59 and figs. 1–21; the relief is there considered the work of a Mileto-Ephesian or a Xanthian school (p. 59). G. Neumann, *AA* 1971, 183–88, favors a Samian origin; E. Homann-Wedeking, at the

10th International Congress of Classical Archaeology in Turkey, Sept. 1973, spoke of a Koan master. See now Hiller, 159–60 (O 14).

For the problem of funerary versus votive reliefs and for possible Ionic gravestones, see Hiller, 132 n. 43, and note her doubts on p. 133.

Kos fragment with cock scene: Berger, 120 fig. 140 n. 297; Hiller, 158 (O 12).

Kos erotic scene: See infra, Ch. 9, 273 and 279.

Other stelai from Rhodes, Kythnos, Tenos, and other islands: See Berger and Hiller, passim.

Paros anthemion, no. 119: Buschor, *AthMitt* 58 (1933) 44, Beil. 16:1; Hiller, 77 n. 36.

Anthemion from Thera: Buschor, *op. cit.*, Beil. 16:2.

Paros Archilocheion: See infra, Ch. 9, pp. 272, 279. On funerary structures, see *Aspécts*, Ch. 3, passim.

Boeotian stelai: *AGA* nos. 9, 28, 68, 75.

Orchomenos stele by Alxenor: "Man-and-dog," 60 fig. 1; Berger, fig. 46; Hiller, 177–79, K 11.

FOR PAGE 176

Finial in Thebes: B. Schmaltz, *AthMitt* 86 (1971) 67–78.

Rider's stele: *Boston Cat.* no. 12.

Lakonian reliefs: A. Delivorrias, *Deltion* 24:2 (1969) 135 pl. 132a; Berger, 107 fig. 128; *Aspécts*, 27–34.

Egyptian motifs in the reliefs: E. Guralnick, *JEA* 60 (1974) 175–88; for the seats, see Kyrieleis, 181–86.

Spartan pyramidal pillar: K. Schefold, *Frühgriechische Sagenbilder* (1964) 78–79 figs. 68–69.

FOR PAGE 177

Horseman stele from Megara Hyblaia: *AA* 1964, cols. 713–17 fig. 32; Hiller, 61 n. 212. Second stele, with warrior: *NSc* 1880, 39; *MonAnt* 1 (1891) 716.

Selinus stele: J. Marconi-Bovio, *Gli Archeologi italiani in onore di A. Maiuri* (1965) 301–14; cf. p. 305 for list of stelai from Sicily. However, P. Zancani-Montuoro, *RendNap*, NS 13 (1967) 33–39, considers the stele a forgery cut on a 6th century block. See also *ArchCl* 23 (1971) 93–107.

Bearded warrior from Camarina: *Sicile Grecque*, pl. 51.

Cyrene stele: Paribeni, no. 18 pl. 28; *AGA*, 53 n. 7a.

PART III

ARCHITECTURAL SCULPTURE

CHAPTER 7

Pediments and Akroteria

THE use of sculpture in high relief, or entirely in the round, to decorate specific areas of public buildings represents one of the greatest innovations and achievements of Greek Archaic masters. Though examples of architectural sculpture can be found elsewhere at earlier times, none can be shown to have been so strictly correlated to the structure they decorated as the Greek material, nor to have been so clearly meant as an important artistic expression in itself, despite relative subordination to the supporting frame.

PEDIMENTS

Pedimental sculpture is perhaps the most distinctive of all Greek forms of architectural decoration. It required the technical feature of a double-pitched roof, as contrasted with domes, hip-roofs, or other possible systems of covering a building. It also implied a specific conception of the tympanon area, which was by no means the same in different regions of the ancient world. We are thoroughly accustomed to seeing figures in action on the narrow pedimental shelf above a facade, but to the literal-minded Greeks this juxtaposition must have seemed surprising, and specific reasons should be sought to account for the first steps in this direction. Solutions adopted in other areas range from leaving the tympanon open, as a sort of window for the cella, to covering the pedimental floor with its own tiles and antefixes, as if it were an extension of the total roof. Decoration can be limited to revetting the projecting ridge pole and beams; or the gutter (sima) can be carried illogically across the pediment in one piece with the horizontal cornice, thus showing that no supporting value was attributed to the triangular space. The Sicilian and South Italian examples will be specifically analyzed below since they have distinctive traits of their own, but it may be useful here to recall Etruscan practices since Tuscan temples resembled the Greek in some architectural forms.

As the excavations at Murlo have now convincingly demonstrated, sculptural decoration in the round could be placed not in the pediment, but on the ridge pole, standing out against the sky in a sort of Indian file which must have considerably hampered the development of narrative compositions. Even the temple of Apollo at Veii, where a story was told, seems to have had the same arrangement and probably relied on the sequence of figures for the explanation of the action involved.

As for Egyptian and Assyro-Babylonian temples, the lack of pitched roofs entirely eliminated the problem of pedimental decoration. Other architectural sculpture in those countries seems to have served almost solely propagandistic purposes. In addition, reliefs were so low, whether on temples or palaces, as to be always closely wedded to painting as an art form, and their frequent indoor location is in sharp contrast to the outdoor display of Greek relief, which implies viewing from a distance and under different lighting conditions.

But one area of the Oriental world has left some evidence for pitched roofs and perhaps even pedimental decoration: Phrygia. The excavations at Gordion have clearly shown that monumental architecture, in poros and mudbrick, though largely reinforced with wood, existed as early as the Eighth century. In particular, doodles scratched on the walls of the so-called Megaron 2 portrayed a number of gabled houses with typical "ice tongs" akroteria over the apex,[1] some of them with vertical scratches in the tympanon area which might stand for some kind of pedimental ornament. In addition, re-used as fillings in the foundations of later buildings, were two carved lion's heads in poros and an akroterion. All three have been assigned to Megaron 2, the lion heads as decoration for the facade at either side. Since the structure precedes the Kimmerian invasion of ca. 690, an Eighth century date should definitely be assigned both to the doodles and to the type of houses they portray. The presence of the akroterion confirms the theory that Megaron 2 also had a pitched roof.

Further evidence of pre-Kimmerian date comes from the great tumulus at the same site, where the inner burial chamber, made of wood, was provided with a pitched roof resting on triangular gables at the ends plus a central one on the interior, carried by beams spanning the width of the tomb. Fortunately, these examples can be dated on the basis of their stratigraphy and contents. Other supporting evidence comes from the well-known rock-cut facades so typical of Phrygia, which unmistakably show all needed elements: akroteria, pediments and possibly apotropaic sculpture within them. But their date is still in dispute. Some authors prefer a high chronology, which would place monuments like the large facade at Midas City (Phrygian Yazilikaya) and Büyük Arslantaş (near Afyon) toward the end of the Eighth century. Other authorities favor lower dates, within the Sixth century, for both examples cited and in general for all such rock-cut monuments. Without entering the dispute over the rock facades and their unquestionably decorated pediments, I believe that Gordion has provided sufficient evidence to assert that gabled roofs, with akroteria and probably pedimental decoration, existed in Phrygia at a time when no such forms are known from Greece.

Our increased knowledge of Greek architecture of the Geometric period shows that building activity was by no means minimal during the Eighth century, but even the earliest temples in stone, for instance the Poseidonion at Isthmia (ca. 690), are restored with hip roofs, which would not allow tympana. Given the already mentioned incongruity of sizable figures resting or moving at high level, literally on the roof of a building, it seems logical to assume that the Greeks found the idea already developed elsewhere and simply adopted it without questioning, as they adopted the lion-head water-spouts. Indeed, one of the main features of Greek art is its ability to absorb disparate ideas coming from different sources, to recast them in a new and thoroughly Greek form which looks plausible and coherent and bears little relationship to the original version.[2]

[1] This form of akroterion may have originated from a structural feature of wooden houses in which the gable roof was framed by timbers that crossed at the apex and were tied together for extra security.

[2] This statement does not mean to imply that all forms of pedimental decoration are inspired by the Orient, but only those involving large-scale figures with apotropaic meaning. For the Gorgon plaques

If this theory is correct and pedimental decoration came to the Greeks from Phrygia or a similar Eastern country, two further assumptions could be made: that the Asia Minor Greeks were the first to adopt it and that the earliest pediments bore mostly apotropaic symbols. Though the second of these surmises seems valid, the first is surprisingly wide of the mark.

An excellent study of the geographical distribution of architectural sculpture in the Archaic period was completed in 1967 by Bookidis, and my own chapters on the subject are almost totally based on her work. Recent finds have added to, but have not considerably changed, the picture as she then saw it, while other studies, for instance by Winter on human-headed antefixes, have provided additional confirmation for some of her conclusions. Briefly stated, on the subject of tympanal sculpture, they are as follows:

DISTRIBUTION OF PEDIMENTS

Pedimental decoration, understood as a group of figures either in relief or in the round, whether in terracotta or stone, occurs abundantly and exclusively in Greece proper.[3] Western Greece completely ignores this concept of tympanon ornamentation in favor of a simpler, more purely apotropaic version, and does not adopt the narrative composition until the very end of the Archaic period. East Greece has preserved only one example of a figured pediment, and that a late one (ca. 530–520), in terracotta, on the temple of Athena at Larisa on the Hermos.[4] Equally late, if not later, is another, more doubtful, example from Kebren in the Troad. It consists of a large terracotta foot, which was found together with fragments of chariot and banquet friezes in the same medium but of smaller scale. Both Åkerström and Cook considered the foot pedimental, and certainly the possibility that terracotta pediments occurred in Asia Minor during the period of the International Style should be kept in mind.

However, pedimental sculpture in stone seems totally absent from East Greece, and the Troad examples are marginal enough to be considered at the fringes of the Greek world. The apparent rejection of a more monumental form of pedimental decoration by the Ionians may be due to several factors: 1) The gigantic temples at Samos, Ephesos, and Didyma would have required the filling of over 50 meters of pedimental space. In addition, the Archaic Didymaion seems to have had a hip roof.[5] 2) The very structure of

which will be mentioned below another origin is possible. They may have stemmed from the practice of hanging victory shields on temple gables, and since such pieces of armor were often decorated with apotropaic devices, the idea may have been retained even when the shield was eliminated. Another theory, which once enjoyed considerable favor, was the alleged *horror vacui* of the Greeks, which prompted them to fill all empty spaces as possible gaps through which evil forces may enter. Minus this rather fanciful explanation, the theory could still stand, and pedimental decoration could be seen as a desire to fill what might otherwise have looked like a rather large undecorated space. Obviously, many other theories could be construed with equal plausibility, and it is perhaps logical to assume that several independent "inventions" may have given rise to pedimental decoration in different areas.

[3] Euboea and Corfu, though islands, are here considered part of the mainland.

[4] One wonders whether the cult may have influenced the choice of some details or even of the Order for the temple. It is perhaps significant that Athena should have been worshiped in a Doric building at Assos, in the Troad, and that her temple at Larisa should be the only one with pedimental decoration.

[5] B. Trell (*The Temple of Artemis at Ephesos*, Numismatic Notes and Monographs no. 107 [New York 1945]; id., *Essays Lehmann* [1964] 344–58) has used numismatic evidence to argue that the Archaic Artemision resembled its Hellenistic successor

Ionic architecture prevents the placing of substantial weight on the cornice, which projects considerably from the facade and even from the underlying dentils of the Asia Minor version of the Order. Recessing the tympanon wall, to distribute the weight of pedimental sculpture over the line of the architrave, would so increase the depth of the pediment as to make its decoration almost invisible from below. When Ionic buildings in Greece proper have decorated pediments, they follow the Attic version of the Order, which substitutes a continuous frieze for the dentils and reduces the projection of the cornice, thus producing a tympanon shelf comparable to that of the Doric Order. 3) East Greek temples, of whatever size, seem to have employed elaborate moldings and bands of continuous frieze in preference to other forms of architectural sculpture. The reliefs of the parapet over the Artemision at Ephesos, while avoiding the problems of uneven weight and decreasing scale created by the pedimental area, must have provided abundant ornament for the upper part of the temple. The very richness of Ionic capitals and carved moldings may have militated against further embellishment, to prevent aesthetic competition. Thus local taste and preferences encouraged the selection of other forms of Oriental decoration (the continuous frieze) technically better suited to their Order.

One should therefore speculate on the problem of how the decorated pediment entered Greece proper and through what channels. Here, surprisingly, the Cyclades, at the forefront of production for freestanding sculpture, have no evidence to offer. Though new excavations may change the present picture, enough is known to wonder why, if pedimental sculpture was ever employed, none of it has yet been found. Even Crete, which so many authorities consider important for the beginning of monumental sculpture, has provided no example of pedimental decoration, or, for that matter, of canonical architecture.[6] A passage in Pindar (*Ol.* 13. vv.20–22) states that Corinth was the first to put the "twin king of the birds over the temples of the gods," with a play on the Greek word *aetos*, which means both eagle and pediment. However, this need imply no more than the use of a pitched roof with the corresponding formation of gables, rather than a reference to actual pedimental decoration. Archaeological remains do not substantiate a claim for Corinthian priority: a small group of poros fragments is so ambiguous in its present state of preservation that none of them can be attributed to a pediment with any degree of certainty, and none can be dated earlier than the earliest known examples from elsewhere. Presumably Corinth, with its abundant supply of suitable clay, was the first to develop an

---

in having three large windows within the tympanon, each flanked by statues in the round which may have represented Amazons. Though the use of windows is well attested for some Ionic temples of the Hellenistic period, we cannot be entirely sure that it existed at an earlier date. As for the sculpture, it may have been added by the die cutters as a further symbol of the site rather than as an accurate representation of what stood in the pediment of the temple. If, moreover, the reconstruction of a parapet around the roof of the Archaic Artemision is correct, the 6th century temple may not have had gables at all, and was perhaps open over the cella.

[6] Some possible pedimental figures have been found in the island of Kea (at Karthaia) within a temple of Athena, but no other information is available (*BCH* 29 [1905] 337–39 and 342–47; Willers, 54 n. 213); in any case, the date is late enough to postulate possible influence from nearby Attica. As for Crete, the island has produced many examples of architectural sculpture, to be sure, but none of them seems to belong to a structure definable in terms of either the Doric or the Ionic Order as we know them from Greece proper. The large stone gorgoneion found at Dreros (*BCH* 60 [1936] 251, figs. 20–21) is not likely to have been part of a pediment since the structure with which it has been connected is not a canonical temple.

elaborate system of roof tiles, which in turn allowed a different method of roofing from that previously employed, thus giving rise to Pindar's statement.[7]

Corfu

As Bookidis convincingly points out, the earliest known pediments (from Corfu, Sparta, and the Athenian Akropolis) not only come from widely different areas but show a certain degree of sophistication which speaks against their being the earliest attempts at this form of architectural decoration. We are probably missing the first steps in the development of pedimental sculpture, but it is perhaps logical to assume that the introduction of the practice may have occurred simultaneously in different places, as is now advocated for perirrhanteria, and probably even along the same routes. On the basis of present evidence alone, our earliest known example is the human leg in relief from a temple to Hera (ca. 600) at Mon Repos, on the island of Corfu. Other architectural elements, and the scale of the leg itself, suggest that the temple was larger than the Artemision on the same island, and earlier in date. But the two carved gables from the Artemision are next in sequence. Very recently in Corfu another decorated pediment has come to light, though smaller and considerably later than the previous two, and terracotta sculpture from two more gables may have belonged to a shrine of Artemis (in the Kanoni area) from the late Sixth century. A total of six decorated pediments from a relatively small island, three among them the earliest known from Greece, suggests that Corfu must have played an important role in the development of pedimental decoration. It has usually been thought that the island's connections with Corinth reinforce the theory of Corinthian invention for the practice. Yet whatever else is known about Corcyran sculpture and architecture shows it more closely related to areas other than Corinth. In particular, its form of terracotta revetments and trumpet spouts finds closer parallels in Sicily than in Greece proper, and Winter has shown that human-headed antefixes, of which both the temple at Mon Repos and some small buildings within the Artemision at Garitsa have provided conspicuous examples, are never used at Corinth or even in Greece proper with the exception of Aetolian Thermon, Kalydon, and Illyrian Apollonia.

This is not the place to discuss antefixes and their role in the sculptural decoration of a Greek temple. Obviously they contributed greatly to the total effect of richness and color, but their very repetitive nature, dependent on the use of a mold, removes them from the sphere of architectural sculpture proper. It seems however that South Italy and Sicily greatly favored and fully developed the form with female or male heads, which appear both at Thermon and Corfu. I would be in favor of de-emphasizing Corinthian influence on both these sites and their temples, though fully accepting a possible Corinthian source for the two late terracotta pediments from Kanoni on the island. But the large pedimental composition of the Artemision at Garitsa should be judged on its own merit since nothing at Corinth appears truly comparable. In addition, the Artemision plan, with a possible adyton rather than an opisthodomos and a pseudo-dipteral arrangement of the peristyle, recalls the Great Sicilian temples at Selinus rather than any of the mainland structures.

[7] Even pedimental sculpture in terracotta, which could have been an obvious Corinthian invention, seems to be consistently late whenever and wherever found, not only at Corinth but also at Delphi, Corfu, perhaps Halai, and Olympia.

From the history of Corfu we know that the earliest Greek colonists there were not the Corinthians but the Eretrians, apparently on their way to Italy in the second quarter of the Eighth century. These Euboeans had branched off from their native island not only in the direction of the West, but also of the East: to Al Mina in North Syria, and to the northern shores of the Aegean, in the Chalkidike. In Eretria itself (as well as in Chalkis, the other major colonizing town on Euboea) Oriental objects have been found in notable quantity. Although the Corinthians supplanted the Eretrians on Corfu in 734, political relations between the new colonizers and the islanders were not always friendly and at times became downright hostile so that independence from Corinth was soon achieved, especially after the death of the Corinthian tyrant Periander around 585. But Corcyran relationships with Euboea and the East on the one hand, and with Italy on the other, continued even after the Eretrians' expulsion, as might be expected from Corfu's position in the Adriatic sea, on the traffic routes from Greece to Etruria and Magna Graecia. My surmise would be that the Euboeans absorbed architectural forms and decoration from the East and in turn passed them on to the Etruscans and the South Italians, but also, *en passant*, to the Corcyrans.

Some vague support can be found in scattered bits of evidence. It is, of course, well known that the Etruscans derived their alphabet from the Euboeans. Recent finds at Acquarossa have shown that a type of akroterion typical of Phrygia was in use in Etruria, though obviously nothing tells us that the Eretrians were responsible for its transmission. I have already mentioned that temple plans and terracotta revetments link Sicily with Corfu, though not necessarily with Euboea. The Swiss excavations at Eretria have however shown that the temple of Apollo Daphnephoros had several phases of construction, some of which go back to the Eighth century, with an early Archaic plan strongly indebted to principles of Ionic architecture.

To be sure, the actual course of transmission cannot be reduced to any sort of schematic statement. The presence of Ionic elements as well as an entire Ionic temple in Syracuse show that Magna Graecian contacts with Ionia were so strong as to have possibly been direct, without Euboean intermediary. As for Corfu and Thermon, their human-headed antefixes may have come from south Italy or, more probably, from a Balkan tradition unknown at present, and this suggests that their sources of influence were not limited to a single important region. In addition, I believe that strong Oriental inspiration was at work on the Akropolis of Athens itself, for the erection of the so-called Hekatompedon. With so many gaps in our knowledge, my present purpose is simply to show that Corfu did not derive its architectural forms from Corinth but perhaps from Sicily and the Orient, possibly through its Euboean connections. If this were indeed the case, it would provide one more example of the selectivity of each Greek area, with Sicily rejecting that form of pedimental decoration which presumably came from the East and which Corfu was eager to adopt.

In one detail, however, the Corfu pediment does show its indebtedness to Sicilian practices: in the way in which the Gorgon's head overlies the molding at the apex of the pediment. In Sicily, in fact, the prevalent form of decoration for the gable was to hang in its center an enormous terracotta gorgoneion, by means of nails or pegs at the corners of the plaque. This method of suspension suggests that originally the entire piece acted as a revetment for the end of the ridge pole to which it was presumably fastened. Thus the terracotta plaque would materially protect the wooden beam from weathering as the Gorgon head would symbolically protect the entire temple from evil influences. In Sicily this apotropaic device did not develop into narrative until, after 480, increased contacts with the mainland of Greece introduced different forms of pedimental decoration.[8] In Corfu we seem to witness the subsequent step: the Gorgon's head has sprouted a body and, in a typically Greek compression of all elements of a story in one tableau, without respect for proper sequence, the entire legend is symbolized by the presence of Pegasos and Chrysaor, the two monstrous creatures which sprang from her decapitated torso. But this is not narrative per se: Medusa remains entirely apotropaic, and her progeny is present solely for identification purposes, almost like attributes which recall her power.

This pediment is so well known that only a few points need be stressed here. First of all, the apotropaic value of the decoration is made clear, I believe, by the fact that both pediments were carved with the same subjects. This could be a feature of the earliest pediments, though, to my knowledge, it remains unique and is not even matched by the central animal-prey groups of the Athenian Hekatompedon.

Though only the west gable of the Corcyran temple is well preserved, enough fragments remain from the east to ensure that at least the central figures (the Gorgon, her children, and the flanking panthers) were repeated on that side, and in even better workmanship. Had narrative been intended, presumably a different subject would have been chosen. The second point concerns chronology. The building has usually been dated ca. 590–580, largely through comparisons with Corinthian pottery for the animals and the Gorgon, as well as anatomical details for Chrysaor. Yet I believe that a date around 570 could be equally defensible on the same evidence and would not be contradicted by the few surviving architectural elements since that shape of Doric capital with "squashed" echinus is found in Sicily as late as ca. 540 or later.[9] As for the sculpture, the Gorgon's face has been intentionally made into a mask and therefore cannot be used as a dating criterion. Her eyes are meant to be disproportionately large since in them resides the petrifying power proper to the monster. But note the emphatic modeling of her cheeks, the elaboration of her spiral curls, which so strongly recall metalwork, the sophistication with which they move around the ear and onto the chest. Her snaky belt makes a deep indentation around which her body bulges naturalistically; her skirt is made to adhere to her legs dipping in between. Her musculature is highly patterned, almost like an Assyrian relief from Nimrud,

[8] The only possible exception would be the terracotta plaque from Syracuse showing the entire Gorgon, running and carrying a small Pegasos under her right arm. Its small size and the four nail holes at its corners suggest that the plaque may still have decorated the end of the ridge pole, thus functioning more as akroterial than as pedimental decoration. The theory that the plaque belongs to an altar has not been generally accepted. Another suggestion is that the plaque was nailed to a wooden board and decorated a metope of the predominantly wooden temple of Athena. If a metope, the seemingly narrative character of the slab would be entirely appropriate and consistent with Sicilian practices. (P. Orsi, *MonAnt* 25 [1918] 614–17 pl. 16; S. Benton, *BSR* 22 [1954] 132–37; Langlotz, *Magna Graecia*, color pl. I and caption.)

[9] G. Rodenwaldt (*Korkyra I*, 89) provides a table of dimensions and proportions among Archaic Doric capitals. The one attested capital from the Garitsa temple is not so different from that of Selinus Temple C. Note that Rodenwaldt dates the capital at Corfu on the basis of the pedimental sculpture and the terracotta sima, not on its own right. Other close similarities between Selinus Temple C and the Artemision at Corfu are mentioned by R. R. Holloway (*A View of Greek Art*, [1973] 61 and note 10) though he concludes that Temple C was therefore built at the beginning of the 6th century, "when the Gorgon temple on Corfu was built." The projected study by G. Scichilone on the reroofing of Temple C may solve some of these problems.

but intentionally, I believe, since the other figures on the pediment do not display such exaggerated knees or swelling arms.[10] These are not signs of early date but rather of attempts to remove her from the human sphere into that of the monstrous or the superhuman. Proof of it is found in Chrysaor, who could be none other than the Gorgon's son, given his facial resemblance; his eyes are equally over-large, his mouth is too wide, his nose is squashed, with dilated nostrils. But that these are not the artist's rendering for a normal youth is shown by comparison with the head of Zeus nearby, where all features are much better proportioned in relation to the total face. Chrysaor *looks* early because he is mask-like, resembling his mother; but note how his spinal furrow has been deflected in an attempt to show the torsion of his body.[11] His glutei are dimpled by the trochanteric depression, and the asymmetrical rendering of the pectorals reflects the differing tension in the muscles of either arm.

Chrysaor's hair is long, much longer than it appears from the front; only a side view reveals the long mass of strands falling down his back. This very length suggests his youth, but could it also be an Ionic touch? A trace of East Greek softness is perhaps apparent also in the smooth transition from face to neck, without a strong jaw line. He is certainly different from the other anthropomorphic figures on the pediment. These have been variously identified and only one can be considered certain: Zeus with his thunderbolt. Whether the others are Giants or Titans, whether the seated figure is Priam or Kronos, is not of immediate concern here. I want only to stress that this latter cannot be female, as sometimes asserted, for a variety of often mentioned reasons: his hair is short, like a man's (rather than a god's?); his skirt clears the feet; his mantle is worn with a triangular tip ending at the back, as typical for men. The figure is active, more than is apparent from his arms because his feet are not aligned evenly, the left one forward as if the man were about to rise under the threat of the spear point directed toward him or perhaps because his opponent is grabbing his right wrist. Unfortunately his face is too corroded for complete certainty, but it looks as if his mouth were open, in a rendering of emotion quite unusual for the early Sixth century. The structure rising behind his seat could not be a backrest, since the outlines of the *thakos* are clearly indicated. It has been suggested that it represents the walls of Troy or the tower of Kronos on the Island of the Blessed, where he retired after the Gods defeated the Titans. Regardless of the correct interpretation, it is important to note the presence of "stage props" on this early pediment: not only a building but also a tree, engraved against the background near the Giant/Titan threatened by Zeus. Usually, Greek pediments deploy their action against a neutral background, painted an even color, with personages taking pride of place to the exclusion of contingent elements. Only one other Archaic composition, to my knowledge (the so-called Olive Tree pediment from the Athenian Akropolis) introduces some elements of landscape which, remarkably, consist of another engraved tree and a larger structure. Whether these two details were utilized at Corfu to label, as it were, the locale of the action, it is impossible to tell now when their meaning is no longer clear, though further thought should be given to this point.

[10] A Gorgon's musculature could be shown in exaggerated fashion as late as ca. 560. Note, for instance, the similarity between the Corfu Pediment Medusa and the running Gorgon on the predella of the stele Athens Nat. Mus. 2687 (*AGA* no. 27). A particularly revealing photograph has been published by Dörig in *AA* 1967, 21 fig. 7.

[11] This detail occurs also on the Zeus.

The composition, in fairly high relief which at times is entirely detached from the background, already tackles the problem of diminishing height within the pedimental field: figures kneel or recline, and bilateral correspondence is obtained without complete symmetry. The corner figures show an awareness of the law of gravity in the way in which their beards curve toward the ground. That the side action seems divorced from the central scene is no definite sign of great age once the main group is seen as apotropaic rather than narrative; the same principle is reflected in the Hekatompedon in Athens or the late Archaic Alkmaionid pediment at Delphi. The only early trait is the use of decorative patterns on the pedimental frames, but this penchant for added ornamentation, which used to be considered typical of high Archaism, has now been found on pediments of the late Sixth century and should therefore reflect local taste rather than date.

A final word on material and surface detail. For all its plastic treatment of masses, the sculptor of the Corfu pediment has also made full use of the engraving possibilities afforded by the soft limestone. Incision reaches incredible complexity, and only close observation reveals the intricacies of the Gorgon's boot feathers, the scaly bodies of the snakes in her hair, the many patterns of costumes and coiffures, the minute detailing of the panthers' bodies. Here perhaps one sees the only touch of Corinthian influence, in the dots scattered over the muzzles of the beasts, in between the whiskers, somewhat like the Loutraki lions in Copenhagen.[12] Technique involves the use of the drill and a good amount of undercutting where necessary, for strong play of light and shadow. Color must have added a great deal to the total scene. Many small bronze pins fastened with molten lead dot the most prominent parts of the sculptures and have been interpreted as meniskoi to hold off the birds, though their effectiveness could be questioned. They are certainly not visible at present and can be seen only in Rodenwaldt's careful publication.

Another important pediment was found on Corfu in 1973. It has received only preliminary publication and therefore cannot be discussed in detail. Suffice it here to note that its subject, a banquet scene, is unprecedented as gable decoration, though obviously an intelligent solution to the problem of the pedimental slope. Only about half of the tympanon is preserved, virtually divided into two horizontal zones by kline, table, and a large standing animal, presumably a dog. Two people recline on the couch: a young naked boy with a diadem on his long streaming hair, who holds a cup, and a bearded man with a drinking horn, who wears an animal skin; each looks toward the missing half of the gable, supporting himself on his elbow. Under the table lies a realistic lion, while a large volute krater fills the left end of the pediment. The soft poros seems to have been exposed to the action of water and has lost some of its original sharpness, but obviously details were plentiful and careful. Engraved patterns decorate the soffit and the corona. Something strange about the figures recalls archaistic works, yet there is no reason to doubt that they are late Archaic. But in their present state they resemble terracotta more than stone. They make me think of Etruscan and South Italian sculpture, rather than sculpture from Greece proper. Perhaps this pediment brings further confirmation of Corfu's artistic ties with the Italian mainland.

[12] For other indications of local style, see, however, supra Ch. 6 n. 7 (a comparison with the so-called Menekrates' lion).

Sparta

A fragment from the neck and mane of a large limestone lion has been attributed to the pedimental decoration of the Archaic temple of Artemis Orthia at Sparta. Unfortunately its publication is early and relatively incomplete, with no dimensions given, but Bookidis has calculated from photographs that the entire beast should be approximately on the scale of the Akropolis lions to be discussed below. Since the temple is relatively small, an animal of that size, if indeed it did decorate the gable, must have filled it almost entirely, together with a possible mate in antithetical pose. According to a recent revision of the Artemis Orthia chronology, the temple should be dated around 570–560, thus approximately contemporary with the Corfu Gorgon pediment and the Hekatompedon in Athens. Too little is known or preserved to discuss this item at greater length, but it is important to note that this emphasis on apotropaic animals within gables seems common to all early pediments in Greece, regardless of location. As the other finds from the Spartan sanctuary clearly show, contact with the Orient was strong in Archaic Lakonia, and the idea of pedimental decoration may have reached the site directly from the East without intermediaries. On the other hand Olympia had several treasuries to which architectural sculpture has been attributed, and one could assume that the idea traveled from the pan-Hellenic to the more local sanctuary. Here, however, the Olympia evidence is too vague, both in terms of chronology and style, to assess priorities.

Athens

We are on firmer ground with Athens, though there is still controversy about nomenclature, location, and attribution of sculpture to the early temple of Athena. It is impossible to give here a complete summary of the various theories on the poros pediments from the Akropolis, and an excellent discussion can be found both in Bookidis' and in Harrison's works. I shall confine myself to an outline of the theory which I find most plausible and to a few considerations of my own.

At the end of the last century, excavations of the citadel brought to light architectural members from several buildings of different sizes, and a good number of sculptures, both in poros and marble, which obviously belonged to pedimental decoration. Though the architectural elements were found in several locations, some of them even re-used in the fortification walls or the Mnesiklean Propylaia, the sculptures basically came out of the fill to the east and south of the Parthenon, presumably put there during the erection of the platform for the predecessor of the Parthenon, while others were buried after the Persian attack of 480. Scholars have tried to distinguish between the first, systematic filling, which implies voluntary dismantling of preexisting buildings (the so-called *Tyrannenschutt*) and the other cache of debris from damaged material (the *Perserschutt*). However, stratigraphy was far from clear and not immediately observed, so that confusion in the records is possible, and some of the early material was found together with marble fragments, thus in the *Perserschutt*, rather than with the purely poros contents of the *Tyrannenschutt*. In addition, some statues which epigraphically and stylistically already belong to the Severe Period, like Angelitos' Athena, were found together with the Kritian Boy, the Athena from the Peisistratid Temple, and the Moschophoros, one of the earliest sculptures from the

Akropolis. One should therefore acknowledge the fact that stratigraphy can be of no help in determining the dates of the pediments.

Architectural connections are equally difficult to prove. The only Archaic foundations preserved in situ on the citadel are those belonging to the so-called Peisistratid Temple, south of the Erechtheion. I accept the argument that the proportions of that temple (both sekos and peristyle) speak for a late Archaic date, and I therefore believe in the contemporaneity of both inner and outer foundations, which some authors would consider instead representative of two building phases. The location of all the other structures, whose existence is based on the architectural fragments alone, is highly conjectural, and no theory can be proven. In addition, some of the poros architecture belongs stylistically to the Fifth century, and therefore cannot go with the Sixth century poros sculpture. It should here be stressed that we seem to have more pediments than we have architectural members to go with them; this is particularly true in the case of small buildings, which were presumably treasuries and thus likely to have only one of their pediments decorated with sculpture.[13] On the other hand, note also that poros architecture seems from the beginning to have been trimmed with marble simas, and even marble metopes in the case of the large temple, so that mixture of materials is equally unhelpful as an indication of date.

The Hekatompedon. How many early and large temples there were on the Athenian Akropolis cannot be discussed at this point. In my opinion, the earliest to be decorated extensively with poros sculpture was quite large, peripteral, and probably stood in the area of the present Parthenon. From an inscription which mentions both the Hekatompedon and the Old Temple of Athena, we know that the two were mutually exclusive; therefore the name of Hekatompedon will be used here for the predecessor of the Parthenon, while the second title will be taken to have referred to the shrine on the site of the Peisistratid temple. The date of the Hekatompedon is likely to have been connected with the reorganization of the Panathenaic games in 566, if we assume that a great religious festival would have virtually demanded a new and imposing structure in stone to replace whatever mudbrick and wood structure may have existed from Geometric times. It is also important to note that no sizable freestanding sculpture from the Akropolis looks earlier than ca. 570–560. Though vases, bronzes, and other objects have been found on the citadel, the site does not seem to have acquired its value as a major sanctuary until the second quarter of the Sixth century, and the new emphasis on the Panathenaia may easily have promoted that value. I therefore visualize extensive building activity on the Akropolis only after 570, with a consequent flourishing of treasuries and independent sculptural dedications around the large temple. If, however, this picture is substantially correct, Athens may have had no great experience with religious stone buildings on a large scale and may have looked for help where such tradition did exist. Many elements in the Hekatompedon, both sculptural and architectural, point in this direction.

To begin with, the marble sima which encircled the building discharged its rain water through trumpet spouts, a feature quite rare in Greece proper, and mainly attested in Magna Graecia and Corfu, though some of the small structures on the Akropolis seem also to have employed it. Though an exact parallel cannot at present be produced from Asia

[13] This statement seems to apply specifically to Olympia. At Delphi, however, some treasuries had sculpture on both gables.

Minor, some terracotta revetments from a Phrygian building have half-trumpet spouts, and perhaps the complete tube will come to light in future excavations.

The Hekatompedon sima continued over each apex into two strips which crossed and formed tongs akroteria. Within the crossing of the "blades" stood a single figure: Perseus on the one side and a Gorgon on the other, chasing each other perennially around the roof. The remains of toes on one of the tongs, as well as fragments of two similar but distinct figures in striped garments, assure the correctness of this reconstruction. As already mentioned, this form of apex decoration seems typically Phrygian, with possible ramifications into Etruria, where examples of figures (animals) between the tongs also exist; it is otherwise unknown in Greece proper.

Another East Greek (and perhaps Etruscan) touch is added by the engraved soffit of the raking cornice.[14] Alternate blocks are decorated with large lotus flowers and flying birds seen from below, of which three species can probably be recognized: a stork, possibly a sea gull, and another equally large and powerful bird. Their portrayal, with legs retracted under the belly, long beaks and eyes bulging out on either side of the head, is most effective and quite sophisticated, suggesting to the viewer that a whole flock is flying overhead; color would have added to the clarity of the representation. This engraved technique, which cannot even be compared with low relief, seems typical of Chios, and perhaps even of Samos and Naxos, as shown by examples on Delos and on the islands themselves. Given the presence of Naxian votives on the Akropolis and the already noted influence of Naxian on Attic sculpture, this correlation cannot be doubted. Historically, it is supported by the knowledge that Peisistratos restored the Naxian tyrant Lygdamis to power[15] The naturalistic subjects (birds and flowers) are more East Greek than Attic.

Another group of "reliefs" has usually been associated with the Hekatompedon. These consist of nine marble fragments for a total of five to six reclining lions and panthers, none of them entirely preserved. Their heads, carved separately in the round, turned outward from the plane of the background to face the spectator. The bodies, made in two pieces, are fully carved on one side but look as if cut in half from the other. This farther side is flat and rough, at times even slightly concave, and two fragments show traces of anathyrosis. That they were meant to stand against a background is shown also by traces of metal dowels secured with molten lead, and by a tenon preserved along the length of the forepaws, which however does not appear on the hind legs. According to the preserved fragments, some animals faced right and some left, the lions slightly smaller and rounder than the panthers. Rough tooling along the spines suggests that they were higher than eye level.

These peculiar creatures have been reconstructed in a variety of ways: as akroteria,

[14] The position occupied by the decoration, under the eaves of the roof, as it were, may indicate a different conception of the entablature from that usually attested on a Greek building. A comparable rendering is provided by the coffers which decorate the soffit of the raking cornice on the Temple of Athena at Paestum. Significantly enough, the excavations at Acquarossa have provided examples of terracotta revetments with relief scenes which belonged to a similar position, though the entire building to which they were fastened is not reconstructed with a corresponding horizontal cornice and therefore has no gable. (For a reconstructed drawing, see E. Wetter, C. E. Östenberg, M. Moretti, *Med kungen på Acquarossa* [Malmö 1972] 141; the building is on zone G.)

[15] This engraved technique is used also for the male and female sphinxes on marble plaques from the Athenian Akropolis, which some authors consider the akroteria of a 7th century temple of Athena. (See also supra Ch. 6 n. 13.) For the practice in Chios, see N. Kontoleon, *BCH* 71–72 (1947–48) 272–301, and *BCH* 73 (1949) 384–97, esp. p. 393. For Samos, see infra Ch. 9.

either near the central Gorgon or at the corners; as decoration attached to poros metopes, though plain marble slabs belonging to the Hekatompedon Doric frieze are also known; and finally as part of a continuous frieze over the porches. All these solutions seem doubtful, especially because of dimensions. The height of the Doric frieze on the facade, and that of a hypothetical continuous frieze over the inner porch, is approximately three times greater than that of the reclining animals, which would therefore represent very meager and unsatisfactory decoration indeed. Even the moldings with which the remaining height of a porch frieze could partially be filled remain entirely conjectural.

My suggestion would be to restore these animals as anta decoration, at the level of the anta capital, for both porches. A minimum of eight reliefs would be needed for these positions, twelve if the front part of the anta were also covered. The creatures would then have had an apotropaic function, protecting the doorways, and would find parallels in some East Greek buildings. For instance, the Artemision at Ephesos had its anta bases protected by bulls; the Samian Heraion of ca. 520–510 had them watched over by winged sphinxes and so did the earlier temple of Hermes and Aphrodite (ca. 530–520) and the Rhoikos Altar (ca. 540). These decorations stood low, at the foot of the antae; comparable sculpture however could be placed higher, for instance at Thasos, where a Pegasos protome may have formed the capital for a small structure. Similarly, on Chios, another Pegasos protome from Phanai was certainly used architecturally; a further peculiarity of Chian buildings is the frequent use of lion's paws as anta bases, which must be part of the same apotropaic conception. Finally, at Didyma, two pairs of large lions are carved in relief on the architrave, flanking the corner Gorgons; but their heads, carved separately in the round and then applied to the building, thus protruded in much higher relief. This contrast between low-relief body and high-projecting head can again find parallels at Gordion, where two marble orthostats were carved with highly stylized lions.

The final touch to this highly complex Athenian Hekatompedon was provided by the poros sculpture of the pediments. Here again there is no agreement as to the combination of the various pieces, but Dinsmoor's reconstruction still seems valid and is supported by the matching color of the few remains of background. It is also the most economical solution, utilizing on a single building all the large-scale sculpture which would otherwise require other sizable constructions of approximately contemporary date on the relatively limited area of the Akropolis. In this solution, the east pediment would have in its center a monumental group of a lion and a lioness over a fallen bull, which they are devouring. The corners would be filled by Herakles fighting Triton on the left-hand side (spectator's point of view), while a three-bodied monster coils away in the right corner.[16] The West pediment has a lioness entirely covering a small bull; of her companion lion only one front leg is preserved, but he would have faced her in the other half of the gable, presumably without prey under him. The corners are filled with two enormous snakes, one facing toward the center, the other turned to look at the viewer.

Objections to this reconstruction stem mostly from the fact that the lioness of the west pediment seems considerably earlier than her mate, especially in the treatment of her

[16] Another figure intervened between the Tricorpor and the central lion group, but not enough is preserved to speculate fruitfully on its appearance. It is sometimes thought that an Athena with an owl might have stood there, on the evidence of a small poros owl now displayed in the same room with the corner figures of the Hekatompedon east pediment (Brouskari, 34 no. 56; Wiegand, 230).

locks. However, a large lion head from the Agora seems to combine the more plastic treatment of the Akropolis lion's hair with the flatter version of the Akropolis lioness, thus showing that the two forms could occur not only contemporaneously but even on the same sculpture. All other reconstructions have to supply a companion either for the lion or for the lioness, for which no sculptural fragments remain, much less a suitable architecture for the resultant, additional pediment. Moreover, symmetry is not always a primary requirement of Archaic compositions, and the small size of the bull under the lioness would have minimized the absence of a comparable prey under the lion, which would have been realistically somewhat larger than his mate. The apotropaic impact of both central groups, showing the felines in the exercise of their great power, is still perceptible today in seeing the sadly fragmentary reconstructions in the Akropolis Museum. An entirely different conception of the central group, and of the entire pediment, by Beyer, will be discussed below.

More difficult is the interpretation of the creatures at the corners of the east gable. Herakles and Triton are obvious enough,[17] but the three-bodied monster, humorously referred to as Bluebeard, is hard to name. Various identifications have been proposed, of which Typhon is perhaps the most plausible; it is largely based on the presence of several attachment holes, filled with lead, which dot the chest and shoulders of the middle torso and which have been connected with the fragments of approximately twelve small poros snakes found in the same context as the larger pieces. The ends of three of these snakes are worked flat, and thus show that they were attached to some surface. Since shield straps from Olympia show Typhon with snakes emerging from his shoulders, near his head, a similar reconstruction for the Akropolis Tricorpor has also suggested a similar identification. Yet not all agree. Other theories see in him Zeus Herkeios, Nereus, Proteus, Erechtheus. Among the most recent suggestions are the Tritopatores, wind divinities of ancestral character; and Boardman's most unusual conception of the body politic, with each torso symbolizing one of the Athenian parties among which Peisistratos had forced a reconciliation. Accordingly, the torso holding a bird would stand for the people of the Hill, the one holding a wave would stand for the people of the Seashore, while a sheaf of wheat (not fire) would symbolize the people of the Plain. The three snaky bodies would allude to the Attic kings, who supposedly were similarly affected in their extremities. The entire theory would see in the exploits of Herakles a veiled allusion to the deeds of Peisistratos himself, so that the struggle with Triton would commemorate the tyrant's amphibious expedition against Megara around 566.

One may hesitate in accepting such symbolic allusions to contemporary politics in works of so early a period; however, the identification of the characters is perhaps of secondary importance compared to that of isolating non-Attic elements in the sculptures. Harrison has already pointed out that the hair of Bluebeard is stylized in an Ionian manner; in addition, the ribbon-like wavy strands end in a thicker mass of horizontal curls, now mostly broken off and thus difficult to note, which terminate in spirals and resemble Assyrian or

[17] The present display in the Akropolis Museum shows Herakles headless, and exhibits separately a poros head which Broneer found on the north slope of the Akropolis in 1938 (*Hesperia* 8 [1939] 91–100). How satisfactory the joining of head and body looked is shown by plate 26 in Lullies & Hirmer. I am convinced that the head does indeed belong to Herakles, as Broneer originally argued. Cf. Bundgaard, 16.

Persian renderings. The very symbols held by the three bodies—the bird, the wave, and either a flame or a sheaf of wheat—resemble the attributes and conception of an Oriental weather monster or personification of the elements, in a philosophical vein which one could easily expect from Ionia.[18] Note that the central torso has a scar on the chest, almost centered between the breasts, which suggests an object stretching forward. Was this one more snake? On the other hand, I am not convinced that all attachment holes were for such additions. Could they have held meniskoi as at Corfu? Yet two lead "puddles" appear on the wave held by the second torso, one in such a position (facing toward the pedimental floor) as to prevent explanation as the bedding for a bird spike. Nor do I find the scattered location of the snakes appropriate for Typhon, especially since the Tricorpor is not in battle attitude. So little remains of another figure which must have stood between him and the lions' group that identification is impossible, but certainly no threatening presence is suggested by the interested way in which the three bearded heads look on.[19] Note the marked asymmetries on these faces, meant for best viewing from below.

To summarize: many details suggest that this major Athenian temple was indebted to the Orient for its architecture as well as for its decoration. Even the name Hekatompedon might have been borrowed from East Greek examples. The tongs akroteria, the trumpet spouts, the engraved soffit (location, technique, and subject matter), the relief felines with projecting heads and, if true, their protective function at the antae, individual stylistic traits and conceptions of the pedimental sculptures, find their best parallels not only in East Greece but even in non-Greek areas like Phrygia, and, to some extent, Etruria. Since no evidence exists for major artistic activity on the Akropolis prior to approximately 566, I would assume that Peisistratos looked overseas for masters who would embellish his citadel and give impetus to a rich architectural and sculptural production for years to come.[20]

Small Poros Pediments. The many other poros pediments from small Akropolis buildings do not contradict, and may actually support, such a theory. None of them, as we have them at present, is definitely earlier than 566, though very high dates have been assigned to some by various authors. Such a high chronology may have been partly influenced by the theory that pedimental decoration began in painting, progressed to low relief, and

[18] Though its reconstruction is highly tentative, a similar winged monster with human head and snaky body may have existed at Samos, perhaps as part of the relief decoration for the great altar (ca. 540—*Samos* XI nos. 111–12, and comments on p. 191 n. 84). Note that Samos has also produced some early examples of engraved design, comparable to the Hekatompedon geison soffit (*ibid.* no. 103, from Hekatompedon II [?] ca. 675).

[19] In the staggering of the torsos the theory that identifies Tricorpor with the Tritopatores finds an allusion to the different quarters from which the winds blow. I believe, however, that no deep meaning motivated the arrangement, which simply parallels the fanning out of the horses of a quadriga, when seen in profile, in order to ensure visibility despite the overlap.

[20] E. Kluwe (*Wissenschaftliche Zeitschrift der Friedrich-Schiller Universität Jena, Gesellschafts- und Sprachwissenschaftliche Reihe* 14:1 [1965] 9–15) argues that the dates of Peisistratos' tyranny preclude the possibility that the great building program was organized by him. The German scholar suggests that such activity either preceded or followed the rule of Peisistratos, and that most of it fell under the tyrant's sons or the young democracy when the economic resources of Athens had been considerably strengthened by Peisistratos' policies. Somewhat the same position is supported by Boersma, 13–15, 18, 19–23. On the other hand, I find it hard to visualize that such an extensive program of major buildings on the citadel could take place without unified sponsorship and control, and at least one tradition in the ancient sources connects Peisistratos with the renewal of the Panathenaia.

then moved to high relief and sculpture in the round. Yet this eminently logical progression is disproved by the evidence; indeed, the one painted gable produced by the Akropolis excavations seems to be the latest, maybe not even Archaic. The choice of technique was determined rather by the size of the building to be decorated and the relative distance of the pediment from the viewer.

The Hydra Pediment, in fact, although the one in lowest relief among the Akropolis examples, is certainly quite sophisticated. Note that this pediment, though usually dated very early, was presumably found in the *Perserschutt*, together with the Red Triton pediment. The snaky monster offers a wonderful solution to the problem of the pedimental corner, and manages to fill half of the entire gable with tapering tail on one side and many threatening heads toward the center. Too little is preserved of Herakles to judge the rendering, but Iolaos' head has been compared to the Boxer's stele from the Kerameikos (ca. 560–550). Note, once again, the short hair for a bearded man, at an early date. The horses look diminutive, in proportion to the human figures, and even so the sculptor had to lower their heads, to fit them under the raking cornice. They seem, however, to be sniffing at the huge crab, part of the story, which again manages to fill the corner plausibly and effectively, without loss of scale. Even Herakles' importance over his charioteer is reflected by his larger size allowed by his position closer to the center of the gable. In sum, the difficult triangular space has been intelligently used to emphasize importance and minimize differences. If vase painting may have provided some inspiration for the scene, the sculptural version is entirely original in its adaptation to the frame.[21]

Approximately contemporary must be the so-called Introduction Pediment. This is well known and well illustrated, and calls for few comments. Note primarily that the beard of Zeus is treated very much like the hair of the Rampin Horseman, with extra strands introduced midway, without visible origin on the cheeks. The minute beads are appropriate for poros carving, though perhaps less so for marble. One wonders whether the same workshop could have produced the rider and the gable. A recent study of masters separates the two works but confirms that a close interrelation existed among sculptural ateliers in Sixth century Athens.

This pediment also shows a certain amount of sophistication. If Zeus, seated in profile, seems to cut off from the scene one entire half of the gable, Hera, seated facing outward, is a good example of compression and foreshortening. Herakles' face at present looks peculiar, and even with restored nose it would be somewhat prognathous. A possible Ionic origin for this sloping profile may find support in other figures if they can be accepted as part of the same pediment. A group of six personages, mostly quite fragmentary, may show the gods coming to meet the new member of Olympos; as such, they would be appropriate to fill the other half of the Introduction tympanon. Some scholars, however, would like to dissociate them and put them in a gable of their own, or scatter them elsewhere, for instance, with the Olive Tree Pediment. One figure in particular, the best preserved, shows a man wrapped in his mantle, with his right arm bent at the elbow visible through a subtle handling of the drapery. The modeled folds created by the tension of

[21] Schuchhardt (*AA* 1963, 812 and figs. 13–14) has attributed the smallest marble sima from the Akropolis to the Hydra pediment and to the architecture of Wiegand's Building B. But this latter was apsidal and fairly substantial, actually the largest by Wiegand's measurements, so that no safe conclusion is possible.

the cloth, as well as the effect of transparency obtained around the arm, recall East Greek renderings. I do not know of equally rippling folds in Attic works until the very end of the Archaic period, while both the Ephesos column drum reliefs and some of the Branchidai can match them.[22]

Compositionally, this pediment may look a bit unbalanced, with the heavy mass of the two seated figures in the center, but the processional theme of two groups of people converging toward the enthroned pair could have unified the scene. In front of Herakles must have stood Athena, now missing, and behind him still stands a figure sometimes called Iris. But to my mind it is definitely male, in view of the short costume, heavy thighs, and masculine ("Parian") chest. There is no definite evidence for attributing to this gable the heavy molding which at present runs along the upper edge of the tympanon wall, just below the raking cornice. Nor is there definite evidence for the total height of the pediment since of the figures themselves so much is restored. However, this would still seem the largest of the small poros pediments recovered from the Akropolis.

A new theory was advanced by Beyer in a lecture delivered in February 1974, as partial result of his study of the architectural material from the Archaic Akropolis. Presumably a more comprehensive discussion and publication will appear later on, and therefore only preliminary summary and discussion can be attempted here. Briefly stated, Beyer's theory consists of attributing the figures of the so-called Introduction pediment to the same gable which housed the large snakes, therefore to the Hekatompedon. His reconstruction includes other poros fragments: a small head of Athena, a sandaled foot from a seated (?) figure, and some pieces which he interprets as the wings of a Gorgon. His total composition strongly recalls the Artemision pediments at Corfu and, from left to right, reads as follows: 1) a large snake to right with head facing outward; 2) some of the gods usually assigned to the left half of the Introduction pediment, moving toward a seated Zeus and a small Athena, in a Birth of Athena scene; 3) a large lion; 4) a Gorgon with the central pedimental joint running through her body; 5) a large lioness; 6) the traditional figures of the Introduction pediment (Zeus, Hera, Athena, Herakles and Iris); 7) a large snake to left, also facing outward. The main reasons for Beyer's rearrangement are his belief that the large snakes should be constructed with fewer coils, and that the pedimental slope needed to accommodate the personages of the "Introduction Pediment" corresponds to that of the Hekatompedon, and not to the steeper angle usually quoted (13.5° instead of 6°). Basically, however, his starting point comes from the attribution of a poros molding to the raking cornice of the Hekatompedon and is therefore based on architectural grounds.

Beyer's theory has several attractive features: the Birth of Athena scene would make a good forerunner for the Pheidian Parthenon, and the presence of mythological figures between the corner snakes and the central group would bring the second pediment more in line with the first. Some objections, however, may also be raised. The most important is perhaps the fact that the Hekatompedon gables require a central vertical joint, but such a line running through the central Gorgon, as Beyer reconstructs it, is hardly feasible. At Corfu, the major part of Medusa's body falls on a central block, and only the outstretched limbs lie on adjacent slabs; the vertical joints, therefore, do not bisect the total figure and

[22] This figure looks almost neckless, with a large roundish head: another East Greek trait? Among the other fragments, one head wears a leafy wreath and has been thought to portray Apollo (Wiegand, p. 206 fig. 223).

are much less conspicuous. To reconstruct an entire Gorgon on the evidence of a few scaly fragments seems somewhat daring at best, and certainly redundant under a Gorgon akroterion. A second objection is that the controversial lioness over the bull would be removed from the Hekatompedon; yet the type of splayed joint which runs through her body occurs also in Bluebeard and Herakles, thus ensuring their connection. In addition, the fragments of background adhering to the lioness are painted blue and thus correspond to the background color of the snakes. Finally, these latter would appear overcrowded by the many divine figures, as contrasted with the snaky monsters of the opposite gable which occupy a much more prominent position. Though the addition of some mythological scene between snakes and central lions is a welcome suggestion, Beyer's reconstruction needs additional reinforcement before it can be accepted, and measurements should be further tested.

Another gable whose dimensions cannot be determined accurately is the so-called Olive Tree Pediment since a few more courses could plausibly be added to the fragmentary pseudo-isodomic structure occupying its center, thus increasing its total height. The composition has been interpreted as Achilles' ambush of Troilos at the fountain; this explanation would see the structure as a fountain house, and the best preserved figure as a hydrophoros because of the rounded pad over her hair and her raised left hand to steady a presumed vessel balanced on her head. A naked leg, carved in relief against the background of the ashlar wall behind the fountain may belong to Achilles in hiding.[23] On the other hand, a tree engraved above the wall suggests that the latter may be the precinct for the Sacred Olive Tree of Athena, with the "fountain" a sort of predecessor of the Erechtheion. Since the female figure is entirely detached from the background, she has been assigned to various positions in relationship to the building: under its eaves (which means she could not be holding a vessel on her head), either facing or in profile; or in front of it, to the right. The remains of at least two more women should also go with this pediment.

So many women would be surprising for an Ambush of Troilos. In addition, one would expect some sign of confusion or terror, even if the moment portrayed precedes the attack proper; but would the scene have been intelligible without such confusion? Moreover, the naked leg wears no armor, though a greave would have been appropriate for an armed Achilles. Finally, at the present state of the reconstruction, Troilos would be relegated to a secondary position at a corner, with little room for himself and his horse. The possibility that the gable depicts the Pandroseion and a pre-Erechtheion is certainly more attractive, and I wonder whether the so-called Hydrophoros could instead be restored as a Karyatid. We would be missing some sort of abacus connecting the pad/echinus over her head with the entablature of the building, but the height would be approximately correct. Her raised left hand need not invalidate the suggestion, since literary sources mention Karyatids as having raised arms, and a few sculptural renderings exist of Karyatids in this position.[24]

[23] Traditional reconstructions (see, e.g., *EAA*, Atlas volume, pl. 181, s.v. *Frontone*) place Achilles at the spectator's extreme right and Troilos at his extreme left, to accommodate horses with bent heads near the corner. The preserved leg would therefore belong to an intermediate figure. However, Achilles should be hiding behind, not in front of, the fountain. Moreover, a Troilos and Achilles displaced toward the corners would receive comparatively little attention since the fountain house in the center, with its many frequenters, would be the central focus of the scene.

[24] Athenaeus, *Ps.* 6.241 has Eukrates saying: "In this place one has to dine with the left hand supporting the roof like the Karyatids." Unfortunately neither the literary source nor any example in the

I have already suggested that there might have been Karyatids on the Akropolis before the Erechtheion, thus providing inspiration for the Fifth century architect. If the Olive Tree localizes the scene on the Akropolis, revolutionary as this topographical intent may be, the pediment could indeed reproduce the area of the tomb of Kekrops with its human supports. Note that not only is the Karyatid an East Greek idea, but the pseudo-isodomic masonry of the "fountain house" is unusual in Attica, though it can be found, for instance, in the Knidian Treasury at Delphi, which also employed Karyatid supports. The date of the Akropolis Pediment has been recently given as no later than 550, but it could probably be slightly lower.

Two more poros gables complete the Akropolis series: the so-called Red Triton Pediment, and another, highly fragmentary, showing a lion ready to attack a boar. The first was found in the *Perserschutt* and forms the right half of a gable showing Herakles fighting the monster. The hero has thrown his arm around Triton's neck, and the latter stretches out one arm, probably begging for help. The unnatural color of red which covers both figures and background cannot be explained and may have been caused by an accident after destruction. Whether the lion and boar filled the missing half of the same gable cannot now be determined, but would seem unlikely.

In summary, it would seem as if several small buildings, decorated with carved poros pediments, stood on the Archaic Akropolis, having all been erected in approximately a quarter century, between 560 and 540. Yet more widely ranging dates have been assigned to the preserved architectural elements, and there are perhaps more carved gables than we have evidence for buildings at present. Certainly, the chronology of the architectural sculpture suggests a growth of treasuries around and shortly after the main temple; their tympanon decoration may have been influenced by the latter's innovation.[25]

The Peisistratid Temple and the Alkmaionid Pediment at Delphi. One more set of pediments, marble this time, should be considered before leaving the Akropolis, those belonging to the so-called Peisistratid Temple.[26] The name is due to the date traditionally assigned to the architecture, approximately 525, therefore too late for Peisistratos who died in 528, but suitable for his sons, Hippias and Hipparchos, who took over the Athenian government until 514–510. On the other hand, recent German studies have suggested a lowering of the dates for the temple, and even the possibility that the Gigantomachy pediment could be the product of the young Athenian democracy. Greek archaeologists have also been working on the composition of the east gable, but their results have not yet been published. In this state of flux, only a few comments can be made.

As already mentioned, most of the sculpture from this building was found in the same general area as the poros pediments, therefore at a certain distance from their original

---

visual arts is earlier than the Roman period (see, e.g., M. Lawrence, *AJA* 69 [1965] 207–8 and note 7; Ch. Picard, *Anthemion,* Festschrift Anti [1955] 273–80). However, note that the Athena of the Atlas Metope on the Temple of Zeus at Olympia holds her hand up to help support the World in a gesture that to a contemporary audience, around 460, may have suggested a Karyatid. For another Athenian monument (the so-called akanthos-column at Delphi) where each dancer/Karyatid lifted her arm, see the recent comments by J. Marcadé, *Mélanges Helléniques offerts à Georges Daux* (1974), 239–54.

[25] Boersma, 14, makes the point that since the Akropolis was not a pan-Hellenic sanctuary, these buildings must have been dedicated by the Athenian aristocrats.

[26] Note that Payne refers to it as the Hekatompedon.

location. Fragments of a marble lion-and-bull belonged to the second gable, but there is no evidence to attribute them to the west side; the animals could easily have decorated the east facade, as a powerful apotropaic device and almost a badge of Athens and her goddess. On the other hand, the Gigantomachy also gives an important position to Athena, and it is highly suited for pedimental decoration since it allows a variety of poses within a unified theme. Unfortunately, the problem of the Peisistratid pediments is complicated by their possible relationship to the so-called Alkmaionid Pediment in Delphi, and the two cannot be discussed independently. The situation is quite complex and no solution can be said to be entirely satisfactory or capable of proof.

The Temple of Apollo at Delphi burned in 548. The Amphictyons promoted a great campaign to raise funds, and money came from various sources, including such non-Greek contributors as Amasis of Egypt, who died in 526/5. Our main evidence is a passage of Herodotos (5. 62) which states that the Alkmaionids, after their expulsion from Athens and their defeated attempt to return (Battle of Leipsydrion, 513) undertook to complete the temple at Delphi in order to secure the help of the priests of Apollo and, through their intercession, of the Spartans. Herodotos also adds that the Alkmaionids completed the temple in marble, rather than in poros, as originally stipulated, and this statement is corroborated by the evidence. In fact, the west gable of the Delphic temple shows a Gigantomachy in limestone, while the east pediment is in marble and has a central quadriga between kouroi and korai, in turn flanked by lion-and-prey groups at the corners.

Despite this correspondence between archaeological finds and literary sources, the date suggested by Herodotos at least for the marble pediment, after the Battle of Leipsydrion, has been doubted by several scholars on stylistic grounds. The best preserved among the kouroi looks earlier than the last decade of the Sixth century, and the korai strongly recall Akr. 681, the so-called Antenor's Kore (Figs. 57–58), whose date is usually placed around 530. Several attempts have been made to reconcile these differences, and the following solutions have been proposed.

a) Herodotos has compressed his information, and the Alkmaionids undertook to finish the Temple earlier than the Battle of Leipsydrion. Thus the pediment dates approximately from the time of Akr. 681.
b) Herodotos is correct, and it is the date of the Akropolis kore which should be lowered, thus diminishing the chronological distance between the freestanding statue and the Delphic pediment.
c) There is no true similarity between Antenor's kore and the pedimental figures; therefore there is no need to connect the two works chronologically.

As far as the relationship with the Peisistratid pediment is concerned, the alternatives can be tabulated as follows:

1) The Peisistratids started the temple on the Akropolis around 525. When the Alkmaionids, after 513, undertook to finish the Delphic temple, they used marble to compete with their Athenian rivals.
2) The Peisistratids started their temple after the Alkmaionids had completed the Delphic gable in marble (before 513), and decided to go one better by having

both pediments of that material. Though later than the Delphic temple, the Athenian building would still date before Hipparchos' murder in 514.

3) Though the Athenian temple was started by the tyrants, it was completed by the Alkmaionids, upon their return to Athens after 510; the subject of the Gigantomachy was their choice. The Delphic pediment was an earlier experiment, actually providing inspiration for the composition of the Athenian Gigantomachy and dating from ca. 520.

From all these solutions, I would tend to favor b) and 1), because of the following objections to the theories above:

a) Though the Alkmaionids' involvement at Delphi may easily be earlier than the Battle of Leipsydrion, no urgency or show of good will is called for before their defeat on the field since they had returned to Athens from exile after Peisistratos' death, as shown by the archonship of Kleisthenes in 525/4.

c) The similarity between Antenor's kore and the pedimental korai in Delphi is limited to details, but these may be significant. Note, for instance, how the folds of the himation are undercut in both works: not by removing the whole pleat from the background of the chiton, but by separating the front layer of the cloth from the part folded under it. This peculiar technique virtually hollows out each fold and results in a tubular arrangement which recalls the pipes of an organ. In addition, similarity can be noted in the vertical accent marking the center of the mantle tip over the right leg. This accent is created by one of the pleats below the breast: it sinks without apparent reason to form an unexpected valley between two sets of projecting ridges. Though similar arrangements occur on other Akropolis korai, none, to my knowledge, is identical. Insignificant per se, this detail may also represent a workshop calligraphy, automatically repeated because basically unimportant but therefore symptomatic of true connection if not of common authorship.

As for the Peisistratid temple, the second alternative seems unlikely since Athenian competition with Delphi would be unnecessary (after all, the Peisistratids *were* in power) and perhaps even somewhat out of proportion, the pan-Hellenic being obviously the more important sanctuary. In addition, Delphi had had marble pediments (for treasuries) at an even earlier date. With respect to the third possibility, the symbolism of the Gigantomachy has been considered typically Peisistratean by at least one author (Boardman) in view of Peisistratos' possible identification with Herakles, whose intervention is crucial to the outcome of the battle against the Giants. Since the other pediment had also been conceived in marble, the likelihood that both gables had been planned simultaneously seems strong. Moreover, this third solution would require an earlier date for the Alkmaionid pediment at Delphi, which I have doubted on other grounds.

According to the solutions designated b and I above, the date of the pediments in Athens should fall approximately between 525 and 513, with possible completion around 510; the Delphi pediment would have been made in marble, after 513, in order for the Alkmaionids to be at least the equals of the tyrants in largesse. Is this chronology possible in terms of style?

The Athena from the Peisistratid Gigantomachy has a very rich and elaborate mantle, with conspicuous double folds which should date no earlier than ca. 520 and could perhaps be somewhat later. Her rounded face, prominent eyes, and strong chin are also in keeping with this chronology. She should definitely be seen from below, so the slant of her features falls into proper position and her expression changes, becoming almost wrathful. The opponent usually placed at her feet has now been moved farther down the gable, more toward the corners which were occupied by two crouching giants straining toward the center. According to a recent suggestion, the middle of the composition should be taken by a frontal chariot, for which evidence is found in some marble half-horses from the Akropolis. This theory is ingenious and would be in keeping with the times. Though compositionally a frontal quadriga would break the flow of battle, it would nonetheless have the value of an apparition. Other reconstructions prefer a split-axis composition, with two diverging major figures near the center, almost a forecast of the Parthenon.

I would be inclined to believe that the Gigantomachy stood on the west gable and that the east was occupied at its center by the time-honored lion-and-bull group.[27] One wonders how its corners were filled, and if the so-called Astragalizontes could possibly belong there. If not, one should assume that small buildings with marble pediments also existed, or that such group compositions stood entirely in the round, as freestanding dedications, which is perhaps just as plausible. In any case, the Peisistratid pediments are the earliest in Attica to have marble figures carved entirely free of the background.

The Temple of Apollo at Delphi also featured a Gigantomachy, on its west pediment. It was carved in very high relief, in poros covered by stucco, so that the final effect would probably have been not unlike marble. Despite attempts to assign both pediments to a date after Leipsydrion, the more decorative rendering of the figures and some difficulty with poses (note especially the hem of Athena's skirt and the awkward twist of her upper torso, fully frontal in contrast with the profile position of her legs) would suggest that the west pediment is earlier than the east, even if not considerably so. Here too a frontal quadriga is reconstructed in the center, with giants reclining at the corners, but the whole is too fragmentary for complete evaluation. The east pediment repeats the motif of the central chariot, flanked by at least three youths and three maidens. The best-preserved kouros admittedly looks early, but is it because we are judging it by Athenian standards? The lack of abdominal partitions would not be surprising in a Cycladic work, and perhaps the sculptor omitted a detail which he believed the gable height would have prevented the viewer from noticing.[28] As for one of the horses, his inserted eyes may again speak for greater effectiveness from a distance, rather than for an early date.[29]

The two animal groups at the corners have been seen by some as a hapless attempt at

[27] Delivorrias (pp. 178–79) would also place the Gigantomachy on the west gable but would accept both a central chariot and animal fights at the corners to increase the similarity with Delphi. He therefore has to split the available lion-and-bull fragments to obtain two groups.

[28] A comparable rendering of the epigastric arch is found for instance on a Samian "kouros" dated ca. 500 (*Samos* XI no. 138 pl. 85) because of its active pose.

[29] This detail is at times interpreted as providing confirmation for a bronze-working tradition in the workshop which made the pedimental sculptures. It may even reflect tendencies of the Severe Style and therefore be a sign of late, rather than early, date. Note, in addition, that a relief from the Akropolis, preserving a horse's head with inserted eye (Akr. 1340; *AMA* no. 475; Brouskari, 52; Payne, 50) has been associated with other fragments and assigned to a continuous frieze decorating the Peisistratid temple.

filling that difficult space, by others as a very impressive use of the old apotropaic symbols. Certainly the neck of the stag brought down by the right-hand lion looks disproportionately long,[30] but the groups are impressive when viewed as a whole. The contrast between the stately scene in the center, all vertical accents and quiet mode, and the lively corners filled with frightening beasts, may be an intentional juxtaposition of civilizing power and primitive force; or both elements may express similar concepts of divine protection. For all its impressiveness, the workmanship may betray haste, and the total effect is rich rather than refined. Obviously several hands were at work on the sculptures, and the "Cycladic" touch may have been contributed by local masters, of which Delphi must have had a number available at all times, to satisfy impromptu commissions. Is the style of the pedimental maidens truly Athenian instead?

Their resemblance to Antenor's kore would suggest it, yet they are not of such high quality as the Akropolis statue. In particular, the one with diagonal mantle looks too slender, as contrasted with the massive build of Akr. 681. Regardless of specific attributions, their date could fit after 513,[31] if Antenor's kore could be placed approximately around 520, and I find this suggestion entirely plausible. In its favor are the rows of snail curls over her forehead, in an incipient stage of the late Archaic coiffure; the inserted eyes, which show the influence of contemporary bronze technique; the articulated chin; the distance of the skirt-holding hand from the body; the relative shortness of the vertical central pleat of her himation and the ruffles over its crossband. Yet other details in the Akropolis statue make it look earlier: the excessive breadth of the shoulders, the wooden appearance of the long tresses falling over the breasts (perhaps somewhat increased by the restoration), the surprising thinness of the composition when viewed from the kore's left side.[32] The sculptor may have been more familiar with metalwork, or perhaps less interested in female figures. Certainly the kore is surprising in its frontal extension and unusual in being made out of a single block of marble despite her outstretched arm.

Though all these traits point in the direction of a bronze sculptor, I hesitate in attributing the kore to the great Antenor, because this attribution would also associate Akr. 681 with the potter Nearchos who dedicated Antenor's work. The attribution is based on the alleged connection between the kore and a base carrying the sculptor's signature, and it has often been disputed on ambiguous technical grounds. Nearchos' votive inscription on the same base qualifies the offering as *aparche*. Yet the expression, meaning first-fruits, seems anachronistic for a potter/painter whose main work is dated around 550 and whose

[30] In animal combat groups, stags are usually represented with head raised, in order to accommodate the voluminous antlers, while bulls can be shown with head lowered if necessary. The need for a different head position in a stag often results in too long a neck, but it also creates an impression that the animal has been overtaken in flight. On the flight pattern, see infra, Ch. 8.

[31] Note in particular that the Nike akroterion from this temple wears a diagonal mantle without crossband, thus representing perhaps a slightly earlier stage than the pedimental korai, transitional between west and east gable.

[32] So thin that Langlotz could compare her with the "Solonian korai built in relief technique" (*AMA*, 80). From still correctly proportioned thickness at the waist, Antenor's kore tapers almost to a feather's edge where the skirt is held away from the body at the left. This diminution of proportions is enhanced by the tight cloth over the legs, which contrasts with the fullness of the himation on the upper body and makes the figure almost top-heavy. From the front the effect is counterbalanced by the additional surface that the pulling aside of the skirt affords, but the topheaviness is still visible in profile and partly also in the rear view, although the kore was to be seen from every point as shown by the careful treatment of details both at front and back.

sons, Ergoteles and Tleson, were themselves no longer very active in the same line by the last quarter of the Sixth century. Epigraphically, however, Nearchos' inscription has been placed ca. 525–510, so that the base may really be connected with Akr. 681 after all. A younger Nearchos, a grandson of the mid Sixth century potter, has also been hypothesized to fit this evidence.

Other Athenian Pediments. Besides the pediments from the Athenian Akropolis, others existed in the city. The poros lion already mentioned must have belonged to a large temple to the northwest of the Agora, perhaps lying beyond the present railroad tracks. Three more possible examples were found in the American Agora excavations; one marble pediment, from the area of the Olympieion, is preserved partly in Athens and partly in New York; and a carved gable in poros belonged to the Old Temple of Dionysos near the Theater. Two comments shall suffice. One pediment from the Agora and the Athens/New York gable repeat the lion-and-bull group, this time on a small scale, once more demonstrating the popularity of this subject for pedimental compositions. Another of the Agora finds shows the head of a man against which presses the paw of a large lion. Harrison reconstructs the composition with the two figures interlocked, the man stretched to the left, the lion attacking from the right, and she suggests identifying it as Herakles and the Nemean lion. It is interesting to note, as she points out, that this horizontal version of the struggle enters vase painting approximately at this time and may have been evolved as a pedimental composition first, and then transferred to the slightly less suitable shape of a vase.[33] Finally, a recent find represents perhaps the first pedimental sculpture from Attica that is not from Athens. Unfortunately, the piece had obviously been removed from its original location and therefore its find spot (Kephissia) is no accurate indication of provenience. It is the headless statue of a naked man who reclined in the left corner of a gable, mortally wounded. In style and size the figure closely resembles "the Aeginetans" and it probably belongs to the very end of the Archaic period if not already to the Severe.

Pediments Elsewhere

All in all, Athens has yielded approximately twelve pedimental compositions, and the number may be greater if some of the figures now assigned to the same gable should instead belong elsewhere. No other site has produced quite as many, but in each of the two great pan-Hellenic sanctuaries, Delphi and Olympia, six survive, and the Delphic total includes two large groups from the Apollo temple. Delphi precedes Athens in the introduction of marble pediments, but these belong to treasuries and therefore do not involve the expense and labor required by sizable temples. It is important, however, that this innovation should have taken place at a sanctuary where many artistic firsts occurred, in a climate of particular splendor and intermingling influences. Among the Delphic pedi-

[33] I doubt, however, that this new schema developed on the analogy of Herakles-and-Triton compositions since there the hero fights *alongside* the monster and therefore fills only one half of a gable, while the confronted schema of the lion fight allows a peaking of both figures at the center of the tympanon. Even a most peculiar rendering of Herakles' struggle with Triton, on a terracotta arula presumably from Gela now in the Louvre, places the hero virtually leaping *above* the monster, but still on his same side (P. Devambez, *MonPiot* 58 [1972] 1–23, ca. 550–530).

ments, the earliest to be decorated, and in marble, is presumably that of the Knidian Treasury (ca. 540) though not everybody agrees in assigning to it a marble slab in high relief with remains of two running animals. The architecture of the Knidian Treasury conformed to the Ionic Order except for the use of Karyatids instead of columns, the omission of the dentils, and the introduction of a plain (?) frieze course. It is interesting that a decorated pediment should occur when this Mainland version is adopted by an Asia Minor building. Next chronologically are the pediments of the Massiliot and the Siphnian Treasuries, ca. 535 and 525 respectively. The former seems to have introduced the first frontal horses if not a chariot; the Siphnian Treasury is of interest for its peculiar technique, partly in relief and partly in the round, with figures adhering up to waist level to what appears to be a bench.[34]

Olympia: Megarian Treasury. The pediments of the Olympia treasuries seem to be exclusively in poros. Many are too fragmentary for interpretation and safe attribution, but the Megarian Pediment is almost complete, despite the poor state of preservation of the figures themselves. It has been recently restudied and republished, both architecturally and sculpturally, with modifications of the original reconstruction, and a lowering of the chronology to the end of the Archaic period, with influence from Aegina. The basic change from the earlier publication consists in placing only one figure (Zeus) on the central axis and eliminating another personage, so that the present number adds up to eleven sculptures. Pausanias (6.19.13) tells us that the pediment represents a Gigantomachy, and this information has been traditionally accepted, especially since that subject seems to have enjoyed particular popularity toward the end of the Sixth century. But technical details make me wonder whether a local battle in Megara's mythical past should not be visualized instead. My suggestion is prompted by the small hole in the chest of the kneeling figure (G) next to "Zeus." From the position of the arms, the warrior looks as if he were trying to grab a spear planted in his body, presumably thrust there by his opponent. But Zeus traditionally fights with a thunderbolt, and is so reproduced in the reconstructed drawing. Since only one foot and lower leg of this central upright personage survive, should he be reconstructed in the process of *spearing* his opponent?

As for the other "gods," only the outline of one foot survives for Athena (figure E), who is restored there because the place in the pediment would be appropriate and the subject unthinkable without her participation. Figure H is considered Herakles, again largely because of the theme though no lion skin identifies him. The armed personage (K) attacking another warrior is called Ares to explain the armor, but basically only cuirassed or naked bodies remain. A single figure shows traces of a skirt, which could easily be a chitoniskos rather than the long stately garment appropriate to Poseidon (figure C). The similarity between the two surviving heads, one of a "Giant" and one of a "God," has always been noted, and the recent publication stresses that if a difference in size exists among combatants, it is due simply to the desire to fill the pedimental space as completely

[34] The central figure in this pediment is not Athena, as originally believed, but Zeus, as shown by costume, build, and remnants of a beard on the chest. The sculptor has therefore employed an intelligent principle of scaling his personages according to importance, utilizing the greatest height of the tympanon for the most prominent character and producing a sculptural version closer to the original myth. J. Boardman and H. W. Parke (*RA* 1972, 57–72; *JHS* 77 [1957] 276–92) have suggested that the Struggle for the Tripod may be an allusion to the First Sacred War at Delphi.

as possible despite the reclining or falling positions. Obviously Pausanias thought he saw a Gigantomachy, but this assumption was easy to make, and the periegetes has been shown mistaken on other occasions. Were this scene really to represent a local myth, it would be important as an example of history used as an identifying label for the city's offering, somewhat comparable to the Deeds of Theseus on the Athenian Treasury at Delphi, or the Nymph Kyrene strangling the lion on the Cyrenean Treasury gable at Olympia if the fragments have been properly interpreted.

Bookidis' study has shown that at Olympia the only form of architectural decoration employed (aside from occasional akroteria) was pedimental, even when the decorated building was dedicated by a city where sculptured gables were not popular. She therefore sees this fact as a reflection of Mainland influence and taste, not on those cities but on Olympia and the purely Doric cast of its building practices. In Delphi, by contrast, sculptured pediments are often associated with other forms of architectural decoration, including friezes, metopes and figured akroteria. This latter sanctuary appears therefore more open to outside influences, especially those of the Ionic sphere.

Elsewhere in Greece, and besides the Corcyran and Spartan examples already cited, pediments occur in scattered fashion, and usually rather late. The following survey does not claim to be comprehensive, but the general picture cannot be too far wrong. The earliest is the gable of a large temple of Athena and Poseidon at Asea, in Arkadia. Only one pediment seems to have been decorated in this structure which combined Doric and Ionic elements, around the middle of the Sixth century. The left hand corner of the tympanon was probably filled by a seated lion, the right by a dolphin which, originally excavated in 1910 and then lost, has recently surfaced among the many fragments in the Tegea Museum.[35] Arkadia is obviously a place which knew unusual sculpture and architecture at an early date and is unfortunately only imperfectly explored. Another carved pediment occurs at Topolia, in Boeotia,[36] and one at Eretria, but both fall presumably within the last quarter of the Sixth century. Corinth has produced two terracotta groups from two different gables, but these too are no earlier than ca. 510–500 and may be later. At least one, if not more, of the pediments from the Temple of Aphaia at Aegina should date from the Archaic period; and another temple on that island, now attributed to Apollo, seems to have been decorated with an Amazonomachy toward the end of the Sixth century.[37] The evidence might be greater if other regions of Greece proper were better known.

[35] One wonders whether the two animals stood for the two deities worshiped in the temple; in that case the reliefs would have purely symbolic rather than narrative or even apotropaic function. This consideration would apply even if, as mentioned in *BCH* 95 (1971) 878, the "dolphin" is a triton instead.

[36] A fragmentary male leg in poros, well under life-size, from the Ptoan sanctuary, is considered pedimental by Ducat (*Ptoion* no. 115, pp. 118–89 pl. 56) because of its piecing technique. However, it is not certain that the fragment came from the sanctuary; if it did, it would suggest the presence of decorated treasuries at the site.

[37] A complete republication of the Aphaia pediments is pending. Preliminary notices and the Munich Glyptothek guide (1972) suggest that not three but as many as four pedimental compositions may have been prepared for the Aphaia temple, all dating before 480. At the other extreme, Delivorrias (pp. 180–81) would reconstruct only two pediments. For the moment I retain my previous position and consider the west gable datable around 490, the east around 480–470 (*Severe Style*, 13–17). The Apollo temple on the same island has recently been published (W. W. Wurster, *Alt-Ägina* I: *Der Apollontempel* [Mainz 1974]) but no mention is made of

Outside the mainland, in North African Cyrene, one more example is equally late, ca. 500, and belongs to the second phase of the Apollo temple, when a peristyle was added to the earlier sekos. The reliefs, in yellow limestone, consist of three fragments, one from a human figure and two from animals, which have been integrated as a scene of a shooting Artemis (why not an Apollo?) and the nymph Kyrene struggling with the lion.

Magna Graecia. South Italy and Sicily, as already mentioned, form a separate group, especially the latter with its strong preference for gorgoneion plaques hung in the center of pediments. The largest known example at present is the mask (ca. 2.75 m. wide) which once decorated Selinus Temple C. Other similar plaques are known from Syracuse, Gela, Akragas, Camarina, Himera, and from a single site in South Italy: Hipponion. Presumably these masks developed from an original revetment of the ridge pole, as already speculated.[38] It is interesting to note that the recent excavations at Murlo have provided examples of a similar practice in Etruria, and at a date earlier than any of the extant Sicilian and South Italian examples, ca. 575. Yet the Corfu pediment, if correctly assessed here, represents an evolutionary step from an earlier mask which therefore presupposes a correspondingly earlier establishment of the practice elsewhere. There is, of course, no way to tell whether Etruria preceded Magna Graecia in this form of gable decoration, and whether the idea came to Corfu from the Etruscans rather than from the Western Greeks. This possibility should at least be considered. Interestingly enough, Thermon is again linked with Corfu and Italy since some circular terracotta gorgoneia have also been attributed to the temples of Apollo Thermaios and Apollo Lysios, as revetments for the ridge pole; but by and large the idea remains virtually a monopoly of the Sicilian sites.

In South Italy, more than in Sicily, the conception of the roof area may have varied entirely from traditional Greek forms. Aside from the peculiar coffers on the soffit of the Temple of Athena at Paestum, and the series of regulae and guttae in the same approximate position on the temple of Apollo at Crimisa, there is now also the possible evidence of the terracotta busts which have been attributed to the gable of the "Basilica" at Paestum. They are female torsos with clear traces of a Corinthian cover-tile attached to their backs; they represent therefore some form of antefix. However, the manner of attachment of the tile to the hand-modeled bust and the horizontal alignment of the tile itself show that such antefixes could not have decorated the edges of the roof, for which other terracotta revetments exist. It has been suggested that these unusual antefixes belonged to the tiled floor of the gable itself, such as we see in the terracotta model from Nemi or in that from Sabucina in Sicily. The Nemi model provides one further link with Etruria; and if indeed the Basilica should be restored with an open gable provided with a tiled floor ending in antefixes, Etruscan influence at Paestum would be equally probable. According to Sestieri,

its sculptural decoration, for which see Bookidis P 32, pp. 117–20; G. Welter, *Aigina* (Berlin 1938) 50, 52 fig. 41.

[38] A type of relief plaque with narrative may also have been used to cover the ends of the roof beams. Aside from the terracotta Gorgon panel from Syracuse (supra, p. 193 n. 8), comparable panels have recently been found at the Archaic sanctuary of Vaglio near Metapontum. These terracottas show two horsemen facing each other, with two figures on foot in between. The excavators suggest that, given the amount of such antepagmenta now found, one should visualize a whole series of religious structures within the sanctuary (D. Adamesteanu, *RA* 1967, 31–33 figs. 38–40). But I wonder whether the plaques should rather be considered as parts of a continuous, though repetitive, frieze revetment, like the Larisa architectural terracottas.

the female busts from the Basilica represent dancers in that they hold up the peculiar ruffled panel of material attached to the front of their "blouses." The costume of these figures is perhaps the most surprising element of the antefixes and cannot be described according to current terminology. The ruffled panel seems to hang free from below the breasts, but to be sewn at the sides; ruffles occur also over the sleeves, at mid biceps and just above the wrist. The earliest in the series belong to ca. 500, with some later replacements.

Apparently, canonical carved pediments began to occur in Sicily and South Italy after 480, presumably because of renewed ties with Greece proper. Bookidis lists five examples, with two additional items less certainly identified. Publications since 1967 have added three more possibilities, two of which are of particular importance because they seem to fall before the fateful 480 watershed. The first is represented by several marble fragments now attributed to the Temple of Herakles at Akragas.[39] They include the naked torso of a helmeted warrior, parts of his arm holding a shield, and pieces of other figures: a draped right arm, and a relief palmette possibly from the shield strap of another and larger statue. Some of the marbles were found in the sandy fill for the foundations of the Temple of Zeus Olympios, others in wells and cisterns not far from the Herakleion, to which they have been assigned mostly because it is the only attested Archaic temple in Akragas and because the dimensions would fit. I feel less confident. To me the warrior looks unmistakably Severe, as the publication itself states, rightly comparing his face with a face from the metopes of Temple E in Selinus (ca. 466–460). In addition, the reconstructed drawing and the anatomical description itself fail to account for all the projections on the warrior's back. Rather than a pedimental composition I would see here a freestanding group, perhaps in the presence of an Athena,[40] with a second figure partly adhering to, and therefore concealing, the extant warrior's rear view. The possibility of a Sicilian narrative pediment before 480 would therefore be eliminated.

The second example occurs in South Italy. Excavations in the Sanctuary of Apollo Lykeios at Metapontum have uncovered a series of poros and marble fragments lying in front of both facades of the Apolloneion and clearly part of its pedimental decoration. The best preserved fragment belongs to the west gable. It is the limestone torso of an archer in shooting position. Many horses' legs and fragments of human figures have survived from the east side. According to preliminary reports, the temple itself dates from ca. 530; but it was extensively repaired and provided with pedimental sculpture around 500–480. One wonders whether the lower margin given is perhaps more probable than the upper although the archer's torso recalls the Eretria pedimental sculpture. As the excavators point out, an Archaic date would make this carved set of gables unique in South Italy.

[39] Some of the same fragments, specifically the warrior's torso, had been tentatively attributed to the Temple of Zeus Olympios, on the strength of a rather obscure mention in Diodorus Siculus (13:82). De Miro was able to connect the torso with a helmeted head and proposed the attribution to the Herakleion.

[40] This idea was also suggested by U. Knigge, *Bewegte Figuren der Grossplastik im strengen Stil* (Munich 1965) 9–14. Attribution to a pediment is based on the following observations (De Miro, p. 149): 1) the presence on the right shoulder blade of a cavity for a tenon presumably anchoring the figure to a tympanon wall; 2) the less accurate modeling of the rear view; 3) the presence of rusty stains on the left side of the head, which therefore should have projected outside of the pedimental cornice; 4) the existence of fragments from other figures. All these points can be explained, perhaps more satisfactorily (especially no. 3), through the hypothesis of an independent group.

The third example, in terracotta, comes from Sicilian Himera, the so-called Temple B on the hill overlooking the site of the Victory Temple. The entire structure has been dated within a relatively large span of time. Erected ca. 575–550, the building's initial decoration consisted of terracotta relief metopes and a Gorgon mask for the pediment. This series of ornaments was replaced some time between 500 and 475 by a new geison and sima, and by relief pediments apparently showing many animals to judge from the many extant fragments. In the late Fifth century, terracotta akroteria of considerable size were added. Given the wide chronological span suggested by the excavators, even these pedimental sculptures could fall after 480, at a time when the erection of the Victory temple (which had decorated gables) may have prompted a renewal of the old building according to new fashions.[41]

SUBJECT MATTER

To speculate briefly on the subject matter of extant pediments, it is interesting to note that initially buildings or temples seemed to prefer apotropaic groups and symbols. When narrative is introduced, it is largely confined to the corners of the gable, until ca. 520 when more unified and entirely narrative compositions are accepted (Delphi, Temple of Apollo, W. Gigantomachy), even if only on one side and that perhaps the rear. The Temple of Aphaia at Aegina offers the first positive example of a temple decorated on both sides with battles, and the choice may be significant for the building's date. Treasuries are more likely to employ narrative, perhaps because no deity or cult statue resided in them, or even because the decoration in being relatively nearer the viewer was more easily understood. It is perhaps significant that pedimental compositions in Classical times petered out as temples became larger and entablatures farther from the ground, with the Parthenon probably the largest building on which narrative sculpture could still work successfully from the spectator's point of view.

Of the subject matter, Athens seems to have had a great preference for the lion-and-prey composition, which appears also elsewhere (Sparta, Delphi, and in a way even Corfu and Asea). The exploits of Herakles lend themselves well for filling small gables, and perhaps Boardman is right in asserting a special Peisistratean liking for that hero. Treasuries at the pan-Hellenic sanctuaries may depict local legends or subjects connected with the host-shrine itself, like the Struggle for the Tripod at Delphi. In many cases, the sculptures are so poorly preserved that no guess as to their subject is possible. Battles offer great possibilities in terms of pedimental distribution since relative scale can be maintained by means of different but justifiable poses; or, preferably, the importance of specific figures can be emphasized by thoughtful placement within the gable (e.g., Siphnian Treasury). Among the Battles, if local myths are excluded (Aegina; Megarian Treasury ?), the Gigantomachy and the Amazonomachy seem most popular after 550, with a possible

[41] One more mention—an Archaic poros pediment with relief decoration and painting, from Megara Hyblaia—occurs in *AA* 1954, col. 539. I have been unable to find confirmation in any of the French reports in *MélRome* or any other official publication. No date is given for the alleged pediment. After 480 pedimental sculpture may also have made its appearance on Samos, since the naked torso of a figure in action, probably armed with shield and spear, has recently been attributed to a gable because of two rectangular dowel holes in its back. (*Samos* XI no. 141 pl. 88; see especially p. 212.) However, no building within the Heraion would seem to correspond to the period 480–470 to which the torso belongs, and therefore the sculpture cannot be attributed to a specific structure.

Titanomachy at Corfu.[42] But since the Gigantomachy appears also in the north frieze of the Siphnian Treasury, I wonder whether political implications (the establishment of a new and rightful order versus earlier or uncivilized forces) can be surmised in all cases. That the implications exist by the time of the Parthenon is no assurance that the idea obtained also during the Archaic period, witness the different interpretations given by Boardman and Stähler for the same Gigantomachy pediment in Athens. Certainly a conscious effort was made to find some kind of logical link between the narrative and the deity worshiped in the building or in the sanctuary, or even between the commission and its commissioner.

AKROTERIA

It would be interesting to investigate the correlation between pedimental sculpture and figural akroteria. A rough survey seems to show that decorated gables did not automatically prevent the erection of elaborate akroteria, but chronology, as well as geography, may be a definite factor.

In general terms, it is surprising to note that no architectural sculpture of any form has survived from Delos, yet Archaic temples there may have had figural akroteria if the Delian Nike is an example.[43] The Naxian style of the akroterial sphinxes found on the Athenian akropolis may also be an indication that such roof embellishment existed on the islands at an early date. East Greek temples employed decoration at the apices, but they were largely abstract in design; volutes are recorded for the Kalabak Tepe temple at Miletos, and a possible palmette decoration for the Rhoikos temple at Samos.[44] The Apollonion at Cyrene, around 500, apparently combined different traditions by enclosing a gorgoneion within lyre volutes as crowning for its apex.[45] At Assos in the Troad, the temple of Athena may have had an abstract central akroterion (one fragment of a volute has been restored after Aegina) and figures in the round at the corners. Only an animal's paw has been found, and therefore the restoration as sphinxes or lions is uncertain, but either would be more plausible than the alleged griffins of the original publication.[46] The same applies to the temple of Aphaia at Aegina, whose lateral sphinxes are somewhat uncertain,[47] though sphinx akroteria in general are second in popularity only to Nikai.

[42] According to F. Vian (*La Guerre des Géants* [Paris 1952] 20) no Gigantomachy occurs in Greek art before the second quarter of the 6th century, but this date is high enough to accommodate the Corfu pediment, regardless of whether a Titanomachy or a Gigantomachy is postulated if a lower chronology for the temple is accepted.

[43] Around 425 the so-called Temple of the Athenians in Delos had elaborate group akroteria over uncarved gables. Are we dealing with a local tradition?

[44] Three fragments of poros sculpture in the round (a right hand, part of a right foot, and a right elbow) have been tentatively interpreted as one or more akroterial figures, because of technique and material (*Samos* XI nos. 135–37). However, their attribution to a specific building remains uncertain, and consequently their precise chronology. Possibly they belonged to the Rhoikos altar or to the Temple of Aphrodite and Hermes, but they may conceivably come from freestanding figures with no architectural connections.

[45] S. Stucchi (*QuadLibia* 4 [1961] 62) calls it a marble antefix, but his reference is to Paribeni (19 no. 22 pl. 30), who calls it a central akroterion and comments at length on its possible stylistic connections.

[46] Akalan in Paphlagonia (not too far from Sinope on the Black Sea) has produced the ears of a terracotta griffin which was probably an akroterion (Åkerström, 126–27 fig. 38), so that we cannot entirely exclude the possibility that the type was used for this function, rare though it may have been.

[47] The two heads which are now attributed to sphinxes as lateral akroteria are larger in scale than the maidens flanking the central anthemion. Furtwängler, who noted this discrepancy, restored griffins at the corners and attributed the female heads

Certainly a terracotta sphinx seems to have formed the lateral akroterion of the Thermon temple though probably not for its earliest stage. Lions, however, occur on Asia Minor buildings during the Classical period,[48] and nothing precludes an earlier appearance, so that when only parts of a feline body or paws are found, sphinxes or lions are equally plausible. Four lions from the Athenian Akropolis, in matching pairs, may in fact have formed the crowning ornament of some building.

Anthropomorphic akroteria occur as early as the Hekatompedon in Athens, ca. 566 (Perseus and the Gorgon), and perhaps earlier, to judge from the larger marble gorgoneion and the fragment of belted torso from the Akropolis. After 550, Nikai seem the more popular form of akroterion, presumably because, like the sphinxes, their wings make them relatively plausible apparitions on a building's roof. Their distribution has been noted before; here I may stress that they seem connected with major temples. At Karthaia (Kea) the Temple of Athena seems to have had a rapidly moving figure, perhaps a Nike, at its apex; of the three bases recovered for the corner akroteria, one is surprisingly inscribed with the name Theseus, thus confirming strong Attic influence on this very late Archaic structure. It is regrettable that no sculpture has as yet been associated with this base. Aphaia at Aegina had a most elaborate central akroterion, consisting of an openwork floral ornament flanked by two korai, whose meaning remains open to speculation. Treasuries had somewhat more freedom of choice, but the most striking instance remains the selection of the Athenian Treasury at Delphi, which had mounted Amazons at the corners, climbing toward the apex of the gable. If correctly attributed, the plinth with remains of feet from a battle group may have formed the (lateral ?) akroterion of the latest Archaic temple of Apollo at Eretria, thus preceding by some fifty years at least a Classical practice.[49]

In the Peloponnesos, except for Corinth, where sphinxes abound, the predominant type of akroterion is the rounded disc, cut to fit onto the peak of the roof and without lateral akroteria. Some of these terracotta roundels assume enormous proportions, like the elaborate disc which surmounted the Heraion at Olympia (2.42 m. in diameter). Comparable discs have been found at Sparta, and at several Arkadian sites. Their dentate outline, rather surprising in terracotta, gives credit to the suggestion that they may derive from an original metal form, perhaps symbolizing the sun. Indeed, one large bronze disc with an *à jour* Gorgon as Mistress of Animals has been found on the Athenian Akropolis and has been explained as the akroterion of a late Geometric temple taken down in Solon's time. Two bronze discs with Gorgoneia, one with a dentate edge, have been found at Cyrene, but their function is still uncertain.

---

to freestanding statues set up in front of the great altar (*Aegina* [Munich 1906] nos. 177–78, pls. 98, 102; see also his figs. 17, 19, 22). For the restoration as sphinxes, cf. G. Welter, *Aigina* (Berlin 1938) fig. 79 and p. 68; P. Wolters, *Münchener Jahrbuch der bildenden Kunst*, NF 11 (1934–36) 211–21, figs. 1–5.

[48] Lions used to be restored at the four corners of the Nereid Monument in Xanthos, but the official publication of the building has shown that the cuttings in the raking sima are too short for the extant lions and would rather fit the smaller Nereids (*FdX* 3 [1969] 150–51 and nn. 10 and 12). On the other hand, the Alexander Sarcophagus (Lullies & Hirmer, pl. 232) suggests that the practice may have obtained in other temple-like tombs. Cf. H. Möbius, *BonnJhr* 158 (1958) 217 and *GGA* 216 (1964) 35, for further examples. The practice seems distinctively non-Greek in origin.

[49] Note that in all these cases (Aegina, Athenian Treasury at Delphi, Eretria) such elaborate akroteria went with complex pedimental sculpture. This should be stressed particularly for the Athenian Treasury, whose carved pediments often go unnoticed since only fragments remain.

Finally, Magna Graecian akroteria. Gela seems to have originated the most intriguing type, with a horse and rider astride the ridge pole, so that the horse's body covers the central beam. That this idea may have been inspired by non-Greek, perhaps Sikel, usage, is suggested by the peculiar model from Sabucina now in Caltanissetta. From Gela, the rider akroterion spread elsewhere. Though largely limited to Sicily, an impressive horse's head in terracotta from the sanctuary of Apollo at Metapontum may show that the type reached South Italy toward the end of the Archaic period.[50] From Gioia Tauro comes a terracotta akroterion (a sphinx supporting horse and rider) which is the late Archaic predecessor of the marble groups from the Marasà and Marafioti Temples at Lokroi. More conventional Magna Graecian types of figured akroteria are also known, including the popular sphinx, the winged lion (?), and the Nike. This last is attested at Syracuse and Tarentum, though somewhat late within the Archaic period. A peculiar bifrontal sphinx (?) decorated the Syracusan Athenaion.

SUMMARY

The idea of pedimental decoration, which the Greeks developed to such aesthetic heights, seems to have had relatively limited distribution during the Archaic period, with most of the examples coming from Athens and the two great pan-Hellenic sanctuaries of Delphi and Olympia. The initial idea may have come from the Orient, perhaps specifically from Phrygia, though spontaneous invention may have occurred elsewhere from different stimuli. Such seems to have been the case in South Italy and Sicily, which developed the form of a gorgoneion plaque in the center of a gable. The Magna Graecian conception of the pedimental area as an open space, or as something independent from the roof proper, may have prevented the introduction of figured scenes until renewed contact with the Greek mainland, after 480, brought about changes in their entire architectural repertoire. East Greece, for local preference as much as for technical reasons connected with the Ionic Order, avoided pedimental compositions until the Late Archaic period, and then produced only one or two examples, in Aeolic territory. The Cyclades have yielded none, while Corfu, with an abundance of occurrences, appears more strictly connected with Italy than with Greece proper.

Anthropomorphic akroteria seem to follow a different pattern of distribution, appearing in Athens as early as ca. 590–580 and perhaps also in the Cyclades and Chios, which may have "invented" the Nike type. Sicily leads in originality, with horse-and-rider in terracotta over the ridge pole, but the Athenian Treasury at Delphi also produces mounted figures, at the corners. The sphinx seems to be the only truly ubiquitous type. No apparent correlation is at present possible between pedimental compositions and the presence or absence of figured akroteria, but thematic affinity is suggested, if not necessarily with the pediments, at least with the metopes of the Athenian Treasury. Akroteria, like pedimental groups, may have originated as a form of prophylactic decoration for various buildings, perhaps developing from originally structural features of the roofing. Some of them remain nonfigural until Classical times, while combinations of the two types are always possible.

[50] Fragments of terracotta horses have been found at Delphi (*FdD* 2:4, 263–65) and at Halai in Boeotia (*Hesperia* 9 [1940] 446–52 nos. 18–31) but their exact architectural use is not known.

FOR PAGE 187

The main work on Greek pedimental sculpture is E. Lapalus, *Le Fronton Sculpté en Grèce* (Paris 1947). See also *EAA*, s.v. *Frontone* (P. Arias), and Atlas vol., pls. 180–84, for reconstructions (some superseded). Bookidis' Dissertation is of great importance.

Murlo terracotta statues over the ridge pole: Edlund-Gantz, especially 179–81 with notes and added bibliography.

Temple of Apollo at Veii: E. Stefani, *NSc* 1953, 50 fig. 25; Schefold, pls. 410–11 and comments on pp. 323–24 with fig. 71 and added bibliography; Edlund-Gantz, 185–86.

FOR PAGE 188

Gordion: *AJA* 60 (1956) 262 pl. 93 (Akroterion), pl. 92 (lion orthostats); *AJA* 61 (1957) 323 pl. 90 (doodles); *AJA* 62 (1958) 144 pl. 21 (doodles and orthostat); see also R. S. Young, *Expedition* 4 (1962) 2–12, on Phrygian constructions, and, id., *Gordion, A Guide to the Excavations and the Museum* (Ankara 1968) 22–24 (Megaron 2).

Gordion, Great Tumulus: *AJA* 62 (1958) 147–49, especially 148 and pls. 23:13, 25:12, for inner gable and section.

For other "ice tongs" akroteria from Phrygia, see also Cummer, 35–36 pl. 6 and fig. 6; cf. also the Cybele relief in Ankara, *KAnat*, 94 fig. 60; Schefold, pl. 324; the carving shows several Oriental elements of interest for Greek art: the gable with a post (?) in the center, the "Chinese roof," the tongs akroterion and a series of maeander spirals on either side of the "doorway" which must represent terracotta tiles.

For the earlier dating of the Phrygian rock-cut facades, see C.H.E. Haspels, *The Highlands of Phrygia* (Princeton 1971); for lower dates, see R. S. Young's review of Haspels, *AJA* 76 (1972) 444–47; see also *KAnat*, 107 fig. 67 (Midas City, large facade, dated 6th century) and 87 fig. 51 (Büyük Arslantaş, dated to the first half of the 6th century).

Greek Geometric architecture: H. Drerup, *ArchHom* 2 (1969) Ch. O; O. Broneer, *Isthmia* I (Athens 1971).

FOR PAGE 189

Larisa pediment: Bookidis, P 34 A; J. Boehlau & K. Schefold, *Larisa* 2 (Stockholm 1940) 117–30, pls. 63–67.

Kebren: J. M. Cook, *The Troad, an Archaeological and Topographical Study* (Oxford 1973) 326–44 on Kebren in general; for the terracotta revetments and the pedimental foot, see pp. 334–36. The chariot frieze is nos. 5–6; the banquet frieze, nos. 7–14; the pedimental foot, no. 15 pl. 62. Cf. also Åkerström, 7 no. 6.

FOR PAGE 190

Group of poros fragments from Corinth: Bookidis, *Hesperia* 39 (1970) 313–25.

FOR PAGE 191

Bookidis on early pediments: 417–18.

Corfu, Mon Repos: Bookidis, P 1; G. Dontas, *Deltion* 18:2 (1963) 161–80, plan 4.

Terracotta pediments from Kanoni: *Corfu*, 57.

Winter's comments on Corinth: 100–2, 106; for Corfu and its contacts with South Italy, see 107, 117–18; also 26–27. By 575–550 Thermon was the only Greek site that continued to use human heads as a form of architectural decoration (Winter, 29).

Corfu, Artemision: See, e.g., Berve & Gruben, 406; for a reconstruction with adyton, see F. Matz, *Geschichte der griechischen Kunst* 1 (Frankfurt am Main 1950) 368 and plan (fig. 19).

FOR PAGE 192

Acquarossa akroterion: E. Wetter, C. E. Östenberg, M. Moretti, *Med kungen på Acquarossa*, (Malmö 1972) 61, upper figure; 116; 140–41. See also *Gli Etruschi, Nuove ricerche e scoperte* (Viterbo 1972–73) pls. 6, 8 nos. 30, 31, 35. I am indebted to K. M. Phillips, Jr., for these references. See also the examples quoted by Edlund-Gantz, 187–93; from Murlo, see *AJA* 78 (1974) 275–77, ill. 14 (akroteria from the lower building, earlier than 650).

Eretria: P. Auberson and K. Schefold, *Führer durch Eretria* (Bern 1972) 113–21, especially 116; P. Auberson, *Eretria* 1 (Bern 1968) 21–22.

Ionic temple in Syracuse: G. V. Gentili, *Palladio* 17 (1967) 61–84. Cf. also infra Ch. 9, pp. 260, n. 9, 266.

Thermon antefixes: For a theory of local (Balkan) tradition, perhaps in wood, see Winter, 107.

For a comparison between Sicilian gorgoneia and Corfu, see P. Montuoro, *MemLinc* 1 s.6 (1925) 276–344 (for Corfu, 315–27). Recent publications have stressed the intentionally narrative rather than the apotropaic character of the Corcyran decoration: J. J. Benson, *Gestalt und Geschichte*, Festschrift K. Schefold (Bern 1967) 48–60, with discussion of previous theories; see also E. Kunze, *AthMitt* 78 (1963) 74–89.

FOR PAGE 193

The main publication of the sculptures is *Korkyra* 2. For the theory of a Titanomachy, see J. Dörig and O. Gigon, *Der Kampf der Götter und Titanen* (Lausanne 1961) 29–37.

FOR PAGE 194

Seated figure: Kranz, 27 and n. 96.

FOR PAGE 195

Bronze pins: *Korkyra* 2, 17–18 and n. 1.

Pediment found in 1973: *AAA* 7 (1974) 183–86; a complete publication is being prepared by A. Choremis, to whom I am greatly indebted for permission to see the sculptures in December 1974. Another pediment featuring a banquet scene was excavated at Sardis and probably belonged to the small mausoleum of a noble Persian or Lydian of the late 5th century. See Hanfmann, 18–19 fig. 42; id., *Mélanges Mansell* (Ankara 1974) 289–301.

FOR PAGE 196

Sparta pediment: Bookidis P 28, 104–7; R. M. Dawkins, *The Sanctuary of Artemis Orthia at Sparta* (*JHS* Suppl. 5, 1929) 21–22 pl. 5; for chronology, see J. Boardman, *BSA* 58 (1963) 1–7.

For summaries of the architectural problems on the Akropolis, see Bookidis, 10–37; *Agora* XI no. 94, esp. pp. 32–33 and nn. 85–89 for the problem of the Hekatompedon. For a recent discussion of the meaning of the lion groups, see Hölscher, esp. pp. 69–74. The latest discussion of the poros sculpture is in Brouskari, but see infra for some of Beyer's ideas. The standard publications of the poros sculpture are Th. Wiegand, *Die archaische Poros-Architektur der Akropolis zu Athen* (Kassel und Leipzig 1904); and R. Heberdey, *Altattische Porosskulptur* (Vienna 1919). For the problems of stratigraphy, see Bundgaard. All present knowledge on find spots should be considered tentative until his work is fully evaluated.

Angelitos Athena and Kritian Boy: *Severe Style*, 29–33.

FOR PAGE 197

On the marble simas, see W.-H. Schuchhardt, *AA* 78 (1963) 797–822; see also Travlos, 258–59.

Trumpet spouts: in Phrygia (half-trumpet): Cummer; on the Akropolis, Travlos, fig. 80.

FOR PAGE 198

On the Hekatompedon Akroteria: Payne, 11 and nn. 1–4 pl. 13; *Agora* XI, 4 n. 13; *AMA* nos. 442–47. Not so Brouskari, who connects Akr. 701 (the large Gorgon head, *AMA* no. 441) with the Hekatompedon, pp. 30–31; cf. also her fig. 53.

Cornice block with incised lotus flower (ca. 40 fragments): Brouskari, 30 fig. 19 (Akr. 4572); birds (ca. 20 fragments): Wiegand, pp. 25–38. For a color reconstruction, see also Schefold, pl. XXVI. For sketches, Heberdey, 129–32 figs. 141, 144–45.

Naxian votive offerings on the Akropolis: Payne, 12–13 n. 1; cf. also supra, Ch. 4 p. 104.

Lions and panthers: Bookidis, 383–92; Brouskari, 29–30 (nos. 552 and 554), also p. 31 (no. 122); *AMA* nos. 462–63; Payne, 11–12 pl. 15. For the reconstruction as metopes, see W. B. Dinsmoor, *AJA* 51 (1947) 149–51 pl. 28:3; for a frieze, see W.-H. Schuchhardt, *AthMitt* 60–61 (1935–36) 102 fig. 18.

FOR PAGE 199

Bulls at antae of Artemision at Ephesos: W. R. Lethaby, *JHS* 37 (1917) 1–2.

Samian anta sphinxes: See supra, p. 179, bibliography for p. 157.

Thasos Pegasos: *GdTh*, no. 8 p. 117 and fig. 58; H. Drerup, *MdI* 5 (1952) 26–27 n. 90.

Chian architecture: J. Boardman, *AntJ* 39 (1959) 170–218; Pegasos on pl. 27e no. 44, pp. 185 and 196. Cf. also *ArchEph* 1939–41, Parart. 24–26 figs. 1–3. For another anta base ending in lion's paw, from Erythrai, see *JOAI* 15 (1912) cols.

66–68 figs. 52–53. See also infra, Ch. 9, pp. 262–63.

Dinsmoor's reconstruction of Hekatompedon pediments: *AJA* 51 (1947) 145–47. See also Brouskari, 25–29 no. 4; 33–34 nos. 41 and 56; 36–37 nos. 37–40; 39–40 nos. 35–36; 46–47 no. 3.

FOR PAGE 200

Large lion head from the Agora: *Agora* XI, 31–33, especially nn. 85–89; no. 94.

For a review of theories on the Tricorpor, see F. Brommer, *MarbWinckPr* 1947, 1–4; more recently, S. Benton, *Studi in Onore di L. Banti* (1965) 47–49; J. Boardman, *RA* 1972, 57–72, who develops further his idea of Peisistratos' connection with Herakles in *JHS* 95 (1975) 1–12.

Shield strap from Olympia: Mallwitz, 31 fig. 29.

Harrison: *Agora* XI, 4 n. 21.

FOR PAGE 201

For the theory that at the beginning of the 6th century Ionia furnished engineers for all major architectural enterprises, see R. R. Holloway, *HSCP* 73 (1968) 281-90.

FOR PAGE 202

Hydra pediment: Brouskari, 29 no. 1; W.-H. Schuchhardt, *AA* 1963, 811–12; Bookidis, 29, P 8, for comparison with the Boxer stele.

Introduction Pediment (= Apotheosis of Herakles): Brouskari, 34–35 no. 9; Bookidis, P 4; Boardman, *RA* 1972, 70–72 n. 3 on p. 69 on the dates of the poros pediments in general. For the comparison with the Rampin Horseman, see Lullies & Hirmer, 41. For the attribution to workshops, Deyhle, 57. For different attributions of figures to pediments, see, e.g., the photographs in *EAA*, s.v. *Atene, Acropoli*, p. 783 fig. 984.

For the other gods, see Heberdey, 41–46; Wiegand, 204–8 pl. 15, reconstructs them in a gable of their own.

Olive Tree Pediment (= Troilos Pediment): Brouskari, 42–43 no. 52; Bookidis P 7; Deyhle, 54.

FOR PAGE 203

Beyer's theory: *AA* 1974, 639–51; see esp. p. 650 fig. 10 for a drawing of the suggested reconstruction.

FOR PAGE 205

Pseudo-isodomic masonry: A. K. Orlandos, *Les Matériaux de Construction et la technique architecturale des anciens Grecs* 2 (Paris 1968) 146–52, especially 150 (b) and fig. 167 for the Olive Tree pediment; the Knidian Treasury is mentioned on p. 147 (a). See also R. Martin, *Manuel d'Architecture Grecque* 1 (Paris 1965) 399–400.

Red Triton Pediment: Brouskari, 37 no. 2; Bookidis P 6.

Lion and Boar Pediment: Bookidis P 5; H. Schrader, *JdI* 43 (1928) 84 fig. 32; Hölscher, 72, G 3.

Peisistratid Temple, lion-and-bull pediment: Brouskari, 32 no. 3831 (should be 3331); *AMA* nos. 471–73; Stähler, 109; Hölscher, 72–73, G 4.

Gigantomachy pediment: Brouskari, 76–78; Payne, 52–54 pls. 35–38; *AMA* nos. 464–70; for a lower chronology, see Stähler, 101–12 (ca. 505); for a reconstruction with a central chariot, id., 88–101; Delivorrias, 178–79. Deyhle connects the Peisistratid Gigantomachy with the workshop of Endoios (pp. 12–39).

For the find spot of the pedimental Athena: Bundgaard, 9 n. 1.

FOR PAGE 206

Alkmaionid pediment at Delphi: For a general summary and chronology, see *Agora* XI, 7–8 and 13. On the problems in general, and the connection with Antenor: Gauer, 130–33; Deyhle, 40–44; Kleine, 34–36 and (on Antenor) 46–51; Stähler, 107 and n. 76; Delivorrias, 177–78 (Apollo Temple 5).

Poros pediment, Temple of Apollo: also attributed to the Alkmaionids by P. de la Coste Messelière, *BCH* 70 (1946) 271–87.

FOR PAGE 208

Astragalizontes: Payne, 47 pl. 124; *AMA* no. 412; Brouskari, 102–3 no. 161 (should be 160); Lapalus, 132–34 and fig. 17. Brouskari and Schrader favor a freestanding composition.

The best photographs of the Delphic gables are in *Delphes*, pls. 140–49. For a reconstruction of the east pediment, see P. de la Coste Messelière, *BCH* 77 (1953) 346–73.

For the east pediment kouros, see *Kouroi* no. 166 figs. 500–3; that he looks Cycladic is noted also by Gauer, 51 and n. 172 with bibliography.

Animal groups at the corners: Hölscher, 74–75, G 8.

FOR PAGE 209

Korai of Delphi, east pediment: *Korai* nos. 106–7 figs. 322–26.

Antenor's kore, Akr. 681: *Korai* no. 110 figs. 339–40; Payne, 31–33, 63–65, pls. 51–53; *AMA* no. 38; *Dedications* no. 197; Brouskari, 78–79; *Agora* XI, 8 and n. 46.

Nearchos' activity has been most recently dated to ca. 570–555 (J. Boardman, *Athenian Black Figure Vases* [New York 1974] 35). For a younger potter by the same name, see, e.g., *EAA* s.v. *Nearchos.*

FOR PAGE 210

The pediments from the Agora are: 1) *Agora* XI no. 95 (lion and bull, poros, ca. 500–490); 2) no. 96 (Herakles and the lion, ca. 530–520); 3) no. 97A (Is head of Herakles with lion skin late Archaic, or copy of a late Archaic work?; cf. also no. 125 and comments on p. 65).

Marble pediment Athens/New York: Richter, *Catalogue* no. 7; Hölscher, 73, G 5 (see her G 6 for Agora no. 95).

Old Temple of Dionysos: Bookidis P 10; E. Coche de la Ferté, *RA* 29–30 (1948) 196–206 (dancing satyrs and a maenad in low relief).

Pedimental figure from Attica (Kephissia): *Deltion* 25:2[2] (1970) 534 pl. 448a.

Delphi pediments: 1) Bookidis P 16 (Knidian Treasury ?); Hölscher, 74, G 7. 2) Bookidis P 17 (Massiliot Treasury); P. de la Coste Messelière, *Au Musée de Delphes* (Paris 1936) 328–81. 3) Bookidis P 18 (Siphnian Treasury); B. S. Ridgway, *AJA* 69 (1965) 1–5. 4) Bookidis P 20 (Temple of Athena Pronaia); Hölscher, 75, G 9. 5) Bookidis P 21 (Athenian Treasury); *FdD* 4:4 (1957) 167–81; Delivorrias, 181–82. 6) Bookidis P 19 (Temple of Apollo). Some of these buildings had a double set of pediments, but the *incidence* of carved gables is here counted as one per structure.

FOR PAGE 211

Olympia pediments: 1) Bookidis P 22 (Cyrenaean Treasury); Mallwitz, 173. 2) Bookidis P 23 (Treasury of the Epidamnians); Mallwitz, 169–70. 3) Bookidis P 24 (Treasury of Sybaris); Mallwitz, 170–73. 4) Bookidis P 25 (Treasury of Metapontum); Mallwitz, 174. 5) Bookidis P 26 (Megarian Treasury); Mallwitz, 174–76, see also infra. 6) Bookidis P 27 (Syracusan Treasury); Mallwitz, 169. See also Bookidis' general comments on pp. 81–84.

Sculpture of Megarian Treasury: P. C. Bol, *AthMitt* 89 (1974) 65–74 fig. 2 pl. 31; cf. also Delivorrias, 180. Architecture: K. Herrmann, *AthMitt* 89 (1974) 75–83 pls. 36–39 Beil. 1.

FOR PAGE 212

Bookidis' comments on the Doric climate at Olympia: 414–15.

Asea Temple: Bookidis P 29; K. Rhomaios, *ArchEph* 1957, 114–63, especially 143–44 figs. 33–34; *Deltion* 24:2[1] (1969) 130 pl. 117a; *BCH* 95 (1971) 878–79 fig. 159.

Topolia, Boeotia: Bookidis P 30; L. Curtius, *AthMitt* 30 (1905) 375–90; D. von Bothmer, *Amazons in Greek Art* (1957) 117.

Eretria: J. Konstantinou, *AthMitt* 69–70 (1954–55) 41–44; Bookidis P 31; Lullies & Hirmer, pls. 66–68; Delivorrias, 179–80.

Corinth Terracotta Pediments: Bookidis P 34; R. Stillwell, *Studies E. Capps* (1936) 318–22; S. W. Weinberg, *Hesperia* 26 (1957) 306–8 pls. 65–66, 74–75.

FOR PAGE 213

Cyrene: Paribeni, nos. 19–21 pl. 29; S. Stucchi, *QuadLibia* 4 (1961) 62.

On the gorgoneion plaques, see Bookidis, 430–31; Berve & Gruben, p. 425 fig. 88 (Selinus); W. Darsow, *Sizilische Dachterrakotten* (Berlin 1938) 12–17.

Murlo plaque: *Poggio Civitate*, 47 nos. 92–93 pl. 33; *AJA* 78 (1974) 266 and nn. 13–14 pl. 55: 2–3.

Thermon: Van Buren, 66–67 and 136 nos. 1–2.

Temple of Athena, Paestum: Berve & Gruben, pls. 122–23 figs. 76–77 on p. 412.

Temple of Apollo at Crimisa: Dinsmoor, 84 fig. 31.

Paestum terracotta busts: P. G. Sestieri, *BdA* 48 (1963) 212–20; see also supra, Ch. 4, p. 92 n. 9.

Nemi model: R. Staccioli, *Modelli di edifici etrusco-italici: I modelli votivi* (Rome 1968) no. 30 pls. 34–37.

Sabucina model: P. Orlandini, *ArchCl* 15 (1963) 86–96, especially 88 pls. 27–28; P. Griffo, *Gela* (Greenwich, Conn., 1968) 74, fig. 47.

FOR PAGE 214

Magna Graecian pediments after 480: Bookidis, 427–28.

Akragas, Herakleion (?): E. De Miro, *CronArch* 7 (1968) 143–56, with previous bibliography.

For a reconstruction, see the drawing on pl. 41.

Metapontum, Apollo Lykeios: D. Adamesteanu, *RA* 1967, 3–38, especially 10–13; see also *AA* 1966, 38.

FOR PAGE 215

Himera: *Himera* I, 162–69, 174–77, and catalogue, 194–202. See also the more condensed account by N. Bonacasa, *Archaeology* 29 (1976) 46–47.

FOR PAGE 216

Akroteria: Marilyn Goldberg is now writing a Ph.D. Dissertation for Bryn Mawr College on the Greek akroteria of the Archaic period. Delivorrias (Appendix II) includes akroteria in his review of Archaic pediments.

Delian Nike: See supra, p. 112 n. 36.

Miletos, Kalabak Tepe temple: *Ruinen*, 40.

Samos, Rhoikos Temple: E. Buschor, *AthMitt* 55 (1930) 90 fig. 44 and Beil. 24; see also supra, p. 157 n. 11, for terracotta sphinxes as lateral akroteria (Berve & Gruben, 453).

Assos: J. Clarke, F. Bacon, R. Koldeway, *Investigations at Assos* 2 (Cambridge, Mass., 1902–1921) 168 and fig. 7 on p. 155.

FOR PAGE 217

Thermon: H. Koch, *RömMitt* 30 (1915) 67 figs. 28–29; Van Buren, 68 fig. 138 (and perhaps a Nike as central akroterion? cf. no. 129).

Akropolis lions: See supra, Ch. 6, p. 153 and bibliography p. 178.

Larger marble gorgoneion from the Akropolis, and belted torso: Akr. 701; Payne, 10 pl. 1; *AMA* no. 441; Brouskari, 30–31.

Karthaia: *Deltion* 18:2[2] (1963) 281–82, pl. 327c; *BCH* 89 (1965) 862 fig. 7.

Aphaia central akroterion: A. Furtwängler, *Aegina* (Munich 1906) 274–95.

Athenian Treasury at Delphi: *FdD* 4:4 (1957) 182–87 pls. 86–91.

Temple of Apollo at Eretria: *AA* 1921, col. 323.

Akroterion of Olympia Heraion: N. Yalouris, *AthMitt* 87 (1972) 85–98; for other disc akroteria, see Van Buren, 179–83.

For an original metal form, see P. Verzone, *Studies Robinson* 1 (St. Louis 1951) 272–94; for the bronze disc from the Athenian Akropolis, see E. Touloupa, *BCH* 93 (1969) 862–84, especially 878–84 with bibliography.

Cyrene discs: *Libya Antiqua* 3–4 (1966–67) 196–97 pl. 72b; *AJA* 75 (1971) 39.

FOR PAGE 218

Gela horsemen: P. Orlandini, *Scritti in onore di G. Libertini* (1958) 117–28.

Horse from Metapontum: V. Zanotti Bianco, L. von Matt, M. Napoli, *La Magna Grecia* (Siena 1973) color pl. XXXIX.

Gioia Tauro terracotta akroterion: E. Gagliardi, *AttiMGrecia* 2 (1958) 33–36 pls. 9–10.

Marasà and Marafioti akroteria: Langlotz, pls. 122–24.

Winged lion akroterion, etc.: L. Bernabò Brea and R. Calza, *ASAtene* 27–29, NS 11–13 (1949–51) 7–102, esp. 83–86. Bifrontal sphinx: G. V. Gentili, *BdA* 58 (1973) 7 and fig. 17 (caption exchanged with that for fig. 18); see also, in general, P. Orsi, *MonAnt* 25 (1918) 622–26, figs. 212–17.

Syracuse Nike: Langlotz, pl. 43. On Nikai in general, see supra Ch. 4. For the Nike akroterion of the Alkmaionid temple in Delphi, see *BCH* 77 (1953) 370 and fig. 6.

Chapter 8

Metopes

PEDIMENTAL sculpture requires for its existence the presence of a pitched roof and a horizontal cornice. Given these two elements, tympanal decoration can occur regardless of the architectural Order, and therefore its adoption or rejection is conditioned exclusively by local taste. Not so for the metope, whether plain or decorated. In its true form, it is strictly connected with the Doric Order, of which it represents the frieze course by alternating with the triglyphs; therefore no metopes are possible except on a Doric building. Since East Greece and the islands preferred the Ionic to the Doric Order,[1] no metopes are to be expected for those areas and indeed, except for the anomalous Doric temple of Athena at Assos, in the Troad, none are found. By contrast the Greek mainland and Magna Graecia, where the Doric order prevailed, have produced many examples of decorated metopes, so that at first no gaps or discrepancies appear on a chart listing all known examples in purely chronological order. Yet the picture becomes decidedly more complex when the evidence is broken down according to distribution.

Here again Bookidis provides an invaluable research tool and many stimulating ideas; even the years intervening between her writing (1967) and mine have not added much that is new or different. But I find myself somewhat at variance with her conclusions, or at least I attribute greater or lesser importance to certain aspects of the evidence. Briefly stated, she suggests that the practice of decorating metopes started in the mainland of Greece, whence it passed on to Magna Graecia, which took it up with great enthusiasm and developed it independently. I think that the examples from Greece proper are either questionable as true metopes, or sparked by outside influences, and I therefore suspect that the idea for this form of architectural decoration may have originated in Magna Graecia itself, or at least that it may have received there its first sculptural form, even if the inspiration may have come from elsewhere. Crucial for this suggestion is the evidence of the so-called metopes from Mycenae.

MYCENAE RELIEFS

These puzzling reliefs have been the subject of a recent study by F. Harl-Schaller, who summarizes all previous opinions on the subject. Besides Doric metopes, the extant eight fragments[2] have been called parts of a pediment, of a continuous frieze, or even decora-

[1] This statement is not quite accurate for pan-Hellenic Delos, which had several Doric buildings. The absence of relief metopes at such a sanctuary is all the more remarkable in the light of the spectacular Mykonos pithos, with its panels depicting the Trojan Horse and scenes from the Ilioupersis so monumental in character that they strongly suggest architectural decoration on a large scale (M. Ervin, *Deltion* 18 [1963] 37–75; Schefold, pl. 11.)

[2] Bookidis (169, no. a) includes one fragment, broken all around, with thighs of a male figure to right, not published and in the storerooms of the National Museum. This piece is not listed by F. Harl-Schaller.

tion for a monumental altar. In effect, the last three identifications can be excluded on technical and stylistic grounds. We know of no altar with such form of decoration in the early Archaic period, the borders around the reliefs prevent them from forming a continuous frieze, and there is no trace of a pedimental slope in the preserved edges. Only the metope interpretation remains still debatable.

As Bookidis had already seen, the reliefs fall into two groups, differing in material (two kinds of limestone), borders, size, perhaps even chronology and subject matter. The best-known fragment, the so-called "Woman at the Window" (Nat. Mus. no. 2869, more probably a deity making the bridal gesture of anakalypsis) goes together with another piece, which Harl-Schaller convincingly reconstructs as a man's body being lifted by two sphinxes with crossing front paws. Because of the Daedalic traits in the woman's face, a date around 630 is usually assigned to the first relief and should therefore be valid also for the other fragment. The second group consists of the remaining six pieces, which probably show hoplites engaged in battle. The Austrian scholar sees in this motif a possible link with the body being lifted by the sphinxes—a sort of Daedalic version of a dead warrior being carried away by Sleep and Death. She would rather divide the subject matter according to motions: one group comprises figures in lively action, while those of the second make significant gestures. Bookidis would accept only her own second group (the six hoplite fragments) as belonging to the Archaic Doric temple of the beginning of the Sixth century.[3] Harl-Schaller accepts both, but refuses to see them as canonical metopes, and can only visualize them as part of a temenos wall, or as decoration for the socle of a small structure of indefinite architectural order.

It is difficult to decide between the two positions, especially since very little remains of the temple on the Mycenaean akropolis. According to some scholars, it was peripteral and built entirely of stone. Others claim that only its Hellenistic successor on the site had a surrounding colonnade. Finally, Harl-Schaller asserts that neither phase of the temple had a peristyle and that there are at present no traces of a structure with which the reliefs can be safely connected. The question therefore arises as to the proper definition of a metope. If by the term is meant exclusively the plaque which alternates with the triglyphs on the entablature of a Doric temple, Harl-Schaller's theory would exclude the Mycenae reliefs from the category. If instead the term is taken to include all self-contained architectural reliefs which did not join in a continuous visual sequence even if connected by their relative proximity and their subject matter, then the Gortyna plaques with the divine triads should also be considered metopes, and the origin of the type be ascribed to Crete and an earlier period.

Yet Crete represents a virtual dead end in terms of the further development of Archaic Greek sculpture and architecture. None of the temples found on early Crete can be described as Doric or Ionic; they are all closed structures with varying interior plans which look back to the Minoan past rather than to the Greek orders of the future. Their use of architectural sculpture is most likely influenced from the Orient, and even the Prinias "frieze" of horsemen, generally restored as part of the temple's superstructure, probably served an entirely different purpose. Though Harl-Schaller refers to the Prinias reliefs as the closest parallel to the Mycenae plaques in terms of function, the visual similarity is relative because the Peloponnesian reliefs are limited by borders and therefore would have

[3] Note, however, some residual hesitation on her part, 467 n. 16.

had a more staccato effect. The Austrian scholar seems to doubt, on the contrary, the architectural use of the Gortyna slabs and calls them votive, though so large as to be closer to cult images.

I would eliminate the Cretan evidence from a discussion on carved metopes and shall use the term in its more restrictive sense, purely in connection with a Doric frieze. I am therefore inclined to exclude the Peloponnesian reliefs from the category, though admittedly without being able to propose a different theory as to their original function. Accepting Harl-Schaller's suggestion, they would not belong to a Doric temple and would therefore automatically lie outside the scope of this enquiry. Accepting Bookidis' theory, we would be confronted with two sets of reliefs, one earlier than the other, though only one building would be available. Yet where would the two earlier fragments go? If those are not accepted as metopes, since there is no evidence at the site for an earlier architectural structure, then one has to admit that reliefs could be employed on the citadel outside the context of a Doric frieze. No compelling evidence then exists to consider the second set of reliefs as metopal; they could just as easily be part of a Heroon or a funerary enclosure and perhaps witness that interest in their Mycenaean past which the Greeks seem to have felt in late Geometric times.

On the other hand, evidence for the Archaic temple at Mycenae is not entirely lacking. Besides the argument of continuity (since a temple stood there in the Hellenistic period), there are blocks from a cornice and perhaps other parts of the building which speak in favor of a stone structure. Given the geographical location of Mycenae, the chances are that such structure would have been in the Doric Order. That the reliefs seem framed on all sides by borders does not automatically disqualify them as metopes since early architecture may not have followed the same conventions of later times, and metopes with comparable frames are attested from Sicilian Selinus. The presence of anathyrosis noticed by Bookidis on at least some of the Mycenae fragments shows that they did not stand in isolation. All these points, however, provide purely circumstantial evidence. Perhaps a final argument shoud be introduced.

METOPES IN GREECE

Granted the danger of deducing earlier practices from later ones, it may still be significant for our problem that for the entire Archaic period no decorated metopes appear elsewhere in the Peloponnesos. This state of affairs is not due to lack of actual buildings since many were erected during that period, especially at Olympia. That architectural sculpture was known is shown by several treasuries there with carved pediments. Yet after the Mycenae "metopes," the next Peloponnesian examples are those of the Temple of Zeus at Olympia, ca. 130 years later. In fact the only carved metopes known for the entire Sixth century on the mainland come from Delphi, the traditional melting pot of influences and practices. Archaic Athens, which produced so many pedimental sculptures, has preserved not a single relief metope. A head of Herakles in high relief excavated in the Agora is difficult to assess and may even be pedimental and Archaistic.[4] Corinth, which some schol-

[4] A painted terracotta plaque with a hunter and a stag comes from the area of Plato's Academy, where it was found together with other fragments and several floral antefixes of ca. 550. J. Travlos (s.v. Akademia, p. 46 and fig. 55) calls it a metope. Bookidis (468 n. 20) questions this identification. The plaque could have served a variety of other purposes without necessarily belonging to a Doric frieze

ars have considered the inventor not only of the gabled roof but also of the triglyph frieze, has yielded only a few fragments of poros sculpture which remain hypothetical at best as part of relief metopes. None come from Isthmia, and none even from the Argive Heraion, virtually the cradle of the Doric Order, until the time of the Classical temple, which a revised chronology would bring down to the beginning of the Fourth century. From the two early phases of the Temple of Apollo at Bassai only architectural terracottas survive, and the metopes which embellished the late Fifth century temple stood over the inner porches. Indeed, one may stress the fact that Peloponnesian temples, even when decorated with carved metopes, tend to locate them over pronaos and opisthodomos, leaving the outside frieze plain, perhaps to eliminate visual competition for the pedimental sculpture. This evidence seems to point to a lack of interest in carved metopes throughout the Peloponnesos, and even to a certain reluctance in accepting the practice at all.

For the rest of the Greek mainland my statement may seem too sweeping, considering the presence of painted terracotta metopes at Kalydon and Thermon. Yet there is a basic difference between a painted panel, which appears all in one plane and is subject to different lighting conditions, and a carved stone metope with all its problems of weight, visibility, shadowing, and relationship with the surrounding triglyphs. It is beyond the scope of the present work to embark on a discussion of the origin of the Doric frieze and its possible derivation from wooden prototypes. The question has been recently debated with special reference to the Thermon temple, by two scholars with different points of view. Certainly the Thermon Apollonion had a wooden entablature which provided an encasing frame for the metopes. These are equipped with tangs projecting from their upper edge, presumably to anchor them to an overlying wooden beam. Beyer, noting the different sizes of the extant metopes, restores two different friezes, the one over the sides higher than that on facade. Kalpaxis assumes differences in the frame to compensate for those of the plaques, which seem to vary somewhat from one another. It should be noted that at least two more buildings around the Apollonion must have had similar painted terracotta metopes, of which fragments have survived. One of these is particularly interesting in that the triglyph is molded in one piece with the metope, which shows traces of paint, indicating that it was decorated in some fashion. And, of course, also Kalydon had painted terracotta metopes, though somewhat different in technique and presumably fastened to stone backers.[5] As an argument in favor of attributing to Corinth the invention of decorated metopes it is often said that the Thermon plaques were painted by Corinthian masters. Yet they were

---

course; indeed a system of painted tiles projecting beyond the walls and visible from below is attested at least in Phrygia and Etruria, and perhaps also in Greece. Yet even if this painted plaque were in fact part of a triglyph frieze it would not affect my general conclusions since it would fall within the category of painted, not relief, panels comparable to votive pinakes, which the Academy plaque may also well be.

Another possible indication of decorated metopes in Athens is given on a cup by the Amasis Painter in the Norbert Schimmel collection; yet the alternation of decorated and undecorated panels is not consistent, and the figures from one of the "metopes" are depicted in the process of escaping from the entablature, thus throwing the reality of the total scene into question. (H. Hoffmann, ed., *The Beauty of Ancient Art* [Mainz 1964] 24.)

A series of four relief slabs, each showing either a rider or a man on foot, seem bordered on only three sides and cannot have been metopes in the canonical sense. They belonged to a funerary monument within the Kerameikos cemetery and have been considered under Ionic influence because of a close parallel from Chios. See supra, Ch. 6, pp. 168, 182.

[5] Bookidis points out (162–63) that this fact is important in showing that the use of terracotta metopes is not necessarily an indication of primitive construction in mudbrick and wood.

certainly made locally, in local clay, even if in imitation of Corinthian vase painting style. Even the inscriptions which label some of the figures are related not only to Corinthian but to Achaian and Dodonian scripts. As Winter has suggested for the human-head antefixes, architectural details at Thermon and Kalydon seem entirely different from the Corinthian tradition as we know it at present, except for a standard way of making tiles. It is therefore risky to reconstruct hypothetical Peloponnesian practices on the basis of evidence from rather unimportant and isolated Aetolian sites.[6]

One more possibility remains: that metopes on the Greek mainland were primarily decorated in different ways, either with metal cut-outs or with bronze relief panels fastened to stone or wood. Indeed a similar theory has been advanced in connection with the large *à jour* relief in thin bronze sheet, found at Olympia: a griffin suckling her young. A more recent find is the fragmentary bronze plaque with two interlocked wrestlers in repoussé relief uncovered in 1966 at Cyrene within the same Archaic deposit which yielded the korai and the sphinx column. Undoubtedly some Archaic buildings must have made great use of applied metal, whether for moldings or other decorative details, few of which have survived to tell their fragmentary tale. On the other hand, no complete certainty can be reached as to the metopal function of the extant examples. Both the Olympia and the Cyrene reliefs, though architectural in nature, could be assigned to different positions on a building. The size of the Olympia cut-out makes it too small for the Heraion metopes, but suitable for a door decoration, a reconstruction further supported by the presence of wooden fragments still adhering to the back of the relief when found. That the Cyrene plaque was made for attachment to another surface is shown by the nail holes along the two surviving edges; yet nothing assures us that such surface was that of a metope. The square shape of the relief, as preserved at present, would be equally appropriate to cover the ridge pole, as suggested by the terracotta plaque from Syracuse with the running Medusa.[7]

Yet, even were we to take for granted the presence of such metal ornaments for metopes, the total effect would not seem too different from that of the painted terracotta plaques. Both repoussé and *à jour* work produce fairly low relief which only color contrast, it is assumed, would distinguish from its background. It could, of course, be supposed that the low grade of limestone or poros available in the Peloponnesos discouraged the production of carved metopes and is therefore responsible for our apparent lack of evidence. Nonetheless Magna Graecia, which largely rejected its poor local stone for statuary in the round, produced great quantities of metopal reliefs, and even modeled terracotta metopes with figured scenes when the more plastic medium was employed, instead of painted plaques. Finally, if terminology can be accepted as significant, the word triglyph seems to emphasize the sculptural nature of the *frame*, not of the metope itself. Considering that the Doric Order, as tradition wants and evidence suggests, may have originated in the Peloponnesos, such terminology could indicate that in that area the tri-

[6] This is in fact one of the points stressed by Bookidis (456): that the earliest mainland metopes, both painted and carved, appear at relatively inconsequential sites, with Mycenae a small settlement of little importance, and Thermon and Kalydon apparently not much more prominent. The truly important centers at this time show instead no evidence of this form of architectural decoration.

[7] Ch. K. Williams informs me that a pre-Roman poros metope from Corinth has holes still filled by bronze nails, apparently to carry relief figures in metal. Whether such figures were however three-dimensionally modeled or simply *à jour* is now impossible to say.

glyphs, and not the metopes, were initially regarded as the sculptural elements within the Doric frieze. Consequently, it is likely that the metopes were left blank, or at least smooth, to avoid competition with their projecting and articulated "spacers."[8]

Corfu

The overwhelmingly abundant evidence from both Sicily and South Italy leads us to believe that the practice of high relief metopes originated in those areas. This theory is not contradicted, to my mind, by the fact that our earliest examples come from the Corcyran Artemision. As already indicated in the discussion of carved pediments, the building itself and the entire island may have been under strong artistic influence from Italy and may therefore reflect Magna Graecian prototypes in this very trait also. The material consists of a series of fragments, most of them too small to be identified except for a relatively well-preserved figure of a long-haired man, helmeted and fighting with a spear. The presence of a hand at the warrior's elbow has suggested that the total scene should be reconstructed as a duel between two hoplites, with interceding or encouraging women standing behind them. This schema is well attested in vase painting to depict the fight between Achilles and Memnon in the presence of their divine mothers, and may have carried the same meaning also in the Corfu sculptures.

Some scholars object to reconstructing the reliefs as part of a Doric frieze for two reasons: 1) some of the preserved metopes from the same temple are obviously undecorated, and 2) the complex scene postulated above requires that the duel be shown on either side of an intervening triglyph since a single panel could not possibly accommodate all four figures involved. An alternate theory has therefore been advanced, that the warrior fragment be attributed to a continuous frieze to be restored over the pronaos. Yet examples of single episodes occupying several metopes in a row are known from both Magna Graecia and Delphi, and even the first objection can be countered by postulating decorated metopes only on the facade, with those of the sides left plain. This distribution, with the reliefs in obvious display over the outer columns, would also be in keeping with Western Greek practices.

It may seem surprising that the earliest example of what I claim to have been a Magna Graecian invention should be found on Corfu around 570. On the other hand, except for vases, nothing much earlier has been found in either Sicily or South Italy, and we may assume that we have not yet uncovered the most ancient architectural remains. Perhaps the first relief metopes were in terracotta and have totally perished or escaped detection. Certainly the Corfu evidence, as it stands, is unlikely to represent an initial experiment. It seems quite sophisticated and provides further argument for lowering the date of the temple to ca. 570. The warrior is seen from the back, so that his spear, carved in low relief against the background, need not cross his face.[9] Though he does not wear a cuirass, the

[8] Drerup (*AA* 1964, cols. 206–7) has actually argued that the entire Doric frieze is so Geometric in nature, that it could have originated only at that time. As on a vase, the presence of space between the triglyphs is therefore necessary to produce the decorative effect. According to this interpretation, a metope on an archetypal wooden building would have been simply an open space, a window, between the triglyphs marking the ends of the ceiling beams.

[9] Were it not for the presence of a tainia above the warrior's head, it would be tempting to connect this fragment with the left half of the west pediment and with the seated figure being threatened by a spear. We would then gain a better understanding of that

figure is unusual in having a forearm guard, rarely represented in art though some actual examples have been found at Olympia. A baldric for a sword crosses the warrior's back, but he fights with a spear: one therefore visualizes a certain distance between him and his opponent. Thus the intervening triglyph may have looked plausible rather than disturbing, as if an indoor spectator were viewing a scene taking place outside two windows. Very much the same effect is obtained in the Sikyonian metopes at Delphi.

Delphi

Sikyonian Metopes. These latter are usually dated around 570–560 and are more difficult to explain in terms of Magna Graecian influence; yet, to all intents and purposes, they are the first examples to have survived from the Greek mainland. Were we sure that they truly belonged to a Sikyonian Treasury, a definite case could be made for mainland contemporaneity, if not priority, in the practice of carved metopes. But the five better-preserved reliefs, and several more fragments, were found re-used in the foundations of the late Archaic Treasury of Sikyon, together with architectural members from two buildings, one of which was certainly round in plan. It is usually argued that the Sikyonians could not have obtained this earlier material for their foundations had they not been the original owners of the dismantled structures. It is also true that the fire of 548 prompted a thorough reshaping of the entire temenos, which would justify the wilful destruction of pre-existing treasuries. Yet one wonders why the Sikyonian replacement (the third structure erected by that city at Delphi, if one follows the above line of reasoning) did not continue the practice of carved metopes, had this been a usual feature of the Peloponnesian town.[10] Certainly toward the end of the Archaic period relief metopes were fairly normal at the sanctuary since they occur on the Athenian Treasury and, very probably, on the newly completed Temples of Apollo and of Athena Pronaia in Marmarià, the latter built with the surplus from the fund drive to rebuild the Apollonion. If a date in the 490's is accepted for the Athenian Treasury, as convincingly argued by E. Harrison, it could even be assumed that the main temple at the site influenced the smaller structure in this specific, and non-Athenian, detail.

One plain poros metope from the temple of Apollo has survived to show that not all metopes on the building were carved. The extant fragments of reliefs are in marble and may therefore belong with the so-called Alkmaionid facade. Yet this possibility does not automatically imply Athenian inspiration: no carved metopes can be found in Athens before ca. 450 (the Hephaisteion), and, as the evidence of carved pediments has shown, the pan-Hellenic sanctuaries are likely to display decorative practices unfamiliar to the dedicating cities. But from where would the inspiration have come to the Delphic melting pot?

---

scene. But the connection seems impossible.

A comparable warrior appears on a metope from an unidentified building at Foce del Sele (Treasury III, *Foce del Sele* I, pls. 63–64). Since the pose is somewhat unusual for the Archaic period, this comparison (which was pointed out to me by George Szeliga) may again point to the connections between Corfu and Magna Graecia. However, the South Italian metope is dated much later by its excavators (first quarter of the 5th century BC).

[10] That the round building, though also thought to be Sikyonian, did not have relief metopes may be understandable because of the difficulty created by curving surfaces though Classical tholoi successfully coped with such problem.

Dinsmoor once suggested that the Sikyonian metopes belonged instead to a Syracusan Treasury. However, this theory was based on incomplete evidence from the Sicilian town. It is now known that the metopes of the Syracusan Apollonion, far from being much wider than tall, like the "Sikyonian" reliefs in Delphi, were instead very tall and narrow, between closely spaced triglyphs. Other technical details adduced by Dinsmoor as further evidence can be paralleled elsewhere and therefore provide no compelling argument. It should be admitted that present evidence does not point decisively in any one direction and that even the attribution of the Delphic reliefs to Sikyon rests on probability alone.[11] Could a Magna Graecian origin be argued on other grounds?

The evidence from Olympia seems negative in this respect. As already mentioned, no carved metopes have survived form that sanctuary, despite the fact that so many of its treasuries were dedicated by South Italian and Sicilian cities, and one even by the very Sikyonians who supposedly made the offering at Delphi. Yet I have also stressed that no immediate correlation can be established between the commissioner and the commissioned product, which rather falls under the influences active at the construction site.[12] All we learn from Olympia, therefore, is purely confirmation that the Peloponnesos was not particularly receptive to the idea of a carved Doric frieze. But Central/Northern Greece was no better disposed toward this form of architectural sculpture, as extant structures seem to show. What, then, was the source of the Delphic inspiration? Here again some link may be missing.

It is important to emphasize the innovative and influential role that this sanctuary played not only in Greek politics but also in Greek art and architecture. As will be discussed in Chapter 9 on continuous friezes, the original idea for this form of architectural sculpture may have come from Asia Minor, but it was at Delphi that the Ionic order acquired its "Attic-Ionic" entablature. Dinsmoor has convincingly suggested that the extra frieze course was added to the Ionic buildings at Delphi because they seemed light at the top next to the Doric structures with their triglyph-metope course above the architrave. Yet this explanation advocates simply the presence of metopes, not of carved metopes. Perhaps a slight case can be made for the suggestion that the continuous Ionic frieze (meant here as a series of contiguous relief figures not separated from each other by architectural elements, regardless of where the sculpture was located on a building) may have preceded in time the practice of decorated metopes. On an uninterrupted band, scenes can easily be depicted which involve several figures and tell a definite episode. But this form of narrative is not ideal for the metope, which allows an optimum of three figures per panel. That more complex representations were attempted in the earliest examples, disregarding, as it were, the intervening triglyphs, may indicate that Ionic practices were known and adapted to the Procrustean bed of a Doric frieze. The ideal place for such an

[11] Even the argument that the reliefs are in Sikyonian limestone is not so strong as it may seem, given the great difficulty in assessing types of stone.

[12] An exceptional case may be that of the Treasury of Gela, which was sent to Olympia prefabricated, as it were, in all its many typical terracotta revetments, to be assembled on the spot. However, Gela itself did not seem to use carved metopes, to judge from the excavated evidence. Cities which have yielded many carved friezes, like Selinus and (indirectly) Sybaris, seem to have been less nationalistic in sending offerings to Olympia, so that their treasuries there did not closely reflect home conditions. On the other hand, there are still numerous Archaic terracottas, belonging to large figures, which have not been pieced together and properly published. When this task is completed, our picture of architectural sculpture at Olympia may well have to be modified.

attempt must have been an area equally open to both influences, the Doric and the Ionic, an area where a strong Doric tradition mingled with a definite Ionic streak. Both Magna Graecia and Delphi fit this description. And it is perhaps significant that the only Asia Minor relief metopes occur at Assos, on a Doric building, to be sure, and perhaps carried along by the cult of Athena, but certainly together with a decorated architrave, which might have prompted the extension of sculptural embellishment to the available areas of the frieze.

In summary, it would seem as if carved metopes may have originated under a certain influence from the continuous Ionic reliefs, in an area open to both traditions. This assertion may be valid even if metopes ornamented in paint or by means of metal reliefs existed in Greece proper since it would have been the invention of this "bilingual" region which translated the flat decorative language of the one area into the high-relief idiom of the other. Spontaneous invention can occur simultaneously in different places subject to the same stimuli, but since our first example of carved metopes occurs on Corfu, with its known Western connections, I am inclined to deny priority to Delphi in favor of Magna Graecia.[13] We do not know enough about its contributions to Delphi's architecture in the first half of the Sixth century, yet the important role which was attributed to the oracle in the colonizing movement may warrant the assumption of Sicilian and South Italian dedications at the sanctuary at an early date. Indeed a recent study of the architectural terracottas at Delphi has identified revetments from at least one Corcyran, one Sicilian, and two South Italian treasuries at the site prior to the fire of 548. Historically, the Western colonies seem to have somewhat loosened their ties with Greece proper after an initial dependence, to strengthen them again after the traumatic experience of the collective wars against the Barbarians (Persians, Carthaginians, and Etruscans). The Sikyonian metopes could easily represent a Magna Graecian contribution to Delphi during the early phase. The difficulty of the form in taking hold at Delphi may reflect a period during which the sanctuary promoted an opening to the East rather than to the West, with the temple of Apollo adding carved metopes during the period of the International Style.

Obviously these suggestions are tentative. The extensive landscaping of the temenos of Apollo at Delphi after 548 eliminated a great deal of evidence which could considerably affect conclusions.[14] But there is nothing inherently implausible in a Magna Graecian origin for carved metopes, and the variety of technical forms adopted for metopes in that area suggests a great deal of experimentation. The very conception of the temple and its entablature seems different in the Western colonies, which showed a high degree of originality in interpreting the canonical architectural Orders, together with a certain amount of independence from one city to the other, as we shall discuss below. Here we should consider one more possible objection: that the Sikyonian metopes bear not the least resemblance to Magna Graecian sculpture, aside from one vague connection in subject matter.

Yet this objection, valid as it is, need not influence the question of nationality. As Book-

[13] Methodologically speaking, one could also assign priority to Corfu itself, which satisfies the same prerequisites advocated for this "mother country of carved metopes." On the other hand, the strong Italian influences on the rest of the Artemision and its decoration, and the relatively advanced stage of its metopes, lead me to believe that the first experiments had occurred elsewhere, on Magna Graecian territory.

[14] According to P. de la Coste Messelière, at least twelve foundations of Treasuries fall within the 590–550 time span. The same author stresses the sanctuary's ties with the Etruscans at the time of the colonization.

idis has argued in her work, there must have been a number of ateliers regularly based at Delphi to execute the architectural commissions coming in from all over the Greek world, which were ultimately responsible for the creation of a local style or manner. Sculptors may have come from elsewhere, but no direct connection need exist between the commissioning city and the nationality of the hired master, as shown by the situation in Athens itself where many foreigners came to work.[15] In addition, if the style of the reliefs is not Western, neither is it Sikyonian, or at least we have to acknowledge that no other example of Sikyonian sculpture has come down to us.[16] I shall continue to refer to the Delphic reliefs as Sikyonian metopes, since this is the name under which they are best known, but I personally believe that they may represent a Magna Graecian dedication executed at Delphi by some local or outside master.

Only four of the metopes are well preserved; a fifth, with Helle or Phrixos riding on the Ram,[17] is so fragmentary as barely to allow recognition of the subject. The relief with the enormous boar is occupied almost entirely by the beast; accessory figures have left minimal traces difficult to read and could never have played a prominent role. This use of the entire metopal field for a single figure has been considered a sign of high Archaism, but, in view of the advanced sophistication of the other panels, it should perhaps be seen as a sign of the importance attributed to the powerful animal. Perhaps it should be stressed that, aside from Europa on the Bull, all other subjects preserved are unique in architectural sculpture of the Archaic period. The Ram of Phrixos (and Helle) appears as a shield device in a sculptural, freestanding group at Olympia, which belongs already to the Severe period. The Cattle Raid of the Dioskouroi and the Apharides (Fig. 59) and the Ship Argo are never seen elsewhere during the Sixth century. The emphasis on the Dioskouroi, who appear also in the Argonauts' adventure, may perhaps suggest a connection of the works with Sparta, where the two sons of Zeus were particularly popular. But they seem to have been prominent also in Magna Graecia, and therefore this argument is not compelling. The point is made here simply to emphasize the originality of the compositions on this Delphic building.

Since the metopes are well known and have been described in masterly fashion by P. de la Coste Messelière, only a few details need be singled out here. In the metope with

[15] In the specific case of the Sikyonian metopes, it has been noted (*Local Scripts*, 101–2) that the painted labels which identify some of the figures are in Phokian script. But the letter forms seem to date from the end of the 6th century and may simply confirm that local workshops existed which could attend to the repainting of faded inscriptions when necessary. On the other hand, this late date may conflict with the theory of a structure dismantled during the landscaping of the temenos and re-used within the foundations of a building which is itself dated around 500. Would the painted inscriptions have been refurbished on a building marked for demolition? (For the date of the later treasury see *BCH* 84 [1960] 412.)

[16] The limestone head in Boston, allegedly from Sikyon (supra 90 n. 6) is so different that it could even be considered Cypriot. And a vague resemblance between Kleobis and Biton and the figures of the Cattle Raid Metope would, if anything, tie the latter with Argos rather than with Sikyon. Geographic attribution based on the selection of subject matter, at this early a date, seems somewhat dangerous. I cannot subscribe to de la Coste Messelière's theory that the myths illustrated on the metopes reflect anti-Argive feelings and Boeotian sympathies, in keeping with Sikyonian politics.

[17] The bracelet on the surviving arm does not necessarily compel identification as a woman. Note the bejeweled draped figure from Sardis (Ch. 3 p. 76) which I believe to be male. Phrixos, because of his later residence in Kolchis, may intentionally have been shown wearing luxury items considered typical of non-Greek men.

the Ship Argo just the prow of the boat, near the shore, is depicted. Since fragments of another metope include further elements of the same ship, the total scene has been reconstructed with the vessel gliding behind the intervening triglyph which hides its central portion. This daring conception is even more remarkable than the Corcyran duel and reflects a more advanced stage of sophistication. In addition, note the many levels established within the composition. Closest to us are the horses' heads, separately attached, which must have protruded considerably from the total metope. Farther in are the Dioskouroi over their mounts: note the horses' manes which fall on either side of the animal's neck in curls resembling human hair. Since the horsemen stand on land, the ship, floating at sea, must be visualized behind them, and its passengers behind the railings of the boat itself with its hanging shields. Once again let me stress the short hair of the bearded Orpheus, who could be a distant relative of the Zeus on the Athenian Introduction Pediment, flattened into a frontal relief.

In the Cattle Raid panel (Fig. 59), realism gives way to aesthetic expression. It is impossible to correlate legs and cattle, profile bodies and sharply turned frontal heads. But the "Savonarola chair" effect of the crossing legs renders the rhythm of the march, and the whirligig on the muzzle of the facing calves, just above the horizontal spears, shows no mere love of decoration but the accurate observation of a true detail. The Apharides are distinguished from the Dioskouroi by their hair,[18] though all figures wear the same costume. This has been used most subtly to produce a sense of perspective. Note the belts which appear through the opening in the chlamys: each may have been depicted in relation to its imagined distance from the viewer, so that the closer the figure, the greater the expanse of belt revealed. A spectator standing in front of the metope has the impression that the troops file before him approaching from his left, so that some are level with his eyes while others are still coming. The depth effect is increased by the diagonal spears which penetrate the background, and by the superimposed heads of the cattle which recall Egyptian renderings.

Finally, the metope with Europa and the Bull. Of all Archaic renderings in sculpture of this legend, this is the most successful, with a fragile looking Europa bending low over her mount so as not to fall during its mad rush and steadying herself by stretching one hand behind her to touch the bull's rump. Her legs are subtly indicated under the drapery.

The date (ca. 570–560) assigned to these reliefs rests partly on a theoretical correlation between the dedication and the exploits of Kleisthenes, tyrant of Sikyon. Once the geographical connection is questioned, the sculptures should stand on their own.[19] I would tend to lower the traditional dating by a decade or so, placing the reliefs around 550. It is, to be sure, difficult to argue without proper parallels to establish even a relative chronology, and some of the five panels are certainly less sophisticated than others. Perspective attempts and experimentation with depth and foreshortening may simply suggest a derivation from painted prototypes, yet the reliefs have a strong plastic quality as well, obvious

[18] At least, this can be assumed to have been the case, though only three of the original four figures are preserved. As the painted inscriptions show, Lynkeas is the missing fourth.

[19] The only other operative date is an *ante quem* of ca. 500, based on the approximate chronology of the Sikyonian Treasury, which used the metopes in its foundations. E. Hansen (*BCH* 84 [1960] 412) states that the Sikyonian Treasury III cannot be much later than 510 and could even be 10 or 20 years earlier.

in the solidity of the bodies and the modeling of surfaces. The medium is treated well beyond the usual possibilities of limestone, which here is compact enough to resemble marble.

Athenian Treasury. How difficult dating can be is shown by the long controversy over the Athenian Treasury at Delphi, whose metopes are the first and only complete series we possess from the Archaic Greek mainland. The problem has often been defined as one of generations, with innovating young sculptors working alongside more traditional masters. The style of the metopes in fact ranges over what would be considered a wide chronological span (from before 510 to after 490), but given the relatively small size of the structure, variant renderings must reflect the differing expression of contemporary artists rather than the passage of time. Attempts to tie the Treasury to historical events on the basis of Pausanias' account (10.11.5), have never met with complete agreement, and architectural analysis has yielded equally uncertain results. The chronological problem has been recently summarized by Harrison, who has suggested the most convincing theory to date: that the building was erected in the 490's, before Marathon but at a time of great economic prosperity for Athens. If such theory is accepted, a further point is gained: that the dedication of a Treasury at Delphi need not necessarily correspond to a specific victory or other important historical event but may simply reflect affluence and piety in the donor city.

The official French publication has provided a close analysis of the preserved metopes, so that few comments can suffice here. It should immediately be stressed that this is the first Mainland structure for which carved metopes on all sides are attested. Except for the Parthenon, this remains an isolated instance in Greece proper, and it is significant that it should occur at Delphi, the sanctuary showing the greatest artistic innovation, and on a Treasury, thus on a building relatively free from religious conservatism. Note also that the same structure had decorated pediments and anthropomorphic akroteria, so that the whole must have presented an unusually rich appearance, somewhat surprising for the sober Doric Order. Obviously the proximity of the even richer Ionic Treasuries (where the very columns could take the shape of freestanding sculpture) is partly responsible for this extensive decorative program.

The metopes depict the deeds of Herakles and Theseus. If the latter may stand for the young Athenian Democracy, the former was certainly a popular subject for the many earlier buildings at Athens, so that both choices may reflect strong Athenian connections. Yet the myths may have been selected because they could be easily adapted to inclusion within single panels, while the repetition of the protagonist insured thematic unity. No obvious link can usually be established between the divinity worshiped in the temple or sanctuary and the entire sculptural program on an Archaic building, nor do the myths chosen always belong to the regional repertoire of the donor city.[20] Here, at the very beginning of the Fifth century, we can assume that the deeds of the two heroes, the pan-Hellenic Herakles and the Athenian par excellence, were also chosen for their immediate intelligibility, since they formed part of a well-known artistic syllabus already diffused through the minor arts.

[20] Some initial connection may have existed between Herakles and Hera, as shall be discussed below.

In this connection, a brief analysis of the compositional patterns of the panels may be relevant. Three major schemata, with inner variations, are adopted: 1) the parallel lines, either vertical or oblique; 2) the pyramid, and 3) the "interlocked c's" pattern. This last could also be described as the superimposition of two semicircles, one formed by the assailant and the other by the prostrate victim. It is usually employed to depict combat scenes, either between two human beings or between a human and an animal. Of particular interest here are the slight variations within the theme, which existed early in the Sixth century and seem to have retained their value as sign language well into the Fifth. In the first variant, the message is that the opponent has been overtaken in flight, and is therefore being subdued through the victor's "flying leap." The winner pushes his victim down with one knee, in a pose that is most effective when the latter is an animal or a centaur. Yet, though the opponent has been overtaken, no immediate harm is necessarily implicit in the pose itself (cf. e.g., Herakles and the Hind). The second variant shows the winner pressing his foot against his opponent's back, usually in preparation for delivering the *coup de grace.* Here too a certain element of chase is implied, but the hostile connotation and deathly outcome of the pattern are unmistakable.

These compositional schemata, which stood out clearly against a unified background, must have been intelligible from a distance, so that the sculptor could rely on them, rather than on the inner structure and torsion of his figures, to convey his message. The various muscles are not depicted in action, either stretched or compressed in accordance with a person's pose, but they are statically rendered within a body frame in motion. Alter the pose, place a body in a vertical rather than in an oblique position, and all impression of movement disappears from the panel. A typical example is given by the metope with the combat between Theseus and Periphetes (S 2), where the body of the hero was once restored in a more erect position, until the addition of another fragment suggested a greater inclination of the figure, with a consequent increase in movement and a stronger effect of violence and animation.[21]

In sculptural terms, the Athenian metopes reflect some Ionic influences. Some figures' eyes are simply a raised almond-shaped surface, without differentiation between lids and eyeball. This same treatment can be found on the Ephesos column drums and other works from East Greece. Perhaps the variations in the rendering of the abdominal partitions, which make some figures look almost flayed and others seem much more naturalistic, depend not so much on antiquated or progressive style as on regional differences, the Attic sculptor tending to over-define the anatomy of his creations, and the "Ionic" preferring the softer renderings and the less detailed modeling. The exaggerated musculature is not consistently used for Herakles alone, nor do all representations of the hero show the same flayed anatomy, so that we cannot interpret such renderings as characterizing attributes of the Superman of antiquity. Obviously several hands were at work on the Treasury, and not all masters may have been Athenian.

Another interesting feature of some of these metopes is an almost miniature-like approach which delights in a wealth of details. The most surprising of all are the inserted nipples, which, given the small size of the holes, may have been in copper. Why such a difficult and time-consuming method was adopted when paint would have produced

[21] Contrast *FdD* 4:1 pls. 46–47:5 with *BCH* 47 (1923) pls. 16–18:2.

similar results is impossible now to fathom. More understandable perhaps are Herakles' tight curls, which seem almost a return to the early Attic beads. Here, however, the more immediate source of inspiration may have been contemporary Attic Red Figure vases, where blobs of black glaze obtained comparable effects. Definite ties can be established between the Athenian metopes and the early Red Figure vases, for example, the "props" in some of the Herakles panels which seem to float in space. But it is then all the more remarkable that such similarities should appear in works carved in very high relief, where the difference between the two media is at its greatest. Yet the very distance from the viewer, and the uneven lighting conditions under the projecting cornice, may partially explain some of the strong accents in the carving, which result in decorative, pictorial effects when the metopes are viewed at eye level.

One final comment on the distribution of subjects. We encounter here the first obvious attempt in a Doric frieze to achieve thematic unity within each of the four sides of the building. So the six metopes of the east facade portrayed the Combat between Greeks and Amazons; the nine panels of the south side (facing the Sacred Way) illustrated the Deeds of Theseus; those of the north side the Deeds of Herakles, and all the six metopes of the west side narrated the story of the Cattle of Geryon, with Herakles shooting his three-bodied opponent across a triglyph. This is perhaps the best Mainland example of a single episode carried across a series of panels, if one excludes the battle scenes which tend to break up into duels. If the Treasury precedes Marathon, as I am inclined to believe, the choice of the Amazonomachy cannot as yet be meant as an allusion to a historical Athenian victory over the Eastern barbarians.[22] This is, therefore, just one more myth connected with Herakles or Theseus which offers to Doric architecture the additional advantage of being capable of expansion over several metopes.

METOPES IN MAGNA GRAECIA

This exhausts the survey of sculpted metopes from the Greek mainland, those attributed to the Temples of Apollo and Athena at Delphi being too fragmentary to be taken into more than statistical account.[23] But we come now to the spectacular wealth of metopes

[22] Indeed the mounted Amazons which formed the lateral akroteria of the Treasury seem to imply no concept of defeat, but rather one of supernatural power, almost like the Valkyries of the German Valhalla.

[23] After the official publication had appeared, metope no. 18 was attributed to a Doric Treasury at Marmarià, and therefore removed from the Athenian Treasury (*BCH* 90 [1966] 699–709). However, this is not enough evidence to reconstruct a sculptural program for the entire building, and the presence of metopes at Delphi at that late a date is not surprising. One more example should perhaps be considered here: a limestone relief in Athens, Nat. Mus. 4468, which the catalogue describes as a metope from Megara. It retains the lower part of a seated female figure who may have held something on her lap. Her feet rest on a footstool with lion's paws. The back of the block preserves a very large and deep cutting, almost for a tenon rather than for a clamp or dowel. The better preserved right edge of the relief (spectator's point of view) is finished and painted and seems to show a border for the main face, which therefore could not have been inserted behind a triglyph. The relief was found in excavating the so-called Fountain House of Theagenes at Megara (*BCH* 82 [1958] 688–92 fig. 36; *AJA* 62 [1958] 324, pl. 86:6); but the building, as discussed by G. Gruben (*Deltion* 19:1[1] [1964] 37–41) had unfinished metopes. Its date, in any case, has been set within the first quarter of the 5th century. My impression is that the piece could not have been a metope; it may perhaps be a votive relief representing Cybele in a naiskos with a lion in her lap, according to the Asia Minor/Anatolian schema.

in both Sicily and South Italy, with their extraordinary repertoire of subjects. Here too, however, the pattern of distribution is peculiar, even when taking into consideration the fact that many Doric buildings are so poorly preserved that their entablatures must be reconstructed almost entirely on paper. Bookidis has pointed out a very high proportion of decorated versus undecorated metopes, stressing that Archaic temples from which plain metopes actually survive are but three: Athena/Ceres at Paestum, Temple D at Selinus, and the Athenaion at Syracuse. On the other hand, when relief metopes are counted, they seem to come from selected sites only, even if often in great numbers.

In Sicily, for instance, aside from Selinus, which has produced sculpted metopes from at least three Archaic temples, other examples come only from Megara Hyblaia, Himera, and an unknown Sicilian source through the antiquarian market (one metope now in Copenhagen). The metopes from Megara Hyblaia belong to a funerary naiskos and are decorated with repetitive floral patterns. Those from Temple B at Himera are in terracotta. In South Italy, Foce del Sele has the widest range: a total of approximately seventy metopes from four buildings are preserved, though only those from the so-called Treasury I remain as a complete (or nearly complete) series. Single items come from Paestum[24] and Rhegion, this latter again in terracotta. In chronological terms, the earliest preserved seem to be the metopes from Treasury I at Foce del Sele (ca. 560–550), but the panel from an unknown Sicilian source now in Copenhagen and the reliefs from Temple Y at Selinus should fall at mid century if not earlier. It is therefore impossible to determine priority, if any, within the generic definition of Magna Graecia. On the other hand, some pattern of diffusion seems to emerge when one considers the relationships within the various towns where metopes have been found.

For instance, Megara Hyblaia was the mother city of Selinus; therefore the presence of carved metopes there does not surprise, even if the earliest hitherto attested at the mother site date from the end of the Archaic period. By contrast, none of the cities directly dependent on Syracuse[25] or Gela[26] seems to have used decorated metopes. The only exception is apparently Himera, where terracotta reliefs occur on the Doric frieze of Temple B between 575/550 and 500. Yet Himera was founded by a mixed contingent, some of the

[24] Two more pieces from Paestum have been attributed to metopes, but I could find no further reference than that quoted in Bookidis, 239 (P. C. Sestieri, *MélRome* 67 [1955] 45). The fragments consist of a veiled head and a hoof, either from a centaur or an animal. Sculptural fragments from Sybaris (Parco del Cavallo) and Metapontum, which had been attributed to metopes in the first notices, are now published as parts of a continuous frieze and two pediments respectively.

[25] Syracuse itself has produced no carved metopes, and one possible candidate, the interesting terracotta relief bordered by elaborate moldings and containing the images of two female figures (Demeter and Kore ?) is at present published as votive (G. V. Gentili, *BdA* 58 [1973] 3–8, reconstructed drawing on p. 5 fig. 1). The dimensions of the pinax (ca. 1 m. high and 0.65 m. wide), and the similarity of its moldings to the metopes from Selinus Temple Y, make me wonder whether this pinax could not have been a metope. A similar suggestion has now been made by L. Bernabò Brea in *Archeologia nella Sicilia Sud-Orientale* (Naples/Syracuse 1973) 79–80 no. 285 pl. 21.

[26] A fragmentary terracotta relief from Gela is now in the Metropolitan Museum in New York (inv. no. 24.97.1; G.M.A. Richter, *Handbook of the Greek Collection* [Cambridge, Mass. 1953] 30, pl. 18f). It shows Troilos riding one horse and leading another to the right; traces of Achilles' thumb appear over his hair. The relief is dated to the 6th century and considered architectural, but it is impossible at present to determine whether it could have been a metope. Throughout Magna Graecia, the great popularity of terracotta arulae in high relief and with strong narrative content makes fragmentary examples difficult to classify when not identified through their context. Gela, in particular, seems to have been one of the manufacturing centers for such altars.

colonists coming from Syracuse, but others from Zankle, therefore being of Chalcidian stock. No carved metopes have been found at Zankle/Messana, but neither have the Archaic levels of the site as a whole, and at least one terracotta metope has been identified at Rhegion (Contrada Griso Labocetta) which had the same ethnic origins and strong ties with its neighbor across the Straits. Finally, Paestum and Foce del Sele are connected through Sybaris.

It would therefore seem as if the practice of decorated metopes originated only in certain specific places within the Magna Graecian territory, and then spread according to the ethnic and political contacts enjoyed by those places.[27] It may be significant that terracotta metopes have been identified at the two cities linked by colonizing patterns (Rhegion and Himera) while the other sites employed stone carvings. On the other hand, this point should not be stressed excessively since other terracotta metopes may have escaped detection elsewhere.

One further aspect should be examined: the possible relationship of carved metopes with the cult of Hera. Here the connection may be two-fold, either in terms of decorated buildings or in terms of subject matter. All the metopes from Foce del Sele would fall under the general heading of dedications to Argive Hera, whether they appeared on the actual temple or on affiliated treasuries. At Paestum, the two Hera temples seem to have been remarkably free of decoration (though the so-called Basilica may have had female bust antefixes in its pediments and terracotta figures at the corners of its cornice); but at least one relief metope is attested from the site. All the other examples come from unidentified buildings; at Selinus, at least one temple of Hera, though having carved metopes, falls outside our survey because dated ca. 460. But here one can perhaps focus on the subject of the Archaic metopes since so many of them depict Zeus-related myths such as Europa and the Bull, or the exploits of Herakles. To be sure, other myths are also represented, but one wonders whether an initial phase of the legends is here attested when the name of the Hero could still mean "The Glory of Hera." In this case one may further speculate whether the idea of mythological tableaux, though *not* of relief metopes, may have come to Magna Graecia even during the Seventh century or earlier, from the Argive Heraion,[28] the Doric center par excellence. This inspiration may then have blossomed into architectural expression under strong influence from Ionia, when proper skills had been acquired and building activity allowed it. This, however, remains pure speculation incapable of proof.

Technique. More concrete, because based on actual evidence, is the suggestion that the carved metopes could not have been "imported" wholesale into Magna Graecia since great variety exists from example to example even within the same site, thus suggesting a good deal of experimentation with this architectural form. At Foce del Sele an interesting technique occurs on the so-called Treasury I, where the triglyphs were carved in one piece

[27] Trade contacts may also have been influential but are now more difficult to assess.

[28] It has indeed been suggested that the myths illustrated on Treasury I at Foce del Sele are all connected with the Peloponnesos and most often with Argive sagas: R. Holloway, *A View of Greek Art* (Providence 1973) 83–84. A tradition of Herakles as the ally, not the victim, of Hera may be reflected on the cup by the Brygos Painter (London E 65, Beazley, *ARV*², 370, 13), where the Hero defends the Queen of Heaven from the attack of four silens, a subject which also appears on the metopes at Foce del Sele.

with one metope, and the next panel was inserted behind the free end of the triglyph in such a way as to lie at an angle to the face of the architrave. A similar technique, though limited to the metopes, occurs on the Temple of Hera at the same sanctuary. At Selinus there is a preference for the very thick metopes, rather than for the more traditional slabs backed by heavier masonry. In general, the panels are taller than wide, but the Rhegion terracotta slab is much wider than tall, and the Foce del Sele metopes from Treasury I taper from top to bottom, while their triglyphs do the opposite. In an unusual feat, the metopes from Temple F at Selinus were carved from two blocks meeting along a horizontal joint; a similar technique is employed for continuous friezes at Sybaris and Samos. Decorative borders may outline the relief panels, and the depth of the background may vary, even within the same series, though nothing ever projects beyond the outer frame.

Foce del Sele

Relatively few comments can be included here about this wealth of material. At Foce del Sele, Treasury I seems to have had decorated metopes all around. It was an unusual building, with a hip-roof and many Ionic elements, but with only one prostyle porch, so that most of the Doric frieze ran above solid walls. After the initial find and publication, three or four more metopes were uncovered, and the present total of 39–40 carved panels is difficult to reconcile with the structure as originally reconstructed.[29] Yet material and technical details assure us that all the reliefs belong together. Interestingly enough, not all of them had the same degree of finish, and it has been suggested that several, which now appear almost like cut-outs, would have received additional touches later, on the building. Be that as it may, this structure decorated on all four sides with carved metopes precedes by approximately half a century Greek mainland examples of comparable richness. Moreover, though commonly called a Treasury, the Foce del Sele building may have been an early temple of Hera, as some authors believe. Its abundant decoration would then be all the more striking.

In sculptural terms, the reliefs betray strong affinities with terracotta works: note in particular the undetailed hairstyles (Fig. 60), the long curls which look like clay sausages, the rippling rendering of folds. In these, as in the large unarticulated eyes and the receding profiles, one detects perhaps East Greek or Ionic influences, but whether the inspiration came directly from Asia Minor or via the Etruscan neighbors is difficult to tell. Though the first hypothesis may seem more plausible historically, certainly the gesticulating poses, the overlarge extremities of many of the figures, the liveliness of gait,[30] and even the selection of certain myths point in the direction of Etruria more than toward the Aegean. Even the gruesome aspect of some subjects, especially the peculiar demon who torments

[29] Several peculiarities among the architectural members attributed to the same building may suggest that we are dealing with material from two rather than from one "Treasury." The sofa capitals for the two antae are different in shape and design, and even the Doric capitals are of two different profiles. Since most of these architectural elements were found re-used in later construction, their attribution to Treasury I is still a matter of conjecture. More could also be done with the interpretation of the myths represented on the metopes, which may also have to be divided between two buildings.

[30] Note in particular the metope with two running girls (Langlotz, *Magna Graecia*, pl. 9) where the one in the foreground, to speed up her flight, lifts her skirt so high that her naked thigh is revealed—an unprecedented rendering of "motivated female nudity" for which we have no parallel until the Stumbling Niobid in the Terme (mid 5th century).

Sisyphos while the King of Corinth rolls his boulder up the slope, is unknown on the Greek mainland and may reflect the gloomier concepts of the Italian neighbors.[31] On the other hand, myths and religious beliefs in Magna Graecia are imperfectly known and seem to have differed considerably from the versions current in Greece proper. A word of caution is therefore in order before attempting to interpret Magna Graecian representations purely on the basis of Greek prototypes. A typical example of difference in popularity is the story of Herakles and the Kerkopes, which occurs both at Foce del Sele and at Selinus (Temple C) but is certainly never used architecturally on the Greek mainland. When it appears on vases, these are usually found abroad, not only in Sicily but, more recently at Tocra in Libya.

The molded look so typical of a malleable medium is no longer quite so strong in the Silaris metopes by the time of the Temple of Hera, ca. 510, but the Ionic influences have become even stronger. These are revealed in the architecture itself, which combines Doric and Ionic columns, but also in the metopal figures, which now wear the Ionic chiton-and-himation combination and have beaded or rippled hair. As on the "Treasury," the same topic extended over several metopes, but here we have no evidence for a mixture of myths on the same side of the building. Only two subjects seem to have been represented. One, involving a group of girls who run (Nereids in flight?) or dance two by two, may have decorated the metopes on facade; a second subject survives in only one metope showing a kneeling archer and a fragmentary companion. It could be part of an Amazonomachy, perhaps to go over the west facade, or at the beginning of the long sides.[32]

Other metopes from the same sanctuary have been assigned to two more Treasuries because their dimensions do not fit either of the previously discussed buildings; they are, however, too fragmentary to be considered here. More interesting is the metope from Paestum, of which enough is preserved to determine its subject. Again, it is Europa and the Bull, a myth which occurs at Selinus (Temple Y), Delphi (Sikyonian metope), Assos, and Pergamon (relief in Berlin). Not too much should be made of this geographical distribution, but once again one receives two impressions, not necessarily contradictory: that the motif may come from East Greece and that it may be part of the cult of Hera, even if it implicates her husband Zeus.

Paestum

Paestum, more than Foce del Sele, seems open to a variety of influences, not only from Ionia but also possibly from Etruria and the rest of Magna Graecia. Pythagorean principles may be reflected in the building criteria of the Temple of Athena; and Sicilian traits in the use of adyta (?) and inner stairways. I have already commented on the coffers in the soffit of the raking cornice of the Athenaion, comparing them to possible Etruscan decora-

[31] E. Simon (*JdI* 82 [1967] 275–95) has suggested that the demon is Thanatos and that some of the metopes show the four Great Sinners in Hades—Tityos, Tantalos, Sisyphos, and Ixion—thus betraying their Achaian tradition.

[32] The official publication advocates an exterior arrangement of decorated metopes comparable to that on the Athenian Hephaisteion (*Foce del Sele* I, 125 n. 1): the first three intercolumniations of the flanks, beside the front, would have carried carved metopes. Note, however, that for this building also some additional metopes were found after the official publication had appeared. The more recent discoveries display definite mannerisms in the rendering of the girls holding their skirts and look almost Archaistic in some features.

tive practices. That building is unusual also in its Doric frieze, where the triglyphs, and not the metopes, are inserted separately; there is no horizontal (Doric) cornice and the tympana are built in horizontal courses. Whether or not these features should be taken as symptoms of the Paestans' approach to the issue of architectural sculpture, I do not know. It is, however, significant that the other two temples at the site, both dedicated to Hera, should have left no evidence of carved metopes. The relief with Europa acquires therefore even greater importance, coming from such a site. Note also the unusual decorativeness of the plaque, with two rosettes of metallic appearance (like nail heads ?) carved on the fascia at the upper edge of the panel, on either side of Europa's head.

Selinus

Temple Y. In Sicily, two metopes were found in 1968, re-used in the late Fifth century fortifications of Selinus. Material and dimensions, as well as their secondary use, suggest that they belonged to that building usually referred to as "Temple Y,"[33] whose original location is unknown but which must have been dismantled to provide material for the walls. Four more metopes from this structure had been known since the last century, though they were built into the wall almost on the opposite side from the location of the new find. These four panels represented: 1) Europa and the Bull; 2) a large Sphinx; 3) Herakles fighting Acheloos and 4) the Delphic Triad. One more panel survives only as a fragment with a human head, impossible to integrate. The subjects of the two new metopes are more startling. One has been explained as Hekate meeting Demeter and Kore after the latter has been returned to her Mother. The other may depict Demeter and Kore in a chariot on their way to Olympos, but the identification is not beyond question. What is surprising, besides the unusual subject, is the specific rendering of a frontal quadriga where the two trace horses appear rampant, in profile, straining toward the center like two pets begging to have their heads patted by the occupants of the chariot.[34]

Though somewhat awkward, the scene is interesting and attractive also for that slight element of asymmetry which prevents monotony. Note, in fact, the uneven distance of the rampant horses from the human figures. This is probably caused by the fact that the sculptor centered his picture on one divinity alone, so that her companion had to be added at her side, disturbing the inherent bilateral symmetry of the composition. Whether this arrangement was meant to suggest the subordinate importance of one personage is no longer clear. Certainly the sculptor had difficulty in providing for the patting hand, which seems to grow directly from the second figure's hair, since there is no available space for

33 Their connection with Temple Y is not entirely assured since the framing elements vary. Specifically, three of the metopes from Temple Y have a beaded molding below the upper fascia, which is entirely missing in the newly found panels.

34 Mary Moore has suggested orally that the right hand of the taller figure on the Selinus metope may be holding a goad, the end of which goes behind the horse's head. An interesting comparison occurs on a fragmentary terracotta plaque from modern Gioia Tauro (ancient Metaurum) in South Italy, now in the Metropolitan Museum in New York (inv. no. 22.139.54). Only two horses survive, the trace horse rampant toward the outer edge of the plaque, rather than toward the center. Over the pole horse one can still see the charioteer's arm, holding the reins. The terracotta plaque was presumably architectural in function. (V. Tusa, *ArchCl* 21 [1969] 166 and n. 35; *BMMA* 20 [1925] 15–16 fig. 4; M. Moore, *J.P. Getty Museum Journal* 2 [1975] 41 n. 24 fig. 17.) The motif of a frontal quadriga with attendants occurs often on Magna Graecian terracotta arulae; cf., recently, *Himera* I, pl. H:1 pp. 338–39 and other examples quoted in note 2.

the whole arm. Yet, for all its naive rendering, the total metope is impressive; the frontal horses are effectively foreshortened and all figures are alert and lively, the animals with their dilated nostrils and the goddesses with their cheerful smiles.

The metope with Hekate, Demeter, and Kore is perhaps the more significant for a stylistic connection with the other panels found earlier. The two deities with tall poloi (one with a pattern of rays which has been compared to the Dorylaion stele)[35] have the same hairstyle as the Europa on the Bull: a solid mass, compact down to the level of the shoulder, then parting abruptly into front and back locks. This almost Daedalic coiffure is chronologically offset by the advanced detail of the "omega fold" (or the incipient swallowtail pattern) which appears at the hem of Hekate's skirt and reappears in the Europa metope. Such a rendering, meant to suggest the bunching of material, seems, in the new metope, almost confused with the fall of the mantle caught by Hekate's left arm. Yet there is no mistaking the zigzag edge to the long mantle of Demeter. A comparable stage is represented by the kore Akr. 593, whose traditionally high dating I should like to lower to the 550's.

Much has been written on the provincial lag of Magna Graecian sculpture and on its retarded stylistic elements. I hesitate to adopt terms which imply inability to keep abreast of new developments or cultural isolation. I find Sicilian art, especially at Selinus, full of a vigor and expressionism of its own. Whatever traits are retained from earlier styles may be favored for religious conservatism, not for lack of information on current trends. In addition, Sicilian artists seem interested in other aspects of sculptural expression: decorativeness, for instance, or the rendering of feelings, even a deliberate distortion of proportions to emphasize the importance of certain elements in a body or in a total episode. To call these traits naive or primitive is to pass a negative qualifying judgment on a form of art which looks different from the norm purely *because* it is different from this hypothetical norm.

The Sicilian decorativeness comes perhaps to its best expression in the metope of Europa and the Bull, from Temple Y. Though the girl's position resembles that on the Sikyonian metope, her upright torso turns the suggestion of a perilous flight into that of a pleasant ride. Her scalloped cape is undisturbed, her right hand on the animal's flank seems to spur him on, rather than to seek for balance, while she glances ahead without fear. The bull is the daintiest of beasts, with his row of curls and elaborate dewlap; though he turns outward to look at the spectator, he does not slow down, as shown by the fact that his four hooves are all off the ground line. That they should be visualized as skimming the waves is suggested by the large fish (dolphins ?) which leap between his legs, stressing speed while suggesting environment. Is that some kind of saddle under Europa, over the bull's back? If so, the impromptu element of the story disappears, and the myth takes on the appearance of a fated event, which explains the fearless attitude of the heroine. This is not an episode in the love life of Zeus but the Myth of Origin of an entire continent. Then the outward-facing bull is not simply a compositional expedient but almost a divine epiphany.

[35] Ch. Kardara (*AJA* 64 [1960] 343–50) has attributed the leaf-crown to the cult of Hera, though mentioning that similar headdresses can be worn by sphinxes and probably by the Lydian goddess Rhea. Perhaps the same type of ornament should be recognized in the Dorylaion stele and the Selinus metopes, thus extending the use of the crown to other Mother-Goddesses: Artemis in Asia Minor (Phrygia) and Demeter in Sicily.

The same emphasis on frontality, on establishing a rapport with the spectator, is shown by the metope with the Delphic Triad. Apollo has an enormous head, disproportionately large eyes, an impossible torsional pose. Yet again I have the impression that these traits are partly intentional, that heads and eyes are enlarged for potency and magnetism and frontality chosen to suggest apparition. Something of the sort is also present in the metopes from Temple C, where Athena and Perseus look away from Medusa not simply to avoid her petrifying glance but to show awareness of their audience of worshipers while slowly performing their ritual.

Temple C. Enough has been written on the metopes from Temple C to include here only random comments. In the better preserved of the two panels with a frontal quadriga, the two side figures actually stand behind the horses, their long robes touching the ground, though the present fragmentary state of the relief makes them appear to share the chariot with the driver. That these two figures are female is shown by the breasts of one, the long garments of both. Tradition interprets the triad as Apollo, Leto, and Artemis, but that is not compelling. What is more interesting is the attempt to show different levels of composition: the horses in front of the quadriga, the driver behind the chariot railing, the women behind the trace horses, in a scansion of space which recalls the Argonaut metope at Delphi. Note that this Selinuntine panel is twice as deep as the other Temple C metopes in order to accommodate such a daring representation, much more plastic than the pictorially indebted scene from Temple Y. Somewhat before the time when the mainland Greeks began to experiment with frontal chariots on their pediments, the Sicilians were obtaining comparable effects in their metopes. Note the forelock of the horses; on Sicilian steeds it is always parted in the center and flung back around the ears. Another detail of interest is the way the mane covers both sides of the neck in the frontal animals. Not too much emphasis should be placed on such a minor detail, but the fact that the same rendering occurs on the horses of the Dioskouroi on the Argo metope in Delphi may provide one more reason for considering it under Sicilian rather than Sikyonian inspiration.[36]

As for the other frontal chariot, which probably stood next to the first metope, on either side of the central axis, a possible interpretation identifies Helios and Phaethon, another Pelops and Oinomaos. It may even depict a local myth of which we have no knowledge, but it is so very fragmentary that no reconstruction is possible. Several other fragments of sculptures from the same series of metopes can no longer be integrated into meaningful episodes. Presumably the carved panels decorated both facades, despite the strong frontality in Temple C's plan.

Temple F. The Gigantomachy on the metopes of Temple F shows that by the end of the Sixth century the subject had achieved popularity also in Magna Graecia; but here the victims, to judge from the one better preserved piece, clearly display their pathos. The

[36] By contrast the relief with a frontal quadriga found on the Athenian Akropolis (Akr. 575–80, *AMA* no. 418; Brouskari, 45 and 109) shows the manes only on the side of the neck opposite the turn of the head. The fragmentary front half of a headless horse from Corinth had been attributed to a metope from the Temple of Apollo, but the most recent study of the sculpture refutes this possibility on the basis of size and suggests that the Corinth horse may come from another votive relief, ca. 530 (N. Bookidis, *Hesperia* 39 [1970] 320–23, no. 8, pl. 78). The first frontal horses on a pediment are probably those from the Massiliot Treasury at Delphi, ca. 535 (supra, Ch. 7, p. 211).

giant defeated by Athena throws back his head and shows his teeth in a scream, while the empty eye-holes of his uptilted helmet function almost as a presage of death. To the Sicilians this myth must have had special meaning since Enkelados, after his bout with Athena, was buried under their own Mount Aetna, from which he roared and spewed lava at intervals, a very tangible and fearful presence. In the metope, the giant's face is long and narrow, the beard incredibly decorative in its fine surface treatment. The style seems entirely different from that of Temple C, and it is hard to explain such difference in terms of time alone. Were the masters of Temple C more at home with stone and clay, and those of Temple F with metal? Technically, the carved metopes are made in two pieces, a difficult method which forces the sculptor to dissimulate a horizontal joint in the center of his panels. Yet plain metopes from the same building seem to have been made in one block, though both the carved and the undecorated metopes are thick enough to function as weight-bearing units within the entablature. Temple F is peculiar also for the ritual which must have taken place in it, with parapets between the columns screening the pteromata from outside viewing.

Other metopes from Selinus cannot be placed into a sequence. One relief from the akropolis, the so-called Eos and Kephalos, is not even certainly a metope. Another, from the Malophoros sanctuary at the Gaggera, showing a man and a woman, may be purely votive. Even the panel in Copenhagen, from an undisclosed Sicilian site, has a good chance of being from Selinus on stylistic grounds. It shows a winged figure in a running or flying position, which could either be a Gorgon or a Harpy, but the face is human, without any of the distorting, exaggerated features typical of Medusa. The figure does not have the bird body usually associated with Harpies though some vases show more anthropomorphic versions of these creatures. I wonder whether a special mythological name should be assigned to this figure, which might just be an apotropaic conception without legendary context, like a hippalektryon or a genius. Theoretically, she could even represent an early Nike (our earliest ?).[37] Her face recalls the Europa from the Y series; her locks, though their centrifugal motion away from the face seems impossible, suggest the idea of speed. Note that her wings are attached to her chest, rather than emerging from her back.

Within the Selinus production, dating is the most difficult aspect. Advanced treatment of drapery folds stands in apparent contrast to the squat proportions of the bodies and the awkward poses. Even architectural elements, when they can be safely connected with the sculptures, offer no great help with chronology. If, as some have suggested, certain details could have been carved later on a metope already in situ, judging by such details might be misleading. Though general agreement would place the series from Temple Y earlier than the reliefs from Temple C, the body proportions in the former set are more naturalistic than those of the latter. One wonders which criterion should therefore predominate in this chronological evaluation. Two more facts deserve consideration: the relatively short span of time in which so many buildings seem to have been erected, and the fact that the appearance of carved metopes may have coincided with the introduction of the peristyle.

The former fact is well known. Not only temples (Y, C, D, F, A and even the gigantic G) were completed or begun during the period 550–480, but also stoas, altars, retaining

[37] This possibility, and even identification as Iris, have been considered in the official Danish publication but were rejected in favor of the Harpy identification.

walls; and a general landscaping project took place on the Selinuntine akropolis around 550–530. It is difficult to allow for logical intervals between each construction and still accommodate them all within a span of approximately 70 years, especially considering the enormous size of many of these enterprises. In general terms, I would consider the Y and C metopes about contemporary, or at most within a decade of each other, on either side of a mid Sixth century date. Temple F, though usually dated much earlier, ca. 560–540, could fall approximately at the turn from the Sixth into the Fifth century.[38]

As for the second fact, we are hampered by the lack of complete publication for Temple M, an important structure near the Malophoros sanctuary. In preliminary mentions, the building is defined as intermediary between the Malophoros megaron and Temple C. Temple M seems to have added to the Gaggera megaron a proper Doric frieze with triglyphs and plain metopes, and an architrave with regulae and guttae, but still no outer peristyle. Though it had a rather deep pronaos, we do not know whether it was closed or in antis. If, as one assumes, no carved metopes decorated Temple M, these must have made their first appearance at Selinus on Temple Y, from which some column capitals have been recovered, also re-used in the later fortifications. Since both the Malophoros megaron and Temple M were constructed entirely in stone, experimentation with terracotta metopes seems to be excluded. Perhaps the answer to this apparent puzzle lies at Megara Hyblaia, or even in South Italy, at Sybaris itself.

Megara Hyblaia

As for Megara Hyblaia, note that the extant metopes[39] from a funerary naiskos are so elaborate that Langlotz could date them to the incipient Fourth century. Yet the contents of the tomb and the presence of a kouros (though fragmentarily preserved) within the naiskos confirm a late Archaic date. Not only the metopes but even the triglyphs are decorated in this unusual building, so that one suspects local sculptors of taking greater liberties with funerary than with temple Doric. The floral ornament carved at the top of each glyph occurs also on an Archaic triglyph from Akrai, in the Syracuse Museum, thus suggesting other areas of diffusion of influence. It is also noteworthy that all the metopes from Megara repeat the same complex motif which seems to serve purely decorative purpose. By the end of the Archaic period, therefore, and at least for funerary structures, carved metopes had already expanded their apotropaic/narrative repertoire to include sheer repetitive ornamentation.

Himera

That narrative metopes occurred at Himera, despite the absence of a peristyle, is shown by the preserved terracotta fragments in high relief depicting figures in action. The myths can no longer be recognized with certainty, but traces of painted labels have been inte-

[38] Our difficulty with the rendering of folds in the metopes from Temple C stems largely from the fact that we are usually comparing them with Athenian rather than with Cycladic or East Greek examples. Yet the chances of Selinuntine sculptors being influenced from Athens are remote indeed. The folds from Temple F are much more elaborate, and the Dionysos from the second surviving metope shows a very low (Ionic ?) kolpos and double curves in the zigzag tips of the voluminous himation.

[39] Reports of a figured limestone metope (a sphinx ?) from an Archaic religious structure appear only in *AA* 1954, col. 539. Neither the French reports in *MélRome* nor the account in the *EAA* Suppl. 1 repeats this information or reproduces the piece.

grated as Herakles and Eurystheus. Once again we would have a tradition of Herakles' exploits, although the divinity worshiped in Temple B cannot be identified. If Himera could indeed be connected with Rhegion and if the terracotta metope from the latter site could be compared to the running girls of the Silaris Heraion, a series of links could perhaps be established around the cult of Hera and South Italian influence on Sicily could be postulated. This speculation, however, is founded on such tenuous evidence that one should do no more than raise the question.

SUMMARY

The distribution of carved metopes seems to suggest that the idea of decorating the Doric frieze with figures in high relief originated in South Italy or Sicily under the influence of cross-cultural currents. Ionia may have provided the example of its continuous bands of relief, while the Peloponnesos may have pointed to the metopal field as a potential area for applied decoration in paint or metal foil. Yet the Peloponnesos, and Greece proper in general, appear to have rejected the practice of carved metopes: the reliefs from Mycenae are controversial as members of a canonical Doric frieze, and no other Archaic examples occur on the mainland except at Delphi. The earliest evidence from that site could reflect Italian practices; the later instances would be part of that general internationalism typical of Delphi. Carved metopes at Corfu fall under that same influence from the West which was already detected in its pediments and terracotta revetments. The odd Doric temple of Athena at Assos in the Troad may have had carved metopes as an extension of its carved architrave. The earliest Magna Graecian examples of relief metopes are yet to be found; they may have been in terracotta since a tradition of decorated panels in that medium existed at some sites. Even within Sicily and South Italy the diffusion of carved metopes seems to have followed specific patterns, with Selinus and Foce del Sele providing the highest concentration of examples and the strongest evidence for experimentation. Because of Magna Graecian preference and conceptions, as well as because of the sheer size of Magna Graecian temples, carved metopes do not occur in conjunction with pedimental figures, which they virtually replace in size and effect. At Delphi, however, such combinations predominate.

FOR PAGE 225

For this chapter, my main source of information has again been Bookidis. In general, see also E. Katterfeld, *Die griechischen Metopenbilder* (1911); J. Fröber, *Die Komposition der archaischen und frühgriechischen Metopenbilder* (1933); H. Kähler, *Das griechische Metopenbild* (1949).

For Bookidis' suggestion, see p. 463.

Mycenae reliefs: Bookidis M 41, 166–76; F. Harl-Schaller, *JOAI* 50 (1972–73) 94–116, with previous bibliography.

FOR PAGE 227

Architectural evidence at Mycenae: Bookidis, 167–68 nn. 2–10; A.J.B. Wace, *A Guide to Mycenae* (Princeton 1949; rept. New York 1964) 85; id., *JHS* 59 (1939) 210.

For the distribution of metopes on the Greek mainland, see Bookidis, 456–58.

FOR PAGE 228

Poros sculpture from Corinth: See supra, pp. 190 and 219.

Thermon temple: I. Beyer, *AA* 1972, 197–226, especially 222 fig. 31, for a reconstruction of the entablature; *contra*, T. E. Kalpaxis, *AA* 1974, 105–14.

Other metopes from Thermon: H. Koch, *RömMitt* 30 (1915) 71; *AntDenk* 2 (1902–8) 3 fig. 7; O. Broneer, *Isthmia* I (Athens 1971) 55 n. 47.

FOR PAGE 229

Thermon metopes in local clay: Bookidis, 154–55; for the inscriptions, see *Local Scripts*, 225–26; H. Koch, *AthMitt* 39 (1914) 251 n. 2.

Antefixes: Winter, 29 and 107.

Olympia, female griffin suckling young: Bookidis, "Metopes, dubia," 251–53; Mallwitz, 90 fig. 79 (where the idea of a door decoration is also advanced).

Cyrene wrestlers: R. G. Goodchild, J. G. Pedley, D. White, *Libya Antiqua* 3–4 (1966–67) 196 pl. 72a.

Syracuse plaque with running Medusa: See supra, 193 n. 8.

For the theory that the Doric frieze originated at Corinth, see R. M. Cook, *BSA* 46 (1951) 50–52.

FOR PAGE 230

Corfu metopes: *Korkyra* 2, 113–26; Bookidis M 42. Rodenwaldt supports the reconstruction as a continuous frieze; Bookidis accepts the metope identification.

FOR PAGE 231

Sikyonian Metopes at Delphi: Bookidis M 43; P. de la Coste Messelière, *Au Musée de Delphes* (Paris 1936) 19–23. For the rearrangement of the Apollo temenos after 548, see P. de la Coste Messelière, *BCH* 70 (1946) 271–87; see also E. Hansen, *BCH* 84 (1960) 387–433.

For the dating of the Temple of Apollo at Delphi (and hence of that of Athena at Marmarià), see supra, Ch. 7, 206–9, and bibliography on pp. 221–22. The Athenian Treasury is discussed on pp. 236–38.

FOR PAGE 232

Dinsmoor's theory on the Syracusan origin of the Sikyonian metopes: *BCH* 36 (1912) 444–46, 460, 467–73.

Temple of Apollo at Syracuse: Berve & Gruben, 416–19 pl. 151 and figs. 79–80.

Sikyonian Treasury at Olympia: Mallwitz, 167–69; on the Treasuries in general, 163–79.

FOR PAGE 233

Assos metopes: Bookidis M 47; F. Sartiaux, *RA* 22 (1913) 1–46, 359–86; *RA* 23 (1914) 191–222, 381–412.

Delphi, architectural terracottas: *FdD* 2:4 (1967) 219 and passim.

For technical experimentation, see here pp. 240–41 and Bookidis, 446–54.

FOR PAGE 234

Bookidis on Delphic workshops: 507–10.

The best photographs of the Sikyonian metopes are in *Delphes*, pls. 40–43.

Olympia shield device: BrBr 779–80, text fig. 4, p. 19 n. 3.

FOR PAGE 235

For a drawing of the two metopes with the ship Argo, see (after *Au Musée de Delphes*) *Hesperia* 35 (1966) 196 fig. 1 and n. 37. Besides the Lakonian cups mentioned in that footnote, other pictorial examples are provided by what Beazley calls "fiction handles" behind which figures disappear. See the description of the François vase in J. D. Beazley, *The Development of Attic Black Figure* (Berkeley 1951) 29.

FOR PAGE 236

Metopes of the Athenian treasury at Delphi: The official publication is by P. de la Coste Messelière, *FdD* 4:4 (1957); some changes, by the same author, *BCH* 90 (1966) 699–709; see also here, p. 238 n. 23. On the metopes, see further Bookidis M 46; for the chronological controversy, with bibliography, see *Agora* XI, 9-11; also Kleine, 94–97.

Theseus as representative of Athenian politics: B. Shefton, *Hesperia* 31 (1962) 330–68; E. Simon, *AJA* 67 (1963) 46; Ch. Sourvinou-Inwood, *JHS* 91 (1971) 97–100.

For the role of Herakles, see also J. Boardman, *RA* 1972, 57–72.

FOR PAGE 237

Ionic eye: See, e.g., *KAnat* figs. 212–13, 218–19, 224, 226.

Nipples inserted in copper: *FdD* 4:4 p. 21 and n. 3.

FOR PAGE 238

Metopes from the Temple of Apollo at Delphi: Bookidis M 44; P. de la Coste Messelière and J. Marcadé, *BCH* 77 (1953) 372–73 pl. 44b.

Metopes from Temple of Athena Pronaia, Marmarià: Bookidis M 45; *FdD* 4:3, no. 6 on p. 3, hors-texte pl. II; no. 38 on p. 9, hors-texte pl. I.

FOR PAGE 239

Decorated versus undecorated metopes: Bookidis, 460–61.

Metopes from Megara Hyblaia: See supra, pp. 150 and 178.

All other metopes mentioned on this page are discussed below.

FOR PAGE 240

Terracotta metope from Rhegion (Contrada Griso Labocetta): Bookidis M 59; Langlotz, color pl. II.

That the Silaris sanctuary was dedicated to Argive Hera is attested by Pliny, *HN* 3.70, and other ancient sources.

FOR PAGE 241

Metopes from Foce del Sele: Bookidis M 52–55; *Foce del Sele* 1 and 2; P. Zancani Montuoro, *AttiMGrecia* NS 2 (1958) 7–26, published additional metopes from the Temple of Hera; id., *AttiMGrecia* NS 5 (1964) 57–59, published additional metopes from Treasury I.

Temple of Hera, rather than Treasury: J. Bérard, *RA* 46 (1955) 121–40, especially 138–40.

For the degree of finish, see the comments by R. R. Holloway, *AJA* 75 (1971) 435–36 and id., *A View of Greek Art* (Providence 1973) 60–61.

FOR PAGE 242

Herakles and the Kerkopes: Besides the references given in *Foce del Sele* 2, pp. 185–95 no. 13, see also J. Boardman and J. Hayes, *Excavations at Tocra 1963–1965: The Archaic Deposits, BSA* Suppl. 4 (1966) 84 no. 934 pl. 57, a Lakonian piece dated ca. 560–55; the scene is otherwise unrecorded on Lakonian ware; see esp. *ibid.*, p. 81 and n. 5 for other comments on the subject matter.

Treasury II: Bookidis M 53, ca. third quarter of the 6th century; *Foce del Sele* 1, pp. 173–80 pl. 62.

Treasury III: Bookidis M 55, first quarter of the 5th century; *Foce del Sele* 1, pp. 32, 181–86 pls. 63–65; also fragments A–D, G, U, on pp. 193–97, 201 pls. 68–69.

Paestum metope: Bookidis M 56; *Foce del Sele* 1, pp. 133–35 fig. 39; the suggestion is made there that the metope belongs to some later phase of the Basilica (ca. 510–500). *Contra*, see Bookidis, 235–37.

Relief from Pergamon in Berlin: Blümel no. 29 pl. 81.

Pythagorean principles at Paestum: For the Temple of Athena, see e.g., R. R. Holloway, *Parola del Passato* 106 (1966) 60–64.

FOR PAGE 243

New metopes from Selinus: V. Tusa, *ArchCl* 21 (1969) 153–71.

Metopes from Temple Y: Bookidis M 49; A. Salinas, *MonAnt* 1 (1892) 957–62 pls. 1–3; Langlotz, pl. 8 (Europa and the Bull); M. Santangelo, *Selinunte* (1966) 72–74 figs. 57–60. The best photographs are in *Sicile Grecque*, pls. 83–85. The fragment with a male (?) head is published by A. M. Bisi, *ArchCl* 21 (1969) 34–38 no. 1 and pl. 10.

FOR PAGE 244

For the comparison of the headdress to the Dorylaion stele, see Tusa, *ArchCl* 21 (1969) 161; see also *ibid.*, pls. 39 and 42:2 (for a detail of Hekate's mantle, pl. 40; for the mantle of Demeter, pl. 41:2).

For Akropolis Kore 593, see supra, Ch. 4, p. 104.

FOR PAGE 245

Metopes from Selinus Temple C: Bookidis M 50; O. Benndorf, *Die Metopen von Selinunt* (Berlin 1873) 38–50; Langlotz, pls. 14–15; Berve & Gruben, pls. 128–29; M. Santangelo, *Selinunte*, 63–67 and fragments illustrated on p. 67 fig. 49; *Sicile Grecque* pls. 93–101. Cf. R. R. Holloway, *A View of Greek Art* (Providence, 1973) 58–60 and *AJA* 75 (1971) 435–36.

Metopes from Selinus Temple F: Bookidis M 51; O. Benndorf, *Die Metopen von Selinunt*, 39–40, 50–52 pls. 5–6; *Sicile Grecque*, pls. 133–35; M. Santangelo, *Selinunte*, 30–35 figs. 14–17. F. Vian, *La Guerre des Géants* (Paris 1952) postulates influence from Delphi. On Temple F in general, see Berve & Gruben, 426–27.

FOR PAGE 246

Eos and Kephalos relief from the akropolis of Selinus: *Sicile Grecque*, pl. 109; M. Santangelo, *Selinunte*, 52 and fig. 35.

Relief from Malophoros sanctuary: *Sicile Grecque*, pl. 167 (the interpretation of a ritual dance is given in the caption by F. Villard); M. Santangelo, *Selinunte*, fig. 67 on p. 92, and p. 90, where she suggests that the panel represents Hades carrying off Persephone.

Metope in Copenhagen: Bookidis M 48; M. Giødesen, *Meddelelser fra Ny Carlsberg Glyptothek* 10 (1953) 22–46; V. Poulsen, *Griechische Bildwerke* (Konigstein im Taunus 1962) 22.

Besides Holloway, the suggestion that some details may have been carved in situ had already been made by Bookidis, p. 212.

FOR PAGE 247

On the landscaping of the akropolis at Selinus, see N. Di Vita, *Palladio* 17 (1967) 3–60.

On the chronology of Temple C, a new study by G. Scichilone may propose a higher date for the original construction; see supra Ch. 7 n. 9.

Selinus, Temple M: *ArchCl* 10 (1958) 58; *FA* 9 (1954) 172 no. 2228 figs. 48–49; *EAA* s.v. *Selinunte.* In *FA* it is mentioned that a *terminus ante quem* for the building is given by the pottery found under its foundations: some Late Proto-Corinthian and some Corinthian, some black glazed fragments and one sherd of Attic Black Figure; but this information is still too vague.

Metopes from Temple B, Himera: *Himera* I, 169–73 and Catalogue, 179–94.

Chapter 9

Friezes

The term frieze can apply either to the portion of entablature which occurs immediately above the architrave in a Greek or Roman building, or to a band of continuous decoration, usually in relief, which may occur at any point on a building—or, for that matter, on any object susceptible of embellishment, such as a chest, a vase, or even a garment. In the context of this chapter, the word frieze refers exclusively to architectural decoration in continuous form regardless of specific location on a structure. Its ornamentation comes under consideration only when it consists of concrete living figures; abstract patterns, even if derived from the world of vegetation, do not here qualify for inclusion within the term.

Despite this distinction, a frieze deserves its name even when it embodies a considerable amount of repetition, provided that the repeated motif consists of individual figures taken from the human and animal sphere. Thus, for instance, an egg-and-dart molding or a Lesbian leaf carved on a continuous band do not qualify as friezes, while the term can apply to a series of mold-made terracotta plaques placed in a sequence and depicting, let us say, hounds chasing hares. To be sure, such a repetitive figured frieze is hardly more than a glorified molding, but this consideration is important in trying to determine the possible origin(s) of the continuous Greek frieze and its function on a building.

THE QUESTION OF ORIGINS

The Oriental kingdoms—Egypt, Assyria, Babylon, the Hittite and neo-Hittite centers—seem to provide the obvious prototype for this form of Greek sculpture; yet second consideration clarifies the many differences. In Egypt and Assyria, to begin with, such friezes decorated mostly the interior of a building, and therefore their relief tended to be extremely low, often hard to differentiate from pure painting. Yet such "sculpture" was highly narrative in character, even when it repeated formalized scenes without individuality. The *raison d'être* of the frieze was not only, or not even primarily, the decoration of the wall surface, but rather the propagandistic or magical value of the scene portrayed. In the case of the Assyrian orthostats, the symbolic protection afforded by the mythical beings carved on them combined with the physical protection provided for the mudbrick walls by the stone slabs themselves. The same double function was served by stone reliefs in Hittite, neo-Hittite, or North Syrian areas, as at Alaca Hüyük or Tell Halaf.[1] From the

[1] Here, however, relief can be relatively high; it is perhaps significant that it usually takes the technical form of "flat relief," which will be discussed below as a typically East Greek rendering. It also often combines relief figures with protomes in the round, emerging, as it were, from the main body of the block. This technique finds its Greek counterpart in the Didyma architrave lions, the Ephesos anta

very beginning, variety predominated in the selection of subjects, even when both figures and scenes were stereotypes or when repetition was introduced to suggest endless numbers—of worldly goods, of servants or of protective beings. Pure mythology found little or no place in Assyria and Egypt; and if more mythical creatures seem to appear in Hittite territory, the stories behind them are not explicitly narrated. Real action occurs only when the deeds of the rulers are depicted, whether the almost ritualistic hunt or the historical battle. In both Egyptian and Assyrian reliefs, ample text usually ensures the total comprehension of the scene for the few who can read.

Not so the Greek frieze. The earliest extant examples have no identifying labels and the selection of scenes implies minimal narrative; when this occurs, it is mythological in character, with intentional repetition of side figures which act like a chorus in a Greek drama. As for the medium, it is not always stone; next to the carved examples many terracotta plaques exist which can rightly lay claim to be considered friezes since they satisfy the requirements of the definition. Their very nature, as a series of mold-made reliefs, produces repetition and uniformity, thus enhancing their purely decorative value. Under the circumstances, one wonders whether different prototypes should be sought as the inspiration for the Greek frieze.

At least a partial answer, to my mind, lies once again in Phrygian territory, and not because of the often advocated etymology: *fregium* = *Phrygion*, which may apply purely to textiles or embroideries. Recent finds have provided concrete evidence that early (Eighth century ?) Phrygian buildings were abundantly decorated with terracotta tiles carrying geometric patterns of some sort. This possibility had already been envisaged in studying the rock-cut facades so typical of the Phrygian landscape, which obviously reproduced in stone contemporary types of wooden buildings with terracotta revetments. In a wood and mudbrick construction such decoration obviously served also a utilitarian function in protecting perishable material from weathering. This material contributed to producing specific architectural features, like the Chinese-roof effect of the eaves projecting well beyond the face of the walls to prevent rain from spattering them. Such projections, and the terracotta plaques which lined them, resulted in decoration not only along the vertical, but also along the horizontal faces, on the soffit of the cornice or sima, to use Greek terminology. Exactly such forms and places for decoration have been recognized in Etruria, both at Acquarossa and Murlo, and it may well be that influences reached Italy directly from the Orient, rather than via the Greek mainland. To be sure, no such terracotta revetments were used thus in Greece proper; and this may seem surprising in view of the abundant evidence for architectural terracottas which has survived from Greek centers.

This vast amount of Greek revetments has prompted the theory, supported by Åkerström and others, that Greece played the leading role in the invention and diffusion of architectural terracottas, which spread from Corinth to all outlying areas, including the non-Greek territories to the East (Phrygia, Lydia) and West (Etruria). But such a hypothesis minimizes the importance of the Oriental tradition, and the vast difference be-

---

bulls and perhaps the "panthers" of the Athenian Hekatompedon. On the Hittite friezes, see M. J. Mellink, *Anatolia* 14 (1970) 15–27 and id., *Anatolian Studies presented to H. G. Güterbock* (Istanbul 1974) 201–14.

tween the Greek and the Phrygian use of such revetments, as exemplified by the rock-cut facades and the Düver and Pazarli buildings. Though the Greeks may have been quick in seizing upon the practice and in stamping the terracottas with their own characteristic style and iconography, I am convinced that the original impetus came to the Greeks (and to the Etruscans) from the Orient, rather than vice versa. The step from geometric to figured decoration must have been relatively easy to make. Thus the first Greek figured friezes may in reality have been terracotta revetments originally used for practical purposes.

It was almost inevitable, according to such premises, that the Greek frieze should first appear in Ionic territory, without being bound to a single definite location on a building, and exhibiting those traits of repetition and decoration which automatically go together with mold production on a vast scale. We are perhaps missing the earliest steps in the development, but whatever figured terracotta friezes survive from Asia Minor, Thasos, and even Phrygia and Lydia, corroborate these assertions. Some of the preserved scenes seem rather incongruous,[2] and it has been suggested that they represent tired versions of what was once a coherent composition. Another possibility is that some crucial element of the narrative has been eliminated, thus making the abbreviated version illogical or incomprehensible. In any case, such modifications to an archetypal composition imply and require the passing of perhaps considerable time, so that even if the low chronology were adopted for the extant examples, a date well before the middle of the Sixth century (the date suggested by Åkerström for some of these "illogical" East Greek terracotta revetments) should be assigned to their hypothesized predecessors. As it is, stratigraphic evidence from Murlo assures us that as early as ca. 575 elaborate figured compositions existed on Etruscan revetments; at the same site, sophisticated architectural terracottas are being found in the earlier levels, in connection with a building *destroyed* around 620–575. The Etruscans are therefore shown to have produced complex revetments, perhaps under direct Oriental inspiration, at a time when none are attested for mainland Greece. Even Åkerström's dates for what is at present available from East Greece should probably be raised.[3]

Yet not all friezes were necessarily in terracotta. Obviously, in mud-brick architecture wood is likely to have played a considerable role in a region well provided with trees. Long beams which acted as a continuous band may have inspired painted or incised decoration. In addition, some of the extant terracotta plaques from Asia Minor were not nailed to a backer-course but stood on their own, as parapet-simas. These characteristic forms are also known from Phrygia, where strange combinations of geison-sima revetments occur (e.g., at Düver). In some cases, East Greek parapets terminate on their upper edge in

[2] For instance, scenes of deer or hare being chased on horseback or in chariots, by warriors in full panoply (see, e.g., a parapet-sima from Thasos, *EtTh* 1, [1944] 37–39 pl. 7). It is interesting to note the diffusion, as well as the adaptability, of the type, which occurs on the top register of a terracotta pinax found at Himera in Sicily (*Himera* I, 119–20, no. Ap. 1 pl. 53:1; dated ca. 610–590). The official publication calls the quarry a fawn, but it looks like a hare to me, because of its large ears; however its size has been increased to the point that the animal being chased is almost as large as the horse of his chaser, as one would expect in a contaminated version geographically and chronologically removed from its archetype.

[3] Åkerström's earliest date, for a Didyma sima (his pl. 55) is ca. 575–560. The scholar's low chronology for the architectural terracottas from Sardis has now been questioned by A. Ramage (*Summaries of Papers presented*, 77th General Meeting, Archaeological Institute of America, December 1975, New York, p. 6).

a series of teeth which resemble the dentate outline of disc akroteria or, with a more modern comparison, the fragments of glass embedded in cement which top the walls of Mediterranean villas. Though this parallel is obviously anachronistic, the original function of the ancient teeth may also have been to protect against human invasion. We must therefore assume that terracotta was not the original medium for this feature, an assumption which had already been made on grounds of impracticality. In fact such triangular projections break easily, thus spoiling the entire effect of the parapet, and in some cases required the elaborate procedure of separate manufacture with subsequent joining by means of metal pins. If terracotta plaques with such dentate edges reflect metal prototypes, the possibility of figured friezes in bronze or other metal should certainly be considered. In recent years evidence has accumulated in that direction, though some of it is still unpublished. No actual figured friezes have come to light, but various other forms of architectural decoration are now known, including the large bronze plaques with gorgoneia and wrestlers from Cyrene and the *à jour* akroterion from the Athenian Akropolis. In combination with allusions in the literary sources, these surprising survivals in a precious as well as perishable medium confirm that metal decoration of various kinds may have figured extensively on Greek temples of the Archaic period.

The Earliest Friezes

It is at present impossible to tell whether the idea of a figured frieze occurred first in terracotta or in another medium. Certainly stone examples seem as early as, if not earlier than, the available figured revetments; yet, as usual, the evidence is somewhat ambiguous. The oldest stone frieze is engraved on a limestone block found in the Samian Heraion. It retains the heads of three male figures facing left, each holding in front a large spear. Though some scholars consider it simply a doodle casually scratched on a wall, the most recent publication of the piece repeats Buschor's suggestion that it decorated Hekatompedon II, around 675. The bodies of the warriors must have been engraved on other courses of the wall, since the lower horizontal joint runs through the faces, which appear at different heights. Color would have unified and strengthened the entire composition. Though no hypothesis can be made as to the original location of this block, its connection with the temple seems assured through its find spot. Presumably the technique of the decoration required a low position on the building, perhaps on the exterior, for greater visibility. Its high date certainly precedes anything extant in terracotta. In view of the fact that the same technique of decoration, spanning several wall courses, was employed in the later Heraion friezes, I am inclined to consider these warriors more than mere doodles and perhaps even evidence of a possible second source of influence for the continuous frieze. Given Samos' strong contacts with Egypt, the island could easily have absorbed concepts of decoration inspired by the availability of a solid surface—a pre-existent stone wall—rather than by a need to protect a perishable medium, mudbrick or wood.

Two different origins could therefore be distinguished, with different patterns of distribution: 1) the frieze as protection, which came from Phrygia or, ultimately, the Near East, and produced the slab-revetment type. This form spread through Asia Minor and eventually to Delphi and Athens. 2) The frieze as wall decoration, which came from Egypt, aimed at the utilization of a pre-existent, self-sufficient wall and produced the many-coursed type. At first adopted only at Samos, this type eventually passed on to South Italy, as we shall see. On the other hand, similarity with Egyptian friezes pales when this same many-coursed Greek form utilizes high relief. It could then be compared to the molded-brick, glazed tile decoration of the Babylonians and Persians. In stone, however, the actual carving must have taken place when the blocks were already in situ, to ensure proper spanning of the joints in free-form compositions which did not permit mass production and automatic assemblage.

If the above speculation is correct, the early date of the Samian example would not per se vindicate priority for the stone over the terracotta friezes, since the two forms may have developed independently. Even our second oldest stone example is somewhat ambiguous as architectural sculpture. It comes from Cretan Prinias and consists of several slabs, including a corner block, which depict a procession of diminutive riders on long-legged horses in flat relief. The men are armed with shield and spear and turn their heads outward to face the spectator. The corner block may show that foot soldiers were also represented frontally in some section of the frieze. The reliefs have been variously interpreted in their architectural relationship to the building. Some scholars see them as a regular frieze course in the entablature, others as a dado at the bottom of the walls, others still as a parapet surrounding a flat roof. Bookidis points out that the large offset at the back and bottom of each slab bespeaks a need for extra resting surface and added balance, as would be required by a parapet. A high balustrade (almost 85 cm.) on a rather flimsy rubble structure seems unlikely to me, and I would rather separate these slabs from the temple itself, visualizing them as an enclosure to a sacred area or a bothros. Although such a feature formed part of the very Temple A to which the reliefs are attributed, another bothros existed in nearby Temple B, and remains of other structures appear in the published plan of the general area. In effect, all extant frieze fragments were found *in front* of Temple A, despite the fact that the corner block and traditional reconstruction would require them all around the building.[4]

Dissociating the horsemen frieze from Temple A may also help in dating the seated statues that adorned the door lintel of the building, the resting block for their feet being itself decorated with a row of animals. These statues have usually been considered later in style than the rider reliefs, yet different dates were inconceivable for architectural sculpture strictly integrated within the same structure. Separate positioning for the frieze would allow us to date it ca. 650, and the lintel sculptures ca. 620–600.

Another Cretan piece, a stone relief from near Khania, may still belong to the Eighth

[4] The bothros within the Archaic temple at Gortyna was lined by upright gypsum slabs, though without relief decoration. The bothros *within* Temple A is 2.40 x 1.40 m. and could easily accommodate the horsemen frieze, which is preserved to a total length of over 3.63 m. However, the stone curbing around the cavity would seem unsuitable to support the frieze slabs. A sacred precinct outside the temple remains a possibility. Several shrines of this kind have been found in Greece proper, for instance in Athens (Agora excavations, on the north side of the railroad tracks, *Hesperia* 43 [1973] 127; also 37 [1968] 58–60; the Altar of the Twelve Gods, H. A. Thompson and R. E. Wycherley, *Agora* XIV [1972] 129–36; the precinct of the Tritopatores, in the Kerameikos, D. Ohly, *AA* 1965, 327–28) and at Corinth (*Hesperia* 42 [1973] 6–9; and *Hesperia* 43 [1974] 1–6). However, the height of the Prinias slabs is ca. 0.84 m., which may be too low for the parapet of a sacred precinct. Another possible objection—that the band with incised floral decoration now placed below the horsemen slabs is unsuitable for a low position—is weakened by the fact that only one fragment of that floral decoration remains, and there is no assurance that the molding should be associated with the figured frieze.

century. It shows a shrine with a cult image inside flanked by diminutive warriors appearing in a stacked arrangement, presumably to suggest depth and perspective. A galloping horse approaching from the right may convey the idea that the warriors are defending the shrine from attacking chariots. The discrepancy between the size of the horse and the defenders is such that Egyptian and Assyrian renderings spontaneously come to mind. Whether the block was part of an architectural frieze is problematical; it is, in any case, so different from other Greek examples that Crete once again seems to lead nowhere in terms of Greek artistic developments.

If the Cretan friezes be eliminated as true architectural sculpture because not demonstrably connected with a building, in chronological sequence the next examples after the engraved Samian warriors are found on the Ephesian Artemision. Though the actual execution of the reliefs may have taken place over a considerable span of time, at least the planning of the areas to receive sculptural decoration may have occurred as early as ca. 560. Yet this is still quite a jump from ca. 675 and one wonders whether terracotta revetments can fill the gap, even if their chronology be raised. More important, the question should be faced whether terracotta revetments, elaborate as their figured decoration may be, can count as full-fledged friezes and as architectural sculpture or should be ranked with lesser elements such as moldings and antefixes.

My answer to this question is ambivalent. I do not doubt that such figured revetments may have provided one of the sources of inspiration for the continuous stone frieze. I am, however, almost as confident that other sources of inspiration existed in other media and perhaps in other contexts. Certainly at one point influences may have gone in the opposite direction, and elaborate stone friezes may have provided material for terracotta plaques, which therefore became cheaper substitutes for the more impressive marble decoration. On the other hand, the development of the stone frieze in its own right is perforce tied to the development of monumental architecture in stone, for which fewer occasions existed. It is perhaps important to note that all major stone temples in Archaic Asia Minor seem to have carried some form of carved frieze decoration. For lesser structures evidence is minimal or nonexistent, so that if the occurrence of carved friezes cannot be proven, neither can it be denied. It is natural that minor buildings should have employed terracotta friezes, not only because more economical in terms of time and money but also because better suited in weight and appearance to more temporary constructions. And even a building of rubble and wood, when properly stuccoed and covered with elaborate terracotta reliefs painted in brilliant colors, must have made a startling and rich effect, in its way quite comparable to the more monumental examples entirely in stone.

Yet there is no denying that a terracotta frieze, because of its method of manufacture, may stifle creativity and cramp narration. Even the Larisa terracottas, a few of which seem to portray mythological subjects, rely on the obvious repetition and alternation of set types, not only on the same building or even in the same place, but also at different sites. Bookidis, for instance, has noticed that the same mold was employed for revetments at Larisa and Phokaia. Therefore only stone reliefs can rise above the level of mass production and qualify as major art. I shall here avoid discussing the many terracotta examples from Asia Minor,[5] except to stress that they must have been crucial in setting the criteria for suc-

[5] In 1967 Bookidis listed (p. 488) a total of 31 friezes from the combined Aegean/Asia Minor area, of which 18 are of terracotta and 13 of stone. This total does not include the very numerous terracotta revetments from non-Greek sites.

cessful continuous decoration in Asia Minor. Of these criteria the most important, both cause and consequence of their technique, was perhaps the secondary role given to narration, which became subordinate to decorative effect. Though only the figured terracotta revetments can be properly defined as glorified moldings, the most successful stone friezes had to incorporate some of the same properties: the ability to cover a long and narrow area without an obvious beginning, center, and end; clarity and intelligibility, even from a distance; repetition and uniformity, mixed with enough variation to arouse interest and dispel monotony but not enough to break the rhythm or distract attention from the over-all effect. These qualities were usually achieved through subject matter.

Ionic "Monotonous Friezes"

Yet the stone friezes from Asia Minor are so sadly fragmentary that even these assumptions may be considered unfounded. The best supporting evidence comes from Myus and Kyzikos, where stone friezes seem to have depicted an endless series of racing chariots. At least ten slabs are represented in the fragments surviving from Myus, in a strange smooth style which recalls metal repoussé. The chariots dash either to right or left, each drawn by two horses. There are many Assyrian details: the eight spokes to the wheels, and the tulip-shaped muscle at the top of the horses' front legs which occurs on the lions of Assurbanipal's hunt in the Seventh century. It is uncertain where the reliefs were placed, perhaps around the cella. The Myus temple, an Ionic peripteral dedicated to Dionysos (?), is dated around 560.

Later (ca. 520) and more ornate, though smaller and fewer, are the chariot reliefs from Kyzikos. There are just enough to tell us that here too the chariots were shown going in two directions, and therefore probably on at least two sides of a building. The slabs are obviously architectural, but their exact position is again uncertain. Note the seated lion which decorates the chariot's side, presumably as metal relief. Though the pose of the animal is attested on the Assos architrave (perhaps under influence from the sphinxes seated nearby) and in Assurbanipal's hunt (though there for a wounded beast), none of the Asia Minor freestanding lions has come down to us in this position, which was instead popular on the Greek mainland. The single long lock trailing loosely behind the charioteer's ear recalls Lydian fashions at Persepolis,[6] but his angular profile is characteristically East Greek. One cannot help recall that the direct descendants of the Kyzikos frieze are the racing charioteers of the Mausoleum at Halikarnassos, approximately 200 years later.[7]

Another East Greek example of what I call the monotonous frieze is the fragmentary dance from Karaköy, near Didyma. Five women form a chain moving to the right, taller women alternating with shorter maidens, each bending forward in their rhythmical move-

[6] K. De Vries (*Expedition* 15 [1973] 32–39, especially p. 35) considers it hair; to me, however, the long trailing "lock" of the Apadana Lydians looks more like cloth, perhaps connected with the spiral binding of the sakkos, when seen in detailed photographs, e.g., Schefold, pl. 354 c–a.

[7] One more chariot frieze (?), from Iasos, is known to me through the paper presented by Dr. Clelia Laviosa at the 10th International Congress in Sept. 1973 (Ankara-Izmir). The charioteer has the sloping profile of the Kyzikos drivers, but the total composition seems closer to the Myus plaques in its over-all simplicity. A hare under the horses and the repetitive outlines of the animals' legs establish strong ties between this sculpture and terracotta revetments. The find is mentioned simply as "an archaic marble relief" in M. J. Mellink, "Archaeology in Asia Minor," *AJA* 77 (1973) 184. It was found on the south side of the Agora. An extensive article on this relief, and on the problem of Ionic friezes, by C. Laviosa, has now appeared in *ASAtene* 50–51, NS 34–35 (1972–73) 397–481.

ment. The shorter figures, wearing only a chiton, raise a flower (?) behind the head of the taller companion who follows them, while at the same time stretching their left hand toward the woman who precedes them. The taller ladies wear a himation over a large-sleeved chiton and bend their left arms to touch the tip of their mantle. The composition works on the alternation of head levels and the subtle undulation between overlapping planes, yet, surprisingly, this is an example of what is called flat relief. This technical term means that the contours of the figures have been cut straight back to the background plane, so that their sides are vertical while their fronts look plastically modeled like figures in the round. The use of the drill to cut channels around each image makes the outlines wavy and lively. I do not believe that the work was left unfinished, as is sometimes claimed, and I would consider this flat relief technique typically Ionic since it reappears on some fragments from the Ephesos column drums and parapet, as well as on two sides of the Siphnian frieze. It is a kind of *trompe-l'œil* that must have been most effective from a certain distance, yet the Artemision drums were more or less set at eye level.[8] Some uncertainty exists as to the location of the Dancing Women slab. That it was part of a larger whole is shown by the joints running vertically through the carved figures, but nothing assures us that it belonged to a raking sima or to a parapet, and its relatively small size (H. 0.53 m.) makes it unlikely for the Archaic Didymaion.

The only other extant example of what could be termed a monotonous frieze is the fragmentary column drum from Kyzikos, which retains the upper parts of three figures linked in a chain dance. A veiled girl in the center is flanked by two naked youths with whom she is holding hands. The figures' backs are against the curving background, but their heads turn slightly toward the viewer's right and there is torsion in their shoulders so that the total impression is one of movement. The relief was a chance find, and it has been suggested that it may be a base rather than part of a *columna caelata*. Certainly what is left of the background is plain rather than fluted, like the Didymaion drums, but the presence of an eccentric dowel on the upper surface seems more appropriate for a column than for a statue, and the restored dimensions of the drum could be adequate for a peripteral temple.[9] Since figured column drums are attested by literary sources and extant examples, the hypothesis is valid also for the Kyzikos relief. It remains to consider the suitability of the rendering for architectural decoration and, in general, the entire question of figured friezes on columns.

FRIEZES ON STRUCTURAL MEMBERS

Since the Kyzikos drum should be restored with at least three additional figures, and perhaps as many as five, the composition certainly qualifies as a frieze, both in extent and

[8] A. Bammer has suggested that the carved drums of the Classical Artemision were placed directly below the column capitals, rather than at the bottom of the shaft as traditionally believed. However, evidence is scarce and the suggestion has not received wide acceptance. From a purely sculptural point of view, the effect of a procession of figures at that high level would have been even more disturbing than at the low one usually assigned to the reliefs. However, this is considered a startling innovation of the Classical period only. Cf. H. Wiegartz, *MarbWinckPr* 1968, 41–73.

[9] It is even possible that carved bottom drums were used for interior columns. Note, for instance, the tall undecorated cylinders which served as bases for the inner Ionic columns of the Naxian Oikos at Delos, and which might have been meant for carving which was never carried out (G. Gruben, *JdI* 78 [1963] 177–82). Uncarved, but probably meant for *columnae caelatae*, are also some remains of peristyle columns from the Ionic temple at Syracuse (P. Pelagatti in *Archeologia nella Sicilia Sud-Orientale* [Naples/Syracuse 1973] 73–74).

in pattern. The dancers, in relatively high relief, face the spectator, and therefore appear almost as if applied against the surface of the drum. Thus the entity of the column is not violated but almost confirmed and emphasized by these encircling figures. The same result is obtained at Didyma through the veiled girls (priestesses ?) who hold offerings and seem to lean against the shafts.

The preserved Didymaion fragments belong to drums of two different sizes. Gruben would place the larger ones (decorated with almost life-size figures, probably 8 per column drum) between the pronaos antae, the smaller ones behind, within the pronaos itself, for a total of eight *columnae caelatae*. There now may be evidence to suggest that the peristyle columns had similar decoration. A recently found fragment with a girl's head, now in Didyma, shows that not all figures were similarly positioned and attired. This relief, which Tuchelt has published for the first time, shows that the girl's head was slightly turned toward her left. In addition her veil, probably fastened in place by a wreath, leaves part of her hair uncovered. The scale of the figure is almost life-size, therefore comparable to that of the "priestesses" which Gruben would place between the pronaos antae. But the lack of frontality in the representation requires a separate location for the new fragment, thus probably on facade. In her stance, the Didyma figure recalls the Kyzikos column drum and, to a lesser extent, those from Ephesos. Unfortunately, not enough of the relief background is preserved to ensure that the newly found fragment belongs to a *columna caelata*, though size, style, and technique may seem to confirm the attribution.

In the case of the other fragments, in Berlin, the connection is assured by the fact that the column's flutes are clearly visible as part of the relief background since they continued down to the base, running in the intervals between the human figures. The resultant appliqué effect must have been even stronger at the Didymaion than at Kyzikos. This form of decoration could therefore be compatible with Archaic Greek architectural principles, which usually left essentially supporting members undecorated, and applied color or sculpture only to those parts which could be mentally removed from the structure without endangering its basic stability. These *columnae caelatae* must have looked as if a glorified wreath had been placed around the bottom of the shaft, in a form of decoration comparable to the more modest anthemion rings below the Ionic capitals at Samos, Naukratis, and Lokroi, or even the smaller garlands on the Doric capitals of the Basilica at Paestum. Such ornamentation in turn may have originated from practical forms: some kind of sheathing to protect the bottom of a wooden column, or a metal band to reinforce or disguise the joint between a wooden shaft and a separately carved echinus.

But what are we to think of the Ephesos drums? Here the figures appear in strict profile, almost as if parts of their bodies were immersed in the column itself, which is therefore conceived as penetrable and inconsistent.[10] Even a small ledge under the figures' feet does not counterbalance the impression that they recede into imaginary space, instead of just moving on the periphery of the shaft. Theoretically this compositional form could have

[10] It should be noted here that the often illustrated reconstruction of one column drum incorporating all major fragments of relief with curved background no longer exists. The British Museum, recognizing the disparate origin of the pieces, now displays them in isolation. In particular, the upper part of a priest (?) wearing a panther skin has been dissociated from the lower torso of a walking man. This latter is remarkable for the plastic treatment of the folds in his lower garment, the catenaries of his upper, which successfully model a figure basically carved in "flat relief." From the drums' fragments I would agree to exclude the fragmentary face B 89 (Lullies & Hirmer pls. 40–41) which differs in style, technique, material, and perhaps even size.

developed from the appliqué type when sufficient time had intervened to weaken the memory of the decoration's original purpose. Yet the visual effect should have been disturbing at any time, given the strong supporting role of the columns. One is led to surmise that architectural decorative principles varied considerably and that only the mainland of Greece may have stressed the distinction between structural and nonstructural members.

Possible confirmation for this theory comes from two votive monuments. The first was found at Sardis, and represents an Ionic pseudo-peripteral shrine with engaged or three-quarter columns; a veiled image of the goddess flanked by two upright snakes fills the facade and suggests the divinity standing in front of her temple. Two maeander fasciae run horizontally around the building, passing behind the columns and forming three registers. In conjunction with the columns, they articulate each side wall into six panels filled by figures in very low relief. Some of these are maidens but some are silenoi and seated lions, and therefore one can hardly visualize them all as members of a procession though the human figures seem to be consistently moving toward the front of the building. The panels on the rear have more complex scenes, perhaps mythological in character: a lion and a boar flanking a tree (Peleus chased up a tree by the animals ?), a charioteer (Pelops ?), a supplication scene (Orestes and Aegisthus ?), and Herakles strangling the Lion. The style of the reliefs suggests a date around 550. Since the goddess over the front holds a lion against her chest, she might be Cybele—or Artemis, who in Anatolian territory is often one in conception with the Great Mother Goddess. Fragments of another naiskos, also from Sardis, show a similar figure who is described as holding a snake, but I wonder whether the latter might not be the edge of the veil being brought forward by the overlarge hand of the goddess. More important than the identification of the divinity is whether the reliefs over the shrine's walls reflect actual decorative practices of Lydian temple architecture or are additional ornamentation appropriate for a votive offering.[11]

The same uncertainty applies to the second example, a freestanding though rock-cut monument at Daskalopetra, on the island of Chios. The so-called Homer's Seat is shaped like the Sardis shrine, but the figure on the facade is seated rather than standing and may have been flanked by human attendants. The antae end in lion's paws and two large felines are carved over the side walls. A gabled roof with akroteria crowns the monument, which could therefore be considered a temple model of sorts. But are the side animals an actual reproduction of wall reliefs, or are they a magnified version of statues which stood in some relation to a temple proper? Whenever dimensions are compressed and reduced, all decoration may be telescoped into whatever space is available, thus playing a greater role in the model than on the actual protoype. If, however, we can assume that both the Sardis and the Chios shrines reflect actual decorative schemata of Ionic temples, then it is likely that such temples had figured walls, thus carrying ornamentation on structurally essential areas.[12]

[11] Note that the "panels" of the Sardis shrine are not of uniform size, and parts of the figures carved on them seem to be hidden by the columns, which are therefore to be visualized as standing *in front* of the walls themselves.

[12] Perhaps similar conclusions can be drawn from the Doric Temple at Isthmia, which seems to have had painted panels on its exterior wall faces as early as ca. 700–675. Less compelling is the evidence of the terracotta models from Perachora and the Argive Heraion, which are painted in contemporary vase-painting styles. By contrast, the interesting marble naiskos from Garaguso, in South Italy, seems entirely devoid of carved decoration though it may

Ionic temples in general, and to some extent also Magna Graecian ones, seem to have embodied different concepts from the Doric, both in plan and superstructure. Gruben has perceptively described the tremendous vital power expressed through the vegetal or quasi-vegetal forms of column shafts, capitals, carved moldings, and other types of decoration permeating an Ionic temple. The Chian antae terminating in lion's paws are a local peculiarity, but they well convey the impression that the entire building is a living entity squatting on the ground in only temporary immobility, as if ready to spring and pounce. The so-called forest of columns of the Ionic giants deliberately screened vision of the inner cella and replaced the linear alternation of Doric voids and masses with a more complex system of shadows created by slanting light filtering through the many rows of columns like trees in the woods. That this imagery taken from the world of nature may not be too far-fetched is shown by the conception of the cella itself,[13] which in some cases (Didyma, perhaps also Ephesos) was not a closed room but rather an enclosed area, probably open to the sky and in its turn containing earlier, smaller shrines which the worshiper may have approached through differences in floor levels. And this maze of columns and walls was peopled, as it were, by carved figures appearing and disappearing through the intervals: at Ephesos the bulls protecting the antae, with heads and hooves projecting in high relief, and the humans in procession around the columns;[14] at Didyma the priestesses around the pronaos shafts; at Samos, winged sphinxes at the antae and carved friezes within the pronaos, perhaps at different levels.[15]

The upper parts of these buildings were equally elaborate: not only rich capitals and moldings but also carved figures on architraves, wall crowns, or parapets. At the Ephesian Artemision a carved balustrade has been variously reconstructed over the two long sides, or all around the building. Yet the scale of its figures is much smaller than that of the column drum reliefs, and one wonders how the scenes could possibly have been visible at the considerable height of the temple roof. Given the great attention to details of these parapet carvings, it would be tempting to suggest a lower location were it not for the shape of the pan-tile visible on the rear of some fragments and the lion-head spouts which intersperse the figured scenes. In addition, the style of the sculptures makes it clear that they were executed at the very end of the building phase, probably well into the Fifth

once have been painted. It differs from the traditional East Greek or Anatolian votive shrines in that its seated cult image is carved entirely in the round and can therefore be taken out of its temple and appreciated in its own right. Langlotz, *Magna Graecia*, pls. 52–53; U. Zanotti Bianco, L. von Matt, M. Napoli, *La Magna Grecia* (Siena 1973) pls. 49–50; M. Sestieri Bertarelli, *AttiMGrecia* 2 (1958) 67–78, pls. 22–26.

[13] Some support for this imagery may derive also from the possible inspiration for the many Greek columns: the hypostyle halls of Egyptian temples which, through their forms taken from the vegetal world and their unnecessarily close spacing, were definitely meant to symbolize a sacred grove.

[14] At Ephesos the fragment of a draped torso walking to the left has a straight, not a curved background, yet its scale makes it too big for attribution to the parapet. Should one restore human figures on the antae, together with the bulls, or assume (as for the later phase of the Artemision) carved square pedestals as well as column drums? See W. R. Lethaby, *JHS* 37 (1917) 1–3.

[15] Perhaps the reliefs on the Sardis shrine are meant to imitate some such frieze, which on a real building would occupy only the lower part of the wall but in a model of reduced scale fills the entire available space. A comparable though perhaps inverse approach might explain the use of Karyatids for small treasuries as compared with the "priestesses" of the *columnae caelatae* for a much larger temple, who could not be made on a gigantic scale and still retain a human connotation.

century, thus suggesting a high position on the temple.[16] Some motifs and details of the sculptures may not even be purely Greek and may reflect Persian influence. Note in particular the Amazon (?) whose garlanded hat looks like a paper cone loosely wrapped around a pony-tail hairstyle, which spills from its open upper end. The two rows of snail curls over the figure's forehead were carved in detail up to a point, then the stone surface, finished but left smooth, was taken straight back to the background level. Another interesting fragment shows the upper torso of a draped female in profile to right, which reminds me of the Penelope from Persepolis. Most impressive of all perhaps is the sensitive head of a horse turning outward until it appears almost frontal: it is fully carved in all details, including the side toward the background and the underside of its jaw.

From the number and complexity of preserved fragments it is clearly impossible to restore a unified subject on the entire parapet, even though the predominance of warriors and chariots does suggest some kind of combat scene. But many other figures would not fit this topic, and the very length of the building to be decorated precludes the possibility of a single theme.[17] Unfortunately not enough is preserved for safe guesses; one suggestion, that a Centauromachy or one of the Deeds of Herakles was included, would be of some interest, if verifiable, in attesting the presence of mythological themes. Fragments of snakes and feathers and of an arm against a wing have prompted a restoration with Gorgons at the four corners; the consequent important similarity with Didyma is somewhat weakened by the fact that the Didymaion formed the basis for the Ephesian reconstruction.

At the Didyma temple the presumed hip-roof had no parapet but a carved architrave.[18] To restore a series of relief animals all around the building seems unwarranted by the extant remains; only three large beasts near the two preserved corner Gorgons are attested. In effect the corners, perhaps more than any other part of a structure would stand in need of symbolic protection. The lions with separately carved heads facing may have been remotely inspired by lion-head water spouts, but their connection with the Gorgon recalls the central composition of the Corfu pediments. In addition, their low-relief bodies contrasting with the high projection of the heads resemble the Gordion orthostats, the Ephesos anta-bulls, and even the Athenian "panthers" from the Hekatompedon, whatever their position on the building. The crossed front paws of the Didyma lions reflect the same Egyptian influence apparent on some freestanding animal monuments from that site.

[16] Conversely, it is usually assumed that the carved column drums were finished around 550–540, not only because of their presumed connection with King Kroisos but also because of their position at the bottom of the column shafts. However the protective surface seen on the bottom drums of the Ionic column at Syracuse (and perhaps also at the Naxian Oikos on Delos) suggests that such embellishments were carved late in the process of construction, presumably to prevent damage to the carvings while materials were being transported in and out of the peristyle. Should this have been the case also at Ephesos, the carved drums may well date later than normally assumed. On the chronology of the Ephesos sculpture, see also my comments in Ch. 1 and in the bibliography to Ch. 4.

[17] That this mixture of subjects on a continuous band may not have been troublesome for the East Greek viewer is shown perhaps by the same variety of themes in the equally continuous band of the Assos architrave. This may be further proof that the main interest in such reliefs was decorative rather than narrative.

[18] This could therefore be another example of Ionic willingness to decorate structural parts. G. Gruben (*JdI* 78 [1963] 176) has indeed advanced the theory that a decorated epistyle in Ionia may be the rule rather than the exception and the ultimate origin of the canonical friezes in Delphic Treasuries. Unfortunately, there remain among Ionic buildings very few entablatures on which to base general statements; and the continuously carved architrave at Assos belongs to a Doric, not to an Ionic, temple.

That the two blocks with relief Gorgons belonged to the temple architrave is attested by the fasciae on one of them; they do not appear on the other, and therefore the two blocks can be restored at diagonally opposite corners of the structure. We thus learn that fasciae may not have been an original feature of the Ionic order but were rather an added embellishment to an initially plain epistyle. This chronological sequence is partly based on the different style of the two Gorgons since the one against the plain background appears earlier than the other in general pose and detail. With a somewhat circular argument, the architectural sequence may be used to confirm our understanding of the development of Archaic drapery during the last quarter of the Sixth century, in that the fascia-less Gorgon has straight zigzag lines to her mantle while the second one wears a himation with double curves.[19]

REGIONAL DISTRIBUTION

Samos

That such changes should occur both at Ephesos and Didyma shows that constant revisions of details were possible, not only for carved figures but also for major architectural features when construction stretched over several decades. Definite stylistic differences are also observable in the Samian friezes. These are so fragmentary as to be hardly worth discussing here from a sculptural point of view. Much more important are their technical features and possible location. The various extant fragments can be divided into three major groups according to size, relief height, find spot, and stylistic dating: 1) One group of three fragments has been attributed to the temple of Aphrodite and Hermes, ca. 530–525, and is probably to be restored within the deep pronaos, running high on the wall. 2) Twelve more fragments form the so-called Small Frieze of the Polykratean Heraion and are dated ca. 510–500. Though their location on the building is far from assured, the fragments in low relief may have lined the interior of the anta walls, while those with higher projection would have decorated the door wall between pronaos and cella. 3) The so-called Big Frieze is attested by eighteen fragments; though it also belonged to the Polykratean Heraion, it may have been carved during the first third of the Fifth century. Its original location is thoroughly hypothetical: the exterior of the cella? In all three friezes, as far as one can tell from existing fragments, subject matter was highly varied, including figures probably divine, people reclining on couches, monsters, horses, and other animals, in a sequence now impossible to recover.

What is more important is that each Samian frieze consisted of several wall courses rather than of single slabs, with a technique already noted for the scratched warriors of

[19] Note the Knielauf pose, so awkwardly rendered in the earlier Gorgon that her raised left knee can escape attention. In the later Gorgon the mantle tip almost completely hides her bent right leg, perhaps as a subtle concealment of the embarrassing pose. The four wings on each Gorgon are of Oriental inspiration. Though the two extant reliefs were obviously meant as matching figures, details vary. Besides the drapery, the later Gorgon's proportions are better than the other's, although her increased height forced the sculptor to carve her head on the molding surmounting the architrave. Or was this his way to integrate various parts of the building and provide them with additional symbolic protection? Cf. the Medusa at Corfu. The mantles of the Didyma Gorgons seem under the influence of the International Style, prehaps specifically of the Cyclades. Could Cycladic influence be responsible also for the introduction of the architrave fasciae? See G. Gruben, *Münchener Jahrbuch der bildenden Kunst* 23 (1972) 7–36.

Hekatompedon II. We have previously discussed the metopes from Temple F at Selinus, which were carved from two superimposed blocks, but as many as five horizontal courses can be postulated for the Small Frieze and comparable numbers are surmised for the others. Yet the courses are relatively low and could have been combined or covered by single relief slabs stretching for the entire height (calculated at ca. 1.25 m. on the scale of the figures), as was the case, for instance, for the Peisistratid frieze on the Athenian Akropolis. One must therefore surmise that the several-course format was adopted because of geographical preferences not through technical necessity. Comparison with Egyptian practices is so obvious that it may have influenced Buschor's suggestion (now discarded) that the Small Frieze represented a procession of offering bearers.

Magna Graecia

This same technique has now been noted in an entirely different area: South Italy. Some large reliefs from Parco del Cavallo, presumably the site of ancient Sybaris, had originally been published as metopes, but the discovery of new fragments has shown that they formed part of a continuous frieze. The thick, weight-bearing blocks were found in a secondary context, and their architecture has not yet been determined. They are carved in high relief, with some parts entirely in the round. Certain details were added in metal and the whole was vividly colored, as attested by traces of blue, red, and yellow. To judge from the extant fragments, the frieze was very long, probably extending along all four sides of the building. The subject matter seems varied but remains uncertain; perhaps a procession of gods and a line of dancing women accompanied by a flute-playing girl can be suggested. Two helmets and some hooves may attest to the presence of warriors, perhaps riding chariots or horses. Stylistic comparison with the Siphnian frieze suggests an approximately contemporary date.

Though the Parco del Cavallo reliefs have been hailed as the first example of a continuous frieze in the West, a possible second instance exists at Selinus. Two main slabs remain, with part of a third and fragments from others; they depict fighting warriors in various poses, perhaps from an Amazonomachy. The limbs of some figures extend beyond the margins of the blocks and must have appeared on adjoining slabs, thus suggesting an Ionic rather than a Doric frieze. The reliefs were found in the vicinity of Temple M, but this building seems to have had plain metopes, larger in size than the carved slabs, for which no architectural context can as yet be suggested. A date around 480 is postulated on the basis of alleged Attic influence.

A continuous frieze at Selinus is at present as unusual as one in South Italy, yet we are gradually beginning to see how strong the Ionic component must have been all over Magna Graecia. Parts of Ionic architecture have been found at Megara Hyblaia, from small structures of the second half of the Sixth century, but a whole great Ionic temple has been discovered at Syracuse near the Athenaion/Cathedral. The building seems patterned after the Artemision at Ephesos, though some elements of its columns are closer to the Polykratean temple on Samos. Yet Syracuse should have been the stronghold of the Doric order, given her Corinthian origin. East Greek influences are less surprising in South Italy, but the Ionic porch within the Doric peristyle of the Athenaion at Paestum and the Heraion at Foce del Sele, and the profusion of Ionic moldings and features at both sites remain striking and unpredictable. Even terracotta revetments present a changing picture. It used to be thought that only abstract ornaments but no figured scenes appeared on Magna Graecian architectural terracottas; now excavations at Metapontum and Vaglio are producing examples to the contrary. From the first site come relief plaques attributed to Temple C within the sanctuary of Apollo; one published example represents two people on a cart pulled by two animals and preceded by a man on foot who holds the reins and turns his head to look back.[20] At Vaglio, square terracotta panels with two horsemen flanking two confronted warriors on foot have been interpreted as antepagmenta for wooden beams; but since several were found, a whole series of religious buildings had to be postulated on the vast platform of the sanctuary. It would perhaps be more logical to restore the plaques as a continuous series on a single structure. Their early date (the beginning of the Sixth century) would make them particularly important for the history of terracotta revetments. Finally, among the colorful architectural terracottas attributed to the Paestan Basilica, parts of a corner sima show a draped figure not above but against the background of the painted moldings, as if moving around the corner of the building. Though its head and torso might have stood out against the skyline, the total effect is not that of a traditional akroterion and recalls the Didyma (and the Ephesian ?) Gorgons.[21] These scattered bits of evidence may suggest strong and direct artistic contacts between East Greece and Magna Graecia, which bypass the Greek mainland.

Greece Proper

Aside from Delphi and Athens, Bookidis lists two examples of possible friezes from Greece proper, but in both cases the evidence is highly fragmentary and uncertain. The sites represented are Thessaloniki and Apollonia in Epiros; chronologically both examples should belong at the beginning of the Fifth century. Neither is likely to add greatly to the entire picture of frieze distribution; they fall within the phase of the International Style and occur at sites under definite East Greek influence, especially Thessaloniki and environs, where several Ionic buildings have been found.

Delphi. The earliest continuous friezes on the Greek mainland appear at Delphi, a fact which again indicates the importance of the sanctuary as a point of confluence for various artistic trends. As an architectural course, whether with or without relief decoration,[22] the continuous frieze seems to have made its debut on the entablature of the Knidian Treasury, around 540. It was soon followed by the relief friezes of three Treasuries: the Massiliot (ca. 535–525), the Siphnian (530–525), and the Aeolic (ca. 520). Architecturally, the appearance of the frieze course spells the elimination of the dentils and produces the so-called Attic-Ionic entablature. Dinsmoor has suggested that this definite position

[20] The discovery of a fourth temple, probably Ionic, within the Metapontum temenos, was announced by D. Adamesteanu at the 15th Congress on Magna Graecia, October 5–10, 1975. See *Archeologia* 89 (Dec. 1975) 73–75.

[21] Besides the floral rings carved on the hypotrachelia of the Doric capitals of the Basilica (which recall the anthemion bands of Ionic columns), it has now been observed that some echini of the same temple were engraved with lotus flowers, an addition that increases their resemblance to Ionic forms (*AA* 1972, 438–40).

[22] A fragment of relief, once attributed to the Knidian Treasury, has subsequently been dissociated from that building. See *BCH* 77 (1953) 360 n. 2; Bookidis, 323–24 and 395–98.

within an established architectural order was achieved by the hitherto fluctuating figured frieze when comparison with the taller superstructure of the Doric made the Ionic treasuries seem light at the top without an intermediate course between epistyle and cornice. He found it logical to assume that such an addition should have been made at Delphi, where the two orders met on equal grounds, around the middle of the Sixth century.

Demangel has plausibly claimed that at Delphi the continuous frieze lost its (East Greek) processional quality and turned into a carefully planned composition with definite beginning, middle, and end. This sense of structure within architectural confines may also have been responsible for the epic, narrative content which was henceforth to characterize all mainland friezes. At Delphi, this was quite possible because of the relatively small scale of the buildings adorned with continuous friezes; in addition, the steep terrain allowed several viewpoints, at different levels. Nonetheless, the narrative frieze had to satisfy the same requirements of clarity and intelligibility that had governed its early stages. This was often achieved through repetition of motifs, and even in late Classical times certain set "units" were used again and again—within battle scenes, for instance—to ensure prompt recognition. Furthermore, once the side of a building was established as the area to be filled with only one topic, the frieze carver had to select a theme which could be stretched to the required length without losing its coherence or plausibility. The earlier repetitive patterns of cavalcades or chariot races could be adjusted at will, by simply adding or subtracting units, more or less like the rolling of a cylinder seal which can be stopped or continued at any point. But a legend had a set number of protagonists, and the solution of adding inactive spectators was not always feasible or aesthetically pleasing. Nor did the Greeks seem to like the kind of historical narrative in which the chief actor, or actors, appears at several points within the same sequence, each appearance representing a subsequent moment in time. Whether within the narrower confines of a metope, or the longer expanse of a frieze, the Greeks preferred an encapsulated version of a story, that is, one that could be comprehended at a glance even when this implied the telescoping of some features in both time and space. Thus a significant moment was usually selected for depiction, and the viewer was required to supply antecedents and consequences out of his own personal knowledge.

This unity of time and space in the continuous frieze could only result in choral scenes, mostly great battle themes which allowed unlimited participants, often anonymous. Even the Gigantomachy was somewhat restrictive in this respect since it required the intervention of specific divinities, some more important than others. It is surprising in fact that this topic, so popular for pediments and metopes, should have been used for a frieze only twice in Greek times: on the Siphnian Treasury, around 530, and on the Pergamon Altar, around 180.[23] To my mind, the north frieze of the Siphnian Treasury is the most successful of all battle scenes from a compositional point of view, because it does not break up into obvious duels and links actions and figures across proportionately wide spans. Yet this positive quality could have been detrimental from an architectural point of view had the building not been so small and relatively low. The opposing factions of Gods and Giants are distinguished by the direction of their movement, with few exceptions which emphasize the rule. But are the two streams clearly discernible against the limited, even if vividly blue,

[23] There are, of course, the above-mentioned Archaic friezes whose topic is uncertain, but the statement can be made with some degree of confidence from ca. 500 onward.

background? The composition is strictly planned, with upright figures framing the beginning and the end, and three chariots interspersed with the fighters on foot at specific intervals. Yet the total effect is one of confusion, most realistic and appropriate for a battle but of difficult reading from a distance. A revealing, if anachronistic, comparison with any section of the Mausoleum Amazonomachy (ca. 350) may explain my point more clearly. Note in particular that the Halikarnassos figures are as three-dimensionally conceived as the fighters of the Siphnian frieze: they turn and act in space with a roundness of form and a freedom of movement which are not only comparable to the Archaic rendering but much more sophisticated. It is therefore not a matter of plastic versus pictorial, nor of high versus low or even "flat" relief, but a matter of spacing and pattern which makes the later frieze much more comprehensible at a glance than the earlier example. Given the size and height of the Mausoleum, these two qualities may have been essential for final success.

To be sure, the two sides of the Siphnian frieze carved in flat relief are more legible than the others, but here again it is rhythm and contours which make the difference, rather than the technique per se. Both the west and south sections of the frieze attributed to the so-called Master A employ sharp outlines carried straight back to the background plane, but the front of the figures is highly, if subtly, modeled and fullness of forms is suggested by the curving shapes selected by the sculptor. All overlapping is virtually absent or rendered as stacked and staggered layers with repetitive profiles, an approach totally different from the free superimposition of figures and perspective arrangements attempted by Master B on the east and north sides.

The Siphnian frieze is so well known and so often discussed that very few comments are needed here. Its overwhelming importance for us rests not so much on its artistic value, great though it may be, as on the fact that it is the best dated monument of the whole Archaic Greek period. I am more than ever convinced that Master A was an Ionian, not necessarily a native Siphnian but certainly someone in contact with the Asia Minor centers.[24] His flat relief technique occurs at Ephesos and Karaköy; his processional approach, with scenes that include many horses and chariots, seems deeply rooted in the East Greek tradition of both stone and terracotta "monotonous" friezes. On the west side, his winged Athena (with her winged horses) is a direct descendant of the Oriental Artemis/Kubaba or Great Goddess in general, as we see her on the Dorylaion stele. But I cannot satisfactorily explain Hermes' over-sized, almost Sicilian calves (Fig. 61), exaggerated even within the sphere of influence of Archaic Attic musculature. Nor do I know why Aphrodite's mantle seems to have no crossband whatever, at this late a date: a deliberate Ionic archaism? She is usually described as adjusting her garment or a necklace (Fig. 62), but the straight line crossing over her locks rather suggests that she is busy with the chariot reins, which she pulls with her right hand.[25]

[24] The same conclusion is reached by J. M. Hemelrijk (*BABesch* 38 [1963] 28–51, especially 44–45) on the basis of some ear ornaments which appear on figures of the west and south friezes and are of Cypriot or East Greek origin; they are distinctive because they cap the upper part of the ear rather than hanging from the lobe; see in particular his figs. 26 and 27, since the former includes a drawing of a west frieze fragment now lost.

[25] A further link between East Greek works and the west Siphnian Frieze is the bird perched on the chariot pole of Aphrodite (and perhaps also of Athena); this finds a parallel on a fragment from the Small Samian Frieze (*Samos* XI no. 118). However B. Freyer-Schauenburg rejects a former interpretation of the Heraion bird as a possible chariot ornament.

Aphrodite's action was considered solved by F.

The subject of the south side has never been identified beyond doubt; The Rape of Helen would unite the entire building in an epic sequence of events that go from The Judgment of Paris on the west to the Trojan Battlefield and the Olympians' Assembly on the east facade. But the Rape of the Leukippidai is also a current theory. I am intrigued by the spare horse held by the single naked rider and obviously meant for someone special, as suggested by its wreath or necklace (blue beads?). The naked horseman tries to control him by sitting well forward on his own mount and stretching out his left arm, while holding on to his own reins with the right hand. In his present damaged state, this man looks too thin and disproportionate, but the ridge of his collarbones shows that his upper torso was turned almost frontally, with the right arm bent at a sharp angle and half his chest sliding behind the horse's mane.

I was once convinced that Master B was an Athenian; now I am not so sure. Not only are the plasticity of some of his folds and his penchant for catenaries paralleled in the Ephesos column drum fragments but the specific hairstyle of the seated Gods on the east frieze resembles that of a head from the "Hermes/Aphrodite Frieze" in Samos, especially in the short strands in front of the ear. Drapery parallels can also be established between another fragment from the same temple group and the work of Master B. Note in addition the unusual rippling of Leto's skirt on the east Assembly of the Gods. Perhaps the solution to this stylistic mixture has been found by Jeffery, who tried to integrate the signature on the Giant's shield (N. side) as "Aristion of Paros." The reliefs would then be the work of a sculptor from the Cyclades who seems to have spent a good deal of his active career in Athens.

One minor point, on variety. Scholars have often commented on the great number of forms which Master B employed on the north side for the warriors' helmets, some of them so fanciful that they can hardly have corresponded to real armor. A similar variety exists in costumes, especially female. Note in particular the peplos with the "canonical" overfold worn by the first Goddess from the left (behind Hephaistos' bellows), the long animal skin over Cybele's chiton, the peculiar smooth garment which Artemis has tied around her waist (another animal skin? but then it is not fastened by knotting the paws), and finally the mantle of Athena. Though she seems at first glance to be wearing the standard diagonal himation pinned along the right arm (Fig. 63), a second edge from the same garment, running parallel to the first and crossing just below her left knee, shows that she must have doubled the cloth, perhaps to ensure greatest freedom of movement in combat.

The Siphnian Treasury must have had, on architectural sculpture, somewhat the same impact that the Geneleos group seems to have had on statuary in the round. Granted that the present picture may be marred by incomplete or missing evidence, no other major mainland building is known to have had an earlier frieze or a more developed example; as far as we can tell, the Siphnian reliefs are the ultimate inspiration behind the Hephaisteion and the Parthenon. The Magna Graecian friezes are either later or, if contemporary, more directly in the tradition of the multi-subject Ionic prototypes, as far as one can judge from their very fragmentary state. It is important to note that the Delphic Treasury was distyle in antis, with Karyatids instead of columns; thus the continuous band of reliefs

---

Courby (*RA* 1911:1, 212–16), who defended the necklace interpretation. But I believe that a thorough reexamination of figures and chariots on the west frieze is in order.

ran largely above solid walls, like a ribbon encircling a box. When the figured frieze appeared over columns, a more strict correlation between sculpture and architecture had to be sought, especially in terms of apparent weight distribution. Except for this last step, however, the Ionic frieze had already found its most complete expression at Delphi around 530.

The Peisistratid Temple. Later in time, presumably between 525 and 510, Athens may also have acquired its first and only attested Archaic frieze.[26] As preserved at present, it consists of one almost complete slab and five fragments with figures in low relief. The dimensions are derived from the major piece and amount to a frieze of considerable size, since the single block is 1.21 m. high and 1.08 m. long. It depicts a charioteer mounting his chariot; of the four horses just the tails and two hind legs appear on the same slab, therefore the relief continued for at least one more block. Furthermore, one of the fragments assigned to the same monument on the basis of marble and style is a corner block, thus showing that the frieze extended over more than one side. Though not all attributed fragments may in fact belong together, it is safe to restore a continuous frieze of some length and size, which included a chariot scene and some seated figures, one of them at least on a campstool. These are the same ingredients to be found in the Siphnian Treasury, and indeed in almost all Archaic friezes as preserved at present; however, they are also found in the Parthenon frieze, and it has been suggested that these Akropolis reliefs represent an Archaic predecessor of Pheidias' Panathenaic procession, on the Peisistratid Temple.

This is an attractive hypothesis, with much to recommend it. As far as is known, the various fragments were found in non-Archaic contexts, and therefore were not buried with the Persian debris. It seems, however, probable that at least part of the Peisistratid Temple was repaired to house the venerable cult image of Athena and that it continued to stand for some time, thus forcing the Erechtheion architect to make specific adjustments in the plan of his building. If, as the shallow depth of its porches suggests, they were Ionic prostyle, the Peisistratid Temple could easily have had a continuous Ionic frieze running either around the entire perimeter of the cella building or over the porches only. Stripped of its Doric peristyle and patched up only at the rear, the surviving ruin might easily have given the Erechtheion architect inspiration for his own Ionic building with prostyle facades, surrounded by a continuous figured frieze. In his turn, at an earlier date, Pheidias may have decided to adopt the same processional theme on a continuous frieze over the equally prostyle, if Doric, porches of the Parthenon, in order to create a visual link with the Peisistratid Temple and to suggest a functional sequence, a sort of spiritual succession, for his own building.

Other possible uses for the Archaic reliefs seem less likely. As decoration for a statue base, for an altar, for a temenos wall, they would all be unprecedented in the Sixth century, and inappropriate in scale. The double-T clamps used on the carved slabs attest to their architectural function and correspond to the type employed on the Peisistratid Temple. The marble is the same. Finally, the height of the carved slabs agrees with that of

[26] A series of relief slabs from the Kerameikos, dated ca. 550–540, could theoretically be considered some kind of frieze in the more general sense of the word. But borders on three of their sides, and the possibility of an intervening architectural member overlapping the unframed fourth side, may speak against a continuous arrangement. See Ch. 6, pp. 168, 181.

the exterior Doric frieze of the temple, when a necessary crowning molding is added. As far as we know, no other structure capable of accommodating such a large frieze existed on the Archaic Akropolis. On the other hand, the strong Peisistratid ties with East Greece make the introduction of a continuous frieze in Athens entirely possible. Inspiration from Delphi is a second likelihood.

One major objection to the attribution has been the presumed chronological discrepancy between the reliefs and the pedimental sculpture of the Peisistratid Temple. Yet recent studies have tended to lower the date of the architecture, and a construction span from ca. 520 to 513 or even 510 seems a plausible assumption. I am inclined to date the pedimental Athena shortly after 520, the frieze around 510. This gap in time could easily be explained if the reliefs were carved in situ (as usually advocated for at least some of the Parthenon frieze), as one of the last building activities for the temple. The same conclusion is almost imposed by the sculptures themselves, which cross the joints at random points, not at obvious intervals in the composition. Two more comments on the reliefs as such. The charioteer has been called an Artemis by at least one author, but it should be male. This is shown by both the hairstyle and the drapery. The former is frequently seen on both Late Archaic and Archaistic men, including the bearded and hatted figure from the same frieze; as a fashion, it may have ultimately derived from Assyrian renderings. As for the drapery, the sculptor seems to have made a conscious effort to show that the group of heavy skirt folds originates from the raised thigh and not from the waist of the charioteer. To be sure, he may simply have meant to suggest the bunching up of material created by the movement, but he may also have wanted to dissociate the effect from the standard paryphe of the female costume, which marks the center of the dress. On the charioteer the folds would then represent only the fullness of the garment and a momentary gather rather than an actual and permanent detail of clothing. The second comment is equally concerned with costume: the sleeveless top worn by the bearded man on fragment Akr. 1343. I know of no exact sculptural parallel for this garment, which looks like a knit T-shirt curling at the edges; even Hephaistos' chitoniskos on the north Siphnian Frieze has short sleeves buttoned along the upper arms. Somewhat comparable renderings in vase painting belong to figures of action: Perseus, or Hermes, who is perhaps the most plausible identification for the Akropolis relief.

The Cyclades

A single example of a frieze comes from the Cyclades, and has been attributed to a Heroon/tomb for the poet Archilochos in Paros. It consists largely of two long slabs with relief scenes, to which a third, smaller block should perhaps be added. The first piece depicts a typical Funerary Banquet (*Totenmahl*), with a bearded man reclining on a couch. His wife sits on a high throne placed in front of the bed, while a young attendant and a dog stand behind it, near a large dinos on a stand. Various objects carved against the background should be visualized as hanging from a wall in what is therefore an indoors scene. Several parts were attached separately by means of metal pins and are now missing. A raised border runs along the vertical left edge; a similar, though wider, tainia closes the right end of the scene on the second block: a lion attacking a bull. Since this is not a corner block, one cannot visualize the reliefs as part of a canonical frieze course, and there is no assurance that the two were joined together.

The third relief shows the front half of an animal, presumably a cow, facing to the right. The rear half of its body is neither portrayed nor meant to be illusionistically suggested as if the beast were just beginning to walk into the visual field, since the carving tapers to background level shortly before reaching the left edge of the block. It has recently been proposed that this peculiar rendering is meant to convey a vanishing act, as the disappearance of a cow is mentioned in a long inscription connected with the same building. This last block, however, is so much smaller than the other two slabs, that its association with them can only be postulated on a different location within the building, or, at the most, as a plug for a diminutive doorway, somewhat like that cut into the west side of the Harpy Tomb frieze from Xanthos. What position the other two slabs occupied is not easy to reconstruct; their size is comparable to the Siphnian frieze, but an "Attic" entablature on an Ionic building in the Cyclades would be surprising, even at the end of the Sixth century. The obvious Oriental flavor of both scenes, as well as the vertical borders to the slabs and the possible association with a door plug relief would invite reconstruction along the lines of the Lycian pillar tombs, but the tradition for such monuments seems so locally limited as to make the suggestion unlikely. The status-symbol value of the banquet scene and the apotropaic potential of the lion-and-bull motif are well in keeping with the idea of a tomb or a Heroon.

Interestingly enough, another late Archaic relief from the Aegean islands, this time from Kos, may have occupied more than one slab and could perhaps have had funerary purpose. Its subject is peculiar, in that it seems to show a bawdy revel: a flute player performs standing at the foot of a couch on which recline a lyre-holding man and an almost entirely naked woman; a naked ithyphallic male seems to have fallen off the bed and is being assisted by a small boy who stretches his hands toward him. Portions of the fallen man and of the two reclining figures have either broken off or crossed the right-hand edge of the slab into an adjoining block. The preserved left edge has anathyrosis, and metal tenons on the upper surface of the slab may have secured it to other architectural elements. This is perhaps sufficient evidence to exclude a votive purpose for the relief, and to attribute it to a frieze on some kind of funerary structure. To be sure, its subject matter would be somewhat unusual for a grave, but it cannot be said to be common for votive offerings either. Who would dedicate such a symposium scene? The naked woman on the couch, as a professional prostitute? or, if one of the male revelers, which one? On an island sacred to Asklepios one could perhaps assume that a miraculous cure is commemorated by a rather unusual ex-voto, but if the total scene necessitated more than one slab, the complete votive monument is hard to visualize.[27] Perhaps the fallen reveler is dead and the relief depicts the moment of his passing. Or a whole series of blocks included more couches and more revelers, in a sequence comparable to some of the terracotta revetments from Larisa. Certainly a banqueting scene appears on the carved architrave of the Assos temple, though more restrained in colorful detail.[28]

[27] Admittedly, the missing parts of the reclining figures might have simply broken off, and one slab could have contained them when complete. Even the architectural details, such as anathyrosis and metal dowels, could be explained in terms of a separately added frame, but the relatively small size of the panel (H. 0.72 m.) would not seem to require such piecing.

[28] Another parallel, presumably architectural in origin, is a terracotta fragment with a banqueter in high relief. The man leans on his left elbow and turns his head to look toward the right, very much like one of the Assos symposiasts. The piece is generally labeled Sicilian, mid 6th century. It is therefore impossible to tell whether it belonged to a metope or a frieze, but the former hypothesis seems more

Be that as it may, two friezes, somewhat doubtful in their arrangement and interpretation, are meager evidence from the entire group of the Aegean islands. Significantly enough, even if accepted as architectural, these two examples would not have belonged to canonical buildings; and as far as we know, the Ionic temples in Paros and Naxos had no frieze whatever, regardless of position.

Particularly surprising also is the lack of friezes in Euboea, where the early temples of Apollo at Eretria seem to have been under strong Ionic influence. Samos is exceptional in this respect and once again demonstrates its strong ties with Asia Minor. Probably some evidence is missing from other likely sites (Chios,[29] Samothrace, Lesbos) or extant fragments have been misinterpreted. As in the case of the reliefs from Paros and Kos, it is often difficult to distinguish between votive and architectural sculpture, and the flexible nature of the East Greek frieze, away from the strict framework of the Attic/Ionic entablature, makes recognition even more problematic. It is relatively easy to recognize a metope from a votive relief because the carving of the latter tends to be considerably lower—as low, however, as that of many friezes, so that only the presence of enframing borders or a contained composition which does not overflow beyond the boundaries of a single slab can be helpful criteria in making the distinction.

In addition, non-Greek areas under Greek influence, or employing Greek masters, used different building types or decorated structures which the Greeks would have left plain. I have already mentioned the Lycian pillar monuments. Another interesting example from the Akropolis of Xanthos is a decorated terrace wall which the excavators date in the 460's, but which looks Archaic in style and composition. Ten fragmentary slabs show several wild animals, a lion attacking a hind, and two satyrs who seem to be fighting against some beasts. The reliefs would have lined a retaining wall for a terrace on which stood the so-called Building G. Since this latter is considered a Heroon or a tomb, the subject matter of the wall sculptures may have had apotropaic meaning. As far as I know, no Greek parallel exists for such a decorated analemma. On the other hand, some East Greek altars may have had elaborately carved friezes; the so-called Rhoikos altar at the Samian Heraion probably had one, and literary sources speak about the extensive sculptural decoration of the Amyklai "throne" which may have included some continuous frieze. Though located in Lakonia, this anomalous altar/tomb was built by Bathykles of Magnesia.

SUMMARY

The continuous frieze seems to have been an East Greek invention from several sources of inspiration: Phrygian terracotta revetments, comparable renderings in other media, and even Egyptian (or Babylonian) wall ornamentation. On present evidence, stone friezes seem as early as the terracotta examples, but first attempts, perhaps even in wood or as

---

likely in view of the height of the relief and the general Sicilian preferences in architectural sculpture (Metropolitan Museum of Art, New York, Inv. no. 13.227.11; G.M.A. Richter, *Handbook of the Greek Collections* [Cambridge 1953] 30 pl. 19a).

[29] A relief with a rider, from this island, must have belonged to the decoration of a funerary structure because of its close similarity to some plaques from the Athenian Kerameikos. But the relief can hardly be reconstructed as a continuous frieze on present evidence. See Ch. 6, pp. 168, 181.

bronze appliqués, may be missing. Though its origin may have been both functional and decorative, the frieze soon became predominantly ornamental, and its subjects were chosen for their legibility and rhythm, often with symbolic, but usually with minimal narrative content or none at all. Within Asia Minor (and Samos) the Archaic frieze never acquired a fixed or exclusive position, but was employed around column drums, at the bottom or top of cella walls, along the walls themselves, as part of the epistyle (both Doric and Ionic), or at the edges of roofs as parapets and simas. The same flexibility probably existed in Magna Graecia, which could have received the frieze directly from Asia Minor, perhaps specifically from Samos, as suggested by the many-courses technique. The Greeks in Italy may have known the continuous frieze at a fairly early date, not only because of their Etruscan neighbors but because they seem to have applied the same concepts of continuity and the same technique of high relief to their Doric metopes. But only two stone examples are as yet known, one (rather late) from Sicily and a relatively early one from South Italy, so that this form of architectural sculpture may never have been very popular on Magna Graecian territory. As far as one can judge, its subject matter remained mixed, at least at Sybaris.

By contrast, when the continuous frieze reached the Greek mainland, it probably acquired at once fixed position within the Ionic entablature, definite compositional structure and highly narrative content. At first made possible by the relatively small size of the decorated buildings, this thematic and structural coherence became a definite requirement of all subsequent Ionic friezes. Yet, even in Classical times, the continuous frieze seems to have had limited distribution in Greece proper, with the notable exception of Athens and her interest in the Ionic order. The Akropolis may have had its first continuous frieze as early as ca. 515–510, on the porches of the Peisistratid Temple.

Though evidence is insufficient for sound judgment, East Greek colonies and the Cyclades seem to have accepted the stone frieze with reluctance. This is especially true for the islands, which may have used the form, if at all, for funerary structures rather than for temples. Friezes in the form of terracotta revetments may have enjoyed somewhat wider distribution.

A brief overview of Archaic Greek architectural sculpture as a whole shows definite regional trends, each major area seemingly having strong preferences of its own.

1. Pedimental sculpture, though possibly inspired by Oriental prototypes, had its widest acceptance on the *Greek mainland*. The many-figured pediments in high relief or entirely in the round are a Mainland monopoly. Sicily used large Gorgoneion plaques in the center of the gables, and South Italy conceived the tympanon space in different ways. Only one or possibly two decorated pediments are known from Asia Minor (Larisa and Kebren) but in terracotta and late. Cycladic Kea may have an example after 500.

2. Decorated metopes may have existed on the Greek mainland, but as painted panels or metal appliqués. The idea of relief metopes, with subject matter carrying over more than one panel, may have originated in certain *Magna Graecian* sites under crosscurrents from Greece and Asia Minor. Certainly those Italian sites seem to have experimented a great deal in their metopal decoration, not only in terms of distribution and composition but also of technique and media. The only terracotta relief metopes known at present come from Sicily and South Italy. Despite the vast production, the number of Magna

Graecian sites using carved metopes remains somewhat limited. From Magna Graecia the carved metope spread to Delphi (and Corfu) but was not accepted in Greece proper until Classical times. In Asia Minor carved metopes occur only on the Assos temple, perhaps as an extension of the carved architrave.

3. Continuous friezes, under Oriental inspiration, predominated in *Asia Minor*, at various positions on a building. Only two examples are known from Magna Graecia. In Greece proper, friezes are attested at Delphi with one example at Athens.

4. Akroterial sculpture is perhaps the only form of architectural decoration unanimously accepted by the Greek world. No meaningful pattern of chronological precedence or distribution can at present be detected for abstract or anthropomorphic types, though regional variants of limited popularity are attested at least for Sicily. This may be the only form of architectural sculpture used on Cycladic temples, if the Delian Nike is indeed a lateral akroterion. It would seem otherwise that the Cyclades, so prominent in the production of freestanding statuary, entirely avoided the traditional forms of architectural embellishment. On present evidence, only at Delphi do all known types occur in combination: carved pediments, metopes, friezes, and figured akroteria.

Figural antefixes or water-spouts, because of the requirements of mass production, cannot be considered within this study, though it would be interesting to correlate them with other forms of architectural sculpture.

FOR PAGE 253

My main source of information is again Bookidis. In general, see P. Demangel, *La Frise Ionique* (Paris 1932); cf. also *EAA* s.v. *Fregio* (H. Kähler). My own views on the development of the Greek frieze are expressed in ampler form in *Hesperia* 35 (1966) 188–204. For all East Greek architectural terracottas, see Åkerström.

FOR PAGE 254

For Phrygian architectural terracottas, see Cummer, esp. 42–43 for tentative chronology. For the Phrygian rock-cut facades, see supra, 188 and 219.

Etruscan terracottas decorated on underside: Ch. 7 n. 14. See the Murlo reconstruction in the Siena Museum: *AJA* 78 (1974) pl. 55: 2–3; *Archaeology* 27 (1974) 133; cf. also *Poggio Civitate*, 37–41 (lateral sima) and *AJA* 78 (1974) 267 and ill. 1. Since terracotta akroteria and other architectural revetments have been found at Murlo in the strata of the earlier building (before 650), Greek inspiration for these Etruscan practices seems untenable, and direct contact with the Orient should be postulated if not native Italian tradition; cf. the comments by Phillips in *AJA* 78 (1974) (275–77). For Murlo in general, *JHS ArchR* 20 (1974) 56–57; *EAA* Suppl. s.v. *Poggio Civitate* (Phillips).

For a review of Åkerström, see N. Bookidis, *AJA* 72 (1968) 81–82.

FOR PAGE 255

Düver: Cummer; see especially his nn. 3–4 for reference to publications of the griffin-rider plaques which have found their illicit way into many European and American collections; only fragments, and most of the non-figural material is in the Burdur museum.

Pazarli: H. Kosay, *Les Fouilles de Pazarli* (Ankara 1941) especially the reconstruction on pl. 40.

For examples of "incongruous" scenes, see "Frieze," 190 and nn. 9–11.

FOR PAGE 256

On dentate terracotta plaques, see "Frieze," 190 nn. 13–14. On the use of bronze in architecture, cf. supra, 217 and 229 with bibliography; also Mallwitz, 89–91; some bronze moldings are on display in the Olympia museum.

Block from the Samian Heraion: *Samos* XI no. 103 pl. 77; with previous bibliography.

FOR PAGE 257

Prinias frieze: Bookidis F 60; L. Pernier, *ASAtene* 1 (1914) 18–111; Davaras, 55 no. 24, with bibliography; cf. also I. Beyer, as quoted in *Isthmia* I, 35 n. 32 (course at foot of wall). Bookidis' observation on p. 272. The parapet theory originated with Dinsmoor, 46–47. For the seated statues connected with the building, see supra, 122, 144.

Relief from Khania: Davaras, 12 fig. 8; 53 no. 9 with bibliography; Boardman, 70 fig. 19a.

FOR PAGE 258

Larisa terracottas: Åkerström, 45–66; Bookidis F 83.

Phokaia: E. Akurgal, *AJA* 66 (1962) pl. 101 figs. 24–25; Bookidis F 84, especially pp. 374–75; the same observation is made by Åkerström, 34.

FOR PAGE 259

Myus frieze: Tuchelt L 41; Blümel, no. 65 figs. 193–211; H. Weber, *IstMitt* 15 (1965) 63–64 pl. 29; Bookidis F 69.

Kyzikos: Tuchelt L 73a and L 107; *KAnat* figs. 207–8; E. Akurgal, *AntK* 8 (1965) 99–102 pl. 28; Bookidis F 70.

Karaköy Dance Frieze: Tuchelt K 86 pls. 79–81; Bookidis F 68. On "flat relief" as a technique, see the comments by L. R. Rogers, *Relief Sculpture* (Oxford 1974) 79–81 and 82–83.

FOR PAGE 260

Kyzikos column drum: Tuchelt L 79; *KAnat* 234 figs. 200, 220; *AntK* 8 (1965) 99–101 pl. 28; Bookidis (F 70) whose observations on dowel and dimensions I have quoted.

FOR PAGE 261

Didyma drums: Tuchelt K 75–81, and general comments on pp. 99–100; pls. 72–75; K 81 is the newly found fragment. Reconstruction by G. Gruben: *JdI* 78 (1963) 105–12, 142–47;

Tuchelt, 221–22, adds decoration also to the peristyle columns on facade (K 81). H. P. Laubscher, *Gnomon* 46 (1974) 500–506, questions the attribution of K 81 to the carved column drums.

Anthemion rings under Ionic capitals at Samos: See, e.g., Berve & Gruben, 448 fig. 112; *ibid.*, pl. 114, for the Doric capitals of the Basilica at Paestum; for Lokroi, see Schefold, pl. 265c. More references in H. Wiegarts, *MarbWinckPr* 1968, 53–54; A. Bammer, *Die Architektur des jüngeren Artemision von Ephesos* (Wiesbaden 1972) 23–24 and notes.

Ephesos column drums: Tuchelt L 45–51, L 54, 56–57; L 60–61, 64, 71–77, 80–81; for the Ephesos drum as originally restored in the British Museum, see S. & S., figs. 265–66. On the Ephesos drums and Archaic *columnae caelatae* in general, see also H. Wiegartz, *MarbWinckPr*, 45–48, with comments on the aesthetic and visual effect.

FOR PAGE 262

Sardis shrine: Most recently, Hanfmann, 12 and n. 43 with previous bibliography; cf. Schefold, pl. 333; *Korai* no. 164 figs. 524–27. The most detailed description is in *BASOR* 174 (1964) 39–43 fig. 25; cf. also *Archaeology* 19 (1966) 93 figs. 4–5.

On Cybele-Artemis at Sardis, Hanfmann and J. W. Waldbaum, *Archaeology* 22 (1969) 264–69.

Second naiskos from Sardis: *BASOR* 174 (1964) 42–43 and fig. 27 on p. 44 (so-called South Kore).

Chios monument (Daskalopetra): J. Boardman, *AntJ* 39 (1959) 195–96 fig. 6 pls. 34–35; cf. supra, 199 and 220.

FOR PAGE 263

On Ionic temples: Berve & Gruben, 453 (Rhoikos Temple at Samos), 458–61 (Ephesian Artemision), 464 (Didymaion).

Ephesos parapet: Tuchelt L 58–59, 66bis, 72, 81bis–83, 109–10. The most complete publication of the fragments is still D. G. Hogarth, *British Museum Excavations at Ephesus* (London 1908). See its pl. 18:25 for the "Penelope." Cf. also Bookidis F 61.

FOR PAGE 264

Restoration with corner Gorgons: W. R. Lethaby, *JHS* 37 (1917) 6–7. *Contra*, Tuchelt, 220–21.

Didyma architrave: Tuchelt K 82–84, and general comments on pp. 104–5; the lion's head K 85, with a tenon for insertion, could belong with K 84. For the reconstruction, see pp. 219–21. A continuous frieze of animals is suggested by G. Gruben, *JdI* 78 (1963) 144 n. 113. The question is left open by Tuchelt. On the basis of the diagonal mantle, Herdejürgen dated *both* Gorgons somewhat later than 530 (p. 48 n. 275).

FOR PAGE 265

Samos, frieze from Temple of Aphrodite and Hermes: *Samos* XI nos. 113–15; for position on the building, p. 195. Cf. Bookidis F 63, 287–88. The scale of the figures is between 1.50 and 2 m.

Small Frieze: *Samos* XI nos. 116–27; from the original grouping by Buschor two fragments have been removed (now nos. 158 and 170) and attributed to the larger frieze, because of scale; the present nos. 125–26 have been shifted from the larger to the smaller frieze, for the same reason. No. 127, which Buschor had interpreted as part of a figure carrying a vessel, is now considered a plain block with only natural breaks and unevenness of surface. See in particular the comments on pp. 201–2, for location and interpretation. Cf. also Bookidis F 64 and pp. 290–91.

Large Frieze: *Samos* XI nos. 155–72; nos. 171–72, however, are undecorated. The scale is between life-size and over life-size. For the location, see p. 229. Cf. Bookidis, F 65 and p. 294.

FOR PAGE 266

Parco del Cavallo/Sybaris: P. Zancani Montuoro, *AttiMGrecia* NS 13–14 (1972–73) 62–66 pls. 29–40 and fig. 5 on p. 65.

Selinus frieze: J. Marconi Bovio, *ArchCl* 10 (1958) 55–59 pls. 16–17. On Temple M, see supra, 247, 251.

Ionic architecture at Megara Hyblaia: *EAA* Suppl., s.v. *Megara Hyblaia*; G. Vallet in *Archeologia nella Sicilia Sud-Orientale* (Naples/Syracuse 1973) 164.

Ionic temple in Syracuse: Cf. supra 192, 220.

FOR PAGE 267

Metapontum, Temple C, terracotta plaque: U. Zanotti Bianco, L. von Matt, M. Napoli, *La Magna Grecia* (Siena 1973) pl. XL.

Vaglio: D. Adamesteanu, *RA* 1967, 31–33 figs. 38–40; cf. supra, Ch. 7 n. 38.

Paestum Basilica, "corner akroterion": M. Napoli, *Paestum* (Serie I Documentari, Visioni d'Italia, Istituto Geografico De Agostini, 1970) 27 and fig. 23.

Thessaloniki: Bookidis F 77; G. Bakalakis, *AntK* Beih. 1 (1963) 30–34 pl. 18:7.

Apollonia in Epiros: Bookidis F 78; L. Rey, *Albania* 5 (1935) 47–48 pl. 16; M. Gjødesen, *ActaA* 15 (1944) 183–86.

For the addition of the frieze course to the Ionic buildings at Delphi: Dinsmoor, 139.

FOR PAGE 268

Demangel, *La Frise Ionique*, 367–481, especially 470.

For the Greek telescoping of a story, see Himmelmann-Wildschütz, *Erzählung*; cf. also the review by J. M. Hemelrijk, *Gnomon* 42 (1970) 166–71.

Siphnian Frieze, Delphi: The most extensive publication remains P. de la Coste Messelière, *Au Musée de Delphes* (Paris 1936) 284–436; the composition of all four friezes can be seen in *EAA* Atlas, pls. 158–59. The best illustrations are in *Delphes*, pls. 66–89, with many details; Gigantomachy on pls. 82–89. Cf. also Lullies & Hirmer, pls. 48 (bottom), 50–55.

FOR PAGE 269

On the Mausoleum frieze, see most recently B. Ashmole, *Architect and Sculptor in Classical Greece* (New York 1972).

On the difference between Master A and Master B, see B. S. Ridgway, *BCH* 86 (1962) 24–35, and "Frieze," 197–98.

FOR PAGE 270

Head from the Hermes/Aphrodite frieze: *Samos* XI no. 114 pl. 80.

Drapery fragment from same frieze: *Samos* XI no. 113 pl. 78.

The attribution to Aristion of Paros was made by L. H. Jeffery in a public lecture at Bryn Mawr College on Nov. 16, 1971. M. Guarducci (*Studi Banti* [Rome 1965] 167–76) has integrated the same inscription with the name of Daippos, whom she considers an Athenian.

For other friezes at Delphi too fragmentary for reconstruction or safe attribution, see Bookidis, 337; *FA* 5 (1950) no. 1661; *BCH* 75 (1951) 136 fig. 32, and *BCH* 81 (1957) 706.

FOR PAGE 271

Charioteer frieze, Akr. 1342: Payne, 47 pl. 127; *AMA* no. 474; Brouskari, 68 and discussion of its location on p. 60 (under Akr. 1343, the fragment with "Hermes"). On the general problem, Bookidis F 76. The six fragments assembled by Schrader as part of the same frieze are *AMA* nos. 474–79, with discussion on pp. 391–99. The figure on campstool is *AMA* 478.

FOR PAGE 272

For the lower chronology of the Peisistratid Temple, see Stähler, 101–12 and supra, 205–8.

Charioteer identified as Artemis: Ch. Picard, *L'Acropole. Le plateau supérieur* (1931) 9. For Assyrian prototypes to its hairstyle, see supra, Ch. 2 no. 26 p. 35.

Akr. 1343: Payne, pl. 127:2; *AMA* no. 475; Brouskari, 60.

Archilocheion in Paros: N. Kontoleon, *Charisterion Orlandos* 1 (Athens 1965) 348–418; Hölscher, 31–36; for the cow relief, see *JHS ArchR* (1956) 28, and *BCH* 80 (1956) 334; M. E. Mayo, *Summaries of Papers presented at the 76th General AIA Meeting, Dec. 1974*, p. 14.

FOR PAGE 273

Relief from Kos: Ch. Karouzos, *AthMitt* 77 (1962) 121–29; Berger, 59 and fig. 59; Ph. Della Croce, "An Erotic Relief from Kos, Kos ArchMus. no. 29," unpublished M.A. thesis for Bryn Mawr College, May 1974.

FOR PAGE 274

Xanthos retaining wall: Br. Mus. B 292–98, with three more slabs found in 1950; *FdX* 2 (1963) 49–50 and fig. 28 pl. 33:1; Hölscher, 23–31.

Rhoikos altar frieze: *Samos* XI nos. 106–12, pp. 191–92.

Amyklaion at Sparta: Schefold, pl. 265a pp. 245–46; for additional architectural fragments, see *BCH* 92 (1968) 815–16 figs. 6–9.

PART IV

SCULPTORS AND THE PROBLEMS OF STYLE

CHAPTER 10

Sculptors and Their Workshops

We are so accustomed today to masters signing their works, and to paintings or statuary selling not by their title but by the name of their creator (a Brancusi, a Cézanne, a Degas) that it is natural for us to imagine that this state of affairs might have prevailed at all times. With specific reference to ancient art, two factors may have contributed to our assumption. The art criticism that has survived from antiquity, whether in Roman or in Greek sources, focuses on the great masters and usually consists of lists of names matched by lists of works. In addition, our increased knowledge of Greek vases has reinforced this impression, not only because vase painters and potters signed some of their works from as early as the second half of the Eighth century onward but also because Beazley and his students have encouraged us to expect that most Attic vases can be attributed with some precision to specific painters or to their circle.[1] But can the same expectation be entertained for works of sculpture?

On first consideration, this would seem to be the case. We do in fact have several signatures of ancient sculptors, either on the statue itself or on its base. In addition, compared to statues, vases were much easier and cheaper to make. Though skill and even artistry were expended in their decoration, their very quantity approximated mass production. Breakable and easily replaceable, vases made their appearance in more or less intimate circles, for banquets and private use; when placed in a grave as funerary offering, they were removed from sight and further use. Yet these expendable objects were often signed. How much more important an Archaic statue would seem to have been! Fewer of them were made and fewer people could afford them. They represented a public statement and were set up in highly frequented sanctuaries or cemeteries for everybody to admire. The material itself was often imported or required lengthy technical procedures. Each work was unique, even when it belonged to a general type, since exact copying and piece casting had not yet been perfected. Yet, despite this intrinsic value, few Archaic monuments seem to have been signed, and few masters seem to have been famous in later times.

This state of affairs may have been abetted by the fact that few or no true copies of Archaic works were made in Roman times, and consequently little echo of their fame survived in ancient sources. Our own knowledge of the period is relatively recent, and it seemed for a while destined to remain impersonal. When E. A. Gardner, in 1910, wrote his *Six Greek Sculptors*, the first name he listed was that of Myron. Early masterpieces, as he

[1] This statement does not mean to imply that all, or almost all, Attic vases have been attributed. That many Black-Figure vases, even after Beazley's *ABV* and *Paralipomena*, remain anonymous, has been recently emphasized by several scholars (see, e.g., M. M. Eisman, *AJA* 77 [1973] 448). It should also be stressed that for vases, as for sculpture, the percentage of signed versus unsigned works remains minimal, and that no rule can be derived from the extant signatures. Certainly no strict correlation exists between the quality of the work and the presence or absence of the artist's signature.

indeed called them, were discussed in a previous chapter, but they were mostly architectural sculpture, and no attribution to masters was attempted. Later, in publishing the Martin Lectures (1948), G. Karo could entitle his book *Greek Personality in Archaic Sculpture*, but he referred to regional traits rather than to individuals. And even A. Rumpf could state (in 1938) that for his and the preceding generation Archaic art was largely "art history without artists," but his statement was expressed in the context of a fundamental study trying to determine the activity and style of a Sixth century master, Endoios. Rumpf's work was followed by repeated attempts, both by archaeologists and epigraphists, to identify and attribute signatures and monuments to Archaic sculptors. And in recent years several studies have appeared in rapid succession, especially by German scholars.

METHODS OF APPROACH

Basically, three methods of approach are possible: 1) the collation of extant signatures, with the plausible integration of those fragmentarily preserved; 2) the examination of ancient sources, especially Pliny and Pausanias, for mention of sculptors' names and their activity; 3) the attribution of stylistically related works to sculptors whose names are either known through other signed pieces or can conveniently be derived from the most representative attribution, e.g., the Master of the Peplos Kore, the Master of the Kerameikos Sphinx, and so on. Of these methods the last is obviously the most feasible, given the very high percentage of anonymous extant monuments; it is, however, also the most subjective, and scholars disagree widely in their attributions.

The second method is largely of academic value since very little correspondence exists between literary sources and preserved sculpture. Only one master is at present attested by extant signatures and monuments as well as by mentions in ancient texts, Endoios.[2] Yet the seated Athena from the Akropolis (Akr. 625) is assigned to him purely on the basis of Pausanias' account and the assumption has recently been questioned; none of Endoios' signatures, as we now have them, gives us any indication of his style since they cannot be assuredly connected with extant sculpture. Though numerous attempts have been made in this direction, they rest either on personal interpretation of the sculptor's manner, or on the tentative integration of partly preserved signatures. For instance, the large votive relief dedicated by a potter on the Akropolis (Akr. 1332) has been attributed to Endoios because the fragmentary inscription includes a sculptor's name beginning in En. But numerous other integrations are possible, and none can be proven.

The first method is probably the safest and the only valid one, though it remains sadly limited by the number of our finds and, to a certain extent, by the erratic signing practices of ancient sculptors. I shall therefore begin by analyzing the available evidence, using the first method.

The standard formula for signing, when preserved in its entirety, usually gives a sculptor's name followed by *epoiesen* or, more rarely, by *ergasato*. The dual form of the verb

[2] A second master could be Antenor, but there is still some question whether Akr. Kore 681 really belongs with the base which carries the sculptor's name. The same applies to Gorgias, who signed a column shaft which may have been topped by the Capital Akr. 3850, on which stood a kore (Akr. 611). Kritios and Nesiotes' Tyrannicides fall beyond the Archaic period and are known only through Roman copies. Archermos' authorship of the Delian Nike is still debated.

is employed when more than one master signed the work. In the Archaic period the aorist tense is more frequent than other tenses, though the imperfect may occur at any time. For bronze works distinction between caster and modeller is not made before the Hellenistic period, but then the technician who poured the bronze is identified by *echalkourgese*. In the Sixth century, the sculptor's name may be followed by the patronimic and, at times, by the ethnic, but no rule can be derived from the preserved evidence. In a few rare cases, which will be discussed below, other formulas were employed to indicate authorship, such as "ergon Aristokleos"—a work of Aristokles.

SIGNATURES IN ATHENS AND ATTICA

In general, most extant signatures come from Athens and its territory, though not all masters are Athenians. According to Deyhle (1969) approximately 300 pieces of Archaic sculpture survive from Attica, but only 37 sculptors' signatures, 23 from the Akropolis and 14 from outside. The extant monuments are therefore almost eight times more numerous than the signatures. Further statistics show that the 23 signatures from the Akropolis represent 16 masters, 12 of them known through only one example, while the other 4 sculptors account for the remaining 11 inscriptions. Almost the opposite situation prevails outside the citadel, where only 3 masters are known through a single signature, while 5 additional sculptors are named in the remaining 11 inscriptions. The total number of masters comes to 22, since Endoios' and Philergos' works stood both inside and outside the Akropolis; yet to our knowledge they are the only two sculptors to have enjoyed such range.[3] Deyhle concludes that a certain amount of specialization existed but that Akropolis dedications were often made by sculptors who did not ordinarily live in Athens and therefore received only occasional commissions.[4]

Because of finds since 1969, Deyhle's actual figures can no longer be considered accurate. In particular, Aristokles' signatures have been increased by three possible additions recovered from the Kerameikos. General conclusions, however, are unlikely to change drastically before publication of this book.

Of the sculptors making funerary monuments at least one, Aristion of Paros, was a non-Athenian who received commissions outside of the city proper (Phrasikleia, for Myrrhi-

[3] In tabulated form, these same figures read as follows:

total extant pieces of sculpture from Attica	ca. 300	
total number of signed pieces (Akr. = 23; outside = 14)	37	(= ⅛ of total)
total number of sculptors known from signatures	22	
sculptors who signed on the Akropolis only	14	
sculptors who signed outside only	6	
sculptors who signed both on and outside the Akropolis	2	
sculptors known through a single signature	12	10 = Akr. 2 = outside
sculptors known through more than one signature (Endoios and Philergos have been included in this total, though they signed only once on the Akropolis, and Philergos signed only once outside)	10	4 = Akr. 6 = outside

[4] In an appendix Deyhle includes (Group III) 6 additional sculptors whose activity extended well into the Severe Period and who therefore, strictly speaking, cannot be considered Archaic. They are represented only by signatures on the Akropolis, thus suggesting that the practice of signing might have increased with time. This consideration is not valid, however, for funerary monuments, which decreased sharply in sumptuousness after ca. 490.

nous). On the Akropolis, two foreigners are definitely attested: Archermos of Chios and Kalon of Aegina. In addition, Pythis was probably a non-Athenian, Bion may have come from Miletos, and Gorgias seems to have been a Lakonian trained by a Samian—his Lakonian origin is mentioned by Pliny, his Samian training is deduced from the technique he used to insert a bronze statue on a stone base.[5] Other Akropolis signatures may also suggest non-Attic origin, but even so the picture is obviously slanted and incomplete, since many more actual sculptures on the citadel can be shown to be imports or at least to have been made in non-Attic style. The same could be said for some funerary monuments.

Numbers alone are misleading in other respects. Not all major works were signed, whereas relatively minor dedications carried the maker's name. Thus not all sculptors' signatures from the Akropolis belong to large-scale statuary. Moreover, two masters may have collaborated for a single offering. Aside from the classic example of Kritios and Nesiotes, we also have Philergos who joined Endoios in signing a pillar which may have supported a kore (Akr. 602 ?). What form this collaboration took is hard to understand, especially since the work was a single marble statue and since it is unlikely that the pedestal itself rated a signature. The possibility exists that one master signed exclusively as owner of the workshop which received the commission while the actual carver of the kore would be represented by the second signature. Recently, similar suggestions have been made for signatures accompanied by *epoiesen* and *egrapsen* on vases, and are still being debated.[6] How valid is the assumption in our case?

WORKSHOPS

On first consideration the assumption would seem legitimate, and several scholars, including Deyhle, speak of The Workshop of the Introduction Pediment, The Workshop of the Master of the Brother-and-Sister Stele, and so on. But the notion deserves some discussion. In particular, what do we mean by a workshop? What does a sculptor's name on a monument identify, his own work or a product of his atelier? If workshops existed, did they specialize in funerary versus votive monuments, or did the same people produce both types of sculpture? Is it true that funerary monuments were more frequently signed than dedications, and if so why? In previous chapters I have used the term workshop loosely, whenever school was too strong a word and a definite master was not determinable. But more precise definition is now needed, and I shall begin by analyzing the evidence for the existence of workshops.

[5] During a Seminar at Bryn Mawr College during the Fall of 1971, Jeffery mentioned that there is evidence of strong connections between Samos and early Sparta, whose bronze casters seem to have been taught by Samians. The entire content of this chapter is heavily indebted not only to Jeffery's publications but to her observations in the above-mentioned seminar. Gorgias' ethnic, based on Plin. *HN* 34.49, is debated. See *Dedications*, 502–3. The presence of foreign artists working in Athens is no surprise; we know that Solon granted Athenian citizenship to foreign craftsmen who agreed to settle in Attica with their families, and I have already suggested that Peisistratos may have called consultants from Ionia when the Hekatompedon was to be built. The same situation prevails in vase painting, where masters like Amasis and Lydos are obviously non-Athenians.

[6] Cook (*JHS* 91 [1971] 137–38) made the initial proposal that *epoiesen* stood for the owner of the workshop rather than for the potter. *Contra*, M. Robertson, *JHS* 92 (1972) 180–83. Concurring with additional reasons involving shipment and trade, M. M. Eisman, *JHS* 94 (1974) 172.

EVIDENCE FOR THEIR EXISTENCE

Such evidence could be: 1) the literary sources which speak of masters and pupils; 2) the presence of more than one signature on a single statue; 3) the fact that the same letterer seems to have worked for more than one sculptor; 4) the long technical process which is involved in the completion of a statue, be it in marble or bronze. In the latter medium, the necessity for specific equipment in a more or less permanent arrangement; 5) stylistic similarities among works that could be by different masters. None of these points, however, offers incontrovertible proof.

1. *The Literary sources.* Written so long after the actual events, reports are likely to be confused. For instance, the undoubtedly historical Endoios is said by Pausanias (1.26.4) to have been the pupil of Daidalos, but though an Archaic master with that name probably existed, certainly Pausanias' account telescopes times and conflates different traditions which refer also to the mythological Daidalos. Ideological ties could also exist between sculptors who may never have met. For instance, in the Fourth century Lysippos could say that the Doryphoros had been his master (Cicero, *Brutus* 86), despite the very considerable interval in time between his and Polykleitos' work. At the practical level, however, it is reasonable to believe that fathers taught sons, in a tradition still alive today in several Mediterranean countries. Many families of sculptors are in fact attested by inscriptions for all ancient periods. In particular, we learn of a whole Chian dynasty, starting with Melas, who was followed by his son Mikkiades, his grandson Archermos, and his great-grandsons Boupalos and Athenis, all of them sculptors datable to the Sixth century and Archermos at least confirmed by inscriptions both at Delos and on the Athenian Akropolis. Antenor's father, Eumares, is also epigraphically documented on the citadel; and though Pliny mentions him as a painter, he seems also to have been a sculptor. These examples could be multiplied if later periods were taken into account.

Outside the family sphere, when people of different cities worked together, workshop connections seem a reasonable assumption. I have already mentioned that Gorgias the Spartan may have been trained by a Samian. This observation need not imply the presence of a Samian foundry in Athens or in Sparta, but it certainly presupposes an established workshop somewhere, perhaps even in Samos, where Gorgias could go and learn bronze casting. In addition, Pausanias (1.26.4) calls Endoios an Athenian, and indeed his signed works have been found in Athens. It has, however, been suggested that he was an Ionian, perhaps a Samian, who migrated to Attica and had an established workshop in the city at the time when Philergos and some of his compatriots left Samos after Polykrates' death. Endoios would have taken in the newly arrived sculptor, who therefore became associated with his atelier. The same workshop ties may have connected Kritios and Nesiotes, since the latter's name could in fact be a nickname to suggest his origin from an island.[7]

2. *Double signatures on single works.* Here the evidence can be expanded to include works outside Athens. From the Ptoan sanctuary we have a possible collaboration of Theokydes

[7] Here also many more examples could be adduced if the Severe or the Classical periods were included.

and Akousilos attested by signatures, and Diodorus Siculus (1.98.5–9) tells us how the Samians Telekles and Theodoros made a bronze statue of Apollo together, though one brother was in Samos and the other in Ephesos. The latter case is the easier to accept since each sculptor is said to have made one half of the total statue which was then joined together. Though such a procedure may be unnecessarily complicated, and the anecdote could have been invented to demonstrate Greek adoption of Egyptian methods, such collaboration is theoretically possible and fully explains the double authorship. Similar explanations have been given for the work of Kritios and Nesiotes, which was largely in bronze. It has been suggested, for instance, that one master was the true sculptor, while the other was purely the technician who supervised the casting operation. However, no such theory is applicable to Endoios and Philergos, if they really made kore Akr. 602; one cannot even assume what is possible in later times: that the more skilled master made the head and the lesser sculptor the body, since the Akropolis maiden was all in one piece, and emphasis on portraiture would be unusual in the Sixth century for such a monument.

Can it therefore be assumed that the two masters were the joint owners of a workshop? Or that Endoios signed as the owner, while Philergos signed as the actual maker of the piece? Though similar theories have been advanced for Attic vases, I find it more logical to assume that both sculptors personally worked on the statue, perhaps one of them finishing what the other had started. This form of joint authorship would still imply some kind of workshop situation but would also account for actual performance. At the most, if one subscribes to the hypothesis of Philergos' late arrival on the Athenian scene, one can assume that Endoios promoted this collaboration (and therefore the double signature) to introduce, as it were, his new assistant to the artistic circle. When Philergos had become better known, he signed on his own.

To be sure, so much preliminary cutting and shaping had to be done on a marble statue that one can readily visualize a number of young apprentices being put to work on a block to prepare the ground before the older master tackled it in person. We have, however, no way of knowing how far these apprentices were allowed to go in their preparatory carving or at what stage they became competent enough to finish and sign a statue. It has been suggested that a sculptor's name on a monument might hide the work of a younger and less renowned collaborator. Yet I still tend to believe that the signing of sculpture was too erratic and sporadic to justify such overshadowing; either a master had to put his name on all pieces from his workshop to increase their value, or he might well have allowed each contributor to take either praise or blame. For vases, trading and shipping considerations may have required the signature of the person who assumed responsibility for a given consignment, but no such problem seems to have existed for sculpture, and the simpler solution—one signed for what one made—remains preferable. Therefore, though a double signature probably stands for collaboration, it gives us no assurance of the existence of a workshop, plausible as this may be.

3. *Letterers.* In an important article on inscribed gravestones (see "Gravestones" in Abbreviations), Jeffery has stressed that inscriptions on Archaic Attic grave monuments were cut by letterers with recognizable hands. These letterers seem to have worked for several sculptors and were often responsible for carving even the master's signature. She recognized a total of between six and ten hands, which for convenience's sake she

named after letters of the alphabet. In particular, she observed that Masons A and B worked for the sculptors Phaidimos and Aristion of Paros, Mason C for Aristion and Aristokles. She therefore suggested that Phaidimos, Aristion, and Aristokles may have belonged to a single workshop, which also employed letterers A, B, and C, though possibly at different times.[8] Her suggestion has been accepted and amplified by Deyhle. Both scholars believe that these letterers may have been lesser artists or apprentices who eventually turned into full-fledged sculptors, but it is unlikely that they may have been the masters themselves since the same hand is attested for different masters. Occasionally a sculptor may have carved his own name, since at least in one instance signature and epitaph are written in different handwritings.[9]

Though her article dealt primarily with funerary monuments, Jeffery occasionally commented on Akropolis dedications or other monuments. We therefore learn that Mason E, who may have inscribed Aristion's stele by the sculptor Aristokles, seems also to have worked on the Akropolis, cutting letters for some votive offerings. Mason A, who worked for Phaidimos, may have inscribed the Moschophoros' dedication. The letterer who carved the base with Antenor's signature may be called the Hekatompedon mason, since he wrote also the long inscription on the Hekatompedon metopes. The same man inscribed the Akropolis dedications of Eumares, Antenor's father, and the so-called Marathon epigram, while the second inscription in the rasura of the same base may be by the mason who worked for Kritios and Nesiotes. Thus the often postulated connection between Antenor and the two younger sculptors would find confirmation in the link between their letterers.

One peculiarity emerging from these observations is the apparent specialization of workshops and masons. The sculptors and letterers of funerary monuments seem by and large different from those who worked on the Akropolis dedications, and this is not a question of chronological sequence. For instance, Aristokles was probably a contemporary of Antenor, but Jeffery sees no connection between the two ateliers. The former man worked in marble, and no votive offerings have yet been found with his signature. The latter, as far as we can see, made no funerary monuments and worked primarily in bronze. Since this medium was probably not used for grave monuments, the apparent separation of the two masters may perhaps be a question of technique rather than of specialization. But what is the relationship among their masons? In particular, can we assume that certain letterers specialized in epitaphs and therefore worked only for certain workshops? Or that well-established workshops had their own letterers who did not accept outside commissions?

Though these connections of sculptors and masons seem significant, I wonder whether this evidence is an adequate basis to postulate workshops. Obviously in Athens there was

[8] For instance, the base for the funerary statue of the Karian Tymnes carried Aristokles' name and was lettered by Mason C, who also inscribed the base of a kouros for Aristion of Paros ("Gravestones", nos. 18 and 8 respectively). Mason A cut the bases for a stele and a kore by Phaidimos, and for a kore by Aristion of Paros ("Gravestones" nos. 2, 44, 46 and p. 151). As for Mason B (an "untidy letterer"), he too worked for Aristion of Paros and perhaps for Phaidimos (nos. 8, 49; no. 48). In tabulated form, this reads:

Phaidimos:	Masons A, B		
Aristion:	Masons A, B, C		
Aristokles:	Masons	C, E	

[9] For instance, the epitaph for the base of Xenophantos, which probably supported the equestrian statue in the Kerameikos ("Grabmalbasen," 136–39 no. 8), is by a different hand from the signature of the sculptor Aristokles on the same block. This observation was made by Jeffery during the Bryn Mawr Seminar mentioned in n. 5 above. Cf. also Kleine, 45 and n. 148.

demand for skilled laborers who could carve inscriptions, not so much for statuary as for public documents and official uses, though this demand became really great after the inception of the democracy. Such masons could have hired themselves out at will, without necessarily belonging to a specific sculptural atelier, as may perhaps be shown by the Hekatompedon Mason who worked both for the City and for Antenor. Conversely, Aristion of Paros, Phaidimos, Aristokles, seem to have been important enough masters to have had their own shop, each perhaps with a few minor apprentices and stonecutters to help out with the preliminary work. Itinerant letterers could have been called in, or bases could have been carted out to their stalls, in a city where concentration of all kinds of marble workers in certain specific locations can be taken for granted.

Jeffery has suggested that epitaphs in which stock phrases recur in the same handwriting may have been composed to order in the sculptor's workshop, the buyer supplying only the basic facts. But this explanation remains valid even if we assume that the text was given ready-made to a mason outside the workshop. That specific guidelines were often provided is in fact shown by the Karian script used together with the Greek in the epitaph for Tymnes, which was however carved by the presumably Attic Mason C. Similarly, the funerary monument for the Samian Leanax was inscribed in the Ionic alphabet, after a text possibly supplied by its sculptor Philergos; yet the master's signature itself seems more of a mixture of Ionic and Attic script. Still another example is the Ionic inscription for the son of Kaletor the Teian, perhaps supplied by the family.

Finally, given the many foreign masters who worked for votive offerings on the Akropolis, it is logical to assume that they would turn to local talent to prepare bases and inscriptions. It is less logical to imagine that they would seek it in sculptors' workshops, rather than in masons' stalls.

4. *Technical procedures and equipment.* The same point of foreign artists raises the question of how important the existence of an established workshop was to their performance. Here two possibilities are open: either the master had his headquarters in one specific place, where all his commissions were executed and then shipped out, or he himself traveled and set up shop wherever convenient, using local facilities. In the first instance we would have a rather elaborate set-up, in the second a much simpler arrangement. I tend to favor the second hypothesis.

An often quoted literary source makes a contrast between the practices in the early Roman Empire, when entire cargoes of statues were being peddled from port to port, and the "sculptors of old" who exported only their own hands and tools (Philostratos, *Life of Apollonios of Thyana* 5.20). Though we cannot be sure that the statement applies to the Archaic period, the simpler methods are also likely to have been the earlier.

This question is particularly important with reference to Endoios, who carved at least two Akropolis dedications and two funerary monuments for Athens but is said by the literary sources to have made a wooden statue of Artemis for Ephesos (Plin. *HN* 16.213–14), a wooden statue of Athena Polias for Erythrai in Ionia (and perhaps also two marble groups for the same city) (Paus. 7.5.9), and an ivory statue of Athena Alea for Tegea in Arkadia (Paus. 8.46.1). Did he travel to these distant cities, or did he remain in his Athenian workshop and ship out the finished products? Especially in the case of precious media, like ivory, one assumes that the commissioning city would have required the presence of the sculptor on the spot to avoid possible embezzlement, or even damage to fragile material in transport. The two Ionian commissions could have been carried out before Endoios migrated to Athens (if indeed he was a Samian). But the Arkadian ivory seems to demand a special trip, whether from an Attic or an East Greek workshop.

The answer becomes particularly obvious in the case of architectural sculpture, which had to be carved in situ. To be sure, the so-called Master B of the Siphnian Frieze has been in turn identified with Endoios, an Athenian Daippos, or even Aristion of Paros. Whoever he may have been, he and his collaborators must have traveled to Delphi to work on the Treasury. Even assuming that Master B represented talent on the spot, the Siphnians are bound to have chosen at least one man to uphold their artistic tradition. This is perhaps best shown by the Cycladic appearance of the Siphnian Karyatid and the pithos on her polos.

Yet architectural sculpture raises another important point. The commission of statues for two large gables, such as those of the Peisistratid Temple, or even for the single marble Alkmaionid pediment at Delphi,[10] must have required more than one hand, to ensure completion of the task within a reasonable period of time. Indeed, in some cases, different hands can be detected in the various pieces of sculpture. Yet such large-scale commissions were not a frequent occurrence. When a master was given the task, and probably only then, he set about looking for collaborators as well as apprentices; I find it hard to believe that he always kept such a work force at hand for routine dedications.

Even a foundry, which involved somewhat elaborate technical procedures, could have had temporary quarters, at times set up near the place where the statue was to be erected if we are to believe the evidence of the Hephaisteion in the Fifth century. Whenever a big task required it, a small number of assistants could have joined the master and his sons to ensure the smooth running of the operations. Toward the end of the Archaic period demand for sculpture seems to have increased, and bronze casting seems to have evolved to the point of creating serious competition for marble works. Workshops and foundries may then have become more complex, with men coming from afar to learn the technique. But, given the strong sense of individuality of the Greeks, I imagine that a sculptor broke loose from his apprenticeship as soon as possible unless family connections held him.[11]

[10] As I have already stated in the chapters on architectural sculpture, I agree with Bookidis' suggestion that the pan-Hellenic sanctuaries must have had local stone carvers with a high level of competence, who could either produce minor works for lesser customers, or could hire themselves out to foreign masters who primarily came to supervise the major commissions and produced the models or cartoons from which the local sculptors could draw.

[11] In a recent analysis (*Essays in Memory of K. Lehmann* [Marsyas Suppl. 1, 1964] 323–38) of the famous cup in Berlin by the Foundry Painter, which shows the activities of a bronze workshop, H. A. Thompson has suggested that the two well-dressed spectators, who lean on the staffs while watching the artisans at work, may be the owners of the foundry, ready to leave at the end of the day and properly clothed and attired for the street. If this interpretation is accepted, it would attest to a sharp difference (in status and activity) between the proprietors and the menial workers. On the other hand, another interpretation is possible. The two elegant men are visitors interested in the artistic production, or simply in the company of the masters, as Sokrates is reputed to have been. That at least one of the men may be a visitor has indeed been now mentioned by H. A. Thompson in a lecture touching on all the above points ("The Philosopher in the Marketplace," Abraham Flexner Memorial Lecture presented on May 22, 1975, at the First Annual Conference of the Association of Members of the Institute for Advanced Study; see especially pp. 8–11). To my mind, all the figures engaged in some activity are the actual members of the foundry, and one may even suppose that the two halves of the cup represent two different moments in the casting activities, rather than a series

Dangerous as it may be to make anachronistic comparisons, Michelangelo's example can be instructive in that the Italian sculptor indeed resembled an ancient master in his versatility and his approach to sculpture. Though at first he belonged to a *bottega* to learn painting, and then to a training workshop to learn sculpture, he set up his own studio whenever commissions were given him, traveling to the towns where his work was required, and dismantling his facilities whenever the work was accomplished. The minimal amount of assistance he seems to have had in his carving, and the surprising volume of his total artistic production may be taken into account in trying to gauge ancient practices.

5. *Stylistic similarities.* Michelangelo had a distinctive style of his own, which might have prevented him from having collaborators. This would not have been the case in antiquity, when originality was not only unimportant but not even desirable. Could the basic difficulty we experience in making attributions to specific masters stem from the fact that workshop training eliminated differences or rather produced similarities? Here my answer is bound to be subjective, but the very disagreement existing among scholars in the matter of attributions makes me consider such speculation unsafe. It is perhaps more accurate to speak of influence and imitation than of actual workshop manner, in a period and place where contacts among sculptors must have been promoted by the very nature of artistic demands.

Therefore, in answer to the question whether the sculptor's signature identifies the master or his workshop, I would reply that it identifies the individual master, whose shop was probably simpler than a Renaissance *bottega* and who was presumably helped by his sons and a few *paidia* in charge of routine preliminary work. This basic force was expanded whenever a complex commission required it.

Specialization (Votive versus Funerary)

Whether shop or workshop, were these establishments specialized? Did some sculptors make only funerary monuments, while others produced the Akropolis dedications? It is, to be sure, quite likely that some masters had their shops close to the main cemeteries, not only because of the general location of the workers' quarters in the Kerameikos but also from a good business sense. The same practice prevails today in many Italian towns. In addition, a certain distribution pattern may perhaps be distinguished in the burials themselves, in that several metics and foreigners, including some women, are found to have been buried around the Peiraeus, the Seaward, and the Phaleron Gates. Obviously visitors to Athens who died away from home would be buried with local facilities. It is

---

of events taking place simultaneously. Note, in fact, that on both side A and side B the two main workers are similarly attired, the sculptor with the "helmet" being consistently naked while his assistant has a garment wrapped around his loins. If this were the case, the entire work force would amount to two main sculptors (perhaps three, if the naked youth with the hammer is a workman rather than a visiting athlete) and two *paidia* (the one behind the furnace being a bit too sizable to be identified with the smaller figure helping the sculptor scrape the large warrior statue). If each side depicts different people, the total work force would amount to seven. To be sure, the small compass of a cup cannot allow too crowded a scene, but certainly more figures could have been added; on the other hand, the total thus reached is in keeping with my idea of an ancient workshop.

perhaps significant that both monuments signed by Endoios (for Nelonides and for Lampito) were found in this general area, suggesting that his shop may not have been far away. People in charge of burying a foreigner could have gone to the section established for foreign graves, would have seen the name of Endoios on existing (and impressive) monuments, and would have automatically thought of giving him the commission, especially if he was conveniently located nearby (perhaps just inside the walls) and, even more, if he was an Ionian himself.

This answer does not mean to suggest that only makers of funerary sculpture had more or less permanent establishments. The same was probably true for other sculptors, and Endoios provides good evidence that the same person could receive both votive and funerary commissions. But perhaps there was a more predictable market in the funerary field, as contrasted with the occasional request for votive sculpture. A grave monument, with its more or less impromptu timing, is likely to have been ordered from whatever local talent was available (which could of course have been considerable), while a foreign master could be called in for the special occasion of a dedication which could choose its own time.[12] On the other hand, we cannot exclude the possibility that Phaidimos, Aristion, and others could, like Endoios, have made sculpture for the Akropolis but without signing it. Masters' signatures do not begin to appear on the citadel until ca. 530, while funerary monuments were already being signed almost thirty years earlier. For instance, Phaidimos' base in New York carries his name around 560, while the almost contemporary Moschophoros, probably lettered by the same Mason A, displays only the dedicant's name. I should therefore attempt to answer the question whether it is correct to assume that funerary monuments were more frequently signed than dedications, and if so why.

On first consideration, the assumption seems incorrect, since Deyhle lists more signatures from the Akropolis than from the rest of Attica (23 versus 14). However, no new evidence has been added to the total from the citadel, nor is likely to be, while at least three more of Aristokles' signatures on grave monuments have been postulated recently, and such numbers are likely to increase. Moreover, what is perhaps more significant is that most of the Akropolis sculptors are known through a single inscription, while the opposite applies to the funerary masters. Aristokles, for instance, has now a total record of 8 signed works.[13] And for the problem under consideration it is the repetition of the name which counts, rather than the appearance of the name per se. With the exception of the two associates, Endoios and Philergos, none of the Akropolis artists is known from the funerary field, yet unsigned dedications are so numerous as to justify the assumption that when a resident sculptor carved a votive monument he did not sign it, relying on local fame. But then, why sign a grave marker? The possibilities may be as follows:

1. Only foreign masters signed on the Akropolis.

This is obviously not true; for instance, Antenor, who signed, was an Athenian. It is usually assumed that when a sculptor's signature is not followed by an ethnic, the man must be a native. That this is not always the case is shown, for example, by Gorgias, who

[12] This argument, of course, is not totally sound since funerary monuments could be erected long after the actual death had occurred, as was probably the case for Kroisos. Conversely, a dedication made as tithe or first-fruits may have followed fairly promptly the lucrative business which motivated it.

[13] Among the artists who signed most frequently on the Akropolis are Gorgias (4 signatures, 2 possible restorations) and Pollias (3 signatures, 3 possible restorations). This information is taken from Deyhle.

was probably a Lakonian but did not so specify in his inscriptions. Should we therefore think that he had set up permanent quarters in Athens? This is a possibility, but Aristion, who probably had a similar establishment, signed as a Parian even when his funerary monuments were for Athens and not for the environs. This may suggest that he was trying to attract foreign commissions, which could more likely be given to another foreigner. But why would he omit to sign altogether if he worked for the Akropolis?

2. The sculptor's signature was usually placed directly on the monument, and was therefore lost in the majority of cases.

This is a possibility, in that some non-Attic statuary was signed this way. But Attic sculptors, as far as we can tell, followed different practices and signed on the base. Perhaps the closest we get to a different way of signing is the stele of Aristion, which carried the name of the deceased on the base, the sculptor's name on the narrow border under the warrior's feet. The loss of the stele would have involved the loss of its maker's name. Note that the total signature reads "ergon Aristokleos," with an unusual emphasis on the actual manufacture of the relief.

3. The dedicant's name had precedence over that of the artist, who therefore remained anonymous.

Since signatures from the Akropolis do exist, this theory is not convincing; moreover, even funerary monuments were a dedication of sorts, since they were usually set up by specific people who were often mentioned in the epitaph (e.g., the stele for Oinanthe, set up by her husband Opsios and her mother Apsynthie; "Stelen," 34–35).

4. To sign one's work on a dedication to the gods was an act of hubris.[14]

This theory could be convincing if no signatures at all were preserved from the Akropolis, but this is not the case. One could perhaps imagine that piety was stronger earlier in the Sixth century, and that this superstitious fear was gradually overcome as the Archaic period drew to a close. It is in fact true that signatures become more numerous with time; but also the number of dedications increases in the last decade of the Sixth and the early Fifth century.

5. It was more profitable to sign a funerary monument which was seen by many than a votive offering which was seen by few.

This is relative of course—in days of festival, masses of visitors must have thronged the Akropolis; but tombs were located along busy arteries of everyday traffic. It is difficult to escape the thought that artists signed as a form of advertisement, to prompt further commissions. If this is the case, then only masters with firmly established shops, rather than itinerant sculptors, could have found it profitable to inscribe their names.

Along these lines one may perhaps explain also the expression: "this too is a work of . . . ." It appears on a base signed by Endoios, which once supported a funerary kouros for Nelonides. On the front face of the base was an incised painting of a seated figure holding a scepter, which was subsequently chiseled out together with the epitaph, for debatable reasons.[15] Presumably the wording may have suggested that Endoios was responsible not

[14] Both the inscription on the north Siphnian Frieze and on the potter's relief have been made illegible by the addition of unnecessary strokes to some letters. A tentative explanation suggests that the master himself may have thus defaced his signature to escape the charge of hubris, but the theory seems unlikely. However other explanations (professional rivalry, political *damnatio memoriae*) seem equally improbable.

[15] For a discussion of the various possibilities, see "Gravestones," 127 no. 19.

only for the sculpture but also for the painting, as some scholars maintain. Raubitschek has pointed out that approximately the same formula had been used on the Siphnian Treasury, to indicate that the same master had carved two adjacent sides (north and east) of the frieze. But another possibility is that Endoios had carved more than one monument in such relatively close proximity that one formula ensured correct attribution to all. In that case, the so-called Ball Players Base and the Hockey Players Base, which were found re-used together with that for Nelonides, could have come from the same family plot and could have supported sculptures by Endoios. However, we now have a base signed by Aristokles which uses the same expression. The block once supported the stele for Oinanthe, and a second base, found re-used in the same stretch of the city wall, is so similar to the first that Willemsen has conjectured that it belonged to Oinanthe's father. However, from remains of letters on the second base, this too seems to have been signed by Aristokles. The expression used on the Oinanthe monument would therefore have been unnecessary, had it referred exclusively to the nearby stele for her father. One could more logically assume that the statement was made in general, without specific connection with other works but as a comprehensive boast of productivity on the part of the sculptor.

Be that as it may, the Attic evidence seems to suggest that a certain element of propaganda was implicit in sculptors' signing practices. But the Athenian picture is unusually rich and basically different from evidence from elsewhere. It is not only that excavation in Athens has been more systematically carried out. Other areas have produced relatively abundant material with much scantier results in terms of sculptors' names. It is perhaps exaggerated to speak of Attic graphomania, but certainly the Athenians seem to have been more inclined to put things in writing than their fellow Greeks.

SIGNATURES OUTSIDE OF ATTICA

The earliest known master's signature comes from Delos and states that Euthykartides the Naxian both made and dedicated his monument. A kouros was supported by a triangular base with a mask at each corner (the head of a lion, a ram, and a gorgon respectively). Base and inscription are usually dated to the second half of the Seventh century, presumably in the last quarter. Thus the monument may have been among the earliest marble sculptures of Archaic Greece, when kouroi were still rare. The dedicant may have been proud of his achievement in a field still open to few, and thus have included mention of workmanship in what was primarily a votive inscription. On the other hand, one could also assume that he dedicated his kouros *because* he was so proud to be a sculptor.

Yet our second example (the signature of [- - - -]otos, whom Ducat considers an Akraiphian since he does not add an ethnic to his name) appears on a limestone statue dedicated to Apollo Ptoios by a second man whose name is only partially preserved. The most recent suggestion dates the inscription (and the statue as well) to ca. 640–620. This means that it is as early as the Delian offering, yet sculptor and dedicant are not the same. One cannot therefore defend the position that in the Seventh century artists signed only their own offerings as part of the dedicatory inscription, and that from this practice developed the Sixth century usage of a sculptor's signature on other people's offerings. Surprisingly enough, the other instances of sculptors' signatures at the Ptoan Sanctuary date from ca. 540–520, almost a century later. Only one sculptor, Akousilos, who was probably another

Akraiphian is attested no less than three times. His signature appears singly, in conjunction with another name (?) of difficult reading (Ptoolamol = Ptoōdamos ?) and together with another master's signature on a dedication by two people. Akousilos, a certain Theokydes, and two other masters form our grand total for the Ptoion, despite the very large number of kouroi preserved from the site. It has been suggested that such kouroi (ca. 120–150 statues) were probably set up on communal bases, sort of vast platforms on the terrace below the Temple of Apollo. In that case, the various inscriptions would have appeared on those platforms. One kouros, however, was inscribed on his thighs; and other dedicatory inscriptions, but without sculptor's signature, are preserved.

Chronologically, after Euthykartides and [- - - -]otos, comes the Argive master who signs the statues of Kleobis and Biton in Delphi (ca. 580–570). His name is preserved only as [- - - -]medes, and has been variously integrated as Agamedes or Polymedes, though the latter form is probably the correct one. The next inscriptions are, to my knowledge, the only ones from Asia Minor sculptors, specifically from Didyma: Terpsikles who signed on a limestone base and Eudemos who wrote his name on the left armrest of one of the Branchidai. Both have been epigraphically dated to the first quarter of the Sixth century.

Finally from Samos we have Geneleos' signature on his famous group, and the name Hortios in a fragmentary inscription to which no monument can be assigned. Note that Geneleos wrote his name along the edge of Phileia's mantle, in a position prominently visible from the front and probably originally enhanced by paint. By contrast, the name of the personage herself is written on a chair's leg, on a recessed plane as compared with the artist's signature. Three more Samian masters, Rhoikos, Telekles and Theodoros, are known only through the literary sources. All the other inscriptions from Samos, and the many sculptures recovered from the Heraion, supply no further information on Samian sculptors.[16]

To round out my survey, I may mention a Domis from Potidaia, who signed at Delphi in the late Sixth century (or later ?), and some fragments of a possible signature in Cycladic alphabet, from Delos. The Chian family of Melas-Mikkiades-Archermos-Boupalos and Athenis is attested by another signature of Archermos in Delos, around 550. The Athenian Diopeithes, who signed on the Akropolis at the end of the Sixth century, signed also at Delphi at the beginning of the Fifth. The Naxian Alxenor put his name on a stele of the man-and-dog type which was found at Orchomenos in Boeotia. In summary form, we have 22 sculptors epigraphically attested in Attica and Athens, one or two who signed in Samos, one Argive and a Potidaian at Delphi, a Chian (who belonged however to a whole family) and a Naxian at Delos, two, possibly four, Boeotians at the Ptoion, a Naxian at Orchomenos, and two Milesians at Didyma. Since this list extends from ca. 640 to approximately 480, a total of 35 sculptors (even 41, if we add those who were mostly active in Athens during the Severe period), seems meager indeed. Obviously many more sculptors worked in this period and did not sign their work.

What is more interesting is that practices seem entirely different in Attica from those elsewhere. All the signatures extant from other sites are on votive offerings. The funerary purpose of some pieces can only be assumed, not proved; nonetheless not even one of the

[16] On the other hand, we seem to have the signatures of two 6th century Samian "tektones," Eurykles and Charmophilos, who erected a bridge and signed it; cf. G. Dunst, *AthMitt* 87 (1972) 124–27 no. 11 pl. 51.

possible candidates has preserved a master's signature. In addition, the sculptors tended to sign on the statues themselves at least as often as on separate bases, especially in East Greek territory. As part of the same "tattooing" tendency one may perhaps consider also the inscription on the shield of a Giant on the north frieze of the Siphnian Treasury. To my knowledge, this is the only example of signed architectural sculpture in the Archaic period. The only other remotely comparable instance occurs in an area which has yielded no sculptors' signatures at all: Magna Graecia. Here two architects (?) signed on the steps of the Temple of Apollo at Syracuse, an event never repeated in Greece proper.[17]

LITERARY SOURCES

To this archaeological evidence one could add that of the literary sources, but not many more names would be gained as a result. The pupils of Daidalos (whether the mythical or the historical master) are perhaps the best known: the Cretans Dipoinos and Skyllis are mentioned by several texts. They in turn taught Tektaios and Angelion, who, according to Pausanias (2.35.5) were the masters of Kalon of Aegina. Since this last name is attested through a signature on the Athenian Akropolis dating from the end of the Archaic period, the sequence of generations could easily go back to the beginning of the Sixth century.

From the literary sources we can learn only that artists traveled, that they worked in several media, and that they made many cult statues or images of divinities. Even assuming that later writers omitted the mention of more "anonymous" pieces in order to concentrate on monuments important chiefly for their religious meaning, there still is a striking discrepancy between the ancient texts and the archaeological finds. We have relatively few images of gods preserved from the Archaic period, and their disappearance cannot be explained entirely on the basis of perishable or precious materials. The Romans may have looted many of these venerable statues for their sacredness rather than for their artistic appeal, but many were still visible in the second century after Christ, when Pausanias visited Greece. Presumably Christian zealots destroyed whatever could be considered a pagan idol, but the present paucity seems remarkable nonetheless, and we may have to re-interpret many of the so-called generic pieces. There is certainly need for a modern study that brings together Archaic statues of divinities found to date.

ATTRIBUTIONS TO SCULPTORS

Whether known through literary sources or from their own signatures, are these sculptors anything but mere names? To this date only four masters are known by their signed works: the Argive (Poly)medes, Geneleos, Aristion of Paros, and Aristokles. The first made

[17] Disagreement exists both on the reading and the dating of this inscription. One version is: "Kleo(me)nes, the son of Knidieidas (?) made (the temple) to Apollo, and Epikles the columns, beautiful works," (Berve & Gruben, 416). Another version has: ". . . Epikles son of Tyletas finished it, beautiful works!" The dates oscillate between the beginning and the third quarter of the 6th century. For a discussion of various opinions see *Local Scripts*, 265 and n. 5; see also M. Guarducci, *Epigrafia Greca* 1 (Rome 1967) 343–44 no. 2.

A second possible example of signed architectural sculpture has been called to my attention by one of my readers. A. Furtwängler (*Aegina* [Munich 1906] 325) integrates as *epoi]ese[n* three letters engraved on a fragment of a chariot rail from the pediment of the Temple of Apollo at Eretria. However, another possible integration, given the subject matter, is *Th]ese[us*. Thus the inscription would be a label rather than a signature.

Kleobis and Biton, two of our few Peloponnesian "kouroi." The second carved a six-figured group with statues in different poses and attires, some of them seemingly innovative and likely to have had some impact on contemporary or later sculptors. The third can be associated with Phrasikleia, a complete statue of a not-yet-walking kore. The fourth made Aristion's stele, with a warrior's image. Only the feet survive of another kore which stood on Phile's grave, a signed work of Phaidimos. Other masters and monuments could be connected, but with less certainty: Antenor with Akropolis Kore 681 (cf. Figs. 57–58), Gorgias with Akropolis kore 611, Endoios and Philergos with Akropolis kore 602, Endoios alone with the potter's relief (Akr. 1332) and perhaps the seated Athena (Akr. 625).

Around this core of definite attributions modern scholars have tried to group others, on the basis of stylistic similarities. Polymedes of Argos has been practically ignored, for obvious reasons: his virtual artistic isolation prevents further attributions. Geneleos lived in a much more vital center of Archaic sculpture, but Samian statues were not thoroughly published until recently, and fewer studies have focused on Samian masters. Buschor, Freyer-Schauenburg, and Schmidt agree in noting stylistic affinities between the Geneleos group and the so-called Calf-leader, now re-dubbed Theseus and the Minotaur. The torso of an offering-bearer from Myli, a battered head, and other fragments have also been connected with the master, but the total is meager and the attributions add little to our understanding of Geneleos' range and style.[18] Schmidt has also tried to group other works around the Samos/Istanbul colossus, but the master remains nameless. The same applies to the two talented sculptors who worked for Cheramyes, one making the Hera in the Louvre, the other making the Aphrodite with the Hare in Berlin. One gets the overriding impact of the regional style, distinctively Samian, rather than the style of individual sculptors.

For the other two artists, Aristion and Aristokles, discussion has been lively but agreement relative. Phrasikleia's discovery is fairly recent, therefore previous suggestions were largely based on guesses, general Parian style, the letterer of Aristion's signatures and plinth forms. Kroisos and the seated "Dionysos" have been often mentioned. Now we have a whole statue to work from, but it is not yet officially published; only one hypothesis has been advanced, for the most part orally: that Aristion is also the master who made the Volomandra kouros. Frel writes that the youth found with Phrasikleia may be by the master of the Lyons kore.

Surprisingly enough, even Phaidimos, with only a pair of feet to his name, has attracted a number of attributions, some of them fully convincing because based on a minor detail: the rendering of toenails. Endoios and Antenor, though less certainly represented through their works, have always received the greatest attention. Among the favorite theories is the one that assigns to Endoios the Rampin Horseman, the Peplos Kore, the lion spout from the Peisistratid Temple, and the marble hounds from the Akropolis; some scholars would add the Ephesos column drum (as if it were a real entity) and the north and east sides

[18] Geneleos has actually been credited with many innovations which seem to have had considerable impact on subsequent monuments, both at Samos and elsewhere. On the other hand, our picture of Samian sculpture is still so incomplete that we may be attributing to one person "inventions" which are rather the product of collective experimentation, simply because the intermediate steps are missing. I also hesitate to accept the idea of a "Geneleos' workshop" even though the master obviously did not carve his signed group singlehanded. However, I take his signature to mean that Geneleos himself was responsible for the general conception and the final touches, while his collaborators probably contributed only the preliminary shaping and roughing out, or executed routine details.

of the Siphnian Frieze. Antenor is usually discussed in conjunction with the Alkmaionid pediment, but Deyhle would see his influence also on the Eretria pediment. Some scholars want to identify one of Antenor's tyrannicides in the original of the so-called Webb head.

Many theories have been advanced in recent years, but basically the same pieces are always discussed and variously attributed to the same few known names, with little general agreement. It would be possible to draw up charts and tabulate results, but to no useful end. Moreover each article usually summarizes all pertinent information, with previous positions and bibliography. Each theory has something to recommend it, and I myself am occasionally struck by stylistic similarities. But I fear that definite attributions may at present be impossible. Certainly a great deal of interaction occurred among sculptors, even if not quite as much as that envisaged by Deyhle. In some cases, this interaction might have taken the form of actual collaboration for a large commission; in others, a master sculptor may have trained apprentices, who later may have set up their own shops, and one may have continued as owner when the original master retired. Certainly, as I see it, workshops in the modern sense of the word did not exist, except for a rather anonymous but highly competent working force at the pan-Hellenic sanctuaries or around the cemeteries. Though private enterprise prevailed, some masters may definitely have influenced others within the set limits of current tradition and experimentation. This latter became strongest at the beginning of the Fifth century and was soon to promote the sharp break with the past that ushered in the Severe style. How much this change was due to individuals of genius and sensitivity, and who they were, we may never know.

BIBLIOGRAPHY 10

FOR PAGE 283

The major work on sculptors' signatures remains E. Loewy, *Inschriften griechischer Bildhauer* (1885), though it is now largely outdated. Two sites have been brought up to date by J. Marcadé, who has collected all masters' signatures from Delphi and Delos (*Signatures* 1 and 2). For the Athenian Akropolis, and more specifically for the Archaic period, the main text remains A. E. Raubitschek, *Dedications*. Information on individual artists can be found in U. Thieme and F. Becker, *Künstler-Lexikon* (1907–1950) and, more currently, in *EAA*.

FOR PAGE 284

A. Rumpf, *Crd'A* 3 (1938) 41–48; the quotation is from the last page.

Endoios' Athena: Attribution questioned by Bundgaard, 16.

Potter's relief, Akr. 1332: Payne, 48 pls. 129–30; *AMA* no. 422; Brouskari, 131–32; Berger, 98 fig. 119. For the attribution, see A. E. Raubitschek, *AJA* 46 (1942) 245–53; *Dedications*, no. 70.

On formulas used by signing sculptors, see the still useful articles by J. A. Letronne, *MémAcInscr* 15:2 (1842) 146–59; D. Raoul-Rochette, *MémAcInscr* 17:1 (1847–48) 101–309. On ethnic and demotic, see *Dedications*, 467–78, and *Ptoion*, 449–50 with notes and references.

FOR PAGE 285

New signatures by Aristokles: "Stelen," 34–41.

FOR PAGE 286

Akr. 602: Payne, pl. 60; *AMA* no. 7.

FOR PAGE 287

On the "Chian dynasty," see *Dedications*, 484–87; *EAA* s.v. *Archermos* and *Mikkiades; Signatures* 2, pp. 21–22 and 75; Jeffrey doubts the connection Mikkiades/Archermos: *Local Scripts*, 173 n. 1, 294–95 and n. 1, with discussion on the Nike of Delos.

Eumares: *Dedications*, 498–500; Deyhle, 61.

For Endoios as an Ionian: U. Knigge, *AthMitt* 84 (1969) 86. Cf. also Deyhle, 12–39, and, on the Master of the Peplos Kore, Ch. Tsirivakou-Neumann, *AthMitt* 79 (1964) 114–26.

Double signatures from the Ptoion: *Ptoion*, 379–84, and esp. 381 n. 61; nos. 232–35.

FOR PAGE 288

Kritios and Nesiotes: Kleine, 129–33; S. Brunnsåker, *The Tyrant-Slayers of Kritios and Nesiotes* (new ed., Stockholm 1971) 135–43; *Severe Style*, 79–83; on double signatures, see also *ibid.*, 76–77, add. Paus. 5.23.7; 6.4.4; 6.19.8 (references suggested by L. H. Jeffery).

The suggestion that one sculptor may have finished what another had started can also be found in Deyhle, p. 14.

Euenor's Athena actually carved by young Pheidias: *Dedications*, 497–98.

The most recent work on letterers is S. V. Tracy, *The Lettering of an Athenian Mason* (*Hesperia* Suppl. 15, 1975), especially its Introduction by S. Dow, "The Study of Lettering," with bibliography (pp. xi–xxiii). See also *Dedications*, 436–37. Though not specifically on the Archaic period, cf. S. V. Tracy, *GRBS* 11 (1970) 321–33 and esp. 325–26 nn. 34–35. For technique, see also U. K. Duncan, *BSA* 56 (1961) 185–88.

FOR PAGE 289

On the workshop connections of Aristion, Aristokles, and Phaidimos, see "Gravestones," 152; Deyhle, 50–53.

On Mason E, "Gravestones," 141 no. 52, and seminar comments.

Mason A and Moschophoros: "Gravestones," 118 no. [2]; cf. also *Local Scripts*, 73 (Phrasikleia).

Hekatompedon Inscription: *IG* I^2, 3–4, dated 485/4.

Akropolis dedications by Eumares: *Dedications* nos. 108 and 244; cf. also no. 51.

Marathon epigram: R. Meiggs and D. Lewis, *Greek Historical Inscriptions* (Oxford 1969) 55 no. 26; cf. *Dedications* no. 58. Jeffery noted that the second inscription in the rasura was by the mason of Kritios and Nesiotes. On these masters' connection with Antenor's workshop, see also *Dedications* no. 112.

FOR PAGE 290

Epitaphs composed to order in sculptor's workshop: "Gravestones," 151; cf. also Ch. W. Clairmont, *Gravestone and Epigram* (Mainz 1970) 10.

Epitaph for Tymnes: "Grabmalbasen," 125–29; "Gravestones," 126 no. 18.

Monument for Samian Leanax: U. Knigge, *AthMitt* 84 (1969) 81–85, esp. p. 84.

Inscription for Kaletor the Teian: "Gravestones," 128–29 no. [21]; E. B. Harrison, *Hesperia* 25 (1956) 38–40.

FOR PAGE 291

On the master of the North Siphnian frieze, see supra, 270 and 279. On the pithos on the polos of the Siphnian Karyatid, see Ch. 4 n. 18.

For foundries and the Hephaisteion casting pits, see H. A. Thompson and R. E. Wycherley, *Agora* XIV (1972) 142 n. 125, 145 n. 144, and, in general, 188–90, with comments on 6th century remains. However, Carol Mattusch, who has recently studied the 5th century casting pit in the Hephaisteion precinct, has found no evidence for the making of large statues and questions the traditional interpretation of this casting arrangement.

FOR PAGE 292

On the distribution of Athenian cemeteries, see "Gravestones," 116 and fig. 1. Note also the articles by U. Knigge and G. Schmidt, *AthMitt* 84 (1969) 76–86 and 65–75 respectively.

FOR PAGE 293

Monuments signed by Endoios: "Gravestones," 127 no. 19 (Nelonides) and 130 no. [24] (Lampito).

Phaidimos' base in New York, MM 16.174.6: "Gravestones," 118 no. [2].

Moschophoros' inscription: *Dedications* no. 59.

FOR PAGE 294

Stele of Aristion: *AGA* no. 67 figs. 155–58; "Gravestones," 141 no. 52.

FOR PAGE 295

For the theory that Endoios was responsible for both the sculpture and the painting, see *EAA* s.v. *Endoios*, p. 338 no. 7.

For Raubitschek's comments, see *Dedications*, 492–93.

Ball Players Base and Hockey Players Base: "Gravestones," 127–28 nos. 1 and 2 respectively; for illustrations of the Ball Players Base (Nat.Mus. 3476), see Lullies & Hirmer, pls. 62–65.

For Oinanthe's stele, and that presumably for her father, see "Stelen," 34–35, where the formula is interpreted to refer to other funerary monuments in the immediate vicinity.

Euthykartides' base: Jacob-Felsch, 106 Kat. I:1; *Signatures*, 2, 45.

Limestone statue signed by [- - - -]otos: *Ptoion*, 79 no. 46 (pp. 77–83). See also *Local Scripts*, 92. The statue is illustrated in *Korai* no. 2 figs. 29–30.

For the theory that 7th century artists signed only their own offerings, from which the practice developed to sign those of others, see Homann-Wedeking, 57–63; Tuchelt, 121.

Other signatures at the Ptoion: *Ptoion*, nos. 232–35 pp. 379–85; note the latest reading suggested, p. 381 n. 6.

FOR PAGE 296

Kouroi set up on communal bases: *Ptoion*, 382, 456–57.

Kouros inscribed on thigh: Nat.Mus. 20; *Kouroi*, no. 155 figs. 450–57; *Ptoion*, 355–62 no. 202; cf. also pp. 457–58 (only two inscriptions definitely for kouroi, one on a poros plinth fragment, the other on the thigh of Nat.Mus. 20; five more probably come from kouros bases).

Kleobis and Biton: *Signatures* 1, p. 115; *Local Scripts*, 155. Though it is sometimes suggested that only the sculptor's signature is in Argive but that the rest of the inscription is in Phokian script and dialect, Jeffery stresses that all the writing is contemporary and Argive.

Asia Minor inscriptions: Tuchelt, p. 121 base no. 2; statue by Eudemos: Tuchelt K 46, Br.Mus. B 273.

Samian signatures: G. Schmidt, *AthMitt* 86 (1971) 40 n. 31; G. Dunst, *AthMitt* 87 (1972) 113 no. 4 pl. 49:1.

On Rhoikos, Telekles, and Theodoros, see the possible stemma in R. R. Holloway, *HSCP* 73 (1968) 285, and contrast 284.

Domis from Potidaia: *Signatures* 1, p. 29; for a later date, see *Local Scripts*, 363.

Cycladic signature from Delos: *Signatures* 2, p. 140.

Archermos of Chios: *Signatures* 2, p. 21; see also supra, 287 and bibliography.

Athenian Diopeithes: *Signatures* 1, p. 27.

Alxenor of Naxos: "Man-and-dog," 63 no. 1; Hiller, 177–79, K 11.

FOR PAGE 297

For inscriptions directly on the statues, see also supra, Ch. 3, pp. 53 and 79.

On Daidalos and the Daidalids, see H. Philipp, *Dädalische Kunst*, 5–13; also supra, Ch. 2, pp. 28 and 41.

FOR PAGE 298

Geneleos, the master of the Samos/Istanbul colossus and the Cheramyes master are discussed by G. Schmidt, *AthMitt* 86 (1971) 31–41.

"Theseus and the Minotaur": *Samos* XI no. 64.

Offering-bearer from Myli: *Samos* XI no. 45.

Aristion of Paros: for Phrasikleia, see supra, Ch. 4, p. 91 and bibliography. The latest discussion, to my knowledge, is Ch. W. Clairmont, *AA* 1974, 220–23 no. 1, with further bibliography in the Addendum on p. 237; see also G. Daux, *ArchCl* 25–26 (1973–74) 239–42.

Aristokles: Kleine, 43–46; "Stelen," 34–41; J. Frel, *AA* 1973, 193–200.

On the kouros found with Phrasikleia, J. Frel, *AAA* 6 (1973) 367–69.

Phaidimos: J. Dörig, *AA* 1967, 15–28; see also Deyhle, 46–57.

On Endoios, see especially Rumpf's article, supra, 284 and 300; also 288.

FOR PAGE 299

For the latest on Antenor, see Kleine, 46–61 and supra, Ch. 7.

On Antenor's Tyrannicides and the Webb head, see infra, Ch. 11.

CHAPTER 11

Archaizing; Archaistic; Roman Copies of Archaic Works

THIS last chapter does not purport to be a comprehensive analysis of one of the most difficult areas within the study of ancient sculpture. Rather it attempts, as a concluding note to an investigation of Archaic sculpture, to present some definitions of terms and to establish some guidelines for determining whether or not a work is truly Archaic. My task is made difficult by the fact that clear lines dividing categories are hard to draw, and no agreement exists among scholars in interpreting works of art which may belong to one class or the other. In addition, the end of the Archaic period witnessed the appearance of a style which could be termed Archaistic despite the fact that it falls within the chronological limits accepted for Archaic proper. Finally, even terminology varies from language to language, and established terms mean different things to different people. I shall set down my own understanding of each term, with the warning that my personal interpretation by no means finds general acceptance.

Harrison has correctly pointed out that *archaizing* represents the verb equivalent of the adjective *archaistic* and that it is therefore at least grammatically wrong to use the two terms with different meanings. Yet I find the distinction necessary to express two different concepts and phenomena, and I shall therefore retain the words for lack of better substitutes.

TERMINOLOGY

By *Archaizing* I mean the style of a work of sculpture which belongs clearly and unequivocally to a period later than 480 and which, for all its differences in plastic treatment of drapery and tridimensionality of poses, retains a few formal traits of Archaic style, such as coiffure, pattern of folds, gestures or the like.

Archaistic, on the contrary, are the works in which Archaic traits predominate, and only a few anachronistic details betray the sculptor's knowledge of later styles. Yet, whatever Archaic form is adopted is rendered in exaggerated fashion, with strong emphasis on linear patterns and decorative effects. Archaistic, as a style, reveals that the theoretical principles behind each rendering are no longer felt as valid solutions to technical or conceptual problems, and Archaic patterns are therefore used in a more mechanical and illogical form which often results in obvious mannerisms.

Lingering Archaic occurs when a sculpture is actually executed after 480 but in a coherent Archaic style which includes only few and minor deviations from Archaic practices, not immediately obvious at a glance. From this point of view, Lingering Archaic is almost the stylistic opposite of Archaizing, since the over-all impression given by an Archaizing work is that it is Classical or later, while a statue in Lingering Archaic style seems at first fully Archaic.

Finally, *Roman copies of Archaic works* are accepted as such when their style is completely coherent with Archaic practices, but either their technique or their material speaks for a Roman date. This is perhaps the most controversial category of all, since we often cannot be sure whether we are dealing with a Roman creation in Archaic style (therefore Archaistic), or with an actual reproduction of an earlier work. Even for works in later styles, it is difficult to tell how faithfully the copyist followed his prototype, and enormous range usually exists among replicas of the same recognizable original. In the case of Archaic copies, any deviation introduced by the copyist is likely to be interpreted as a sign that the work is Archaistic, rather than truly Archaic, so that many scholars have asserted that no Archaic statues were ever copied in Roman times. This extreme position has been somewhat modified in recent years, but basic attitudes have not greatly changed.

THE ARCHAISTIC STYLE

To take first the line of least resistance, I shall begin by discussing points on which more or less general agreement has been reached. I shall therefore describe what are usually considered the most distinctive traits of the Archaistic style, and analyze later its possible motivations and chronology.

The Traits

Both Harrison and Herdejürgen have recently focused on Archaistic costume as one of the main features which enable us to determine whether a sculpture was made before or after 480. Since these two authors have described Archaistic dress in detail, only a brief listing of clues need be mentioned here, without discussing the various items of clothing per se.

1. The most popular late Archaic costume, the *short diagonal mantle*, after 480 is usually *fastened over the shoulder only*, rather than along the entire arm.[1]

2. *The "ruffle" of the diagonal mantle* no longer looks like part of the material pulled over the crossband but often seems a separate valance, thickly pleated and added *below* the crossband, or in its place, for purely decorative effects.

3. *The long himation with overfold* is introduced. This is at first glance so similar to the short diagonal mantle that one has to note the length of the lower part to realize that the upper edge, at mid body, simply marks the end of the overfold. The diagonal draping, which actually represents the point where the mantle is folded double, is ornamented by an illogical ruffle, so that the similarity with the true Archaic rendering is made even greater. This long himation too is pinned over only one shoulder, and it is always worn with a chiton underneath.

4. The chiton often has a *smooth border* not only along the neckline, which is a good Archaic fashion, but also at the hem and at the edge of the sleeves (Fig. 64).

5. The crinkly folds of the chiton indicate *texture*, rather than gathers, so that at times such wavy lines can occur *over* larger folds plastically rendered. Different ways of carving the chiton are introduced.

[1] This rendering occurs on a Nike from the Akropolis (Akr. 694 supra, Ch. 4, 113) which is usually considered one of the akroteria of the Peisistratid temple. However, the statue shows traces of extensive repair, so that the present fastening of the mantle is probably the result of alterations made to the figure after it was damaged during the Persian invasion. See Herdejürgen, 67.

6. The *peplos* worn in Archaistic fashion is belted over the overfold in such a way that the edge of the latter can form a central swallowtail or even two. The swags on either side of the central pleat tend to swing out. The rendering can be distinguished from the more common diagonal himation (either the short version, or the overfold of the long) by the fact that the swallowtail pattern starts *below* the belt and that the costume is pinned over *both* shoulders. This peplos is usually worn over a chiton.

7. *Skirts*, whether lifted or hanging straight, are often bisected by a *heavy central pleat*, while catenaries appear on either side of it, over the legs, sometimes accompanied by thick vertical folds which form the outer contours of the skirt.

8. *Scarf-like shawls* are often worn, their tips emphasized and usually bifurcated. In general, each tip or edge of costume tends to be marked by sharp zigzags.

Speaking now in more general terms, we can stress the over-all liveliness of Archaistic drapery. When the style is at its most obvious, garments have a windblown appearance which makes them stand away from the bodies, often going in opposite directions as if caught in a swirling motion. Particularly in reliefs, drapery is treated as transparent over the often muscular and projecting bodies, and is virtually flattened in very low relief against the background as soon as it leaves the figure. Whenever a mantle swag or the hem of a skirt swings free, it describes a scimitar-like curve with the virtual rigidity of metal. This impression is heightened by the serrated zigzags of the edges, which revert to the early Archaic straight lines, rather than to the late Archaic double-curves.

The artificial elegance of this "motion drapery" is reinforced by proportions and poses. Bodies tend to be elongated and waist lines may be high, though some stocky builds do exist. Gestures are overemphasized and affected, made by hands with long thin fingers curving up at the tips.[2] Normal walking poses turn into tiptoe stances which suggest dancing, even when none is involved.

Facial features may give additional dating clues. Hairstyles, for instance, are often revealing. In female figures, the long tresses spreading over the chest are frequently carved as spiral locks. Also forehead curls twist, usually in three rows, and end in tight ringlets with drilled centers (cf. Fig. 69). This rendering, favored for male figures and herms, forms a virtual shelf overhanging the smooth plane of the brow. The loop hairdo, which is a genuine late Archaic fashion, is popular with Archaistic deities, especially male. In general Archaistic coiffures tend to be very elaborate and often illogical, juxtaposing plastic renderings and linear decoration. Eyes often show the upper lid overlapping the lower at the outer corner, and may have inserted pupils in contrasting material. When an Archaistic mouth smiles, it does not describe the upward curve typical of a truly Archaic statue but has a more enigmatic expression, probably caused by the fact that the lips themselves can be straight but curl up at the corners, usually marked by drill holes. Beards, when present, are pointed; bare chins may jut out.

Chronology

These are the most explicit traits of Archaistic style. But was there a gradual elaboration of these stylistic features, or did they appear all at once as a coherent whole? In other

[2] Comparable affectations appear in the vases by the Andokides Painter though his style is genuinely Archaic and as early as ca. 525.

words, what is the chronology of the Archaistic style? Three main theories are current at present.

The first would see Archaistic as the logical evolution from Archaic, without interruption in time (Hauser, Herdejürgen). The second would place the beginning of a continuous Archaistic tradition in the late Fifth century (Harrison). The third would lower this date to ca. 300, limiting the style to two-dimensional manifestations and, in sculpture, to relief (Becatti, Havelock).[3]

This last position was largely determined by an acknowledgment of the strong decorative quality inherent in Archaistic works. Becatti saw them as the invention of Hellenistic designers and painters who around 300 started to produce decadent, if skilled and learned, re-elaborations of Archaic forms for ornamental purposes. The types and compositions thus created had original content, different from the Archaic, of which they could by no means be considered a continuation. The vivacity of the first creations soon became dulled by mechanical repetition in the so-called Neo-Attic workshops, which started producing in terms of commercial art, but, at its inception, Archaistic was a new and coherent style in its own right. As such, it could not have derived from the mannered renderings of the Athena on the obverse of Panathenaic amphoras of the Fourth century, since these vases were shop products, often of inferior artistic quality, which could not have set a style.

Becatti's theory was recently upheld by Havelock, who pointed out that many Archaistic reliefs utilized the same body silhouette for each figure, which could then be varied through the addition of individual costumes and attributes: long drapery for Dionysos, a swinging peplos for Athena, a chlamys for Hermes, and so on. The use of cartoons, cutouts, and pattern books implied by such mechanical repetition seemed to Havelock compatible only with the advanced Hellenistic period, and, in particular, with Neo-Attic workshops, in the wider geographical meaning of the term. She therefore suggested dates in the Second century BC for a number of monuments traditionally placed within the Classical period.

By virtue of their definition, both Becatti and Havelock excluded from their consideration works in the round with comparable stylistic traits, even if made less linear or windblown because of their different technique. Indeed, Becatti considered them Archaizing, and saw this last as a tendency, rather than a style, that intentionally set out to repeat in cold and antiquarian fashion the formal and external appearance of Archaic, not for decorative but for conservative and religious purposes.

Harrison, on the contrary, eliminated any distinction between Archaistic and Archaizing, and could thus consider a much greater body of material in which Archaic features appeared in varying proportion, from actual copies of Archaic originals to Neo-Attic creations. She pointed out that one of the typical Archaistic features, the heavy central fold accompanied by symmetrical catenaries and lateral framing pleats, was a Classical elaboration of an Archaic formula which did not include the side folds. These were added by the modeling tendencies of the late Fifth century, which wanted to emphasize the legs

[3] Willers' book became available to me after the present chapter had been written. The author distinguishes between what he calls "sub-archaic" (my Lingering Archaic) and archaistic sculpture proper. Basically he believes in 5th century Archaistic and argues against Becatti's and Havelock's theories. Like Harrison, Willers seems inclined to believe that certain types of gods and of monuments are more susceptible of archaizing traits than others, but he leaves the question open (p. 69). Though I cannot agree with all examples mentioned by Willers, basically I accept his general premises and conclusions.

through drapery, and were probably transferred to Archaistic art by Alkamenes in his creation of a triple-bodied Hekate. Since no other extant Archaistic sculpture can be securely dated earlier than the late Fifth century, Harrison concluded that the style originated at that time, at least in sculpture in the round. Archaistic votive reliefs may not have started before the middle of the Fourth century but increased in popularity around the last quarter. Some specific mannerisms of the style, such as the swinging tips of the swallowtails in the overfold of the mantle, may however have originated in the world of two-dimensional art, as shown by Red Figure vases of the late Fifth century.

The first theory, which would see the Archaistic style as a continuous development from Archaic, has been recently defended by Herdejürgen, who however limited her enquiry to representations with diagonal mantles. Here too the problem is largely conditioned by terminology since works like the seated goddess from Tarentum, which I would consider a case of Lingering Archaic, she calls Archaistic. In addition, most of her examples for the early Fifth century belong to the sphere of statuettes, and therefore cannot assure us that a comparable production existed in large scale. Finally, Roman copies of possible Fifth century Archaistic prototypes are difficult to assess since Roman sculptors often patterned their own original creations in Archaistic style after post-Archaic rather than true Archaic works. One point indeed she emphasized: that Archaistic sculptures of the Fifth century are difficult to recognize because of their similarity to Archaic proper. Several pieces included in her discussion have in fact been variously dated by other scholars, some to the Hellenistic period, some to the late Sixth century, or at least to the decades before 480.

Most of the discrepancies among supporters of the three chronological theories mentioned above seem to stem from a different use of terminology. I have already defined my own understanding of the terms, and shall now attempt to outline the development of the Archaistic style as I see it. Basically, mine is a position of compromise between the first and second theory, and takes its premises from the belief that Archaistic forms and mannerisms had appeared already in the late Archaic period. I refer in particular to exaggerated gestures, illogical drapery, swinging folds, and decorative elaboration.

Manifestations in the Late Archaic Period

Perhaps the most typical of these mannerisms is what we might call "the multiplication of the swallowtails." This motif had been introduced into Archaic drapery to suggest the gathering of cloth and the layering of concomitant folds. Its most prominent appearance had been as part of the draping of the diagonal mantle, on or near the central axis of a figure. At the height of its popularity, the kore type had only one such swallowtail over the front; the richness of its zigzag edges was often balanced by corresponding zigzags on the swags of cloth hanging from the arm along which the diagonal mantle was fastened, but no true swallowtail was possible there since the material joined along two edges and the two tips fell on either side of the arm. Toward the end of the Sixth century this basic pattern became increasingly elaborate. At times a balancing mass of folds hung from the opposite arm, despite its obvious incongruity in terms of actual clothing. In some cases, minor swallowtails appeared along the arm where the mantle was fastened. Finally, extra swallowtails were introduced over the chest, on either side of the main one. When the skirt was not pulled aside, the central paryphe was terminated high enough over the ankles to produce a swallowtail pattern at hem level.

Some of this elaboration occurs, for instance, on the Leto of the Dodekatheon group from Delos (Athens N.M. 22) where the diagonal mantle forms two sets of stacked folds; but in this Cycladic figure the richness of the total effect is largely obtained through the superimposition of various items of clothing. An even clearer example, because basically simpler, is therefore provided by the central Athena from the west pediment of the Temple of Aphaia at Aegina (ca. 480). Her diagonal himation is treated almost as if it were the overfold of a Classical peplos, ending along a virtually horizontal line accented by three swallowtail patterns. Those masses of folds could be fully understandable, even significant, if they marked the projection of the breasts on a smooth peplos panel, with the consequent gathering of the material away from the body. In a diagonal mantle they make no sense except as decoration, and manage to flatten the torso rather than to increase its tridimensional appearance. The sculptor seems to have experimented with a modeling device which was to find its true expression in the Severe period; here it was rendered within an Archaic costume, in Archaic terms—therefore incongruously.

The large paryphe of the pedimental Athena forms a plausible, if unusual, swallowtail. The lower fragment of a striding akroterial figure found within the Archaic temple of Athena at Karthaia (Keos) shows *two* such patterns, in a more illogical rendering which presumably tried to emphasize the motion as well as the fullness of the skirt. Were it not for its context, the piece could easily be considered Archaistic in its linear and calligraphic appearance.[4] Greater expressiveness within the Archaic idiom seems to lead inevitably to meaningless elaboration.

Somewhat the same problem occurs with a gesture which was aesthetically and technically useful in the Sixth century but was no longer necessary in the Fifth and therefore turned into mannerism: that of a kore pulling her skirt aside. When Archaic sculptors were experimenting with ways of making their female statues appear to walk, this rendering managed to suggest a sufficiently wide skirt for the stepping pose, while at the same time providing a reinforcement for the advanced leg by means of the thickened marble at the gather. The motif could also be exploited to obtain interesting contrasts of patterns: deviations to the course of vertical folds, textural differences between the smoothed and the bunched material, decorative edges of pleats versus straight hem, and so on. In certain areas it was also used to create transparency effects, in that the pulled skirt, adhering to the legs, could conveniently reveal them in outline. But by the end of the Archaic period daily fashions were changing and taste seems to have undergone a comparable change. The motif was no longer necessary to suggest a motion pose which was fully within the sculptor's means of expression, either in a different medium, bronze, or through shifts in balance and manipulation of folds. Therefore the gesture of pulling the skirt aside turned into one of pulling it forward and became gracious and artificial, rather than practical. The material, pulled well away from the body, was stretched into a veritable peak; the farther this peak was held, the thinner it became, and the deeper was the curve described

[4] More plastic but equally over-elaborate is the fragment of a gravestone (?) from the Akropolis (Akr. 1350; Payne, 50 pl. 125:4; *AMA* no. 433; Brouskari, 83) where the chiton hem has 7 omega-folds, if not true swallowtails. The date traditionally assigned to this fragment is 480–470 and the pose is comparable (in reverse) to the girl on the Esquiline stele.

by the cloth between leg and fist. Yet the skirt could not be made unreasonably wide, for reasons of economy and aesthetic balance; therefore the material was made to fall back toward the legs as promptly as possible. The obvious consequence of this treatment of the marble was that many of these tenuous peaks could not withstand pressure and have broken off almost without exception. What the total effect would have been can be either visualized from the extant fragments (Fig. 19), or understood from contemporary reliefs. In the round, the typical example of this mannerism is the otherwise Severe Euthydikos' kore, in relief, the votive plaque Akr. 581 (Athena and the Pig sacrifice: Fig. 66) and Nat. Mus. 36, a possible gravestone.

In a recent discussion, both reliefs have been attributed to an experimenting master of the early Fifth century. Herdejürgen believes that the gravestone is post-Archaic. I am inclined to date the Akropolis ex-voto also after 480 because of its many incongruities. Note for instance the swallowtail below Athena's right arm, an impossible rendering since her diagonal mantle is buttoned along the same arm and cannot form an unbroken expanse capable of a central gather. Indeed, the total appearance of her mantle is peculiar since it does not stretch from chest to arm as in a true Archaic kore, but part of it behaves like a fitted bodice which can cling to the waist and outline the buttock, and it is clearly separate from the mass of material hanging from the arm. In this detail the relief betrays its derivation from a drawing, where the silhouette of the goddess' body could be marked under diaphanous drapery, somewhat like the white-ground vases by the Achilles Painter.[5]

Though this pose is obscured by the break in the relief, note also how high Athena holds her skirt, away and in front of her body and almost level with her pointed breast. The goddess' face has a non-Attic sloping profile and an Ionic eye; her right hand is clenched but her little finger is held straight out, in another mannered gesture. As for the family of worshipers approaching Athena, the break has taken away the upper part of the taller figures, but enough is preserved of the mother to show that the way in which her mantle circles the neck compares fairly closely with the same detail on the Esquiline Stele, definitely later than 480. The sculptor of the Akropolis relief seems to have been somewhat cavalier in his rendering of the mother's garment; it is difficult to separate the mantle's edge at the sleeve from the skirt area, and the long low kolpos of the crinkly chiton seems peculiarly divorced from the rest of the figure.[6]

In the second relief, the panel in the National Museum, the same mannered gesture of pulling the skirt high can be seen in the maiden standing in front of the seated matron. This latter achieves a comparable effect in pulling (presumably) her veil or mantle away from her face (note the vertical lines along her left arm), though the actual motion is difficult to reconstruct at present. Both women have high pointed breasts, though only one

[5] This peculiar rendering of the diagonal mantle has also been noted by von Graeve (*IstMitt* 25 [1975] 63–64) who attributes it to the sculptor's desire to give the impression of a freestanding figure. He too, however, stresses the Archaistic qualities of the relief.

[6] Willers (55–56) believes that the Athena on the relief has been made to look more Archaic than her worshipers in order to emphasize that she is an apparition, the divinity herself in her superhuman quality which finds expression through larger size and hieratic-Archaistic rendering. By the same token, the second relief, in the National Museum, must be votive, according to Willers, who refutes the possibility of a gravestone, not only on chronological grounds (if the date is indeed ca. 490) but also for the Archaistic character of the representation. Since, however, I find *both* figures (the seated matron and the standing girl) equally Archaistic, I am not so sure that divinity is implied, beyond the standard heroization element of funerary art.

per figure is actually shown in the awkward profile poses. Clothes are difficult to define. If the girl is wearing a simple chiton, the diagonal lines across her breast are surprising in their course and texture, different from the wide crinkly sleeves. The matron wears a diagonal himation over the chiton, but the former is pinned only over the shoulder, not along the arm, in a fashion which is usually not found in the Archaic period. The whole mantle is incongruous, however, and the swallowtail lying on the woman's lap is inexplainable in terms of actual draping. Note also the wide smooth band running vertically in the center of her chiton sleeve. The crinkly folds on either side are no longer rendered as originating from the sleeve buttons and are therefore purely an indication of texture, rather than an explanatory motif.[7] Finally, the seated lady must have worn her hair high, as contrasted with the streaming tresses of the maiden, another suggestion that the date of the relief should be lower than 480.

These two reliefs share a calligraphic approach much more in keeping with drawing than with carving yet their total effect is still Archaic, and their mannerisms can be seen as the logical elaboration of earlier stylistic premises. For instance, both panels employ double curves for zigzag edges, even if these occur in somewhat illogical positions. Nonetheless the reliefs are also highly decorative, therefore fully in keeping with one of the main features of Archaistic art. In particular, one of them may help raise the dating for the inception of what may be considered the hallmark of the style: the swinging tips. On the Akropolis plaque, in fact, Athena's mantle swings definitely backwards as it hangs in two swags from her right arm. That this is not an isolated instance is confirmed by two more or less contemporary examples. One is the already mentioned central Athena from the west pediment of the Aphaia temple, even if her free-hanging folds are partially restored. The second, and to my mind the most convincing because irrational, is the Seated Goddess from Tarentum in Berlin.

Though Herdejürgen calls it Archaistic, the statue seems to me a clear case of Lingering Archaic.[8] It is in fact so completely coherent in its total appearance that only prolonged observation reveals the minor asymmetries in its pose, the non-Archaic shape of the sakkos, the diagonal mantle with kolpos, belted at the waist. The frontal view is not especially revealing, but from the side one can see the swinging tips of the shawl hanging from the Goddess' arms and safely drawn back because basically rendered in high relief against the throne. Yet a seated pose, especially if in a cult statue, would hardly justify such movement, even if Demeter's hands held libation bowls.

It is easy to see how such convention may have started in the late Archaic period to convey an increased sense of movement, once the stepping forward pose had lost its novelty and therefore its impact. Vase painters may well have pioneered in this research, in-

[7] Von Graeve (*IshMitt* 25 [1975] 64) gives a different explanation for this arrangement. He believes that the apparent chiton sleeve is instead the normal diagonal mantle fastened along the right arm, with a broad border where the buttons were rendered in paint. The erroneous impression is created by the mass of folds which belong in reality to the rear of the figure and should not have been visible in the side view presented by the relief. Here again, as in the Akropolis relief, the master's intent would have been to recall Archaic freestanding statues, and especially to show the back contour of the seated lady. Though I see von Graeve's point, I still cannot properly visualize the relationship of the folds since, according to his explanation, they should have been hanging from the elbow.

[8] The same position is held by D. Willers (18) who calls the statue "sub-archaic."

troducing the swirling drapery of their frenzied Maenads.[9] Bronze sculptors probably followed, with the freedom granted by their medium but with the restraint imposed by their more conventional subjects. Perhaps the motif originated with a large-scale statue of Athena Promachos, where the battle attitude of the goddess required some suggestion of movement. Indeed, some small bronzes from the Akropolis repeat the trait, though in the more limited fashion dictated perhaps by the strictures of mold-casting a one-piece statuette. It would seem, however, that the practice was well established by the end of the Archaic period, if the above-mentioned marble sculptures reflect it in figures where the trait is either unmotivated (on the Seated Goddess) or made dangerous by the brittle medium (the Aphaia Athena). In later works, the "swinging drapery" motif could turn into mannered decoration, repeating the process outlined above: what had begun as a logical mode of expression was superseded by more successful devices, but was retained for a variety of other reasons and therefore changed into pure and often illogical pattern.

If the two Athenian reliefs can be accepted as Archaistic works of the immediate post-480 period, then we begin to fill the gap, and gradual transition can be more readily accepted. Harrison herself expressed the difficulty of dating non-Roman Archaistic works by placing a question mark after each suggested period in her Catalogue entries. The fragments of Archaistic korai found on the Athenian Akropolis are not dated at all in the official publication, and could theoretically belong to the Fifth century. Since korai had been traditionally offered to Athena, after the Persian destruction worshipers who were accustomed to the "real thing" in Archaic times may have insisted on having the same type of statue to give.[10] In addition, the Severe style seems to have emphasized characterization and to have personalized its creations. An Archaic kore was an anonymous type, while a Severe peplophoros seems to have stood for a specific woman or divinity. The increased humanity and naturalism of Severe statues may have made them seem ill-suited for a generic offering, especially when donated by a man. This could mean that the first Archaistic statues on the Akropolis had little of the flamboyancy which distinguished later products; only slight changes in costume and minor illogicalities in renderings may have revealed the difference, as Herdejürgen claims. Here the line between Archaistic and Lingering Archaic is most difficult to draw, and the two trends perhaps merge in intention and formal expression.

Going down in time documentation becomes more concrete. Aside from the triple-bodied Hekate and the Hermes Propylaios by Alkamenes, which I would consider Archaizing, we have the often cited idols in the Xenokrateia relief in Athens, the Bassai frieze, and the pediments at the Argive Heraion and at Epidauros. The last example is firmly assigned to the early Fourth century; for the other three works, chronology is still debated and at times lowered to the very end of the Fifth or the beginning of the Fourth century, but

[9] The White-ground tondo on a cup by the Brygos Painter (Munich 2645; *ARV*², 371, 15) shows a dancing Maenad with many elements which were to be adopted by the Archaistic style.

[10] A comparable example of religious conservatism for identification purposes can be established with church architecture, which, until a few decades ago, followed set patterns and was modernized only in recent years and always within certain conventional limits. It has however been pointed out to me that, instead of repeating the old types, the Archaistic korai from the Akropolis seem often to have been changed into perirrhanteria and therefore into functional statues. Images of Athena herself may have taken on the prominence as votives enjoyed by the earlier korai.

cannot at any rate precede 425. Absolute dates for Fourth century Archaistic exist in at least two cases. The first is a record relief of the year 356/5, which depicts a Classical Athena approaching an Archaistic Neapolis/Parthenos with spreading overfold. The second is a fragmentary panel from a similar document, this time dated to 321/20, which was found in the Athenian Agora. It shows the lower part of a female figure, probably a goddess (Athena ?), wearing the typical flaring skirt with incurving sides; she is confronted by the snout of a large dolphin, presumably the symbol of some divinity or town. Finally, though chronology cannot be so precisely determined in this case, a developed example of Archaistic style appears on the Frieze of the Dancing Maidens from the Propylon at Samothrace. Though Havelock would place them in the Second century BC, the architectural setting of the reliefs precludes such a late date. A recent study of the slabs restores them above the architrave, on the exterior of the building, under a dentil course which makes the Samothracian propylon the earliest example of such a combination. The suggested date is ca. 340.[11]

Because the frieze is so distinctively Archaistic, it represents a veritable milestone in our understanding of this difficult style. The maidens engaged in a chain dance are obviously part of a ritual, and therefore their Archaistic dresses are meant as an allusion to the venerable past; their poloi remove them from the sphere of common mortals and assimilate them to the Great Goddess. Here we find most of the formal elements of the style: the long mantle with overfold and ruffle, pinned over only one shoulder (which varies according to the direction of the movement); the chiton underneath; the scarf-like shawl with bifurcated ends; the strong axial pleat in the skirt; the tiptoe pose, on rather stilted legs; the thin, elongated proportions of the body. Even the spacing of the figures, the emphasis on repetition with minor variations, the rhythm of the composition, bring us back to the "glorified molding" type of frieze so popular in East Greece during the Sixth century. And this effect is not simply produced by the chain-dance motif; to have a clear understanding of its willfullness, contrast the Samothracian slabs with the mid Hellenistic frieze from Sagalassos, where the same topic is treated in heavy Baroque style.

During the Fourth century, Archaistic sculpture in the round was certainly produced, and indeed it has been claimed that this period is the richest in terms of Archaistic production. But once again, chronology is most difficult to determine without help from external elements, such as architecture or epigraphy. A feature which recalls non-Archaistic renderings may have been introduced at this time: the ruffle of the mantle which passes under both breasts and ends over the arm as if it were a voluminous himation normally wrapped and thrown over the bent left arm for support. In addition, high waists and the general proportions of some figures seem to fit best within this artistic phase; but once Classical prototypes are accepted as a possible source of inspiration, it is hard to tell whether a specific rendering influenced a comparable Archaistic version during the same period or much later. Herdejürgen and Harrison, who have most recently discussed some of the same material, seem at variance in dating some of the key monuments, thus con-

[11] The chronology of many Samothracian buildings has been revised in recent years (see, e.g., J. McCredie, *Papers presented at the 1974 Annual AIA/APA Meeting*, Chicago, p. 24), but the date of the Propylon rests assured, as Professor McCredie kindly confirmed in December 1974 (oral communication). P. W. Lehmann connects the carved frieze with Skopas and suggests that the widely traveled sculptor may have been influenced by Persian renderings, which always retained a "lingering Archaic" style (*Skopas in Samothrace* [Northampton, Mass. 1973] 13).

firming the difficulty of the task. Since a chronological analysis of Archaistic is beyond the scope of this book, suffice it here to stress that the style continued into the Hellenistic and Roman periods, receiving added strength by its infiltration of Neo-Attic workshops and especially of those producing religious art for the Romans.

Reasons for Its Development

This last point brings up the whole complex question of the reasons behind Archaistic art, which obviously cannot receive a single answer. If my assumption is correct, Archaistic began within the Archaic period proper as a symptom of stylistic fatigue. Patterns and motifs were being used beyond their normal life-span, when the theoretical premises behind their existence were no longer accepted or even remembered. To put it in other terms, Archaic formulas, developed to their utmost potential, inevitably resulted in Archaistic. Increased knowledge of anatomy (perhaps through the experiments of the medical schools) and greater skill in the undercutting and modeling of folds, could produce only a multiplication of patterns, with consequent greater artificiality, or could trigger the stylistic revolution of the Severe style, which used its increased knowledge to eliminate and select rather than to add. We now know that the Severe style prevailed, but Archaistic remained as a limited form of expression.

What it expressed after 480 varies according to the period. Obviously in the Classical examples mentioned above, figures distinguished by Archaistic dress were meant either as apparitions or as statues in contrast to other figures meant to represent living beings. We can be sure of this assumption in the case of the Bassai frieze, or at Epidauros, where harassed women are seeking help at the feet of an idol, and basically the same idea may apply to the record reliefs, where statues may stand for a specific city.[12]

In more general terms, and especially for a later period, old-fashioned dress and style stand for antiquity and venerability. As in the late Sixth century the Peplos Kore probably stood for a xoanon in her outmoded attire, so the Archaistic Athenas or other deities stood for the Archaic past in the eyes of the Hellenistic Greeks or the Romans. It has indeed been pointed out that the well-known Archaistic Artemis in Naples was found at Pompeii in a context which clearly revealed the statue as an object of cult beyond the restricted family circle, and certainly not as a piece of garden decoration. It is significant that Archaistic statues, when their origin is known, seem to come from sanctuaries which could claim great antiquity themselves or where an old divinity was worshiped. Several Archaistic korai holding holy water basins have in fact been found at Eleusis, and a fragment of a female figure in this style was recently excavated near the Athenian Eleusinion, close to the Agora. On the Athenian Akropolis itself, these Archaistic creations may have represented statues rather than human beings, but may also have emphasized the antiquity of the tradition of giving korai to Athena. And the Archaistic repertoire was not lim-

[12] This meaning of "statue" must have continued also in Roman times, since a recently found base at Corinth shows, on each of three faces, an Archaistic figure of a deity standing on a platform. This rendering was probably meant to convey that not the divinity itself was represented but its image. (C. K. Williams, *Hesperia* 44 [1975] 23–29 no. 28 pls. 9–10.) Statuary was also implied when Archaistic figures were used as struts or supports for sculptures in Classical or Hellenistic style; the basic concept was to create a striking juxtaposition between the traditional, and antiquated, image of the divinity and its own epiphany in contemporary terms (cf. *Agora* XI, 134–35).

ited to female figures. Aside from the somewhat grotesque Priapi and Dionysoi in Roman collections, we have several examples of Archaistic Apollos or more generic kouroi. An Apollo, which may date from the Fourth century, has been recently excavated in a sanctuary at Halieis, and a kouros-like figure (Dionysos ?) was found in the Athenian Agora. As for the Archaistic dancers on the Samothracian frieze, their connection with the Great Mother Goddess has been repeatedly stressed by various scholars.

Can the same venerability attach to all Archaistic reliefs? The Samothracian frieze is our sole example of this style in a large-scale architectural context, and some of the Neo-Attic products seem more closely related to decorative than to religious art. Certainly a strong desire for elegance and ornamentation forms a definite component of Archaistic style, but, to a certain extent, this consideration applies to genuine Archaic art as well. I am in fact convinced that every Archaic pattern was motivated not only by the need to express an elusive natural feature but also by the wish to express it neatly and decoratively. As Harrison has properly stressed, the artificiality of Archaistic works should not make us overlook the importance of their content and, in most cases, the propagandistic message that old-fashioned forms are meant to convey. When coins, Panathenaic amphoras, tripod bases, votive reliefs and cult images display Archaistic style, their political or religious purpose is to advertise themselves as the latest items in a long and venerable series. Seen in this particular light, it is more than understandable that Archaistic should have flourished particularly under Augustus.

Perhaps the same motivation should be sought even for Archaistic works which seem more narrative than religious in content. A typical example is the so-called Creeping Odysseus in Boston (Fig. 69), which at times has been considered a forgery but which has an unassailable pedigree certificate in a Roman excavation report. The statue was found in September of 1884, at a depth of 12 m., together with other marble fragments and bases, in Regio VI, in the new Sallustine quarters, not too far from a nymphaeum. The Greek hero is obviously shown in the act of stealing toward the Palladion, in the well-known episode of the Trojan war. Such a composition can hardly have been an object of cult in itself, but the distinctive shape of the statue suggests that it may have filled one corner of a small pediment for some kind of shrine. The center of the gable would have been filled by the Palladion itself, obviously rendered as an Archaistic kore, and the other corner may have contained the balancing figure of Diomedes. The subject could have been appropriate for a naiskos of Athena/Minerva or for some other divinity, and the Archaistic style may have earned the stamp of approval of a Roman congregation accustomed to a different form of pedimental decoration. Harrison has suggested that some Archaistic fragments from the Agora may have been Roman repair or replacement figures for Archaic pediments re-erected in later times, but I wonder whether we need postulate survival and repair rather than outright creation.

ROMAN COPIES

This brings us to the problem of Roman copies of Archaic works, as contrasted with Roman creations in Archaistic style. Admittedly, this is a most difficult problem, definitely in need of further study. Since original Archaic sculpture is plentiful, possible Roman copies have been neglected as a source of information or briefly dismissed as Archaistic manifestations. Indeed some scholars could categorically state that no true replicas of Archaic originals ever existed. On the other hand, some recent studies have begun to accumulate possible evidence and, although individual pieces may remain debatable, the general practice should at least be acknowledged, limited though it may have been.

A most convincing example is the unfinished relief of a man leading two horses from the Athenian Agora. Were it not for the measuring points and the tool marks, the work could be taken for Archaic, as one would expect for any accurate replica of an earlier work. Harrison suggests that the Agora relief may have been copied from Greek metalwork, which the Romans may have admired for its own sake rather than for its religious content. She also "demotes" to Archaistic a perirrhanterion kore from the Akropolis (no. 628) considered Archaic by Langlotz and Payne because of its heavy weathering and the pattern of its chiton folds (sets of two shallow furrows separated from the next pair by a thin incised groove) which reoccurs on a definitely Archaistic piece.

Other possible examples are mentioned by Herdejürgen, who seems to imply that no work earlier than ca. 530 was ever copied by the Romans, though such copying increased for works after 500. This, of course, is quite likely since only an advanced Archaic style could have had any appeal for that kind of clientele. She further believes that a number of Roman works copy more or less faithfully the same East Greek prototype and considers most reliable replicas the Guicciardini Kore in Florence (Figs. 67–68) and a headless statue in the Rodin Museum, Paris. Close, but less exact reproductions are the Castelporziano Kore in the Terme Museum and a statue in Munich. The similarity of these collected works is so striking that Herdejürgen's assumption cannot be doubted. What perhaps needs further probing is whether the prototype was indeed Archaic or Archaistic.

That the answer is difficult is shown by the fact that both the Guicciardini and the Castelporziano statues were at some point considered Greek originals, until Bianchi Bandinelli's penetrating analysis pointed out the minor discrepancies which effectively marked them as Roman products. But the question goes beyond the actual date of manufacture. For instance, are the plastically modeled stretch-folds on the skirt the copyist's rendition of a motif which Archaic art rendered with less chiaroscuro and greater linearity, or were they part of a prototype which betrayed the conquests of a later artistic period? Is the swallowtail under the right elbow of the Guicciardini kore the misunderstanding of a copyist who had never seen an actual diagonal mantle, or the intentional elaboration of an Archaistic master who disregarded plausibility in favor of decoration?[13] The same question could be asked of the groove which bisects the central pleat of the himation in the Castelporziano statue since it does not appear in the Guicciardini kore and is multiplied into many grooves in the Munich replica. These variant renderings seem to suggest copyists' improvisations. On the other hand, that Roman antiquarian creations could be copied as much as Greek prototypes is shown by the typical example of the Stephanos Athlete, even if its style imitates the Severe rather than the Archaic.[14]

[13] This detail cannot be verified on the other replicas since the portion of drapery where the swallowtail appears on the Guicciardini kore is broken off and missing in the others.

[14] Note in particular that there exist two more replicas of the Walking Artemis from Pompeii. One of these is in Florence and one in Venice. Yet the Artemis was created in the 1st century BC, even if one scholar has suggested that the type was patterned after an actual Archaic original at Segesta (A. Giuliano, *ArchCl* 5 [1953] 48–54). Other Archaistic works known in multiple copies are, e.g., the Munich Tyche and the Herculaneum Pallas (see *Agora* XI nos. 115 and 124 respectively).

In favor of Archaic originals is J. Dörig, who has specifically reopened the question of Roman copies. His answer is decidedly positive, and he lists several examples. Most of them seem however to belong to the Severe rather than to the late Archaic period proper, and there is certainly no doubt that Severe originals were copied in Roman times. More to the point is the Webb head, which Dörig has recently restudied. He convincingly dates its workmanship to the Flavian period but wants to see in it a replica of the Harmodios by Antenor.

The idea is not new, but this careful analysis points out how heavily restored the Webb head was in modern times, so that an Archaic original may be easier to accept once these disturbing features are understood as recent alterations. However, should the British Museum piece truly be a copy of Antenor's bronze, I would be inclined to think that this latter too was somewhat Archaistic, even if made around 500. Dörig, for instance, seems to attribute to the Flavian copyist the peculiar mannerism of the rosettes which form the forehead curls of the Webb head. But very similar rosettes with wavy contours appear over the forehead of Kore Akr. 682, that controversial piece of undoubtedly Greek sculpture. The kore has been usually dated within the last quarter of the Sixth century. I wonder whether it may be later and already Archaistic, even if technically falling before the 480 deadline. We could then explain her peculiar eyes, her enigmatic mouth, her excessive thinness and elongation, the spiral curls over the chest[15] and that certain mannered and artificial impression that the total statute gives.

Finally, I may mention another Roman copy (possibly also Flavian) because it has been considered a close replica of a specific cult statue, the bronze Apollo Philesios made by Kanachos of Sikyon for the Didyma sanctuary. Here too the original must have belonged around 500, even if definitely before 494 when the site was sacked by the Persians and the Philesios removed to Ecbatana. This Roman copy was found in Rome itself and may have been the object of some veneration. The same pious intent probably inspired a relief of Apollo found in Delos in a building which may have been the seat of a religious fraternity. The sculptor surrounded the replica of an Archaic Apollo, perhaps that by Tektaios and Angelion, with the symbols of other divinities, in a surprising combination of miniscule, attribute-like figures around a major image. These smaller creatures were probably the sculptor's invention, after all sorts of prototypes, but the Apollo looks Archaic, not so much in his awkward stance as in the distinctive, rectangular outline to his fist. This minor work deserves mention as representing, therefore, the other end of the range in the series of Roman copies after Archaic originals: from the accurate to the approximate, from the full-scale in the round to the reduced size in relief, from the major work to the mediocre, commercial reproduction.

[15] Comparable spiral locks appear on the Athena from the Pediment of the temple of Apollo at Eretria (S. & S., fig. 281), which has several other mannered traits and can qualify as Archaistic, as also mentioned by Willers, 54 n. 231. Yet, unless the Athena is part of a later repair, its date should precede the Persian destruction in 490. In a much flatter version, spiral curls occur also on the Gorgon of the Corfu pediment, ca. 570. For all their implications of remote antiquity, these twisting locks present a problem. They appear often enough on late Archaic or classicizing works to assure us that they stand for earlier fashions, yet technically they are implausible for bronze statues (not much bronze casting on a large scale was done in the early 6th century) and are not truly rendered in marble before ca. 500. Since their appearance strongly suggests a metal prototype, we should probably suppose that bronze (or lead) curls were added to the early wooden xoana venerated in cult.

Before leaving the topic of Roman copies, one final question should be asked. Were these late works always acknowledged for what they were, or were they ever passed off as originals? That a certain number of forgeries in the modern sense of the word might have been current on the ancient antiquarian market is perhaps shown by the case of the so-called Piombino Apollo. Though the issue is still being debated, the high lead content in the bronze seems to confirm the theory that the statue was made in the First century BC. Whether it was a new creation in Archaic style sold as a Sixth century Greek original or a fairly accurate copy of an Archaic prototype, may perhaps be still disputed, but a late Archaic or Severe date for the casting of the bronze itself should probably be rejected. I still support the theory of a late creation, skillfully made to look coherently Archaic but actually incorporating several elements of later styles.

THE LINGERING ARCHAIC STYLE

Two more categories deserve brief consideration: the works in Lingering Archaic and those in Archaizing style. The first class is limited and perhaps a bit nebulous since its members often tend to be classed as genuine Archaic or as outright Archaistic sculptures. What basically differentiates them from the Archaistic group is their lack of affectation, even if fashions and poses have been modernized according to Fifth century trends. I have attempted elsewhere to collect a few examples, and have mentioned above the Seated Goddess from Tarentum, as typical of this style. Also the seated deity from Grammichele, now in Syracuse, briefly discussed in Chapter 5, qualifies for inclusion in the group. In general terms, examples are scarce in the major artistic centers, where one can logically expect innovations to make their most rapid strides or where Archaic most readily turns into Archaistic.[16] But obviously not all masters shifted manner overnight, and several may have continued to carve in an Archaic tradition from force of habit if not necessarily from religious conservatism or reluctance to accept new forms. Certain types of art, and in some areas certain media, seem particularly retardatory; for instance, in Lakonia and Thessaly, gravestones, and in Magna Graecia the terracotta sculptures, are often in Lingering Archaic, while stone and bronze seem more readily imprinted by the new Severe style. In outlying areas, such as Thasos and the Northern colonies, and of course Magna Graecia, the usual excuses of time lag and provincialism are often adduced by modern scholars to explain what might well have been a deliberate choice, since other works from the same regions show their ability to keep up with the general stylistic pace. Even more conserva-

[16] Very much the same point is made by Willers (17) when he says that "sub-archaic" is provincial art in the wider sense of the term. In particular, he isolates a group of male torsos for which he advocates a western Cycladic origin. These sculptures betray conflicting elements of style in that the backs are more advanced than the fronts in expressing the shifts in balance and the incipient contrapposto of the pose (Willers, 9–17). For another example of Lingering Archaic in the peripheral regions, see the interesting relief (fragmentary) with a male figure sitting on a stool and playing (?) with a goat, which stands on its hind legs leaning against the figure's knees: K. Kostoglou, *Deltion* 24 (1969) 118–26 (German summary on pp. 249–51) pl. 58, from near the village of Martino in Lokris. Of particular interest also is the seated figure from Miletos, found in 1967 (see V. von Graeve, *IstMitt* 25 [1975] 61–65). The author has clearly perceived the "transitional" style of the sculpture, between Archaic and Severe, and dates it after the reconstruction of the town in 474, perhaps under some influence from Paros. But instead of showing sub-archaic tendencies, in von Graeve's judgment, the statue is an example of Archaistic in that its effect is intentional and its allusions (to the older type) conscious.

tive are the sculptures at the fringes of the Greek world proper, of which an entire class is formed by the so-called Graeco-Persian stelai. With their flat surfaces, clear outlines, simplified details, large frontal eyes, stumpy proportions, the figures on these stelai look thoroughly Archaic, and it is difficult to place them in their proper time-slot, as the controversy over the Daskyleion stelai reveals. This is perhaps the only area where the Lingering Archaic style may have continued almost to the end of the Fifth century or even later; elsewhere it is reasonable to assume that the trend may have ended with the full flowering of High Classical.

THE ARCHAIZING STYLE

Archaizing, on the contrary, may be found at any time since it could be limited to a few details or could inform the whole statue. Typical are the Karyatids of the Erechtheion, which are thoroughly Classical in pose and treatment of drapery but recall the Archaic in the long spiral locks over the chest. Here the allusion is probably motivated by the function since a human figure supporting an entablature, light as it might have been, must have looked incongruous enough to deserve the support of tradition.

Though Lingering Archaic and Archaistic ensure continuity of motifs from the Archaic period proper, the inception of Archaizing can perhaps be pinned down to a specific moment through the work of Alkamenes. His Hermes Propylaios is still a debated subject since two different types of herms claim its paternity through ancient inscriptions. They are known as the Ephesos and the Pergamon types, after the find spot of the inscribed replicas, but copies of both have been found in Athens, suggesting that both originals stood there, though not necessarily in Mnesikles' Propylaia on the Akropolis. Whether one type or the other, or even neither, were made by Alkamenes is basically beside the point of this inquiry. What matters here is that we have a Classical face, with modeled cheeks and sharply lidded eyes, framed by a shelf-like series of spiral curls over the forehead and long locks on either side of the neck. In addition, the fluid wisps of the beard are Classical, but its jutting outline, at times squarish, imitates Archaic fashions. All in all, both types could be described as a Classical facial island surrounded by a sea of Archaic hair; the pillar-like body with atrophied arms increases the dichotomy and adds to the strangeness of the total appearance. Indeed, it may have been the convention of the Hermaic pillar which inspired Alkamenes to archaize, since a normal head in advanced Fifth century style would have looked out of place on such a body. A certain element of religious conservatism, as well as the general desire to suggest the venerable tradition behind the incongruous type, may again have played an important role in this decision. Alkamenes' creation must have set a pattern for all future herms to imitate since most of them archaize in some fashion.

A second work by Alkamenes, the triple-bodied Hekate, may well have been Archaizing in style, perhaps for the very same reasons. Again, whether or not the standard Hekataion type goes back to Alkamenes' original, we can focus on the significant details. In this case we have three female figures with their backs against a pillar-like core. They wear the Classical peplos belted over the overfold, but the Archaic touch is given by the curve at the edge of the apoptygma, which creates the pointed tips reminiscent of a diagonal mantle. In the most strongly Archaizing examples, this rendering turns into an outright swallowtail pattern. In addition, the skirt is marked by a strong axial pleat, like the paryphe of an Archaic costume. Usually, catenaries festoon the transparent drapery over the legs, and two heavy folds frame the sides. As mentioned above, this basic pattern is Classical (witness the so-called Frejus Aphrodite), but the central pleat and catenaries over the legs are good Archaic motifs, which first appeared on mid Sixth century seated statues in East Greece. From them the convention extended to standing figures, but without the accompanying outer folds since these latter would have obscured those contours so necessary for the clarity of Archaic compositions. In the enriched Fifth century version the skirt pattern became equally at home in Archaizing and Archaistic. But while Archaistic drapery had the dryness and linear sharpness typical of the total style, Archaizing statues could enjoy the full chiaroscuro of their periods. Thus catenaries could become veritable folds in their own right, catching light over their sharp ridges and trapping shadow in their deep pockets; the vertical pleats could be emphasized by deep grooves acting as dark outlines. In brief, the drapery could acquire the full plasticity, chiaroscuro, and flamboyancy of High Classical and then Hellenistic style, while retaining that bilateral symmetry caused by the axial pleat which provided a definitely old-fashioned flavor.

From the Hekate of Alkamenes (if this really was its origin), the pattern passed to many other types and found its widest use in the mid Hellenistic period, for instance in semi-draped statues of Aphrodite (the so-called Pudica type). Another logical extension of the motif was supplied by Isiac iconography, in which both the Goddess and her priestesses wore a fringed mantle knotted in the center; this produced a central fold which the artists then carried down into the chiton skirt. In abbreviated version, with short skirt, the motif found favor with Roman cuirassed statues and, if I am correct in my assumption, in a Classicizing/Archaizing Amazon of Augustan date, the so-called Lansdowne type.

SUMMARY

Lingering Archaic, Archaistic, and Archaizing are stylistic trends in need of further study and sharper definition. It would seem at present that Archaistic, as here understood, probably began within the Archaic period proper, as a mannered version of a current if exhausted style; it continued, with greater decorativeness and exaggeration, well into Roman times. It encompassed both reliefs and statues in the round, not as purely ornamental sculpture but as part of a religious expression which sought its roots in the remote past. As such, it was capable of vital creations which ranked as valuable originals worthy of reproduction in several replicas. Truly Archaic works were also copied, but apparently only those in an advanced, late Sixth century style, and presumably solely for religious reasons, perhaps with few exceptions taken from the realm of minor arts. In any case, the practice may never have been widespread.

Archaizing may have begun in the last quarter of the Fifth century, but it too continued into Roman times, with a period of renewed liveliness in the Mid to Late Hellenistic period. Lingering Archaic, on the contrary, was rather short-lived, since it was the purest expression of Archaic style and therefore could not survive the conquest of new stylistic principles and formal development.

BIBLIOGRAPHY 11

FOR PAGE 303

The most recent work on Archaistic sculpture is by Willers, with previous bibliography. Most important are the discussions by Harrison in *Agora* XI (on Archaistic per se, on Herms, and on Hekataia) and by Herdejürgen on the diagonal mantle in Archaistic sculpture. Recent articles on specific Archaistic monuments are too numerous to be mentioned individually; note, however, Herdejürgen, *JdI* 87 (1972) 299–313, for some Roman Archaistic heads which reflect the coiffures of Roman ladies of the Claudian period, and F. Harl-Schaller, *AthMitt* 87 (1972) 241–53, who discusses an Augustan pier in the Athens National Museum as a copy of a late 5th century Archaistic work of different (frieze-like) format.

On Neo-Attic works and their prototypes, see the important work by W. Fuchs, *Die Vorbilder der neuattischen Reliefs, JdI* ErgH. 20, 1959.

On Archaistic sculpture in the round, the most comprehensive gathering of monuments remains H. Bulle, *Archaisierende griechische Rundplastik* (*AbhBayerAk* 30:2, 1918).

Harrison's terminology: *Agora* XI, 50, Cf. Willers, 19–20.

FOR PAGE 306

Hauser: F. Hauser, *Die neu-attischen Reliefs* (Stuttgart 1889).

Herdejürgen: Passim, but especially 63–66, with summary of previous positions on 65–66.

Harrison: *Agora* XI, 63–64, 66 (on chronology).

Becatti: *Crd'A* 6 (1941) 32–48; id., *RendPontAcc* 17 (1940–41) 85–95; id., *EAA* s.v. *Arcaistico, stile*, and *Arcaizzante, stile*.

Havelock: "Archaic as Survival" and "Archaistic Reliefs."

A summary of previous literature and opinions can also be found in Willers, 21–28. The names I have quoted are representative of the respective positions, but are by no means a complete list of the scholars who have dealt with the problem.

For the use of cartoons and pattern books, see especially "Archaistic Reliefs," 46–49.

FOR PAGE 307

Late 5th century Red Figure vases: See especially the oinochoe from the Agora, illustrated in *Agora* XI, pl. 63b. See also *ibid.*, 62–64 and especially 63, for comments on two-dimensional traits.

FOR PAGE 308

Leto from Delos, Athens Nat. Mus. 22: supra, Ch. 4, pp. 110 and 118; cf. also Willers, 54 and n. 211, for the Athena in the same group, with comparable comments.

Athena from west pediment of Aphaia Temple: *Severe Style*, 15–16 n. 4, fig. 1.

Striding figure from Keos: *BCH* 89 (1965) 862 fig. 7; Willers, 54 n. 213; cf. also supra, Ch. 7 n. 6.

FOR PAGE 309

Euthydikos' kore (Akr. 686 + 609): supra, Ch. 4, pp. 106 and 118; see especially *Korai*, figs. 569–572, for an appreciation of the pose.

Akr. 581 (Athena and the Pig relief): Payne, 48–49, pl. 126:1; *AMA* no. 424; *Aspécts*, 16–17; Willers, 55–56; V. von Graeve, *IstMitt* 25 (1975) 63–64. Brouskari, 52–53, dates the relief around 490, but calls it the earliest example of Archaizing or Archaistic, and points out details in Severe style, "which appear to have escaped the attention of the artist."

Nat. Mus. 36: Supra, Ch. 6, 166 and bibliography. For the attribution of both these works to an experimenting master, see J. Frel, *AA* 1973, 198–200 figs. 6–7.

Herdejürgen: Akr. relief, p. 57 n. 339; Nat. Mus. stele, p. 68 n. 425.

Willers (55–56) attributes both reliefs to the same master and dates them both to 490–480, finding in this chronology support for the interpretation of the National Museum stele as votive.

Esquiline stele: *Korai* no. 194 fig. 611; most recently, Hiller, 168, Catalogue I 1, with further bibliography.

FOR PAGE 310

Seated Goddess from Tarentum in Berlin: Herdejürgen's whole book focuses on this statue, but see in particular 9–36 and 90–92, with the date given on this last page. Cf. also *Severe Style*, 93–94 fig. 125; Willers, 18.

FOR PAGE 311

On 5th century statues of Athena Promachos see Willers, 58–60; cf. also H. G. Niemeyer, *AntP* 3 (1964) 7–23, for the bronze statuettes from the Akropolis; cf. Cl. Rolley, *RA* 1968, 35–48. On the Promachos type as coming from Ionia, see H. Herdejürgen, *AntK* 12 (1969) 102–10.

Archaistic works in the Agora: *Agora* XI nos. 108–9, 111–15.

Archaistic korai on the Akropolis: *AMA* nos. 138–41, 143.

Hekate and Hermes Propylaios by Alkamenes: see infra (bibl. for pp. 318–19).

Xenokrateia relief: *Agora* XI, 53 n. 27; Karouzou, p. 57 no. 2756.

Idol in Bassai frieze: H. Kenner, *Der Fries des Tempels von Bassae-Phigaleia* (Vienna 1946); pl. 5; B. Brown, *Anticlassicism in Greek Sculpture of the Fourth Century B.C.*, (New York 1973) fig. 5.

Idol in Argive Heraion: F. Eichler, *JOAI* 19–20 (1919) 30–31, G, fig. 23 (note a second idol, *ibid.*, 32 fig. 24, in xoanon form).

Idol in Epidauros, Temple of Asklepios: J. F. Crome, *Die Skulpturen des Asklepiostempels von Epidauros* (Berlin 1951) 46 no. 35 pl. 39.

For a discussion of these idols, see, e.g., "Archaic as Survival," 333, nn. 9–14; and *Agora* XI, 51 nn. 7–8; 53 n. 26; 61–62.

For the dating of the temple of Apollo at Bassai, see N. Yalouris *AAA* 6 (1973) 39–55, especially p. 44 and (in translation) p. 54. The Argive Heraion burned down in 423 (Paus. 2.17.7) and its replacement must of necessity postdate this event.

FOR PAGE 312

Record relief of 356/5, Athens Nat. Mus. 1480: "Archaic as Survival," pl. 74:8.

Record relief from the Agora, 321/20: *Agora* XI no. 133 pl. 31.

The Archaistic frieze from Samothrace has been discussed most recently by P. W. Lehmann, *Skopas in Samothrace* (Northampton, Mass. 1973) 4–5, 10–13. For the 2d century dating, see "Archaistic Reliefs," 50 n. 28.

Sagalassos frieze: *JOAI* 50 (1972–73) 117–24; additions in *AJA* 79 (1975) 211 and pl. 40:13–14.

Fourth century as peak of Archaistic production: Herdejürgen, 78.

FOR PAGE 313

Archaistic Artemis in Naples, location: L. Richardson, Jr., *AJA* 74 (1970) 202. See also supra, p. 315 n. 14.

Archaistic korai from Eleusis: *Agora* XI, 56 and nn. 50–55; see also *Korai* figs. 683–85. Harrison mentions at least six korai from that site, all of which probably held perirrhanteria.

Kore from Athenian Eleusinion: *Hesperia* 35 (1966) 85 pl. 30 a–b.

FOR PAGE 314

Apollo from Halieis (Porto Cheli): *AJA* 75 (1972) 301–2; *JHS ArchR* 17 (1971) 11–12; *Scientific American* 231:4 (October 1974) 110–19 and drawing on p. 117. This very interesting statue will be published by Bookidis.

Dionysos (?) from the Agora: *Agora* XI no. 109.

Creeping Odysseus, I. S. Gardner Museum, Boston: G. Lanciani, *NSc* 1885, 516; V. Poulsen, *ActaA* 25 (1954) 301–4.

For the traditional form of Roman pedimental decoration, see P. Hommel, *Studien zu den römischen Figurengiebeln der Kaiserzeit* (Berlin 1954). See also the comments by S. Lattimore, *AJA* 78 (1974) 55–61, especially p. 57.

Archaistic "replacements" in the Agora: *Agora* XI nos. 97 A and 125; cf. p. 65.

FOR PAGE 315

The position that no true replicas of Archaic originals exist is taken, e.g., by Ch. Picard, *Manuel d'archéologie grecque: La sculpture classique*, 2 (Paris 1939) 106; A. Giuliano, *ArchCl* 6 (1954) 21.

For recent studies on Roman copies, see J. Dörig, *AntK* 12 (1969) 41–50, and especially 45ff. Cf. also bibliography in B. S. Ridgway, *AntP* 7 (1967) 58–62; Herdejürgen, 73–74 (Archaic or Archaistic originals ?); Willers, 61–65.

Unfinished relief from Agora: *Agora* XI no. 127 pl. 29.

Akr. 628: *Agora* XI, 51; *AMA* no. 36; Payne, pl. 96:4.

Herdejürgen, on copying: 52–54, also 63.

Guicciardini kore: R. Bianchi Bandinelli, *CrdA* 6 (1941) 91–96 pls. 52–55; B. S. Ridgway, *AntP* 7 (1967) 62 figs. 30–31.

Kore in Rodin Museum: Herdejürgen, 53 pl. 8c.
Castelporziano kore: *Korai*, figs. 675–78.
Munich kore: Herdejürgen, pl. 8 a–b.
Stephanos Athlete: Most recently, P. Zanker, *Klassizistische Statuen* (Mainz 1974) 49–70.

FOR PAGE 316

Akr. 682: supra, 94, 117; cf. also p. 107.
Apollo Philesios, Roman copy: E. Bielefeld, *AntP* 8 (1969) 13–17, with previous bibliography; Dörig, *AntK* 12 (1969) 47.
Delos relief: J. Marcadé, *BCH* Suppl. 1 (1973) 351–57, no. 11; cf. also id., *Au Musée de Delos* (Paris 1969) 166–67.

FOR PAGE 317

Piombino Apollo: The latest opinion I have seen is Willers, 17 and n. 37, who still tends towards a dating around 470 BC. This is also the opinion held by Richter in her third edition of *Kouroi* (1970) with epigraphic discussion on pp. 152–53. For the later date, see B. S. Ridgway, *AntP* 7 (1967) 43–75.
Lingering Archaic: See *Severe Style*, 93–96. In particular, see now Willers, 9–20, and V. von Graeve, *IstMitt* 25 (1975) 61–65.

FOR PAGE 318

Graeco-Persian stelai: See supra, Ch. 6, p. 173 n. 32.
Erechtheion Karyatids: *Korai*, figs. 669–70.
Hermes Propylaios and Hekate by Alkamenes: *Agora* XI, 86–98, and 122–24; Willers, 33–47 (Hermes), 48–52 (Hekate). On the Hermes Propylaios, see also D. Willers, *JdI* 82 (1967) 37–109.

FOR PAGE 319

For Archaizing traits in Isiac iconography, see *Agora* XI, 56 and n. 56; cf. also D. B. Thompson, *Ptolemaic Oinochoai and Portraits in Faience* (Oxford 1973) 114–15 and n. 6.
For a discussion of the central fold, see *Agora* XI, 62; for different conclusions on the "Amazon of Kresilas," see B. S. Ridgway, *AJA* 78 (1974) 1–17; id., *AJA* 80 (1976) 82.

Index

I gratefully acknowledge much help by Ann Steiner and Fred Albertson in the preparation of this index.

PLATES

1. Seated Figure from Prinias. Herakleion Museum

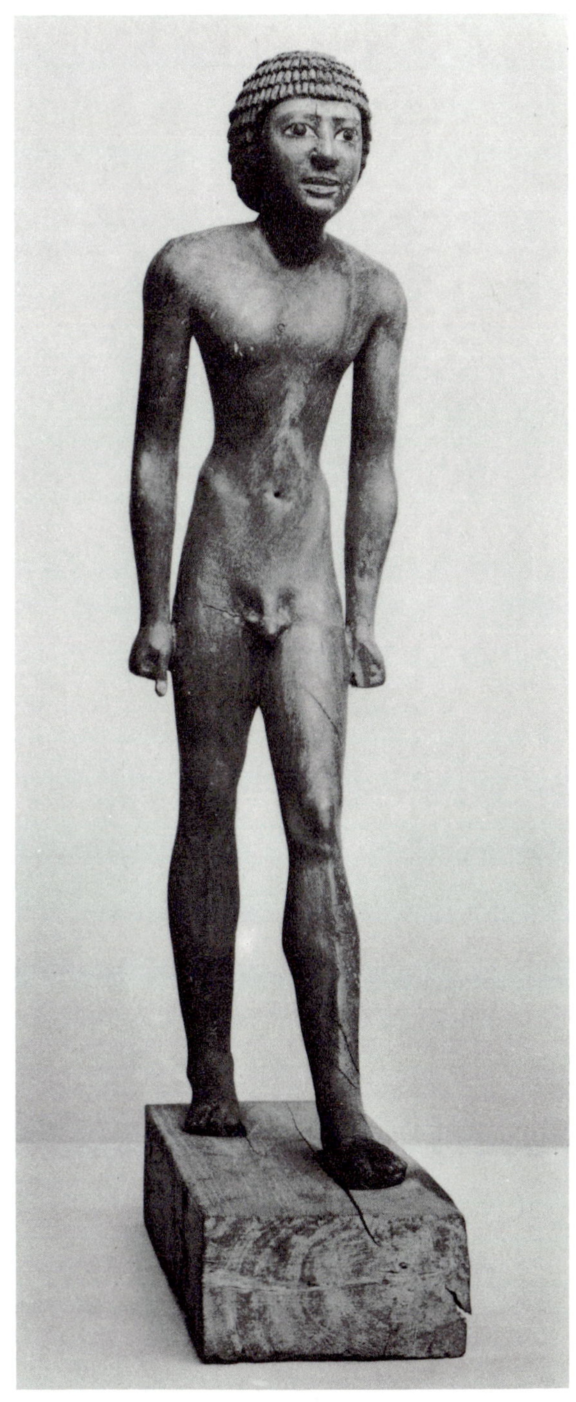

2. Wooden Figure of Meryrehashtef from Sedment, Egypt, ca. 2200 BC. London, British Museum

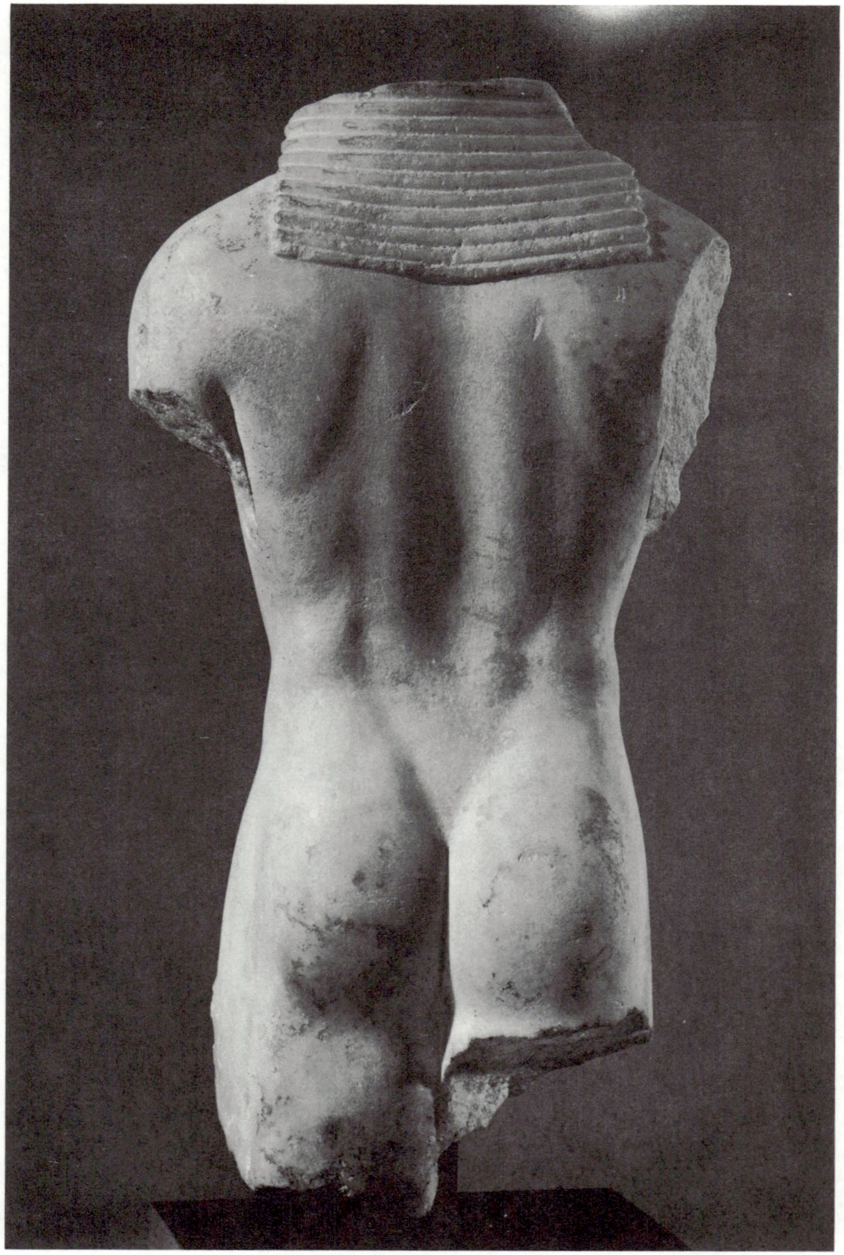

3–4. Kouros. Cleveland Museum of Art

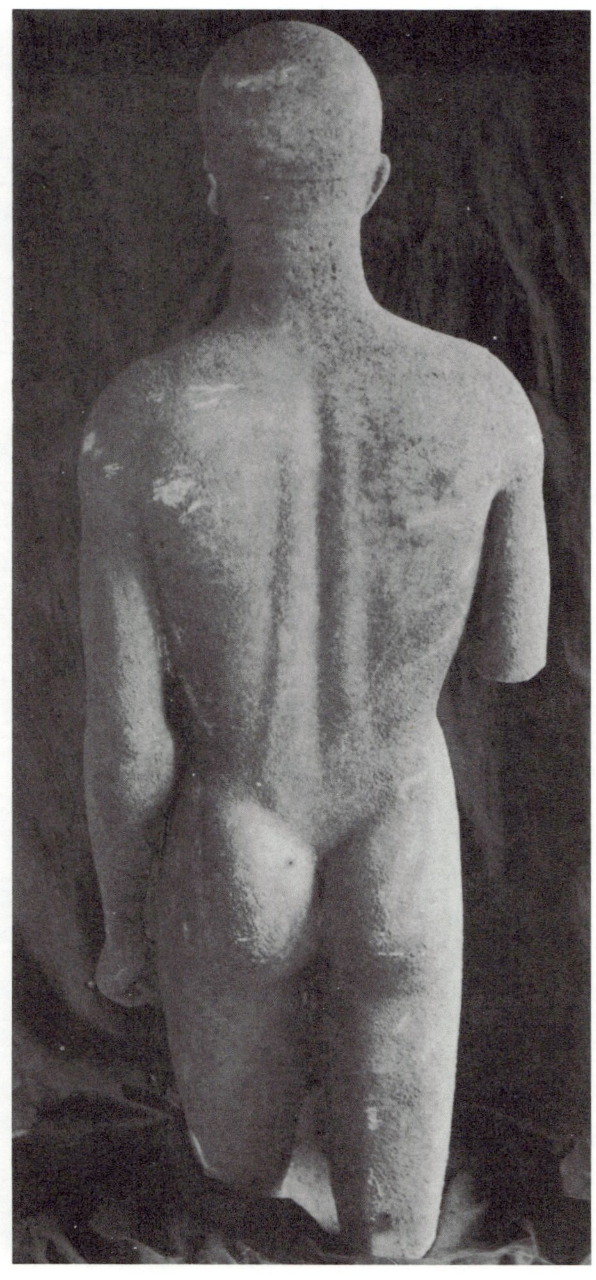

5–6. Kouros from Eunopos. Kilkis Museum (Height 1.82 m.)

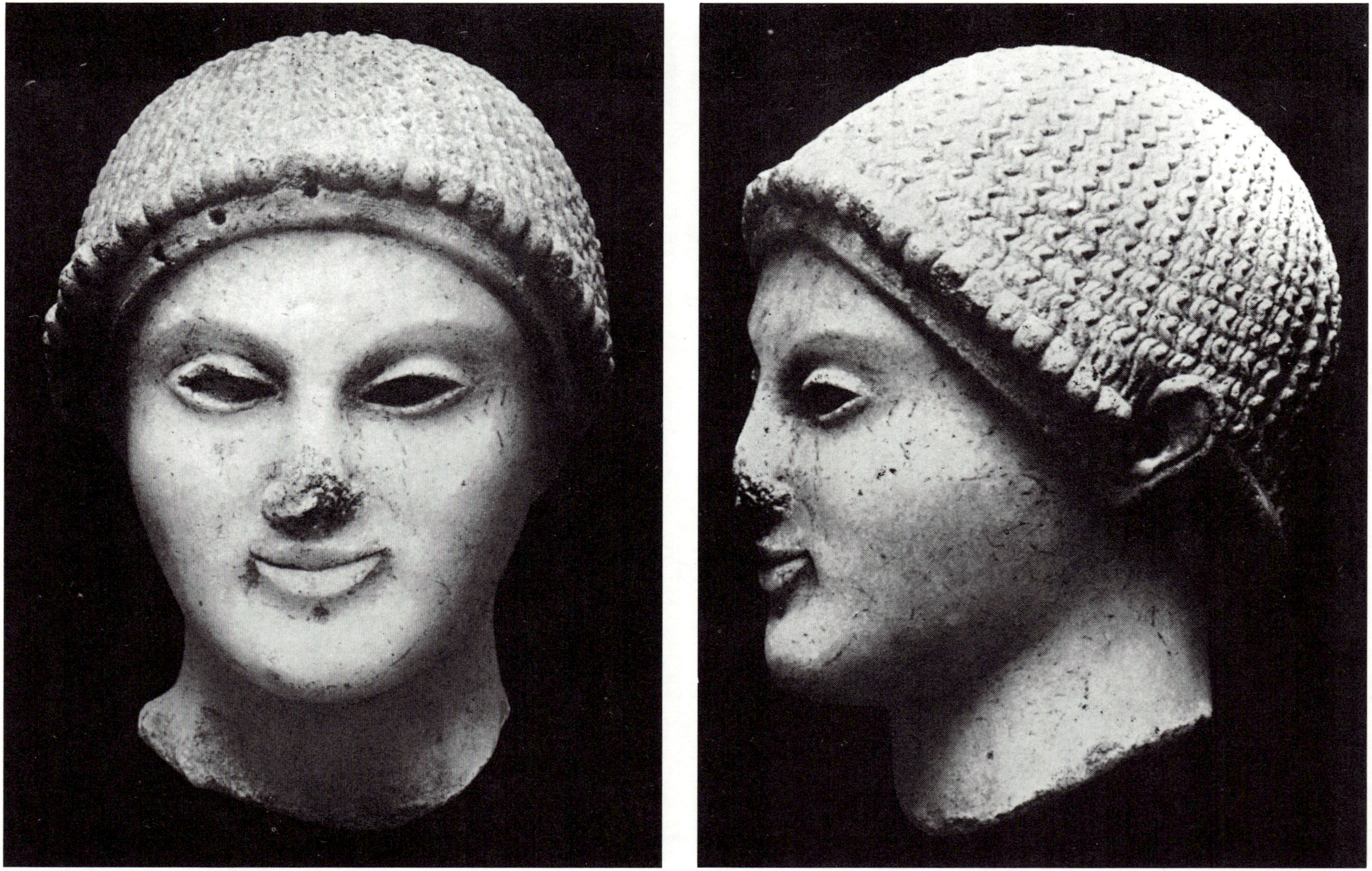

7–8. Head in Cyrene Museum, from Sanctuary of Apollo

9–10. Turkish Peasant Girls

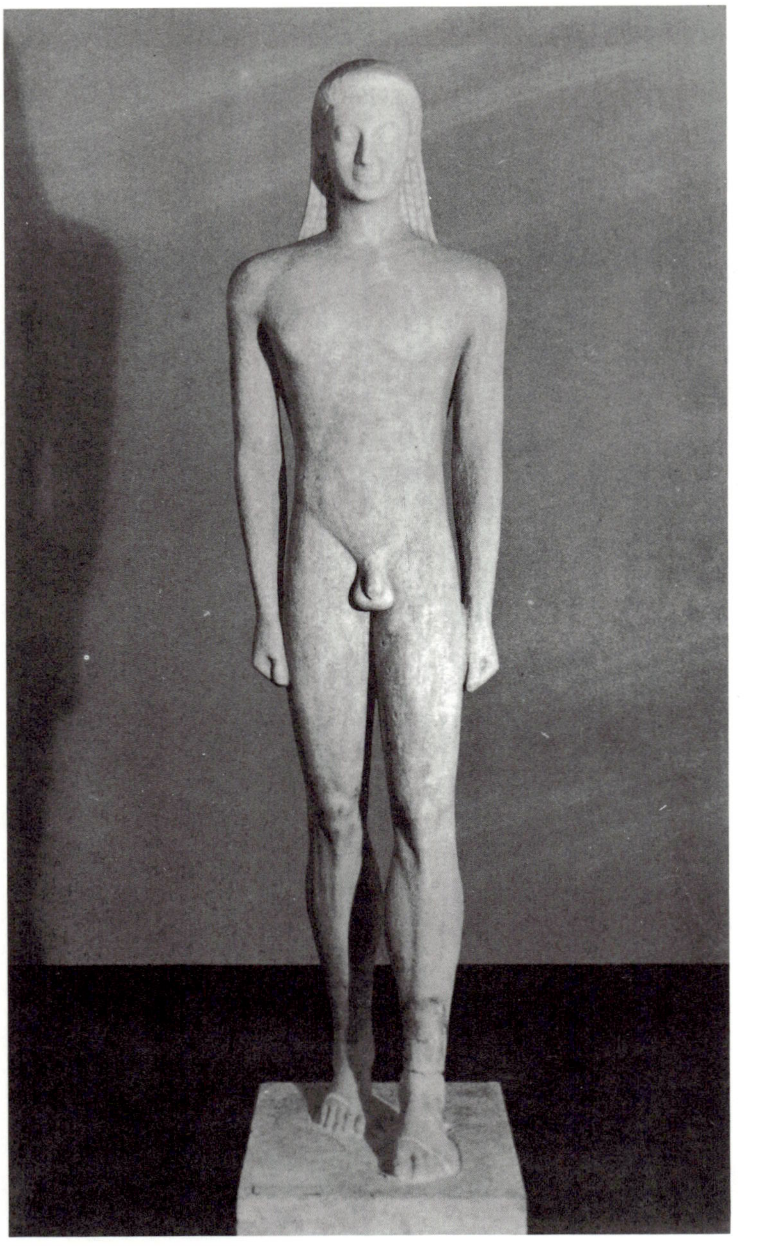

11. Kouros from Melos. Athens, National Museum

12. Bronze Head from Akropolis. Athens, National Museum

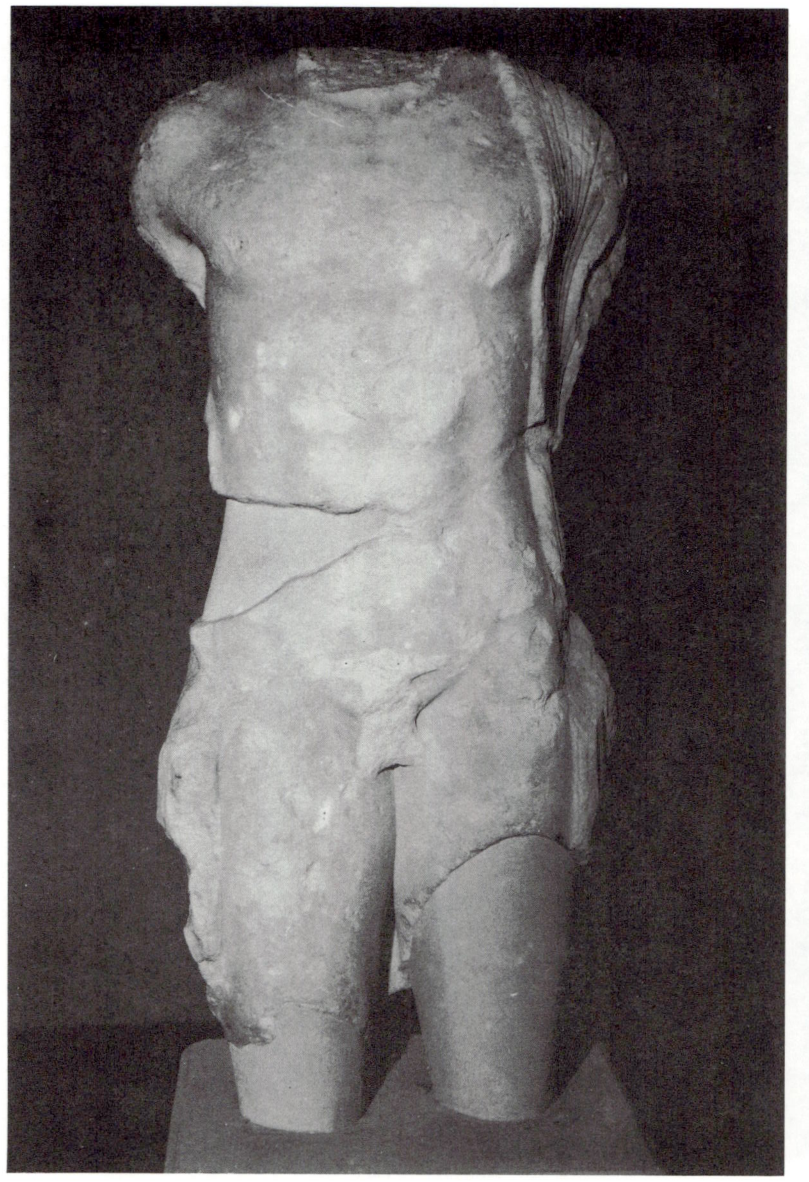

13–14. Draped Kouros from Syracuse. Syracuse Museum

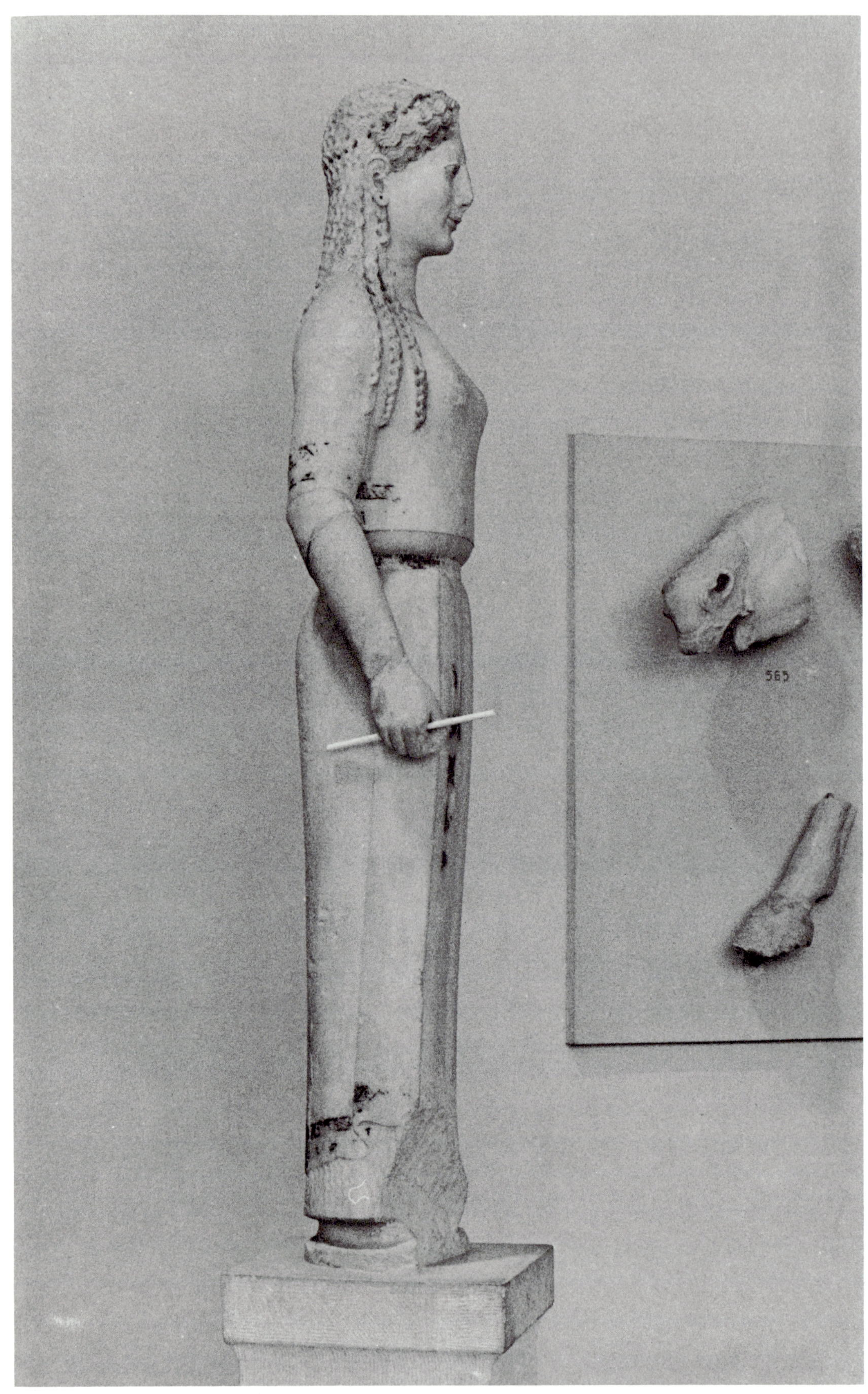

15. Kore Akr. 679 (The Peplos Kore) with insertion in right hand. Athens, Akropolis Museum

16. Kore Akr. 678. Athens, Akropolis Museum

17. Kore Akr. 611. Athens, Akropolis Museum

18. Kore Akr. 673. Athens, Akropolis Museum

19. Kore Akr. 683. Athens, Akropolis Museum

20. Kore Akr. 680. Athens, Akropolis Museum

21. Kore from the Heraion.
Samos Museum (*Samos* XI no. 16)

22. Kore Head. Museum of Art and Archaeology, University of Missouri

23. Kore I, Cyrene

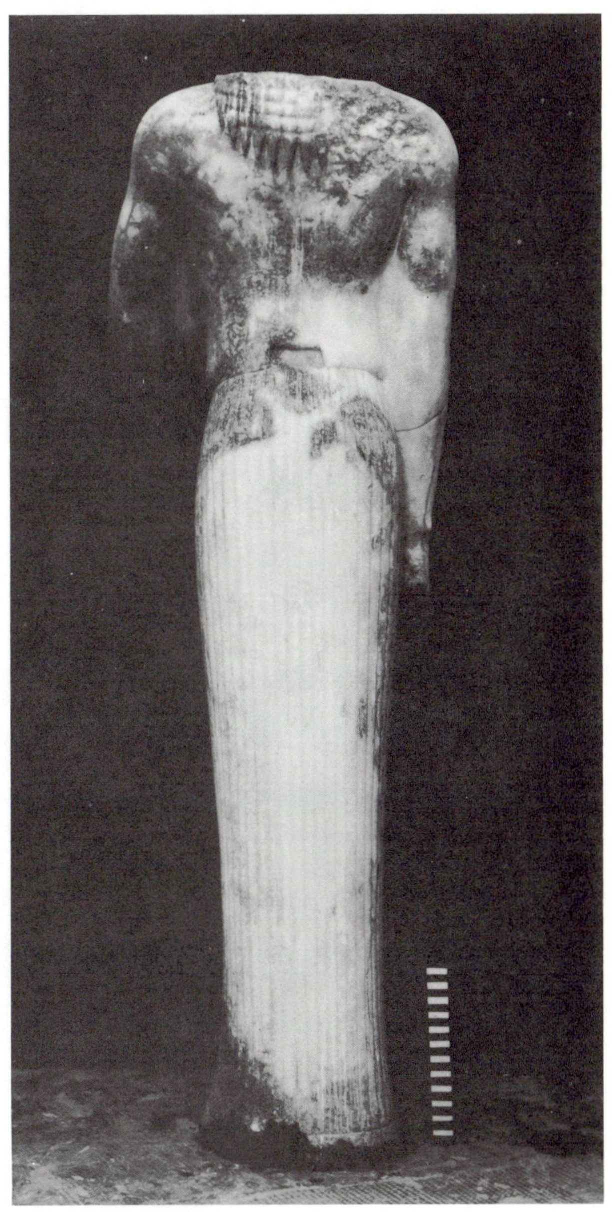

24. Kore II, Cyrene

25–26. Kore from Rhedesto. Thessaloniki Museum (Height 0.57 m.)

27–28. Lyons Kore. Lyons Museum (upper part); Athens, Akropolis Museum (lower part)

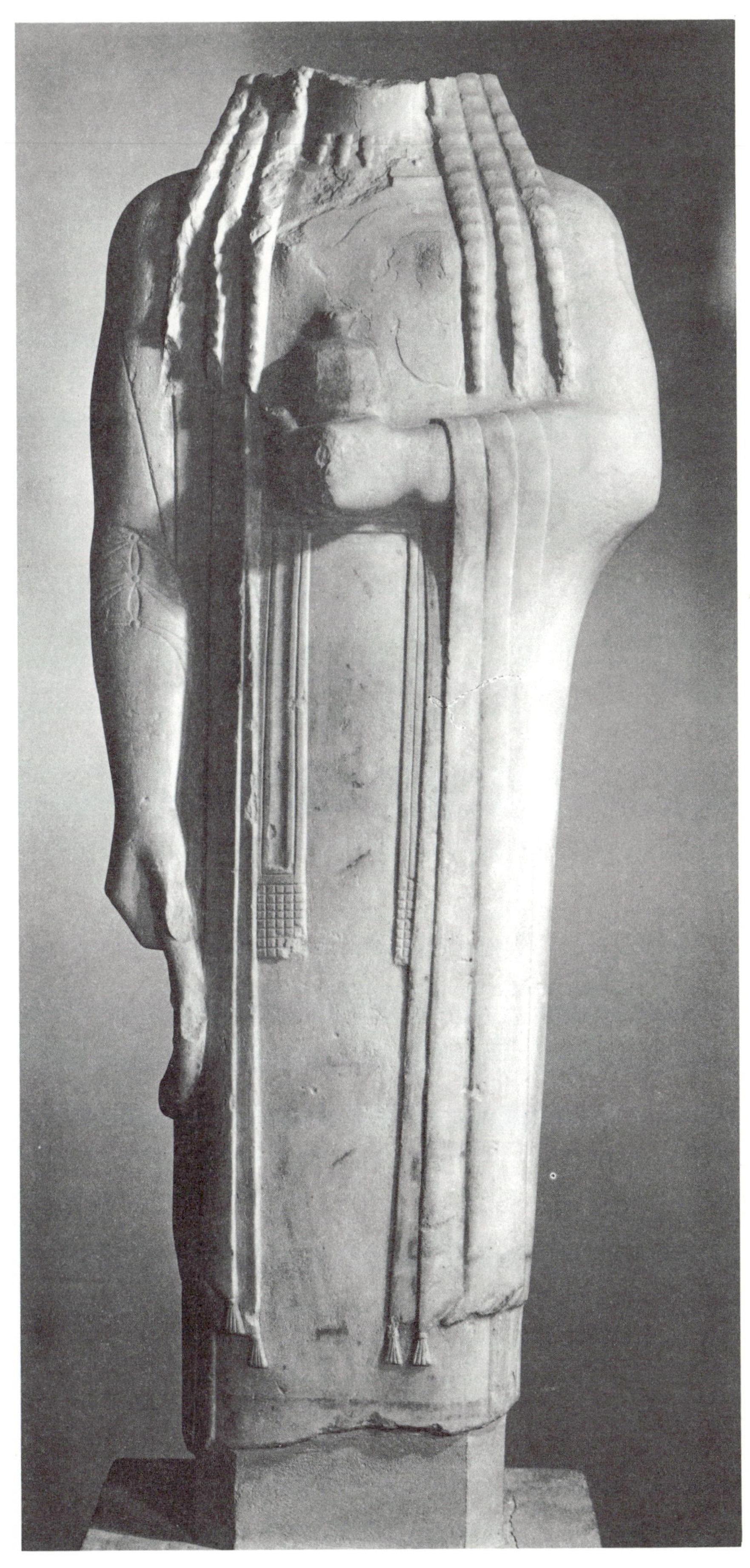

29. Kore Akr. 593 (The Pomegranate Kore). Athens, Akropolis Museum

30. Kore Akr. 674. Athens, Akropolis Museum

31. Chares of Teichioussa. London, British Museum B 278

32–33. Seated Figure. Athens, National Museum

34–35. Dionysos from Ikaria. Athens, National Museum

36. “Scribe,” Akr. 629. Athens, Akropolis Museum

37. Seated Man. Athens, Kerameikos Museum

38–39. Seated “Dionysos.” Athens, National Museum

40–41. Equestrian Statue. Athens, Kerameikos Museum

42. Pink Granite Lion from Soleb, Sudan, ca. 1350 BC. London, British Museum

43. Lion from Perachora. Boston Museum of Fine Arts

44–45. Head of Sphinx. Cleveland Museum of Art

46. Head of Sphinx, Cyrene

47–49. Poros Siren. Corinth Museum

50. Limestone Head of Goat. Cleveland Museum of Art

51. Stele from Crete. Museum of Art and Archaeology, University of Missouri

52. Sphinx and Capital from Attic Gravestone. New York, Metropolitan Museum of Art

53. Stele of "Marathon Runner." Athens, National Museum

54. Rider Stele from Boeotia. Boston Museum of Fine Arts

55. Stele from Velanideza. Athens, National Museum

56. Stele of Warrior. Cyrene Museum

57–58. Kore Akr. 681 ("Antenore's Kore").
Athens, Akropolis Museum

59. Cattle Raid, Metope from Sikyonian Treasury. Delphi Museum

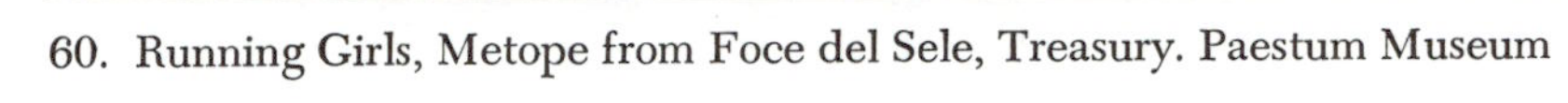

60. Running Girls, Metope from Foce del Sele, Treasury. Paestum Museum

61. Detail of Hermes' Legs from West Frieze of Siphnian Treasury. Delphi Museum

62. Detail of Aphrodite from West Frieze of Siphnian Treasury. Delphi Museum

63. Detail of Athena's Mantle from North Frieze of Siphnian Treasury. Delphi Museum

64. Archaistic Athena. Corinth Museum

65. Hand, from matching piece. Corinth Museum

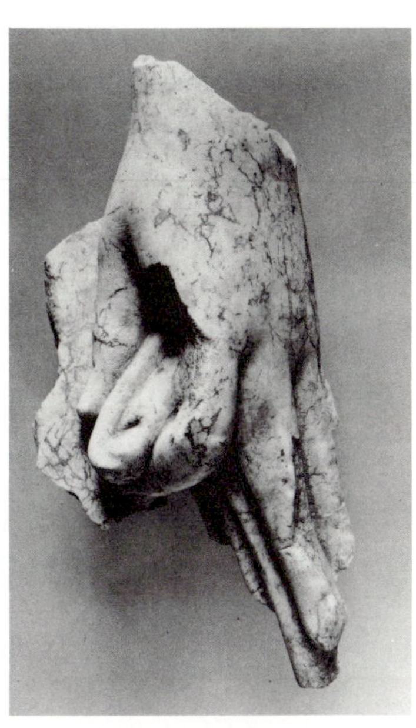

66. Athena and Pig Sacrifice, Votive Relief, Akr. 381.
Athens, Akropolis Museum

67–68. Guicciardini Kore. Florence, Palazzo Guicciardini

69. Creeping Odysseus. Boston, Isabella Stewart Gardner Museum